ENCYCLOPEDIA
OF
SOVIET LIFE

Ilya Zemtsov

Transaction Publishers
New Brunswick (U.S.A.) and London (U.K.)

Library of Congress Catalog Number: 89-77891
ISBN: 0-88738-350-5
Printed in the United States of America

Library of Congress Cataloging-in-Publication Data

Zemtsov, Ilya.
    Encyclopedia of Soviet life   /   by Ilya Zemtsov.
       p.   cm.
    ISBN 0-88738-350-5
    1. Political science—Dictionaries—Russian.   2. Propaganda, Communist—
Dictionaries—Russian.   3. Soviet Union—Politics and government—20th century—
Dictionaries—Russian.   I. Title.
JA64.R8Z44   1990   89-77891
947.084′03—dc20   CIP

To my wife, Maya.

Contents

Acknowledgments

I wish to express my thanks to my colleagues, research workers of the International Research Center for Contemporary Society, Dr. Yisrael Cohen and Ms. Esther Rofe for the editing of the book and its preparation for print, and to Prof. Shlomo Mogilevsky and Ms. Faina Perlova for their valuable comments.

Introduction

An important, perhaps the most important specific feature of the contemporary Soviet life is the magic or words. The USSR has been engulfed by a wave of newly coined terms (e.g., *uskorenie* [acceleration], *demokratizatsiya* [democratization], *perestroika* [reconstruction], *novoe politicheskoe myshlenie* [new political thinking])—tens or even hundreds of terms and phrases with new meanings. A new sort of language has arisen, based on the illusion that one only had to invent and introduce new terms into mass circulation to bring to life—immediately—new, desirable phenomena. And when the latter did not materialize, when social change in the Soviet Union proved to proceed much more slowly and painfully than expected, disillusionment and dissatisfaction ensued. Society expected, even demanded, decisive and rapid changes, such as the attainment of real democracy and a rapid rise in the standard of living. Newly awakened political activism was something totally out of the ordinary in a society accustomed to order and based on fear and silent endurance. Now, the long-suffering Soviet people are finally expressing their rejection of the existing system with its inefficient decision-making and its naive rituals and slogans along with their meaningless rhetoric and groundless optimism.

It became clear that there is a real danger that the Soviet leadership will lose control over events. Thus, out of desperation they may turn to force and terror. The potential for such a course finds its reflection in the Soviet language in which there coexist words and phrases reflecting recent social tendencies toward stagnation and decay alongside words and phrases that more or less realistically reflect current trends toward increased liberalization. The latter comprise what I have chosen to refer to as the "lexicon of glasnost," despite the fact that the vocabulary of glasnost itself is only a thin layer within the broad stratum of the Soviet language, a layer of very recent provenance. It is an echo and reflection of Gorbachev's reforms. Although it has managed to accumulate no more than a small number of new words, the new terms and their meanings have already initiated a process of reconceptualizing the entire remainder of the Soviet language. This reconceptualization has included relieving it of some of its excessively ideological ballast and reducing its distance from social realities. This is why the entire Soviet political language can be viewed as a "lexicon of glasnost."

However, this Soviet language remains faithful to its original purpose. Its terms and phrases refer less to objects and events of the real world than to the world of fiction as posited by communist doctrine. The Soviet political language is self-contradictory. Although its meanings tend to be devoid of ambiguity, its fracture of the world into polarities of good and evil destroys whatever coherence and inner logic it might have otherwise possessed. This axiomatic polarization has a curious consequence: it projects a socialist form toward the outside world, and, simultaneously, an authoritarian essence toward the Soviet people.

The words and phrases of the Soviet language act upon the unconscious and become triggers of political manipulation. Through them fabrication replaces reality.

The Soviet language has two basic components: fictions that communist ideology proclaims as reality and realities that are portrayed in the guise of fictions. This has led

1

to two diverse but not opposite categories in the Soviet language. The first consists of phenomena-words, which, even if they distort fact, bear some correspondence to Soviet realities: e.g., "Party," "collective farm," "ongoing production meeting." The second category consists of fiction-words, which project images devoid of any correspondence to Soviet reality: e.g., "vanguard," "fighting spirit," "internal Party democracy," "friendship between the peoples," "idealism."

Terms belonging to the first category refer to actual facts of Soviet life. This circumstance limits and, at times, renders impossible total fictionalization. Terms belonging to the second category serve as prefabricated building blocks that may be used with some imagination. It suits the authorities to preserve the vagueness of such terms for the purpose of various successive manipulations. In each case, depending on the current political situation, the requisite social coloration or association is imparted to the words. Since life doesn't stand still, each manipulation tends to differ from the preceding one. Nevertheless, all manipulations are strictly determined in accordance with the communist view of the world, which allows for a very limited range of ideological variation.

The terms of the first category are basically fixed formulas: they are unaffected by contact with reality, since the devaluation (or collapse) of the stereotypes they give expression to would entail the collapse of the communist worldview.

Fiction-words and, even more so, fiction-phrases have the merit of versatility; they can be swiftly readjusted to changing political currents. If one ingredient of a composite phrase of this type loses its persuasiveness, it can in no time be replaced by another, better suited to the task of the moment. In this manner, "Hegemony of the Proletariat" gave way to "Hegemony of the People." Such an operation leaves intact the original function of the phrase, which was to camouflage the fact that real hegemony is that of the party bureaucracy. Yet when real social change occurs, fiction-words and phrases can

be altered radically. Such was the case when "dictatorship of the proletariat" was superseded by "State of All the People." Similar processes were reflected in the succession of adjectives attached to the noun phrase "Way of Life": first "Proletarian," next "Soviet," then "Socialist" and finally "Communist." In contrast, the phenomena-words lend themselves far less easily to manipulation since they are rooted in some concrete social experience. As such, they are less useful than fiction-words which, due to their abstractness, offer practically limitless possibilities to Soviet propaganda. Not all of them are totally contrived. At the historical point in time when they first appeared, a certain number of fiction-words reflected emergent developments that were subsequently aborted. Ideological reinterpretation of such developments is as a rule a later occurrence. Other phenomena-words arose out of ideology, and only later made their way into real life, where they could affect the latter.

Nevertheless, these two categories of the Soviet language are not mutually exclusive. With the demise of realities they denote, phenomena-words can become fiction-words. Conversely, fiction-words can become realities when an ideological construct happens to acquire some counterpart in real events. In the final analysis, the two categories differ only in the scope and manner of ideological manipulation they typify. In the case of phenomena-words, reality is superimposed on ideology, while in the case of fiction-words, ideology is superimposed on reality. The efforts of communist propaganda are focused on maintaining the stability of the phenomena-words and revitalizing fiction-words.

The Soviet language contains a multiplicity of subtle psychological snares. It limits the freedom of thought and action of the individual. Conformist thinking is ensured not just by impoverished expression and by clichés. Obfuscation and the cryptic nature of certain expressions also play a considerable role. Conversely, other phrases are notable for their informational overload. The overburdened content of the latter and the minimal content of the former both deprive the individual of the capacity to integrate a huge mass of variegated factors, and to construct a coherent explanatory system.

The Soviet language fully exploits the devices of rhetoric. It seeks to rouse people to spiritual exaltation. Typical examples of rhetorical usage are: "by the will of the Party" (*voleyu partii*), "activist attitude (*aktivnaya zhiznennaya pozitsiya*), and "guards of labor" (*gvardeytsy truda*). The Soviet language frequently euphemizes concepts. In the context of communist reality, as reflected by the official Soviet lexicon, there are no "unemployed," there are merely "jobseekers." There are no "crises," merely "temporary difficulties." Dictatorship as such would appear not to exist; rather, there is "democratic centralism." Association, both by analogy and by contrast, plays a key role in the Soviet language. Thus, when "Soviet labor" is mentioned, the following associations are expected to be evoked: "heroic" and "selfless"—or, at the least, "meritorious." At the same time, labor in the West is depicted as "forced," "backbreaking," and "degrading." The Soviet people are invariably "great" and "heroic," whereas the American people are "long-suffering."

The Soviet language is capable not only of distorting the proportions and contours of reality but also of concealing certain phenomena by failing to name them. Thus, the official Soviet lexicon lacks names for phenomena as ubiquitous in Soviet society as "closed stores," "government *dachas*," and "Kremlin rations." In addition, many Soviet words lose their original meaning when their referents become symbols of veneration. Thus, the "Party" has been deified, "labor" vested with spiritual qualities, and "plan" and "socialist competition" made sacrosanct.

A further characteristic of the Soviet language is its extensive stock of substitute words and expressions intentionally coined by the authorities to conceal their true policies and actions. For example, Brezhenev's rule of decline and disintegration is referred to as *epokha zastoya* ("the period of stagnation"),

totalitarian methods of rule as *komandno-direktivnoe rukovodstvo* ("command-directive leadership"), informers as *osvedomiteli* ("information-providers"), and the mass annihilation of Soviet citizens in Stalin's prisons and camps as *likvidatsiya* ("liquidation") or *izyatie* ("removal") as if it concerned not people but inanimate objects.

Some Soviet words do not simply denote, they also "unmask" or condemn. Thus the words "renegade," "opportunism," "apoliticality," and "dregs" are shorthand for a verdict of guilty rendered as per provisions of specific sections of the Criminal Code. The same holds true for branding someone as an "enemy of the people" or an "anti-Soviet element."

The Soviet language has reached a level whereby the process of apperception of reality has been replaced by catchwords that encapsulate key values of Marxist dogma: "Forward to Communism," "Glory to the Party," "Everybody out for a Communist subbotnik."

The destruction of the dual-signal system of human perception of reality inevitably ensued. People learned not to react to the conventional meaning of Soviet slogans and exhortations since their referents had become devoid of all contents and thus incapable of stimulating action. Soviet vocabulary became in this way dissociated from human behavior. There appeared two parallel worlds divorced from each other: the real world, even if not free of contradictions and conflicts, and the fictitious kingdom of words.

Through the process of adaptation, human behavior likewise underwent a split. The public domain, where people learned to conform strictly to the expectations of the Soviet rulers, had little in common with the private domain where the same expectations were notoriously disregarded. It was necessary to somehow overcome this duality that adversely affected both the performance capacity of Soviet political and economic institutions and the ethical values of Soviet society. The rational thing to do would have been to reject reliance on fiction-words altogether. This, however, would have posed a threat to the future of Soviet socialism, which relies on symbols and is itself an ideological symbol lacking real content.

In the second half of the 1980s the Soviet leadership embarked on a compromise course. It began to create words referring to a middle ground between fiction and reality. This is the origin of such terms as *perestroika*, *uskorenie*, *demokratizatsiya*, etc. What was new in them was not just their meaning, but also the underlying principle of their formation. They were not created out of thin air, but in conformity with the already existing semantic models borrowed either from entirely nonpolitical everyday life speech (*perestroika*, *uskorenie*, etc.), or from commonsense political concepts suitably narrowed and restricted in scope (*demokratizatsiya*, *novoe politicheskoe myshlenie*, etc.).

This mode of concept formation explains both the advantages and disadvantages of the neologisms noted above. On the disadvantage side, the meanings of the new terms tend to be indeterminate, poor in content. On the other side, however, being only partly fictions they allow actual processes or phenomena behind them to be discerned. Thus a new range of meanings, a "vocabulary of glasnost" originally emerged.

This new vocabulary has already begun to interact with the majority of words in the Soviet language in an intricate and even challenging manner. The former began to supersede the latter but also faced the prospect of ultimately being superseded by it. Time will provide the resolution of this historic contest that, far from being a merely linguisitic matter, reflects a major social struggle. Its outcome will show whether Gorbachev's *perestroika* will continue or will be curtailed by the same party apparat that previously succeeded in quashing the reforms of Gorbachev's predecessors, Khrushchev and Kosygin.

Meanwhile all is in flux in the Soviet Union, as the old blends with the new, the advanced with the retarded, the progressive with the conservative, pluralistic democracy which may be emergent with totalitarianism desperately clinging to the past. On the eve of the 1990s Soviet society lacks clear political contours or a stable social content. The Soviet language immediately responds to the overarching confusion. Terms are appearing and disappearing; meanings expand, contract or become altered otherwise. Much as this book aims at capturing lexical change throughout the period of turbulence, it cannot engage in missions impossible. Unlike most dictionaries, it cannot aspire to provide knowledge reasonably detached from historical moment, let alone to set historical semantic standards. It must be open to revisions which are certain to come with each turnabout in Soviet politics, economy, popular culture. It must not fear but indeed welcome invalidations of its contents contingent on social change as rapid as that in the USSR of Gorbachev's time. Accordingly, its readers, instead of expecting to find a body of knowledge frozen in time, will face an exacting task of critically determining, on the basis of their grasp of Soviet realities, which of its contents will have retained their validity and which will have stood in need to be revised.

The Dictionary

A

Absenteeism (*Progul*). Failure to appear at work without valid reason. Absenteeism is viewed as violation of work discipline subject to administrative sanctions. Penalties for absenteeism range from reprimand, transfer to a lower-paying job, denial of such benefits as bonuses, an extra month's salary paid once a year, summer vacation, allowances for length of service, etc. In cases of repeated absenteeism the absentee (*progul'shchik*) is subject to dismissal from work. In reality, however, highly skilled and not easily replaceable workers are treated with forbearance, even if they fail to appear at work for weeks on end due, for example, to heavy drinking. At the same time, the more expendable workers can be easily categorized as absentees and fired on the spot. Unexplained and repeated absenteeism is referred to as "willful" (*zlostny*) in contrast to absenteeism explicable on grounds of health or family problems, which is referred to as "forced" (*vynuzhdenny*).

Absenteeism is a grave and apparently insoluble social problem that stems from the absence of a work ethic, lack of incentives, and bad working conditions. From time to time campaigns are launched against absenteeism—with some Soviet leaders wanting to put an end to absenteeism, and others to get rid of the absentees. However, neither repeated condemnations of absenteeism nor punishment of the absentees—even by measures as severe as banishment from urban areas or imprisonment for parasitism (*tuneyadstvo*)—have had much effect. What is required here is drastic reorganization of the Soviet system of labor management and work incentives, and ultimately of the entire Socialist economy. Naturally, the Soviet leaders cannot agree to such measures, which would threaten to undermine the very foundation of their power.

Additional vacations for an uninterrupted record of work in the current year may be completely or partially denied to absentees from work: to those who absent themselves without valid reason, or who report to work intoxicated. (O dal'neyshem ukreplenii trudovoy distsipliny i sokrashchenii tekuchesti kadrov v narodnom khozyaystve [Ways to further consolidate working discipline and reduce personnel turnover in the national economy]: Resolution of the Central Committee of the CPSU, Council of Ministers of the USSR and All-Union Central Soviet of Trace Union, Izvestiya, 12 January 1980)

It is particularly difficult for a collective to work if it shuts its eyes to drunkards. As a rule drinking is responsible for their absenteeism and for disruptions of public order. (Agitator, no. 19, 1980, p. 25)

Acceleration (*Uskorenie*). A method and process of developing and improving the socialist system, offered as an alternative to its political and social stagnation. The strategy of acceleration concerns itself with both current problems and developmental goals for Soviet society (which are defined for the next fifteen years) as well as with the means by which development is to be pursued (the intensification of production, structural reform of the economy, and the implementation of effective forms of management). But this is not all. The essence of acceleration is conceived of in terms of reaching a higher quality of life, of profound changes in the character of labor, and of changes in material and spiritual values.

In historical perspective, acceleration is seen as a prerequisite for progress, which manifests itself in socio-economic development, particularly in transitions from earlier to more advanced stages of that development. Each successive stage of development releases more numerous and more powerful productive forces than those known to previous generations. This process has unfolded in Russia naturally and freely until it was first fettered and then paralyzed by the political and economic institutions of Soviet socialism. Then the contradictions and imbalances of that system became manifest as some branches of industry were developed at the expense of others and at the expense of the welfare of the masses. In the late 1970s Soviet economic development ground to a halt.

Disproving its slogan of the "historical law of progress," Soviet socialism was idling. This was due not to the immobilism or incompetence of Soviet leadership (bad administration merely aggravated the deeper social crisis) but rather to inherent features of the system itself. As a result of the dictatorship of the party, extreme centralization, and the command economy, Soviet society found itself in a bind. There was only one way out—to borrow Western methods of management and social organization. This historical shift, or drift, toward capitalistic practices in the USSR in the mid 1980s began with the ascent to power of Gorbachev and his cohorts.

However, Gorbachev's innovations are being carried out inconsistently, timidly, and, most importantly, within the institutional framework left over from a totalitarian society. The entire program of acceleration, its social goals and economic means, is based on the premise of building an "improved" socialism—the latest utopia in the endless succession of Soviet myths. The goal of acceleration is highly specific, even if not realistic: to win in the "historic" contest between the two competing systems of socialism and capitalism. Prerequisite for such a victory, however, would be the most impressive leaps forward in a number of respects: nothing less than doubling Soviet national income and industrial production and realizing an economic potential equal to that reached over the entire previous period of Soviet rule.

To reach goals of such scale, however, appropriate means have to be found. Acceleration relies on a combination of both direct and indirect methods of development. The direct means would entail the simple (which in fact would not at all be simple) establishment of order and discipline and of a sufficient (although it will never be sufficient) degree of organization of the production and labor processes. The indirect means of acceleration would include high rates of economic growth to be attained through a radical transformation of the existing material-technological base, which in turn would increase the production of high-quality goods sharply enough to meet the current aggregate demand.

A crucial implication of the concept of acceleration is the idea that the entire economic structure needs to be radically revamped. By means of perestroika (cf.) an attempt is being made to assess the performance of enterprises, not according to the resources they expend and their gross production output in rubles, but according to their actual contribution to the creation of national wealth. In this process, quantitative indicators of production output (in rubles) are to be replaced by indicators of its quality.

Theoretically, the Soviet leadership could effect certain economic achievements without resorting to mechanisms of a free market. One possible approach would require a reassignment of capital investment priorities from heavy, particularly military, industry to light industry, the production of consumer goods, and the expansion of the service sector. This would allow a significant increase in the salaries of both blue- and white-collar workers and a consequent increase in labor productivity. The discussed reassignment of priorities, however, would be possible only if the Soviet Union were to abandon its global ambitions, which is not yet in the cards. Thus, the bulk of the surplus continues to be invested in machine-building and in the development of the most up-to-date technology for missile production and electronic technology, i.e., in areas vital for the development of modern weaponry. Meanwhile, in light industry acceleration proceeds via minor managerial improvements and attempts to "raise the consciousness" of workers, but without additional resources invested.

The shift to radically new forms of economic development is marked by the present Soviet leaders' excessive caution and insufficient consistency. They reject the methods of acceleration applied by Stalin, like the use of forced labor and the merciless exploitation of the peasantry. But while rejecting Stalin's options they are nevertheless reluctant to do anything decisive to modernize production management out of fear of weakening the regime and undermining their own authority.

As could be expected, Gorbachev's rejection of the most backward forms of management, as well as personnel changes that brought in younger cadres, initially injected a degree of vitality into the country's economy. However, quite soon acceleration began to be stifled by the weight of interference from above, the continuing flow of government directives, and the binding centralized planning.

Limited changes thus far effected have not been sufficient to change the Soviet system. This, however, does not mean that changes within the system are impossible. Some of the reforms already carried out, like the introduction of self-employed labor and family contract-work brigades or the autonomization of enterprises, provide grounds for believing that acceleration will continue in the Soviet Union—at least for the next few years.

What do we mean by acceleration? First of all—increasing the rates of economic growth. But not only this alone. The essence of acceleration lies in the new quality of growth: intensification of production in all ways possible on the basis of scientific and technological progress, the structural reorganization of the economy, effective forms of management, organization and encouragement of labor. (M. S. Gorbachev, Materialy xxvii s"ezda Kommunisticheskoy partii Sovetskogo Soyuza (Materials of the twenty-seventh Congress of the Communist Party of the USSR) (Moscow: Izd. politicheskoy literatury, 1986, p. 21)

Under conditions of acceleration every Party functionary simply must be able to look ahead and boldly solve problems which only yesterday seems insoluble. (Kommunist, no. 17, 1986, p. 32)

Scientific and technological progress is the main way of advancing the innovative strategy of acceleration endorsed by the Party. (Kommunist, no. 14, 1986, p. 20)

Accepting decisions enthusiastically (*Voodushevlennye resheniyami*). A definition of the emotional response that the masses are obliged to display toward newly announced Soviet policies. The phrase implies social consensus, infallibility of the CPSU, and willing acceptance of its authority by the masses. The Soviet citizen has a duty to feel enthusiastic only about the decisions of the higher echelons of the party and government apparatus, such as the Politburo, Party Congresses, and government conferences. In regard to decisions made by city and regional bodies, the citizen does not need "to be enthusiastic," as long as he or she abides by them.

Similar to "enthusiastic" are: "inspired by" (*vdokhnovlenny*), "uplifted by" (*okrylenny*) and the more forceful term, "armed by" (*vooruzhenny*). Occasionally, the adjective "historic" (*istorichesky*) is added to create the phrase "accepting historic decisions enthusiastically" (*voodushevlennye istoricheskimi resheniyami*). The intention here is to stress the momentous character of the resolutions that mandatorily call for enthusiastic acceptance.

Soviet fighting men, enthusiastically accepting the decisions of the July Plenum of the Central Committee of the CPSU and the first session of the tenth convocation of the Supreme Soviet of the USSR, are tirelessly improving their training on land, sea and air. (Kommunist vooruzhennykh sil, no. 13, 1979, p. 3)

Enthusiastically accepting the decisions of the XXVI Congress of the CPSU, Moldavian writers will taken an even more active part in the noble work of Lenin's Party. (Literaturnaya gazeta, 29 April 1981, p. 2)

Enthusiastically accepting the decisions of the XXVI Congress of the CPSU, the Thirtieth Congress of the Communist Part of Azerbaijan, as well as the May and November 1982, and July 1983 Plena of the Central Committee of the CPSU, they are constantly increasing their contribution to the economic might and defense capability of the multi-national socialist Motherland. (Vyshka, 22 December 1983, p. 2)

Accomplishments (*Sversheniya*). Achievement of goals intended to perpetuate the Soviet system. The word "accomplishments" is used in reference to both exceptional deeds and quite ordinary events. The fulfillment of production targets and five-year plans, success in socialist competition, and the completion of construction of industrial installations, housing projects, and the like are all extolled as accomplishments. Moreover, Soviet propaganda never fails to stress that all accomplishments of the Soviet people (in fact their entire lives, in so far as they are based on these accomplishments) are possible only because of the infallible guidance provided by the party leadership in the pursuit of the "great purpose" (*velikaya tsel'*).

Accomplishments are spoken of in a variety of different contexts: "collective accomplishments" (*kollektivnye sversheniya*), "creative accomplishments" (*tvorcheskie sversheniya*), "accomplishments of the party and the people" (*sversheniya partii i naroda*), "accomplishments of the Soviet people" (*sversheniya sovetskogo naroda*), "accomplishments of the human spirit" (*sversheniya chelovecheskogo dukha*), and "accomplishments of our heroic reality" (*sversheniya nashey geroicheskoy deystvitel'nosti*). The lofty nature of all accomplishments is underscored by vivid attributes such as glorious, great, mighty, heroic, magnificent, historic, and supreme.

The figures testify to the scale of the current accomplishments of Kabardino-Balkaria. (Izvestiya, 1 September 1981, p. 3)

The present period in the history of our country is marked by significant events and great accomplishments. (Agitator, no. 19, 1983, p. 20)

Later, veterans try to keep in contact with the youngsters, and by encouragement and personal example stimulate them to accomplishments in their work. (Krasnaya zveda, 26 October 1983, p. 4)

Activist Attitude (*Aktivnaya zhiznennaya pozitsiya*). Participation in various social undertakings imposed on the Soviet citizen by communist morality and implying the "voluntary" assumption of greater responsibilities than required by conventional morality. Activist attitude is conceived of as internalized civic duty that implies disinterested service to the state and dynamic involvement in the production process or in efforts to educate others in conformity with the ideals and expectations of the Communist party.

The ideology of activist attitude and its concomitant ethics imply the relegation to secondary importance of all personal interests, dispositions, and concerns in favor of the implementation of programs and instructions of the party. In practice, activist attitude involves the traditional imperatives of Soviet ethics: idealism and loyalty, communist conscientiousness, civic responsibility and the priority of collective over individual interests. The only social role permitted is that of a fighter for communism or, what is essentially the same thing, of a champion of the policies of the communist leadership. All other roles (for example, that of a critic of totalitarianism or of Soviet society or advocate of reforms) are proscribed. Thus, the philosophy of activist attitude, while theoretically entailing a freedom of choice, in fact denies individuals the right to any choice.

As a concept, activist attitude gained currency after the Twenty-fifth Congress of the CPSU in 1976, which sought to halt the decline and degeneration of communist values. Mass consciousness had begun to reflect widespread indifference toward official ideology, apathy about public affairs, political skepticism, and disbelief in both the rationality and the humaneness of party policies.

The public apathy of people who had lost whatever illusions about communism and confidence in the Soviet system they might have once had was generally accompanied by a shift to private concerns and the wish to give short shrift to imposed social obligations.

Along with the political skepticism and apathy in various segments of society, there emerged an overt consumer psychology, expressing itself in acquisitiveness and an interest in comforts and amenities to be amassed by means both lawful and unlawful. However, in Soviet society only the ruling elite has the right to enjoy comforts and amenities. The interest of the Soviet man-on-the-street in improving his material well-being signals a danger to the regime, for it indicates the existence of dissatisfaction with the living standards of the whole society. Besides, the retreat to private concerns implies a certain emancipation from official doctrine.

If communist ideology is to maintain its hold over people's hearts and minds, it cannot afford even a mite of freedom. This is why official propaganda strives to hammer home the idea that the interests of the state come before personal happiness. It explains the current propaganda emphasis upon activist attitude and the recurrent fierce denunciations of any preoccupation with private affairs, which is portrayed as a manifestation of petty bourgeois egotism and individualism alien to communism.

Parallel to the rise of consumerist tendencies in the 1970s and especially in the 1980s, there has been a noticeable growth of social ferment, which has manifested itself in a search for independent social and moral values. Heterodox cultural and political initiatives have mushroomed; they include nationalist and religious movements as well as informal social groupings. Many Soviet people, particularly youth, became involved in types of activities that the regime regards as posing dangers to its very existence. Hence the frantic efforts of official propaganda to convince the Soviet people that there is room

for spiritual quest and moral choice within the existing system.

In this futile effort to combat the erosion of ideals and maintain faith in communism, uncritical acceptance of the party line, and social conformism, the authorities insist on preserving intact the whole body of rigid and increasingly outdated ideological tenets that have not proved reliable guides for human conduct, much less sources of inspiration. Ultimately, the advocacy of activist attitude is intended to conceal the striving of the authorities to maintain thought control, discredit all forms of dissent, and continue channeling the energies of their citizens into prescribed modes of activity.

> An activist attitude entails implacable opposition to the enemies of socialism and all deviations from the principles of Marxism-Leninism and proletarian internationalism. It is tempered in struggles against bourgeois and revisionist ideologies, remnants of individualist psychology, and forces opposed to communist morality. (Kommunist, no. 8, 1979, p. 28)

> Soviet citizens' knowledge of revolutionary theory and Party politics must be transformed into the activist attitude of fighters for Communism, ready to oppose all manifestations of alien ideology. . . . (Partiynaya zhizn' no. 10, 1979, p. 7)

Activist Ranks (*Aktiv*). Functionaries in state and public organizations who systematically and actively conduct propaganda work, disseminate communist ideology and carry out the social and economic policies of the party. Thousands of meetings of activist ranks are regularly held in the USSR in all possible types of units: party, Komsomol, trade union, and management. The most prestigious among these various kinds of activist ranks are those which operate in the party. Their role is to directly implement the decisions of Soviet authorities. The designation of party activist ranks is broad. Besides party functionaries, the category includes heads of state institutions, departments, and ministries, all of whom are obligatorily party members. Komsomol, trade union, and economic activist ranks consist of employees holding responsible positions.

In its nature the concept of activist ranks overlaps somewhat with that of nomenklatura, but is not identical with it, since many members of activist ranks do not enjoy the rights and privilege of the nomenklatura.

Activist ranks hold periodic meetings at which information is relayed on the resolutions adopted by various party organs. At these meetings, decisions are made on the basis of preset agendas and speeches are made only by prescripted speakers who invariably approve party resolutions and "voluntarily" accept the obligations assigned them. Meetings of the activist ranks have a superficial semblance of democracy, but they really follow a prearranged scenario for the enthusiastic approval of higher-level party decisions in solemn speeches, and for the distribution of responsibilities that really have been assigned in advance. The procedure of the meetings is strictly regulated: they have to follow one another in descending order of party and administrative competence, as each meeting is supposed to conclude with "unanimous approval" (*edinodushnoe odobrenie*) of decisions taken at one level upward in the party hierarchy. When the meetings of activist ranks are completed, there comes another chain of party meetings for reporting on the resolutions passed. The elevation of party activist ranks above other activist ranks and the preprogramming of the former provides the Soviet leadership with a convenient means of manipulating the party membership.

The innovators are those from among our Activist Ranks who place themselves at the crossroads of theory and practice. (Pravda, 11 may 1978, p. 2)

For the Party organizations of collective farms, for their Activist Ranks, and for their agitators it is imperative to improve the situation, to mobilize reserves, and to further increase farm output. (Agitator, no. 5, 1983, p. 18)

The Activist Ranks of agitators are called upon to elucidate in greater detail the opinions and the feelings held by the public. (Agitator, no. 22, 1983, p. 2)

Afghan (*Afganets*). A soldier who has fought in Afghanistan. The primary, most substantive meaning of the word is the veteran of the Afghan war. But it has a quite different secondary meaning. It refers to someone with an acutely developed sense of social justice, who is honest, resolute and capable of holding his own even in the face of extreme adversity. The connection is that it is presumed that only those with a highest moral fiber could have been sent to serve in Afghanistan in the first place. Those who come back from there are automatically regarded as epitomes of moral integrity.

The word *Afghan* was not always value-loaded. For some time, it simply referred to those who had fought in Afghanistan, and to nothing more than that. Gradually, however, it began to acquire a moral meaning, but quite different from the one currently advocated. The word then referred to a misfit, hardly able to control his temper, easily falling into trouble, prone to resort to violence or commit outrages.

Alarmed, the mass media tried to divert attention from such popular notions of the personal characteristics of an Afghan. The existence of a Soviet military "contingent" in Afghanistan, which, according to official version of things, was strictly "limited" in size, was no secret. This "contingent" was described in the most impersonal of phrases, as if it had no human attributes at all. In fact, it was mentioned as seldom as possible. The media stressed that the Afghan war was nothing more than a local conflict and that there was no reason to inflame people's passions by describing battles or dwelling upon the losses. It came to the point where dead soldiers were brought back home secretly and buried at night. Their graves were marked with a standard gray tombstone bearing the inscription "Fell in the Line of Duty . . . " without mentioning where and how.

It is not difficult to understand the Soviet government's motives for treating the Afghan war in such a low-key manner. The war dragged on for a long time, longer than the Great Patriotic War (i.e., World War II). Under these circumstances the question of why men were sent to their deaths had to be avoided at all costs. The nation was not prepared for this tragedy, which was exacting such a huge toll of killed and badly maimed.

The Soviet people had to be psychologically primed to accept the decision to go to war. The phrase "internationalist fighters" (*voiny-internatsionalisty*) was coined to glorify both the cause of the war and the motives of the soldiers fighting in it. It was supposed to explain why Soviet soldiers were fighting in the war (in response to an appeal by the Afghan nation), and to describe what they were doing there (fulfilling their international duty by defending the revolution). The whole concept, although perfectly orthodox from the ideological point of view, utterly failed to sway the public, the best proof being that soldiers on their way to Afghanistan were not given any kind of festive send-off nor accorded an honorific welcome when they returned. At best, they achieved recognition only after their deaths as those who had proved faithful to their oath of allegiance and had done their duty. They were pitied but not respected as had been their predecessors in 1945.

The talk about the "internationalist fighters," in a way intended to serve as a loose reminder of the "International Brigade" of volunteers who fought in Spain between 1936 and 1939, proved to be of no help to the soldiers' morale either. The opposite was true: the mental connection only served to weaken morale even further. People did remember, after all, that the war in Spain was a defensive one, against fascism. Compared to that, the war in Afghanistan was being waged against simple peasants. This prompted the propagandists to coin a new term for soldiers fighting in Afghanistan, the laconic but expressive *Afganets*. Immediately thereafter, efforts were mounted to give the newly created term inspiration content. Here, psychologists were put to work. Ever mindful of the "image," they began to expound on the supposedly "natural" traits of the Afghan. He was construed as a man who, after facing death and after experiencing true comradeship and real bravery, seeks perfection rather than acquiescing to ordinariness. When he returns home he finds a society unchanged: untroubled, complacent, pampered. As against such a society he who has come to know the highest meaning of life is different—demanding, determined, and uncompromising with his conscience. He and his army comrades are eager to change society, to make it more rational, just, and humane. The implication of all this runs that these soldiers, with their noble inclinations and pure aspirations, should not be alienated from society, however strange and disconcerting their behavior may be. Rather, they should be taken as a source of inspiration and emulated by others.

In this way, the veterans of the Afghan war have gradually come to bear the image of spiritual giants, endowed with uncommon moral qualities. The appearance has been created that, finally, the long-awaited new Soviet man had been found. In line with Soviet practice, this hero of our time was quickly granted suitable privileges. Their red or green certificate (red for the officers, green for ordinary soldiers: no equality in the Soviet army) give them automatic access to special shops where they can obtain a monthly order of foodstuffs, with the red certificate holders offered, to be sure, a wider choice of goods. Every five years they can buy furniture without signing up for it in advance; they can acquire living accommodations on favorable terms and are given preference over other candidates seeking admission to educational institutions. Afghan veterans also enjoy other, less material but more visible benefits: the right to an extra vacation pass and (once a year) a 50-percent rebate on a rail journey, as well as the right (envied by everyone else) to buy goods in shops without standing in the queue (cf.).

All in all, these privileges are paltry compared to the blood and years of his youth that the Afghan sacrificed, but Soviet citizens see them differently, for in a society that lacks everything, privileges are considered more important than human values. Thus, men will go to great lengths of deceit to pass themselves off as Afghans. They procure for themselves army shirts, buy medals, and forge the appropriate documents. The Soviet people still do not shower the Afghans with particular affection. But, in the typical spirit of Soviet socialism, they do envy the rights and privileges to which the Afghans are entitled. These, rather than the real or imaginary moral virtues, spur people to pretend to be Afghans. And they fail to realize that they have once again been deceived by the system. The crux of the matter is not that a real Afghan in no way resembles the propagandistic concoction about him, but that young men back from Afghanistan have to wait years before they find a job, gain admission to a school, or obtain an apartment. Here too, the realities of Soviet life are not what they are made out to be.

> For teenagers, the word "Afghan" is a by-word, the embodiment of bravery and prestige. (Literaturnaya gazeta, 3 August 1988, p. 11).

> All our trade-unions organizations, particularly the trade-union committees in factories, organizations and collective farms are obliged to do their utmost to ensure that "Afghans" are warmly welcomed into every workers' collective. (Pravda, 20 August 1988, p. 6)

> Now we have finally lifted the taboo from the subject of the "Afghans'" privileges. But what about those of the "Chernobylites"? (Izvestiya, 25 August 1988, p. 6)

Agitation (*Agitatsiya*). Ideological, moral, and psychological indoctrination designed to make people's minds and wills responsive and submissive to the policies of the Soviet leadership. The declared purposes of agitation are explanation and popularization of decisions made by the party apparatus and the government, and mobilization of the Soviet people for the fulfillment of predetermined social and economic goals. Agitation is intended to stimulate the population's productivity and its involvement in officially approved initiatives, and to subject the minds and behavior

of Soviet citizens to the control of the Communist party.

Agitation is accorded high priority in the Soviet Union. Its importance is stressed in many resolutions of the Central Committee of the CPSU. Ways and means of conducting it are constantly being refined and improved. There is even a specialized literature for "agitators" (*agitatory*) with specific information about the most up-to-date techniques. Characteristic of this literature is the monthly *Agitator* (The Agitator).

Agitation work (*agitatsionnaya rabota*) can be classified into three types: verbal agitation (*ustnaya agitatsiya*), which comprises meetings, talks, and radio and TV broadcasts; visual agitation (*naglyadnaya agitatsiya*), comprising slogans, posters, and charts; and written agitation (*pis'mennaya agitatsiya*) comprising special articles in newspapers, journals, and books.

Verbal agitation is designed to maintain constant direct contact between the agitator and the recipients of his ministrations and is conducted by groups of speakers who give their briefings or lectures to primary party cells and regional and district party organizations. One form of verbal agitation that began to be widely used in the 1970s is known as "tutoring" (*nastavnichestvo*) and consists of meetings of youth with "honored" party functionaries, military men, scientists, and creative artists. Traditional means of verbal agitation are so-called "oral journals" (*ustnye zhurnaly*), i.e., brief oral information about current events presented at work places, at meetings on the occasion of Soviet holidays, and special meetings in honor of winners of "socialist competitions."

The underlying task of the agitators is to extol communist principles and ideas, to glorify the Soviet way of life, to exhort people to live up to the proclaimed standards of communist morality, and to propagate the view that the communist way of life is right beyond any doubt, as well as to discredit capitalist mores and values. The official information agitators are provided with must be accepted by them in toto, as they have no right to analyze or comment on it, or to add to or subtract from it. Its content is set by party instructions.

In addition to his regular duties, the agitator is required to attend various conferences and conventions periodically convened for the purpose of explaining decisions adopted at party congresses and plenums; discussing the directives for the consecutive five-year plans; organizing agricultural work, etc. The agitator is responsible for the organization of commemoration ceremonies such as jubilees, state holidays, and "commemoration dates" (*znamenatel'nye daty*). He is also expected to deliver periodic lectures on communist values and give talks expounding the tenets of atheism.

Great importance is attached to the display of visual agitation such as banners, slogans, posters, and boards of honor (*doska pocheta*). It is considered indispensable for virtually every street in every town, village, or settlement throughout the Soviet Union to be thus adorned. The portraits of Lenin and the current members and candidate members of the Politburo, for example, are considered requisite ornaments of every Soviet industrial or agricultural enterprise, office, and army headquarters.

For all the importance of verbal and visual agitation as a means of influence, highest priority is assigned to written agitation. This form of agitation gains wide circulation through the press, fiction, scientific publications, and even children's literature. Every type of publication contains the obligatory dose of agitation. Depending on the mentality, tastes and educational level of the expected readers, this may consist of ideological exhortation, quotations from the "founders of scientific communism," or thoughts or aphorisms of Soviet leaders. Similarly on this basis, the limits of what is permitted and acceptable to print about Soviet realities are also determined in advance. From the cradle (in nursery schools) almost to the grave (in the pensioners' clubs), the Soviet citizen is constantly exposed to one or another kind of "agitation campaign." Such thorough indoctrination does have some effect, but, being stereotypical and devoid of

all originality, it rarely succeeds completely. Instead of increasing public activism, overexposure to the sloganeering of agitation often results in inertia and passivity. Instead of strengthening communist belief, it breeds skepticism and alienation.

Despite all its failures, however, agitation is an effective tool of ideological and political manipulation of the masses, contributing to a certain extent to the stability of the regime by promoting stereotypical patterns of both public and private behavior.

Much concern was expressed at the Congress about underestimating such an effective tool as verbal political Agitation, which (unfortunately) often lacks specificity and a fighting spirit. (Pravda, 1 February 1982, p. 2)

Posters are widely used in verbal propaganda and Agitation. (The Agitator, no. 20, 1983, p. 59)

Visual Agitation at harvest time must be militant, concrete, and to the point. (Agitator, no. 14, 1983, p. 32)

Anonymous Letter (*Anonimnoe pis'mo*; colloquial variant *Anonimka*). Denunciation or complaint addressed to party or state authorities or some public institution without the signature and address of the sender. As a social phenomenon anonymous letters were a frequent occurrence in the USSR during the period of mass political terror. These were the years when physical destruction of the opposition and prosecutions of "enemies of the people" (*vragi naroda*) helped Stalin consolidate his dictatorship. Bloody "purges" accompanied by constant appeals for "vigilance" and the eradication of complacency in the struggle against wreckers (saboteurs), spies, and "internal" counterrevolution created throughout the entire country an atmosphere of mistrust and suspicion. Many Soviet citizens in constant turmoil over the threat to their freedom and their lives, turned to informing as a means of self-preservation by proving their "reliability." They were no more amoral in their attitude toward society than society was toward them. Informing was then extolled as a "moral duty" of the Soviet citizen.

Anonymous letters were written not only by those who retained their belief in the rectitude and infallibility of communist ideals but also by those who, by victimizing as many others as possible, hoped to stay safe; and by those who were seeking revenge against personal enemies among their acquaintances and colleagues.

Anonymity protected the informers not only from the vengeance of friends or relatives of those whom the letter victimized but also from the charge of complicity with the "disloyal elements" on whom they were informing. The latter precaution was not superfluous, since state security organs viewed all citizens as potential criminals. The method the state security organs used consisted in first selecting their victims, and only later accusing them of crimes which, although invented, were supposed to "fit" the criminal. It was this practice that gave rise to the revealing saying: "Let us first have the man—the appropriate clause of the law can always be found later."

The work of the security services was meticulously planned. Lists of those to be arrested were compiled, along with deadlines. In accordance with procedures accepted in the Soviet economy, the set quotas of victims had to be outstripped ("overfulfilled") in practice. Moreover, the quotas had to grow: each month more people had to be arrested than the previous month. The implementation of these targets for arresting "enemies of the people" depended to a great extent on the number of anonymous letters received. The latter were considered sufficient grounds for indictment and were used as evidence of the "crime." The campaign of mass denunciation permitted the Soviet authorities to divide the entire population into those who were already in detention and those who might be detained in the future. It was immaterial whether a crime had actually been committed or not and, if so, by whom; it was also immaterial whether the punishment fitted the crime. All that mattered was to produce a sense of diffuse guilt toward the state and to permeate the consciousness of the entire population with this feeling. As soon as a new twist of the general line or a political reorganization began, the state security organs would receive a flood of anonymous letters and would proceed to mass arrests on the grounds of "information" they contained. The practice of anonymous letters reveals that indifference, unprincipledness, corruption, career-mindedness, and sheer venality affected all strata of Soviet society from top to bottom.

Since Stalin's death, in the 1950s and especially the 1960s anonymous letters have been less considered as evidence of guilt. They were, however, for many years still used by the authorities as grounds for opening criminal investigations. Anonymous letters persist as a social phenomenon that the communist regime once generated and still encourages. The intensity of this phenomenon varies from one historical stage in the development of the Soviet state to another and is related to various propaganda campaigns, like the "struggle against drunkenness," or against "hoodwinking," or the campaigns against infringement of "socialist legality" and for work discipline and the like.

Soviet propaganda tends to attribute the institution of anonymous letters to the presence of some (allegedly sporadic) cases of malfunctioning work collectives, whose malfunctions tend in turn to be attributed to insufficient indoctrination, the weakness of a local party organization, etc. Actually, the very existence of anonymous letters proves that something is wrong with the very structure of communist society. The absence of opportunities for independent public expression for democracy and the unlimited and uncontrolled power of the bureaucratic apparatus are responsible for the emergence of very peculiar individual adaptations to the totalitarian system or individual defenses against the system. Anonymous letters are merely one of such peculiar adaptations.

Anonymous letters are convenient for, and probably indispensable to, the authorities. Information about concealed aspects of citizens' activities compels the appropriate organizations to adopt from time to time certain corrective measures aimed at the elimination of the shortcomings. Thus additional opportunities were created for manipulating popular consciousness: from time to time certain steps would be taken to remove particularly egregious abuses so as to show that the party was concerned about the people. However, with the passage of time the surfeit of anonymous "creative writing" began to prove embarrassing. For one thing, the lives of millions of people were poisoned; for another—which from the point of view of the authorities was even more important—the content of the anonymous letters paralyzed the activity of the administrative organs, resulting in a tremendous waste of their time and resources. Most importantly, however, encouragement of anonymous letters did not square with the policies of Gorbachev.

Such were the disadvantages of anonymous informing. Thus in February 1988 the presidium of the Supreme Soviet of the USSR declared that "complaints against people and citizens' proposals [to investigate or prosecute others] presented in the form of anonymous letters would not be considered by the authorities." Nevertheless, the system of anonymous denunciation does have permanent value for the Soviet authorities. It permits them to keep society constantly under surveillance, provides them with important information about the moods and private lives of people and helps them keep everything under control. Thus there is room for skepticism about how long the Soviet regime will deny itself the advantages of anonymous letters, especially since the latter add hosts of volunteers to the ranks of professional informers.

But for the authors of anonymous letters, victory is not the triumph of justice, or even of elementary decency. (Bakinsky rabochy, 13 August 1980, p. 2)

Furthermore, he had done vile things even before: he had written an anonymous letter about a college friend. (Pravda, 28 December 1983, p. 3)

Upon checking, in a majority of cases the facts cited in anonymous letters are not corroborated and this rebounds against those who write such letters. (Bakinsky rabochy, 4 February 1984, p. 4)

Anti-Alcohol Campaign (*Antialkogol'ny kurs*). Policy comprising legal enactments and practical measures aimed at the eradication of alcohol abuse. The current anti–alcohol campaign had a precedent in the pre-revolutionary period, during the introduction of the "wine concession," when the Russian government established a monopoly on the retail sale of alcoholic beverages. The pertinent law of 1895, however, did not lead to a decline in alcoholism. On the contrary, it led to the proliferation of new wine stores and inns by the thousands and to drunkenness on a mass scale that was difficult to control. The essence of the problem lay not in some national propensity of the Russians for vodka but in the greed of the government, which received fantastic sums—up to a fourth of all its revenues—from the sale of alcohol.

The educated classes, primarily the intelligentsia and the clergy, very quickly understood the drastic consequences of the alcohol revenues for social welfare and launched the first anti–alcohol campaign in Russia, which led to the convocation in 1910 of the first anti–alcohol congress. Public protest against the alcohol monopoly influenced the tsarist government to enact the prohibition (the so-called "dry law" of 1914) initially intended for the mobilization period only, but subsequently extended for the duration of the war. Forced sobriety was therefore due to the special circumstances of wartime. Once enacted, however, it had the quite unforeseen consequences of stimulating higher labor productivity and better family relations. Gradually life style began to change as well: hooliganism declined, "thirst" for education was whetted, and new, "dry" customs began to be observed at weddings, funerals, baptisms, etc.

However, the authorities proved to be inconsistent and gradually began to retreat from their uncompromising stand. First beer was permitted, then some low-proof wines. Such relaxations were dictated by economic considerations: the state treasury was depleted without revenues from alcohol sales. The Bolsheviks keenly recognized this fact of economic life, and consequently, after seizing power, began to gradually get rid of prohibition. Initially, they proceeded cautiously and without consistency, since party circles were still mindful of how the classics of Marxism had anticipated that once the proletariat became liberated it would no longer need to poison and drug itself with alcohol. But once secure with the sense of power resting firmly in their hands, the communists began to act more resolutely. In 1923 half-strength (20 percent alcohol) vodka was back on sale, while one year later the state monopoly on the sale of alcoholic beverages was officially enacted. However, the Soviet authorities found it advisable to guard their "revolutionary" profile, and toward that end they justified this compromise with their principles in terms of imperatives of the international situation. A dilemma was contrived: was it preferable to fall into bondage to foreign capital or to avoid that fate by repealing the ban on vodka? In the name of "building a bright future," the communists chose the latter alternative, preferring, as Stalin put it, "to soil oneself for a while in filth." The "while" however, lasted a full sixty years—until Andropov became general secretary.

The real reason for pushing the sales of alcohol was not to be sought, of course, in any fear of international capital, but rather in the inability of the Soviet authorities to provide a decent life for Soviet citizens. In order to suppress civil unrest, the communists found alcohol handy as a means of dulling the populace's wits and stifling its criticism. Since it is easier to manipulate the masses when they are not sober, drinking sprees were found preferable to rebellions. The Soviet authorities created an atmosphere of tolerance for inebriates, even of sympathy with them. The use of alcohol became the obligatory feature of many social activities. Drinking became a pattern of Soviet culture.

Gradually alcohol became a prime budget item: urban families spent up to half of their earnings on it, while their rural counterparts up to one third. People drank to escape from their stupefying work, to become oblivious to social inequalities, to distract themselves from the burdens of daily life. Vodka blocked out the oppressive feelings caused by constant exhaustion, poor nutrition, and uncertainty about the future.

Soon the USSR gained the dubious distinction of having the highest consumption of alcohol per capita in the world. The Soviet Union now consumes three billion liters of vodka annually, which amounts to a per capita (children counted) quota of over eleven liters. This is fifteen times more than was consumed in prerevolutionary Russia, and five times more than in the United States or England. Even this figure, however, has to be qualified, as it covers only the consumption of state-manufactured alcohol. In reality, a considerable amount of the alcohol consumed comes from the black market (cf.) via a widespread network of "moonshiners." Real consumption is therefore higher than cited, but it is impossible to estimate how much higher.

As a consequence of intemperate drinking, the Soviet rates of infants with either physical or mental birth defects grew from nine per 1,000 births in 1972 to eleven in 1976, thirteen in 1981, and fifteen in 1986. No less devastating were the effects of alcohol on the family, "the main cell of Soviet society." In 1965 there were twenty divorces per 100 marriages; twenty years later the figure had risen to thirty-five. Of these, two thirds were related to alcoholism.

The most recent Soviet anti–alcohol campaign might have been a relative success if it had been carried out seriously and conscientiously. However, the anti–alcohol campaign is one of those characteristically Soviet ventures that tend to develop into absurdities when put into practice. After the bureaucracy launched this campaign, varieties of vineyards were destroyed, rare vines cultivated for decades were burned out, while grapes remained an unaffordable luxury for most Soviet citizens.

Another anomaly of the anti–alcohol campaigns were the huge lines in front of liquor outlets that involved an incredible waste of everybody's time, either the work time of those who skipped their jobs or the free time of others—both alcoholics and simply those who wanted to celebrate a holiday or another occasion with the traditional bottle of wine. Yet, despite all the propaganda to the contrary, the amount of alcohol available has not declined as the shortfall in official production is more than made up for by privately produced "home-brew." One side effect is the shortage of sugar on the market as vast amounts of it are cornered by moonshiners for their industry.

The "rhythm" or frequency of drinking determines the Soviet man's alcoholic demands and defines the category to which he or she belongs in respect to alcoholic consumption. The first category is that of "table consumption," under the pretext of whetting the appetite. The representatives of this category are largely members of the communist ruling class—the party and state bureaucracy and the artistic elite. The second category is the "social" or "ceremonial drinkers" whose philosophy is: "everyone else is drinking, I'll drink too." Such an approach is characteristic of broad segments of the intelligentsia. A third category of drinkers are attracted to the psychotropic properties of alcohol, to its numbing capacity, to its power to distract from life's troubles. This category is largely comprised of workers and peasants, although representatives of other social groups may also find themselves in this category.

Each of the listed modes of drinking has its social function and value. "Table consumption" is an inevitable feature of official receptions and banquets. "Ceremonial drinking" marks the celebration of the conclusion of a contract, the assumption of a new job, the receipt of a prize, the successful defense of a dissertation, etc.

"Psychotropic drinking," indulged in so as to forget one's woes, was thought to be an outlet that allowed citizens to while away free time in a social activity that posed no threat to the regime. People under the influence of alcohol tend to socialize, and inebriation prompts them to speak somewhat more freely than usual and to confide their usually "bottled up" thoughts. Finally, in the Soviet Union alcoholic beverages serve as a universal means of barter in exchange for favors rendered: a bottle serves as a recompense for after-hours work someone does privately for someone else or for services one receives "under the table."

Only gradually did the realization dawn on the authorities that widespread drinking harmed not only the health of individuals (this was hardly news), but also the Soviet system as a whole—as it contributed to the decline of interpersonal relations, industrial production, the birthrate, and life expectancy. As these conditions became aggravated, sporadic ventures in anti–alcohol campaigns were undertaken, which gathered and then ran out of steam. Stalin did not want to admit the existence of alcoholism because it would have contradicted the facade of happiness that covered the realities of his grim rule. Khruschev, in contrast, both recognized the problem and the danger that alcoholism posed to social cohesion, and he advocated several remedial measures, some at the beginning and others at the end of his rule. His successor, Brezhnev, could never really decide whether drinking or abstention from it was more advantageous to the system. Hence, he simultaneously encouraged the masses to drink and launched an anti–alcohol campaign in which he had little success (as in much else of what he did). Brezhnev neither gained pubic sympathy for the anti–alcohol cause, nor did he succeed in coining any memorable slogans for this purpose.

It took Andropov to fully recognize the extent of the calamity on a nationwide scale. The former KGB head resolved to fight it in his own way, dictated by his own views and experience: via formal administrative methods, backed by threats, sanctions, and punishments. He was prepared to apply the same punitive measures to sick individuals whose alcoholism required treatment (and whose right to receive treatment was guaranteed by law) as to the drinkers who committed crimes while "under the influence" (as if the criminal law were not enough to curb them) and those who just liked to get drunk without doing anything antisocial or unlawful. Early death, however, prevented Andropov from doing what he wanted to do to all drinkers alike.

Gorbachev is approaching the problem of alcoholism differently. He understands that this problem stems from specific socioeconomic causes that he traces to stagnation inherited from the past. Glasnost (cf.) has made it possible for him to admit that drinking in the Soviet Union fulfills the latent function of helping individuals adapt to society. In accordance with this diagnosis, a composite remedial strategy was adopted, aiming at radical transformations. A series of important organizational measures and special resolutions was adopted concerning the struggle against alcoholism. These resolutions sharply attacked the entrenched and custom-backed patterns of social interaction prevalent in the country. Still, conditions do not yet appear to be ripe for the eradication of alcoholism: the public, for so long the passive object of successive legislative fiats, is not inclined to actively participate in the state-sponsored campaigns. To encourage genuine popular participation, the entire power system and patterns of mainstream culture need to be radically overhauled. This, however, cannot be done within the framework of Soviet socialism, and whatever the revolutionary slogans of the new Soviet leadership, it is not ready to discard socialism. Thus it has begun to substitute propagandistic efforts for a real, effective campaign. As a result, the vital matter of the current anti-alcohol campaign is beginning to founder and run aground amidst numerous bureaucratic initiatives (the most publicized of which are the anti-alcohol clubs and "sober societies" that have already enrolled in their ranks millions of people) and exhortations expressed in such slogans as "Tea Instead of Vodka," "Put Down the Glass," "Alcohol Is as Deadly as a Bullet," etc.

Meanwhile the Soviet public, with its feelings of being no more than cogs in a political machine, has heard many unfulfilled promises and consequently retains little faith in them. It would thus be no wonder to find Soviet citizens standing in long lines in front of wine stores muttering bitterly, "For decades they have been turning us into drunkards and now they won't let us have a drink to relieve our hangover."

> For more than two years we have been waging a struggle against drinking and alcoholism. But recently private distilling of liquor has posed a grave threat to the anti-alcohol campaign. (Pravda Ukrainy, 27 December 1987, p. 2)

> Basically the moonshiner is issuing a brazen challenge to the anti-alcohol campaign, in his search for self-enrichment he causes great economic and moral damage. (Agitator, no. 14, 1987, p. 40)

> Make no mistake: in the anti-alcohol movement [i.e., campaign] there is still much paper shuffling and many attempts to produce impressive figures. (Pravda, 11 January 1988, p. 3)

> The struggle against drinking and alcoholism has grown into a mass movement for a healthy, sober way of life. (Agitator, no. 23, 1987, p. 24)

Anticommunism (*Antikommunizm*). The totality of doctrines and consequent policies incompatible with the Communist world view and Soviet interests. Quite diverse and mutually incompatible ideas and ideological orientations are referred to by this term. For example, any critical analysis of the theoretical heritage of Lenin which refuses to accept the claim that this heritage constitutes the only and perpetually valid explanation and resolution of all fundamental social issues will be pronounced anticommunist. The same is true for economic theories which either reveal how out-of-date and inappropriate is the Marxist approach to the solution of problems of developed industrial society or which demonstrate that a system of state administration like the Soviet one cannot be efficient. The anticommunist label will also be pinned on all ethical and religious teachings which point out the fundamental inhuman nature of Soviet totalitarianism. Any political or social activity against the establishment of new Communist regimes is referred to as anticommunist as well. Finally, any opposition to various communist-dominated movements, such as "national liberation movements," "peace campaigns," and "disarmament movements," as well as any manifestation of nationalism, is also declared to be anticommunist.

The Soviet rejection of anticommunism, and of all independent thought in general, reflects the regime's fears of any criticism, and its desire to isolate the Soviet people from any foreign, in particular Western, influences and attractions.

The term anticommunism is often modified by adjectives such as "unprincipled" (*besprintsipny*), "rabid" (*makhrovy*), and "frenzied" (*ogoltely*). Such adjectives help brand manifestations of anticommunism as embodiments of reaction, obscurantism, and inhumanity. The ideals of classical Marxism are constantly referred to in order further to discredit any criticism of the Soviet regime and to automatically link anticommunism with imperialism, fascism, Zionism, etc.

Soviet propaganda attempts to impress upon the masses that their well-being, as well as national security and stability necessitate continuous resistance to and rejection of anticommunist propaganda (*antikommunisticheskaya propaganda*) and activity. This enables the Communist party to present itself as the savior of the nation. The supposed necessity to fight anticommunism has served and continues to serve also as a convenient apologia for the arbitrariness of the regime. The struggle against anticommunism is conducted not only on the ideological plane but also in relation to the leadership's policies toward its own population. Any disagreement with the leadership can be conveniently dismissed as a manifestation of anticommunist consciousness and dealt with

accordingly. Thus fear of anticommunism which affects the entire Soviet world view testifies to the inability of the Communist leadership to create a viable alternative to democracy, its spiritual values and social praxis.

Anti-Sovietism and anti-Communism have been transformed into instruments of heating up the arms race, into weapons directed not only against the USSR and other countries of the Socialist community, not only against Communists, but also against all opponents of war, peace-loving forces, into means of subverting detente. (Partiynaya zhizn', no. 13, 1980, pp 8–9)

We must be uncompromising in the struggle of ideas, actively unmask anti-Sovietism and (anti-Communism, decisively oppose any traces of alien views. (Literaturnaya gazeta, 22 April 1981, p. 1)

The policy of anti-Communism is doomed to failure. (Pariynaya zhizn', no. 11, 1983, p. 72)

Anti-Semitism (*Antisemitizm*). National and racial intolerance toward Jews proclaimed by communist ideology to be one of the methods used by the "exploiting classes" in their struggle against revolutionary movements. In accordance with such an understanding of anti-Semitism one must gain the impression that the social and political basis for anti-Semitism has been completely eradicated in the Soviet Union. The reality is quite different, much less clear-cut and categorical. After the October Revolution, Jews were officially granted equal rights with other nationalities. Legal restrictions placed on them by the tsarist government were abolished, together with the Pale of Settlement (restricted area of residence), and quotas for entry into professions and into educational institutions. During the first years of communist rule, the attack on Judaism as a religion was not perceived as a manifestation of anti-Semitism, but rather as a part of the general struggle against religious worship and belief.

Moreover, Soviet leaders, then intent on fomenting world revolution, took a strong stand against popular anti-Semitism. As the Soviet regime lacked support among the

Russian intelligentsia, it had an interest in attracting to its fold assimilated Jews who culturally were already remote from their Jewish origins. Although the vast majority of observant Jews did not take part in the Communist coup and were even hostile to it, many assimilated Jews supported the new regime enthusiastically and actively. By 1922 the latter comprised more than 5 percent of the Communist party membership and more than 26 percent of the party's Central Committee. Some of the most important power positions in the country were held by Jews: Trotsky was head of the Red Army and second only to Lenin, Sverdlov was chairman of the Soviet State, Zinoviev was chairman of the Communist International (*Komintern*) and governor of Petrograd, and Kamenev was Lenin's deputy in the Soviet of People's Commissars (*Sovnarkom*).

These facts were more than sufficient to inflame anti-Semitic passions in Russia, a country where anti-Semitism was already a centuries-old tradition. Anti-Semitism grew in the USSR, over and beyond the forms it had assumed in prerevolutionary Russia.

The official anti-Semitism of tsarist Russia expressed itself in regulations: it precisely defined the rights and obligations of the Jews. Quotas for high school and university entrance, the Pale of Settlement—all such restrictions undoubtedly humiliated the Jewish population, and limited the possibilities of Jewish national self-expression, but did not necessarily lead to the destruction of Jewish culture or forced denial of national identity. Nor were such measures racist. Conversion to Christianity would to a significant degree open otherwise foreclosed options: an ex-Jew could become an officer, gain the right to own land, etc.

Neither party membership nor renunciation of Jewish religion protects Jews in the Soviet Union from discrimination. Many educational institutions of the Soviet Union remain closed to them (the Institute of Foreign Relations, the Diplomatic Academy, the Institute of Foreign Trade) while in others there is a tacit, but effective quota for Jews. Similarly there exist quotas limiting the number of Jews who can be appointed to top posts.

From the 1920s onward, the growth of anti-Semitism became apparent against the background of the rapid integration of the Jews into Soviet society and the hardships experienced by the population in the process of the "building of a Communist society." In the eyes of the lower classes, hunger, deprivations, political repression, and the breakdown of traditional patterns of life were all attributable to Jew-Bolsheviks. The active participation of Jewish businessmen in ventures of the New Economic Policy added to the existing hostility against Jews. The Jew came again to be identified in the Russian and Ukrainian consciousness with the money lender, the merchant, and the tradesman. The employment of a considerable number of the Jews in the governmental and economic bodies was interpreted as evidence that the Jews alone had gained from the revolution. The influx of Jews into educational institutions, science, technology, and industry was seen as proof that economic and public life were dominated by them. When communist domestic policies led to forced collectivization, Chekist repression of "class enemies" (*klassovye vragi*), and rural policies that brought famine to the Ukraine, Kazakhstan, and the Volga region, hatred was generated against the Jews (some of whom were indeed involved in these policies) who were perceived as a whole as supporting and implementing them.

The rising anti-Semitism worried the authorities and forced them to explain to the masses that it was incompatible with the principles of communist internationalism. A special law was even enacted instituting penalties for anti-Semitism. However, in the 1930s and 1940s this struggle against anti-Semitism slackened. Even earlier, at the Fourteenth Party Congress (near the end of 1925), Stalin had dealt Jewish communists a severe blow by removing from leadership the entire Jewish faction of Trotsky, Zinoviev, and Kamenev. At that time, however, this was not considered as an anti-Jewish step. What was stressed rather was the intraparty opposition and the ideological nature of the struggle against it. After Hitler came to power, Stalin, anticipating the possibility of a military confrontation with Germany, did not wish to alienate the Jewish world. Thus, the dismissals of Jews from the upper echelons of power were not succeeded by such dismissals at the lower levels. In the years before World War II Jews still occupied many important positions in the government, for example as members of the Board of People's Commissars (*narkomaty*) and as members of the Central Inspection Commission.

The origins of the first great wave of official Soviet anti-Semitism are traceable to the Nazi-Soviet pact of 1939. Nazi anti-Semitism and the Nazi measures against the Jews ceased to be mentioned in the Soviet press from the signing of the pact until the German attack on the USSR in June 1941. From the German invasion onward, strongly nationalistic attitudes began to appear and grow in the Soviet Union, like the widely propagandized official notion of the superiority of the Russians over other peoples. These tendencies provided fertile ground for the growth of anti-Semitism, and it was at this time that the abolition of the Jewish educational system took place, along with massive repression of the Jewish religious intelligentsia.

After World War II, anti-Semitic sentiments were no longer voiced only by the lower classes. They became a component of official ideology. From being merely a "relic of the pre-revolutionary past," anti-Semitism became part and parcel of Stalin's nationality policy. In 1948 all Jewish organizations, theaters, and publishing houses were closed down, while leading Jewish cultural figures were subject to persecution and eventually shot. In 1949 a campaign was unleashed in the USSR to expel "cosmopolitans" (*kosmopolity*)—80 percent of whom were Jews—from the party and banish them from public and scientific life. Measures limiting employment of Jews and access of Jews to institutions of higher education were adopted and with time stiffened. The decisions of the party apparatus to enforce these measures were never openly publicized but were brought to the attention of executive agencies only through internal channels: classified communications, instructions, and special "trust" talks. Stalin began to conceive a scheme for the complete extermination of the Jews. The outcome was the "Doctors' Plot" of 1953. Nine doctors, six

of them Jews, were arrested and charged with conspiring against the state and premeditated murder of party leaders. People were incited against the Jews. The direction of the "wrath of the people" against the Jews for being guilty of all the failures of the regime and all the deprivations of the postwar years was designed as a safety valve to channel popular disaffections toward a safe outlet. The death of Stalin halted plans to deport the Jews to the Far East and Siberia but did not lead to their public rehabilitation. Anti-Jewish restrictions in employment and in enrollment in institutions of higher education were maintained. Jewish schools, theaters, and publishing houses were not reopened.

In the early 1960s, numerous trials for "economic crimes" (*ekonomicheskie protsessy*) were held and widely publicized in the press. Jews were not the only or chief ones charged with illicit business practices, but Soviet propaganda used their presence among the defendants to inflame existing anti-Semitic sentiments. The papers printed satirical commentaries and cartoons depicting Jews as mischievous plunderers of state property, economic wreckers, speculators, bribe-takers, and "currency dealers" (*valyutchiki*).

After Israel's victory in the Six-Day War, the Soviet authorities began methodically to spread anti-Israel propaganda that was eagerly swallowed by the adherents of traditional Russian anti-Semitism. Soviet newspapers, radio, and television unleashed violent verbal attacks on "world Zionism." The Soviet public was systematically encouraged to associate Zionism in the USSR with heterodoxy, dissidence, and anti-Sovietism. Quite often the "enemy," domestic and foreign alike, was depicted as a "Zionist": an accomplice of imperialism and a spreader of ideological corruption.

The intriguing question is what makes Soviet anti-Semitism persist at a time when official anti-Semitism has virtually vanished from all civilized countries? As has been noted, the party eagerly used the Jews in the early period of the communist regime when the shortage of qualified cadres for economic, party, and government administration was acute. Educated Jewish masses which at that time were already largely remote from Jewish traditions constituted a non-negligible base of social support for the new regime. Subsequently during the period of Stalin's terror communist cadres appeared eager for personal advancement, positions of prestige and power had to be vacated for them. Anti-Semitism thus became a convenient (and also popular) instrument of Stalin's purges. In the process it turned out, however, that the Bolsheviks had not entirely succeeded in eradicating the Jewish propensity for dissent and insubordination. Jews turned out to comprise a significant proportion among the numerous opposition groups which attempted to oppose Stalin's tyranny. The price they paid for it was their gradual but firm ejection from the power apparatus. In the process, the communists realized that anti-semitism was a convenient ideological lightning rod. It was not possible to grant political rights to peoples when all political rights were in the hands of the party. Granting any freedoms could only breach the party's monopoly of power and thus spell danger to the regime's very existence. Also, rigid planning and centralized administration of the economy stymied all hopes of abundance. In this situation, the Jews could serve as convenient scapegoats. By appealing to base instincts and prejudices of anti-Semitism, the authorities attempted to stifle mass discontent. Compared with the debasement of the Jews, the denial of rights to other Soviet peoples did not appear quite so blatant.

The combination of rabid anti-Semitism in practice, despite official denials of its existence and any causes for it, along with strident anti-Zionist propaganda, which clearly included all Soviet Jews as its target, contributed to the reawakening of a national consciousness among Soviet Jews. The Jewish protest movement expressed itself in attempts to study Jewish culture and history and in the struggle for the right to emigrate to Israel. The ensuing Jewish emigration, however, led to a new upsurge in anti-Semitism among the chauvinist masses, who were outraged by the sight of Soviet citizens renouncing their allegiance to the country where they were born and educated.

With the ascent of Gorbachev to power a change occurred. Official anti-Semitic tendencies began to be somewhat muffled: in the press one could read about the contributions of the Jews to the nation's culture, science, and economy. Yet the popular anti-Semitism, which had previously been held in check, made its presence felt even more forcefully than before. By permitting a modicum of free speech, glasnost also permitted expressions of anti-Semitic prejudice. Hence blaming the Jews for aiming at world domination and trampling upon the ideals of the Revolution can now be heard. Overall, anti-Semitism has therefore not been reduced in the USSR. As previously, it serves the country's leadership equally in the pursuit of its domestic and foreign policy objectives. On the domestic scene, it helps channel the dissatisfaction of the masses away from the authorities to a traditional scapegoat that the party is not loath to victimize. In terms of foreign policy, the strident campaign against Zionism helps fortify Soviet influence in the Arab countries.

At the same time as previously, the Jewish interest in emigrating from the USSR that has been sparked by Soviet anti-Semitism means that the granting or denying of exit visas to Jews can be used as a bargaining chip to win trade concessions from the West.

Anti-Semitism serves exploiters like a lightning conductor, rescuing capitalists from the wrath of the working masses. Anti-Semitism is dangerous for the working masses as it represents a false path, guiding them away from the right road and leading them into the jungle. Therefore, Communists, as consistent internationalists, cannot fail to be the implacable and sworn enemies of anti-Semitism.

Anti-Semitism is severely punished in the USSR as a manifestation that is deeply hostile to the Soviet system. (From Y. V. Stalin's reply of 12 January 1931 to the Jewish Telegraphic Agency's question from America, in V. M. Molotov, Konstitutsiya sotsializma [The constitution of socialism]; Moscow, 1936, p. 27)

The real state of affairs totally refutes Western propaganda's slander that official anti-Semitism exists in the Soviet Union. (Novoe vremya, no. 46, 1983, p. 26)

Unforunately, in the recent writings of some

Soviet authors criticism of Zionism has not always conformed to the class point of view. Scientific analysis has been replaced by ambiguous inuendos, with the terms "Jew" and "Zionist" often confused. Anti-Semitism and its social roots in a number of such publications have been passed over in silence or not properly described. (Ogonek, no. 23, 1988, p. 7)

Anti-Sovietism (*Antisovetizm*). An ideology or activity incompatible with the political stance and social goals of the Kremlin. Within a philosophical framework, anti-Sovietism represents a form of class struggle, directed against the economic and social foundations of the Soviet state as well as against its morals and culture. As interpreted by the Soviets, anti-Sovietism slanders and falsifies historical experience in order to weaken the influence and authority of the USSR in the modern world. It adapts itself to different conditions and situations, constantly changing its form and appearance, while invariably pursuing an anticommunist line.

On the moral plane, the development of anti-Sovietism can be seen as a continuum, ranging from "slander" and dissemination of "subtle" and "deceitful" fabrications about the Soviet Union to policies of ideological subversion. On the political plane, it can be identified as subversive activity, military threat, or actual intervention.

Anti-Sovietism is regarded as inseparable from anticommunist ideological movements which are hostile to the USSR. Attention is focused on "epistemological" interpretations of anti-Sovietism. Actual analysis of its social nature is carefully avoided, in that no distinction is made between one's criticism of the Soviet Union, its regime, its politics, and the activities of its leaders, on the one hand, and one's attitude toward communism as an ideal, on the other. Several versions of anti-Sovietism are said to be gaining ground and becoming established. Each one cunningly disguises its underlying motives and goals:

1. Bourgeois Anti-Sovietism (*burzhuanzy antisovetizm*): Its socio-political function is to prove the superiority of capitalism over communism. It specializes in the false interpretation of the Kremlin's foreign policy, distortion of the economic development

of the USSR, misrepresentation of Soviet reality, etc. Soviet philosophy claims that this form of anti-Sovietism reflects the essential features of modern Western ideology, which is deeply engulfed in crisis, and attempts to hide the historically inevitable doom of capitalism from the working masses.

2. Reformist Anti-Sovietism (*reformistsky antisovetizm*): Soviet propaganda claims that this has the same goal as bourgeois anti-Sovietism, namely the defense of capitalism. It simply uses socialist (or "pseudosocialist") phraseology for this purpose. Reformist anti-Sovietism is considered the more dangerous for the Soviet system since it supposedly claims that problems confronting the working masses can be solved quickly and efficiently without revolution and fundamental sociopolitical changes. The attitude toward reformist anti-Sovietism has altered under Gorbachev, as many of the ideas once deemed hostile have been included in the program of perestroika. Particularly successfully incorporated into the new Soviet policy was the idea of reformist anti-Sovietism that the problems of Soviet society can be rapidly and effectively resolved without revolution, and even without major disruption of the existing social system.

3. Trotskyist Anti-Sovietism (*trotskistsky antisovetizm*): Distorting the essential features of Trotskyist anti-Sovietism, Soviet ideology had long depicted its adherents as enemies of communism. In reality, they are closer to classical Marxism than the Soviet rules themselves. They were banished from the ranks of "world communism" precisely because they argued that there was neither socialism nor rule by the *soviets* in the USSR. From such arguments stemmed the Trotskyists' pessimistic forecasts for the Soviet Union and their skepticism about the Soviet Communist party's ability to build a "classless society" there.

In the process of the recent revision of Soviet history and open admission of historical facts never officially mentioned before, a reevaluation of the intellectual heritage of Trotsky has been taking place. Disagreements with Trotsky have thus come to be pursued in substantive terms, without resort to invective such as "enemy of the people" and "agent of imperialism" which used to preclude all possibility of confronting his ideas.

4. Maoist Anti-Sovietism (*maoistsky antisovetizm*): This is a relatively new concept in Soviet ideology, born of the struggle that has raged for years between the USSR and the People's Republic of China for hegemony in the world communist movement. Chinese communists, acquainted with the Soviet "experiment" from the inside (the Soviets spread it intensively in China in the 1940s and 1950s), did more to discredit and compromise the Soviet system fundamentally and comprehensively than was done in decades by al the diverse currents of anti-communist thought in the West. The Soviet Union, in an unsuccessful attempt to excommunicate China from the communist movement, branded Chinese leaders with the epithet "anti-Soviets" (*antisovetchiki*). They were accused of scheming to disrupt "socialist cooperation," undermine the "anti-imperialist front," weaken the national liberation movement, etc. Under Gorbachev, however, criticism of Maoist anti-Sovietism has been somewhat muted in an effort to normalize relations with the People's Republic of China.

5. Right-Revisionist Anti-Sovietism (*pravorevizionistsky antisovetizm*): Like the Trotskyist and Maoist forms of anti-Sovietism, this can be described as a domestic criticism of Communism, as it springs directly from the ranks of the Socialist movement. Trotskyist anti-Sovietism attacks the Soviet order precepts "from the left," while advocating orthodox Marxist-Leninist tenets. Right-Revisionist anti-Sovietism tears the "socialist masks" from the Soviet system and appeals to the concepts of democracy and liberalism. This provides the basis for Soviet branding of Right-Revisionist anti-Sovietism as an attempt to restore capitalism in socialist countries. It is blamed for misrepresenting the Soviet "experiment" and denying the leading role of the proletarian Communist party in the revolutionary process.

6. Zionist Anti-Sovietism (*sionistsky antisovetizm*): This is a quite flimsy concept, since neither anti-Soviet nor anticommunist content can be found in the precepts and goals of Zionism. Zionist anti-Sovietism is defined not only in terms of imperialist ideology, but also as a movement which seeks to move "the war of ideas into the sphere of practical activity." Zionist anti-Sovietism is charged with striving to divert world public opinion away from the "aggressive" designs of imperialism in the Middle East, to weaken the Soviet Union's "revolutionary" influence on the workers of the entire world, and to cast doubt on the peace-loving intentions of Soviet foreign policy. Additionally, Zionist anti-Sovietism is identified with fascism, but with one difference. The former allegedly preaches the superiority of the Chosen People, in the same way as the latter preaches the superiority of the Aryan race. The root of Soviet propaganda's acute fear of, and hostility toward, Zionism can be explained by the revival of nationalist ideas and sentiments in the Soviet state. These have destroyed the myth of the "new historical community of the Soviet nation" that was supposed to have been built in the USSR.

The need of the communist authorities to conceptualize and distinguish the various forms of anti-Sovietism goes together with their vital interest in obscuring the fact that the reality of Soviet life itself is sufficient reason for the emergence of anti-Sovietism since it leads to an increased understanding of the evils of totalitarianism.

Notwithstanding the whole network of myths erected around it, "anti-Soviet activity" (*antisovetskaya deyatel'nost'*) cannot qualify as treason (antistate activity) because it does not exceed the bound of the constitution of the USSR. The communist regime, however, sees fit to present such activity as antisocial, anticommunist, and antinational in order to discredit intellectual dissent. The anti-Soviet person (*antisovetchik*) is depicted as a renegade, torn away from communist ideology and morality, a pathetic, insignificant adventurist who has no roots in Soviet society and who has fallen under the influence of bourgeois propaganda. This ideological portrait of the *antisovetchik* has been created to hide the fact that his nonacceptance of the Soviet regime stems not from a hostile attitude toward the USSR, but from

the realities of Soviet society and the existence of democratic societies and movements
which, in the pursuit of their commitments
and independence, refuse to take orders from
Moscow.

> The United States is betting on the growth of
> anti-Sovietism in China. But what if this anti-
> Sovietism in turn is no more than a token in
> the rearmament game which China is now
> playing? (Literaturnaya gazeta, 5 August 1981,
> p. 14)

> We are warning those who sow the seed of
> anti-Sovietism. They will reap the fruit of
> shame. (Izvestiya, 1 September 1981, p. 5)

Apoliticality (*Apolitichnost'*). The evasion,
real or perceived, of participation in political
activity or social life, practiced by "certain
individuals" or circles to justify their own
anti-social, egotistical views and interests. The
assumption is that in Soviet society, where
the state of "moral and political unity of the
people" has already been established, there
is no place for indulgence in apoliticality.
People have an unalterable obligation to engage in political activism, to participate
unanimously in public life as it is organized
and regimented by the Communist Party of
the Soviet Union (CPSU). A rejection or
abandonment of such activism, which in the
USSR encompasses quite diverse spheres of
activity (such as party and Komsomol meetings, production conferences, demonstrations, rallies, etc.), is considered a serious
breach of the morality of Soviet society.

Various expressions of cultural creativity,
such as objective scientific analysis, which
refuses to follow party instructions, or unbiased literature or art, which defies the narrow confines of socialist realism, are often
condemned as exhibiting apoliticality.

In the 1930s and the 1940s apoliticality was
defined as a criminal offense which could
lead to prosecution, while in the 1970s and
the 1980s the charge of apoliticality has usually led to administrative sanctions, such as
expulsion from the party or artists' unions
or deprivation of honorary titles and awards.

Gorbachev's policy of glasnost has somewhat altered the forms of struggle against
apoliticality, as political controls have by and

large been replaced by social controls. However, as previously, the authorities force participation in prescribed forms of acclamatory
social activism. The latter, to at least some
degree, entails the coresponsibility of every
forced participant for the arbitrary actions
of the regime, and such involvement significantly contributes to the regime's stability.

> In the arts anti-Socialist theories manifest
> themselves primarily in attempts to separate
> form from content, i.e., in the explicit es-
> pousal of formalism which is responsible for
> unprincipledness, apolitically [and] poverty of
> content in the art it inspires. (L. Timofeev,
> Problemy teorii literatury [Problems of the
> theory of literature], Moscow, 1956)

> Contemporary anti-Communism is attempting
> to exploit the economic, cultural, and scien-
> tific-technological contacts now developing on
> a large scale between the Polish Peoples' Re-
> public and capitalist countries as channels for
> sneaking in anti-socialist ideology to stimulate
> attitudes of apoliticality, desire for property,
> and other sentiments alien to our society.
> (Problemy mira i sotsializma, no. 6, 1979, p.
> 24)

> Each military man, and in particular each of-
> ficer, is obliged to be vigilant, to the point of
> refusing to condone any manifestations of
> apoliticality. (Kommunist vooruzhennykh sil,
> no. 3, 1984, p. 31)

Assault (*Naskok*). A political attack on the
USSR or other communist countries is seen
as crude and baseless. The word is used (usually in the plural) to describe the aims of
social and political groups, organizations and,
at times, even countries that for one reason
or another do not suit the Soviet leadership
or serve its interests. In wide usage are such
phrases as "assault upon international detente" (*naskoki na mezhdunarodnuyu
razryadku*), "assault upon rights of the
working people" (*naskoki na prava trudyas-
chikhsya*), "assaults of the military clique"
(*naskoki voenshchiny*). In Soviet political
terminology, the term "assault" has clearly
disparaging, even ironic overtones, although
in colloquial speech it tends to be value-neutral, meaning "surprise and swift attack"
(*neozhidannoe stremitel'noe napadenie*) or
"raid" (*nalet*).

Assault is frequently qualified by such adjectives as "coarse" (*gruby*) and "hostile" (*vrazhdebny*). The opprobrium attached to the term saves Soviet propaganda from the need to argue, let alone substantiate arguments. The term does not appeal to the reason of the reader, but to his emotions, offering in place of proof a cliché.

> We shall resolutely oppose assaults upon the rights and interests of the Soviet state, but will not let ourselves be provoked. (Kommunist, no. 14, 1978, p. 8)

> For much of this year, crude assaults were made against socialist countries. (Pravda, 31 December 1978, p. 1)

Atheistic Education (*Ateisticheskoe vospitanie*). Education intended to instill an atheistic worldview and an attitude of ideological hostility toward religion and religious ways of life. Education in atheist attitudes, like communism as a whole, is targeted at every age group in the population, from preschool children to pensioners. The party regards this as one of its crucial propaganda tasks.

Following the October Revolution, the Bolsheviks proclaimed freedom of religion, and the separation of religion from the state and its educational institutions. Religion was proclaimed to be, as Marx had declared, the "opium of the people" (*opium dlya naroda*) and a "relic of the Past" (*perezhitok proshlogo*). According to Marx, this relic was supposed to disappear with the advent of socialism. Atheistic education was assigned to a major role in speeding up this process.

Rather than waiting for this "disappearance," however, the Bolsheviks applied atheistic education with force. In the first years of Soviet rule, many churches, synagogues, and mosques were closed, while property and valuables belonging to religious institutions were confiscated. Clergymen were branded counterrevolutionaries and enemies of the people, and a majority of them were persecuted.

In 1919, the Soviet government legislated freedom of conscience, i.e., the right of a citizen to practice any religion, but reserved for itself the right to carry on the struggle against religion with every means at its disposal. Furthermore, after proclaiming the separating of church and state, the communists put the former under the latter's administrative and financial control: clergymen had to be appointed or approved by Soviet authorities, the churches' activities were subject to strict political control, criticism of the Soviet system was banned from sermons, clergymen were forbidden to carry on charitable work, and the publication and circulation of religious literature was suppressed.

Violent methods of struggle against religion and the religious communities were pursued along with less violent ones. Lenin demanded consistency. Atheistic education required the elimination of manifestations of religious "prejudice." Nevertheless he recognized the danger of extremism in the antireligion campaign. Thus, Party Congresses periodically passed resolutions calling for the correction of "intolerant distortions of the Party Line in the struggle against religion" (1929) and criticized mistakes "in carrying out of scientific-atheistic propaganda among the population" (1954).

Atheistic education is viewed as a struggle to create people who will fight in the front ranks of ideological combat, according to Lenin. This "struggle" is waged by various means, including popular atheistic propaganda, lectures, radio broadcasts, the establishment of antireligious associations to further atheism and "unmask" religion, the publication of pamphlets and periodicals on atheistic education, and the substitution of socialist holidays for religious ones, etc.

According to official Soviet figures, the communists succeeded in reducing the number of religious believers in the Soviet Union from 80 percent of the population in 1917 to 30 percent in 1988. This decline (which had been basically reached by 1939) cannot be attributed to the success of atheistic education. People were hardly convinced or "educated" by dull lectures or discussions on atheism. The spread of atheism was rather achieved by many years of political terror, intimidation, and persecution. To some degree the success of the communist authorities can be attributed to the sophistication of their techniques of sociopsychological manipulation that have so thoroughly integrated the mass of citizens into socialist society that it has become almost impossible for them to adopt any belief other than Marxism.

The totalitarian regime strove to destroy all influences, including religious ones, which might open the popular consciousness to alternative values. Thus, although the Soviet constitution grants religious believers the "freedom of religious practice" (*otpravlenie religioznogo kul'ta*) it prohibits the dissemination of religious propaganda.

The authorities, however, went much further by attempting to enlist the support of religious believers in promoting the communist ideal of a world of material achievements and abundance, a utopia in which there is allegedly no room for either God or religion.

In the clash between state and church, however, religion has not been destroyed. Soviet society, forcibly pushed toward the future—to Communism—felt emotionally drawn to the past, to its spiritual and moral roots. The metaphysical worldview patched together from the themes of "evolution," "the development of matter," and "the laws of history" came increasingly to reveal a lack of coherence and ideals, while the irreligious humanism, devoid of any concept of a relation to divinity, turned out to be a humanism without humanity—constricting, impoverished in content, and out of touch with everyday life. This has been tacitly recognized in the Soviet Union over the years, until the popular rejection of the atheistic substitutes to religion emerged into the open in 1988 during the celebrations of the millennium of Christianity in Russia. After some hesitation, the authorities decided to participate in these celebrations in order to show that they hadn't lost touch with the feelings of common people. What ensued was a grandiose spectacle with numerous prayers to the sound of church bells, and receptions for and awards to Christians. This spectacle was calculated to serve several goals—first, to stress the tolerance of the Gorbachev leadership in the spirit of perestroika and second, to mobilize the support of the Russian Orthodox Church for Gorbachev's reforms. This, however, was tactics rather than strategy. The latter did not notably change, as it continues to rest on a political ideology which has always viewed atheistic education as an inalienable part of the Soviet way of life. Hence any compromise between state and church is inevitably temporary. Their coexistence can last only until the new soviet leadership succeeds in consolidating its power and authority.

The effectiveness of atheistic education depends on the conditions in which it is carried out and on the degree to which means are used to ideologically influence people. (Agitator, no. 6, 1983, p. 60)

In reforming atheistic education, we have distinguished two main factors which prevent its pursuit on the level of contemporary requirements. The first is the absence of a firm material basis and the shortage of trained cadres of atheists. (Agitator, 1988, no. 7, p. 57)

Unfortunately, there is no real, systematic, competent, and well-organized work on atheistic education of the population, and [no real effort] to reduce and neutralize the influence of the clergy. (Agitator, 1988, no. 5, p. 58)

Berezka. A special store selling goods in short supply in exchange for foreign currency or checks certified by Vneshtorgbank (the Foreign Trade Bank). The chain of Berezka shops emerged in the early 1960s. Ostensibly founded to provide foreign visitors with scarce goods, these shops actually catered to the ever-growing needs of a certain segment of the Soviet population.

Berezka shops had their heyday in the 1970s, that is in what is now called the "period of stagnation." Within Soviet society, a new class was beginning to thrive. It was made up of enterprising activists of the countereconomy who possessed plentiful means but lacked privileges, especially the most valuable one: access to restricted government shops. Their readiness to pay anything for "scarce consumer goods" enabled the government to drain the market of some of the money it had previously lost to black marketeers.

At the same time, it became apparent that the Berezka network had unintended consequences. The stores caused drastic raise in demand for hard currencies in the black market and thus contributed to a further devaluation of socialist ideals. The ordinary citizen used to chronic shortages can hardly be expected to maintain whatever loyalty he may have had to the regime in view of the (for him unattainable) luxury of Berezka display windows.

More than any western propaganda, Berezka contributed to exposing the poverty and drabness of Soviet life. Eventually, in order to avoid inflaming popular indignation, the Berezka shops were relocated to remote alleys, and their windows covered with blinds. Yet Berezka shops continued to exist and the streets in their vicinity continued to attract the usual crowds of hard-currency speculators ready to pay high prices for fashionable imported goods.

The whirlwind of Gorbachev's reforms also caught the Berezka shops. A number of stores selling their wares for Vneshtorgbank checks were closed, yet the ones accepting only foreign currency remained inviolable. On the contrary, their number kept growing. Every republic ended up having its own chain of Berezka shops whose names reflected a local touch: "Chinara" in Azerbaijan, "Aragvi" in Georgia, and so on. And in addition to these, there were opened a number of jointly owned Soviet-foreign enterprises, particularly cafes and restaurants offering their services for foreign currency only: Italian pizzerias, Japanese sushi-bars, and American "MacDonald" restaurants. These ventures proved so lucrative that the country's most prestigious resorts and hotels began to be leased out to foreign companies. Gradually the Soviet Union was creating a kind of absurd and isolated "home away from home" for foreign visitors.

> For example, checks from the foreign parcel authority selling at the rate of 1:2 can be easily bought at the Berezka shops. It is transparent that people who sell them lost all their civic virtue long ago . . . . (Ogonek, no. 36, September 1987, p. 7)

> When the girls got in the car, the man told them that exactly at noon he had to be on the Grazhdanskaya Avenue . . . to buy an enamel work of art for 2510 rubles. The girls, however, suggested going instead to a Berezka shop. (Nedelya, no. 42, 1988, p. 10)

Black Market (*Cherny rynok*). Illegal commerce carried out under conditions of government rationing and state regulation of trade. In contrast to state-managed production, the black market is well-attuned to the existing demand. Rationality, practicality and serious thinking about consumer needs reign there. Ugly and unfashionable junk ceased to be peddled there long ago.

The conventional notion of the Soviet black market conjures up images of speculators noisily and obtrusively bustling around entrances to hotels and department stores, of dilletantish amateurs whose brash appearance marks them as shady characters. In fact, such operators are only the most visible segment of the black market and conceal its true essence. It has penetrated the system of state trade and has at its disposal broad underground channels of supply such as resale of goods brought in from abroad and of goods obtained in the restricted government stores for the privileged elite. One does not simply enter the Soviet black market, first one has to make the necessary "connections." The network of interpersonal "connections" of this sort gives rise to yet another variety of the black market—the so-called "gray market." Goods are exchanged for services there, and vice versa, on a barter basis, according to the principle: "you scratch my back, I'll scratch yours."

Illegal commerce in the USSR has its own strategy, geography, and standard operating procedures. First rate, top quality goods are imported from abroad, primarily from the West, but sometimes from Eastern Europe. The goods are purchased by officials who go abroad on business trips or are stationed abroad. They "import" items—for themselves whatever they want and for sale whatever brings the largest profits. In contrast to state commerce, the black market is remarkably responsive to demand. In the 1960s there was considerable demand for mohair woolen goods and transistor radios from Holland or Japan. Twenty years later, at the time Chernenko came to power, the greatest demand was for stereo systems, video recorders, and computers. Profits from resale of such goods could run to ten times their cost. The nature of goods determines with exactitude the division of labor. The principle of specialization, which does not find consistent application in the state economy, thrives in the black market. Sailors, chauf-

feurs, train conductors, stewardesses bring in from abroad various "small calibre" items which can be concealed in their luggage or clothing, such as gold pins, silver chains, watches, bras, stockings, and scarfs. The smuggling of such items usually brings quite handsome pay-offs. The turnover in such items runs to millions of rubles, with profits amounting to 80 to 90 percent. This is quite an incentive to run the risk of being caught. If a smuggler is caught, he may be banned from travelling abroad for many years, in some cases jailed, and, in any case, he is expelled from the party. In much the same way working capital is accumulated by "moving" goods. In this case the "movement" goes not from West to East but in the reverse direction, from the USSR westward. Such trade involves antiques, rare coins, stamps, religious objects, including valuable icons and paintings, etc. The profits on these run to 4- and 5-digit figures.

Soviet officials of higher standing, from the Ministry of Foreign Affairs or the Ministry of Trade, for instance, or party officials of corresponding levels tend to import radio and electronic equipment. The profit on the resale of two stereos can buy a two-room apartment in a Moscow housing cooperative.

Athletes, performing artists, and writers tend to prefer to deal in clothing that can be bought abroad cheaply on sale or in discount stores. The profit from such items is not high, but it requires little investment. Since Soviet tourists are allowed to take only a minimal amount of cash abroad with them, this type of "business" is an option for many of them.

In contrast to government-set prices, the prices on the Soviet black market follow supply-and-demand shifts swiftly. When supply becomes massive, prices fall or, as happens much more frequently, capital moves to areas of higher demand.

Goods can be sold via several channels. The simplest and most convenient (although not the most profitable) channel is the commission stores. Such operations are perfectly legal and the profit there comes from the difference between the prices of foreign goods (which the demand will set) and of domestic goods (which are fixed by the state). However, commission stores do not deal with all types of goods. This is why the bulk of illegal imports of value are marketed via other "black" channels, which again means "through connections." There exist apartments specially rented for the purpose of effecting such transactions. Usually anonymity is observed in such transactions: the not too frequent exceptions are "orders" placed in person. Profit is then higher, but so is the risk.

However, the most important operations of the black market take place on a solid business basis, conducted not directly but via a wide network of middlemen. Their ranks are recruited from all walks of society (depending on the nature and quality of goods dealt in), but mostly they come from among people of respectable standing: sedate pensioners, for example, or adroit journalists, clever jurists, members of the creative professions like writers, actors, or other artists; in short, from people seeking decent living standards above those affordable on their paltry overt incomes. To sell their merchandise they spend much of their time in lines in commission stores, or in travelling to places where the goods they can offer may be in demand, if they cannot sell it profitably at their work place.

The black market boldly and deeply infiltrates state commerce and state services. There exists in the USSR a broad range of goods and services for which a "supplementary" payment is charged. The latter consists of a form of "surcharge" which may amount to 100 percent or more and is imposed on the bulk of goods in high demand, e.g., fashionable clothing, good quality footwear, furniture, household appliances, jewelry, and much more. The same holds true for state services. Whoever seeks attentive and conscientious service from a physician, a jurist, a hospital orderly, a barber, a locksmith, or taxi driver has to pay more than the official price. Needless to say, the same goes for special services such as receiving an apartment ahead of one's turn, for buying a burial place (that too is a business in the USSR), for being assigned a hard-to-get hospital bed, and for placing a small child in a desirable nursery or an older child in a prestigious school, etc.

There is no opprobrium attached to black market involvement. On the contrary, the population gives its full support to the black market as it is the only institution that provides tasty food, good-looking clothing, and attractive home furnishings. However, Soviet citizens can also be drawn into covert forms of back marketeering against their will when in stores and workshops they receive short shrift in value, weight, or measure. The possibilities for "ripping off" the ordinary Soviet consumer abound. Both meat and milk products are sold in frozen form, which adds to their weight; many goods are misclassified, with second best being sold as top quality, and downright defective ones as of certified quality. Many products are adulterated, e.g., milk is added to sour cream, or water to milk.

The primary reason for such deceptive practices has to do less with the quality of Soviet manufactures or constant commodity shortages and more with the ways Soviet commerce is structured and regulated. The latter rests on a maze of minute legal regulations. Without swindling and circumventing these laws, it would be impossible to maintain the whole Soviet system of "income padding." This system ties the seller to the store manager to the director of the supply base and onward to the head of the division, and to the bosses in the ministry, and party leadership on local, district, urban, republic, and national levels. Trade employees in the Soviet Union are linchpins within the chain of such mutual interdependence and exchange of mutual favors. Otherwise they could not make up for numerous shortages or receive (even if in insufficient quantities) goods they require to meet the turnover targets set for them by the state plan. Their participation in the system of corruption also provides them with considerable income. Even according to purposely lowered figures which can be found in Soviet statistical publications, income of trade personnel exceeds their official salaries by 60 percent.

The state trade network as a whole is deeply immersed in the "gray market," i.e., in rare goods for hard-to-obtain services exchanges. This mechanism relieves many hardships and helps solve many problems of ordinary people. Thus, a kilogram of sausage may be exchanged for a theater ticket; a set of imported furniture or a car for "facilitating" the admission of a child into some institute; or special attention from a teacher or a physician or a medical orderly for a placement in a rest-and-recuperation facility or a reservation in a good hotel. Favors are reciprocal in this market: he who has nothing to offer will not receive anything.

The basic principle can be summed up as "If you do something for me, I'll do something for you." Only on this basis can one participate in yet another of the illegal markets, the "pink market" in which rare goods and services (or entitlement priorities) restricted to the privileged class of Soviet officials, can, through appropriate "bending" of the regulations, be obtained by others. In other words, this provides unauthorized "rear door" entry into the network of restricted supply establishments, catering only to the nomenklatura (cf.).

The black market including its gray and pink branches, undermines the regimentation and strict hierarchy in allocation of goods according to one's social status. By so doing, it undermines the entire social structure in the USSR. The illegal market could be overcome only by eliminating the causes responsible for its rise and development. However, these causes are interwoven into the warp and woof of the Soviet economy, inseparably linked to the persistent shortages and supply disruptions. Consequently the need to take concrete steps to fight against the black market coincides with the need to radically restructure Soviet society from top to bottom.

Each of us has had and still has the opportunity in varying degrees to encounter the black market but only now under conditions of glasnost

is it possible to examine it in its full "flower." (Ogonek, no. 36, 1987, p. 6)

The black market in goods and services to the population is the obverse side of the shortages that are constantly appearing. (Ibid.)

Bloc of Communists and Unaffiliated (*Blok kommunistov i bespartiynykh*). Literally, bloc of communists and non–party members—a slogan employed primarily during preelection campaigns to create the impression of a unity and harmony of interests between the government and the people. The concept entered the Soviet language during the campaign preceding the first election of deputies to the Supreme Soviet of the USSR in 1937. By that time the intraparty opposition had already been crushed, and all social groups and organizations that tried to preserve a modicum of creative or ideological independence from the CPSU had been destroyed. Total power was concentrated in the Apparatus of the Central Committee, actually in the hands of Stalin. Then, in order to conceal the dictatorship of the party, it was felt necessary to convince the public that the terror and the "purges" served the best interests of the state and would lead to the establishment of democracy. This purpose was served by the introduction of the concept of the bloc of communists and unaffiliated.

During the electoral campaigns the lists of candidates for deputies for every region are drafted and approved by party organizations, even though unaffiliated citizens also have the right to propose candidates. In order to maintain the illusion of popular participation, a certain number of people who do not formally belong to the party, but serve it loyally and enjoy its confidence, regularly are "elected" to Soviet bodies. In reality, the communists of the USSR do not have anyone to form a bloc with since there exist no other parties. Such organizations as the Young Communist League (*Komsomol*) or the trade unions (*profsoyuzy*) are as communist as the CPSU, as indicated by the fact that in the program of the CPSU the Komsomol is referred to as the reservoir for the party and as its auxiliary body, and the *prof-soyuzy* were called by Lenin the "transmission belts" of the party and "schools of Communism." The activities of both these organizations, as of all others, follow exactly the instructions of the party; no initiative and no independence are permitted. Far from forming any bloc with the party, such organizations are its subservient tools. Thus, the bloc of communists and unaffiliated can in no way refer to a real accord or alliance formed on the basis of a common political program.

This important political campaign should be conducted under the banners of the further development of socialist popular rule, strengthening the bloc of Communists and unaffiliated, [and] the even broader involvement of citizens in the management of affairs of state and society. (Bakinsky rabochy, 20 December 1983, p. 1)

The important task of the republic Party organizations, provincial, city, and regional committees of the Party is the exemplary preparation for and conduct of the very important political campaign of elections for the Supreme Soviet of the USSR which, as stressed in the resolution of the CC of the CPSU, are supposed to be conducted under the banner of the further development of popular rule, (and) the strengthening of the bloc of Communists and unaffiliated . . . . (Vyshka, 24 December 1983, p. 3)

The electron campaign is being conducted throughout the country under the banners of the further development of socialist popular rule, (and) of the strengthening of the bloc of Communists and unaffiliated. (Vyshka, 7 January 1984, p. 3)

Board of Honor (*Doska pocheta*). A form of "visual agitation" (*naglyadnaya agitatsiya*) intended to encourage increased productivity and participation in public activities. Usually, a board of honor is in the form of a brightly decorated placard covered with red material or decorated with red wood (in the USSR, red symbolizes revolutionary struggle and self-sacrifice). In the upper left corner of the stand one invariably finds a portrait of Lenin, while on the right side there invariably are slogans, appeals, or other inspirational messages. Below the inscriptions, the photographs of a number of party and trade-union officials, as well as of local activists and high-speed, high performance "shock-workers" (*udarniki truda*), are neatly arranged in rows, with captions listing the functions, honors, and awards of all of them.

Boards of honor are exhibited in the most conspicuous places: in shops, factories, and institutions they are placed near local party committee or director's offices; regional city or republican boards of honor are placed in clubs, parks, or in the middle of public squares. The "All-Union" board of honor containing the names of winners of the "socialist competitions" (*sotsialisticheskoe sorevnovanie*), is set up in Moscow at the Exhibition of Achievements of the National Economy of the USSR (*VDNKH: Vystavka dostizheny narodnogo khozyaystva SSSR*).

The distinction of having one's name and photograph placed on the board of honor by itself confers no status or prestige, and no rights or privileges—not even a higher salary, bonuses, or longer vacations. Nevertheless a recipient of this honor may feel symbolically compensated for the constant humiliations of life in the USSR, and the authorities skillfully exploit the resulting competition for the distinction. Hence the preoccupation of mass propaganda with boards of honor and constant talk about them in the media.

The "membership" of boards of honor is renewed periodically, usually before the holidays of 1 May, 7 November, and 8 March (International Womens' Day). For a good month before these "commemoration dates," cf., the machinery of electoral hypocrisy, popularly referred to as "show-off" (*pokazukha*) is set in motion preparing to yield a crop of new names and new photographs.

A board of honor with portraits of victors in [socialist] competition can be seen in every town and even in every village. (Agitator, no. 19, 1983, p. 58)

Here, thought was also given to devising a system of measures to encourage winners in [socialist] competitions. They are presented with Red Banners, challenge pennants, and diplomas, are awarded the title of "Best in the profession," are photographed next to the flag; decorative five-pointed stars are set on fire in their honor, the names of the best of them are entered on a book of honor and on the board of honor, and they are awarded prizes named after distinguished sons and daughters of the Motherland. (Agitator, no. 22, 1979, p. 60)

The portrait of Vitaly Rodionov, a roller of the fourth workshop, hangs on the board of honor at the factory entrance. [He is] among the best of the very best of thousands of workers of our collective. (Agitator, no. 19, 1983, p. 2)

Brainchild (*Detishche*). A product ascribed to the social activity of the Soviet state. In ordinary usage the association with "child" is lost. As in English, the concept becomes a metaphoric term for the "result of human labor." Soviet propaganda favors the use of this term because it can capitalize on the residual association between "product" and "offspring" to humanize the former. For example, the *Komsomol* is proclaimed to be the brainchild of the party; construction projects worked on by youth as the brainchild of the *Komsomol*; and the "new man" as the brainchild of youth construction projects. The *Komsomol*, the youth constructions, and the new man are supposed to be as close to the heart of the communist authorities as children are to their parents. Such an image helps foster the illusion of the family-like close-knit nature of Soviet society, which does not exist in reality.

Occasionally, the term brainchild is severed from the positive connotations stemming from its connection with communist ideology and takes on instead negative connotations when applied to phenomena which Soviet authorities appraise negatively. Thus, facism is proclaimed to be the brainchild of capitalism, war the brainchild of imperialism.

The planning system is the brainchild of socialism and an expression of its fundamental superiority. (Kommunist, no. 5, 1979, p. 3)

The Comintern became . . . the brainchild of

the revolutionary work of the masses. (Kommunist, no. 5, 1979, p. 20)

Cultivation of virgin lands is the brainchild of the indestructible unity of the workers, the peasantry, and the intelligentsia. (Komsomol'skaya pravda, 15 March 1979)

Bribery (*Vzyatochnichestvo*). Bribing of public officials, widespread in all areas of Soviet society. Bribery is an inescapable feature of the Soviet way of life. It is a common way of getting oneself appointed to a public office, enrolled at a university or entitled to receive various privileges. The practice flourishes everywhere: in industry, science, commerce, services, health care, the judiciary, and at all levels of Soviet social life.

Forms of bribery are diverse. The payment may be in money, valuable, or scarce goods. The commonest form, however, is the mutual exchange of favors. For helping someone to obtain a prestigious appointment, for example, an ailing minor official may be offered admission to a recuperation home.

In the first decade of communist rule bribery was still considered to be a legacy of capitalism, a "relic of the past," certainly not an intrinsic trait of the new system. From the 1960s onward, however, bribery as a social phenomenon grew to such an enormous scale that the press began to discuss this phenomenon while insisting that this "isolated drawback" (*otdelny nedostatok*) is somehow "unrelated" to other traits of the system. By the 1980s it had become clear that bribery was central to a whole historical period of Soviet society (1965–85: the long rule of Brezhnev and the brief one of Chernenko), which is now pejoratively referred to as the "era of stagnation."

Bribery qualifies as a serious crime subject to severe penalties. Fear of penalties has led to the emergence of cautionary adaptations of vocabulary. No one says "bribe" (*vzyatka*) any more: the word has become taboo. Instead of saying, "I offered a bribe" or "everyone takes bribes," the common parlance is "I gave," "every one takes."

Bribery helps ease some of the problems of Soviet society. It protects people to a certain extent from crushing social pressures of exploitation, discrimination, and personal humiliation. Thanks to bribery, many categories of Soviet employees with wretchedly low salaries, like teachers, physicians, or commodity distributors, are somehow able to make a living. A teacher can raise his students' grades, a doctor cover up absenteeism at work by issuing medical exemptions, a trade union official enables someone to jump queue to get an apartment, or a party functionary helps someone advance his or her career or shows leniency to a criminal.

Without bribery the socialist economy could not function. Production plans do not take into account the requirements and potential of industrial plants. This is why plans need to be constantly "adjusted" by reduction of projected outputs or by camouflaging nonfulfillment, which can be done through bribery. Also, for factory managers bribery is the only way of getting the supplies of ever-scarce raw materials at the right time and in sufficient amounts. An entire network of supply agents (*tolkachi*) operates in Soviet enterprises for this sole purpose. What they actually do is to distribute bribes to the appropriate officials in the state apparatus.

The net of bribery encompasses the entire Soviet Union, from the regional to the republic and national levels. But it is a complex phenomenon. In the Transcaucasus, Central Asia, and the Baltic area, bribery is a long-hallowed tradition. Bribes are given and taken widely and believed virtually lawful, at least as long as a case doesn't wind up in court. In the Russian and Ukrainian republics, where black market money is not as abundant as in Georgia or Azerbaijan, bribery is somewhat less widespread.

However, due to the disorderly state of social and economic planning, in every Soviet city and town a well-organized and elaborate system of bribery operates, and revenues from black market business are distributed widely. An experienced secretary of a city party committee would never question the "right" of a district secretary to receive bribes from within the latter's jurisdiction. Although the district secretary is his subordinate, he would conveniently presume that district cadres are none of his business. After all, he himself gets his due from city institutions and enterprises. In complicated situations, as, for example, when there is "up for grabs" a top or lucrative position that fits within two administrative categories, that is, belonging territorially to the district but coming under the nomenklatura authority of the city party committee, the bribe accepted from the aspirant to the office is "honorably" split between city committee and district committee officials.

Thus it is the established practice that if an organization or enterprise has importance for the city, but is located beyond its boundaries in the surrounding district, the district official (district committee secretary or chairman of the district executive committee) appoints whichever candidate is recommended by the city boss (secretary of the party city committee or chairman of the city executive committee). However, the local boss does not lose out. As soon as the new appointees named by the city authority begin operating and receiving illegal funds or bribes, the money will, according to previously agreed-upon terms, be delivered not only to the city, but also to the district authorities.

Of course, no exact figures are available on the sums received in bribes by city officials, but there is no doubt that the annual figure is in five digits. As for national "partocrats" (ministers and Central Committee Secretaries), their profits are virtually endless. They do not stoop to trifles. For them, money is no longer of great concern. As long as they are in power, as long as their position is firm, they have at their exclusive disposal nature preserves, dachas, and resplendent trips with large retinues. Consequently, their main goal is to maintain their positions and attendant privileges as long as possible. Toward that end, what is decisive is not money, but intimidation, blackmail, and intrigue. However, for their supporters, or rather their underlings, money is far from a trifle: it guarantees independence during one's term of tenure as well as a carefree retirement. The greedy hands of Soviet administration officials of all ranks are stretched out to receive all types of bribes but foreign currency—especially American dollars and British pounds—are particularly appreciated along with such luxury items as diamonds and gold.

During Gorbachev's rule a whole phalanx of ambitious young careerists seized positions of power, pushing aside from party "thrones" an encrusted and totally corrupt cohort of old bureaucrats. This process was accompanied by exposures. For a while one was able to get a peek through cracks in the hypocritical ideological façade of "developed socialism" at the typical features of the state mafia. The country's jails began filling up once again; both bribe-takers and those forced to offer them were appropriately sharing the same "facilities." In prisons one could see high officials and black market wheelers and dealers who had amassed millions sharing cots with waiters, taxi drivers, and shop clerks who had taken a couple of rubles on the side.

Scandalous exposures reached the level of ministers and secretaries of the central committees of the union republics. However, on a higher level—that of the Politburo or secretaries of the Central Committee of the CPSU—the punitive arm of the Soviet law was impotent. If any of these top men got into trouble, they were allowed to vanish quietly into oblivion. If any of them were dismissed, in the course of a campaign against corruption, all that was condemned was either the style of their leadership or (more rarely) the character of their methods of work—but never the universal system of venality and corruption in which they participated. In any case, such matters were not discussed in public. By the very character of their activity, such top officials are not liable to public prosecution, since very high party officials not only perform functions, but also serve as symbols of Soviet authority, which is supposed to be faultless.

There is also another, more prosaic factor which protects Soviet leaders from public ex-posure. Opportunity and continuity of exploitation of elite positions for personal gain needs to be preserved. Thus, bribery has developed into an all-pervasive corruption and reached the level of a major social malignancy.

It is high time for us to persistently pursue a major public educational effort to create an all-pervasive atmosphere in which such negative aspects of our life as acquisitiveness, bribery, slovenly attitudes and living at someone else's expenses will not be tolerated. (Literaturnaya gazeta, 3 June 1981, p. 11)

To live in a worthy manner means to fight against petty bourgeois and consumerist tendencies, careerism, and bribery. (Komsomol'-skaya pravda, 27 October 1983, p. 2)

All those getting rich from gifts, sops, generous donations and quite material expressions of friendly feelings, all of which can simply be called bribes, are sentenced to long terms of imprisonment. (Izvestiya, 27 January 1984, p. 3)

The system of bribery and corruption was exposed and is continuing to be exposed in Uzbekistan, Kazakhstan, Tadzhikistan, Turkmenistan, in the three Transcaucasian republics, in Moldavia, in the Krasnoyarsk Territory, in the Ukraine, and in Moscow. . . . (Ogonek, no. 26, 1988, p. 27)

Bright Future (*Svetloe budushchee*). Euphemism for communism. This notion of the future is based on Marxist-Leninist concepts of social progress, whose trajectory culminates in universal well-being, abundance and the triumph of reason. Moreover, the road to the bright future is held to have been opened by the communists, and in our day all of "progressive mankind" (*progressivnoe chelovechestvo*) is supposedly "striding" (*shagaet*) forward on it to its inevitable destiny.

In colloquial speech the expression "bright future" has been stripped of its high-flown rhetoric and acquired instead an ironic connotation. It is used to poke fun at the absurdity of communist schemes for the social reorganization of the world. As a result, "bright future" is now employed less, and more staid phrases are used like "classless society" (*besklassovoe obshchestvo*) or "communist formation" (*kommunisticheskaya formatsiya*), which are less likely to evoke ironic reactions.

> Each day brings news that the campaign of the masses of the world, numbering in the millions, for a bright future of the planet is growing stronger and stronger. (Novoe vremya, no. 15, 1980, p. 1)

> The color red . . . symbolizes the struggle for a bright future. (Novoe vremya, no. 18, 1980, p. 13)

> Soviet literature is in the front ranks of those who build a new life; it makes people confident of a bright future and it encourages them to work and dream. (Literaturnaya gazeta, 8 July 1981, p. 6)

Business (*Biznes*). Any industrial or commercial activities that are at variance with the norms of "Soviet morality" and/or in conflict with "socialist legality"; always used in a pejorative sense. In this sense "business" is often qualified by the adjectives "underground," or "illegal" in order to stress its reprehensibility. Business refers specifically to the networks of illegal manufacturing enterprises, whose production depends either on private home workshops or on larger establishments ostensibly running as state or cooperative plants, but which keep no reliable records of their real output.

This "second" economy bears a certain resemblance to what in the West goes under the name of the black market (cf). The term business covers the totality of such practices as bribery, tax evasion, falsification of documents or reports, illegal industrial enterprises, theft of state property, and abuse of one's position. Far from being exceptional, sporadic, or alien to the communist economy, these practices are part and parcel of the Soviet way of life.

Although the black market is not an exclusively Soviet phenomenon, in the Soviet Union it is rooted in peculiarly Soviet structural conditions, such as the chronic shortages of goods, poor quality of services, and near starvation level wages. These factors act as powerful incentives to illegal economic pursuits capable of providing supplementary income. The ideologically grounded lack of flexibility on the part of Soviet managers in setting production and distribution quotas further encourages industrial enterprises to search for illegal ways of circumventing imposed rigidities in order to fulfill production plans by ensuring the flow of requisite supplies or to distribute their products. Thus, Soviet business forms a symbiotic relationship with the legitimate economy by performing important and useful functions. It redistributes what has been extorted, and reallocates what has been misallocated. It takes from the exploiters and gives to the exploited. It supplies the population with foodstuffs and consumer goods which the state is unable to provide. It creates a web of personal relationships encompassing the entire social structure from top to bottom, helps many people earn a minimally tolerable living, and provides ways to circumvent unfair and counterproductive laws or regulations.

Thus, business fuels the engine of the Soviet state and permits it to continue functioning. Without it public life would come to a standstill. It constitutes the only form of participation in the governance of the state that is not downright phony. Since the legitimate economy is weak, any serious attempt to crack down on business would made that dependent legitimate economy collapse. This is why the campaigns against business, which the authorities launch from time to time, can only be limited in scope, no matter how violent the threats or forceful the actual reprisals. Indeed, from such campaigns business generally emerges strengthened, in a position to claim new spheres of economic activity. One reason that business cannot be suppressed is that every human being yearns for non-alienating labor and for opportunities to display initiative, in short, to be his own master.

The term "business" has another meaning as well. In this sense it is used sarcastically to refer to policies of Western states or actions of foreign politicians out of favor with Moscow. When media employ the term in this context, they invariably qualify the noun by adjectives like "filthy" (*gryazny*), or "bloody" (*krovavy*). However, even without such pejorative qualifications, business retains its derogatory connotations. In the Soviet lexicon, in all contexts and all circumstances, business is considered morally reprehensible.

A person of not very strong moral fibre, he abandoned two families . . . and took up with people who made slander their business. (Belaya kniga [The White Book], Moscow: Yuridicheskaya literatura 1979, p. 22)

For the first time in the history of the modern Olympic movement the games have been completely farmed out to private business. (Literaturnaya gazeta, 21 December 1983, p. 11)

We have learned that the cemetery business is flourishing in relation to absolutely everything connected with funerals. Grief-stricken, the mourner is defenseless in the face of the dictate of various wheelers and dealers who have no qualms about taking advantage of a person's pain when there is profit to be made. (Literaturnaya gazeta, 31 December 1983, p. 14)

By the Will of the Party (*Voleyu partii*). An ideological cliché intended to remind people of the leading role of the CPSU in the life and development of Soviet society. "By the will or the party" echoes traditional Russian sayings such as "by the will of the destiny" (*voleyu sudeb*) and "by the will of heaven" (*voleyu nebes*). Common to these sayings is the notion of an omnipotent and irresistible power which cannot be influenced by ordinary mortals. The phrase "by the will of the party" ascribes this same power to the party and implies its ability to transform the face

of reality. The archaic form of the instrumental case ("*voleyu*" instead of *voley*) lends a degree of elevation to the expression.

In propaganda messages, the phrase "by the will of the party" is as a rule followed by expressions such as, "by the labor of the people" (*trudom naroda*) or "by the feats of the working masses" (*podvigom trudyashchikhsya*). For example, "by the will of the party and by the labor of the people the virgin lands have been reclaimed." This sequence symbolizes the social hierarchy of the Soviet system where power is vested in the party and the role of the people is to carry out the will and instructions of the party.

A widely used variant of this term is "according to the will of the party" (*po vole partii*) which is less rhetorical and applies to the current political, economic and administrative activities of the Soviet leadership, as in the phrase: "According to the will of the party the construction of a huge plant was begun in the desert."

By the will of the Party, in the process of overcoming class distinctions, Communist consciousness . . . is being developed and internationalism is being strengthened. (Stroitel'stvo kommunizma i razvitie obshchestva [The construction of communism and development of society]; Moscow: Nauka, 1966, p. 172)

By the will of the Party we are strong. . . . (From a Soviet song)

All speakers noted with satisfaction that the extraordinary February Plenum of the CC of the CPSU once again demonstrated convincingly the unbending will of the Party to firmly and consistently transform into reality the strategic course set by the XXVI Congress. . . . (Komsomol'skaya pravda, 23 February 1984, p. 2)

C

Cadres (*Kadry*). Party, trade union, and state officials who implement the policies of the soviet government. The training and placement of cadres (*kadry*) in the Soviet Union take place under the strict supervision of the authorities. The primary criterion of recruitment is unconditional obedience (*bezzavetnaya predannost'*) to the regime, irrespective of what the latter may demand or claim. In the early years of Soviet statehood government and party cadres were primarily recruited from among the workers and declassé intellectuals who had been directly involved in the communist coup and the civil war. People thus elevated became "red directors," managers of Soviet enterprises and institutions and party leaders. They were brimming with revolutionary enthusiasm, but innocent of any knowledge or professional experience of managerial and organizational techniques. Thus, after launching the slogan "the cadres decide everything" (*kadry reshayut vse*) the party apparatus had no choice but to send the very same cadres to study at accelerated courses at special "workers' faculties" (*rabfaki*) of universities and institutes.

During the collectivization of agriculture, tens of thousands of communist cadres were sent to the countryside in order to forcibly wrench from the peasants the compulsory deliveries of crops. In industry, cadres imposed "voluntary," i.e., unpaid days of labor (*subbotniki*) and formed the "shock-worker" (*udarniki*) movements. Contrary to the quoted slogan, the cadres decided nothing: the Politburo decided everything. Thus, instead of being exhorted to make decisions, from the 1930s on, the cadres were exhorted to master Marxist-Leninist theory (*kadry obyazany ovladevat' marksistsko-leninskoy teoriey*). The eligibility criteria were strict: the cadres had to be of worker or peasant extraction and have no relatives abroad and no record of affiliation with any opposition. After World War II the criteria became even stricter, as all upward mobility was strictly blocked for anyone who had been captured by the enemy or had lived in enemy-occupied territory. Added to this were secret restrictions on the employment and promotion of national minorities, including a numerous clausus specifically for Jews.

Stalin's pronouncement that the cadres were to be treated as the party's "gold reserves" was hogwash pure and simple. In reality, the most capable and best-qualified cadres of the Communist party were exterminated in the successive purges.

Responsible for overall coordination of cadre (manpower) policy is the Organizational Department of Central Committee of the CPSU. The actual implementation of this policy is, however, entrusted to special departments of the KGB, namely to the First and General Departments, which respectively deal with production enterprises and institutions. In selection for managerial cadres (*rukovodyaschie kadry*) political loyalty and unquestioning obedience remain primary considerations. Competence is considered secondarily, if at all.

Our Party is constantly displaying an authentically Leninist concern for the selection, placement, and training of cadres. (Partiynaya zhizn', no. 19, October 1980, p. 11)

The June 1983 Plenum of the Central Committee of the CPSU stressed that the key factor in ideological work is cadres. (Agitator, no. 20, 1982, p. 2)

The training of cadres has been set up on solid foundations. (Partiynaya zhizn', no. 4, 1984, p. 34)

Censorship (*Tsenzura*). Government control over printed matter, public statements, and contents broadcast over radio and television. Censorship in the Soviet Union also refers to the Chief Directorate for the Preservation of State Secrets in Publishing (*Glavlit*), attached to the Council of Ministers of the USSR. *Glavlit* has a virtual monopoly on deciding whether or not to authorize the publication of all printed matter: books or candy wrappers, journals or bottle labels, postage stamps or newspapers, invitation cards or billboard notices. All radio and television broadcasts, film, plays, and exhibitions must also receive authorization from the same source. All printed matter entering and leaving the USSR, as well as personal correspondence, is subject to censorship as well.

Glavlit is a powerful and complex organization. Although officially attached to the Council of Ministers of the USSR, it effectively operates under the authority of the Central Committee, its Ideological Department, and the KGB, which together appoint and remove the director of *Glavlit*. This director has at his disposal a staff of secretaries, advisers, deputies, and dozens of senior censors. In addition to this "general headquarters" of Soviet censorship there exist republic and regional *Glavlit* and censorship bodies attached to all the central, republic, and provincial newspapers, with never fewer than two representatives on each editorial board. Similar groups also operate at the TASS and Novosti news agencies; in all publishing houses, printing establishments, and radio and television studies; at the Academy of Sciences; and in all research institutes that have permission to publish the results of their research and thus possess printing facilities.

There are many different categories of censorship: general, military, international (Ministry of Foreign Affairs), atomic energy, KGB, and others. Censorship can also be classified according to mode of control, as preventive or punitive censorship. The former, "cleaning" (*razreshitel'naya*) censorship, functions as a supervisory authority, in charge of deciding what should be published. The latter, acting in concert with state security organs, marks deviant authors and editors for the whole gamut of penalties, which may range from confiscation of manuscripts and dismissal from work to arrest and internal exile.

Soviet censorship is an institution that closely follows tsarist tradition. In Russia, censorship was introduced in the eighteenth century and operated up to the early twentieth century. However, tsarist censorship had limits—it was possible to appeal bans to higher government authorities. The very liberal reforms introduced by Alexander II in the 1860s significantly curtailed the powers of censorship. A telling illustration was the fact that even Marxist literature calling for the overthrow of the monarchy could be published legally in Russia (works by Marx himself were published in the 1870s). In 1905, preventive censorship was abolished, and after the February 1917 revolution, censorship in general. In fact, even earlier, during World War I, censorship no longer existed, except for military security.

A few days after the October Revolution a Decree on Freedom of Speech and the Press, bearing Lenin's signature, was promulgated. In fact, however, censorship, which had been abolished by the provisional government, was soon reintroduced as a "temporary" measure to suppress all hostile comments published by the bourgeois press. This was done with the understanding that once Soviet power was consolidated, censorship would be abolished and a press charter legislated. In fact, no press charter was ever promulgated and censorship continued.

Nevertheless, at the beginning of the 1920s censorship became more lax. Nonparty independent publishing houses were allowed to exist, and the publications of the Academy of Sciences were not subject to censorship. Ten years later all independent publishing houses were liquidated and censorship was reimposed on the Academy's publications; it has not yet been lifted.

To justify the new and increasingly stringent restrictions of the 1930s, the authorities referred to the danger of "hostile encirclement" (*vrazhdebnoe okruzhenie*) of the country by bourgeois powers. With the end of World War II, the USSR was girdled by pro-Soviet regimes, but censorship persisted. Moreover, political control intensified from year to year rather than abating.

The Soviet constitution guarantees freedom of the press, which the existing multiplicity of publishing houses, newspapers, journals, and the like is supposed to ensure. In actuality, all these institutions together are free only to purchase paper (if it is available). This is the limit of their freedom, since putting anything on that paper requires prior approval of the censor.

Glavlit representatives—censors—are active in every city and town of the country and in every regional center. Newspapers, printers, and local radio stations must obtain approval for every item they wish to publish or broadcast. The decision of the censor are guided by a special index called the "List of Information Not for Publication in the Open Press" (*Perechen' svedeny ne podlezhashchikh opublikovaniyu v otkrytoy pechati*), which *Glavlit* issues annually and periodically updates by circulars and instructions marked "secret." This list includes a general section defining the scope of military and state secrets the publication of which is prohibited, and detailed sections (dealing respectively with industry, transport, agriculture, construction, manpower, economy, finance, history, literature, art, etc.) specifying which particular data in each of these areas are classified. For example, the number of workers at a given factory or the volume of production output and its cost may be forbidden items. Likewise, there is a list of factories which cannot be mentioned and enterprises which may only be named but not discussed in any specific detail.

Until quite recently there had been a ban on publication of reports on fires, hurricanes, earthquakes, and other disasters inside the USSR. Likewise prohibited was all information on crop yields and salaries of high officials. Despite glasnost there is still a ban on revealing the identity of state security personnel (except with KGB permission). There are also rules against making "invidious" comparisons (even if inadvertently) between Soviet and Western living standards. Even the juxtaposition of photographs of Soviet and Western cities falls under the *Glavlit* ban. The publication ban extends to the publication of information about Soviet diplomats working abroad other than the names of ambassadors and their closest assistants.

The censors are bound by strict rules that prohibit personal contact with the authors under review. Recommendations are conveyed by go-betweens (usually the chief editor or his deputy), who inform the authors of what is presented as the decisions of the "editorial board" or "publishing house." The decisions of the censor are not subject to appeal. The entire process of publishing is regulated by censorship. Usually, two copies of every manuscript to be published are submitted to *Glavlit*. They must be accompanied by all documentary material to be included in the publication (drawings, tables, diagrams) and by a special form stating the name of the author and the title of the manuscript. In the process of censorship, a signed statement is attached to the work that the work does or does not contain any classified information, and an additional form signed by authorized experts confirming the statement must also be attached. In the event that the censor clears the manuscript, he stamps it "permitted for print" (*razresheno k pechati*). Without such stamp, no publisher has the right to process any manuscript. But the censor has not yet completed his job. Once the galleys appear, they are referred to him for collation with the manuscript he previously approved. Only if he finds no discrepancies does he stamp the galleys as "permitted for distribution" (*razresheno k vypusku v svet*). Without this stamp, no printing shop has the right to print the full run.

Manuscripts dealing with military matters fall under the authority of military censorship, the sole institution that overtly refers to itself as censorship. The approval stamp of military censorship reads: "From the military point of view, there are no objections to the publication of this material. For our comments, see pages . . . . Regarding other matters, publication must be approved by *Glavlit*."

Works that deal with atomic energy (however peripherally) must be submitted to the Atomic Affairs Censorship Board of the State Committee for the Use of Atomic Energy attached to the Council of Ministers of the USSR. Manuscripts that touch upon activities of the organs of state security need to be passed to the KGB for approval (usually this is done by *Glavlit* censors).

In the seventy years of the existence of the Soviet state, no single word, on any topic, has been printed without being first screened by censorship. In the USSR, censorship is an inseparable part of everyday life. Its nearly unlimited power over intellectual life has had a devastating effect upon science, literature, and art. The extensive powers of Soviet censorship have created an atmosphere that makes people prefer to censor themselves first, rather than risk the wrath of the censor.

The institution of *Samizdat* (self-publishing)—typewritten uncensored publications that are widely distributed in the Soviet Union—developed in response to Soviet censorship. *Tamizdat* (publishing there, i.e., abroad)—manuscripts published outside the USSR—appeared soon after. These two types of publications enjoy great popularity in the Soviet Union. However, authors who are part to their distribution are liable to criminal prosecution or rather were liable until two to three years ago, when, due to perestroika, relaxations appeared in the structure of censorship. It is not that the new, more liberal leadership has decided to abandon its censorship monopoly, but rather it has used it more tactfully and selectively. Glasnost has led to the important discovery that Soviet citizens can be allowed to read subversive books, or view previously forbidden films and plays without their immediately rushing to overthrow the regime. It is now clear that the type of person who has been formed in the Soviet Union, whatever drawbacks and moral deficiencies he or she may have from the point of view of the authorities, still adheres to the fundamentals of the communist

worldview. He or she can be trusted to the extent of being informed about natural disasters, accidents, etc. and even propitiated by such show of trust on the authorities' part. Other social control remains available in abundance. Citizens can even be allowed to establish a cooperative publishing house which can cause no great harm since information considered vital will continue to be available only to official agencies, newspapers, and journals that remain subject to censorship. These can be trusted to see to it that anything of real importance passes through the channels controlled by the party.

> Censorship is not a horrible feature of the transitional period, but rather something inherent in a collectivized and orderly life under socialism. . . . (Pechat' i revolyutsiya no. 1, 1921, p. 7)

> The Great October Socialist Revolution put an end to both tsarist and bourgeois censorship . . . Censorship in the USSR is of a totally different character than censorship in bourgeois states. It is an organ of the socialist state, and its purpose is to prevent military and state secrets from appearing in print and to prevent the publication of materials liable to damage the interests of the working people. (Bol'shaya sovetskaya entsiklopediya [Great Soviet encyclopedia]; Moscow: State Scientific Publishing House, 2d ed., vol. 46, 1957, p. 519)

> Marx compared censorship to slavery and saw in it a manifestation of a lack of confidence in the people. (Komsomol'skaya pravda, 2 April 1989, p. 2)

Character Reference (*Kharakteristika*). An official document that describes the personality and activity of Soviet individuals and evaluates their standing in the eyes of the authorities. People in the USSR require a character reference from childhood. This document accompanies them all their lives. It is needed at school and at major junctures of their lives as admission to a university. The need to present a character reference in applying for work contradicts the resolution passed by the council of Ministers on 25 February 1960, which stipulates that an identity card, work record (*trudovaya knizhka*), and certificate of an educational degree are the only documents required. Thus it appears that personnel departments that require character references are not bound by the law. A character reference is also needed for admission to the Komsomol and to the party, for advancement to post-graduate studies or to a new administrative position, for receipt of an academic degree, professional accreditation or a state award, and for permission to travel abroad, whether for business or pleasure.

Character references report the extent to which a given person conforms or does not conform to the prescribed modes of behavior in the USSR, that is, whether he or she is or is not politically "reliable." They are authored by a person's immediate superiors— at work or at school—who sign them, but they also require the signatures of the secretary of the party organization and chairman of his local trade union council. The document contains the usual data, such as birth date, nationality, party membership, occupation, length of employment, qualifications, and attitude toward "voluntary public work" (*obshchestvennaya rabota*). Such data, however, are typically given in jargon, which imparts to the character reference a stilted style. Examples of such expressions are "highly qualified specialist" (*vysokokvalifitsirovanny spetsialist*), "has a conscientious attitude toward his work" (*dobrosovestno otnositsya k rabote*), "actively participates in public life" (*aktivno uchastvuet v obshchestvennoy zhizni*), "politically aware" (*politicheski gramoten*), "morally stable" (*moral'no ustoychiv*), and "respected by his colleagues" (*pol'zuetsya avtoritetom v kollektive*); or, conversely, "inadequately qualified" (*nedostatochno kvalifitsirovan*) and "does not participate in the public life of the collective" (*ne uchastvuet v obshchestvennoy zhizni kollektiva*). By combining such clichés, the authorities gain an overall picture that is quite sufficient for their needs.

The character reference often yields a picture far from realistic: a careerist, a drunkard, a cheat, or an idler may well be described in a character reference as a well-educated, competent, and efficient worker. This is because the character reference is basically concerned not with a person's morality or ability but rather with his conformity. A conscientious, capable, and industrious worker may well be given a very negative character reference if it has been decided to get rid of him. The character reference serves not only as a tool of party and government control but also of self-control. The evaluative standards of the character reference are internalized by many people simply because their internalization helps one function successfully in the Soviet bureaucratic environment.

A positive character reference establishes a bond of mutual interest between a person and his or her work establishment. It is of incalculable value for the worker in gaining promotions, and it also helps him or her secure an apartment, gain access to a health resort, etc. At the same time superiors at the place of work have a stake in one's character reference. If one commits a crime, the management of his or her enterprise and the party organization there are likely to omit such a stain from one's character reference so as not to be considered guilty by association.

Thus, the character reference can function either as a kind of indulgence that grants absolution from sin or as a pitiless excommunication that drives people from their professions and bans them from public life.

His marks for the eighth grade were average, and included merely a "satisfactory" in conduct. There also were many reservations in his character reference. . . . (Partiynaya zhizn', no. 21, 1983, p. 59)

The editorial board has received a letter with the notification that the Party character reference of a [certain] Party member was examined at a meeting. . . . (Partiynaya zhizn', no. 23, 1983, p. 73)

If [your] Party character reference is required by the regional Party committee, the latter may request it from the Party office. (Partiynaya zhizn', no. 24, 1983, p. 65)

Chauvinism (*Shovinizm*). The ideology of national exclusiveness and social superiority. In the Soviet Union, chauvinism is viewed as an inherent feature of capitalism, rooted in the era of bourgeois nation-building and the formation of colonial empires. Its development is associated with the suppression of national liberation movements, and thus it is often referred to as "great-power" (*velikoderzhavny*) chauvinism, diametrically opposed to "proletarian internationalism" (*proletarsky internatsionalizm*). Chauvinism is declared to be incompatible with the Soviet or any other socialist society and, if it does manifest itself in the attitudes of Soviet citizens, it is described as a mere "relic of the past" (*perezhitok proshlogo*), (cf.).

During its formative years the Soviet regime established what was proclaimed as a voluntary union of nations that "would not permit the coercion of one nation by another." In November 1917, the Bolshevik government adopted a "Declaration of the Rights of the Peoples of Russia," which affirmed the right of self-determination of every nation, including the right to secede from Russia, and which included the guarantee of autonomous development for every ethnic minority group. Yet when the Soviet government proceeded from lofty promises to action, chauvinism appeared in the very way in which the USSR was established. There were two approaches to the establishment of a Soviet federation: that of Lenin and that of Stalin. Lenin's design envisaged a union of more or less equal republics, with some attributes of independence, while Stalin called for Soviet republics to join the Russian Federation and become subordinated to the central authority in Moscow, which implied that the *Union* of Soviet Socialist Republics would become a purely symbolic term.

Ultimately, it was Stalin's view that was adopted and put into practice, but it was founded on Lenin's doctrines of "democratic centralism" (cf.) and the submission of the minority to the majority, which soon led to the development of Soviet, or socialist, chauvinism disguised as "Russian patriotism." This patriotism proved a useful coun-

terweight to poverty and hunger while costing next to nothing, and it appealed to the basest human instincts.

The "scrap heap of history" was scoured for "great forebears": with the result that Alexander Nevsky, Dmitri Donskoy, Ivan the Terrible, and Peter the Great were taken and made to undergo a peculiar transubstantiation. These despotic and arrogant rulers were transformed into national heroes, the heralds of the people's "honor" and "wisdom." This was the "prologue" to the chauvinistic brainwashing of the Soviet people. The popular mind was inundated with xenophobia. A country that only a short time before had been quite open to the world began to exhibit signs of fear and hostility toward the West. Western countries began to be scorned as "immature" and "backward" from the point of view of class struggle, and were presented in a lurid light, of which these lines by Mayakovsky are a good example:

> If your eye
>   does not see the foe,
> and you're sated
>   with NEP and pork,
> if your hatred is running low,—
>   take a trip
>   down here,
>   to New York.

This was accompanied by unabashed praise of everything Soviet, from the Dnieper hydroelectric station to potatoes. The bloodier Stalin's terror became, the louder sounded the paeans to the "Motherland," which were used as a cover for the crushing of the opposition and the annihilation of Russian peasantry.

The war against fascism gave a powerful boost to chauvinism. The Great Patriotic War of 1941–45 stirred up the nation, bringing hope for positive change, making Soviet people believe that life would really become "better" and "happier." Yet such expectations, being unsponsored by the government, were viewed as undesirable and dangerous: Soviet people were supposed to believe in and worship only the genius of their leader. Stalin dispelled their hopes using the well-known principle of "divide and conquer."

The victorious Soviet army became his first target. The military personnel that returned from encirclement or captivity were dispatched to labor camps. Then Stalin went on to "divide" the Soviet nations. The Crimean Tatars, Chechens, and Ingushes were deported to the east and the north. Dozens of ethnic minorities and millions of people were evicted from their homes and scattered through remote areas of Russia.

Next, Stalin undertook another step by depriving the nation of its spiritual "brain center"—the intelligentsia—whose liquidation was carried out under the guise of the blatantly chauvinistic slogan of "the struggle against cosmopolitans" (*bor'ba s kosmopolitami*) (cf. Cosmopolitanism). Scores of prominent Soviet writers, musicians, artists, and scientists were subjected to abuse, reprisals, and forced self-abasement.

"Cosmopolitan" was largely a code name for Jew. The campaign of official anti-Semitism was in full swing, and the wave of persecution and extermination swallowed up thousands of Jews. Although the Jews were the main victims of this campaign, they were nevertheless not the only victims. The category of "antipatriots" included quite a few representatives of other nationalities as well. The reasons behind these programs were mainly ideological, even though they were racist in outward form. Still, views and convictions rather than peoples' origins were the basis for the selection of victims. Stalin was willing to tolerate Jews among his retinue, but he never forgave any encroachments on ideological myths. Through no fault of their own, Jews had the misfortune of perceiving and interpreting these myths in ways that were not to Stalin's liking. The bogey of cosmopolitanism in the 1940s was primarily a political weapon in Stalin's hands, just as were "Trotskyism" in the 1920s and "rightist opposition" in the 1930s. Each time Stalin felt his regime threatened, he would seek out "enemies" and persecute them savagely. The struggle against "cosmopolitans," i.e. peo-

ple seeking to transcend the borders of national culture, was one of the means used by Stalin to safeguard his despotic power. The concept of "cosmopolitanism," however, was not Stalin's own original invention.

Almost two centuries before Stalin, Catherine the Great exhibited hostility toward cosmopolitanism. Frightened by the French revolution, she ordered all Russian citizens residing abroad to return. In the same vein, Stalin's attempts to exterminate displaced persons after the war were dictated by his fear that they might carry seeds of freedom from the West into the Soviet Union. In order to achieve this goal, he deliberately distorted the concept and essence of "cosmopolitanism." Lenin, who saw cosmopolitanism in a positive light as a way of sharing in the world's experience, encouraged it and used it for the Marxist "enlightenment" of Russia.

Stalin transformed the notion of cosmopolitanism, and, to suit his chauvinist proclivities, defined it as the "obverse side of bourgeois nationalism." This viewpoint is still concealed behind the discourse of perestroika. Chauvinism is proving to be a hurdle too high for the new policies to leap over. At first it looked as if the rebirth of national spirit had evoked a favorable reaction from the new Soviet leadership. Demonstrations were no longer dispersed with the previous ruthlessness; gestures of goodwill were made toward national republics by recalling the harshest Russifier officials and redeeming national languages. Even national symbols and flag were allowed in some of the republics. Yet the national issue proved incapable of being solved through initiatives coming from above. The Baltic republics demanded national sovereignty, even if limited for the time being, while the Armenians clamored for the redrawing of their borders and the reunification of Nagorny Karabakh.

Gorbachev found himself in a difficult dilemma. Suppressing national unrest by force is wrought with dangers and bound to inflict irreparable damage on perestroika. On the other hand, meeting national demands would create a perilous precedent and pave the way for the claims of other aggrieved peoples. Thus, Samarkand, inhabited by the Tadjiks, may want to secede from Uzbekistan, while Southern Ossetiya may try to break away from Georgia and rejoin Northern Ossetiya, which belongs to the Russian Republic, etc.

However, these political and administrative complications are only a part of the broader nationalities issue. There may well appear the need to grant cultural autonomy to peoples living outside their national territories, such as the Kazan Tatars in Moscow, the Georgians in Azerbaijan, Azerbaijanis in Georgia, or the Ukrainians in Russia. Further aggravations may arise in relation to the problems posed by the Jews, the Crimean Tatars, the Koreans, the Greeks, and the Chinese.

In order to stay in power, Gorbachev could conceivably curtail official chauvinism, but renouncing it entirely would mean not only the loss of his own power, but also that of the party over the state. Thus perestroika has skidded and come to a halt before the nationalities issue. Chauvinism has emerged once more, proving that it is the genuine ideology of the Soviet regime, while all the declarations of international brotherhood are nothing but empty propaganda slogans.

The essence of the Great-Russian chauvinistic deviation is the attempt to ignore national differences in language, culture, and everyday life. . . . (Stalin, Sochineniya [Works]; vol. 12, 1949, p. 362)

Chauvinism is an aggressive reactionary policy of the imperialistic bourgeoisie aimed at the subjugation and enslavement of other nations. (Bol'shaya Sovetskaya Entsiklopediya [Great Soviet Encyclopedia]; Moscow: State Scientific Publishing House, 2d ed. vol. 48, 1957, p. 181)

The most reactionary and chauvinistic circles of the upper bourgeoisie of Jewish origin render extensive support to Zionist and pro-Zionist organizations. (Agitator, no. 19, 1979, p. 46)

Cheka (*Ch.K.*). An abbreviation referring to the Soviet state security services. Hence Chekist: an employee of these services. The original term in full was *Vserossiyskaya Chrezvychaynaya Komissiya* (All-Russian Extraordinary Commission), whose Russian initials are *V.Ch.K.* or *Ch.K.* (the latter pronounced "che-ka"). Such was the name of the agency established in 1917 and charged with combating "counterrevolution." A network of Chekas, or extraordinary commissions, soon spread throughout the whole country, and they existed in cities and other settlements, in the armed forces, in ports, and railway facilities. They had only one task: to mete out reprisal against anyone who resisted the new regime. Under the Chekas' purview were all stages of repression, including arrest, investigation, adjudication, and the execution of its own verdicts.

Unknown in prerevolutionary Russia, the practice of taking hostages and executing them was originated by the Cheka. Another "historic" innovation of the Cheka was the establishment of concentration camps in 1918. The Cheka did not care much about the revolutionary spirit of the times. Although the Revolutionary government abolished capital punishment, the Cheka decided that *it* would not be bound by any such restrictions in its war against counterrevolution. In fact, according to official, undoubtedly pared-down, figures, more than 6,000 people were liquidated in Cheka torture chambers without investigation and without trial in the first year of its existence alone. The Cheka became the first agency in the Soviet state to cast off the already trampled and threadbare trappings of socialist legality. It was not subordinate to either the Commissariat of Justice or to the *Sovnarkom* (the Soviet, i.e., Council, of People's Commissars), but operated under the personal control of Lenin and, subsequently, of Stalin. As a tool of terror and repression, it enjoyed total independence and immunity to criticism. A special government resolution ("decree") prohibited any criticism of its activities. It was free to determine the degree of guilt of anyone: workers who refused to work as required, peasants reluctant to deliver compulsory quotas of grain for free, members of the intelligentsia guilty of having once maintained ties with the "exploiting class," and the few representatives of that "class" who had managed to survive the Revolution. The guilt of all of them was a foregone conclusion, and the Cheka merely determined its gravity. The Cheka was not satisfied with a narrow mandate of fighting "counterrevolution" if the latter term was to mean only armed resistance to the revolutionary regime. Hence the term was suitably "expanded" to include all those who acted against Soviet rule, even if "unintentionally." Consequently, the Cheka had unlimited opportunities for meting out reprisals arbitrarily depending on the current policy or the dictator's whim.

The Cheka also waged war against the Russian exile communities, undermining and subverting them from within by infiltrating into their ranks terrorists and agitators. Most open to infiltration by its agents turned out to be those emigré circles which sought contacts and ties with their countrymen in the USSR. The methods used by the Cheka were clever; the degree of its success being best indicated by the fact that the term "Cheka" soon became a synonym for model, well-organized, and well-executed work.

Domestically, whenever some disaster or disruption occurred, the Cheka was immediately delegated to step in. Thus it became involved in such problem areas as disparate as the supply of foodstuffs, snow removal, rail transport, aid for homeless children, and labor disputes. There were dozens, even hundreds of extraordinary commissions dealing with such matters. As a rule they were headed by professional Chekists—whose participation spread fear in the population. The Cheka then suddenly changed its name, not because the organization changed its nature through some reform, but merely in order to camouflage its activities during the more peaceful period of the NEP (cf.). In 1922, the Cheka was renamed the GPU (*Gosudarstvennoe Politicheskoe Upravlenie*—the State Political Directorate). However, this was not the last time that the Soviet security apparatus would change its name. With the formation of the Soviet Union (from 1922 to 1934) it became the OGPU (*Ob'edinennoe GPU*—the United GPU). In 1934, it assumed the innocuous name of the NKVD (*Narodny Komissariat Vnutrennikh Del*—The People's Commissariat of Internal Affairs), while in 1946, it proudly emerged to claim ministerial status as the MGB (*Ministerstvo Gosudarstvennoy Bezopasnosti*—The Ministry of State Security). With the death of Stalin in 1953 and the exposure of the sinister crimes of those "valiant Chekists," the state security apparatus once again sought to lower its profile, becoming the MVD (*Ministerstvo Vnutrennikh Del*—Ministry of Internal Affairs), only to reappear one year later under the even more modest appellation of KGB (*Komitet Gosudarstvennoy Bezopasnosti*—Committee of State Security).

"What's in a name?" Shakespeare asked. In this instance, all the changes of name entailed no essential change of substance. Under any of its names, the distinct trait of the Soviet security organs was the arbitrary use of force, unfettered by legal restraints or qualms about the use of terror—although Cheka successor agencies have displayed concern about their "image" and have used different, more refined methods than those used by the old Cheka in the bloody years after the Revolution. However, they did not succeed in improving their reputation: a sinister aura stuck to them for good, no matter how they tried to dispel it. Moreover, the pretense of "liberalism" assumed by the GPU ended almost as soon as it started when, in 1922, the GPU (and subsequently the OGPU and the NKVD) was allowed to mete out extrajudicial punishments, including life imprisonment and execution.

From the Cheka, the GPU inherited the concentration camps. The latter organ also followed its predecessor in meddling in intraparty power struggles. In the early 1930s, the GPU set up show trials for alleged sabotage in industry (the Shakhty and Promparty [Industrial Party] cases) and in agriculture (the Worker-Peasant Party). Another show trial was intended to eliminate the last surviving Mensheviks who were accused of subverting the Soviet central planning system.

In order to convict suspects, the Cheka needed neither material evidence nor witnesses. Confessions extorted by torture or blackmail from hapless victims or faked testimony of provocateurs entirely sufficed. As the concentration camps began to fill up with hundreds of thousands of inmates, the Cheka gradually became a wholesale supplier of slave labor. Nevertheless, despite all the Cheka's best efforts, there was still a shortage of labor for the construction of gigantic industrial enterprises in the Urals and the Kuzbass, of the White Sea-Baltic Canal, and of the huge electropower station on the Dnieper River. So the arrests intensified in scale as more and more class enemies were discovered among the supposed "master" of the Revolution—the proletariat—which accounted for the bulk of the slaves of Soviet socialism.

Fear pervaded and paralyzed all of Soviet society, all of its 170 million citizens. The peasants feared confiscation of their property and enforced collectivization: the workers—accusations of sabotage; party functionaries—purges; state employees, engineers, and technical personnel—accusations of a lack of vigilance or helping the enemy; the artistic intelligentsia—being branded as ideological enemies influenced by bourgeois ideas; academics—being branded as "idealists." Even the children lived in a state of constant fear as legislation on the collective responsibility of members of a family for each other held them responsible for the "crimes" of their parents, with the legislated punishment for such family association being from two to five years.

The machinery of terror was being steadily improved while its victims changed. At first, the "enemies" were counterrevolutionaries, then Mensheviks, kulaks (cf.) and eventually, the "wreckers" or saboteurs, i.e., potentially anyone. The work of the Cheka proceeded rapidly, strictly according to plan. Each region and city received from Moscow its "quota for the delivery of enemies," which was ten, twenty, or thirty thousand depending on the size of the area's population. The terror penetrated all of society when Stalin's attack on the party also encompassed numerous relatives of party members. Thus, millions of people perished. The Cheka's bloody rule, which lasted almost twenty years, proceeded through several stages: the show trials of the old Bolsheviks (1935–37), the decimation of the top military brass (1937–38), the campaign against the "cosmopolitans," i.e., Jews (1946–48), reprisals against leaders of the state (1949–51), and finally the "Doctors' Plot" directed against the (Jewish) "murderers in white coats" (1952–53).

When the USSR became an empire by subjugating Eastern Europe, hundreds of thousands of citizens of the socialist countries were tossed into the meat-grinder of repression according to the Soviet recipe. Even the ranks of the Cheka itself and its successors were not immune to terror. Many of its functionaries, including almost all its successive chiefs, were purged by the usual methods, their execution having been preceded by neither investigation nor trial.

One of the tragic paradoxes of Soviet history was that the Cheka has always waged a relentless war not only against its own people but also against humanity at large. Its domestic and foreign activities have always been intertwined. With every attack against the free world via demonstrations, provocation, sabotage, encouragement of coups or assassination the Cheka could strengthen totalitarianism at home; while suppression of free speech and of public opinion, repression of dissidents, and mass terror directed against the entire Soviet people could contribute to the adoption of a more aggressive Soviet stance toward the West. Tens of thousands of agents, well disguised or protected by diplomatic cover, subvert democracies by demoralizing them and undermining their ability to survive and to resist communism. In the seventy years of its existence, the Soviet Union has changed its foreign and domestic policy a number of times, but the security services have remained unchanged—they always dominated the Soviet state and have always used their domestic power in a bid to dominate the entire world.

The GPU or the Ch.K. is the punitive organ of Soviet rule. . . . It concentrates on punishing spies, plotters, terrorists, bandits, speculators, and counterfeiters. It is a kind of military-political tribunal established for protecting the interests of the Revolution from attacks of counter-revolutionary bourgeoisie and their agents. . . . This agency was established right after the October Revolution, as soon as all kinds of conspiratorial, terrorist, and espionage organizations financed by Russian and foreign capitalists were discovered. (J. V. Stalin, Sochineniya [Works], Moscow: Gosudarstvennoe izd-stvo politicheskoy literatury, 1950, vol. 10, p. 234)

Worker in state quality control, the qualities required of you are the same as those of a chekist—a cold head, a fervent heart, and clean hands. (Pravda Ukrainy, 27 January 1988, p. 2)

On January 21, 1919, V. I. Lenin sent a directive to the V.Ch.K. demanding that "stern and merciless measures be taken in fighting the bandits." (Agitator, no. 20, 1987, p. 23)

Classified Communications (*Zakrytye pis'ma*; literally "closed letters"). Secret briefs drawn up by the Central Committee of the CPSU for exclusive use of party activists to clarify some urgent problems of Soviet domestic or foreign policy. These briefs are stamped "Top Secret," "Not for Publication," or "For Official Use Only." Classified communications have the appearance of large exercise books of varying color, and they range from fifty to two hundred pages of printed text. They are authored by high officials of the various departments of the Central Committee of the CPSU, highly qualified experts and scientists, who have received the requisite instructions from the party apparat and are in a position to provide "scientific" explanations of contemporary sociopolitical events and phenomena.

There are several types of classified communications. Leaders of republics and provincial party organizations receive classified communications in a red cover with red type and marked "Top Secret." These contain recommendations that are to be considered as party instructions not open to discussion. Their gist can sometimes be guessed by reading related *Pravda* editorials, but not their textual content, which the newspaper obfuscates behind a facade of phrases and generalities.

Classified communications in a blue cover with red type and marked "For Official Use Only" are distributed to high republic and provincial party and government officials. Their aim is to provide selected circles within the party with guidelines clarifying the Central Committee's political line. Carefully sifted selections from these classified communications are drafted in republic and provincial party organs and passed on to the directors of factories, institutions, and educational establishments, as well as to lecturers and propaganda agitators.

Classified communications addressed to party activists (*partiyny aktiv*) come in white covers with red type and are marked "Not for Publication." Their contents—half truths about the social and political realities of Soviet society—are divulged to party members at closed party meetings, and their function is not so much to explain political events as to appease the masses. Classified communications of this type extol the party and its "wisdom," "genius," and ability to overcome all obstacles in its path. In general terms, they define long-term tasks of the party apparatus. Such classified communications are extremely rare, usually appearing only in the wake of a major disruption in the top leadership, caused by such events as the death of a general secretary, or a brewing intraparty or international crisis.

The ruling elite requires the institution of classified communications to absolve itself of responsibility for recurrent political and economic failures (e.g., price increases, severe food shortages, or poor harvests) by periodically explaining to party officials of various ranks their causes. Blame for the disastrous state of agriculture and the collapse of industrial production is usually laid on individual managers. Thus doubt is never cast on the merits of the system, which involves the party's monopoly not only of political power but also of economic management.

The information value of classified communications is limited, owing to their inherent lack of objectivity and to the demagoguery they employ to explain the sources of crises and failures. The uprisings of workers of the industrial towns of Tamirtau and Nizhny Tagil was explained in classified communications by the "unsatisfactory" provision of supplies. Simultaneously, it was noted that these "anti-Soviet" demonstrations stemmed from deliberate provocation of hostile social elements which justified arrests and reprisals. No less self-serving are the claims of classified communications on foreign policy matters. For example, classified communications dealing with the communist parties of China and Albania contained "proofs" that the leaders of these countries had abandoned Marxism-Leninism.

The content and form of classified communications had specific features during each successive period of Soviet history. In Lenin's time they were written in an emotionally stirring style and contained relatively accurate information on military and economic subjects. Under Stalin, classified communications had an authoritative tone of omniscience, and smacked of bigotry and hypocrisy. In terms of content their chief concern was the unmasking of "enemies of the people" and the struggle against various "deviations" within the party. Only relatively small and relatively trivial sections of classified communications were published in the press.

When Khruschev came to power, classified communications became more critical of Soviet realities. They revealed the disastrous situation in industry and agriculture, and explained the splits occurring in the international communist movement. Occasionally, commentaries appeared in the newspapers based on the contents of classified communications.

Under Brezhnev, and then under Andropov and Chernenko, classified communications to party members increased in frequency and all categories of classified communications began to treat a broader range of topics. They began to include negative evaluations in regard to many aspects of Soviet life. This should be attributed not to the extension of democracy in the USSR, but to the impossibility of concealing any longer the lack of achievements or foresight on the part of the leadership, in particular, its failures in economy and politics. Many of these exposures eventually appeared in the press. As in the past, however, all cases of negligence or abuse, along with their underlying causes, were pronounced to be "isolated" and "atypical" of Soviet society. One reason for the increased objectivity of classified communications was that it became less possible to ignore the foreign media and the increasingly accessible uncensored publications (*samizdat*, cf.).

With the ascent of Gorbachev to power a decrease in frequency of classified communications was for some time evident. The policy of glasnost pushed them to the fringes of party life. However it took the first serious crisis of power, namely the national ferment in the Caucasus to quickly revive this practice. Twice during 1988 (up to late October of that year) the Central Committee of the CPSU resorted to classified communications: in connection with the pogrom of Armenians in Sumgait and with the resolution of local organs of Nagorny Karabakh to secede from Azerbaijan. Thus, despite the reforms of Gorbachev, classified communications remain a tool of public opinion manipulation through appropriately measured doses of information.

Dr. Boff's source is a classified communication of the Central Committee of the CPSU directed to local Party organizations with an account of exactly what went on during the discussion of controversial questions in the presidium of the Central Committee of the CPSU and how the actual condemnation of the Molotov group proceeded at the Plenum of the Central Committee of the CPSU (A. Avtorkhanov, Tekhnologiya vlasti [The Mechanisms of Power]; Frankfurt A.M.: Possev-Verlag, 1976, p. 694)

The restricted circulation Party instructions: classified communications, and classified directives are disseminated by top Party authorities by means of an entire network of special sections which exist in every regional, city, and provincial committee. (Posev, no. 7, 1982, p. 39)

Clique (*Klika*). A group of people engaged in anti-Soviet or antisocialist activity. This broad term is used by the Soviet propaganda machine to brand political opponents as gangs of criminals who betray the Soviet people and flaunt both law and common morality, e.g., "the clique of Trotskyites" (*klika trotskistov*), "the clique of warmongers" (*klika podzhigateley voiny*), and "the Maoist clique" (*klika maoistov*). The object of the invective depends on ideological requirements and political circumstances. In the 1950s, during the period of strained relations between the Soviet Union and Yugoslavia, the Belgrade leadership was called the "Tito clique" (*klika Tito*) or the "Tito-Rankovic clique" (*klika Tito-Rankovicha*). After the reconciliation, Tito and his associates were called "true sons of Yugoslavia."

Any democratic government that opposes Moscow may be called a clique. At the same time, rulers who assume power by force, with the support of the USSR, are recognized by Soviet propaganda as perfectly legal. However, if such a Soviet supported government falls, the CPSU may subsequently find it convenient to describe the former ex post facto as a clique, to condemn its "unseemly" policies (*neblagovidnaya politika*) and "antidemocratic" rule, and to try to convey the notion that its "antinational" aims had been unsound. An example of such relabeling can be seen in the case of Afghanistan. After the communist government of Amin was overthrown by a Soviet force, it became in retrospect a "clique which had sold out to world reaction."

As part of the general investigation into the criminal activities of the clique of Amin, who, as has been indisputably proved, is an agent of the imperialist circles and CIA, an additional inquiry into the "Dabs affair" is being held by the Ministry of Internal Affairs of the Democratic Republic of Afghanistan. (Izvestiya, 2 April 1980, p. 4)

Those countries which had decided to boycott the Olympics represent a most curious collection. They include fascist Chile; the dictatorial regimes of Haiti, Honduras, Paraguay, South Korea (the people of which fervently oppose their own reactionary ruling clique), China, Israel, and Pakistan. (Komsomol'skaya pravda, 25 May 1980, p. 4)

Humanity will not forget the tragedy the Kampuchean people experienced during the rule of the Pol Pot clique. (Agitator, no. 5, 1983, p. 52)

Closed Stores (*Zakrytye magaziny*). A wide variety of stores that serve the Soviet elites and are off limits to the ordinary shopper. Closed stores can be found throughout the USSR. They exist in every republic, province, and town in order to protect the privileged sectors of society from shortages and chronic irregularities in the supply of consumer goods. Their shelves, unlike those of the open stores, are always well-stocked.

The clientele of closed stores determines the quality of their merchandise. The most prized are those which dispense (hence their other name *raspredeliteli*—"dispensaries") their stocks to the most elect, the beneficiaries of Kremlin rations (*Kremlevsky paek*). They serve the chosen few: members of the Central Committee, ministers, and chief editors of Moscow newspapers and magazines. Their fare includes hot meals prepared by the best cooks, which can be delivered directly to their customers' homes. They are located well out of sight of the public, on the Kremlin grounds (in Moscow) or on the premises of republic and provincial party committee buildings, so as not to attract public attention and provoke the resentment of the Soviet working masses.

Special stores (*spetsmagaziny*); abbreviation of *spetsial'nye magaziny*) offer discount prices and are considered quite prestigious. They serve the top strata of Soviet officialdom, that is, officials working in the Central Committee apparat, heads of major departments, and top army brass. Although these do not qualify for Kremlin rations, they enjoy a sufficiently high status to be spared the hardship of endless waiting in lines that is the lot of ordinary shoppers. Special stores offer a wide variety of goods, which, although less spectacular than the merchandise in the "dispensaries," far outstrips what is available to the ordinary Soviet consumer. The latter does not have access to these closed stores without "special distribution coupons," which a Soviet official in a managerial position is allocated for an allotted sum proportional to his rank.

There is a kind of social limbo in Soviet society between the ruling elites and the middle classes. This limbo is occupied by deputies to the soviets, various party and Komsomol activists, and trade unionists, all of whom were elevated to their positions in accordance with Soviet protocol's requirement of a token representation of workers, peasants, and intelligentsia in elective bodies and executive committees. While a few of these people find their way to the ruling class, the vast majority are absorbed by the middle class upon the termination of their sojourn in this fuzzy area of the Soviet hierarchy. The temporary nature of their incumbencies means that these people are awarded only temporary privileges. Accordingly, their access to closed stores is limited in duration to periods in which the institutions they are members of hold plenary sessions. During sessions of the Supreme Soviet of party provincial, city, and regional committees, they receive one-time coupons for use in closed stores in addition to their salaries. For such recipients these coupons are a reminder of privileges that loyal subjects can expect. At the same time, they serve as a reminder of what those who fail to live up to expectations will be denied, for access to closed stores is prized more than money and is a major dividend—and a major status symbol—offered to loyal servants of the partocracy.

A network of stores known by the name of *Berezka* serves the strata of the population that, while not part of the ruling class, are the latter's faithful and trusted servants. The *Berezka* stores sell imported and short supply Soviet goods in exchange for certificates, rather than for worthless Soviet rubles. These certificates are distributed as part of the salary of Soviet citizens who work abroad, or have foreign work contacts. This network of stores was a specific target of Gorbachev's liberalization. since he did not dare attack the perks and privileges of the elite, he decided to abolish the most visible (and hence the most hated) segment of closed commerce. He ordered the closure of most of the *Berezka* stores, effective from 1 July 1988. Furthermore, in the few which were not abolished the range of available products was narrowed down significantly, and only foreigners are now welcome there as customers. However, all other types of special stores remained unaffected, providing ample evidence of the rights and privileges of the Soviet ruling class and of the castelike structure of Soviet society, with the masses strictly separated from those holding any authority positions.

Certain of these closed stores provide the Soviet upper crust with foreign goods which the man on the street never lays eyes on. (H. Smith, The Russians, New York: Ballantine, 1978, p. 55)

Writers have closed clinics and their own network of rest homes, and are allowed access to closed stores. (Novoe russkoe slovo, 21 January 1984, p. 3)

They receive all the necessities of life at symbolic prices in closed stores. (Posev, no. 7, 1975, p. 48)

Club (*Klub*). A meeting place where soviet people can gather for rest and relaxation. Clubs are always for a specific occupational category: there are clubs for seamen, Army officers, railwaymen, typesetters, medical staff, and members of the KGB, to name just a few. Often, they are called "houses," as in "Journalists' House," "Writers' House," or "Artists' House." Clubs for the highest elite, however, do not generally have names, so as not to attract attention; it is a matter of principle that the less known about their existence the better. They are located, as a rule, near secluded government *dachas*, behind imposing doors and frosted glass windows. They may be disguised as "preventive medicine centers''' (*profilaktorii*) in Moscow, Kiev, and Erevan; as "guest houses" in Baku, Dushanbe, and Tbilisi; or as sauna baths in Riga, Tallin, and Petrozavodsk. Every town and even every district has at least one club or "house."

The clubs that serve the elite help to cement the standing of the ruling class at the apex of the pyramid of privilege. Moreover, by virtue of providing Soviet officials with an informal place to meet, the clubs play an important role in the life of the country. Contacts are made between party bureaucrats and technocrats, diplomats and prosecutors, presidents of academies and heads of artists' unions, in short between all kinds of policy setters and policy executors. While final state and party decisions are made at meetings of the Politburo, ministerial cabinets and offices of provincial, city, and regional, party Committees, preliminary consideration is given to them at the elite clubs.

To gain admittance to these "sanctuaries," a chauffeured car with a government license plate is all the identification that is required. Members are greeted by a servile porter who flings open the club's heavy doors and takes coats and hats. Crossing the threshold, club members find themselves in luxurious surroundings. The cuisine and liquor are of the finest quality. The fruit is imported, the service unobtrusive, and the atmosphere is informal, in the Western style: billiard tables, polished pianos, gold candelabra, color televisions, stereos, and cozy libraries filled with foreign newspapers and magazines that are not available to the general public. Here the loud slogans and obnoxious behavior that are permanent features of workers' clubs and factory "red corners" do not offend the refined sensibilities of the patrons. Original canvases by well-known artists and old lithographs that are banned for public exhibition give a sense of cultural elevation. Finally, the prevailing informal style of social interaction and the customary *tutoyage* leave no doubt that this is a special world—the world of power.

The houses and clubs of the Central Committee of the CPSU are the most prestigious. Open only to a handful, they include private rooms set aside for exclusive use of members of the Politburo. The cream of Soviet society congregates within their walls.

Artists' clubs or "houses" for writers, artists, journalists, and composers make possible encounters between members of the top elite and the slightly-below-the-top elites. The sedate secretaries of the Central Committee come to these places to gape at the eccentric goings-on, see banned movies, or simply mingle with the bohemians. Everybody rubs shoulders like buddies. Habitués of these clubs are known for their passionate allegiance to their world. Although timid criticism may be expressed, this is done with an air of saying something risque, rather than of calling Soviet society into question. Even members of the party bureaucracy let people make fun of them at their club, provided the joke doesn't go too far. Tired of the insipid atmosphere of official meetings, they seek out wit and irony.

All habitués of these "houses" adopt the prevailing intellectual and behavioral code, even though each has his own fiefdom—one a provincial one, another in the Moscow headquarters of the Writers' Union. Strict hierarchy is observed. The higher the officials are on the ladder, the less modest they tend to be and the more undemocratically they behave. Conversation in regional clubs consists basically of gossip about the size of bribes, family matters, and chances of being promoted. Clubs frequented by the members of the Central Committee and the Council of Ministers are different. Their elegant surroundings, service, and the food served provide the proper atmosphere for intimate conversations about the direction of party politics or the consequences of governmental reorganizations. The ascending spiral of privilege in regard to the allocation of positions and authority reaches its highest level at candle-lit dinners in these buildings. Prior to their implementation, decrees and resolutions of the Central Committee of the CPSU are thoroughly appraised, thought out, and analyzed in the privacy of these clubs, far from the maddening crowds.

One might even term these clubs the true loci of power. But that would perhaps be an oversimplification of the complexity of Soviet political life. Not everyone who frequents these establishments is a policy decision-maker, but as a group the members command exceptional political influence, even when they don't act together. They may include political figures who have retired or men on the sidelines of the power game who can still be used for various purposes.

Government clubs fulfill strictly defined sociopolitical functions. First, their membership is an indicator of where and in whose hands power is currently concentrated. Second, they provide a backdrop against which to stage intrigues and jockey for power. A list of regular frequenters to these "houses" may well suffice to show who is currently in control and what is the mechanism of top policy decision-making.

Occasionally, people who are not regular members can be seen in government clubs. If they are factory or department store managers, their presence hints that an illegal transaction may be in the making, and sometimes one may guess that a party bureaucrat is clinching a deal with a black market millionaire. For besides providing members of the Soviet ruling class with a place to "let their hair down," government clubs serve as a center for conducting shady business deals. Moreover, government clubs can be launching pads for the ambitious, particularly for artists dreaming of big roles, solo opera parts, and the like. Women whose sole asset is their attractive bodies can use the clubs to meet "the right people." And partocrats are all too willing to seize the opportunities for pleasure the clubs provide, since outside the clubs pleasure is so rare.

. . . On the territory of the USSR, bombs were thrown at a Party club in Leningrad by English spies and saboteurs. (Istoriya VKPb, Kratky kurs [History of the All-Union Communist Party of the Bolsheviks, Brief Course]; Moscow: State Publishing House for Political Literature, 1950, p. 270

At places of residence various clubs and associations of people with common interests represent a form of organization which the working people can profitably use for the sake of spending their leisure time. (Agitator, no. 23, 1980, p. 39)

Social-political clubs recommend themselves as an effective means of systematic educational work. (Agitator, no. 23, 1980, p. 38)

Collective Farm (*Kollektivnoe khozyaystvo*; commonly abbreviated as *Kolkhoz*). An agricultural production unit, established through forced alienation of peasants from their private farms and through institution of compulsory labor. The communist reorganization of agriculture, consisting of the amalgamation of private farms into collective ones, was carried out primarily between 1917 and the mid-1930s. Collectivized farms were at first referred to variously as agricultural communes, cooperatives (*arteli*) and land cultivation collectives until the name "collective farm" became popular in the late 1920s.

"Collective farm" was thus a new term, designating a new Soviet-created reality: the mass integration of peasants into collective farms following Stalin's announcement of a plan for the liquidation of the *kulaki* (the prosperous section of the peasantry) as a class (*likvidatsiya kulachestva kak klassa*). Collectivization entailed the transfer of the land, farm implements, and the fruits of the farmers' labor into public property, and the complete subordination of the peasants to the state.

The collective management of agriculture operates according to priorities set by the state, which include deliveries of agricultural produce to the state and the payment of taxes imposed on any individually farmed plots (*priusadebnye uchastki*) of the collective farmers (*kolkhozniki*). State interests always take precedence over the interests of the cooperative, such as the promotion of the collective farm's own crops and the accumulation of its financial reserves. Satisfaction of the personal needs of the peasants is accorded the lowest priority: nothing is done for that purpose except for the distribution to them of the remainder of agricultural produce according to their days of labor (*trudodni*). After state procurement plans are fulfilled, this remainder invariably turns out to be very meager. Hence, Soviet peasants for many years lived in extreme poverty: for the most part their only means of subsistence being the produce of their heavily taxed individual plots.

From the time of its inauguration in the 1920s, the collective system of farming proved inefficient. The peasants opposed the system in any way they could. At that time the Soviet state was hardly in a position to subsidize agriculture, much less modernize it by providing machinery and chemical fertilizers. The party leadership's decision to force enrollment in the collective farms totally ignored the peasant's wishes and their attachment to their land. Not only the land, but also all the livestock was collectivized. Private plots were greatly reduced in size. All this scarcely made the collective farms attractive to the peasants. Created by administrative fiat, they were not viable; their productivity was too low to vindicate their existence.

Consequently, at the beginning of 1930, the Central Committee was compelled to issue a special directive slowing the furious pace of collectivization and enabling several million peasants to leave the collective farms. Simultaneously a high level of taxation was levied on individual farmers outside the collective farm system, and their mandatory deliveries of agricultural produce to the state were set at a rate 50 percent higher than for collective farmers. Those who failed to fulfill their quotas were labelled as well-off peasants (*kulaki*). Their land and property were then confiscated and they were exiled to Siberia. For Soviet peasantry the choice thus came down to: exile or the collective farm.

Although the lack of any prospects for individual farming contributed to the growth of the collective farms, it did not contribute to their stability. Grain, vegetables, and seeds continued to be confiscated from the peasants. The collective farms remained undeveloped. Continuing to rely mostly on manual labor, they were not able to raise production substantially. There was a severe shortage of qualified manpower, and the size of collective farms was subject to constant changes. (After the period of giant collective farms, they were broken down into small-size units, only to grow subsequently in size again.) Repeated attempts were also made to abolish individual plots, which the authorities regarded as "relics of capitalism" (*perezhitki kapitalizma*). Collective farms that did not manage to meet their delivery quotas were subjected to criticism and repression.

By 1940, collectivization had taken over 96 percent of the peasant farms; the casualties of this process amounted to approximately ten million dead, in addition to the paralysis of agricultural production. The centralization of planning and management of agriculture stifled peasants' initiative. High taxes and low procurement prices (which did not even cover production costs) severely limited the opportunities for investment and growth of productivity. In addition, Stalin demanded that crackpot biological and agronomical theories, which had a highly detrimental impact upon agricultural development, be followed to the letter.

Khrushchev made an attempt to improve this state of affairs by massively allocating modern machinery and chemical fertilizers to collective farms, by reducing taxes, by paying wages to collective farmers, and occasionally issuing identity cards to the collective farmers, which would allow them some motility within the country. At this time, the public image of the peasant also underwent a change. Originally, a collective farmer had to perform all types of work. Only later did his labor become increasingly specialized. New specializations arose in the countryside: dairyman (*doyar*), pig-tender (*svinar*), combine harvester operator (*kombayner*), or tractor driver (*traktorist*). Specialization paved the way for the transformation of the peasant mentality. The peasant who had to cope with all kinds of tasks as best he could became, instead, a specialist. Yet he has never become the master of the land and has continued to live in poverty. This is why hardly any collective farmer desired to remain on the farm and few would resist an opportunity to run away to town and take the first job available.

Collective farms nevertheless continued to exist though hardly flourish. All their activities remained strictly regimented and controlled by the authorities who periodically staged various "campaigns," like the sowing, weeding, or harvesting campaign, or the campaign to donate grain to the "motherland's granaries." Through its directives the party leadership constantly "coordinated" the work of the collective farms to the point of interfering with their day-to-day management, and these directives often contradicted each other. In regard to sowing, for example, they at the same time called for grassland, spring crops, autumn ploughing, and double cluster sowing all across the country. The delivery of produce to the state ahead of schedule and for a symbolic price remained the primary task that the collective farms were assigned regardless of harvest yields. To make up for the chronic shortages of basic necessities, the collective farmers had to sell the produce from their private plots. Between 40 and 50 percent of the cabbage, meat, milk, and eggs that were supplied to the towns came from these diminutive plots, cultivated without the benefit of either tractors or chemical fertilizers. The 3 to 4 percent of the land that these plots constituted accounted for almost as much agricultural produce as all the collective farmlands. This fact alone suffices to assess the entire Soviet collective farming system as an utter failure. The compulsory labor "donated" to the collective farms by workers, engineers, scientists, students, schoolchildren, and other urbanites during the harvest time is an additional proof of the system's inefficiency.

Nevertheless, Soviet leaders extol the collective farms as both the required and optimal way for developing modern "production forces" (*proizvoditel'nye sily*) in agriculture. They reiterate that "the collective farm is the School of Communism for peasantry." At the same time they purchase millions of tons of grain from the West in order to save the country from famine and their rule from being endangered by popular discontent. They maintain the collective farming system by all means they have at their disposal, because that system alone can guarantee the maintenance of their control over the countryside.

The liberal reforms of Gorbachev had gone no further than tentative changes in the form of work organization on collective farms. Rural inhabitants have been offered the opportunity to work as family brigades, taking on lease land and equipment for the collective farms. In effect in the country the feudal system of production has been revived in the quitrent variety, which is undoubtedly more progressive than the collective farm corvée. However, it remains less effective than private property, which is still considered incompatible with the principles of socialism. Consequently a compromise has been reached that entails neither private nor pubic production but something in between. It is called "lease contract" (*arendny podryad*). It provides the farmers with the property they request for temporary use. This new system of organization allows the farmers to farm independently but still within the collective farm system and under its auspices. The authorities hope that via such leasing arrangements they will succeed in turning price and cost— which thus far were sheer abstractions—into incentives to more productive work. This is what now goes under the name of "real economy" (*real'naya ekonomika*) in the countryside.

The authorities expect that the transition to "real economy" will eventually transform the collective farms into a mosaic of specialized production units that are expected to be capable of redeeming the heretofore lagging segments of production. Instead of centralized collective farms and unmanageable labor brigades, streamlined, well-organized collectives with high labor motivation are thus expected to appear. The institution of the collective farm will undoubtedly remain and even its formal status will not change, but its character is supposed to change because production relations within it are expected to approximate those within cooperative federations. The bureaucratic apparatus of the collective farms will have to be curtailed: not simply due to their size, but rather due to their changing functional requirements: collectives of leasees will have no need for workmates who do not do any productive work. Bureaucrats will have to find productive employment. However, the authorities are in no hurry to assign any new responsibilities to collective farm heads who form the base of the authorities' support in the countryside. As for the bureaucrats themselves, they are in no rush to roll up their sleeves and pick up hoes or mount tractors. Reform fever continues to express itself primarily on paper—in declarations and statements. In early life very many of those who have signed lease contracts hardly have skills, competence, or personal qualities qualifying them for entrepreneurial activity. They have been corrupted by Soviet socialism, which for years has encouraged habits of irresponsible and mindless execution of orders from above. People in the USSR have little initiative or independence left.

The best proof that the collective farm as an idea and an institution is discredited is the reluctance to use the term "collective farmers" in propaganda. The current tendency is to rely on synonyms such as "land cultivators" (*zemledel'tsy*), "toilers of the fields" (*truzheniki poley*), "Soviet peasantry" (*sovetskoe krest'yanstvo*), and "rural toilers" (*truzheniki sela*). In colloquial speech, "collective farm" and "collective farmer" have even become expressions of scorn, epitomizing backwardness and abasement.

There are fine collective farms and State farms in the province of Perm and in the Mari Autonomous Soviet Socialist Republic. (Komsomol'skaya pravda, 22 December 1983, p. 2)

On the "Rossiya" collective farm in the Komrat region, the productivity of collective laborers grew 1.6 times over ten years, as a result of specialization and the wide application of industrial technologies for crop cultivation. (Agitator, no. 14, 1983, p. 22)

We speak of the collective farm (Rodina) but is it a collective farm now if its whole property is hired out to leasees?" (Izvestiya, 26 July 1988, p. 2)

Collective Leadership (*Kollektivnoe rukovodstvo*). Governing power shared among a group of leaders: a frequently hailed principle of party governance. If Soviet society is seen in terms of the realities of its political history rather than according to the image proffered by its propagandists, it is obvious that the idea of collective leadership is radically at variance with the real nature of the communist regime and even with the communist doctrine of "democratic centralism." Collective leadership in the USSR has never been more than a transitional form of government, out of which a dictator has always emerged. Periods of collective leadership have never lasted more than a few years and they had characteristic dynamics of their own. Stalin had to share authority with Rykov (government), Dzerzhinsky (state security), and Bukharin (ideology). Khrushchev ruled together with Bulganin (government), Zhukov (army), and Saburov and Pervukhin (economy); while Brezhnev's authority was divided with Kosygin (government and economy), Suslov (ideology), Kirilenko (party apparatus), Shelepin (state security), and Podgorny (Supreme and local Soviets).

Not being an unchallenged maestro who can follow his own impulses, Chernenko conducted a sextet on the Kremlin stage. He had to stay in tune with Ustinov (army), Gromyko (foreign affairs), Aliev (political and criminal police), Gorbachev (party apparatus), and Tikhonov (economy).

The previous collective leadership "duet" of Andropov and Chernenko sought to ensure orderly succession after Brezhnev so as not to endanger "national unity." Their idea was to play melodies loud and clear, especially the "unity" theme, to prevent panic and disorder in the country. It was a particularly instructive example of collective leadership, which is touted as the most effective and fruitful form of "popular rule." The Andropov-Chernenko duet subtly publicized its collective nature. At the end of 1982, regular reports entitled "In the Politburo of the Central Committee of the CPSU" began to appear in Moscow, republic, and provincial newspapers, and these were the first publications of Politburo sessions since the death of Lenin. This was a message that a genuinely collective leadership was operating in Moscow and was restoring Leninism.

Such reports, together with other information on the work of the Politburo published in the Soviet press indicated a temporary suspension of one-man rule. However, it would be a mistake to equate this with a democratization of the Soviet system. Soviet leaders only "consult" with the people when they feel that their positions have become shaky, and then this is done for the sole purpose of buttressing their power, generally at the expense of rival leaders' power. People are quick to forget the lessons of the past, and the Soviet people are grateful for an easing of the dictatorship, however short-lived. Although those events revealed only cosmetic changes, many viewed them as evidence of a political thaw. The "Politburo reports" (*V Politburo TsK KPSS*) seem to have succeeded in fostering an illusion of popular participation in government decision-making. While this participation should certainly not be overestimated, there is significance in the fact that the Soviet public is now being presented with hitherto classified information—not overly substantial to be sure—and is free to analyze it without the guidance of "authoritative bodies."

Gorbachev made better and more skillful use of this innovation than his predecessors. His ascent to power took place against the background of a dramatic struggle in the Politburo in which not simply rivals for power clashed, but two generations of partocrats—one consisting of old Bolsheviks of the 1917 revolution generation about to depart already from the political stage, and the other, of young technocrats, proud and cynical pragmatists ascending that stage. A strange and paradoxical situation ensued at the very beginning of Gorbachev's effort to consolidate his power. After having reached the post of general secretary, the relatively young Gorbachev had the best chance to win the contest, but the only way he could effectively consolidate his power was by gaining the support of the old guard: Gromyko, Solomentsev, and Sokolov who headed, respectively, the Supreme Soviet, the party control apparat, and the armed forces. During the closing stage of the struggle for one-man rule, Gorbachev had to cope with a difficult and prolonged challenge: he had to find ways to retire the old guard who still controlled the government (Tikhonov) and the Moscow party organization (Grishin). Gorbachev solved the problem by bending the rules of the party game: by moving the contest from the intraparty stage to the wide one and thus involving broad segments of the public in the process. What was supposed to be an internal party affair became, through glasnost, a game played out in public view, with the public participating in it.

Every Soviet leader either had to retain or establish his or her own power base. Lenin appealed to the proletarian masses and leaned on the party. Stalin no longer treated the party as his power base; instead, he sought support in the party bureaucracy that he built up. In the process, he was appealing not to the masses, but to the security organs. Under Khrushchev, the power structure was broadened to include two foci—the party apparatus and the army, which supported him against the opposition. Khrushchev also sought ideological support for his policies in the peasant masses whom he attempted to emancipate from their semislavery. The division of power changed again when Brezhnev became general secretary: it then assumed the form of a triangle with the party apparat at its apex and the armed forces and the organs of state security at its two bottom corners. The courting of the popular masses that began under Lenin and continued under Khrushchev was discontinued. This triangle-like structure of power was maintained under Andropov and Chernenko, but with one difference; the former increased the influence of the security organs in political decision-making and the latter that of the party apparat. Gorbachev "opened up" the triangle by including the scientific and technological intelligentsia within it as well. The character of the leadership was thus transformed as the party bureaucracy that had previously shared power with the general secretary now came under the blow of harsh public criticism. Although the power base had been extended, the maneuverability of the general secretary within the collective leadership also grew when the latter's mode of officiation became subject to popular control. The inevitable effect of this was the weakening of the party's monopoly on power. Gorbachev, however, decided to counteract this process by increasing the prerogatives of the party leader—the general secretary—and thus indirectly strengthening his own power. For this aim he introduced in the fall of 1988 the law that mandated the ex officio assumption by the general secretary of the post of chairman of the Supreme Soviet of the USSR, and thus vested in him formal authority over the entire government. As a consequence, the general secretary was becoming independent of the Politburo, even if only to a degree. By manipulating his two jointly held posts, their incumbent could use his government authority to impose his will on the party (the Central Committee and Politburo alike) or, by accumulating power and influence due to his party leadership position, effect measures of his choice in government administration. On top of that, the general secretary gained additional legally vested powers in the armed forces (which he previously had held only de facto) by becoming chairman of the Defense Council. Due to the joint incumbency of these three posts Gorbachev can now hope to attain the always desired, but hitherto unattained, goal: namely the invulnerability to conspiracies within the collective leadership. Such conspiracies have been a threat feared by all party leaders. They drove Khrushchev out of power, but their mere threat was sufficient to drive all other general secretaries, from Lenin to Chernenko, prematurely into the grave.

The Party is carrying out all its activities on the basis of full compliance with the Leninist norms of Party life, the principle of collective leadership, and the multifaceted development of inter-Party democracy. (Kommunist, Kalendar' spravochnik za 1977 [Communist, reference calendar for 1977]; Moscow: Publishing House for Political Literature, 1978, p. 37)

Not only the local soviets as a whole, as an organ of collective leadership, but also each individual soviet member, particularly the Communists among them, should be vigilant and indefatigable in protecting state interests. (Kommunist, no. 13, 1981, p. 12)

The efficiency, energy, selflessness of the members of the elected Party bodies, their faithfulness to the principle of the collective leadership, their efforts to be first on the "front line" and to be exemplary in their work—all these are keys to a successful solution of the major and complicated tasks in building Communism in every field. (Pravda, 27 February 1984, p. 1)

Colonies (*Kolonii*). Penal settlements with hard labor regimes and compulsory ideological indoctrination. The colonies are an inseparable part of Soviet life. Created immediately after the Revolution, they have remained a constant while constantly changing form and name. In the beginning they were officially known as "labor camps." The Soviet Union's descent into the hell of labor camps, however, was paved with good intentions. This institution was rooted in the conviction that labor and labor alone was capable of redeeming the criminal, and that it was time to do away with prisons, which Lenin considered to be a vile "remnant of the past." Thus, prisons began to be replaced with camps where "free" labor performed by the not-so-free people would bring reformation of the criminal and his or her restoration to society. Thus, labor camps were originally conceived of as models of "socialism in action," complete with their own people's committees (educational, surveillance, administrative) and lack of guards because the convicts were supposed to guard themselves. They were also supposed to provide themselves with services and food. Yet Soviet reality ended up distorting this ideal image beyond all recognition. The humane idea of redemption by labor gave way to inhuman brutality.

The inmates of the first labor camps belonged to classes singled out for destruction: the nobility, the clergy, and the intelligentsia. Later, the camps were resupplied by scores of White officers, kulaks (cf.), political dissidents, and ordinary criminals. Very soon there was engendered a phenomenon which, however unnatural, was, under the circumstances, logical: the alliance of the security forces with hardened criminals. The purpose of that alliance was to secure firm control over the convicts. As a result, the guards assumed the norms of conduct of their charges. The law of the jungle of the criminal world began to gain the upper hand within the camps. The inmates (in Russian, *zaklyuchennye*—which gave rise to the abbreviation "*zek*," "jailbird") were ruthlessly victimized. The smallest act of disobedience served as an excuse for brutal punishment. The victim might be stripped and left outdoors to be devoured by mosquitos (as so-called "mosquito bait"), or have a log tied to his back and then be thrown down stairs, reaching the bottom as a bloody, unrecognizable pulp (this "game" was known as "making a beefsteak").

Authorities refused to see the *zeks* as human beings. Not satisfied with giving them jail sentences that for many years deprived them of normal life, of the right of see relatives, and to perform professional work, they invented additional punishments, which cynical jailers transformed into cruel moral and physical tortures. Convicts in the Soviet Union are obliged to shave all their hair so that for many years they lose their normal appearance. This is convenient for the camp administration because it makes it easier to recognize fugitives. Convicts live behind barbed wire as if in cages. At one time their movement was restricted to the camp zone, but later the barracks began to be isolated from each other by solid fences that turned them into prisons within a prison. Until 1953 prisoners had to wear numbers, with the effect of effacing their identities. Later, during the more "humane" Brezhnev period, the numbers were replaced with names on badges. These were introduced, however, not for the purpose of identifying the prisoners, since the wardens knew everyone by sight, but to further humiliate them.

Prisoners exist in a state of constant malnutrition on a "special food ration" (*spetsial'naya norma pitaniya*), which costs sixty kopecks per day. Their life is at the mercy of their convoy guards who may shoot them in the case of an attempted escape (perhaps "inspired" or encouraged by the guard himself) or even without any reason, since "for preventing an escape" the guards are rewarded with ten days vacation. The *zeks* are continually being robbed—by the cooks who steal food from their modest rations, by doctors who appropriate for themselves alcohol, and by other staff members who make off with their mattresses and sheets. The prisoners' lack of rights is clearly reflected in prison argot: wherein even the most junior supervisor is called "chief" (*nachal'nik*), and the camp's chief officer is called the "master" or "boss" (*khozyain*). The latter is indeed their master, and his power over their bodies and souls is unlimited: at will he can throw anyone into a tiny isolation cell or "slap on" (*pripyat'*) an additional jail sentence. There is no help for prisoners either from appeals or from the public prosecutor, who always covers up any arbitrariness or petty tyranny. When the self-esteem of a convict is at its low point, his life loses its value. By the end of his sentence nearly everyone develops one or more chronic diseases, one of them invariably being tuberculosis caused by the constant malnutrition.

The early Soviet regime, bursting with youthful optimism, entertained the hope that labor camps were but a passing evil, bound to dissappear as soon as the Revolution would be consolidated. The camps were openly referred to as being either "concentration" or "forced labor" ones. They were built in a hasty and haphazard manner, in the vicinity of cities, on the grounds of ancient monasteries or deserted estates. Soon, however, it became apparent that socialism could not afford to dispense with the cheap labor that the camps provided. The means justified the end, and so the people, in the name of the people, began to be herded off to the camps. The wave of mass arrests created an army of slaves, millions strong and always replenishable. The dead were replaced by fresh reinforcements of convicts on their way to "social redemption." The nature of the camp empire was changing; it became part of the basic social structure and sprouted countless archipelagos and islands of correctional, labor, closed, special, and other kinds of camps.

After Stalin's death, the sinister meaning of the word "camp" was revealed, and in the autumn of 1956 the term was hastily removed from circulation and replaced by the word colony, which sounded more respectable and gave no hint as to the reality behind it. Russian dictionaries provide various definitions for the word "colonies": communal settlements, dormitories, associations. Yet no dictionary mentions the existence of its fundamental meaning, which in colloquial speech became its only meaning. This meaning is grasped intuitively, needing no elucidation or commentary, while all other meanings need to be explicitly specified. That is how the Soviet Union became "free" of labor camps. A few years later, in 1960, the *zaklyuchennye* (inmates) also disappeared, becoming known as *osuzhdennye* (convicts), so as not to offend the ear with the word "zek."

The multilevel penal administration in charge of places of detention was also reorganized. First, the names were changed: GULAG, *Glavnoe upravlenie lagerey* (the chief directorate in charge of labor camps) became ITK, *Ispravitel'no-trudovaya koloniya* (correctional labor colony), and later ITU, *Ispravitel'no-trudovoe uchrezhdenie* (correctional labor institution). In the official vocabulary the word "colony" was replaced by "institution," which is a neutral, innocuously sounding term used in the USSR to denote many diverse agencies. The inner structure of these bodies also underwent a series of transformations. They were merged and reorganized into several different categories.

The educational labor or children's colonies are intended for teenage delinquents between the ages of 14 and 18, while the correctional labor colonies are for adults. Each of these two categories is further subdivided into ordinary-regime colonies for first-time offenders, and special-regime colonies for hardened criminals. From the time of Stalin's terror the USSR has retained one or two colonies (somewhere on the Kolyma River or Vrangel Island, as rumor has it) where convicts are deprived of the right to correspondence and hence kept in total isolation from the outside world. The continuity between the period of mass repression and the present relative liberalism is revealed in the regulations enforced in today's colonies.

Imprisonment is a sufficiently heavy penalty and there would seem to be no reason for aggravating it by humiliation. Yet law and morality have no place in the colonies. Once inside, one is no longer considered a human being. A convict's life in a colony begins with a *"propiska"* ("residence permit"), i.e., a cruel beating supposed to test the "rookie's" mettle. If he breaks and begs for mercy, he will be branded as second class; the others will degrade him, exploit him, and attempt to force him into homosexuality. If, however, the newcomer, mangled and mutilated, passes the test, he will then be initiated into the life of the colony, and be able to learn its "wisdom" and laws. He will earn some respect among the criminals, acquire a certain freedom of action and, after passing various trials, begin to impose his will on others.

Penal institutions reflect the society that created them. Thus the inmates of the colonies model their community after the Soviet regime, which represents a system of values they identify with, even if they are its first victims. The camp hierarchy, perhaps even more brutal than the power hierarchy outside, is ruled by a dictatorial figure who used to be called *"pakhan"* ("old man") and today is known as *"avtoritet"* ("authority").

Directly below him are "*muzhiki*" ("guys"), who passed the "*propiska*" and thus earned their right to various privileges. The bottom rung is occupied by "*opushchennye*" (the "downtrodden"), who make up the hard-working core of the colony, and "*obizhen-nye*" (the "harassed") who serve as flunkeys at others' beck and call.

The camp authorities approve and encourage this stratification. Gradually the modes of political conduct practiced outside begin to be applied inside the colonies, albeit in a more candid fashion, unadorned by any ideology or layers of obligatory hypocrisy. In both settings, the suppression of freedom is achieved by granting all power and all privileges to a small elite that uses brute strength to keep itself on top. A semblance of order is thus maintained, which in the camps assumes a cynical and inhuman shape. Of course, the value of privileges also differs: inside the "little zone" of the camps it amounts to getting a cushy job, an extra bowl of soup, or a more comfortable bunk; while out in the "big zone" of Soviet society the privileges consist of honorary titles, dachas (cf.), personal limousines, and access to the exclusive shops. Yet inside each "zone" the subjective value of rank remains the same in that it sets it holder apart from the crowd, confirming his status and influence.

Life outside the camps is also mirrored inside them in other ways. One of them concerns the avenues for self-assertion. It is hard to assert one's identity on both sides of the barbed wire. On either side one must learn to put up with all kinds of humiliating experiences and elbow one's way to the top. Another parallel between the two "zones" can be seen in the ways ordinary mortals are exploited by those in power. In both settings this is done through sophisticated extortion: miserly salaries and numerous taxes outside the colonies, underpaid labor and various methods of expropriation inside. As Soviet citizens are obliged to contribute part of their wages to "social welfare funds," the convicts too are forced to pool their shares into their own unoffical mutual aid fund. These "funds" are the holy of holies in the colonies. They

are used to help those convicts, such as those who face transportation to other camps, to bribe the authorities or to obtain vodka and drugs. They are the mainstay of the leaders' authority, and around them revolves the dismal life of the colony. Those who want to avoid doing the dirtiest work possible must contribute ten rubles out of their salary. The convicts who are served by lackeys ("*shus-triki*") have to pay fifteen rubles for them. Ten rubles a month are collected from those who are clandestinely engaged in doing odd jobs in their spare time, making chess sets or knives, which will be smuggled out and sold on the outside.

The convicts are reluctant to part with their money, and the leaders occasionally have to persuade them by force. Whenever these coercive methods diverge from the prisoners' notions of justice, the colonies explode in violent riots. Long-exercized patience is suddenly exhausted, and the camp hierarchs can be beaten to death by others venting months of accumulated rage and pain. The administration is reluctant to intervene in such brawls. Whatever passions flare up inside the colonies are none of its concern, as long as the production quotas are fulfilled. Promotions and bonuses of the jailers depend only on the latter factor: hence their only worry is that the criminals might be reeducated, and not return to the colonies. As to the convicts, after cooling down and licking their wounds after a riot they elect new leaders. They do so hoping against hope that the new electees will turn out to be more humane and fair than their predecessors. Their hopes are naive for the camps never change. While physically excluded from Soviet society, psychologically the convicts remain a part of it, unwittingly recreating its evils inside the penal colonies.

The same ancient principle of "divide and rule" is successfully applied by the administration in other colonies as well, except that here, because of the specific nature of the inmates it assumed the most ungainly and lurid forms. (Ogonek, no. 32, August 1988, p. 27)

What was initially discussed was the position

of a dozen convicts in a correctional labor institution . . . whom the American author named "prisoners of conscience." (Moskovskie novosti, 28 August 1988, p. 7)

According to my estimates, about fifteen percent of all the released convicts not only retain the mores of the underworld, but quit the colonies anticipating their eventual return to them. (Moskovskie novosti, 18 September 1988, p. 11)

Commemoration Dates (*Znamenatel'nye daty*). Soviet public holidays, celebrations, and historical anniversaries. Commemoration dates are included in Soviet calendars and observed in honor of events viewed as important "landmarks" of communist history. They occur on the anniversaries of the birth and death of prominent Soviet leaders, victories in the civil war and World War II, and also Russian feats of arms in the more distant past.

Commemoration dates first began to be observed by order of Lenin in 1918, on the first anniversary of the October Revolution. They were intended as a substitute for tsarist and religious holidays, as new traditions to supersede the old ones. The most solemn commemoration dates came to be called "resplendent holidays" (*svetlye prazdniki*), a phrase borrowed from the language of the Orthodox Church, where it meant the commemoration of the period associated with Jesus' resurrection. The phrase, precisely because it conjured up religious associations such as "Holy Week" and "Holy Matins," was used in order to lend a special aura to Soviet commemoration dates. The phrase "Soviet Holiday" is reserved only for official celebrations such as the anniversary of the October Revolution, "Victory Day," and "Soviet Army Day." Other celebrations fall under the category of commemoration dates.

Commemoration dates have become an established tradition in Soviet society. They are observed on the basis of government decision, and the ceremonies are regarded as a political means of educating the populace. Celebration of commemoration dates is showy, costly, and labor-consuming. The streets are decorated and cleaned, and festive meetings are held. Factories, institutions, and schools prepare for them thoroughly and well in advance.

Commemoration dates and the modes of their celebration are subject to change. The ritual attached to them depends to a large measure on the political situation and social circumstances. When Stalin's "cult of personality" was exposed, commemoration dates connected with his name were abolished. His birthday and the anniversary of "the Stalin Constitution" ceased to be observed.

In the 1960s new commemoration dates were introduced and given much publicity. Among these are: "Cosmonaut Day," "Miner Day," "Geologist Day," and "Fisherman Day." When such a "day" comes, the mass media devote considerable attention to hailing "the achievements" and "the successes" of workers and employees in the respective branches of industry, while "shock-workers," factory managers, and party activists are rewarded with decorations, certificates, and bonuses. Official bodies encourage a festive atmosphere and, at the same time, attempt to arouse enthusiasm for work. Enterprises undertake obligations to boost production and keep "labor watches" (*trudovye vakhty*). Ordinary working men, however, welcome the opportunity to rest, have a good time, or seek oblivion in drinking (which often leads to brawls) in a break from their gray and joyless existence.

A republic exhibition entitled "Monuments to the Fatherland in the Works of Artists of Russia" was opened in Tula on a commemoration dates. (Literaturnaya gazeta, 10 September 1980, p. 1)

In the past year, our country and the whole progressive world celebrated an important commemoration dates of Russian literature, the 100th anniversary of the birth of Alexander Blok. (Literaturnaya gazeta, 5 August 1981, p. 6)

We are planning to conduct street festivities every year according to the calendar of commemoration dates, and to charge party organizations with this responsibility. (Agitator, 22 November 1981, p. 50)

Communism (*Kommunizm*). The socioeconomic doctrine of orthodox Marxism; the classless, conflict-free society that it forsees for the future; and also a contemporary totalitarian sociopolitical system. The doctrine referred to as scientific communism was authored by Karl Marx and Friedrich Engels. According to their writings, a classless communist society was to be built as a result of class struggle, spearheaded by "the most revolutionary class," that is, the proletariat. The latter was to effect worldwide revolution in the interests of the overwhelming majority of people and thus bring about equality and social justice. With the advent of communism the means of production were supposed to become the common property of all the people, the economy to be balanced and geared to steady growth, society's needs to be satisfied to the maximum, and class conflicts to disappear. Soviet propaganda claims that with the advent of communism, which is theoretically still in the future, contrasts between industry and agriculture and between mental and physical work will vanish. Each citizen will be able to work according to his or her capabilities and be paid according to his or her needs. The need for a state as an instrument of coercion will fade away, and the reign of universal well-being and prosperity will begin.

In the Soviet Union creative development of Marxist theory is the exclusive prerogative of general secretaries of the Party Central Committee. It was they who defined the characteristics of the first, lower or transitional (*nizshaya-perekhodnaya*) phase of communist society—socialism. They outlined "the successive tasks" (*ocherednye zadachi*) in the building of communism, set the goals for communist upbringing, and devised methods for overcoming the "survivals of capitalism" (*perezhitki kapitalizma*) in people's consciousness. Moreover, the leading role in the building of communism has been assigned to the party, which is considered to have foiled all attempts of "enemies of the people" (*vragi naroda*) to frustrate the peaceful development of the USSR, and to be "steadfastly" (*tverdo*) leading the people

toward communism. This path, which has already exacted millions of victims and dreadful human suffering and deprivation, is referred to in Soviet propaganda as the struggle for a "bright future" (cf.), or *svetloe budushchee*. The wholesale extermination of social groups (the aristocracy, bourgeoisie, and prosperous peasants [kulaki, cf.]), genocide, and ruthless suppression of dissent have all been explained as serving the interests of the "building of communism" (*stroitel'stvo kommunizma*).

Over time the faith of the Soviet people in the communist system has considerably weakened, a process accelerated by the discreditation of Stalin at the Twentieth Congress of the CPSU. In an effort to stimulate communist zeal, Khrushchev promised that communism would be built by 1980. Under Andropov and Chernenko, the Soviet rulers no longer even bothered to hazard a date for the advent of communism, although they continued to reaffirm the party's task of leading the people toward communism. Under Gorbachev there is less talk about building communism and more about perestroika, which like communism, is supposed to bring about "equal opportunity and the general welfare."

Just as the advent of communism has failed to materialize, so have all the hopes pinned on its first stage (socialism) proven delusory: severe shortages continued instead of promised affluence, inequalities persisted, and people were not any freer. Even technological progress proved more apparent than real. The struggle of socialism against capitalism has amounted to the struggle of totalitarianism against democracy or to the struggle of a closed society against an open one.

The noun communist (*kommunist*) basically means no more than a "member of the Communist party," although occasionally it is used to denote any dynamic and active person. Following this usage the adjective communist (*kommunistichesky*) has become a synonym for "conscientious," "moral," "honorable," "just," or "noble." In such contexts, it serves as a general term emphasizing ideological aspects of Soviet life. Thus, "communist teams" (*Kommunisticheskie brigady*) always lead; "communist ideals" (*idealy*) invariably hold bright promise for the future, "communist morality" (*nravstvennost'*) is infallible, "the communist future" (*budushchee*) is most promising, "communist initiatives" (*initsiativy*) are the most effective and "communist labor" (*trud*) is invariably conscientious, constructive, heroic, and ennobling.

Such expressions constantly appear in the newspapers and are invariably heard in speeches of Soviet leaders and resolutions of party congresses, plenums, and meetings. However, such expressions are no longer common in popular usage as they evoke associations of hypocrisy rather than ideals.

> Comrade L. I. Brezhnev's report to the XXVI Congress of the CPSU was a significant contribution to the theory and practice of scientific Communism. (Partiynaya zhizn', no. 18, 1981, p. 8)

> Communism must be learned not only from textbooks but also from practical experience. (Komsomol'skaya pravda, 27 October 1983)

> There can be no doubt that the preparations for the elections to the Supreme Soviet of the USSR will be accompanied by new successes in the struggle to implement the Party's plans and the great ideals of Communism. (Izvestiya, December 1983, p. 2)

Communist Labor Team (*Brigada kommunisticheskogo truda*). A type of organization of a production group at Soviet enterprises. Communist labor teams date from the mid-1950s. In contrast to ordinary Soviet work brigades, they are charged with the responsibility of fulfilling and overfulfilling plans and production assignments, participating in socialist competition, and manifesting political activism, communist consciousness, and conscientious labor discipline.

The communist labor teams were envisioned by the authorities as model production cells that would function as prototypes of a communist society. They were given a modicum of autonomy, and even some self-government, specifically the right to partic-

ipate in management discussions and thus to affect planning decisions. They were also given responsibility for certain social tasks, including reeducation of offenders guilty of petty infractions of regulations and the granting of probation to former criminal offenders.

The state's expectation was that communist labor teams would be the schools where there would be created a new Soviet man, whose entire conduct would live up to the "moral code of the builders of communism." During the period of Khrushchev (1953–64), collectivism was stressed as the highest value, and the slogan was "all for the collective." Self-sacrifice at work, appreciation of spiritual rather than material rewards, the sharing of needs and interests, and communal recreation complete with political study were all intended norms of conduct for members of communist labor teams. Also, communist labor teams were meant to provide all Soviet citizens with a model of a conscientious attitude toward production, of the harmonious merging of intellectual and physical endeavors, and of professional creativity requiring considerable general education, specialized training, and broad intellectual horizons.

In reality, the communist labor teams have been distinguished neither by outstanding productivity nor by outstanding conduct, nor have they become "cells of the communist future." Under conditions of the exploitation of the individual by the state, where the ruling party-government bureaucracy has a monopoly over the means and processes and where production is regimented no less completely than are other areas of human conduct, one can scarcely speak of *voluntary* labor for the common good. Labor—both within and without the communist labor teams—has a character no less coercive and regimented than before the creation of communist labor teams, and the distribution of material benefits continues to be carried out not according to work performance, but according to the social status of the employee.

The drive to establish communist labor teams was quickly transformed into a propaganda campaign. In effect, the authorities took advantage of the communist labor teams to create more refined forms of exploitation. After the fall of Khrushchev, the communist labor teams, which had discredited themselves, began gradually to be done away with. First, from the pages of newspapers, then from the actual praxis of Soviet life itself. They were replaced by other efforts just as stillborn as were the communist labor teams.

> The Zaparozh'e Silk-Spinning Plant's Communist labor team, headed by N. Mokeeva, has fulfilled the socialist obligations it assumed for the Tenth Five-Year Plan. (Sotsialisticheskaya industriya, 11 August 1978, p. 2)

> It is for good reason that this comradely collective holds the title Communist labor team. (Agitator, no. 23, 1980, p. 41)

> Shock-workers and Communist labor teams are broadening and improving the practice of concluding agreements in regard to mutual obligations between cooperating factories. (Agitator, no. 20, 1983, p. 16)

Consumer Goods in Popular Demand (*Tovary narodnogo potrebleniya*). Commodities and products intended for sale to the public at large. "Consumer goods in popular demand" became part of Soviet officialese in the 1950s when it supplanted the term "basic consumeer goods" (*tovary shirokogo potrebleniya*). The latter, abbreviated to "*shirpotreb*," had become a popular byword for low quality and defective goods and, subsequently, for anything found crude, primitive, and in bad taste. Hence derive such phrases as "poetic *shirpotreb*," "moral *shirpotreb*" or "ideological *shirpotreb*." Undaunted by the irony of using a term relating to its own shortcomings to characterize other societies, Soviet propaganda employs the word in its campaign against contemporary Western culture, i.e., communist writers on aesthetics refer to European and American literature as "bourgeois *shirpotreb*."

Ultimately, the need was recognized for a new word for domestically produced consumer goods that would be devoid of sarcastic connotation. The new term "consumer goods in popular demand" was supposed to express the idea that consumer goods are produced for the working masses to satisfy their needs and raise their living standard.

However, consumer goods in popular demand remain *Soviet* consumer goods in popular demand, i.e., usually of inferior quality and always in short supply. To remedy the endless malfunctions of the consumer goods supply network, much regulatory legislation has been enacted. There have been numerous government decrees and also the introduction of a special state food supply program. This remedial effort, however, has largely proved futile as reflected in the currency of such contemporary terms as "shortage" (*defitsit*), "temporary difficulties" (*vremennye trudnosti*), and "to unearth" (*otorvat'*), meaning "to buy."

> Our production of consumer goods in popular demand today amounts to 13 rubles for each ruble we earn in wages. In the sector of light industry, this is a national record. (Izvestiya, 9 December 1983, p. 2)

> A new item has been added to the list of consumer goods in popular demand manufactured by the A. A. Zhdanov Izhory Plant connected to the Leningrad Productive Trust. (Izvestiya, 19 December 1983, p. 1)

> On the basis of a study of popular demand and of the supply potential of the industrial enterprises, measures are being adopted in the republic to organizationally expand the production of consumer goods in popular demand. (Pravda, 25 December 1983, p. 2)

Contract (*Podryad*). (1) An agreement reached between the supplier and the performers of work. (2) Work carried out on the basis of such an agreement. "Contract" implies various forms of contractual ties depending on which contracts may be collective, family, individual, or rental.

The collective contract is not a new concept in the Soviet Union. It was first tried out in the early 1960s with independently operating (literally, "undirected"—*beznaryadnye*) work brigades. The manner in which these brigades worked differed from the accepted norm. Rather than working according to the mandatory instructions imposed by authorities in charge of assigning labor, they worked on the basis of contractual labor agreements. When this happened, a brigade collective would undertake to produce a certain quantity of goods, while the management of the factory ordering these goods had to supply the requisite materials and equipment. In this way, the workers became contractors while the management of a factory, *kolkhoz*, etc. became their customers. Under this arrangement, an enterprise would pay workers not according to their input (e.g., time or effort), but according to their output.

Although it was economically justified, the contract experiment of the early 1960s was not in itself capable of solving the problems of the Soviet economy. A conflict arose between industry as a whole and the enterprises working on the basis of a collective contract. In order to consolidate and expand the new work system, it was not sufficient to overcome or at least undermine the prevailing bureaucratic mindset. More was needed: a cost accounting system, self-financing and, most important of all, state guarantees for the protection of the new form of labor. But none of these were then available. Yet, without all these preconditions, the collective contract system simply would not work. It would be impossible to mobilize a labor collective around a single-minded pursuit of production goals, to create incentives and enhance collective responsibility for the finished product, or allow worker participation in the managerial decision-making.

The experiment in the collective contract, which in fact amounted to a revival of the old Russian tradition of *artel'* (i.e., small groups organizing themselves for the purpose of working together), was alien to a society ideologically shaped by Khrushchev and Brezhnev. Consequently, for more than twenty years "undirected labor" was viewed with the utmost suspicion, as an eccentric attempt to restore some forms of bourgeois economy. Real official recognition of the principle of the collective contract came only with Gorbachev's reforms. Henceforth, it was approved on a nationwide scale and protected by laws issued to facilitate its widespread adoption as an essential form of economic activity.

However, the adoption of the collective contract was to be phased in over many years since it conflicted with the very essence of the Soviet economy with its centralization and command planning. According to official figures, out of the one million work brigades operating in Soviet industry in 1988, more than 20 percent (and almost 85 percent in the construction sector) had gone over to the collective contract system. Yet a closer examination of the actual situation reveals that its apparent massive scale is an illusion since most enterprises that have formally adopted the collective contract continue to operate as they did previously.

The collective contract became widespread (in real terms) in agriculture. By 1987, more than 500,000 work brigades and teams had converted to this system. These work units were cultivating three-quarters of the country's arable land and husbanding more than half its cattle, sheep, and goats. In this context, it should be noted that the collective contract has developed into individual and family contracts of which there are several forms. Firstly, there are contracts concluded with laborers of agricultural enterprises (who work either individually or in family groups) with the consent of the enterprise's management. The contracted work is usually done in the workers' free time. Secondly, there are contractual units formed by families from outlying settlements that are interested in working on contracts for the local collective or state farm (*kolkhoz* or *sovkhoz*). Thirdly, contractual units also exist in the form of cooperative peasant labor.

Contractual work on a family basis also includes people not necessarily bound by kinship, but its main nucleus remains the family (up to the time of this writing at least). In this sense, kinship provides the motivation for their efficient operation—the workers involved are closely acquainted and do not usually have disputes regarding work discipline and distribution of earnings. The family contract represents a distinct and inevitable concession on the authorities' part to a natural human yearning for private ownership and for being master of one's own labor. Such yearnings in the past had been carefully concealed but not entirely extinguished.

The state, however, is not completely relinquishing its controls over the activities of family collectives. It continues to own all the means of production, and this allows it to establish production norms and determine the amount of a collective's earnings. When production norms are surpassed, the income of the family collective does not grow proportionately. This is because accounting ploys are then used. For example, in the event of a productive year with a good harvest, the family collective's pay rates are computed not for that single year but in correspondence with its average productivity over several previous years. If the family collective's mean income is then still judged as too high, a supplementary tax is imposed for "exceptionally fertile land," i.e., for fertilizers used and agricultural equipment depreciated.

In other words, a family or individual contract very often turns out to be an old type of *kolkhoz* arrangement in a new guise. This explains their frequent inefficiency and insolvency. Family and individual contract workers have their own kinds of problems. The advantages of a small collective whose members are all related are obvious: they are more homogeneous and cohesive than larger, unwieldy collectives. Yet the former are dependent on the changing family situations of their members (marriages, births, decisions to move elsewhere, etc.). While these problems may have only a minor impact on the workings of a large collective, for a small one they can be disastrous. The main problem of family collectives, however, is still the fact that they are not masters of their economic fate. For example, their operating expenses and profits are hardly ever taken into account when their earnings are calculated. Enterprise managers are constantly breaking contractual agreements by refusing to pay the workers of family con-

tracts the money they have earned. The claim is that the collectives' earnings are too high; this perception is shaped by the ideology of egalitarianism, which has been trumpeted since the time of the Bolshevik Revolution.

The Soviet government manipulates contracts with the objective of turning them into tools faithfully serving the interests of the state. The needs of the workers are regarded as of only minor importance. The spread of family and individual contractual work is hindered by a psychological factor—the disbelief of their members in any sort of assured future.

Agricultural workers are ever mindful of the possibility that in the future a leader (a successor of Gorbachev or even Gorbachev himself) will come and tell them: "enough of your *kulak* ways, share your riches with the state." Such fears are far from groundless, not only in view of historical experience, but also because of present day realities in the Soviet Union. Family and individual contracts are a burden for the managers of *kolkhozy* and *sovkhozy*, who have to reach some kind of accomodation with them and supply them with materials and equipment. Essentially, family and individual labor contractors actively oppose interference "from above" in their affairs. Their opposition challenges the principle of the leading role of the party.

Yet Soviet agrarian policy-makers, as long as they still want to foster change in their country's farming methods, have no serious alternatives to contract work. In order to keep themselves in power, Soviet rulers have to feed the people. Hence they support the establishment of contracts out of dire necessity, rather than out of free choice. This is why contracts were not only established but have been encouraged to grow.

In 1988, peasants were given the right to lease land. As a result, a new term appeared in the Soviet Union: a leasehold contract (*arendny podryad*). Under this form of contract, a labor brigade or detachment receives land from a *kolkhoz* or *sovkhoz* and all the equipment necessary to farm it. The members then sell their produce to their leasor, as agreed, either for money or for goods. Whichever is the case, due account is taken of the leasehold payments. *Kolkhoz* or state property—land, machinery, and buildings—become thus in a very tangible way closer to the worker while the worker becomes a temporary owner of these resources. Through this arrangement, Soviet man's deep alienation from the land and state ownership is to a certain extent overcome.

Socialist cooperation in the countryside is becoming to all intents and purposes obsolete. For people working according to contract the cumbersome and incompetent administrative apparatus is not only unnecessary but harmful. It hinders their ability to choose their own production items and blocks their marketing outlets. Yet the breakup of the *kolkhoz* and *sovkhoz* way of life is proceeding haltingly, and thus far not on a large scale. For the future of the Soviet system, however, this change could be decisive.

The creation of a significant private sector in agriculture, which would amount to a decisive social and economic factor, would lead to a weakening of the party's economic monopoly. Eventually, political democracy would be bound to follow. This would have little in common with the current regimented, strictly controlled process known as "democratization (cf.). It would be genuine democracy, entailing far-reaching social reforms. Private ownership could not remain without an impact on the country's politics. It would be likely to result in the formation of a new party to represent the interests of private entrepreneurs. Understanding the implications of this matter thoroughly, Lenin warned Soviet communists about petty, private enterprise "continually daily, hourly and spontaneously giving birth to large-scale capitalism."

However, labor contracts are another matter. Operating within the framework and under the auspices of collective and state farms, they present no danger to the Soviet regime, for they can be abolished at any time and the peasants can lose their newly won relative independence to again become hired day-laborers.

Thus, progress in Soviet agriculture, which began with the establishment of contractual collectives, will stop short of improving the lot of the farm worker, the main actor in the drama of agricultural production.

> The basic principles on which the collective contract is today being set up are self-financing, self-support and self-management. (Agitator, no. 16, 1987, p. 20)

> What is the meaning of a leasehold contract? In this form of work a brigade, a team or a unit, lease land and all the resources necessary for yielding produce from a kolkhoz or sovkhoz. (Agitator, no. 7, 1988, p. 35)

> A family contract in the agricultural sector implies a diversity of contractual agreements between an individual family, which works or lives in a rural location, and a kolkhoz or sovkhoz. (Agitator, no. 14, 1988, p. 44)

Conviction (*Ubezhdennost'*). A firm belief in communism and in the correctness of the course the Soviet leadership is pursuing. Since conviction is said to be the very foundation of Marxist morality, the frequency of this word in propaganda messages is high. Typically, it appears in combination with attributes like "communist" (*kommunistichesky*) and "Bolshevik" (*bol'shevistsky*) or, for added emphasis, with such adjectives as "unshakable" (*nepokolebimy*), "steadfast" (*nezyblemy*), and "ideological" (*ideyny*).

Conviction is supposed to shape the mental habits of Soviet man, his attitude toward society and work, his relationships with his fellow workers, his conduct with his family. It is supposed to make him loyal to the party and active in carrying out its policies. Conviction is associated with such characteristics as conscientiousness, love for work, and helpfulness to others. It is supposed to encourage a sense of personal responsibility to society, involvement in public activities, and the readiness to put state interests above one's own. The shaping of conviction is seen as one of the main tasks of communist education.

Nonetheless, it is precisely conviction that is less typical for the Soviet man than other qualities he is expected to have. This is because he typically accepts Marxism only for lack of alternatives, or merely pretends to accept it. Thus he lacks a deep commitment to Marxist aims and standards of personal conduct. By contrast, the "conviction" that communism is bankrupt is indeed firmly held in the Soviet Union by very many.

Authoritative Soviet documents recognize the rarity of true (i.e., communist) conviction, but explain it by shortcomings of ideological and political work. The propaganda machine has been talking about improving this work for nearly seventy years, while either remaining silent or lying about manifestations of anticommunist conviction and while contriving to suppress any such manifestations.

Unshakable ideological conviction and steadfastness rooted in his class position are the qualities of the agitator-fighter which are bound to guarantee his success. . . . (Agitator, no. 4, 1984, p. 61)

I admit that reading Nabi Khazri's books, listening to the music of those verses permeated with civic conviction filled me with love for the poet. (Izvestiya, 12 March 1984, p. 3)

Cooperative/Co-op (*Kooperatsiya/Kooperativy*). (1) A voluntary association for joint activity. (2) A way of organizing labor. Under socialism, cooperatives are subordinate to its law of development, which means that they are exploited by the state. However, this phenomenon evolved and spread in Russia long before the Revolution. At the beginning of the century, the country had some two thousand cooperative organizations, while by the time of the Bolshevik Revolution, their number exceeded sixty thousand. The speed with which these organizations developed and their efficiency, both in industry and agriculture, made it possible (in the words of one Russian scholar, Alexander Chayanov) to view the cooperative as an innovation on a par with man's most consequential discoveries.

Lenin also considered the cooperative to be very significant, although he related to it strictly from the standpoint of a communist, valuing it to the extent to which it was capable of serving that system. In this context, he wrote: "ten to twenty years of correct relations with the peasantry will give us victory on a worldwide scale" (Lenin, *Sochineniya* [Works], 4th ed., vol. 43, Moscow, Izd-vo politicheskoy literatury, 1961, p. 382–83). This was how Lenin saw the international meaning of cooperatives. For domestic consumption, he said, "a network of civilized cooperatives" together with "public ownership of the means of production, and the proletariat's class victory over the bourgoisie" ought to lead to "the building of socialism." However, "a civilized network of cooperatives" never materialized in the Soviet Union.

"The cooperative plan," according to Lenin's (and subsequently Stalin's) interpretation was quite different from the original concept of cooperative, which implied democracy, independence, and self-management. Stalin's so-called "great breakthrough" in Soviet agriculture was great only in terms of the famine and mass repression it brought about, which together accounted for the death of millions of peasants. In reality, the "great breakthrough" meant nothing other than "management by administrative fiat" which is now being criticized as resoundingly as it was then extolled. What was supposed to be the gradual, voluntary collectivization of agriculture turned into the rapid and universal establishment of collective farms (cf.) (*kolkhozy*), by force.

The Soviet economy, although ideologically purporting to represent joint interests of the workers, the collectives, and society, actually amounted to a new form of serfdom, where the *barshchina*, or corvée, was termed "socially useful labor" and the *obrok*, the quit-rent, "contract work" (*podryad*) (cf.). Cooperatives—*kolkhozy* as well as a few surviving traders' cooperatives—were relegated to the status of wretched, backward, organizations. A campaign was waged to "uplift them" to the level of "national" state enterprises, while the ineffective manner in which they had supposedly developed was stressed. Raising them to the level of the "national" sector was done in a typically Soviet manner, by reorganizing cooperatives as state organizations. This happened with many *kolkhozy*, which became *sovkhozy* or state farms, as well as with consumers' cooperatives, all of which were funnelled into a centralized trading network.

The biased and prejudicial notions about cooperatives proved so entrenched that they rendered futile all subsequent efforts to reanimate them. The problem of cooperatives has twice assumed a political significance in Soviet history. The first time this occurred was in the early 1920s, when the communists sought to extricate the economy from the morass of "war communism," (cf.) At that time, they had to redefine socialism somehow and resolved to base it on the idea of cooperation. The cooperative movement once again entered the agenda in the 1980s when the government began to see it as a salutary method of revitalizing the country after more than a decade of economic and social stagnation. It was stagnation that made reform necessary in the country. This time, however, changes were directed not at particular sectors of the economy, as attempted under Khrushchev and Kosygin, but aimed at bringing about an entirely new, macroeconomic approach to management.

New legislation (the 1988 "Law on Cooperatives") was enacted "to provide ample room for initiative, independence, genuine self-supporting, and personal interest to ensure the best results for individual and collective-social labor" (*Agitator*, no. 9, 1988, p. 8).

If Lenin aspired to integrate cooperatives into the body of socialism, Gorbachev's goal is exactly the opposite, namely to refashion socialism into cooperation, without, however, openly contradicting Lenin. Because of the latter factor, the tenet of the leading role of state ownership continues to be upheld: This means that the idea of the cooperatives is being sneaked in via the back door.

No cooperative has the right to buy anything from or sell anything to state enterprises or to accept any kind of technological commission from them. A common problem faced by cooperatives is the difficulty in finding premises for their productive activities, which prevents them from working effectively. Inflexible regulations obstructing the flow of supplies needed for their production are responsible for illicit activities in which, according to an estimate from the mid-1980s, some 18 million people were involved.

Cooperatives also need to cope with the irrational Soviet pricing (cf.) system. Because of their difficulty in obtaining raw materials and because of the long hours worked by their members, (typically, fourteen or even sixteen hours a day), the prices of the goods they manufacture are quite high. In a situation of acute shortage of nearly everything, markets also contribute to raising their prices. The major factor pushing up the price of cooperatively manufactured goods is the state trading network, which takes a 20 percent commission on co-op sales. The corresponding commission taken on state-produced goods is only $7\frac{1}{2}$ percent. This situation is a clear example of the principle that "the worse it is for the customer, the better it is for the state."

Soviet economic policy is effectively aimed at rechanneling consumer discontent against the cooperatives. The state hits cooperatives with crippling taxation. In itself, this taxation shows how the state goes about "meeting the wishes of the working masses." Taxes comparable to those which, since 1 April 1988, have been levied at a rate of up to 90 percent on the revenues of cooperatives exist nowhere else. The growth of cooperatives was immediately halted. Then a retreat was sounded, at least for the time being: the Presidium of the Supreme Soviet decreed that in the future taxes would be levied "on the members of cooperatives . . . according to the rates fixed for taxing the earnings of workers and employees" (*Izvestiya*, 30 July 1988, p. 3).

Another obstacle to the proper functioning of cooperatives is the widely held belief that they lure the best qualified workers away from the state sector. There is a grain of truth in this. The state might halt the outflow of manpower from its industries by restructuring wage scales. This would enable the state to successfully compete with cooperatives to the advantage rather than to the detriment of the workers. Meanwhile, however, all efforts are being made to turn cooperatives into yet another sector of an economy steered by command from above.

This explains the low productivity of cooperatives. Out of the overall range of goods and services supplied to the population during the first quarter of 1988, cooperatives accounted for less than 0.3 percent or, in absolute terms, 300 million compared to the 99.5 billion rubles worth of goods and services supplied by the state sector. This resulted even though the state sector is still unable to satisfy consumer demand. In fact the shortage of goods, far from declining, is actually growing—to the extent that the population has accumulated the enormous sum of 267 billion "unspent" rubles.

Cooperatives are afflicted by the same malaise that pervades the entire Soviet economy: corruption (cf.). In this particular case, many experienced, dishonest operators from the shadow economy (cf. second economy), have taken over the most lucrative and promising branches of the cooperative sector. Not wanting to be left out, many ministries and directorates take advantage of their right to turn unprofitable enterprises into cooperatives in order to pocket profits on the side. For that purpose a quite profitable state enterprise can be misclassified as unprofitable. The gimmick works. Since the output of such cooperatives is considered to be part of the overall production volume in a given sector and since the prices cooperatives charge are far higher than those of the state enterprises, the financial indicators of a given sector's performance skyrocket, and hence, the managers are duly rewarded.

Under such conditions, it is doubtful whether Soviet leaders will succeed in effecting the transition from primitive cooperatives to modern cooperatives. Hence their slogan "the attitude toward cooperatives de-fines the attitude toward *perestroika*" is meaningless.

It is no secret that in our country, cooperatives have not, as they say, made it. To say that their road has been hard and rough, and that our society has sustained much material loss as a result would be an understatement. (Agitator, no. 9, 1988, p. 8)

This is the real course of action, not just a temporary detour, as some would like to believe. This is the Party's long-term strategy. As long as 65 years ago, Lenin wrote of cooperatives: "This is the building of socialism." But we must fight for it. (Komsomol'skaya pravda, 26 May 1988, p. 8)

Socialist cooperation represents a constantly improving, progressive form of socially useful activity. (Izvestiya, 8 June 1988, p. 1)

Corruption (*Korruptsiya*). The buying of favors from highly placed persons or political officials through various forms of bribery. Such is the Soviet notion of corruption, which roughly corresponds to the notion commonly accepted elsewhere, except that in the USSR it is invariably qualified as "taking place in the capitalist countries." It is true that corruption is quite advanced in the free world, but there it is viewed as a deviation from the legal and moral standards. However, in the socialist countries corruption is more or less accepted as an indispensable extension of the single-party system, ubiquitous secrecy, and suppression of democracy. Even more importantly, however, corruption is bred by the very character of the communist power elite.

Communism has institutionalized a system of double standards, one for the masses, the other for the ruling class. The later live in fashionable mansions, country villas, and resorts built by Western craftsmen and located in forest areas or by the sea. They receive special medical services, unavailable to others, in facilities to which no one else is admitted. Ordinary people must be kept in the dark as to the nature (and indeed the very fact) of their leaders' illnesses. Members of the ruling class stay in the best hotels ("for the exclusive use of party officials"), travel in special sections of airplanes and by deluxe railway cars, and relax in closely guarded VIP lounges in railway stations and airports. To set the ruling class apart from the people, its members are granted special passes enabling them to attend concerts and movies without the need to wait in the ticket-lines. They have at their disposal chauffeur-driven limousines and private shops offering a wide selection of consumer goods unattainable for ordinary mortals.

The rights and privileges enjoyed by the ruling class cannot be made universal, to benefit the entire Soviet society. Distributions in the USSR is subject to hierarchical considerations; within this system, one-third of the gross national product is allocated to 10 percent of its privileged citizens. These 10 percent end up receiving one-quarter of all the cars produced, half of all the new apartments, and one-third of all subsidized vacations. Anything that is left over is then distributed among the people in accordance with their meager rights: the closer one is to the top, the larger and better the rewards.

Initially it seemed that increases in salaries and privileges would eliminate corruption among the ruling class. Yet such hopes did not materialize. Salary increases only whetted appetites. The privileged perceived the state as a stock market: they thought that the higher the stakes (i.e., their social status), the larger should be the profits. Thus corruption is not incidental to the Soviet system. It is rather a social compact of the "haves," whereby self-enrichment is done not in an isolated manner but within a well-organized and closely-knit framework of association.

It is difficult to pinpoint the exact motives of the Soviet ruling class. There is no doubt that their value system attaches considerable importance to the enjoyment of life, to love, to the family. Yet beyond these needs, there looms an all-consuming drive whose objective is the acquisition of money by any means available. It is not easy to estimate the size of their illegal profits. The "black" income of Soviet officials is amassed through various sorts of bribes extorted from the ministries

and departments under their authority. Their amount is largely determined by the opportunities provided by the city or republic where a given official holds his post. In any event, the amounts of money obtained by such officials run to tenfold and sometimes even hundredfold their salaries, which in themselves are not insubstantial as (after taking into account various bonuses such as the deputy bonus, overtime pay, subsidized trips, etc.) they approach 900 to 1,000 rubles a month, which is five times the official minimum wage.

The data on the side earnings shown here are derivable from various sources, primarily from periodical literature dealing with crime. Recently, Soviet leaders have been exposed to public censure—for being greedy. Particularly noteworthy is the recent process of the dismissal and even prosecution of party officials compromised by their involvement in giving or taking huge bribes under Brezhnev. In this context, there have been revelations about the buying and selling of various positions, including the prices for specific posts. The going prices for positions were as follows: managers of factories, schools, and technical schools paid four-digit figures; secretaries of district party committees and university rectors, five digit figures; and ministers and secretaries of city party committees, six digit ones. There are also, or at least have been until recently, price lists for receiving honorary titles. There is one golden rule: a profitable position should justify the investment in it within one year, two at the most, and in a few years time begin to yield a steady payoff at 200 to 300 percent interest. There is logic here in that the future of a Soviet VIP is too precarious to be counted on for more than a few years.

The geographical variations in Soviet corruption follow many subtle and idiosyncratic patterns. For instance, in the southern and eastern republics the tradition is to hand baksheesh in a wallet (with all the money it can hold, be it fifty or a hundred thousand). Local residents have considered such a method of transaction quite legal; however, now criminal laws sometimes operate to prove the contrary. In the Ukrainian, Russian (excluding Moscow), and Baltic republics corruption is somewhat milder. There, the stakes do not exceed twenty to thirty thousand rubles.

Thus we are dealing with a special kind of corruption, one that is integral to the domination of the entire society by one privileged class—the communists. This system is based on the principle "You scratch my back—I'll scratch yours." In such a society, material comforts are strictly proportional to one's hierarchical rank. That determines not only the size but also the sources of one's income; not only the opportunities for amassing benefits but also of distributing them.

One of the most important consequences of power-wielding in the USSR is the accumulation of capital, which itself is a source of power. In other words, capital can buy power. The more money one has, the more power one can acquire. Power and the acquisitive urge is what makes the communist elite tick. This trait sets this elite apart from any other class within the Soviet society. On the whole, the Soviet state resembles a monarchy, albeit not an enlightened one. It offers no independence to anyone, either to those who hold power and seek wealth or those who produce the wealth and want power.

There was a time when the Soviet leaders received the rewards—proportionate to their position—directly into their own hands. Later, the methods of bribery were perfected. For instance, the authority to receive bribes was delegated to personal secretaries and assistants who would retain a certain percentage as a "service charge." The same function is often entrusted to officials' wives or children. An example was provided by Brezhnev's son and son-in-law, both large-scale swindlers, the former in the Ministry of Foreign Trade, where he held the post of First Deputy Minister, the latter in the Ministry of Internal Affairs, where he held an analogous position. Brezhnev's daughter also busied herself with illegal transactions. Once, when she had her heart set on some diamond jewelry owned by a famous circus per-

former, she arranged to have it stolen. The theft was sanctioned by the KGB, not gratuitously, of course; there must have been some compensation for the "favors" extended on that occasion by the deputy chairman of the KGB, General Tsvigun, Brezhnev's brother-in-law.

It is not easy to calculate precisely the "supplementary" income of republic, territorial, and provincial leaders. This would involve the use of all four arithmetical operations; addition—of cities and districts under their jurisdiction; subtraction—of the parts of the profits passed on to the superiors; division—distribution of income among subordinates intended to ensure their cooperation; and finally, multiplication—since the amounts received steadily increase manifold. The highest-ranking leaders—secretaries of the Central Committee and ministers—would never accept less than a million, the estimated price for being awarded the title of Hero of Socialist Labor.

As a result of generational change in the Kremlin and elaborate intrigues within the party, the pinnacles of authority in the USSR were seized by young and vigorous men. They began to jostle and push the old, fossilized bureaucrats away from posts of any importance. Public exposures began to be trumpeted, and some cracks and gaps suddenly appeared on the contrived "socialist" facade, allowing a glimpse into the true nature of the ruling mafia. Hundreds of prominent officials were charged with accepting bribes and fired, forced to retire, or sent off to busy themselves with academic pursuits. The purges spread to every republic and included even Moscow.

By and large, the exposures were a by-product of political feuding at the top. Yet there was more at stake. Casting dubious light on the conduct of the Soviet elite amounted to a legitimacy crisis that threatened stability of the regime. This did not happen overnight but through a gradual process that, paradoxically, gained momentum concurrently with the new leadership's desperate attempts to solidify its position. The process of the Soviet communist elite's formation as a class was being completed; its lifetime privileges were becoming hereditary. The fragile psuedosocialist veneer was crumbling, with authority passing over to the elite's scions, not as smoothly as might have been wished, but just as surely.

Money was attracted to the powerful. The Soviet leaders had accumulated capital that subsequently had to be "laundered." Because of this, the interests of the communist elite coincided with those social groups which functioned outside the pale of legality: e.g., the underground shop operators (*tsekhoviki*) who had amassed huge fortunes by dealing in the "countereconomy." The latter had what the communist elite craved: money—while the communist elite possessed the things coveted by the underground racketeers: status and the privileges that go with it.

Cooperation between the communist class and the underworld has been flourishing for years. Privileges were sold and respectability bought. But, gradually the communist class ceased being patrons of the countereconomy and became its operators, while the underworld bosses shouldered their way into the ruling class.

The racketeers achieved amazing social mobility. Gradually they began to fill key government positions, while the more inert communist class was getting bogged down in shady wheeling and dealing. Nominally, it still held power, while the country was increasingly ruled by racketeers and black marketeers. These people came to wield so much power that, had they wanted to, they could have dispensed with the partocracy entirely. To do that, they would only have to destroy the old communist fiction and create a new one designed to provide their actual power with some legitimacy. That would mean communism's total collapse. Under these circumstances, the new Soviet leaders decided to save the communist system from itself. This explains their rigid and often ruthless treatment of corruption not out of moral but out of pragmatic considerations. The country's future hinges on the clear-cut issue of who will be the winner—the communists or the racketeers. However, Soviet corruption has advanced so far as to develop immunity against the measures devised to fight it, which actually only add to its growth. That is one of the reasons for the powerlessness of the anticorruption campaign. But a quite nonideological factor also plays a role. The new leaders want to preserve the mechanisms of corruption for their own future use.

> A network of bribery and corruption had been and still is being exposed in Uzbekistan, Kazakhstan, Tadzhikistan, Turkmenia, the three Transcaucasian republics, Moldavia, the Krasnodar Territory, Ukraine, and Moscow. (Ogonek, no. 26, 1988, p. 27)

> Yes, the struggle against corruption and embezzlement has reached the point akin to the one which made Marshal Foch in WWI dispatch his famous report: "Our left flank has collapsed, our right flank is crushed, I am launching an attack." (Moskovskie novosti, no. 11, 13 March 1988, p. 15)

> Heads of the team investigating the Kamalov case told me about one of the provincial Party committee secretaries who had paid one million rubles for the title of a Hero of Socialist Labor. (Nedelya, no. 29, 1988, p. 14)

Cosmopolitanism (*Kosmopolitizm*). An affinity for universal culture interpreted by the communists as indifference toward Russian national traditions. Ideological condemnation of and political reprisals against cosmopolitanism help the Soviet Union affirm the superiority of the Russian nation and preach mistrust and hostility toward other nations and, in this sense, can be viewed as an antithesis of the "proletarian internationalism" that masks the expansionist designs of Soviet imperialism.

A campaign against cosmopolitanism and cosmopolitans (*kosmopolity*) was conducted in the late 1940s. It began with an attack on culture and art in the well-tested style of the "Great Terror." In 1946, the exposures and condemnations of "rootless cosmopolitans" (*bezrodnye kosmopolity*), depicted as "degenerates" kowtowing before the West, opened with the publication of two party resolutions. The first concerned the magazines

Zvezda and *Leningrad*, while the second dealt with theatrical productions. The campaign against cosmopolitans took place in a country devastated by war, with a paralyzed economy and backward industry. The Soviet leadership found attacks on cosmopolitans useful for distracting the miserable masses from the privations of daily life and at the same time for stimulating them to higher productivity. The goal was to revive the fading patriotism and Russian national consciousness that had played so crucial a role in defeating Germany.

There was more to the campaign against cosmopolitanism, however, than just reasserting Russian "uniqueness." Propaganda about the exceptional contributions of the Russian people to science, literature, and art was meant to serve, and did actually serve, as an ideological "fuse" to set off a new wave of terror. The scope of the purges expanded rapidly. Starting with literature (the persecution of the writers Akhmatova and Zoshchenko), the purges spread to linguistics (the campaign against Academician Marr), and then to physiology, history, political economy, and biology. From arts and sciences the purges moved to the sphere they had been targeted on from the very beginning of the campaign: the government administration. Dismissals, arrests, and executions then decimated the ranks of top party and state officials.

However, a dress rehearsal for the struggle against cosmopolitanism had taken place earlier, at the time of anti-Jewish reprisals that culminated in the murder of the famous Jewish actor Mikhoels, the dissolution of the Jewish Anti-Fascist Committee, and the closing of Jewish schools, theaters, newspapers, and publishing houses. Although Jews were not the only victims of the cosmopolitanism campaign, its anti-Semitic character soon became evident. Public figures, scientists, and artists who had concealed their Jewish origin under Russian names or pen names were publicly exposed as Jews and castigated in the most virulent and debasing terms in the Soviet press. Readers were informed that in Soviet society there was no

social basis for cosmopolitanism, which was merely a legacy of prerevolutionary capitalism and amounted to admiring everything European and denigrating everything Russian. The public was called on to "stigmatize" (cf. *kleimit'*) cosmopolitans.

The term itself became a general term of abuse. In colloquial speech it became associated with Jews, who were viewed as "rootless outsiders" (*lyudi bez rodu i plemeni*) or "Judases who commit treachery for thirty pieces of silver." Soviet anti-Semitism reached its apex in the winter of 1953 with the arrest of a number of Jewish physicians—"the murderers in white coats"—in connection with "the Doctors' Plot" and the planned mass deportation of Jews to Siberia.

At this point, Stalin died and the anti-cosmopolitan campaign was cut short. However, the conditions that gave birth to "the struggle against cosmopolitanism" persist. Xenophobia is rampant in the USSR and influences government policies. Depending on the expediencies of the power struggle at the top, this sentiment may yet be exploited or fanned. From the corridors of power, anti-Semitism may be channelled into the street where extremist groups like "Pamyat" will be only too willing to take advantage of it. In that case a revival of the anticosmopolitan campaign of the early 1950s could again engulf Soviet society.

Under present conditions cosmopolitanism is used as an ideological tool of imperialist reaction, as an ideological cover for the aggressive policies of the monopolistic circles of the USA and England. (Bol'shaya sovetskaya entsiklopediya [Great Soviet encyclopedia]; Moscow: State Scientific Publishing House, 2d ed., vol. 23, 1953, p. 114)

. . . It's not very far from political naiveté to cosmopolitanism. (Agitator, no. 3, 1984, p. 47)

The falsifier and pseudo-academic speaks about Jews as if they were some cosmopolitan commercial-industrial group. . . . (Novoe russkoe slovo, 13 January 1984, p. 3)

Counterplan (*Vstrechny plan*). A production plan, worked out by the local management of an enterprise, which raises the targets and shortens the time schedules for tasks envisaged by the state plan. Counterplans, which upon being drafted have to be approved by party organizations, are part and parcel of "socialist competition" (*sotsialisticheskoe sorevnovanie*). They are looked upon as a major form of worker participation in the search for improved use of manpower, equipment and raw materials in industry.

Counterplanning is intended by the authorities to remedy flaws in the Soviet economy. It is seen as a way to boost productivity, lower the costs of production, and increase the efficiency, and thereby the profits, of enterprises. In theory, the task of counterplans is to adjust state planning to the existing potential of an enterprise and to coordinate the activities of raw material suppliers and trade organizations. The counterplans nevertheless fail to make a significant impact on the national economy because they are powerless against the prevailing atmosphere of inertia and apathy. This is also why the stepped-up financial incentives to both individual workers and industrial enterprises fail to achieve their purpose. Thus all the exertions of the party apparatus in propagandizing the need for designing and implementing ambitious counterplans (*napryazhenny vstrechny plan*) have not helped.

Counterplans are particularly intended to remedy the practice of enterprise managements of concealing resources they have at their disposal; thus the very existence of counterplans bears witness to the incompetence and bankruptcy of centralized planning. While boosting output to a certain extent, the counterplans are responsible for a decline in quality. This explains the phenomenon of a constant and frantic "storming" (*shturmovshchina*) in Soviet industrial enterprises. As a rule, instead of growth in actual output, there is "growth" in targeting output in the plans ("showing off"—*pokazukha*) and in reporting it afterwards ("cooking the books"—*pripiski*).

When counterplans are worked out, attention is focused on the improvement of quality

standards, on prompt and complete delivery of goods ordered by customers, and on comprehensive savings in material, labor and financial resources. (Pravda, 28 November 1983, p. 1)

One of the most important objectives is to ensure the fulfillment of counterplans which are drafted at the beginning of the year, when hidden resources are most accurately accounted for. (Pravda, 13 December 1983, p. 1)

The counterplans for 1984 are the very embodiment of [economic] logic. (Pravda, 25 December 1983, p. 2)

Counterrevolution (*Kontrrevolyutsiya*). Any opposition to the communist regime or Soviet policy. Historically, the concept of counterrevolutions is connected with the Bolshevik coup (the October Revolution) of 1917. Political bodies and their actions inside or outside the country were appraised as revolutionary if they contributed to the consolidation of communist power and counterrevolutionary if they were perceived as posing any threat to communist domestic or foreign policy aims.

Around 1930, millions of peasants who opposed forced collectivization were accused of counterrevolution and exterminated or sent to concentration camps. Under the pretext of the struggle against counterrevolution, in the 1930s, 1940s, and 1950s the state security services started a series of trials of top party and state figures who were charged with conspiring with the forces of international reaction to restore capitalism in the country.

In order to intimidate the people and thus maintain the regime's stability, Soviet ruling circles have often fabricated reports of counterrevolution, foreign or domestic, overt or covert. Repeatedly, they have justified resorting to military force, as in Berlin in June 1953, in Hungary in October 1956, in Czechoslovakia in August 1968, and in Afghanistan in December 1979 by the alleged need to oppose counterrevolution.

The distinction between the concepts of "revolution" and "counterrevolution" in Soviet usage tends to be less than absolute and sometimes depends on political circumstances. For instance, as long as the Chinese government acted in accordance with Soviet interests, Soviet propaganda praised the Chinese revolution; but when the leadership of the Chinese People's Republic began to show signs of self-assertion and independence from Moscow, the Soviet press began branding Mao Tse-tung and other Chinese leaders as counterrevolutionaries (*kontrrevolyutsionery*). The transparently opportunistic use of the word counterrevolution can be seen in Soviet commentaries on recent events in Nicaragua and Guatemala. The pro-Soviet line of the Nicaraguan authorities is represented as "revolutionary," while Guatemala's opposition to the USSR is described as counterrevolutionary.

The adjective counterrevolutionary (*kontrrevolutsionny*) is often used together with such derogatory nouns as "putsch" (*putch*), "junta" (*khunta*), and "gang" (*banda*). Sometimes the adjective is replaced by a synonymous one, such as "antinational" (*antinatsional'ny*) or "reactionary" (*reaktsionny*). As if mere counterrevolution were not enough, Soviet propaganda often adds to it qualifications such as "covert" (*tikhaya*) or "creeping" (*polzuchaya*) in order to stress further the dangerous and despicable nature of the alleged threat.

> There is a growing threat from counterrevolution to the existence of the socialist system in Poland. (Pravda, 13 June 1981, p. 4)

> While the USA has provided the Afghan counterrevolution with $218 million in aid over the past five years, in the current financial year alone this figure has reached $105 million. (Pravda, 19 November 1983)

> Deceived by counterrevolution, these people fled Afghanistan. (Komsomol'skaya pravda, 12 December 1982, p. 3)

Cult of Personality (*Kul't lichnosti*). In the wide sense, blind worship of authority; in the narrow sense, the glorification and idolization of Stalin. Historically, the cult of personality took shape in the Soviet Union in the process of its transformation from a dictatorship of party bureaucracy into a dictatorship of party leaders. The cult of personality's main ideas and features, such as arbitrariness, oppression, and terror, were in germinal form present in the communist system from its inception. It was Lenin who insisted that "to raise the question of any contradiction between a dictatorship of the Party and a dictatorship of the masses attests to an incredible confusion of ideas . . . . To reach the conclusion that there is a contradiction between the dictatorship of the masses and the dictatorship of their leaders is a laughable stupidity and absurdity" (V. I. Lenin, *Sobr. soch.* [*Collected works*], 3d ed., vol. 25, p. 188). Once Lenin consolidated his power, he paved the way for the cult of personality by initiating the resolution banning all factionalism within the party, which was passed by the Tenth Party Congress in March 1921.

The slavish adulation of communist leaders and the glorification of their wisdom, superior insight, and infallibility were established and encouraged while Lenin was still alive—and with his approval. From there it was but a short step to creating the image of Stalin as a human deity. This notion was established and propagated by many members of Stalin's entourage, friend and foe alike. Some did it out of servility, others—out of fear and the determination to hold onto the power that could slip out of their grasp any moment. Stalin himself did much to promote the cult of personality by emphasizing and flaunting his authority, experience, and superior knowledge in every possible context. However, the syndrome known as the cult of personality cannot be accounted for by acts of individual will, not even the will of Stalin. For the real explanation, one has to refer to the nature of Soviet history. In order to elucidate and justify its goals and the inhumane means needed to attain them, the Communist party had to rely on some supreme, absolute, and supposedly infallible intelligence. The cult of personality catered to a belief in the existence of such a quasi-supernatural being, all but immortal, omnipotent, and omniscient. The place left vacant by the dethroned and deconsecrated Divinity was not taken by a new transcendental deity, but rather by a pagan idol, an avatar of the distant past. It was endowed with the power to castigate, punish, and kill. As the Christian religion was replaced by the communist one, the content and object of worship underwent a drastic change. The new deity, i.e., Stalin, instead of exhibiting the attributes of love and mercy, was ruthless, merciless, and inaccessible in his grandeur. He rose from oblivion via the magic of dialectical materialism. In place of the Christian churches that he destroyed he erected new, Marxist ones: the mausoleum with the enbalmed body of Lenin in Red Square and the imposing monuments in bronze and granite dedicated to himself, the self-appointed spiritual descendant of Lenin.

In developed societies, Christianity was modified by the principles of individual freedom and justice. Such a worldview was unacceptable to Stalin since he waged war against all rival claimants to divinity, as well as against a large segment of humanity. His moral code justified baseness, violence, slander, and lies. He was aggressive and spiteful. For him a human being, in his uniqueness and spiritual dimensions, did not exist. For him all that mattered was a black-and-white division into followers and enemies, rationalized by the philosophy of the "class struggle against imperialism." He was feared and revered. He remained inaccessible, surrounded by an aura of secrecy and mystery, avoiding contact with the masses, thus leaving wide room for speculation about him. This wall of secrecy and evasiveness, erected around Stalin in order to conceal his intellectual inferiority and lack of skill in public speaking, facilitated the perpetuation of the cult of his personality. The lack of information about him gave rise to all kinds of fanciful and incredible legends and myths. Stalin was credited with extraordinary genius in every possible sphere of human endeavor—politics, military strategy, industry, agriculture, science, etc. Countless works of music and poetry were composed in his honor, prefaced by passionate professions of

devotion such as, "To the greatest friend and leader of all peoples—from a worthless poet, son of a faithful nation" (*Izbrannye stranitsy armyanskoy literatury* [Selected pages of Armenian literature], Moscow: Gosizdat, 1946, p. 1004).

However, the true object of these panegyrics was not the real, live Stalin, but his image reflected in countless statues and paintings, which provided a focus for imagination whereby human dissatisfaction sought and found its faith in another kind of life, a better and more just one than Soviet reality could offer.

Those were the sources of the ebullient and unbridled glorification of Stalin. He was depicted as the greatest genius of all times and peoples, the champion and savior of the downtrodden. To create this image, no expressions were spared. The semantic range included nouns like "leader," "father," and "brother," embellished by bombastic adjectives like "unfailing," "radiant," "wise," "bright," "mighty," "brave," etc. All that official propaganda had to do to maintain this image was to occasionally introduce additions or modifications.

Soviet society had a vital need for Stalin. His tangible image, widely reproduced in paint and stone, was more comprehensible than the fervidly but unsuccessfully propagated notion of a "bright future" (cf.). Stalin appeared to be the main source of light in the cheerless present and, for the uncertain future, the only point on the road to communism (cf.).

The cult of Stalin's personality was regulated by an elaborate code of symbols and rituals: public buildings, parks, boulevards, and town squares were decorated with portraits of "the father of the peoples." Party conferences and plenums commenced and concluded with salutations to Stalin and pledges of love, loyalty, and respect for him. Stalin was symbolically "elected" chairman of conferences and meetings to tempestuous rounds of long-lasting applause.

Nevertheless, the expected leap of the Soviet people and, with it, all mankind, from the realm of necessity to the realm of freedom did not take place. The force of coercion embodied by Stalin, with its tens of millions of victims, turned out to be too devastating. The survivors were systematically degraded to a subhuman state not only by being enslaved or permanently tied to the farm or the factory, but also by being corrupted from within by the cult of personality. By hailing Stalin as "great" and "all-powerful," the Soviet people were implicitly acknowledging their own wretchedness and helplessness. By proclaiming him "father," they proclaimed themselves obedient "sons." By accepting Stalin as a "genius," they accepted for themselves the role of pitiful cogs in his machine. By submitting themselves to his leadership, they revealed their moral and spiritual dependence, which afforded them the kind of security that slaves have. Their adherence to the set code of behavior freed them from all sense of responsibility. As a result, they became either passive onlookers or active accomplices who wrote denunciations and joined in the "struggle" to ferret out "enemies of the people."

The cult of personality was psychologically effective. It functioned as an intangible specter, constantly hovering over people, intimidating them to the point that they were mortally afraid to speak out, to trust their neighbor, or to display any kind of initiative.

After Stalin's death the logic of the succession struggles dictated the need to discard the cult of personality and consequently to revive a form of collective leadership. In order to secure his position in the Kremlin, Khrushchev needed to elevate himself to the party olympus occupied by his predecessor. But to displace Lenin would have entailed too great a risk to the very integrity of the state. Therefore, Stalin became his target. He launched an offensive against the cult of personality, which implies a notion of return to the sources of genuine socialism and promises to observe the norms of democracy and socialist legality. Concurrently, the process of exposing the cult of personality and its attendant crimes conveniently helped Khrushchev in defeating the opposition against him. The social causes of the cult of personality were not eliminated, however. The regime remained coercive and the omnipotence of the party apparatus remained intact.

Collective leadership (cf.) has been, at best, a transitory form of government in the Soviet Union. Periods of "collective leadership" have lasted for no more than a few years, before the glorification of a Khrushchev, Brezhnev, Andropov, or Chernenko again become the order of the day. Criticism of the cult of personality, which dwells on Stalin's personal failings, confuses a surface phenomenon of Soviet politics with its essence.

The violence of Stalin's rule (*stalinshchina*) was not just Stalin's personal legacy to life in the USSR, but rather an inevitable consequence of the communist system. The cult of personality is the other side of the coin of the impersonal cult of communism. A communist leader is the beneficiary of the cult, but never the mainspring. He cannot exist without a cult, and the cult of communism cannot propagate itself without a leader who embodies the unchanging will to "change and transform" the world. Transmutations of the cult of personality in communist society are boundless. The glorification of Stalin as the personification of communism was one version among many. A Maoist cult of personality was no less rampant. The cult of personality of Kim Il Sung in Korea thrives as did that of Ceausescu in Romania. The cult of personality of Andropov and Chernenko proved to be possible no matter how short-lived, and the possibility should not be excluded that the future will also see a cult of personality of Gorbachev.

Regardless of any historically known personal characteristics, a standard set of ossified clichés is indiscriminately applied to each and every communist leader. They have all been called "great and remarkable," "steadfast," "unflinching," "principled," and "brave." They have all been referred to as "ardent fighters for the happiness of the peoples" and "thoroughly experienced leaders of the party and the state." They were endowed with "revolutionary experience," "brilliant foresight," and "wisdom." And when they die, like Brezhnev, Andropov, and Chernenko, they are proclaimed to be "eternally alive" in the hearts of the Soviet people and progressive humanity at large.

When a new ruler takes power, he tends at first to be somewhat hesitant about the pomp and circumstance of office. Subsequently, however, after having consolidated his power in the Politburo, he graciously acquiesces in his own glorification. The propaganda machine goes to work churning out low-key cant as a general secretary (cf.) builds up his power base, and then, upon the consolidation of his rule, goes into full gear. The number of quotations from the "leader's" speeches, the length of the ovations he receives, the number of decorations he is awarded, and the size of his portraits all grow by leaps and bounds. In Soviet history, the cult of personality recurs again and again since it provides the mystique that legitimizes the rulers' authority. This is why it cannot be permanently discarded.

The cult of personality reflects the sociopsychological character of the Soviet state. The endowment of the party leader with superhuman capacities is just a variant of the myth of socialism's infinite possibilities for human development. Thus one should not be surprised that the shadow of Stalin also looms over the Gorbachev era. It is present not as a past to be overcome but as a requirement of an authority system in quest for legitimacy. The plan of political reform advanced by the new Soviet leader ingeniously included the idea of altering the form of his or her personal power. The proposed formula for separating the powers of party and state agencies actually signified their merging under the authority of the general secretary. Thus the "genetic code" of the cult of personality, far from having undergone a mutation, is merely being adapted to suit the latest Soviet leader. In accord with the logic of Soviet history at its current stage, the perennial Soviet dilemma of "What is to be done?" is being replaced by the question of "Who is guilty" of the crimes of the regime? Yet in stark contradiction to the scale of the events in question, only one person—Stalin—is blamed. Gorbachev could not help joining in the denunciation of Stalin; in fact,

he needed it to check the decline and degeneration of the system. However, he had not gone so far as to admit that the personality of Stalin was a reflection of the pernicious nature and goals of the system itself.

The limited nature of Gorbachev's criticism of the cult of personality goes together with the limited nature of the reforms he has undertaken. Gorbachev wants to preserve the myth of the party's infallibility and grandeur so as to leave its authority unchallenged, and, at the same time, to lay the fundaments on which a new cult of personality—his own—might be erected. The first bricks for this ideological construction are already being introduced into the Soviet language: it is claimed that *perestroika* (Gorbachev's) is being buttressed by the "new political thinking" (cf.) (also Gorbachev's) and being shored up by Gorbachev's supposedly distinctive humanity. One may recall here that when Stalin's cult of personality was launched, it also was accompanied by claims of the leader's progressive ideas.

The cult of personality cannot be overcome, since the communists need it badly to legitimize their authority. It is, in fact, the only remaining legitimacy they have.

> Stalin is no longer alive but we feel it necessary to refute the shameful methods of leadership which flourished under the conditions of the cult of personality. (N. Khrushchev, Zaklyuchitel'noye slovo na XXII s"ezde KPSS [Concluding speech at the Twenty-second Congress of the CPSU]; Moscow: State Publishing House for Political Literature, 1961, p. 24)

> In criticizing the cult of personality, the Party dedicated itself to the goal of removing its harmful consequences and strengthening the position of socialism. (Kratkaya istoriya SSSR [A short history of the USSR]; Part 2, 3d ed., Moscow: "Nauka" Publishing House, 1978, p. 478)

> In the past there were definitely many ideologues who helped establish the cult of personality of Stalin. . . . They presented various kinds of "arguments" for the practice of jingoistic self-glorification. (Druzhba narodov, no. 6, 1988, p. 195)

D

Dacha (*Dacha*). An out-of-town summer house. A dacha can be anything from a squalid one-room hut, without water, electricity or heating, to a palatial mansion complete with servants, watchmen, and a private beach and wood.

Some dachas are privately owned dwellings, built by housing cooperatives and bought on the installment plan, or renovated from inherited old country cottages. Others belong to the state and are used free of charge or for a symbolic fee in strict accordance with party protocol.

For well-known scientists, directors, writers, composers, and operatic soloists, often more renowned for their services to the regime than for their creative achievements, dachas are usually built in special settlements, far from main roads in secluded locations surrounded by pine woods.

The party elite and those who protect it, i.e., high-ranking members of the secret police and army officers, receive villas with grounds of several hectares that sometimes include a grove of trees, a tennis court, a swimming pool, and a sauna. Private roads, guarded by police watchmen, protect residents from the curiosity of passers-by. To enter, one needs a special pass or prior permission of the dacha resident. Many dachas are located in the area twenty to thirty kilometers southwest of Moscow, near the railroad stations of Barvikha, Zhukovskiy, and Vnukovo. Similar villas can be found in picturesque spots outside every major Soviet city.

Dachas are allocated according to rank; the type, size, decor, and location all depend on the owner's status. It would, for example, be unthinkable for a Politburo member to own the same type of dacha as a Politburo candidate.

Gorbachev's summer residence is a ten-room flat-roofed, California-style dacha, which previously belonged to Chernenko, who inherited it from Andropov, who inherited it from Brezhnev. It is located twenty-five kilometers west of Moscow in the settlement of Usovo, near the Moscow River. It is surrounded by a three-meter-high cast-iron fence. In addition, the Soviet leader has an estate in Zavidovo, where he can hunt and fish. For rest and relaxation he also has villas at Oreanda in Crimea and Pitsunda on the Black Sea coast, plus another on the Baltic coast, and a Finnish-style cottage on the Karelian peninsula.

Nor are other members of the Politburo left out in distribution of dachas. Theirs too, whether located by calm or rushing rivers, in valleys, or in mountainous areas, are inevitably isolated from the rest of the world. Their luxury is hidden behind a wall of secrecy: all of the Soviet elite have things to hide, particularly the privileges they stand to lose.

From time to time the dacha-dwellers may recall some of the communist "commandments" which they expounded before the people and by which they themselves are supposed to stand in their lives, e.g., according to Engels, "Private property should be abolished, all property should be held in common."

The Leninist CPSU district Party buro severely unbraided the Communist A. Khokhlov, and had a reprimand inserted in his personal file, for having abused his official position while building his dacha. (Partiynaya zhizn', no. 20, 1983, p. 72)

A landowner's house that was burnt down during the revolution once stood on the plot now occupied by five cooperative dachas. (Yuriy Trifonov, Starik [The old man]; Moscow: Soviet Writer Publishers, 1979, p. 132)

In the 1960s dacha construction in Baku became very widespread. Who built these dachas? For the most part, managers and intellectuals. Under what circumstances were they built? In many cases, as a result of abusive practices, which included the illegal use of building machinery, transport, vehicles, building materials, manpower from factories. . . . We had to severely punish several managers, some of whom were expelled from the Party. (Literaturnaya gazeta, 18 February 1981)

Deal (*Sedlka*). An agreement that is considered immoral, i.e., antagonistic to Soviet interests. The word is used to discredit commercial transactions and political accords which take place in the free world. The word "deal" is almost synonymous with "collusion" (*sgovor*) and has a sinister ring to it, suggesting existence of improper and reprehensible objectives which need to remain secret and are hypocritically misrepresented. This meaning of the term is routinely underscored by such qualifying adjectives as "base" (*podlaya*) and "despicable" (*nizkaya*).

The connotations of selfishness and baseness attached to the term "deal" are transferred to the states that conclude such agreements. Propaganda about deals of this sort is calculated to arouse "waves of protest" among Soviet workers who often have very little idea of the reality of such international understandings.

Thus far, the loudly proclaimed anti-Arab collusion has not yet resulted in a "peace" deal concluded on American-Israeli terms. (Pravda, 31 December 1978, p. 7)

The Palestinian problem has a long and dramatic history. Its origins lie in the deal made between Anglo-American imperialism and Zionism. (Mezhdunarodnaya zhizn', no. 11, 1979)

Both the Arab world and progressive people everywhere see the Camp David accords as a neo-colonialist deal. (Novoe vremya, no. 42, 1980, p. 289)

Death Penalty (*Smertnaya kazn'*). Capital punishment. The Death penalty is claimed to be used in the Soviet Union in exceptional cases only, yet in fact it is commonly accepted and extensively applied as a means

of deterrence to crime. Its use is stipulated for seven criminal, eleven political, and sixteen military offenses. A close look at the Soviet Criminal Code, together with supplementary clarifications, reveals that the death penalty is also applicable to a dozen other articles.

The Soviet authorities have always striven to mask the cruelty and arbitrariness of Soviet justice, trying to reconcile it with the claim that in the socialist society all people are "friends, comrades and brothers." This gave rise to the subjection of the term "death penalty" to various semantic modifications. In order to avoid calling it by its real name, the authorities came up with such euphemisms as "the extreme penalty" or "the highest penalty" (hence the slang term "*vyshka*," literally a high tower). During the period of mass executions there was an attempt to cover up the truth through the use of the downright sadistic euphemism "ten years without the right to correspond."

This hypocrisy about the death penalty has been manifest through all stages of Soviet history. Until they came to power, the Bolsheviks had been adamant in their opposition to the death penalty. Consequently, they decided to abolish it immediately after the October Revolution (by a decree passed at the Second Congress of Soviets on 10 November 1917). Yet, even at that time it was clear that the decision was only on paper, as the party and Lenin vowed to execute without mercy and trial anyone opposing the regime or undermining production efforts.

According to incomplete data, during the civil war, from 1918 through 1920, more than 50,000 people were executed by the Special Committee for State Security (Cheka). In contrast to that, during the last one hundred years of the imperial rule of the Romanov dynasty in Russia, less than 7,000 people were put to death. In January 1920 the government passed another law abolishing the death penalty. But already in May of that year, a directive was issued reinstating it in localities placed under martial law, and subsequently all over the country. The Soviet government's decree of 26 May 1947 replaced the death penalty with a twenty-five-year prison term. Yet between 1920 and 1947 millions of people throughout the Soviet Union were executed in secrecy. The roster included: the sailors of Kronstadt (1921)—10,000; religious believers and priests (1921–29)—100,000; "counterrevolutionaries" of all kinds, including the White guard, "Antonovtsy," "Makhnovtsy," Central Asian "basmachi," etc. (1920–27)—120,000; striking workers and rebellious peasants (1922–30)—110,000; political prisoners (first the class enemies—Constitutional Democrats, Mensheviks,—and later the class allies—the Socialist Revolutionaries and Trotskyites) (1922–33)—70,000 to 80,000. From then on the executions became wholesale. The kulaks (cf.) (1930–33) supplied close to a million victims. During the "great purge" (1937–39) a series of obviously false charges led to the death of more than two million people. The eve of World War II was marked by hundreds of thousands more deaths: 14,000 Polish officers in the spring of 1940, added in the fall by 10,000 Baltic nationalists and 200,000 prisoners "summarily" executed when the hasty retreat allowed no time for their evacuation. Germany's defeat sparked another wave of executions, this time of Soviet POWs returning from captivity.

For three years the Soviet regime managed to function without the death penalty on its books. Unofficially, however, it was meted out. In the city of Ashkhabad in 1948, militia officers surrounded prison buildings destroyed by an earthquake and mowed down those inmates who had not managed to escape. Scores of convicts were killed in labor camps in 1948–49, during the suppression of strikes. Finally in 1950, the death penalty was reintroduced in response to the supposed "demands" of the "workers." New waves of terror were planned, except that Stalin died. The respite that followed his death, however, did not last long. A decade had barely elapsed after fifty years of relentless slaughter, when the Soviet regime once again resorted to the bludgeon of the death penalty. This time it began to be widely used as a deterrent to economic crime, such

as theft, corruption, and speculation in foreign currency.

The phenomenon was paradoxical: the state, which had been devastated by terror, resorted to terror again. This time it was backed by the tacit consent of the citizens who, having been brought up on cruelty, developed an instinctive urge to administer it to others. Worn out by their own hopeless lives, they derived a cynical satisfaction from knowing that prosperous and highly successful people were facing the firing squad. Their consciences did not bother them: they perceived the death penalty as a just retribution.

Moreover, there was some skepticism as to whether death sentences were actually being carried out. Soviet criminal folklore abounds in stories about prisoners sentenced to death who were "shot" with blank bullets and, after surviving this mental ordeal, were sent to the uranium mines. Unfortunately, those tales bore no resemblance to reality. Only in a distant past had Russian rulers indulged in such impressive spectacles as sparing prisoners' lives at the foot of a gallows or a guillotine. The Soviet law, on the other hand, knows no mercy: as soon as the prisoners' appeal for mercy is denied, the execution is carried out. However, during the two or more years it takes for his appeal to be processed, the doomed prisoner waits in agony for his execution. Decked out in a striped uniform, he is kept apart from other prisoners in a solitary cell with barred windows, in total isolation from the outside world. Yet the most horrible thing is that the inmates of these death cells are often innocent. This happens because Soviet investigative organs, like the rest of society, operate according to central planning and are issued quotas of capital crimes solved. To fill the quotas, the accused were forced to confess to crimes they had never committed. They were beaten or blackmailed, intimidated, or driven insane. The interrogators repeated to them: confess—and we will let you live; persist in pleading your innocence—and you will be surely sentenced to death. Gripped with a sense of anguish and impotence, isolated from the outside world, the prisoner tended to see himself as a pitiful wretch. His deranged mind might suddenly conceive the desperate thought: "what if I actually am guilty?" And then, bereft of all hope, he would sign his "confession," with the effect of immediately entering a maze of distorting mirrors where he admitted to crimes he had never committed and perhaps even began to see his tormentors as benefactors.

The court, faced with the obligation to meet its quota of verdicts, automatically churned out guilty sentences. Soviet judges, despite their professed objectivity, belong to the government apparatus. They depend entirely on the party, which controls their appointments, promotion, and transfer. A ruined human life has for them no meaning except as a token toward their possible promotion one rank upward. As a result, they virtually never decide in favor of the defendant. Until recently, 99 percent of all trials in the Soviet Union ended in "guilty" verdicts. Instead of determining the merits of a case, the Soviet court only decides how harsh the punishment should be. Like everyone else, Soviet judges must fulfill the targets of "assigned work" against which their "productivity" is measured. This allows for a certain proportion of "preventive" penalties, to be meted out with moderation, so as to neither exceed the predetermined quota (lest the harmony of "advanced socialism" is upset), nor fall short of that quota (lest crime is encouraged). This cynical bookkeeping system determined the optimal number of death penalties. They were publicized only rarely—when required by propaganda considerations.

The legal reform has dispelled the mist of secrecy surrounding the issue of death penalty. For the first time in Soviet history, consideration is being given not merely to the utility of executing a specific criminal but rather to the very legality of the death penalty. Nevertheless, capital punishment has not yet been rejected. Capital punishment perhaps offers the regime some hope for dealing with organized crime, which has now emerged as a threatening phenomenon

marked not only by massive economic corruption but also by audacious murders.

It is silly and hypocritical to talk (as some people tend to do) about humanizing the death penalty, but the conditions prevailing inside death cells must clearly be alleviated. (Ogonek, no. 41, October 1988, p. 21)

Her son, her only child, through an unfortunate "error" ended up being sentenced to . . . the "extreme penalty." (Literaturnaya gazeta, 2 November 1988, p. 12)

Ten years without the right to correspond. That was the Machiavellian euphemism once used to disguise the word "execution." (Literaturnaya gazeta, 28 September 1988, p. 12)

Deceleration (*Tormozhenie*). A euphemism referring to manifestations of stagnation in the Soviet economy and society. The term "deceleration" became accepted as a scientific concept in January 1987, when it was first used by Gorbachev in his speech at the Plenary session of the Central Committee CPSU.

An analysis of the sociopolitical aspects of what passes for deceleration gives rise to a series of questions: How widely has stagnation afflicted Soviet society? Why have the traditional explanations of the ills of socialist society proved inadequate, making it necessary to apply new concepts? How deeply rooted is deceleration, and what are its origins?

The Soviet reality has continued to engender facts and events incompatible with the socialist blueprint, such as callousness, apathy, and crime. For many years such "unsocialist" phenomena were explained away as "relics of the past." It was taken for granted that they would fade away as the system progressed and perfected itself. Reality, however, proved more complicated: it turned out that there was no correlation between technical progress and morality, just as a high level of formal education provided no guarantee against crime.

Soviet society witnessed a steady increase of shortcomings and vice—labor discipline declined, alcoholism tainted all sections of the population, bribery and protectionism became widespread. Moral ties regulating relations between individual and society loosened: people began to lose their sense of decency, duty, and self-respect. Meanwhile, the authorities continued to triumphantly proclaim the achievements of socialism, but propagandistic imagery and rhetoric diverged considerably from reality.

The new Soviet leaders headed by Gorbachev were unable to admit the failure of the regime since their power rested on its totalitarian nature. But neither were they in a position to ignore the country's progressing decay. Popular discontent could explode at any moment. Furthermore, in international competition, the economically backward country with its outdated technology was falling behind twentieth century standards and thus being relegated to the position of a minor power, with a possible consequence being the disintegration of the communist bloc.

It was then that the concept of deceleration was invented. It provided an inconsistent and contradictory explanation of the crisis afflicting the Soviet Union. It was claimed that on the whole the socialist government acted in the best interests of the people. To this, however, a qualification was added—that the government was made up of concrete individuals whose principles could conflict with their personal interests. In other words, the idea of socialism is wonderful, it is only the particular leaders that are imperfect. They were named Stalin, Brezhnev and Chernenko. It was claimed that they lacked general culture and the strength of character to resist numerous temptations. Their very first concessions to such temptations entangled them with criminal groups. The country's economic development was paralyzed by the bureaucratic methods of administration, and the progress of socialism was obstructed by the power of organized crime. As a result, not only the leaders themselves became slaves to the spirit of profiteering and acquisition, but the latter managed to corrupt virtually the entire bureaucratic apparatus: party officials, the militia,

the public prosecutor's office, and other law enforcement agencies. That is what is commonly considered in the USSR to be the underlying cause of deceleration. What remained unrecognized (and therefore unmentioned) was that socialism itself produces and encourages antisocial tendencies, giving rise to cynicism, indifference, and lack of concern about values. What emerges is either the thirst for power or selfishness and greed.

The described psychological mechanisms operate, as it were, synchronically, within the system of relations between individual and society. Yet they can be understood properly only diachronically, from a historical point of view. Deceleration has its source in the single-party government structure and personal dictatorship, which began to be formed under Lenin. Deceleration was prompted by the centralized methods of administration established in Russia in the wake of the Communist Revolution. The same factors paved the way for all the aberrations of Stalin's dictatorship, for mass terror and for what in fact amounted to the first Soviet "perestroika," consisting of ruthless industrialization and forced collectivization. A further contributory factor to deceleration was the fear of the leader and the fabrication of charisma and quasi-religious worship around his or her person. If the Soviet system still continued to function with a modicum of efficiency, it was due either to people's misguided faith in communism or to their fear of reprisals.

Following the war with Germany, Stalin's power structure became a blueprint for export. Accordingly, deceleration spread beyond Soviet borders and began to operate on an international scale, destroying the social initiative of other nations. The fault did not lie with idiosyncratic defects of the particularly change-resistant Soviet socialism but with the defects inherent in socialism as a system. In fact, within this sytem Stalin was the ideal helmsman, since by simplifying it and adjusting it to his level, he made it easier for Soviet citizens to comprehend. Therefore, the question (recently often asked) as to whether the extension and development of deceleration was, under socialism, inevitable, should be answered in the affirmative.

Quite another question is whether deceleration could be somehow reduced or prevented from extending any further. Such a possibility appeared in the Soviet Union around 1957, when Khrushchev attempted to change the country's ideological foundations. Yet the regime proved too inert for a purposeful change. Having recovered from Khrushchev's reforms, it resumed its traditional inertia. The wave of tentative democratization and inconsistent economic reorganization subsided. Once again, socialism produced its usual fruits: red tape, indifference, opportunism, mutual favors, and disrespect for law. Khrushchev's "thaw" failed to evolve into a spring of "revival." The government was back to exercising power for the sake of power. Bureaucracy and dogmatism, joined and fortified, became part of Brezhnev's worldview and philosophy, protecting his inertia and incompetence, and providing him with the arguments against any reforms and any social change. Under such conditions, people were unwilling to reveal their true interests. Human creativity and civic spirit were paralyzed and frozen.

An analysis of socialism shows that deceleration, rather than being a by-product, is an intrinsic trait of Soviet society as historically conditioned, with its rigidly devised *nomenklatura* hierarchy at the centralized and firm controls of the country. The *nomenklatura*'s economic power is based on the ever-increasingly "nationalized" government property, which is disguised as common property, but which, far from turning the workers into owners or masters, merely turns them into units of manpower. The results are visible in workers' passivity, inertia, and uninvolvement in economic development.

The transformation of deceleration into acceleration (cf.) will not be achieved through any socialist "renewal." The introduction of an additional modification—even such as enterprising and dynamic people—will not change a thing. Quickly and inevitably, they

will slip into the old patterns of behavior and work as dictated by the system. Thus Gorbachev's blows directed at deceleration are futile. Just as dragons in folklore grow new heads in place of those that have been chopped off, so Soviet society breeds new metastases of deceleration. In order to kill this monster, socialism itself would have to be destroyed.

The mechanisms of deceleration operate not only on the scale of the whole society; they also function on the level of specific production colletives, within the network of administrative, scientific and other institutions. (Mekhanizm tormozheniya [The mechanism of deceleration]. Moscow: Izdatel'stvo politicheskoy literatury, 1988, p. 21)

More often than not, acceleration attempts encounter magnetic zones of deceleration in ministerial offices far away from the Far East. (Ogonek, no. 32, 1988, p. 6)

And what about the forces of deceleration, whether local or not? Are they trembling in fear? Not as far as we can see. (Moskovskie novosti, 25 September 1988, p. 4)

Democratic Centralism (*Demokratichesky tsentralizm*). The organizational principle determining the way of functioning of the CPSU and the state administration of the USSR. Centralism in Soviet society is reflected in the existence of a single party operating under a single leadership, the Politburo and the Central Committee. In the absolute subordination of the lower party organs to the higher ones; and in the absolute subordination of minority to majority within the overall framework of strict "party discipline." In state administration, centralism manifests itself through subordination of the republic ministries and provincial soviets to the All-Union Council of Ministers and the Supreme Soviet, respectively. It is this mechanism that secures the complete and systematic control of the central governing apparatus over its subordinate branches. State planning of the Soviet economy is structured similarly.

The "Democratic" claim is pure fiction, both with regard to the party and with regard to the state administration. The election of governing bodies, from the top to the bottom of the hierarchy, the accountability of the representatives to the electorate, and the deliberations of Party Congresses and of the Supreme Soviet sessions are pure formalities, intended to create the semblance of popular mandate. In reality, total power, with no personal or institutional restraints, resides in the Politburo of the Central Committee of the CPSU. It is the joint command of the party and state administration that determines everything at the lower levels of both hierarchies.

Democratism also disguises the domination of the Russian "Federal Republic" and its imperial designs over the other republics. This configuration, which, in official Soviet documents, bears the name of the "unity of centralism and federalism," in effect completely nullifies the sovereign rights of the national republics. Nominally, each one of these has its own soviets and ministries. The centralist subordination of everything to the top leadership in Moscow, however, transforms the republic authorities into mere appendages of the central state machine. Their responsibilities and their powers are the same regardless of whether they are formally accountable to the republic or to the All-Union Soviet. Although each republic has its own language, all official documents are written in Russian. Russian is also the language of all republic party conferences and congresses, and all republic Soviet sessions.

The decentralization of decision-making within the party and state administration is permissible only to the extent to which it ultimately furthers centralism and makes it more effective. If one disregards some specific aspects of the reform of the political system currently underway in the Soviet Union, avoids an emotional evaluation of the reform, and considers its main aspects, then it becomes clear that democratic centralism in the party and government remains unshaken, and no dismantling of the command-administrative system is taking place. Rule from above and centralization remain keys to the structure of administration, and society continues to be swaddled in layers of detailed regulations. Given the existence of a single party and state leadership, state security organization, internal security armies, and centralized planning, the tenet of democratic centralism is no more than an ideological justification for the maintenance of the Soviet state's totalitarianism, which tolerates no real democracy and no nationalist aspirations.

The relationship between central and local Party bodies is based on the principle of democratic centralism, which is the main principle of the organizational structure of the CPSU. (Kommunist, Kalendar'-spravochnik, 1977g [Communist, a reference calendar, 1977]; Moscow: Political Literature Publishing House, 1976, p. 38)

A range of Party organizations . . . instills Party mores and the foundations of democratic centralism in the course of their practical work . . . . (Istoriya VKP(b), Kratky Kurs; Moscow: Political Literature Publishing House, 1950, p. 133)

The very first task is to fully restore the Leninist concept of democratic centralism which envisages freedom of discussion at the stage of considering issues and unity of action after a decision is reached by the majority. (Izvestiya, 5 July 1977, p. 2)

Democratic Socialism (*Demokratichesky sotsializm*). A new way of presenting and defining the Soviet political system. The expression reflects the changes that have occurred in Soviet socialism, in its conceptual foundations, and in the development of humanistic features within it. It is characterized by (1) glasnost (cf.) ("openness")—a certain degree of openness in public life; (2) legality and adherence to the constitution; (3) democratization (cf.)—limited, with the one-party system and centralized leadership left intact, yet apparent in the liberalization of the electoral procedures, primarily in the right to nominate alternative candidates and the existence of comparatively broad opportunities for discussing their merits and demerits; (4) the proposed separation of the executive, legislative, and judicial authorities, which may result in a broader base of popular power (apart from the traditional power pillars of Soviet society—the party, army, and the government—certain activistically-minded segments of the population are thus expected to be drawn into the policy decision-making process, albeit only in a consultative capacity); and (5) economic pluralism—the introduction of certain aspects of free-market forces and private enterprise into the economy, in the form of leasehold businesses and cooperative industries.

Since its first appearance on the political scene, the concept of socialism has undergone a long and unique process of evolution. Its creators, Marx and subsequently Engels, spoke of the possibility of socialism's triumphing simultaneously throughout the world or, at least, in the most industrially advanced countries. When the worldwide socialist revolution failed to materialize, Lenin, in order to avoid catastrophe, was forced to take a step backwards via his New Economic Policy (NEP) (cf.), which allowed a partial restoration of capitalism to the economy.

This state of affairs did not suit Stalin, who wanted a one-man dictatorship for himself. Under the guise of communist ideology, he advocated the possibility of building "socialism in one country." In the name of this doctrine, which assumed that the victory of socialism could not be final because of the presence of hostile "capitalist encirclement," a brutal wave of terror began to sweep the Soviet Union, consigning to the grave forty million people (not counting victims of the war with Germany, for which Stalin could be blamed to a considerable extent and which caused the loss of another thirty million lives). These seventy million can be counted as the price actually paid for attempting to create a socialist utopia. (This figure concerns the Soviet Union alone. If "popular-democratic" countries are taken into account, it should be at least doubled.) The price was found exorbitant even by the standards of the post-Stalin Soviet leadership. As a result, they have sought a more "embellished" concept of socialism.

Khrushchev put forward the idea of "mature" and subsequently "developed" socialism. In order to make it more attractive, he offered an "enticement," declaring that "the classless society" could soon follow the "developed" ("mature") socialism. He expected such society to materialize within fifteen or twenty years and launched the slogan "The present generation will live to see communism." This was a reckless and a risky promise. Previously, the Bolsheviks had never deceived the people in such a vulgar manner. Consequently, Khrushchev ended up being accused of "voluntarism" ("hare-brained schemes"). His successors (Brezhnev, Andropov, and Chernenko) determined that the existing form of socialism was "real," which meant that it had some "known" deficiencies and that it should be accepted as it is, without vain hopes or illusions. As for the advent of communism, they tried to avoid mentioning the topic.

"Real socialism" turned out to mean stagnation in every domain of social and economic life, while the USSR found itself on the verge of political bankruptcy. To forestall disaster, the new Soviet leadership was forced to rapidly adopt a program of perestroika (cf.) and to carry out social and economic reforms. This led to the birth of yet one more description for socialism: democratic socialism. The concept was to a large extent copied from the Czech "socialism with a human face," which had been crushed by Soviet tanks in 1968.

Democratic socialism should not simply be understood in the sense in which it is claimed in the USSR. Even Marx noted that a differentiation should be made between political reality as appraised by a particular class and the practical significance of that appraisal. There is a clear difference between the theory and practice of democratic socialism. In particular, the idea that democratic socialism and its reforms are attributable to the party's concern "for the people" is a clear illusion. In actuality these reforms are being implemented because the state needs them.

The existence of the Soviet system has for

long been based on a paradox. The system works badly and inefficiently, yet the communist regime has flourished and grown stronger. However, below a certain threshold its foundations become untenable and begin to crumble. Since the time this point was reached, Soviet society has been paralyzed from top to bottom. In order to prevent the transformation of society under pressure from below, the authorities hastened to carry out reforms from above, without taking any interests but their own into account. In order to salvage their vital interests, the Soviet leadership occasionally had to sacrifice some of its secondary interests. However, the designing of reforms has thus far been basically the job of a narrow circle of the country's leadership. It is there, not among the ordinary people, that the question of *what* should be rejected and *what* should be accepted and implemented is being discussed.

In reality, there are no mythical "enemies of perestroika who must be sought out and unmasked." The main enemy of perestroika is the socialist system and the people at its helm. It is their corporate interests that are blocking and paralyzing the process of reform. The majority of the new leadership has come to champion old ideas, in accordance with what the system demands. As a result, the number of liberals in the corridors of power is constantly declining, while the strength of conservatives is growing. Ordinary people do not trust the leaders nobody really elected, who have long since failed to repay the political credit they once might have been granted. Only part of the intelligentsia support Gorbachev, and it is their voices that constantly resound from the pages of the press; the masses remain silent, waiting to see what will really change.

Certainly, the significance of glasnost should not be belittled: the articulation of bold and progressive ideas is helping to cleanse the country's politics. But it should not be exaggerated either. A revolution of words (and words alone) will not help refashion the fabric of society. A tangible achievement of glasnost has been the gen-

eration of controversy. For a long time, ever since the death of Lenin, political debate in the USSR was kept away from the public eye. The people were presented with matters that had already been decided, by behind-the-scenes political battling and compromises. Today, political infighting has been brought out into the open. This, undeniably, is progress but not yet democratization, as long as policy decision-making and policy implementation remain prerogatives of the communist ruling class. Yet, at the same time, signs of liberalization are clear: liberalization of censorship, the controlled right to strike, the creation of voluntary associations unsanctioned by law but not illegal, partial freedom of speech, and restrictions imposed on the powers of the bureaucracy (which is incapable of restraining itself). Gorbachev's reforms have reached the limit of the change that is possible under the communist system. Further reforms would lead to a change of the system itself. Gorbachev is now standing at a crossroads. The demands he is facing from the left, to broaden the extent of reform, would, if acceded to, signal a defeat for the regime. Demands from the right, to retreat from the path of reforms, would signal his personal defeat. Either way, he faces the terrifying risk of losing power. Because of his reformist impulses, Gorbachev is already perceived as a danger by the increasingly conservative regime. For the conservatives, a quiet and cautious leader would be more acceptable. The victory of a radical faction within the leadership, however, would make him superfluous, as a more resolute and daring leader would be preferable. Reactionary tendencies within the government would spare neither Gorbachev nor society, while liberalization would spell the end both of the party and of Gorbachev.

Gorbachev's choice will ultimately depend on his evaluation of the danger to his political survival. Considerations of social progress would, at best, be of only secondary importance to him. His choice will be a function of "historical compromise": with the conservatives, if they consent to keeping him in power, or with the radicals, if they need him as a leader while they pursue changes in the nature of the regime.

Currently, with the hour of crisis approaching, Gorbachev's good intentions are hindered by the bureaucracy at the top of the power structure and apathy at the bottom. The opposition of the former stems inevitably from the very nature of the regime, while the attitudes of the masses are a product of the incessant indoctrination of seventy years, which in the end produced a modal personality devoid of creative awareness, initiative, and activism. This is why the extent of Gorbachev's changes is less far-reaching than real reform would require and possibly than he himself would like. The primary attention has been paid to secondary matters, like the reorganization of industrial management, even though it is now known from the experience of other communist countries (Hungary and Yugoslavia, for example) that such reorganization is bound to be a palliative measure leading to a short period of prosperity, followed by a new recession.

The main watchword of democratic socialism is decentralization. But decentralization is being implemented only partially and rather meaninglessly by transferring a few rights and prerogatives to local organizations and associations. These have not achieved full independence, however. As before, the plans, now foisted on the enterprises from above in the form of *goszakazy* (state orders for goods), often contain targets exceeding an enterprise's production capacity. Ownership remains unchanged, in the hands of the state, which precludes the emergence of market forces and minimizes the influence of supply and demand as economic regulators. As before, prices remain unrealistically low, with the effect of obstructing industrial development. "Acceleration" (cf.) is only achieved by the production of unwanted goods. Industry is caught in a double bind: on the one hand production has to be accelerated and increased at any price (to achieve the *val*—gross output as an indicator of industrial efficiency, in contrast to profit), while on the other hand it must con-

form to state approval (*gospriemka*), which requires a high (and until now unusual) level of product quality.

The economy and society as a whole have turned out to be torn by contradictory demands: enterprises are obstensibly given the right to freely conclude agreements on a self-supporting basis while their production is simultaneously allocated by state diktat; much is said about industrial profitability, yet this is achieved at the public's expense by raising prices rather than by modernizing industrial technology and increasing the choice of goods available. It is stressed that reform is aimed at the citizen, at raising his or her standards of living, while in reality it envisages the dismissal of ten million workers. The state, which has become embroiled in a "moonshine vodka" (*samogon*) war with the populace, has lost a significant proportion of its revenue to "moonshiners." (In the early 1980s, the state received two-thirds of the proceeds from sales of spirits; moonshiners received one-third. Today, however, this proportion has changed in the moonshiners' favor.)

"Self-supporting socialism" (as some economists call democratic socialism) stopped before it ever reached the countryside. There, the principles of forced labor still hold but fail to vindicate the abnormalities of the economic system prevailing in agriculture, which rests on compulsory planned deliveries to the state. This policy is dictated by the conviction, which, to be sure, is never made explicit, that Soviet man is lazy and inert and that he won't work except when prompted by carrot-and-stick methods. It cannot be said that the kolkhozes and sovkhozes have outlived their utility, since they have never been viable in the first place. However, in the event of their abolition, agriculture will grind to a halt and the country will be devoid of produce. Under the existing system they may operate inefficiently, with many disruptions, but they do somehow manage to produce something.

The logic of economic compulsion is also applied to industry, which is subject to preestablished and unreviewable norms whereby the state takes up to 90 percent of an enterprise's profits. This explains why Soviet economists are pleading for help: "create a *cheka* (special commission) for perestroika" (*Sovetskaya Rossiya*, 14 February 1987, p. 2). (The harsh image of the Cheka lives on.) Economics in the Soviet Union is still regarded as a field for enunciation of various whims and pretentions rather than as a discipline that deals with objective laws (much as the latters' presence is invariably noted). Meanwhile, the conflict between man (i.e., the manager) and economics goes on. Exhortations are made to go over to self-supporting and self-financing status, while unprofitable and unsought output is increased; five-year plans for industrial growth are fixed and the reconstruction of factories is urged; and enterprises are required to increase their rate of output and expand when they are not even in a position to supply the market with enough basic commodities.

Paradoxes are not confined to industry. As part of the fight against drunkenness (over the propriety of the administrative methods used, doubts have already been raised), vineyards are being cut down. Nothing is done, however, to eliminate the social causes of the nationwide weakness for the bottle, such as people's despair at having to live in continual mendacity, at the disruption and insecurity of everyday life, at stagnation and hopelessness about one's future. Another incongruity of perestroika is that the budget is balanced mainly by cutting subsidies on staples and social services rather than by curtailing military expenditures. The fact that the majority of the population needs such subsidies in view of their low wages is not taken into account.

Inconsistencies abound in democratic socialism. Government bonds (the population supposedly holds 260 billion "unspent" rubles) are being increased while confidence in banking institutions is being undermined—a price reform stands to lower their real value by 40 to 50 percent. Cuts in government expenditure are called for, but in the absence of objective cost indicators, no one knows how much anything is really worth. Metaphorically speaking, the coun-

try's economy resembles a hall of distorting mirrors, where large and important events are made to look small, while matters of secondary importance are represented as essential.

The existing financial system in the Soviet Union generates inflation. Revenues and expenditures of the state are illusory as the value of money is not sufficiently backed by supplies in the market. Enterprises are taxed without consideration to how much of their produce is sold and whether it is sold at all. They are, in effect, financed on the basis of nonreturnable credit. (Industry's debts to the state amount to 300 billion rubles and will obviously never be repaid.) The country has no single exchange rate. There are more than ten different indexes in operation: one for domestic use, another for the COMECON bloc, still another for exchanges with the West, etc.

There is much latent hostility toward private and cooperative enterprise ventures, which are accused of various machinations, of raising their prices for the sake of excessive profits, etc.—all of which results in periodic outbursts of antagonism.

But issues of economic administration are only part of the problem. The principle that operates in the USSR is that only reforms conforming to the spirit of socialism (or rather democratic socialism) are possible and permissible. The nature of ownership, which should be the most important aspect of any reorganization, remains unchanged. As before, state ownership is proclaimed as the inviolable foundation of any social reconstruction, while private ownership is assigned a merely secondary and temporary role. Such an approach presupposes, as in the past, state monopoly of all economic and political activity.

Thus, the essential features of democratic socialism show that the Soviet government has decided to relax its controls only over peripheral aspects of economic and social life. As it surrenders some of its controls, the socialist state tries to gain other ones in the hope of improving its operation. In a situation where all other forms of socialism have exhausted themselves, the Soviet Union is attempting democratic socialism, which, in short, is a doctrine of restructuring totalitarian society for the sake of its gradual transformation into an autocratic rather than democratic society.

> Which is the new model of a more effective, democratic, humane socialism? Currently, only a few of its features are visible. These are: planned economy of consumer goods, based on self-financing and diverse forms of collective ownership; raising state ownership to the level of national ownership; and the growth of cooperative, family and private ownership forms. This is economic (socialist) competition. This is the development of a civil society and the subordination of the state to society . . . . This is the division of authority, power and functions between party, state and public organizations. (Literaturnaya gazeta, 22 April 1988, p. 2)

> The logic of "self-supporting socialism" dictates that district committees should be deprived of economic functions as quickly as possible . . . . (Novy mir, no. 4, 1988, p. 164)

> A search is underway for a socialism adapted to present conditions. (Izvestiya, 22 August 1988, p. 3).

Democratization (*Demokratizatsiya*). The process of limited liberalization being carried out in the Soviet Union within the framework of perestroika (cf.). Democratization is a distortion of democracy. True democracy manifests and tests itself in popular rule and equality of rights and duties for all citizens. In contrast, Soviet democratization is one of the tools that ensures that Soviet society will continue to be ruled in accordance with the ideology of the communist class and the latter's goals and interests.

Democratization also provides certain points of departure for the further social and economic development of the socialist state. It endorses self-management of enterprises and elections of managers and allows a degree of glasnost (cf.) in various sectors of public affairs. All this is intended to facilitate perestroika, the reorganization of administration. Democratization helps shake the country out of its condition of economic and political stagnation and establish an administrative infrastructure for carrying out economic reforms.

Subjectively, however, the party leaders have been and remain advocates of authoritarian methods of administration. Nevertheless, the future of socialism—and consequently the chance of the present leadership's survival—has been staked on democratization. The Soviet leaders are no longer in the position to mobilize and organize the masses with their traditional slogans and exhortations, which have lost all impact. Nor can those leaders revert to methods of terror that have lost their utility and become dangerous for the regime, with the possible political gain not justifying the social price: constant fear and uncertainty in the country. This means that it was practical necessity rather than socialist theory that made the Soviet leadership opt for democratization. In production relations democratization is intended to facilitate the transition from strictly administrative to more economically oriented forms of management. Furthermore, it implies expanding the autonomy of enterprises as well as their full cost accountability and self-financing.

However, as with much else in the Soviet Union, appearance is substituted for real change. Electoral competition between candidates for managerial positions is no more than a propaganda ploy. In order to show that he or she is already "reconstructed," each director rushes to demonstrate his or her eagerness to sponsor elections. At one enterprise, six candidates are proposed to run for top posts; at another, nine; at a third, twenty. Democratization is in demand, like a precious object at an auction that prompts ever higher bids as if the one who outbids the other in the number of proposed candidates will walk off with the prize. Those who are elected are not the best and the brightest, but rather the most complacent and manipulatable. This is why democratization does not lead to democracy but remains its parody.

The Soviet leadership can safely embark on democratization precisely because it does not really entail any freedom of choice. The candidates continue to be preselected and nominated by party committees. Nevertheless, the authorities have succeeded in rousing society, in galvanizing the masses, in playing on what in Soviet parlance is referred to as the "human factor." In this, their success was impressive: to the extent that it carried them, unmindful of the risk involved, toward democratization of social life.

In elections to local councils (soviets) in 1987, a number of electoral districts had multiple candidates running for a single office. This was supposed to be a trial experiment. Multicandidate elections would definitely mark a progress, if not toward democracy, then at least toward respect for the formalities of the electoral process. Voting for a single candidate is, needless to way, an election without a choice; but several contenders, even if selected from the same party deck, already make for a political contest that ostensibly follows democratic rules. This type of election is not new. It existed in the Soviet Union in the distant (forgotten) past, in the years right after the Revolution. Then, however, the elections were more democratic than they are now since in the elections to the soviets, including the Supreme Soviet (which was then called the All-Union Central Executive Committee), candidates ran not only from the Communist (Bolshevik) party but also from the opposition parties—the Left Social Revolutionaries, the Menshevik Internationalists, etc.

In the Soviet Union today neither the state structure, the political system, nor the foundations of the economy has changed—at least as yet. There is only an illusion of change. The Soviet leadership has begun talking about merging socialism with democracy. The idea of such a merger, however, has a major drawback: it implies that in the entire Soviet past thus far, more than seventy years, socialism has been built without democracy. This was true enough, and far from a chance occurrence. For democracy is antithetic to the essence of socialism. The more "developed" socialism is the less freedom society has. And conversely, the broader the extent of democracy, the weaker become such features of socialism as the monopoly of power in the hands of the party and the resultant inequality.

The attempts of Gorbachev to improve socialism are naive. The Soviet-type of socialism cannot be better or worse: it will always remain based on dictatorship, repression, and arbitrariness. A symbiosis of socialism and democracy is bound to be short-lived: either socialism will devour democracy or democracy will predominate, with the effect of the gradual extinction of socialism. In society, no less than in nature, there are no mixed breeds. This precludes any half-and-half "blend" of socialism and democracy.

The crisis of the Soviet system is a crisis of socialism, a logical result of the pursuit of its policies entailing a refusal to recognize the laws of value, disregard for cost accounting, arbitrariness in price-setting, toleration of no more than limited democracy in management, and the alienation of the worker from the products of his or her labor. The USSR is a closed, single-party-ruled society, rigidly hierarchized and hypertrophically centralized. A way out of the crises it generates is not to be sought in its extension or in its renewal, not in building a "bigger" or "better" socialism, but in transcending its confines; not in the reconstruction of the socialist system, but in transforming it into something else.

Socialism was forced to turn to democratization to save itself from a self-engineered doom. This is why, for the first time since the brief period of revolutionary romanticism, the Soviet leaders brought the working masses onto the political stage, meeting with them, appealing to them, even "consulting" with them. However, the significance of democratization in the Soviet Union should not be exaggerated: the people are, as previously, being assigned a quite modest role, that of extras in the socialist drama.

Nor is the breach of the party's monopoly on power unprecedented in Soviet history. Only under Stalin were all political decisions taken exclusively in party corridors. This was where economic plans were drawn up, social norms determined, and decisions made to purge officials. After Stalin, the power structure in the USSR began to change. The first to turn for support to an "outside," nonparty body—in this case the army—was Khrushchev, who would not have retained his general secretaryship otherwise. Subsequently, however, the army, rather than saving him, facilitated his downfall by taking the side of his opponents.

Brezhnev attempted to restore the party monopoly of power, but he was ultimately forced to share power with the military. In his struggle for power, Andropov turned to another extra-party body: the state security service, or KGB. Since then, there has developed in the USSR a peculiar power triangle consisting of the party, the army, and the KGB. The party, however, remains politically dominant in the triad, while the other two subsidiary members play a role in certain political decisions. The significance of this redistribution of power in the Soviet Union should not be overestimated. The party retains the decisive voice; the other two factors are permitted to directly influence political events only in crisis situations, when factions contending for power within the party are forced to seek allies outside of it. Such crises cannot be resolved within the party and therefore transcend its power monopoly. However, once admitted to the political arena, the armed forces and the KGB are reluctant to withdraw. This explains why the party remains the dominant but no longer the sole source of power.

By inaugurating his democratization policies, Gorbachev introduced a new element into the complex equation: the masses. If the latter should free themselves of party control (either under Gorbachev or under his successors), the described power triangle is bound to come apart. It could take on the form of a complex, multifaceted geometric figure in which new forces, like the intelligentsia or national minorities, might assume significance. Such new power-sharers emerging from the masses might well pursue goals not compatible with democratization.

Such a development seems all the more likely since Gorbachev has broken the taboo of the infallibility of the party. Before him one could criticize individual party leaders (even top-ranking ones), but the party as such remained immune to criticism. Even Khrushchev, who came closest to breaking this rule, cast all blame on one person—Stalin—and at that he only condemned one period, the last, of Stalin's long rule. Nevertheless, the inevitable spilling over of the blame from Stalin to the party and the system caused tremors throughout Soviet society.

One of the consequences of this upheaval was the emergence of dissidence, with which the successors of Khrushchev have had to attempt to cope. However, the opposition movement today, weakened by persecution and consequent disarray, poses such minimal danger that the authorities felt secure enough to release several hundred dissidents from incarceration.

The Soviet leadership could afford to pardon some dissidents since, thanks to democratization, their critique had lost its force. The Soviet leadership had co-opted the dissidents' slogans, including even the most radical of them: "Abide by your own constitution and your own laws." Such calls coincide with the program of perestroika and serve its goals. Naturally, the authorities know the difference between the goals of the dissidents and their own: while for the authorities democratization and the criticism generated by it is meant to strengthen the system, for the dissidents democratization means opportunities to denounce Soviet society. This is why for the dissidents democratization should have no limits, whereas for the communists their determination to maintain the party power intact sets very definite limits on democratization.

However, perestroika has confounded the intentions of the Soviet leaders to such a degree that democratization often exceeds the limits that they have set for it. For the first time in Soviet practice, criticism, engendered or inspired by democratization, has been aimed at the Politburo and the Central Committee secretaries, thereby calling into question the presumption of the unassailability of the party. The authorities had attempted to restrict criticism to the lower echelons of the party, but democratization broke though the barriers they had set. In the end even Gorbachev himself became a target for satire. At this point the traditional Soviet dilemma of "Who-Whom?" (i.e., who will come out on top of whom, or which force will predominate) arises again. Will the party curb democratization or will democratization gradually evolve into democracy? Developments of the coming years will provide the answer to this critical question.

> We need the best possible work from the therefore full rights to be given to all social organizations, all production collectives and artists' unions; we need novel forms of citizen involvement and the renewal of those which have been forgotten. In brief, there is a need for a broad democratization of our entire social life. That will best guarantee the irreversibility of the processes which have been inaugurated. (M. S. Gorbachev, Perestroika i novoe myshlenie dlya nashey strany i dlya vsego mira [Perestroika and the new thinking for our country and the whole world], Moscow: Izd. politicheskoy literatury, 1987, p. 27)

> Democratization, understood as a process which occurs in the human mind, and as the affirmation of both socialist and universal values is the main and in practice the sole way of carrying out perestroika. (Pravda, 18 July 1987, p. 3)

> The mechanism of exerting pressure by force has been worked out masterfully and precisely by those who use democratic enthusiasms for their own purposes. No, under democratization dictatorship is still required. . . . Otherwise unscrupulous demagogues with their loud voices will dominate the collectives. (Pravda, 16 November 1987, p. 2)

Denunciation (*Donositel'stvo*). A form of legalized and idealized betrayal of trust, considered in the USSR a symbol of devotion and class consciousness. As a social phenomenon, denunciation was a product of Bolshevik philosophy. The Bolsheviks, whose clandestine existence produced a psychology of siege mentality, upon coming to power applied this psychology to interpersonal relations. Corrupting people, paralyzing their will to resist and overcoming their moral qualms, denunciation enabled the Soviet rulers to defeat hostile classes, exterminate—by slaughter or exile—whole categories of "undesirables," and erect an elaborate dictatorship. Denunciation served as a peculiar kind of feedback, keeping the government informed as to the population's moods, opinions, and doubts.

The first manifestation of denunciation in the postrevolutionary period was the wave of political libels. They were extensively used by Lenin in order to discredit his opponents. His associates—Trotsky, Kamenev, and Zinoviev—also specialized in informing. Yet the one who by all standards excelled in it was Stalin. Denunciation was Stalin's original profession: as head of RKI (*Raboche-krestyanskaya inspektsiya*—Workers' and Peasants' Inspection), his job was to collect rumors, gossip, and anonymous reports from all over the country. Later, when he was appointed general secretary, denunciation became Stalin's forte.

It was Stalin who suggested the idea of setting up a network of agents among party members back at the time when the Cheka (the Soviet security agency from 1918 to 1922) still had no power to deal with internal party matters. He encouraged and channelled the flow of denunciation through the Complaints Department founded under the Central Committee and personally eavesdropped on his associates' conversations, amazing them with the extent of his "insight" and knowledge.

The "explosion" of denunciation in the USSR, however, was not caused by Stalin's evil genius, much as his venal character helped in the process. The phenomenon was attributable to objective processes underway in Soviet society. Hunger, social instability, and economic stagnation undermined the party's position, causing ferment and unrest. In an attempt to halt this process, Stalin decided to administer some political "bloodletting" by annihilating Lenin's cohorts. Denunciation helped compromise the required victims. In order not to deter the timid and the hesitant by denunciation's repulsive nature, it was surrounded with a halo of heroism and sacrifice. People were exhorted to follow the example of Pavlik Morozov, the martyr pioneer (Soviet boy scout) who informed on his father and then testified against him in court. Many Soviet people, misled into self-debasement, eagerly welcomed government-inspired encouragement of betrayal, while their mindless and enthusiastic servility encouraged more betrayal, which turned out to be profitable and praiseworthy. However, during the early postrevolutionary years, most people were still honest and proud. They found the inner strength to refuse to collaborate with the authorities, keep an eye on people, and eavesdrop. Yet with time, the ranks of nonconformists dwindled, and more and more people were ready to turn informer, agent-provocateur, and stool-pigeon on demand.

The word *stukach* (literally, one who knocks on a door), or informer, along with many other terms, reached the Soviet vocabulary from labor camps (it had the same negative connotation as "stool-pigeon") and immediately took root. This notion accurately expressed the essence of life under Soviet socialism, where one could not succeed without "knocking." *Stukachestvo* (knocking) was part of the nervous system of the "new" society. It was embodied in its principles and "commandments": e.g., "betrayal is one's duty" and "to inform is to help society."

Thus from being a *mass* phenomenon, denunciation was transformed into one that was *universal*. It replaced patriotism, becoming a state-fostered symbol of vigilance, courage, and conscientiousness, with children informing on parents, wives on husbands, students on teachers. Universal denunciation turned society into millions of isolated, helpless human cells, driving them into shells of loneliness and fear. Society as a sum total of interrelated, conscious individuals ceased to exist. Denunciation became uncontrollable. It confused and complicated the work of government agencies, which found themselves buried under millions of notices and reports. It completely disoriented the security organs, preventing them from carrying out focused and well-designed investigations and purposeful reprisals and drawing their attention instead to secondary and fortuitous matters. Hence the campaign of denunciation had to be called off.

Then, for some time, denunciation went out of style. The "quota" of arrests had been over-fulfilled to such an extent that the flow of people was reversed—not to but from prisons and labor camps, back into the confines of Soviet society as a whole, i.e., the so-called "large zone" rather than the "small zone" of the prisons. Furthermore, war was looming, relegating the hero-informer to the background. His or her place was taken by another hero: one ready to respond to the call of "the party and the government" to lay down his or her life. Still, killing of his subjects remained Stalin's primary goal, otherwise he would not have retained power. Thus, as soon as the war was over, millions of files were opened on prisoners-of-war, residents of temporarily occupied territories, and plain soldiers who had fought and survived. There were unlimited possibilities for accusations: aiding and abetting the enemy (i.e., being taken prisoner); collaboration with the Germans (i.e., failure to join the partisans); cowardice (i.e., staying in the rear); etc. Without denunciation, it was impossible to achieve so important a goal.

The rising tide of denunciation deluged the country until nothing was spared by it. It was swelled by the induced hysteria of spymania and by the endless calls of the authorities for vigilance. These techniques appeared so convincing (or contagious) that its victims even included people in Stalin's intimate circle. The wife of his elder son Yakov was arrested, while his youngest son Vasily informed on his superior, Marshal Novikov. Moreover, Stalin's comrades-in-arms Molotov, Voroshilov, Kalinin, and Poskrebyshev were all forced to give consent to their wives' arrests. This wave of denunciations also had its heroes. The greatest of them, Lidiya Timashuk, informed about the Doctors' Plot, the "murderers in white robes"—for which, shortly before Stalin's death, she was awarded the Order of Lenin.

After Stalin's death, mass terror was condemned. The practice of denunciation fell into disrepute, hastily replaced by the loftier-sounding term "signal" (and the derivative verb *signalizirovat*—to give a signal). The concept of denunciation had to be reconsidered during the relatively liberal Khrushchev period. Henceforth denunciation was to be the exclusive province of the appropriate officials—activists and social workers—without any "spontaneous initiatives" on the part of the masses and under strict party supervision, intended to keep denunciation within prescribed bounds and prevent it from ever again turning against the party.

The heroes of denunciation were no longer promoted and glorified. Gradually (and unexpectedly for the authorities) they became "antiheroes." Recruitment of informers (there was no question of dispensing with their services) ran into difficulties. As there were few volunteers, there was increasing need to resort to hiring. The old ideological catch-phrases ("It is your duty," "The homeland counts on you") no longer carried any appeal. Candidates therefore had to be forced into informing by intimidation, blackmail, or bought with promises of promotion, a better apartment, or work abroad.

Plenty of people were thus lured into collaborating. The machinery of denunciation went back into motion and picked up speed. Eventually, the informer's image again began to be spruced up. The Soviet press again ran reports of how children had helped the organs expose their parents' unlawful earnings (Pavlik Morozov's "grandchildren" were closing ranks to wage heroic battle), and of how mothers had informed on their children (one of them caused her son to be sentenced to death). The Soviet legacy of denunciation retains its force. It has successfully overcome the pitfalls of glasnost and placed itself at the service of the regime. It is now apparent that even the new Soviet leaders can rely on denunciations, since the closed social system cannot offer any other, more efficient means of gathering information needed for managing the country. Furthermore, many of today's leaders (if not all) were educated in the philosophy of denunciation. Without practicing it themselves, they could have never reached their high offices; so it is only natural if they tried to use it to their advantage. In fact, they already are doing so: Soviet newspapers are now calling upon the population to give signals of any unearned incomes of citizens and to report on "enemies of perestroika." The form of denunciation may be different, yet its essence remains unchanged.

Every citizen knew that a denunciation to the court is not a denunciation but a duty. If you want to cultivate the feeling of trust . . . then develop the ability to denounce, and do not make anyone afraid of [repercussions for conveying] a false report. (Sovetskaya yustitsiya, no. 15, 1927, p. 18) [Note date.]

What was common to the 30s? False denunciations. Many characters with anti-Soviet tendencies, opportunities, and simple slanderers began to settle accounts with anyone they held grudge against. (Sotsiologicheskie issledovaniya, no. 3, 1988, p. 88)

. . . The first model figure presented for millions of pioneers to emulate was an informer on his own father, Pavlik Morozov. From the ethical point of view this figure is so vulnerable that the film about the boy-traitor, "Bezhin Field," directed by Sergei Eisenstein, was suppressed on Stalin's orders. (Ogonek, no. 31, July 1988, p. 24)

The "boss" [Stalin] was already living out his final days when, in the wake of a denunciation made by a filthy agent-provocateur, Professor Serafim Pokrovsky, who directly corresponded with Stalin, one of the most talented and promising scholars and lawyers was sentenced to death. . . . (Literaturnaya gazeta, 27 January 1988, p. 13)

Deprived (of Rights) Person (*Lishenets*). A social stigma that the Soviet authorities, very soon after coming to power, began to impose on various categories of citizens. The term "deprived person" reflected the situation established in the first Soviet constitution (enacted in 1918) of inequality before the law—the deprivation of a group of people of various political and citizen rights.

The term "deprived person" was broadly and vaguely defined as including "everyone living on income not earned by his own labor or derived from hiring the labor of others." With such a definition, the term could be applied to many millions of people, e.g., private entrepreneurs and merchants, clergy, former gentry, and peasants who employed even a single farmhand or seasonal worker. The imposed restrictions affected the deprived persons themselves and the members of their family. The latter were denied the right to study in institutions of higher learning, to receive rations, and to vote. Until 1936, being deprived effectively, barred those thus stigmatized from any upward mobility or merely from escaping the severe restrictions imposed on them.

> Lishenets (deprived): . . . until the promulgation of the 1936 constitution—a person who belonged to the exploiting classes, or a political opponent of Soviet rule, deprived of electoral and other citizen rights. (S. I. Ozhegov, Slovar russkogo yazyka [Dictionary of the Russian language], Moscow: Gosudarstvennoe Izd-stvonatsional'nykh i innostrannykh slovarey, 1960, p. 318)

> The People's Commissariat of Social Welfare confirms that all kulak and bourgeois elements of countryside and town should be deprived of rations. (Pravda, 27 September 1919, p. 1)

> In the USSR the people were deprived of electoral rights during the first period of the existence of the Soviet state, this affected the overthrown exploiting classes. (Bolshaya Sovetskaya entsiklopediya [The great Soviet encyclopedia], Moscow: Gosudarstvennoe nauchnoe izd-stvo Sovetskoy entsiklopedii, 1954, vol. 25, p. 310).

Devotion (*Priverzhennost'*). A moral quality implying allegiance to communist ideals. To amplify the emotional impact of cells for devotion, the term customarily appears together with the adjectives "selfless" (*bez-*

zavetny), "unflagging" (*nepokolebimy*), and "integral (*organichesky*). Such sentiments are by definition related only and exclusively to the Soviet government. Therefore, in any other noncommunist society, there is no room for this quality: there is only room for mercenary motives, selfishness, and egotistic individualism.

> The firm devotion of the fraternal socialist states to the policy of peace is recognized and supported by all progressive and peace-loving forces of the planet. (Zrubezhom, no. 36, 1979, p. 3)

> For Communists of the Soviet Armed Forces selfless devotion to great ideals acquires special significance. (Kommunist vooruzhennykh sil, no. 15, 1979, p. 4)

Dictatorship of the Proletariat (*Diktatura proletariata*). The absolute rule of the party apparat established by a revolutionary coup, maintained by force, and unrestrained by law. The idea of the dictatorship of the proletariat was first expressed by Marxists of the nineteenth century who anticipated a seizure of power by the proletariat, the abolition of bourgeois exploitation, and the creation of a proletarian state. They expected that, with the onset of a classless society, the dictatorship of the proletariat as an instrument of state control would automatically wither away.

Russian Bolshevism broadened the concept of the dictatorship of the proletariat, which came to refer to a particular form of class bond between the industrial proletariat and the poorest peasantry. Despite this bond, the industrial proletariat was not expected to share political power with any other class. Thus, the participation of the peasantry in the revolution was viewed as conditional on its full acceptance of the program and the political leadership of the working class.

From the Paris Commune in 1871 to the death of Stalin in 1953, it was dogma that the dictatorship of the proletariat would last until the complete transition to communism.

Beginning in 1961, party documents started to restrict the dictatorship of the proletariat to the "epoch of Socialism." The latter, however, turned out to be endless: succeeding the stage of "developed socialism," the heirs of Khrushchev (who released the country from Khrushchev's so-called period of "transition to communism") led the USSR into "mature socialism" and began to sensibly maintain that socialism would become "complete" and "final" only when it becomes global. The triumph of socialism in individual countries was then referred to as "complete" but not "final" since, as long as the world capitalist system continues to exist, the possibility of the restoration of bourgeois regimes in socialist states cannot be excluded. Despite the changes in communist interpretations of the dictatorship of the proletariat, one idea has remained constant: the idea that the authoritative and guiding force behind the dictatorship of the proletariat is and always will be the Communist party. Only under the "guidance of the Communist Party" and "armed with Marxist-Leninist theory," can the working class carry out its historic mission of building a "just society."

Before the communist coup in Russia, attempts were made to interpret the dictatorship of the proletariat as "the rule of the workers," organized into spontaneously evolving self-governing bodies. Doctrines of direct governance, not by the party but by congresses of the "toiling masses" (*s"ezdy trudyashchikhsya*), were formulated and advocated. But the dictatorship of the proletariat as the rule of the working class was rejected as inefficient by the Bolsheviks when they gained control over the machinery of state.

During the first years of Soviet power, the dictatorship of the proletariat retained some of its original ideals of popular rule. For example, administrative personnel were recruited mainly from among the workers, who remained a major reservoir of the Communist party's rapid growth after 1917. However, the concept of the dictatorship of the proletariat in the original meaning of the term was already being rendered meaningless by the emerging power structure of the new state, in which "the guiding and driving" force of

society was the Communist party. The Workers' Opposition, espousing the idea of a state administration by proletarian masses, rebelled against the creation of a bureaucratized party-state apparatus to rule over the working class. It demanded the participation "of all the workers" in government, citing the prerevolutionary slogans of Lenin to support its case. Trade union leaders fought for social privileges for the workers on the assumption that they were the ruling class. These privileges included free municipal services, full control over the production process, and a shortened work week, exactly as the pre–October Revolution version of the Program of RKP (B)—Russian Communist Party (Bolsheviks)—had demanded.

The rule of the proletariat, "organized to a man into the ruling class," quickly revealed itself to be a utopian fantasy. The creation of the communist state gave birth to a multitude of administrative, governmental, organizational, and military functions that could not be executed by workers, especially if they were concurrently to carry out their everyday tasks in the factories and plants.

The dictatorship of the proletariat, as a dictatorship of the working class, also proved to be utopian when, after the exploiting classes had been suppressed, the workers' rights and freedoms were suppressed as well. Democratic principles turned out to be incompatible with the principle of the party's dictatorial rule. Shaken by peasants' protests and workers' strikes in the early 1920s, the Communist party felt itself in no position to grant any political freedoms (including the right to free elections) to the trade unions, or to tolerate a Workers' Opposition within the party. Critical in this development was the Kronstadt sailors' mutiny. Immediately after the Kronstadt crisis, the Tenth Congress of the CPSU in 1921 adopted a resolution on the unity of the party that outlawed any kind of opposition, the Workers' Opposition, of course, included. The Communist party consolidated its exclusive rule, abolishing all forms of democracy in the state, within the party, and within working class institutions. The rights of the working class in the Soviet

Union were reduced to the level of the rights of classes like the peasantry and the intelligentsia; that is, they disappeared. But the slogan of the dictatorship of the proletariat, hailed as the most advanced form of democracy in the history of mankind, was retained as window dressing for the party dictatorship.

In order to reconcile the mutually incompatible notions of dictatorship and democracy in a single definition, the communists proclaimed the dictatorship of the proletariat as a dictatorship of the overwhelming majority of the people, namely of the toiling masses (*trudyashchiesya*) over the minority of exploiters. As a dictatorship of the majority, it was claimed to constitute the most fully developed form of popular rule (*narodovlastie*). The facts, however, do not bear out this contention. In Russia in 1913, blue- and white-collar workers comprised 17 per cent of the population, while in 1920–22 the percentage of workers in the population dropped to a mere 3 per cent, and in China on the eve of the communist takeover it was less than 3 per cent. Even in the most highly developed industrial states of the west, the workers still do not comprise the majority of the population.

Stalin's regime embodied two of the ideas that the doctrine of the dictatorship of the proletariat implied: the use of violence to maintain power and the principle of absolute power subject to no legal restraints. These implications had already been spelled out by Lenin in his writings about the dictatorship of the proletariat. Consequently, Stalin was able to draw from Lenin justification for his despotism, arbitrariness, violence, and repression, which, far from affecting the exploiter class alone, also affected broad segments of the working class and peasantry, whose interests the dictatorship of the proletariat was supposed to represent. In this revised version, the dictatorship of the proletariat amounted to the dictatorship of the party elite, supported by the government and its repressive apparatus. The Soviet regime, still nominally exercising the dictatorship of the proletariat, proceeded to assume, in addition to the usual law-and-order enforcing functions of any state, the following tasks: account-settling with the political opposition, control of the entire national economy, totalitarian control over social, political and cultural life, and monopoly of compulsory indoctrination.

The maintenance of the facade of the dictatorship of the proletariat in the contemporary communist theory is essential for the authorities to pursue their expansionist policies because the dictatorship of the proletariat serves as the ideological foundation for the Soviet bid for leadership over the international communist as well as the international working class movements. The countries of the developing world, which lack a substantial proletariat, are on this basis encouraged to look for support to the international working class movement, first and foremost to the Soviet Union. Newly independent states are urged to develop heavy industry and create their own working class. However, in encouraging communist takeovers, the USSR does not always have the patience to wait for the appearance of a local proletariat to create a government that would act in the workers' name. Hence the Soviet Union may act on the basis of a "presumed" social development, which is to "actualize" only in the future.

The dictatorship of the proletariat concept also has ideological functions in domestic propaganda. In 1961, the Soviet Union was proclaimed as having become a "State of All the People" (*obshchenarodnoe gosudarstvo*), but, at the same time, notice was served that in this State of All the People, the leading role of the working class was being maintained and even enhanced.

The professed reliance of the state on the working class, accompanied by strident glorification of the real and imaginary historical "merits" of the workers, helps conceal and at the same time justify the monopoly of the party bureaucracy's power. However, the prospect of the Soviet working class gaining power on account of its sheer size exists and is taken into consideration. This is why the authorities carefully scrutinize all manifestations of political and economic consciousness of working masses.

The new Soviet leadership attentively oversees workers' self-expression as it is coming to the fore on the waves of perestroika. Workers' demands for increased salaries and improvement of work conditions, as well as their spontaneous drive to revive trade unions, are not repressed as previously.

They are silenced by subtler means: through petty concession and *cooptation* like the enactment of residual enterprise autonomy or raising of payments for performance of production assignments. The main goal for the Soviet leadership is to preserve its monopoly of power, though the forms of that power are allowed to change. In the process, these forms have changed from personal, tyrannical dictatorship under Stalin, directed against the people and the party itself, through totalitarian dictatorship of the partocracy under Stalin's successors, to the autocratic regime of Gorbachev, which contains elements of limited popular rule.

On the basis of the conceptions of class struggle and dictatorship of the proletariat enunciated by Marx, Lenin comprehensively developed the theory of socialist revolution, elaborated a scientific strategy of broad class alliances of the proletariat with the peasantry and other classes of workers in the struggle for democracy, national independence and socialism. . . . (Kommunist, no. 4, March 1980, pp. 13–14)

When speaking about the socialist type of personality, Lenin noted some of its features, such as ideological firmness, Communist conviction, loyalty to the ideals of Communism. . . . The development and spreading of these traits on a mass scale turned out to be possible only after the establishment of the dictatorship of the proletariat. (Kommunist, no. 8, August 1980)

It should be considered a hard and fast rule that countries engaged in building socialism must first of all take into consideration the experience of the USSR where, for the first time in history there was established a dictatorship of the proletariat, and created a new type of state—a Soviet socialist state. . . .

(Mirovaya ekonomika i mezhdunarodnye otnosheniya, no. 9, 1980, p. 142)

Direct Dialing (*Vertushka*). A telephone that allows one to place direct calls without going through the municipal network. Available only to top bureaucrats, it has become something of a status symbol.

"One of a hundred" (*sotka*) is the nickname for direct dialing telephones, which date back to the time when there were only a hundred of them in the whole of Moscow. Today there are several thousand. These first automatic telephones in the USSR, with lines that did not pass through a switchboard, were installed in the offices of highly placed party officials on Lenin's orders. His intention was to prevent the confidential conversations of Politburo members and ministers from being overheard by telephone operators or anyone else. Stalin found a way to break this system. He installed a subsidiary exchange in his office to monitor the direct dialing lines and thus kept abreast of the intentions of his political rivals.

Direct dialing telephones were installed in the union republics after World War II. "Government telephones," as they came to be called, were part of the capital style that local government officials were keen to ape. Obtaining a direct dialing line is a matter of well-defined privilege like having an official car with a chauffeur or a pass to a closed store. Members of the Politburo and the government, top commanders of the armed forces and republic leaders are entitled to have direct dialing lines in both their offices and their apartments. Their deputies, city party secretaries, district and regional party secretaries, chairmen of the district and regional executive committees, Central Committee department heads, and newspaper editors are provided with a direct dialing line only at work. Access to a direct dialing line is a symbol of social status that marks a person as belonging to the upper crust of Soviet officialdom.

Direct dialing should be distinguished from the other government telephone network, known as *V Ch* (pronounced "veh-cheh," an abbreviation of *vysokochastotny*: high frequency), *V Ch* serves the same purposes as direct dialing, but involves a different technology used exclusively for long distance calls. It appeared at the end of 1941 to facilitate contact with the front. At present, *V Chs* are placed at the disposal of Central Committee secretaries and department heads, ministers, top commanders of the various branches of the armed forces, and leaders of republics and provinces.

I went to the Pravda Editorial Board, where there is a special Kremlin telephone, so-called direct dialing. (Leonard Vladimirov, Rossiya bez prikras i umolchaniy [Russia without embellishment and omission]; Frankfurt a.M: Possev Verlag, 1969, p. 243)

Finally, there is the fourth type of telephone which operates on the direct dialing network. It is automatic and available to very few. . . . (B. Bazhanov, Vospominaniya byvshego sekretarya Stalina [Memoirs of Stalin's former secretary); Frankfurt a.M.: Possev-Verlag, 1980, p. 56)

So, in short, they prohibited me from staging this performance and reprimanded me. My response was to throw myself into a whirl of activity. I talked to them through direct dialing. I talked, as the popular expression goes, with all the big shots [of the Politburo]. (Strana i mir, no. 1–2, 1984, Munchen, p. 131)

Discipline (*Distsiplina*). Obedience to whatever the norms and regulations of the CPSU statutes, state laws, and labor codes say. In precommunist Russia, as well as in present-day free countries, the word "discipline" was normally reserved for military discipline. But under the communists, phrases such as "state discipline" (*gosudarstvennaya distsiplina*), "labor discipline" (*trudovaya distsiplina*), "trade union discipline" (*profsoyuznaya distsiplina*), "party discipline" (*partiynaya distsiplina*), and "Komsomol discipline" (*komsomol'skaya distsiplina*) gained linguistic legitimacy.

Each of these notions essentially echoes the precepts of military discipline. The organizational structure of the Communist party, and simultaneously, relations within

the labor collectives, began to be largely governed by a set of military-type regulations. In addition, whenever party, state, or trade union documents use the term "discipline," they add qualifications like, "iron," "inviolable," or "strictest," which themselves evoke military associations.

The most important type of discipline in Soviet society is party discipline, simply because the Communist party as the supposed "guiding and decisive force" has centralized and subordinated to itself all forms of social and political activity. Its leadership, the Politburo and the Central Committee, possess supreme authority and virtually unlimited powers. Since their decisions are binding on all Soviet state and public organizations, the implementation of these decisions requires party discipline. Acceptance of such discipline is said to stem from "selfless devotion" (*bezzavetnaya predannost'*) to the people, "loyalty" to the party, and a "high level of communist consciousness."

In reality, the strict observance of "party discipline" is insured by the severity of the punishments meted out to those who fail to toe the line. Those who do not abide by the will of the party are expelled from its ranks and dismissed from their jobs. The practice of informing also makes for obedience. A party member is obliged to inform the leadership of all instances of disobedience and discontent, which reach his notice.

Fundamental for the conduct of the party affairs is the notion (traceable to Lenin) of breaches of party discipline as criminal acts. "He who weakens party discipline in any way is objectively helping the enemies of the working masses" (Lenin, *Sochineniya* [Works], 4th ed., vol. 4, Moscow: Publishing House for Political Literature, 1946, p. 27).

Infringements of "labor discipline" are also equated with treason. The idea behind this view is that "labor discipline" in a socialist society is a form of communist consciousness, patriotism, heroism, selflessness, and mutual aid.

The Soviet concept of "labor discipline" is full of contradictions. Marxist morality considers work to be an a priori necessity (that is, an inherent part of the human individual's socialization). On the other hand, work discipline is conceived of as a prerequisite for the organization of labor: a concept that provides ready-made justification for constant recourse to coercion and restrictions. In order to bypass this contradiction, Soviet ideologists enlist a theory that sees the individual as lagging behind social consciousness. Thus, the argument runs, although labor has been freed of the alienating effects it had under capitalism, some members of the Soviet work force continue to feel alienated nevertheless. For their own good—which is held to be identical with the good of society at large—labor discipline needs to be imposed on them as a therapy aiming to speed up their journey to communism. Labor discipline is presumed to be capable of strengthening the bonds between the worker and his place of work, regulating productivity, guaranteeing plan fulfillment, and providing motivation for participatory involvement.

"Labor discipline" rests on the same foundation as "party discipline"; the unquestioning execution of one's assignments, the unquestioning compliance with regulations, and the unquestioning obedience to authorities. The only problem is that a conscientious (or communist, as it is routinely called) attitude toward work has proved a total fiction. Soviet industry is afflicted by rampant absenteeism and tardiness among workers, low labor productivity, a disinterest of producers in what they produce, pilfering, drunkenness, mendacious and self-exonerating reporting, and money-grubbing. The authorities try to shift the blame for the "breakdown of labor discipline" from the system to the public at large, accusing it of laziness, apathy, inertia, and inefficiency. The struggle for labor discipline (in effect, a struggle against the people) is carried out by using the people themselves in a transparent pretense of popular rule.

The suggestion that drunkards should be sentenced to hard labor is put forward in the name of the working masses, as their supposed "will." Wages and vacation allowances are also determined according to the "will of the working people." The same pretense is used when workers are deprived of bonuses and summer vacations as a punishment for tardiness and absenteeism. Not long ago, on the initiative of the now deceased General Secretary Andropov, in order to find shirkers and other offenders against socialist discipline, roundups were staged in shops, cinemas, and public baths. Collective farmers on their way to a nearby town for shopping expeditions were dragged out of the commuter train. Everyone was constantly exhorted to be vigilant. Eavesdroppers (*slukhachi*) became full-time operators; equipped with tape-recorders, they overheard and recorded "seditious" utterances.

But the new Soviet leaders have few illusions about the efficacy of the labor discipline they are so eager to inculcate. Their goal is simply to prove to the public that infringements of labor discipline do not pay in view of the political or economic sanctions in store. Nevertheless, resistance to the all-pervading regimentation is not an isolated phenomenon, but an integral and organic aspect of the situation in the USSR.

> The unity of word and deed is, perhaps, the most reliable determinant of conscientious discipline and the best guarantee of fulfillment of our plans. (Pravda, 13 December 1983, p. 1)

> Strengthening of conscientious discipline and increasing the sense of reponsibility for the task in hand are major reserves at the disposal of every place of work. (Pravda, 29 November 1983, p. 2)

> The attention of the Communists was focused primarily on improving management, strengthening discipline and increasing labor productivity. (Pravda, 13 December 1983, p. 2)

Distinguished (*Znatny*). An attribute applied to persons engaged in physical labor who have been selected for publicizing. This term has an archaic meaning of "noble" in the sense of "belonging to the nobility" (*prinadlezhashchy k znati*). It is precisely this origin of the word that the authorities are drawing upon by bestowing this title on ordinary working persons in order to idealize their labors and create the impression that workers have a high status in Soviet society. Thus, it has become customary to speak of "distinguished lathe operators," "distinguished miners," "distinguished weavers," "distinguished hog-breeders," "distinguished brigade foremen," etc. By no means is this appelation extended to all conscientious Soviet proletarians. An artificially created stratum of workers, comprising various "winners of socialist competition," "shock-workers of communist labor," and "innovators," is being sifted out of the main body of the Soviet working class. They alone are distinguished. However, although they are entitled to certain material benefits and accorded special prestige and corresponding honors, they have neither political power nor influence.

Since, in zealous deference to official ideology, the Soviet vocabulary is designed to camouflage the existence of profound social inequalities in the USSR, the term distinguished is not used to refer to the real latter-day nobility of Soviet society, the party and state elite.

The distinguished miner skillfully supervises the work of the collective. Our workers' productivity grew by 778 t/month. (Sotsialisticheskaya industriya, 6 August 1978, p. 2)

Agitator N. M. Sisukina, the distinguished spinner of the Kamensk Synthetic Fiber Factory, is sharing her work experience. . . . (Agitator, no. 12, 1978, p. 11)

The distinguished builder Demidenko, a brigade foreman, said, "In the name of the builders' collective, I can assure you that we will not let you down." (Izvestiya, 26 October 1983, p. 1)

Document (*Spravka*). An official form, with either typed or handwritten text, certifying certain presumed facts or information about a person. Documents hound the Soviet citizens through their entire lives, and even follow them after death. Once existent, they

assume a life of their own, independent of either those who draft them or those who read them. They are sustained by a vast array of decrees, directives, and circulars. Some documents, like a birth certificate, make sense since it is important to know when and where a person was born. Documents that list the members of one's family can also be justified since it is important to know the person's social status. Yet scores of other documents constitute flagrant invasion of privacy, describing the most private aspects of one's life, in total disregard of one's self-respect. Such are the documents specifying one's salary, apartment space, additional income, amount of the bank account savings, etc. (As soon as the concerned citizen becomes aware that documents about him or her are in circulation, he or she cannot but begin to worry about whether it is "good" or "bad" to have so little money or a certain amount of apartment space or the like.) The huge collection of such official papers even contains a document authorizing someone to grow a beard. Many documents indicate blatant and insulting suspiciousness. Most of them violate one of man's basic human rights: the presumption of innocence.

Soviet citizens often react with fear and loathing whenever they hear the word "document." It means having to spend days and weeks in various waiting rooms, standing in long lines in order to be received by some government bureaucrat and issued the necessary papers.

Soviet life is governed by documents. The government, busy drawing up its next "directive," is totally preoccupied with paperwork, to the point of having absolutely no regard for human feelings aroused in the process of filling out all these forms. Government officials are concerned with making sure there are enough decrees and regulations around to provide a formal basis for every conceivable measure they may undertake. The principle of "playing it safe" is the cornerstone of Soviet government performance. The more papers there are, the easier it is to create the impression of importance and efficiency. Once the bureaucrat is deprived of his "paper power," his uselessness will become patently obvious. Thus, in addition to the passport, which is the "main" document certifying one's identity, everybody's life is encumbered by a steady flow of hundreds of "secondary" documents: from the housing committee, the district soviet, the police, one's place of employment, and party organization. Their proliferation is a major feature of the Soviet way of life, as accurately attested by a ditty that in free translation emerges as follows: "Without a form you are just a worm."

Incidentally, my expanded collection even includes a document granting me "the right to permanently wear a beard. . . ." (Pravda, 7 August 1988, p. 1)

Those are the kinds of details that have to be included in the documents required to update the personal file of head of the Institute's personnel department. What I would like to know is why should anybody need information concerning my relatives? Are we back in Stalin's time? Who needs such documentary "glasnost" about members of my family? (Ogonek, no. 24, 1988, p. 7)

We have become more dispirited and oppressed. Like a schoolboy waiting for his chemistry exam, we wait for our turn in today's, tomorrow's, and next week's line for a document, a pair of winter shoes, a kilo of tomatoes, a tomb-stone. (Pravda, 3 August 1988, p. 3)

Dogmatism (*Dogmatizm*). (1) A way of thinking embodying never-changing precepts and formulas. (2) An uncritical acceptance of reality, an adherence to outdated attitudes and theories. Dogmatism typifies many reactionary, detached-from-reality and past-revering ideas of the unchangeability of the world. In the Soviet Union, it originated with the advocacy and spread of Marxist concepts demanding blind obedience and subordination to (practically religious belief in) the dogmas of communism, which were expounded as an eternal and absolute truth ("Marxist-Leninist teaching is omnipotent because it is true"). Independently of this, dogmatism is deeply

rooted in the structure of Soviet society: in its closed nature, self-containment, the longevity of its antidemocratic institutions, and its suppression of freedom. Thus it often happens that even the champions of radical change, the advocates of perestroika, as they are now called, prove to be no less intolerant of any opposition than their opponents.

Dogmatism has penetrated into human psychology. It has already become an integral feature of "homo sovieticus," an inalienable part of his personality and the basis of his world view. His consciousness has become totally compartmentalized and resists any attempt to assimilate new facts. The center of the Soviet man's mental universe is formed by the formulas backed by the permanent authority of Marx, Engles, and Lenin, and by the transient authority of successive leaders of the party. All information he receives and any opinion he holds conforms to those formulas. If he is programmed to accept a piece of information or an opinion, he recognizes it as "progressive." If he is denied access to a particular piece of information or opinion, and if he runs across it nevertheless, he immediately recognizes it as backward and reactionary.

"Homo sovieticus" is short of historical perspective: he regards the present as a transition to the future. Dogmatism is more than a worldview for him: it is his innermost need. He can only tolerate others to the extent that their behavior coincides with stereotypes prescribed by the authority to which he bows, usually a Marxist authority, but not necessarily to the exclusion of other authorities such as nationalist or religious, for example. He is so dependent on an authoritarian style of thought that he needs not only an idol to emulate, but also its opposite, an enemy to whom anything opprobrious can be ascribed. He needs such an enemy in order to blame him for defeats, disorder, and misfortune. This is true in general, but in the Soviet Union the ramifications are broader than elsewhere. Contrary to the official claim that dogmatism has its roots in capitalism and the spirit of individualism, capitalism never managed to develop in tsarist Russia, which means that dogmatism could have evolved only from precapitalist lifestyles, typical of the feudal system and serfdom, and of its primitive, communal social structure, which entailed strict controls over minute details of people's lives. These tendencies grew even stronger in the USSR after the communist revolution, which deprived people of the means of defense against the total penetration of ideology into their lives. Economically, they became completely dependent on the collective and thereby on the state. Legal guarantees for the protection of individual rights were abolished to the point that any attempt to shield one's private life from prying eyes came to be regarded as proof of his or her suspect intentions and disloyalty to the state. Individualism was proscribed. The state (often misrepresented as "society") was made more important than the individual. Authoritarianism rapidly intensified and took root in the country in various forms to the point of permitting mass exterminations. The first mutually contradictory attitudes of love for ideas, combined with hatred for people or of freedom for the party and slavery for the people, which were the hallmark of ascendant dogmatism, began to assert themselves in social consciousness.

By relegating all individual differences to the realm of privacy, the communist collectivization of consciousness inadvertently elevated the latter into the primary (perhaps even exclusive) area of human initiative. Under those circumstances "shameless" egoism could not but evolve into the first principle of human conduct, as a counter-reaction to ideology and to coercive collectivism. This egoism was perfectly candid, professed in the open, and was unfettered by any code of ehics. It was fast becoming a moral code itself, based on precepts that today define the Soviet way of life: "Your own shirt is closest to the skin," "You help me and I'll help you" [get something useful], "If you want to live, learn how to operate," "My hut is the farthest away," meaning, "It's no concern of mine." As a result, Soviet man has been caught in a double bind between individualism and collectivism. Individual-

ism has been helpful in preserving his self-esteem, while collectivism has provided him the means of adaptation and survival. Society is therefore governed by two moralities: one individualist for private use, and the second, collectivist for public use. Both have proved to be indispensable, and their alternation according to circumstances has proved to be indispensable as well. This has shaped a personality type addicted to duplicity. But such a personality has tended also to be addicted to dogmatism already since the 1930s, when two forms of truth, two parallel realities to be more accurate, first developed in the USSR. One of these competing realities derived from the transformations brought about by the Revolution, from enthusiasm and solidarity, in general from the "bright" side of life. The other derived from the shady, "dark" side of life, with its increasingly arbitrary rule, interrogations, torture, and executions.

The masses, well aware of repression that was too widespread to be effectively concealed, led a dual existence, believing in both the "bright" and the "dark" truths. (Their rulers were hardly different in that respect.) The realities of joyless, poverty-stricken everyday life under communism became totally divorced from propagandistic fictions of prosperity. The two mental worlds were never to converge. Accordingly, dual standards pervaded Soviet society from the top to the bottom. This could not have been different even for the country's rulers, who taught that nothing elevated the individual more than an "activist attitude" (cf.) and a sense of "obligation to society" (Brezhnev) and who shamelessly plundered the people, who were left with no choice but to emulate their example, that is to play the hypocrite and believe (or, like their leaders, pretend to believe), all evidence to the contrary notwithstanding, that the battle for discipline would save Soviet industry and that rationing would lead to prosperity. Likewise, despite all the boorishness they encountered in everyday life, the people were left with no choice but to see (or pretend to see) others as their friends, comrades, and brothers.

Soviet man's life experience taught him to be intolerant. Intolerance is an essential feature of dogmatism. From the very beginning, intolerance was a weapon in the class war, during the Revolution and the civil war. It served the regime quite well as it helped to unite the masses under its banner. When the class war abated, intolerance was artificially stimulated in order "to exploit the revolutionary awareness of the working classes." Categories of people not yet completely wiped out—the nobility, clergy, and merchant class—were the first victims of this intolerance. After these had been exterminated, the regime began to persecute the purely "socialist" elements of society: the proletariat, the working intelligentsia, and the party itself. World War II once again provided a natural object for hatred: the Nazis. Once they had been defeated, the system renewed its attacks on imaginary enemies: the "cosmopolitans," the "geneticists," party officials yet again ("the Leningrad affair"), and Jewish doctors ("the murderers in white robes").

In accordance with the laws of dogmatism, Stalin searched not for the causes of ills but for culprits. Contrived hatred for Stalin's enemies, real and imaginary, served to stabilize society, diverting the attention of the masses away from their lack of freedom, their poverty, and their deprivations. After Stalin's death, however, intolerance did not disappear; it only acquired more "civilized" forms. It came to be instilled in other ways: by increasing differences in the standard of living and distances between social strata. It is now expressed in the whole complex system of social antagonisms, whereby officials snub workers, workers scoff at intellectuals, intellectuals despise workers, and they all hate bureaucrats.

In Soviet society, dogmatism is also reinforced by the hardships of everyday life, by all the years of waiting in order to obtain living space (cf.), all the ordeals one has to go through in order to obtain a pay raise, or place children in a nursery school, have a telephone installed, or buy basic provisions. People's depressing, monotonous lives instill

in them passivity. This is why there is so much boredom and stagnation in Soviet society, not just in the sense of spiritual malaise, but also as a symptom of social conditions.

Dogmatism is not endangered by public criticism, because the latter is usually aimed at secondary and therefore perfectly evident ills. Thus, one criticizes the destruction of vineyards wrought in order to eradicate drunkenness; or the zeal in branding decent earnings as an obstacle in the path toward socialism; or the perception of each member of a cooperative as an enemy of the Soviet regime. Stalin understood the "safe" character of such criticism well, noting that "Marxism is not a dogma but a guide to action." Such a "dialectical" critique of dogmatism did not prevent Stalin from setting the mills of intolerance to grind. As they revolved, they rendered sterling service to a series of "personality cults," the first definitely tragic, the subsequent ones more farcical.

Dogmatism is perpetually in search of new targets for victimization: the *stilyagi* (cf.) in the 1960s, the hippies in the 1970s, and the freemasons in the 1980s. Its latest victims are "the enemies of *perestroika*." Dogmatism sadistically calls for incarcerations and executions as "solutions" to social problems. Soviet society always needs an object for hatred in order to justify its existence. The question is, who will be branded its next victim?

Dogmatism is social: it appears and grows in relationships between people. Its constant companions in interpersonal relations are fanatical intolerance toward any heterodoxy and the authoritarian manner in which opinions are foisted on people. (Ogonek, no. 31, July 1988, p. 14)

In contrast to dogmatism, Marxist-Leninism is the creative development of theory, a dialectical assertion of the concreteness of truth. (Kratky politichesky slovar', Moscow: Political Literature Publishing House, 1988, p. 110)

From the standpoint of traditional dogmatic precepts, the slogan 'More Socialism' raises quite a few questions. (Ogonek, no. 36, September 1988, p. 9)

Dormitory (*Obshchezhitie*). A communal residence for people working in the same factory or studying at the same educational institution. As a result of chronic housing shortages, more than ten million people are currently in more than seventy thousand dormitories scattered throughout the USSR. On top of this, nearly 60 percent of the dormitory residents have only "limited registration" rights (cf. "registration") (*limitnaya propiska*), which means that their dormitory residence is conditional on their working in the factory or studying in the educational institution that owns their dormitory. Leaving their job or terminating their studies deprives them of the right to live in a dormitory and automatically of the right to reside in a given town.

Dormitories are uncomfortable and overcrowded, with each person having no more than three to four square meters of living space. Between four and twelve people live in a single room devoid of requisite furniture and basic comforts. The authorities are, however, in no hurry to relieve the overcrowding in dormitories by dispersing their inhabitants. The concentration of large numbers of people in one place facilitates ideological manipulation and brainwashing. It makes it easier to organize "communist leisure" (*kommunistichesky dosug*), to recruit audiences for propaganda lectures, and to control people and interfere with their private lives.

In many dormitories there is no canteen or dining room, and when there are, their patrons are dissatisfied with their service, and the range and quality of their food. (Komsomol'skaya pravda, 17 September 1980, p. 2)

In our country today there are 37,000 worker dormitories in which there reside five and one half million people. The average age of the residents is 25, hence such workers' dormitories can well be called young peoples' dormitories. (Komsomol'skaya pravda, 17 September 1980, p. 2)

Just recently young people from the country

have been coming to work in factories, but dormitory-space is lacking. (Komsomol'skaya pravda, 18 October 1980, p. 1)

The rate of satisfaction of demand for dormitory-space for small families is only 15%. (Komsomol'skaya pravda, 24 March 1989, p. 2)

Draconian (*Drakonovsky*). Cruel, merciless. The attribute is used as a standard designation of political or social measures undertaken by governments hostile to the USSR. This word originates from the name of the ancient Greek statesman Dracon, whose laws were notable for their harshness.

Draconian is usually used in phrases such as "Draconian measures" (*drakonovskie mery*) and "Draconian regime" (*drakonovsky rezhim*). The term has a particularly expressive quality derived from its phonetic similarity to the word "dragon" (*drakon*). Expressions containing the word "Draconian" carry connotations similar to those of such common clichés as "the sharks of capitalism" (*akuly kapitalizma*), "the hydra of counterrevolution" (*gidra kontrrevolyutsii*), and "the tentacles of Zionism" (*shchupal'tsy sionizma*).

The actions of the Soviet government and the arbitrariness of Soviet laws are never described as Draconian but rather as "just," "necessary," "extraordinary," or "indispensable."

No matter how Draconian the measures which the Israelis have taken in Lebanon itself to create preconditions for a "post-Palestinian" era, they will not succeed. (Literaturnaya gazeta, 7 July 1982, p. 14)

From the very first days of the strike at the beginning of August, the American authorities resorted to Draconian measures in order to break it. (Izvestiya, 2 August 1981, p. 5)

In response to the Draconian measures instituted by the [Pakistan] authorities last February-March, a wave of mass protest demonstrations and strikes by students, teachers, lawyers, and physicians swept the country. (Izvestiya, 27 March 1981, p. 4)

Dregs (*Otreb'e*). An extravagant invective applied to opponents of the Soviet regime, which implies their utter spiritual corruption, moral degradation, and well-deserved social marginality. The term can be also applied to voluntary associations and political groups committed to an anticommunist ideology.

The word "dregs" usually appears in hackneyed phrases such as "counterrevolutionary dregs" (*kontreevolyutsionnoe otreb'e*), "White Guard dregs" (*belogvardeyskoe otreb'e*), and "emigré dregs" (*emigrantskoe otreb'e*). After the October Revolution such phrases were in common use in reference to social classes and political groups that opposed the establishment of Soviet rule. Later, the scope of this term expanded markedly. Thus, in the 1970s and 1980s, organizations founded by expatriates from communist countries who worked for human rights came to be called "emigré dregs." Within the Soviet Union, it is the dissidents who are called "anti-Soviet dregs" (*antisovetskoe otreb'e*), alternative appelations being "tools of world imperialism," "tools of Zionism," and "agents of international reaction."

As for expatriates, communist propaganda does not recognize their right to consider themselves political exiles. The Soviet people are told that the only political exiles are communists who flee from reactionary regimes. For those leaving the Soviet Union a different terminology is reserved: "traitor to the Fatherland," "criminal," "dregs." The period of glasnost is marked by a certain verbal restraint. A selective approach to emigrés has appeared: some were graciously forgiven, and granted (as a rule, posthumously) the honor and rank they deserved, while others were shown pity and sympathy for their real or alleged hardships. Nevertheless, there remain some whom the Soviet Union continues to consider "dregs" although the term itself may be avoided.

The meeting indignantly denounced the endeavors of emigré nationalistic dregs to organize ideological sabotage and to smuggle in hostile literature. (Kommunist, no. 5, 1979, p. 49)

Under White House pressure, the American press continues its massive campaign to increase assistance to the counter-revolutionary dregs now entrenched in numerous bases in Pakistan. (Mezhdunarodnaya zhizn', no. 9, 1980, p. 11)

The fabrication of Western propaganda, that counter-revolutionary dregs are using weapons captured in Afghanistan itself, has finally collapsed. (Izvestiya, 27 September 1981, p. 5)

E

Edicts (*Prednachertaniya*). Instructions and plans of the party. The word belongs to a sophisticated literary vocabulary, and in colloquial Russian sounds somewhat archaic. Nevertheless, communist ideologists have borrowed the word and rely on it in order to stress the exalted nature of the policies and activities of the party. Traditionally, the term "edict" conveys the notion of a distant power elevated high above man and determining his destiny. In accordance with the ritual of communist ideology, the notion of a "distant power" ascribed to the party is meant to sanctify the soulless Soviet regime, to emphasize its almost supernatural ability to foresee and control the future. The party apparatus, which is the sole source of edicts, is supposed to appear as an unchallengeable authority, steering the people toward their true goals.

Thus, the edicts of the party are described as "historic," "great," "epochmaking," and "scientifically grounded." In fact, imbuing the term "edicts" with a mythical aura is an indispensable measure, since the party directives and plans are misconceived and unrealistic and therefore ignored by the public.

> Today it is abundantly clear that the Party's edicts are becoming reality in all the spheres of building [Communism]: governmental, economic, social, and cultural. (Agitator, no. 1, 1979, p. 3)

> The Soviet people, fulfilling the Party's edicts, are raising the land of the Soviets to new heights of progress. (Agitator, no. 3, 1979, p. 3)

> All the working masses of the Latvian Soviet Socialist Republic are doing their utmost to carry out fully all the edicts and decisions of the Report of the Central Committee of the CPSU and to successfully transform into reality the edicts of our dear Leninist Party. (Izvestiya, 27 February 1981, p. 3)

Elected Representatives of the People (*Narodnye izbranniki*). A propagandistic term for deputies to the local soviets and the Supreme Soviet. In contrast to the semantically related concept of "deputies" (*deputaty*), the term "elected representatives of the people" is not neutral. In fact, both the constituent Russian words are value-loaded. The word *narodnye* ("of the people") suggests the existence of popular sovereignty and a general popular orientation in regard to public policy. The word *izbranniki* ("elected representatives") suggests the existence of democratic elections in the USSR and equality before the law. In reality, the elected representatives of the people are appointed rather than elected, and they possess neither real power nor the right to exercise effective control over the executive bodies.

Since the first Soviet constitution was enacted, deputies have been permitted to discuss only secondary matters, and that only with the party's permission. Until quite recently (until Gorbachev's reforms, to be precise), there had never been a case of the Supreme Soviet rejecting draft legislation or sending it to be revised. This, of course, does not prove the infallible nature of all government decrees. On the contrary, many of them have in time been acknowledged as mistaken and repealed, but initiative in such cases has never been taken by the elected representatives of the people. It has always come from the party and its apparatus.

Lenin viewed the soviets as the highest form of democracy. In this he differed from Marx, who saw a parliamentary republic as the prototype for the government of the future. The formula of "the rule of the soviets" (*vlast' sovetov*) was enunciated by the Bolsheviks during the revolution of 1905, and in the 1920s it was included in the program of many communist parties. Since then, the soviets, as the organs of state power in the USSR, have undergone a complex evolution. For example, their function as a representative body organized according to industries disappeared, the line of command between the local soviets and the Supreme Soviet was severed, and multistage elections were replaced by direct elections. As a result, the soviets became a mere appendage to the party machine.

Initially, the elected representatives of the people were elected only to local soviets, which in turn nominated deputies to the Supreme Soviet. Elections were held at work places, and the choice of candidates was open to discussion. With the advent of direct elections, the population no longer had the right to choose: it was offered a single candidate (until recently, when more than one candidate is possible), for whom one automatically voted. Thus, the deputies were no longer accountable before the electorate but only and exclusively before the collectives or organizations that had nominated them. Along with these changes, the soviets lost all of their distinctive role without acquiring one characteristic of the parliamentary system of government. As a result, the prestige of the soviets as organs of popular power declined not only in the Soviet Union but elsewhere as well. One by one, workers' parties began to drop the call for " power to the soviets" from their political programs.

The nomination (or, more precisely, the selection) of candidates to the soviets is carried out in strict accordance with the social hierarchy of Soviet society. Every more or less important position in the USSR has its appropriate level of representation in the soviets: high officials at the district level are nominated for the district soviets, and those at the city level for the city soviets. The party's elite—secretaries of the Central Committee, ministers, newspaper chief editors, top army commanders, presidents of academies, etc.—are nominated for the Supreme Soviet. Of course, workers and peasants are represented at all levels of the pyramid of soviets by "extras," used to maintain the fiction of the "popular" char-

acter of the Soviet government, whose sole function within the elected organs is to rubberstamp party directives and government decisions. To prevent deputies from developing a collective inferiority complex, their total lack of any power or influence is compensated by the lavish privileges heaped upon them.

In addition to the wages they receive from the places of their employment, deputies to various soviets receive what by Soviet standards amounts to substantial financial privileges and fringe benefits. During sessions of the soviets they do not pay for rides on public transportation. They get access to closed shops (cf.) and rest homes, and receive exclusive medical treatment from doctors assigned to the special medical facilities for the elite. Of course, the volume and quality of privileges enjoyed by the elected representatives of the people is directly proportional to the level of soviet in which they participate. Still, even deputies to local soviets receive their share.

Last but not least, deputies are entitled to wear the deputy's badge, an important symbol of social distinction and prestige. There are different forms of such badges, depending on the rank in the hierarchy of the soviets. The social value of the deputy's badge is not negligible: it offers tangible evidence of one's position on the social ladder, guaranteeing its bearer the opportunity to gain power or the right to obtain an apartment, to enter a restaurant without queueing (cf. queue) or to purchase a theater ticket ahead of the line. Social inequality is so deeply ingrained in Soviet society that a person who lacks any external distinctions indicative of his or her social standing is treated as a nonperson, and neither his or her intellect, knowledge, or education are of any avail. By equipping deputies with badges and special IDs, the party apparatus thereby ensures that they will follow a pattern of social behavior useful to itself.

As far as the Soviet voter is concerned, his or her interests were not at all taken seriously until 1987. Voters would receive a ballot with the instructions "Leave the name of the one deputy for whom you wish to vote;

cross out the names of the rest." Ironically, however, there was no one to cross out: the ballot contained the name of only one deputy! A voter who might think about entering the privacy of a polling booth, rather than immediately handing in his ballot, would be kept back by the watchful and suspicious eyes of electoral commission members. To them, a voter walking toward the booth was a clear sign of his intention to cross out the name of the only listed candidate. The safest thing to do was to drop the ballot into the nearest box without even looking at it.

The candidates showed no particular concern about the elections either. They knew that their election was a foregone conclusion. Thus, the electoral process was equally senseless for the voters and the nominees. Nevertheless, for many years attempts were made to attract the population to the polling booths by colorfully decorating the polling stations and handing out free snacks and drinks. This proved to be too cumbersome and costly, so attempts were made to combat the apathy of the electorate by sending election personnel with ballot boxes to voters' homes. Finally, a clever decision was reached: let those who want to vote do so. The figures to be reported would, in any case, be determined in advance and always be the same: 99.99 percent of all eligible voters. Thus, the elected representatives of the people were elected neither by the people nor from the ranks of the people. The Soviets came to be largely filled by high officials whose authority was contingent not on their deputy status but on their position within the party or government. This situation remained virtually intact for seventy years. It suited Lenin's political ambitions and adapted itself well to the existing regime from Stalin to Chernenko. It was only under Gorbachev's rule that the facade began to show signs of crumbling. Gorbachev endorsed the original communist slogan "All power to the soviets," but he had in mind an interpretation of his own that could be understood: "All my power will be in the soviets."

At first glance, this concept would not seem at all original. After all, every Soviet leader,

each in his or her own fashion, imposed his or her will upon the soviets. However, before Gorbachev, this had been done from the outside, through the party apparatus. Gorbachev, on the other hand, decided to control the soviets from the inside, by exercising his prerogatives as the general secretary (cf.). In order to achieve this goal, the usual decision of the Politburo to concurrently appoint him chairman of the Supreme Soviet was not enough. He had to merge this post into that of the general secretary, turning the former into one of the functions of the latter. This led to the new Soviet law mandating joint incumbency of the posts of general secretary of the CPSU and chairman of the Supreme Soviet. Now Gorbachev can safely remove the soviets from the tight control of the party. Such emancipation of the soviets not only presented no threat to his power monopoly, but, on the contrary, made him less vulnerable to intrigues and conspiracies.

Gorbachev conferred on the soviets numerous administrative and supervisory prerogatives, granting them the authority to deal with some major economic, social, and cultural issues and restoring their superordinate position over the government. He also took care to free the deputies to local soviets from their ordinary work duties during sessions and also the deputies to the Supreme Soviet for the duration of their terms. He also introduced major changes in the electoral system by providing for an excess of candidates on the ballot over the number of the posts to be filled and therefore for a choice between a number of candidates, in addition to the possibility of extensively discussing their candidacies. He also reorganized the soviets themselves. From now on, the highest government body is the Congress of Peoples' Deputies, which elects the relatively small and permanently deliberating bicameral Supreme Soviet.

The Congress of People's Deputies of the USSR comprises 2,250 deputies. Out of that number, two-thirds are nominated by territorial and national-territorial electoral districts and one-third by various organizations:

one hundred candidates by party organizations, one hundred by trade unions and one hundred by cooperatives, and seventy-five each by the Komsomol and public unions (the women's groups, war and labor veterans' groups, artists' unions, etc.).

This system of representation cannot be viewed as democratic. Candidacies from public unions are not determined by their membership, but only the heads of the unions. Furthermore, the members of bodies represented in the congress actually vote twice: at their polling stations as well as through their representatives in the public organizations they belong to. This creates electoral inequality: members of the party, the trade unions, artists' unions, and scientists' organizations are represented by six or more deputies each, two from their territorial and national districts, and one from each public organization; while the rest of the Soviet population, who are neither party members nor social activists, are only represented by two deputies, nominated at their place of residence.

The principle of electoral equality is also prejudiced by the rules for nominating candidates from political and social organizations themselves. No grounds are given for the unequal representation of party and Komsomol bodies or the trade unions and artists' unions. It is not specified on what basis the mandates are subdivided within the quotas assigned to various organizations, whether equally or according to their membership or depending on how vital a given profession is. Furthermore, the election of deputies from various unions totally disregards the interests of the multinational Soviet population, since only All-Union organizations centered in Moscow are represented in the top government organs. Thus, less important associations, like the hunters' or the stamp-collection associations, will be able to send their deputies to Congresses of People's Representatives and sessions of the Supreme Soviet, while unions and organizations on local and even republic levels, often having distinct political or national orientations (for example, the *"Narodnye Fronty"*—the

"Peoples' Fronts"), will end up being unrepresented.

Those are the gravest flaws of the new Soviet law on amendments to the constitution. Its separate articles are also open to various interpretations. One of the articles, in fact the most important one, stipulates that deputies will be chosen by direct elections: ". . . the deputies to all soviets of peoples' deputies will be elected directly by the citizens" (article 98 of the Constitution of the USSR). Indeed, Soviet elections, while being neither universal nor equal, for many years remained direct. Not quite, of course, since the deputies were divested of all authority, which was held instead by the soviets' executive committees, which were not elected but rather appointed. Still, at least nominally the principle of direct elections to soviets on all levels was upheld. It was this principle that fell the first victim to the political shuffle by which the Congress of Peoples' Deputies now determines the composition of the Supreme Soviet.

This concept necessitates indirect elections, of two stages or, insofar as the head of the government is concerned, three stages. From the democratic point of view, or even from the point of view of the moderate democratization (cf.) now underway in the USSR, there is no reason why the voter should have no right to decide for him- or herself without mediating agents, who would represent him or her in the Supreme Soviet or who would be elected as the head of state. The reasons for this reform are easily understandable in terms of the interests of the leadership as can be seen even in the wording of the new law on amending the Soviet constitution.

The chairman of the Supreme Soviet is now elected at the Congress of People's Deputies, not during a session of the Supreme Soviet as before. At first glance, this seems to be a minor amendment, yet it has far-reaching political consequences. The chairman is thereby set apart from and above the Supreme Soviet. He or she can now be removed neither by the Presidium of the Supreme Soviet (now called the chairman of the Supreme Soviet and not of the Presidium as in the past) nor by the Supreme Soviet itself. The chairman therefore comes to wield such immense power that he or she is practically no longer answerable even to the all-powerful Politburo, the apex of Soviet authority. In his or her capacity of the chairman of the Supreme Soviet (not that of the general secretary!) he or she is now considered to be the "highest official of the Soviet state, representing the Union of Soviet Socialist Republics both within the country and in international relations" (article 120). The chairman also sets the overall course of Soviet foreign policy, receives the diplomatic representatives of foreign countries, coordinates the activity of permanent commissions, committees and chambers of the Supreme Soviet, conducts negotiations and signs international agreements, and heads the Defense Council.

The question of whether one person is capable of combining the extended powers of the chairman of the Supreme Soviet with the complicated and numerous duties of the general secretary, the party head, is carefully glossed over in the Soviet Union. The Soviet leader is not subject to the principles of glasnost but is above all criticism. The only expression of doubt is timidly ventured in regard to the right of republic and provincial leaders to concurrently be heads of soviets and chiefs of local party organizations. Furthermore, what is questioned is not so much the legality of amassing such power as the pragmatic issue of its practical consequences. In other words, the real question is whether individual party officials, accustomed to the authoritarian leadership style, have the character and experience suited for heading the soviets. At the same time, the problem of the constitutional propriety of merging together the (supposedly separate) powers is passed over in silence.

The first secretary (and in theory the general secretary as well) of a party committee can be removed from the soviet by the electorate. In such a case, the chairman will lose his or her status as deputy. The opposite can also happen: a party leader may not be elected as chairman of a soviet, which will necessitate nomination of another candidate. However, the latter could not be nominated, since according to the new law only a secretary of the party committee at the corresponding level can be elected to the post of the chairman.

Many of the liberal principles of the current Soviet political reform are being eroded by technicalities and minor points of procedure. The law on amending the constitution states that in the Soviet electoral process the nomination of candidates for deputies must remain unlimited. At the same time, it stipulates (article 37) that the minimum number of five hundred votes is needed for each nominee. Thus, while endorsing the right of each citizen to be elected, this law effectively precludes any nonconformist group that fails to get the required quorum of votes from nominating their candidates. Or consider article 56, which states: "A candidate to the post of deputy is considered to be elected if he receives more than 50% of the total votes in his electoral district." Yet this ruling is effectively annulled by the following addendum: "Elections are rendered null and void if the turnout amounted to less than 50% of all voters registered on the election lists. . . ."

Whoever drafted and passed this clause must have based it on the idea of compulsory participation in the elections, in accordance with the motto "I am, therefore I vote." Thus it becomes clear why the dying Chernenko was conveyed to the polling station, where he had his cramped fingers unclenched, was handed a ballot, and had to cast his vote. In the Soviet Union, the constitutional voting right has been transformed into a constitutional duty. It probably never even occurred to the Soviet legislators that the notion of electoral rights includes not only the options of voting "for" or "against," but also a third option—that of abstaining, i.e., of "voting with one's feet" by refusing to come to the polling station.

Nevertheless, the political reform carried out by Gorbachev, with all its imperfections and inconsistencies, has managed to significantly circumscribe executive powers, including that of the party. This became apparent with the proposal to exclude the heads of the soviets' departments and boards from being nominated as deputies. This applies to judges, procurators, and arbitrators, and it has been suggested to extend this rule to government members and heads of government authorities.

Still, the role of the party as the leading authority in Soviet society has not been affected. On the contrary, the power of the party has to some extent been even strengthened due to the increased influence of the general secretary. The general secretary will be automatically elected chairman of the Supreme Soviet (so the secret ballot will actually be of no avail), and the first secretaries of party committees will just as automatically become chairmen of corresponding soviets. Thus, the authority, as well as representative power of the new soviet, has been conferred on party leaders. Therein lies the main, covert intention of Gorbachev's political reform.

The flaw of this reform lies in the single-party character of the Soviet regime. Only political pluralism, implying the existence of an opposition, could provide Soviet society with a viable political alternative. Such pluralism would have to include the possibility of selecting alternative deputies and forcing the ruling party (which might even be communist) to pursue a policy reflecting the people's needs and demands. Naturally, in such a hypothetical situation the issue would no longer be restoring forms of government that existed under Lenin but rather a basic reform of the Soviet political system. Only then would the soviets become real representative organs, and only then could deputies to them be truly considered elected representatives of the people.

Alexey Stakhanov and Maria Demchenko, Alexandr Pokryshkin and Ivan Kozhedub, Ivan Papanin and Yury Gagarin, as well as numerous other distinguished citizens of the Soviet state, have been honored by receiving the high distinction of becoming elected representa-

tives of the people. (Agitator, no. 20, 1983, p. 26)

Natalya Anatolevna Stenina, deputy to the Supreme Soviet in the USSR, is informing us about the work of an elected representative of the people, about the ways of carrying out the popular mandate. (Komsomol'skaya pravda, 14 Feburary 1984, p. 4)

Elites (*Elity*). The groups and strata within the communist class, whose relative social and political standing is determined by functions they perform in service to the Soviet regime. Soviet elites can be viewed as a pyramid with a clearly defined hierarchy. The party elite is at the apex of that pyramid; the government elites, bureaucratic elites, and military and police elites occupy the middle level, followed by Komsomol, trade-union and industrial-technological elites, and, at the very bottom, the scientific, artistic, and literary elites.

Social mobility in the USSR is programmed. Family, nationality, social connections, and money are the surest means of attaining high positions. Very few people can propel themselves upward by dint of their talents and capabilities alone. yet eligibility criteria vary; each elite has its own.

Scientific, literary, and artistic elites, due to their low status, are relatively open to newcomers. Although recruitment to their ranks depends on talent, initiative and originality are not attritubes that are prized. Instead, the decisive criterion is an entrant's willingness to serve the ruling class.

The technological and industrial elites, occupying the middle level of the pyramid, are harder to penetrate. Class origins and party membership limit the selection. Nationality is a major consideration, but ability also counts. The decisive factor for admittance is, again, loyalty.

Recruitment into the ranks of the party, government, military, and police elites, which occupy the top level of the pyramid, and into the associated Komsomol and trade-union elites, is highly discriminatory in terms of social origin and nationality. Talent is not required, and creativity, originality, and independent thought are definite drawbacks. Nor does personal reliability count for much. It is no exaggeration to say that the Soviet elites are generally made up of robotlike, indifferent, and unprincipled people. Upward mobility within them is possible. Downward mobility, on the other hand, is quite rare, occurring only when someone has fallen out of favor. The top-level elites operate in an autonomous fashion. The party elite holds the dominant position, in the sense of having tremendous power over all the other elites, determining both their activity and mobility.

Family and personal ties are an important factor of elite composition and in the relationship between different elites. Soviet elites periodically stage shake-ups and rid themselves of those who are no longer useful to the ruling class. New people take their places, and the elites then consolidate themselves for a time, becoming more homogeneous and less torn by friction.

Each elite expects its members to behave with reticence and maintain solidarity when dealing with outsiders. In maintaining the common front against others, their chief motivation is to defend their privileges and augment them if the opportunity presents itself. Because of their interest in maintaining their power and privileges, they have a vested interest in the preservation of the existing system as a whole and are united around that goal.

On a deeper level, Soviet elites are made up of people who have become highly similar in outlook, personality traits, and life-style. They conform to a stereotype that leaves no room for personal variations and thus makes for a high level of functional interchangeability. And it is precisely their colorlessness and their interchangeability that account for the measure of genuine—not faked—unity they can muster.

The rise and fall of an elite is determined by the stage of Soviet society's development. The exception is the party elite—whose position at the apex of the pyramid is not allowed to fluctuate. But apart from this exception, elite fluctuation is constant. In Stalin's time, the state security forces vied with the party elite for the top power position and influence in formulation of development policies. The militarization of the USSR and its global interest during Brezhnev's reign entailed the advancement of the military elite to positions close to the pyramid's very top. This showed that the armed forces was then functioning in the USSR not only within the Soviet borders but also beyond them as an important, and, perhaps, the ultimate support of the regime.

However, control of communist society has always been, and remains more than ever under Gorbachev, the *sole* prerogative of the party elite. It grants the other elites whatever status and privileges they have. It coalesces with the other elites to a certain extent, but it jealously guards its monopolistic position.

Only an infinitesimal proportion of the population of the country, i.e., its ruling elite and black market operators, enjoy reasonably high standards of living. (Posev, no. 12, 1973, p. 48)

Our theater was not art for connoisseurs that relied on technical wonders as does Sergey Obraztsov. We performed not for the children of the capital's elite but for the children of the textile factory region, and for the starving populace of the Volga region. (Novoe russkoe slovo, 18 January 1974, p. 5)

But business grew, and cassettes appeared in the homes of a new economic elite. (Novoe russkoe slovo, 15 January 1984, p. 8)

Emigration (*Emigratsiya*). Eviction, escape, resettlement, or departure for the purpose of taking up permanent residence abroad. In regard to the term's various shades of meaning, the main emphasis for many years fell on the first two: "eviction" and "escape." These meanings imbued the term with overtones of contempt and fear, making it near-synonymous with such concepts as "treason" or "anti-Sovietism" (cf.). This gave rise to expressions like "emigrant rabble" (*emigrantskoe okhvost'e*) or "emigrant den of iniquity" (*emigrantskoe logovo*), which were part and parcel of a mindset in which emigration would be considered a distinct phenomenon of an "exploiting society [*ekspluatatorskoe obshchestvo*], prevailing especially in the capitalist world" (*Slovar' inostrannykh slov*, [The dictionary of foreign terms], Moscow: "*Sovetskaya Entsiklopediya*" Publishing House, 1964, p. 755).

All such ideas are, of course, tendentious and farfetched. Emigration even existed in Russia in the pre-capitalist period. As early as the Middle Ages, serfs would leave Russia in order to escape the petty tyranny of their landlords, while religious dissenters left in order to escape the persecution of the Russian Orthodox Church.

Emigration became especially widespread, reaching mass proportions precisely when, in the wake of the October Revolution of 1917, exploitation seemed to be a thing of the past. The socialist revolution rid the country of its most active and educated classes: the enlightened nobility, the bulk of the intelligentsia, and a significant part of the peasantry. They left Russia in sorrow, pursued by hatred and fear. Yet their native Russia, racked by terror and bled by violence, forever remained the focus of their longing and devotion. Far away from their homeland, they tried to resurrect Russian art, culture, and even life-style. They found Russian-language publications, composed Russian music, and wrote Russian poetry. Whenever driven by nostalgia and misled by false promises, they came back—and were met by prison cells and barbed wire as enemies of the people.

The communist hostility to emigration is not entirely explainable by the slogan "those who are not with us are against us." Rather, it was the result of cold and sober logic, which dictated that a person who had experienced Western life could no longer be an easy mark for Soviet propaganda. He would not be duped by patriotic hogwash and naive visions of the future "classless society." Stalin's annihilation of millions of Soviet POWs, who had returned home after being imprisoned in enemy territory, had a similar, sadistic, logic. In the eyes of the Soviet regime, such people were no longer malleable ma-

terial. Thus, they were either executed or imprisoned, despite the fact that they were totally blameless. On the contrary, it was their country that was to blame for the incompetence that had led to their capture by the enemy. It was the regime's fault that some of the soldiers opted to "side with the enemy" against the Soviet government, which had earned their hatred through its practices of indiscriminate repression and bloody terror.

Military victory did not bring peace to the relations between the regime and the people. The first chink in the Soviet borders triggered a new flood of emigration, which was the third mass wave. The first wave had consisted of the remnants of the White army, joined by the thousands of scholars, engineers, doctors, and artists who had managed to slip out of Soviet Russia during the early, still relatively liberal years right after the Revolution. The second wave was made up of millions of people displaced during World War II, who subsequently scattered in many foreign lands.

The core of the third wave consisted largely of the Jews and the Germans seeking to regain their national identity in their historical homelands as well as Armenians who had been deprived of their identity in their own country. This wave also included a number of dissidents stripped of their citizenship and forcibly deported for having dared to express independent opinions. The custom of deporting native dissidents originated in Lenin's time; it took a major stride with the 1929 expulsion of Trotsky and reached its peak during the 1970s, when scores of prominent figures (scientists, musicians, artists, and writers) were deported from the Soviet Union. Among them was the one—Solzhenitsyn—who had already won the Nobel prize and another—Brodsky—who would win it twenty years after being expelled from the Soviet Union.

The first wave of emigration was political in nature. It was forced to leave Russia as a result of the lost battle. The second wave was mostly involuntary, with only a fraction of it political, prepared to take up arms against the communists. It continued to reside in the West out of fear of Stalin's retaliation. The third wave was primarily nationalist, motivated by the desire to be reunited with its respective peoples, but in part also economic, driven by the aspiration for better living conditions and a life free from the restrictions and indignities of Soviet existence. There is only a marginal, though high crucial, sense in which this wave can be considered political: it had been encouraged by a movement of dissidents who could not be tolerated by the Soviet regime, and hence were forced to emigrate.

Until recently, the Soviet government's attitude towards all three waves of emigration remained unambiguously negative, as expressed via laconic and uncompromising epithets like "renegade" (*otschchepenets*) (cf.) or "turncoat" (*perebezhchik*). The present period, however, is marked by a tendency to distinguish between different varieties of emigration, so as to sift and recover human resources usable for perestroika's purposes. However, the Soviet leaders find it hard to break the fixed patterns of old mentality. Hence, the process of reevaluating emigration is cautious and highly selective.

The first to be "rehabilitated" are prominent writers and artists who are dead and therefore no longer dangerous to the system, which can now afford to admit that their "art was and remains Russian." The search for supporters of *perestroika* also includes some living emigrants, who are called upon to join in the common cause and return (as some of them have done already). Their talent, integrity, and civic spirit are expected to contribute to Gorbachev's efforts at reform.

The Soviet government is also not above exploiting the spiritual, moral, and financial support of millions of emigrants, who have taken root in Western society, by trying to ingratiate itself with them and win their support. Yet the "civil war" against emigration is far from over in the Soviet Union; it is now only at a cease-fire stage. The Soviet leadership is still separated from its former compatriots abroad by the unbridgeable gap of its intolerance toward political emigra-

tions. Political emigrants are still viewed as enemies, perhaps even more so than in the past, for they are the only ones who are immune to the allure of the present reforms.

> The turning point that drastically changed the former . . . meaning the term emigration was the October revolution. (Literaturnaya gazeta, 28 December 1988, p. 14)

> This may seem paradoxical to some, but if we establish an undemocratic procedure for leaving the country, we will only have a rise in emigration. (Ogonek, no. 5, January 1989, p. 29)

Enemy of the People (*Vrag naroda*). A sinister appellation summarily applied to any opponents of the Soviet regime. The very vagueness of this term made it suitable for use in political infighting precisely because it admitted very broad application. The expression could be applied to various actions (or inactions), modes of behavior, or even mere intentions. Via dialectics, this label was foisted on millions of people, with the result that the Soviet people appeared to be its own enemy.

The expression did not appear in the Soviet language immediately. It was preceded by less sweeping and censorious terms. The first of these was *kaery* ("C.R.'s," i.e., counterrevolutionaries). Right after the Revolution, the authorities realized that socialism could never be implemented in Russia, with its vast population and mosaic of social classes. Thus began a deadly "game of terror." The initial wave of reprisals was directed against all political parties other than the communist one. First to be dealt with were the *kadety* ("C.D.'s"—Constitutional Democrats), i.e., those who had formed the largest and strongest opposition to tsarism. In late 1917, they were outlawed. To ensure that the breakup of their party would be permanent, the Bolsheviks tried to liquidate its members physically. They began by arresting them and incarcerating them in prisons across the country. Then, they were secretly killed in deserted fields or cemeteries. The executions had an educational purpose: people were cowed into obedience by fright, and fright turned out to be a more effective deterrent than punishment.

Beginning with the spring of 1918, "social traitors," as well as "brother" socialists, such as Mensheviks and *esery* ("S.R.'s"—Socialist Revolutionaries) began to be included under the expanded definition of *kaery*. Very quickly, the authorities proved their "bourgeois" nature. Following violent outbursts of discontent, riots, and strikes (in the early postrevolutionary period, these had still not been banned), their "ringleaders," who just happened to invariably be S.R.s or Mensheviks, were exposed and punished. At the beginning, they were treated leniently: their offenses were considered political rather than criminal. They were even described to the public as opponents rather than as criminals. Then, in order to prevent them from obstructing the building of a "new society," they were scattered through the concentration camp archipelago. It was said (and perhaps believed) that they would stay there only as long as the struggle between labor and capital lasted; that as soon as the Revolution was fully consummated, they would be freed. But for some reason, this moment never came.

Thereafter, the turn came for the anarchists, and after them for politically nonaffiliated people. At that stage, the ranks of the *kaery* became legion, including one social group after another: craftsmen, merchants, homeowners, members of cooperatives, clergymen, and monks. By now, the authorities were no longer even capable of abiding by legality, because drawn-out investigations could only hinder the effectiveness of the purges. Accordingly, extra-judicial investigations became widespread. These were more effective, but still too slow. A criminal code was badly needed.

Help came in the form of "a revolutionary sense of justice," which worked unfailingly. This infallible intuition about the guilt of accused parties was supplemented by the Extraordinary Commission (*Cheka*), which dealt with all stages of Soviet justice: arrest, investigation, and execution. It proved to be

particularly tough on former officers of tsarist or White armies who were apprehended and executed en masse, by the hundreds and thousands. But not just them, as the *kaery* population also included quite innocent people, e.g., hostages killed in order to intimidate or take revenge on enemies, real or imaginary. In such ways, the number of victims defined as *kaery* soon passed a million.

Numbers so vast posed a need for a new, more flexible definition of the next victims of the revolution. The term was quickly found: "wreckers" (*vrediteli*). It could be effortlessly applied to the entire nation—to workers who were shirkers (a strange paradox of communism is that on the way to becoming a "dictator," the working class was proclaimed to be a wrecker), to peasants who had opposed the *prodrazverstka* (the forced seizure of grain), and to the intelligentsia, whom the communists never trusted but had to rely upon. All failures and crises were attributed to the wreckers. In no other way could such events be reconciled with the communists' "class" standpoint, for the revolution was supposed to be infallible. Hence electricity stoppages and the shortages of fuel or consumer goods were said to have been caused by wrecking.

The grain shortage was so acute that people were swelling up and dying from malnutrition. This made it imperative to find and expose the wreckers responsible for the famine. Accordingly, wrecking was depicted in the form of a huge, evil monster with millions of arms ensnaring and strangling the Revolution. As soon as they were cut off, new arms appeared and these too had to be cut off. In order to stifle the cries of the victims, popular enthusiasm was whipped up against them. Anticipating the verdicts of the courts, the popular masses demanded blood.

At this juncture in Soviet history, a new concept, "enemy of the Revolution" (*vrag revolyutsii*) emerged in place of counter-revolutionaries and wreckers. This term could be manipulated even more easily than its predecessors. Its all-encompassing scope came to include: Nepmen (enterprising people who prospered under Lenin's New Economic Policy or the new Soviet bourgeoisie), officials whose loyalty was doubtful (who "by deceit" found places for themselves in Soviet institutions); returning emigrés; and nationalists of various persuasions, such as *mussavatisty* (Azerbaijan nationalists), *dashnaki* (Armenian nationalists), and *basmachi* (fighters in an anti-Soviet insurrection in Central Asia). Invariably classified as enemies of the Revolution were religious believers, members of the intelligentsia, and class "brother-enemies"—Mensheviks, S.R.'s, along with any White officers who somehow had not been killed earlier.

Over the years, however, the word "Revolution" lost its potency, and so "enemies of the Revolution" gradually gave way to "enemies of the people." This proved to be quite advantageous. When the time came to imprison members of the ruling party, it would have been inappropriate and implausible to accuse them of being "enemies of the Revolution." But they could plausibly become "enemies of the people." And so they did.

The first to be declared enemies of the people were members of "the workers' opposition," due to their ideological differences with the "workers'" party. Next in line were the Trotskyists, on account of their imprudent choice of a leader. Then came the turn of the "right" opposition, on account of their "petty bourgeois degeneration." Afterwards came loyal communists who had never strayed from the party line or even doubted its wisdom. It was at this stage that the Great Terror of 1937 began, which culminated in the incarceration, prosecution, and extermination of the entire Bolshevik Old Guard of Lenin, i.e., hundreds and thousands of communists who had fought in the Revolution. Yet even this was not the peak of the enemies of the people story. More massive and cruel waves of terror had been unleashed earlier, in 1930, when millions of peasants ("kulaks") who did not want to enter collective farms (cf.) were shot or exiled with their families to Siberia. During World War II, Soviet prisoners of war, five or six million soldiers—many of whom had survived Nazi camps, were pronounced enemies of the people upon their return home. It was then that Stalin conceived the idea of declaring entire nations as enemies of the people. In 1943, the Kalmyks, Chechens, Ingushes, and Kabardinians, and, in 1944, the Crimean Tatars were banished from their lands when their loyalty became suspect to the Soviet authorities (i.e., basically to Stalin). They were convicted without having done anything other than belonging to the wrong nationality.

The expression "enemies of the people" is linked to one of the greatest tragedies humanity has ever experienced. Yet it also contains an element of irony, as its promoter Stalin apparently intended. This became clear when the hammer of terror was brought down on its organizers and instigators in the party, the state security apparatus, and the army. The way in which arrests were carried out at the time seemed to follow a certain plan: firstly, to destroy the apex of the state's leadership; then, to get rid of its middle rung; and finally, to strike at the entire mass of the *nomenklatura* (cf.) by humiliating, frightening, and in the end annihilating many of them. Those people were killed en masse by the tens, hundreds, and even thousands. Competition was established between districts and provinces to see which one would excel in meeting quotas for arrests, convictions, and executions. Such quotas were fixed by plans that were expected to be overfulfilled. The crimes that serves as pretexts included resisting collectivization, opposition sympathies, refusal to accept the party line, and slandering Stalin.

Even though the party might have had a chance to stand up to Stalin, its officials did not protest even when signing their own death warrants. This happened in 1934, at the Seventeenth Party Congress, where the Central Committee's assent was required to arrest its own members. It consented, handing over whole lists on the principle that "you die today, I die tomorrow." No one tried to resist: at most, there were a few cases of suicide. Nor were there abject confessions obtained through torture alone. They agreed to go along with their torturers and hangmen in the name of "the common good." They bowed to the idea that the Revolution called for their humiliation and death in order to strengthen its cause. Refusing to confirm an investigator's "evidence" was regarded as treasonous "antiparty" activity. Even while facing death, most of the purge victims were unwilling to incur such opprobrium.

None were greater masters in changing opinions and principles than the communists, who managed to come up with "reformed" views even in the last minutes before execution. They went off to penal servitude without understanding why, and if they survived, they still learned nothing from their ordeal. This can only be explained by the fact that they had no other meaning to life apart from their blind faith in communism.

One should mention here the millions of refugees from Nazism, from Poland, Greece, Czechoslovakia, and Hungary, as well as those from fascist Spain, who had sought shelter in the Soviet Union. They were all sent to Siberia as enemies of the people (without any clarification ever being offered as to which people were they enemies of). Nor were ordinary Soviet citizens spared. After the victorious war and with all their blind admiration for Stalin, they certainly had not entertained any thoughts of overthrowing the Soviet regime.

Once drawn from the scabbard, the avenging sword of the Revolution was unable to stay idle and refrain from cutting down new enemies of the people. These were the "cosmopolitans" (1946–47), selector-geneticists (1945 and 1949), party officials yet again (1951) and, finally, physicians, "the murderers in white robes." The plan to settle accounts with the latter was never implemented, since Stalin, the inventor of the concept of enemies of the people, died in the meantime. Without its creator, the concept proved to be no longer translatable into action. This is not to say that innocent people have no longer been arrested tried, and imprisoned in the USSR. True, they can no longer be numbered in the millions, but they

still can be in the thousands. The term "enemies of the people," however, is usually avoided. It was discredited by too much innocent blood shed in its name.

On the other hand, quite unexpectedly (for everyone except the authorities), the concept has reappeared in the rather original mutation of "enemy of perestroika." In the era of glasnost, it transpires that Soviet leaders are still unable to manage without enemies. The principle that "He who is not with us is against us" is still operative.

If one views the issue of the enemies of the people apart from history and an atmosphere of fear and suspicion, then there can be only one conclusion. The whole thing consisted of a shameful arbitrariness, and a violation of the fundamental principles of justice on which the state is built. (Sotsiologicheskie issledovaniya, no. 3, 1988, p. 98)

"Accomplice of the Kulaks" [proto-Kulak, podkulachnik] during the years of collectivization (cf.) and "enemies of the people" during the thirties are clear examples of artificially fashioned images of the enemy. (Ogonek, no. 31, 1988, p. 15)

One of the agent provocateur informers then proudly declared from the rostrum of the writers' meeting that, despite his poor health, he had personally exposed 26 "enemies of the people." (Ogonek, no. 19, 1988, p. 25)

Epoch-Making (*Vsemirno-istorichesky*, literal meaning: universally historic). An attribute that serves to stress the unique and indisputable significance of the ideas and practice of communism. The term "epoch-making," as well as its variant, "historic" (*istorichesky*), applies only to the "classics" of scientific communism, to events leading to the establishment of the Soviet regime in Russia (such as the October Revolution), to stages in the consolidation of the regime (for example, industrialization, or collectivization of agriculture), and to the extension of socialist ideas in the world, as in World War II.

Historical events or processes, which from the vantage point of the Kremlin's interests are not desirable or advantageous, cannot be termed epoch-making. Not even the weaker variant of the term, "historic," is then applicable. Thus, the achievements of Western technology and social science, the Allies' contribution to the victory over fascism, and the American exploration of space are neither epoch making nor historic.

The term "epoch-making" is therefore devoid of all objectivity, its entire meaning being reduced to a reflection of Soviet political ambitions.

Janos Kádár emphasized that the XXVI Congress of the CPSU has an epoch-making significance. (Izvestiya, 28 February 1981, p. 2)

Soviet writers welcomed the extraordinary CPSU Congress as an event of epoch-making significance, heralding a new stage on the road to building Communism. (Literaturnaya gazeta, 1 July 1981, p. 5)

The epoch-making economic competition between the two systems goes on. (Pravda, 21, February 1982, p. 4)

F

Farsighted Policy (*Dal'novidnaya politika*).
A phrase of commendation often used to
describe the political course of the CPSU
and decisions of the Soviet leadership. Both
the general policy orientation of the Soviet
leadership and its specific policies (for example, in regard to administrative, economic, or educational reform) are referred
to as "farsighted."

All the policies of Soviet leaders during
their lifetime are invariably referred to as
farsighted, though in historical perspective
they may well turn out to be mutually incompatible. For instance, Khrushchev's policy of restricting private farming of plots of
land by collective farmers was at the time
hailed as farsighted—but so was the later
policy of Gorbachev to encourage cultivation of private plots.

Since Soviet leaders can be criticized for
their policies only after they fall from power
or die, the "General Party Line" remains
farsighted regardless of specific content.

The policies of the leaders of states hostile
to the USSR are always referred to as "not
farsighted" (*nedal'novidnaya*) or, alternatively, as "blind" (*slepaya*) or "short-
sighted" (*blizorukaya*).

> The Soviet people express their fervent ap-
> proval of and deep appreciation for the con-
> structive, farsighted, and consistent foreign
> policy carried out by the Leninist Central
> Committee of the CPSU, its Politburo and
> Comrade L. I. Brezhnev himself. (Partiynaya
> zhizn', no. 13, 1979, p. 5)

> The considerable international authority of the
> Soviet Union stems from the consistently far-
> sighted policy of the party. (Kommunist, no.
> 5, 1979, p. 17)

> The whole world can see in the example of
> Kazakhstan how farsighted is the agricultural
> policy of our Party. (Literaturnaya Rossiya,
> 22 June 1979, p. 8)

Fartsovka (racketeering, trafficking). The illegal practice of buying goods and currency
from foreigners. The fartsovka practitioner
is called a "fartsovshchik." Fartsovka is rooted
in the high esteem in which the Soviet people
hold foreign goods, anything from a car to
a ragged pair of pants or a fountain pen.
Another contributing factor is the official exchange rate of the dollar to sixty-five ko-
peks—which bears no relationship to the real
market situation. In fact, on the Soviet black
market a dollar costs ten times as much.

From the official Soviet point of view, fartsovka is not only an unworthy occupation
but an unrewarding one as well. However,
this commonly accepted idea is contradicted
by reality. In the early 1960s, the dramatic
trial of Rokotov and Faibishchenko proved
that through fartsovka one can become a
multimillionaire.

As a matter of fact, fartsovka does imply
an unabashed pursuit of petty deals, like
buying a hundred or ten dollars or acquiring
all kinds of trifles—jeans, shirts, ties, even
chewing gum. However, the smalltime operators are a front for the real bigwigs, who
deal in huge amounts of currency and entire
shipments of merchandise. Fartsovka is their
full-time profession, which brings them an
income of many thousands of dollars. As a
rule, they keep a low profile and take no
risks. Instead, small retail buyers—students, laborers, office clerks—can be seen
lounging about hotel and museum entrances, near theaters, and other tourist sites,
using fartsovka to make ends meet and get
a little taste of Western life. They hope to
meet some interesting people, exchange information or, if they are lucky, marry a foreigner. The fartsovshchik usually speaks some
foreign languages, so there is no language
barrier between him and the tourists. The
chain of illegal deals also stretches in the

opposite direction, as paintings, jewelry, and antiques find their way abroad. In this impromptu "bank"—operating out of the fartsovshchik's pocket—foreign tourists will always find ready cash that will enable them to make a handsome profit selling foreign-made goods and hard currency.

> Today organized crime is setting off on a new course, mastering new criminal techniques, such as racketeering, blackmail, gambling, and fartsovka. (Literaturnaya gazeta, 12 October 1988, p. 14)

> Many of us perceive fartsovka as reprehensible activity engaged in by foolish teenagers who coax foreign tourists into giving them used trousers and plastic bags. (Moskovskie novosti, 16 October 1988, p. 4)

> The negotiations were broken up by the appearance of two militia sergeants who for the entire forty minutes of the scheduled trainstop had to shoo away, like chickens from a vegetable patch, the scores of young fartsovshchikis and speculators that kept sneaking back to the platform. (Literaturnaya gazeta, 2 November 1988, p. 9)

Fighting Spirit (*Boevitost'*). An expected standard of Soviet way of life, consisting of ideological principledness, enterprise, no-nonsense approach, and diligence at work. Paradoxically, fighting spirit (*boevitost'* is derived from the word *boy*—combat) is used exclusively to describe peaceful activities. However, the military connotations of the term imply the latently warlike nature of overtly peaceful pursuits. Fighting spirit reflects the authorities' desire to keep society in a state of permanent mobilization and "combat readiness" and thus elicit repeated surges of enthusiasm and creative activity. The concept of fighting spirit also reflects the constant tension in Soviet society and the continual need to cope with disruptions and system-generated failures. The concept of fighting spirit, however, was not coined in order to cope with social problems. Rather, it is intended to give the impression that the party is dynamic, competent, and vigorous in leading and directing the masses.

The "democratism" of the concept (in the sense that all Soviet citizens are obliged to display a fighting spirit) fosters the illusion of the party as being close to the masses and of its constant involvement in life in the vanguard of social developments. Activists (said to be imbued with a fighting spirit) are depicted as having close ties with ordinary people, only being more dynamic and, or course, more knowledgeable of the party line than the rank-and-file.

Although the term "fighting spirit" has been established in official propaganda, it has not attained much currency in colloquial speech. In colloquial use, fighting spirit is usually replaced by the terms *aktivnost'*, *energichnost'*, and *initsiativnost'*, that is, being "active," being "energetic," and having "initiative." The artificiality of the phrase "fighting spirit" is indicated by the fact that when the term appears in print, it is usually buttressed by additional words, such as "self-discipline" (*organizovannost'*), "effectiveness" (*deystvennost'*), "solidarity" (*splochennost'*), and "responsibility" (*otvetsvennost'*), etc.

> It is necessary to raise the fighting spirit of Komsomol organizations in order to help them more. (Kommunist vooruzhennykh sil, no. 13, 1975, p. 6)

> The success of instruction and educational activities is directly proportional to . . . the fighting spirit of the Party and Komsomol organizations of the collectives in the institutions of higher learning. (Kommunist, no. 8, 1979, p. 36)

> Our multi-national Soviet literature is imbued with . . . solidarity and a fighting spirit . . . . (Literaturnaya gazeta, 8 July 1981, p. 3)

Filial Gratitude (*Synovnyaya blagodarnost'*). An attitude that the Soviet people are expected by the authorities to exhibit toward the state. The term is intended to convey the notion of Soviet society as one big family—a "fraternal family of nations," as Soviet propaganda would have it. The implication is that the "family" takes good care of its individual members who, in return, remain forever grateful to it. Thus the Soviet people are exhorted to show filial gratitude to the party and government on as many occasions as possible.

The nexus of filial gratitude is less rooted in the communist worldview than in the traditional Russian concept of paternalism. According to this concept, a state authority (in the Soviet case, the party) assumes the role of a "father" to the people. For example, just as the tsar was called *batyushka* (dear father), Stalin was known as *otets rodnoy* (one's own father). Thereby Soviet society has imposed on it an ostensible model of family relations—which is actually one of subordination—with the people playing the role of "grateful" and obedient children of the state.

The Soviet people ardently approve and unanimously support the domestic and foreign policies of our Motherland's Communist Party and express their *filial gratitude* to the Central Committee of the CPSU and the Politburo for all their untiring efforts to strengthen the might of our Motherland, improve our well-being, and establish peace on earth. (Izvestiya, 9 February 1979, p. 1)

The Plenum of the Central Committee of the All-Union Leninist-Communist League of Youth, in the name of the Leninist Komsomol, declare that all Soviet youth wholly and fully approve and support the decisions of the XXVI Congress of the Communist Party of the Soviet Union, its domestic and foreign policies, and wish to express their unbounded filial love and gratitude to our Motherland's Party. (V. Ivanov, V partiynom rukovodstve—sila komsomola [In party leadership lies the strength of the Komsomol], Moscow: Publishing House for Political Literature, 1981, p. 55)

First Department (*Pervy otdel*). The state security office within Soviet industrial enterprises and other institutions. In party organizations, the First Department is camouflaged as the "General Department" (*Obshchy otdel*), while within the army and the police it is referred to as the "Special Department" (*Spetsotdel*). Large military factories and scientific research institutes that work for the Ministry of Defense generally have both a First Department and a Special Department.

The First Department has extensive powers and responsibilities. Its members keep track of workers' loyalty, compiling dossiers that detail the political views of all workers and the trips abroad (including conduct thereupon) of the select few. It also grants or denies permits (*dopuski*) for employment in secret work.

So-called first departments exist in all institutes, regardless of whether their research is classified or accessible to public. The entire staff of these first departments consists of secret police agents. Occasionally high-ranking KGB officers are among them. (Leonid Vladimirov, Rossiya bez prikras i umolchany [Russia without embellishment and omission], Frankfurt a.M.: Possev-verlag, 1969, p. 135)

In 1971 in the State Research and Design Institute for Processing Nonferrous Metals in Moscow, there was a single Party member who spoke up against the re-election to the local Party Bureau of the head of the Institute's first department, a man with the appearance and manners of an agent-provocateur and a patent KGB protégé. (Posev, no. 7, 1975, p. 47)

Flagship (*Flagman*). An industrial or agricultural enterprise that has been proclaimed outstanding and therefore exemplary for the development of an entire branch of industry. "Flagship" is one of the many words of the Soviet language borrowed from the military or naval lexicon. The transfer of this word from naval to political usage helps romanticize Soviet reality. The state and its subdivisions are seen as huge naval squadrons, each led by a proud vessel bearing the commander and his or her flag and manned by an eager crew—their workers. This idea is illustrated by such expressions as "flagship of our country" (*flagman nashey strany*), "flagship of production" (*flagman proizvodstva*), and "flagship of machine building" (*flagman mashinostroeniya*).

The word "flagship" itself is not applied to anything in countries independent of Soviet influence. However, antiimperialist invective often does contain other borrowings from the naval lexicon. For example, the imperialist countries have "set their course on aggression," or are "taking a ruinous, dangerous course." Their "ships" (*not* "flagships") will often "lose their way in the fog," be "forced against the reefs" or "become stranded upon a shoal," while Soviet flagships always pursue the "right course" (*idut vernym kursom*) by following the "guiding star of communism" (*putevodnaya zvezda kommunizma*).

> The Lenin Skoda Trust, the flagship of Czechoslovak machine-building, is actively participating in the implementing of a complex program of socialist integration. (Izvestiya, 25 October 1980, p. 5)

> The Lvov "Elektron" Trust, which produces color and black-and-white television sets, is a flagship among plants of this type. (Izvestiya, 28 October 1983, p. 1)

> The Likhachev factory: who does not know this flagship of machine-building of our fatherland! (Agitator, no. 20, 1983, p. 55)

Flunkey (*Podpevala*). An epithet branding someone as an accomplice of imperialism. In the USSR, imperialism is regarded as an embodiment of universal evil. This makes it possible to present any evil as somehow being connected with imperialism. Consequently, not only foreign political figures, but also Soviet people who do not fit communist models can be described as flunkeys of imperialism.

Flunkeys have been designated at each stage of Soviet history. During the struggle against "the Opposition," "Trotskyist flunkeys" (*Trotskistskie podpevaly*) were constantly referred to; during the collectivization period "kulak flunkeys" (*kulatskie podpevaly*) became a standard epithet, and the postwar years saw the emergence of both "Cold War flunkeys" (*podpevaly kholodnoy voyny*), and "Zionist flunkeys" (*sionistskie podpevaly*).

Flunkeys are characterized as individuals who, totally lacking any convictions of their own, are susceptible to harmful influences and capable of ignominious and treacherous actions. The derogatory connotation of "flunkey" is often enhanced by combining the term with adjectives, as in the phrases "corrupt flunkey" (*prodazhny podpevala*), "hired flunkey" (*naemny podpevala*) or "unprincipled flunkey" (*besprintsypny podpevala*).

> As was expected, the supporters of the (Trotskyite-Zinovievist anti-Party) bloc managed to get out on the street only a pitiful handful of their flunkeys. (Istoriya VKPb, Kratky Kurs [History of the All-Union Communist Party of the Bolsheviks, brief course], Moscow: Publishing House for Political Literature, 1950, p. 272)

> The Beijing leaders and their West European flunkeys are now hailing the "progressive nature" of corrupt cliques. (Komsomol'skaya pravda, 15 March 1979, p. 3)

Fraternal (*Bratsky*). An attribute of a state or people dominated by the Soviet Union or dependent on it and invariably behaving in conformity to Soviet will. As a value category, "fraternal" is widely used in reference to relations between the USSR and its satellites. It conveys the impression of close, altruistic, friendly interstate ties. Beyond the boundaries of the communist system, "fraternal" is often used to refer to social forces that are completely subservient to Soviet policy. Hence, leftist movements, including communist ones, which pursue a line independent of Moscow, are not considered fraternal. Likewise, countries are nonfraternal if their regimes, although pro-Soviet, are not considered stable, or their leadership has not been fully certified as communist. Thus, Angola and Ethiopia have not yet been granted the status of being fraternal, and Afghanistan has been accorded the honor only recently, although it may soon lose that honor.

The use of the term "fraternal" entails not only political and economic subordination to the USSR but also common ideology. In combination with various nouns, "fraternal" is used to refer to a broad range of social phenomena, including "ties" (*svyazi*), "relations" (*otnosheniya*), "support" (*podderzhka*), "cooperation" (*sodruzhestvo*), "friendship" (*druzhba*), "solidarity" (*solidarnost*), and "unity" (*edinenie*).

The phrase "fraternal help" (*bratskaya pomoshch*) is used to conceal the brashness of the Kremlin's interference in the affairs of other communist states. On the basis of such fraternal help, for example, the Warsaw Pact military bloc was formed. Similarly, the creation and exploitation of the COMECON are also justified on the grounds of providing fraternal help. The limitation of the sovereignty of the East European communist countries has been attributed to "fraternal relations" (*bratskie otnosheniya*). Under the pretext of "'fraternal solidarity" (*solidarnost'*) with the other members of the communist camp, the Soviet Union had done its best to foster the growth of its own national economy to the detriment of the economies of the states it controls.

Soviet "fraternal help" should not be described as altruistic, even when it entails considerable material loss, since it is dictated by global imperialistic aims, that is, the desire to establish new communist states or to support shaky totalitarian regimes. During the periods of political crisis in East Germany (1953), Hungary (1956), Czechoslovakia (1968), and Poland (1970, 1981), the USSR provided these states with considerable economic aid. The Soviet Union is not daunted by the cost of supporting Cuba or of assisting incipient communist regimes in Asia and Africa.

However, if political and economic pressures prove ineffectual, the USSR is not averse to resorting to open military intervention, which is also referred to as "fraternal help." In order to legitimize the provision of "fraternal help" in its military guise, the Soviet leaders have advanced the thesis of the responsibility of the USSR for the national and political development of communist countries (that is, the theory of the limited national sovereignty of socialist states). This doctrine was used to explain the Soviet intervention in Czechoslovakia (1968) and the occupation of Afghanistan (1981).

The concept of fraternity is no less inappropriate when used in relation to the Soviet domestic scene. Despite claims to the contrary, in Soviet society there scarcely exist "fraternal relations," "fraternal friendship," "fraternal cooperation," or "fraternal mutual aid." What does prevail is inequality and hostility between individuals and nationalities, all alienated from the state and largely from each other as well.

With the victory of the Great October Socialist Revolution there began the era of new, truly fraternal relations between the peoples of the former tsarist empire. (Kommunist, no. 12, August 1980, p. 11)

The meeting was conducted under the banner of indissoluble friendship and solidarity of the Communist Party of the Soviet Union and the Communist Party of Vietnam, and of the fraternal unity of the Soviet and Vietnamese people. (Komsomol'skaya pravda, 1 November 1983, p. 3)

Representatives of the Soviet and Afghan public have declared their intentions of furthering the friendship and fraternal solidarity between the peoples of their two countries. (Pravda, 29 November 1983, p. 4)

Friendship between the Nations (*Druzhba narodov*). Harmonious relationships among the nationality groups that make up the Soviet Union—a communist tenet that is strikingly belied by Soviet politics and the Soviet economy and the spiritual and moral values on which they are based. The mutual relationships between the more than one hundred nationalities of the Soviet Union, which the expression "friendship between the nations" defines, developed and crystallized during the five hundred years of Russian imperial expansion, from the fifteenth to the twentieth century. As a result of this expansion, the Russians have become a minority in the country they rule.

Once the Soviet regime inherited "the prison house of nationalities" created by the tsars, it had to deal with the situation bequeathed to it by history. When the communists came to power in 1917, they proclaimed the right of each nation to self-determination, which theoretically included the right to secede from the Soviet state. In reality, advocacy of secession was soon banned by law and viewed as an infringement of the principle of friendship between the nations.

On a number of occasions during the history of the Soviet Union, the communists retook by force territories that they had lost during the Revolution and civil war. In 1920 and 1921, the republics of the Transcaucasus and Central Asia were forcibly Sovietized. Twenty years later, the independent states of the Baltic Region, as well as parts of Romania and Finland, Western Byelorussia, and Western Ukraine were annexed to the USSR. After the Second World War, the same was done to parts of East Prussia and the Kurile Islands.

In the early 1940's the autonomous republics of the Volga Germans, Crimean Tatars, Kalmyks, and Chechens were wiped off the political map of the Soviet Union, together with their respective populations. Millions of people were deported to Siberia and scattered to the far corners of the Soviet empire.

The idea of friendship between the nations in Marxist cultural policy was defined by the principle of a culture that was to be "national in form and socialist in content" (*natsional'naya po forme, sotsialisticheskaya po soderzhaniyu*). What the formula meant was that the values of communist society as determined by the central leadership were to be shared by all nationalities, while the expression of these values would be allowed to follow in external, superficial ways each nationality's tradition. In fact, however, tolerance was shown only toward those forms of expression which coincided with the political interests of the authorities. As soon as the authorities detected any manifestation of nationalism or pronounced ethnic flavor in peoples' creative work (*narodnoe tvorchestvo*), it would be suppressed. Thus, the Soviet tolerance of national forms of cultural expression was allowed only as long as ideological boundaries were not approached.

Religion was for many decades suppressed among all nationalities alike. This proved to be particularly damaging to the cultural development of the smaller nationalities, which were often spiritually sustained in a hostile environment by their religions. The persecution of religious beliefs was in such instances perceived by the believers as an alien occupier's attempt to destroy distinctive features of their national way of life.

All public life in the Soviet Union has been permeated with a standardized ideological content. Standardization embraces everything: central economic planning, collectivized agriculture, collectivized industry, surveillance of behavior, and ideological brainwashing. The nations of the Soviet Union are powerless vassals of a foreign state, ruled by the imperial lords in Moscow. These lords are not necessarily ethnic Russians, though. Some are Georgians, Armenians, Ukrainians, or members of other minorities. Whatever their nationality, however, they unfailingly pursue the interests of the central authority, which the subject peoples associate with Russian rule. This rule imposes upon each nation the duty to learn the Russian language and assimilate Russian cultural and historical traditions. In the efforts to keep nationalist tides from rising, the Soviet leadership deliberately divides national populations. For example, the Ukrainian-populated stretches of the Voronezh and Rostov provinces were truncated from the Ukraine; the originally Armenian territories of Karabakh and Nakhichevan were included into Azerbaijan; and Abkhaziya and Ossetia were incorporated into Georgia.

The diversity of ethnically specific modes of thinking and of the actual experience of various ethnic groups nevertheless turned out to be stronger than either ideology that had denied the existence of any differences between them or power that had suppressed such differences. The Soviet rulers tried to find a way out of this dilemma via the policies of glasnost and perestroika. However, history played an ironic trick here. The Soviet nationalities have taken Gorbachev's liberalization seriously and are demanding an extension of their rights of self-expression: the Latvians, Lithuanians, and Estonians began their demands in the realm of culture and ended up demanding national independence and secession from the Union.

Demands for national independence have also been increasingly voiced in the Moldavian and Caucasian republics, while the Crimean Tatars have requested restoration of their national rights, which were finally acknowledged in 1989. Most insistent of all have been the Armenians, who passed a resolution in Nagorny Karabakh province about secession from Azerbaijan. National solidarities are proving more powerful than the unity that the tenet of friendship between the nations presupposes: the Supreme Soviet of Armenia has demanded that Nogorny Karabakh be united with Armenia. The myth of friendship between the nations has been buried along with the corpses of dozens of Armenians who were slaughtered in the streets of Sumgait and Baku. The masses demonstrating in the Armenian city of Erevan debunked this myth with a bang rather than a whisper. Perestroika may yet fall victim to the stirring of national passions in the USSR, and the latter may yet engulf the former. To concede to the demands of the Armenians would amount to a precedent for the dismantling of the multinational Soviet empire. To quell by force the uprising in Armenia, with its thousands of protesters and comprehensive strike, would amount to undermining glasnost and democratization. The Soviet government is resolved to revitalize the Soviet state, to enable it to exist as a multinational amalgamate. The amalgamate, however, does not seem to find it acceptable to continue as such.

Under Stalin the amalgamation of Soviet nationalities had appeared to have been achieved at whatever cost, which needs to be estimated in terms of the decimation of the party by purges, of the destruction of the economy by forced industrialization, and of the annihilation of millions of human beings. It is still anyone's guess what price Gorbachev is willing to pay or willing to make his country pay to attain the same goal. Ineluctably, friendship between the nations commands a price.

Noteworthy measures for educating the working masses in the spirit of internationalism and friendship of the nations are being carried out jointly by the Dagestan and Kabardino-Balkar Provincial Party Committees. (Partiynaya zhizn', no. 24, 1983, p. 56)

Soviet Armenia is a remarkable school of internationalism, friendship, and brotherhood between the nations of the land of the Soviets. (Partiynaya zhizn', no. 24, 1983, p. 56)

A constant theme of mass-agitation work has been and remains the explanation of the Leninist nationalities policy of the CPSU, the upbringing/education of the workers, especially the young generation in the spirit of fraternal friendship between the nations of the USSR . . . . (Agitator, no. 3, 1984, p. 54)

Frugal (*Rachitel'ny*). A term used to laud conscientiousness and honesty in regard to work and state property. As a rule, the term appears in party appeals and slogans addressed to managers, workers, and peasants. Recent Russian dictionaries define "frugal" as an obsolete bookish word used to express peasant notions of prudent husbandry. However, the word was revived when standard appeals exhorting the Soviet public to a greater degree of on-the-job responsibility proved ineffective. Constant admonitions are considered necessary because of the Soviet worker's and collective farmer's indifference with regard to productivity, waste of work time, and the theft of state property. Such attitudes are attributable to the status of the workers at the bottom of the social ladder and their exploitation manifest in the denial of both work rewards and "side benefits" (which the elites have access to). Confronted with such attitudes, the Soviet leadership has not decided to change this situation via radical reform of the economy but is limiting itself to reforms that do not challenge the essence or basis of the social system. Thus, they must continue to rely on propaganda, seeking to combat apathy and wastefulness by appealing to the traditional values of the common man with words like "frugal," which connote the proverbial thriftiness of peasant life. When the term "frugal" is used in reference to the property of the state, it is intended to foster the illusion that the common person has a share in its ownership and should care for it as his or her own.

In actuality, state property in the USSR is not at the disposal of the masses but rather of the communist elite. Considering the degree of deprivation of basics in the USSR, it would be unrealistic to expect that repeated exhortations to be frugal would change the Soviet people's attitude toward property that obviously does not belong to them. Constant repetition devalues slogans and makes it necessary to revise them periodically. The adverb "frugally" is used in phrases such as "frugally and economically" (*rachitel'no i berezhno*), or "conscientiously and frugally" (*dobrosovestno i rachitel'no*) with the added synonym serving as "insurance" that the meaning of the uncommon word is properly understood by all.

> Leisure time belongs to society and can and should be frugally and economically utilized. . . . (Kommunist, no. 8, 1979, p. 35)

> . . . We all know the importance of using our time frugally. Every minute counts. In evaluating our work and the achievements of the Motherland, it is important not to forget this. (Pravda, 1 February 1981, p. 2)

> Our plans will not be fulfilled unless frugality for the sake of the national good becomes a standard of our behavior. (Agitator, no. 9, 1983, p. 4)

Further (*Dal'neyshy*). An attribute that stresses the progressive nature of communism and at the same time exposes the insurmountable contradictions and inescapable degradation of capitalism. "Further" is often used to qualify various synonyms of progress and development, such as "further improvement" (*uluchshenie*), "further ascent" (*pod'em*), "further growth" (*rost*), "further success" (*uspekhi*), "further progress" (*prodvizhenie*), "further expansion" (*rasshirenie*), or "further increase" (*narashchivanie*). In combinations of this type, "further" may be replaced by another attribute of similar content, such as "undeviating" (*neuklonny*), "increasing" (*narastayushchy*), "offensive" (*nastupatel'ny*), "steady" (*ne-*

preryvny), or "unceasing" (*neprekrashchayushchiysya*). When used to describe Soviet affairs, these attributes, as a rule, relate to the activities of the party leadership, the unceasing inspirer and initiator of further development, prosperity, and improvement. The reason for the repeated use of the term "further" is a need to strengthen the image of the CPSU as a great constructive force. Lenin stressed the party leadership's unlimited potential for molding men and society, and by manipulation of simple words like "further," people are subtly influenced to believe that the advancement of Soviet society cannot be halted.

In conformity with the myth of the omnipotence and infallibility of the party, the "interruption in progress," i.e., the stagnation that dominated the Soviet economy and society from the early 1970s to the mid-1980s, was blamed on factors allegedly independent of the nature of the Soviet system, i.e., on "voluntarism" or "subjectivism" of specific Soviet leaders. Thus the basic party line and pretense of further success and progress of the USSR was salvaged. All that apparently was needed for this was to promote the further development of socialism.

Another use of the term "further" is in the descriptions of social processes in capitalist states, such as, "further strengthening of the class struggle in the capitalist countries," "further impoverishment of the working masses in the clutches of capitalism," and "further deepening of the crises in the world imperialist system." All this social deterioration in capitalist countries is claimed to have been predicted by the "classics" of scientific communism, (*klassiki nauchnogo kommunizma*). This alleged predictive success of these communist sources is taken as an additional confirmation of the universal validity and infinite wisdom of Marxist-Leninist teaching.

Occasionally, the term "further" is applied to the growth of something that, from the Soviet viewpoint, is undesirable, e.g., "further growth of imperialist military might" and "further strengthening of the aggressive NATO bloc." But even here, "further" retains its positive connotations through dialectical logic. Used in such contexts, "further" serves as warning to the world of the dangers posed by bourgeois politics.

The working people of our country are exhibiting constant concern for the further strength-ening of the economic and military might of their native country. (Pravda, 1 December 1983, p. 1)

The maintenance of the American military presence on Lebanese territory is dangerous because it might lead to a further escalation of US involvement. (Vyshka, 16 December 1983, p. 2)

G

General Secretary (abbreviated GENSEC [*General'ny sekretar', Gensek*]). The CPSU leader, simultaneously elected Chairman of the Supreme Soviet, i.e., head of state. The general secretary is a specific product of the Soviet system. His power has no basis in law or democratic practice. He is elected according to the Politburo "recommendation" by a narrow circle of party officials at the Plenum of the Central Committee of the CPSU. The only foundation of the general secretary's power is the power itself. Thus it must be maintained by the constant demonstration of the regime's successes and a constant struggle against the party apparatus. Otherwise the question would come to the fore: by what right does the general secretary rule the country and dispose of its resources and human fates?

The idea and the office of general secretary developed gradually in the Soviet Union. It was preceded by the Secretariat of the Central Committee—which was established soon after the February Revolution of 1917 but acquired political importance only in August of that year, when the recognized party leadership was forced to go underground. At that point the secretariat's first leader (not yet called either "first" or "top" secretary of the Central Committee), Ya. M. Sverdlov, began to play a significant role in party life. However, his responsibilities at that time were mainly of a technical rather than a political nature, e.g., compiling and preserving documentation, preparing preliminary materials for plenums, and collecting party membership dues. The same functions, but no more, were fulfilled by those who after Sverdlov's death inherited his office, which by this time was already called "top secretary" (*otvetstvenny sekretar'*); E. D. Stasova, N. N. Krestinsky, and V. M. Molotov (until Stalin gained his post in 1922).

Due to Stalin's reputation within and services to the party, the title "top secretary" was replaced with the more impressive "general secretary."

In the early 1920s, no one in Lenin's circle, including the leader himself, paid much attention to this office. The leadership of the party and the country was concentrated in the hands of the Politburo. Stalin, however, managed to imbue the post with new meaning. He gradually extended its powers. Letters, circulars, and resolutions at first began to be signed with two signatures—those of Lenin and of Stalin, then with Stalin's only. He strengthened his personal influence by placing in the Central Committee and in the party periphery people who were loyal to him alone. At this time the party apparatus was expanding by leaps and bounds. In October 1917, on the eve of the Revolution, only thirteen officials worked in the Secretariat; by 1924 there were already hundreds. Under Lenin the bureaucracy was completely subordinate to party policy; Stalin, however, succeeded in subordinating party policy to its bureaucracy. He appointed and replaced party officials without paying the slightest attention to the opinion or will of the Politburo. When he was terminally ill, Lenin finally realized that the domination of the party by the general secretary posed a mortal danger. But it was too late. The members of the Central Committee, seeing in Stalin a resolute leader, did not follow the recommendation of their deceased leader to replace Stalin. They didn't surmise the extent of the ruthlessness of which he was capable. For Stalin, the rejection of Lenin's recommendation was a sign that his time had come. He turned Lenin's resolution "On the Unity of the Party," passed at the Tenth Party Congress (1921), into an instrument of his own autocratic power, which allowed him to interpret any attempt to criticize him as an attempt to split the party. The idea of "democratic centralism" (cf.), which he reinterpreted as totalitarian centralism, was used as the justification for administrative repressions—expulsion from the party and exile of its recognized leaders. In historical perspective these repressions can be seen as a rehearsal of the mass terror that overwhelmed the party and, subsequently, during the 1930s, the entire nation. This cost the country about fifteen million of victims while consolidating and ultimately making unassailable the power of the general secretary.

After Stalin's death the party apparatus tried to prevent the general secretary from holding the reins of power too firmly. The drive of the general secretary toward autocracy is opposed by attempts to disperse power among the people who are pillars of the Soviet regime. The ingenious device for ensuring such dispersal is called, in party jargon, "collective leadership" (cf.). For a time, before he finds himself in a position to establish his absolute rule, every new general secretary has to bow to the "collective leadership." During that period, the general secretary has to keep balancing between rival factions in the split Politburo—a faction that opposes and will fight him on every conceivable issue and a faction that supports him and will usually, although not always, back him up. The ensuing maneuvering will decide the fateful question of survival for each individual Politburo member. Some will fall; others will achieve reasonably secure power and prestige.

The general secretary's power or potential is inversely proportional to the influence of the Politburo members, who aim at maintaining a delicate balance between his power and theirs. They cannot afford to let the general secretary accumulate too much power, for they would then find themselves devoid of influence in decision-making, but neither can they afford to let his authority dwindle too much, since that would obliterate their chances of promoting their own ambitions through him. Thus, while according the gen-

eral secretary the levers of power, the members of the Politburo attempt to keep the transmission chains in their own hands. And precisely at this point a contradiction appears between the subjective intentions of the Politburo members and the objective consequences of the concentration of power in the general secretary's hands due to his function.

The general secretary takes care to get rid of both those who supported him and those who opposed him during his ascent to the pinnacle of power. He depends on the former, while the latter depend on him. This double dependence obstructs the transformation of the general secretary's status vis-à-vis other Politburo members from "first among equals" to "first among unequals." His dependence on the members of the Politburo limits his freedom of action: their dependence on him entails the risk of a potential coup. Hence his aim is to fill the Politburo with people on whom he can completely rely. This is how the power system functions in the Soviet Union, unifying rival government cliques and party mafias.

Stalin needed fifteen years to fill the Politburo with a majority of his faithfuls. He was in no hurry, however, because he became general secretary at age 43. Khrushchev became head of the party when he was nearly old enough to be a pensioner, at 59, and therefore had to work twice as fast, achieving the same aim in seven years. Brezhnev, who came to power when he was only one year younger than Khrushchev had been, ruled for a considerably longer time. He therefore had time to purge the Politburo twice, first filling it with the "Dnepropetrovsk Clan" (1969–72) and then with the "Moldavian Mafia" (1971–1980). Andropov and Chernenko knew that they were in a desperate scramble for time, one was close to 70 (but did not attain that age); the other had passed it. They tried to restack the Politburo within one or two years. Without enough time at their disposal, neither could possibly succeed. The speed record for attaining absolute power was beaten by Gorbachev. He succeeded because in the Politburo (and in the party apparat as a whole) the biological process took its toll. Gorbachev's allies were the infirmity and deaths of his rivals. His far older rivals could present no real opposition. Thus he became the acknowledged leader by the end of his first year as general secretary.

Neither the party statutes nor the Soviet constitution prescribe any rules of succession. When one general secretary succeeds another, the succession is inevitably followed by a rejection of the predecessor's policies, accompanied by the latter's censure and disclosure of his failures. Such a rejection of the past forms a systematic pattern conditioned by circumstances. Each general secretary operates within the strictly confined social environment of the totalitarian state: he can not move beyond it without ceasing to be a communist leader, recognized as faithful to the basics of the system. Hence any admissible social change, be it in the realm of politics or economics, basically amounts to some rearrangement of a few variables that are always the same, like party monopoly of power, central planning by administrative directives, state monopoly over the economy, and the labor market. After reaching the pinnacle of power, or rather after being brought to power by the system in accordance with its needs, every new Soviet leader is in a position to demonstrate his individuality and creativity only within the confines of a narrow pattern, of the so-called "building of socialism."

He has few alternatives between which to choose. To follow the path of one's predecessor is not wise since that would imply acknowledging responsibility for the latter's mistakes and failures. In this respect, the options essentially boil down to one: to distance oneself from the predecessor's policies and from his person as well. By the 1950s, the middle of the twentieth century, the communist system did not provide "building materials" prerequisite for achieving progress that would be actual rather than fictitious. By then, it had already exhausted its dynamic capacity. Consequently, a rejection of the stagnant past by a new general sec-

retary without success in finding a suitable "affirmative" program in its place, however warranted by the logic of power, still can undermine the authority of the new incumbent as it amounts to his acknowledging that something hardly on the level of the most advanced state in the world is occurring in a state that is supposed to be the most advanced in the world.

Communist leaders have no alternative but to fabricate affirmations, in imitation of what is done in mathematics, by multiplying two negations. In social life, no less than in mathematics, two minuses make a plus. Khrushchev's negation of Stalin by itself was not yet a plus, but Khrushchev not only negated Stalin, he also negated Stalin's negation of Lenin. Thus Khrushchev's double negation led him to the affirmation of the origins of communist mythology—to Lenin, whose name and authority he invoked both in his struggle against his opposition and in justification of his own adventurist experiments.

Brezhnev acted on the same principle. By censuring Khrushchev, he distanced himself from the wholesale condemnation of Stalin. Thus, out of the fabric of "double negation," the rulers of the USSR weave themselves the suits of "positive" heroes. In this way social change in the Soviet Union has become circular: from Khrushchev skipping over Stalin back to Lenin, from Brezhnev skipping over the deposed Khrushchev to Stalin, from Andropov skipping over the late Brezhnev to Khrushchev, and from Chernenko skipping over the brief-reigning Andropov back to Brezhnev. Each time the more or less forgotten past was proclaimed to be a novelty.

The main goals of Lenin were world revolution and the communist international. Stalin, in contrast, once in power, preferred to concentrate on the internal problems of the USSR—primarily on the economy and his personal power. His hold on power, however, turned out to last long enough to permit him to become increasingly involved with foreign policy. Upon realizing that the building of "socialism in one country" had not succeeded, Stalin began to lay the foundations for the international communist expansion.

The range of possible social and economic policy variations within the Soviet system is therefore quite narrow, to the point that Lenin, together with Stalin, had already exhausted all available options. All that remained for their successors was to imitate either or both, or else to synthesize elements borrowed from each into various combinations.

The first to do this was Khrushchev. Realizing that steering the vessel of the Soviet state forward was a hopeless task—when it could never reach its destination since the transition to communism, which he had promised, could not occur—and also realizing that the attempt was dangerous (since the depths of ideology long in the doldrums had spawned opposition and dissident shoals), Khrushchev claimed to be moving forward while actually only moving back and forth between Leninism and Stalinism. This lasted until the directors in the Politburo decided that his captaincy had run out of steam. They then removed him from the helm and pensioned him off.

Khruschev's successor, Brezhnev, was so appalled by the results of his predecessor's "hare-brained schemes" that he began by ignoring domestic problems almost completely, burying proposed economic reforms and preoccupying himself instead with foreign policy initiatives. This shift was also reminiscent of an earlier period of Soviet history. Brezhnev brought to conclusion what Stalin had begun: he made inroads for communism on all continents, and transformed the USSR into a global imperial power, first in the world in military strength, while remaining in the ranks of the less developed countries in per capita consumption.

The "de-Brezhnevization," which first helped Andropov reach power, eventually produced a reordering of national priorities away from foreign policy, where Andropov would have found it difficult to match Brezhnev's achievements, to domestic affairs—first of all to the economy (the reorganization of production and the improvement of plan-

ning and management) and then to social problems (intensification of state controls in general and the campaign against corruption in particular). This explains Andropov's interest in within-the-system reforms that would be capable of strengthening the state and promoting socialism. After Andropov, Chernenko again turned to a negation of his predecessor's policies.

Chernenko's rule turned out to be a mere episode in the struggle for power in the Kremlin, but after his death the history of the Soviet state began to significantly deviate from its traditional course. This was because the helm of the country came into the hands of new, young leaders who were better educated, more independent and self-confident, more modern in their thinking, and more familiar with the West. Being pragmatists, they were quick to realize that the Soviet Union's problems could not possibly be solved by merely manipulating outdated Leninist or Stalinist ideological rhetoric and that any further reliance on such rhetoric was bound to bring disaster upon their society. They have thus chosen the path of attempting to revive "socialism" by injecting into its decrepit, moribund body some ingredients of capitalism and democracy—e.g., private enterprise, market mechanisms, competition, and democratization. Only in regard to monopolization of power by the general secretary does the new Soviet leader remain true to the model of his predecessors. Moreover, the political reform that he designed and began to implement has added a completely new dimension to the power of the general secretary. Previously, from the time of Lenin, the statutory functions were always purposefully defined vaguely so as to allow whoever became general secretary to grab the power of both executive and legislative organs. To attain the same purpose, Gorbachev used strictly legal means. At the June 1988, Nineteenth All-Union Party Conference, a resolution was adopted that made mandatory the election of first secretaries of party committees as chairmen of executive soviets (councils).

This resolution cleared the way for restructuring the pyramid of government power. At its peak, basking in the aura of full legality, there now stands the general secretary, graced with the office of chairman of the Supreme Soviet. His power is almost absolute, above that of the party. He controls the government, the armed forces, and the organs of state security. Lord Acton once observed that "power corrupts and absolute power corrupts absolutely." Time will tell whether this maxim also proves true in the case of Gorbachev and his successors.

Democratization (cf.) and glasnost will have to stop short of infringing on the general secretary's unlimited authority, which is inviolable and can only grow. In the wake of the Nineteenth Party Conference, there was a formal extension of the general secretary's prerogatives in relation to government organizations. Thus the head of the party is now also the head of state as chairman of the restructured Supreme Soviet with expanded powers. This absolutization of the power of the general secretary appeared somewhat counterbalanced by a parallel resolution limiting the tenure of the leader of party and state to two five-year terms. This resolution, however, cannot be treated too seriously since after ten years of power in the Kremlin the general secretary should have no trouble in inspiring enough popular support to ensure his staying in power for life, irrespective of any legal basis.

As general secretary L. I. Brezhnev noted at the Plenum, imperialism apparently undertook to challenge the determination of the peoples throughout the world to live in peace. Agitator, no. 19, 1980, p. 36)

The Politburo is certain that Konstantin Ustinovich Chernenko in his position as general secretary of the CPSU will be best qualified to have the honor of heading the militant command of our party. (Za rubezhom, no. 8, 1984, p. 3)

At the general consulate of the USSR in Milan the book Glasnost: Questions of and Answers to Journalists of the Whole World, which contains the texts of the press-conferences of M. S. Gorbachev from the time he was elected general secretary of the CC CPSU, was pre-

sented to the public. (Pravda Ukrainy, 7 December 1988, p. 2)

. . . Stalin was able to introduce grave content into the, at first glance, harmless word gen sec. (Trud, 22 December 1988, p. 6)

Give (*Davat'*). A colloquial, truncated form of the verb *prodavat'* "to sell." Usually all that is readily available in stores in the USSR is low-quality goods or outmoded brands not in demand. In the rare cases when high quality (usually imported) popular goods come onto the market, the Soviet citizen is less apt to say that they are being sold (*prodayut*), as easily available items are, but rather that they are being "given." The implication is that the very appearance of such high-demand commodities is a smile of fate, like an unexpected charity handout. Needless to say, the goods in question are hardly "given" to the consumer but, on the contrary, tend to be overpriced. This latter fact, however, little affects the gratitude of the Soviet populace for the "gift" of, for example, butter, meat, brassieres, blouses, neckties, etc.

The goods in short supply are not only said to be "given," but "thrown out" (*vybrosit'*), which is an even stronger term that implies that commodities in short supply are never seen on the counters or shelves of the shops. This is a rare event, generally reserved for major holidays. Goods suddenly appear from "under the counter" (*iz-pod prilavaka*), i.e., from stores where they have been warehoused for a long time to be sold to secondhand dealers (*perekupshchiki*) or from "closed distribution stores" (*zakrytye magaziny-raspredeliteli*) serving the restricted clientele of privileged officials, where demand for them is low. In this case, the "thrown out" and "given" commodities are not said to be "bought," (*kupleny*). Rather they are "gotten" or "obtained" (*dostal*), since it is not enough to have money, and one must often spend long hours in line "to get" an object. Getting hold of a prized item may also entail elbowing one's way to the front of the line. Thus it is not surprising that such acquisitions are often experienced as personal success, warranting feelings of joy and satisfaction.

Accustomed to permanent shortages of nearly everything, the Soviet citizen typically first takes a place in line whenever he sees one and only then inquires about "what is being given?" (*chto dayut?*). Such behavior is deeply conditioned by Soviet reality: the very sight of people gathering in front of a store is immediately interpreted to mean that some attractive commodity is being "thrown out."

> At the entrance to the shop the long line is twisting like a snake. "What is being given?" asks a woman perspiring from the heat, with heavy bags in both hands. The answer comes back from the line: crystalware. (Izvestiya, 16 September 1980, p. 6)

> On October 9, there appeared the photo of a Soviet shop in front of which a large crowd was visible: something was being "given" something was "thrown out." (Novoe russkoe slovo, 21 November 1983)

> The readers of Novoe russkoe slovo belonging to the older generation have already noticed that newcomers have brought in the baggage of their native language new meanings for the words "to give" and "to throw out," which were totally unfamiliar to them. (Novoe russkoe slovo, 28 November, 1981, p. 3)

Glasnost (candor, frankness, openness, criticism). The extent of openness and accessibility to public debate and popular control allowed by the Soviet authorities to their people. The word "glasnost" in its modern sense (i.e., accessibility to public knowledge and debate) gained currency in the mid-nineteenth century on the eve of the emancipation of the serfs, which sparked the need to define rudimentary civil liberties. But as a trait relating to modern society, the term began to be used only during the reforms of Gorbachev. The current attempt to revive the Soviet economy gave glasnost a certain momentum. This is because the attempted economic reforms envisage the growing role of popular initiative in the process of production and therefore the formation and gradual development of public opinion. Ad-

ditional impetus to glasnost derives from the struggle for power in the Kremlin: the new Soviet leadership has utilized glasnost as a weapon in its attack on its opponents. In the process, glasnost has also come to serve as a means for severe criticism of the party and government bureaucracies, which are blamed for inertia, resistance to change, and disinterest in reforms that they are supposed to be implementing.

Traditional control from above over the performance of local bureaucracies has proved ineffective as massive indulgence in whitewashing (cf.) and write-ups (cf.) on the part of local authorities threatened to drown Gorbachev's reforms. This is why Gorbachev decided to bring the masses into the game and thus to place the bureaucracy under public scrutiny. His assumption is that once the governing apparatus is exposed to both administrative and popular controls, it will find it much harder to resist perestroika (cf.).

Glasnost emanates from the Soviet press (where the limits of glasnost are set by party directives), public meetings (at which its extent and direction are regulated by the administrative authorities), and a handful of informal groups (cf.) or associations committed to testing the possibilities and limits of glasnost.

Glasnost is a typically Soviet institutional arrangement. It facilitates social regulation, helps strengthen social discipline, and fosters internal controls (i.e., self-censorship), while posing hardly any danger of disclosing the full truth or giving the masses any real control over their rulers. Since glasnost is hedged in and defined by the party, it neither envisages nor allows the expression of free opinion, nor does it provide individuals with free choice. The degree of criticism allowed by glasnost is severely limited. Only targets preselected or preapproved by the authorities can be subject to criticism. It would be naive to suppose that glasnost is dictated by any moral considerations or imperatives on the part of the Soviet leadership. However, it may well reflect the leadership's intention to use popular feedback on party performance as an aid in implementing policies. Thus glasnost basically should be viewed as an instrumentality (at present, a rather effective one) of governing: it helps the regime (and Gorbachev personally) to control developments they find not to their liking and to deprive of influence people who stand in their way. In other words, glasnost is only one in a wide assortment of psychological and tactical devices the Soviet leadership uses to mobilize the masses for its own purposes without yielding any real power to them.

The first immediate goal of glasnost is to decrease the amount of disinformation in reports from lower rungs of the bureaucratic hierarchy and thus reduce the probability of decision-making errors by central authorities. The second goal of glasnost is to stimulate people's interest in their work and the third is to provide the rationale for a purge of the apparat.

As yet there are no grounds for claiming that the campaign of glasnost has affected the great masses of the Soviet population. If anything, the majority of the population still remains skeptical, unwilling to believe that any ex cathedra pronounced political change is for real. Only among the intelligentsia has glasnost elicited some support. However, the significance and potential of that support should not be overrated either. For glasnost is not intended to transcend the narrow interests of intelligentsia as a pressure group.

The faint response to glasnost, its failure to arouse the masses, is now prompting Gorbachev to cautiously expand its limits. This means that glasnost is acquiring a logic of its own. Its development may run amiss of the original purposes the Soviet leadership attached to it and generate changes more radical than was intended. In that case, the leadership may yet find it difficult to control this process. Meanwhile, there is a certain amount of hypocrisy and pretense, even though a genuine struggle against stubborn traditions, habits, and, in some cases, against current rules and customs can also be detected.

There is also a psychological aspect to glasnost. For the elite, it serves as a kind of stimulant to arouse interest in improving their performance. However, in ordinary people,

long denied any outlets for social or political self-expression, it is likely to engender a deeper resonance insofar as it may encourage them to voice their dissatisfaction and protest. Together with slight political relaxation (and improvement in the availability of foodstuffs), glasnost is having the effect of raising expectations rather than labor enthusiasm as Gorbachev hoped.

A clearly outlined program of glasnost does not exist. Glasnost proceeds by trial and error as the authorities tentatively stake out the boundaries of change they feel they can allow without running the risk of losing control over events. Besides, the forms of glasnost vary in different walks of life. In economy, glasnost has fairly broad applications as the light it sheds illuminates various problem-ridden complexities of industrial performance and production relations. In that sector, there are few noticeable limits to the spread of glasnost.

In social areas, glasnost has more restricted applications. Its criticism is dosed out and targeted at malignancies already recognized as such: stagnation, moral decline, alcoholism, miseducation, ineffectual indoctrination, and various problems of literature and art.

Glasnost is subject to severest restrictions in political debate, where candor is considered to be rife with dangerous consequences. Applying glasnost is regarded as suspect not only in discussions of current political realities but also in discussions of the Soviet past, where many events remain unmentionable, precluding their objective examination. These include numerous myths and fictions about Lenin and his life. Subsequent developments in Soviet history, e.g., the forced industrialization, the tragic collectivization, and the Great Terror of the 1930s are likewise either passed over in silence or distorted.

In regard to current politics, the stifling of criticism is the rule. Glasnost is very selective here: the little that is "selected" is regulated by the canon of party-mindedness (cf.), which either commands a "responsible" attitude toward the "accomplishments of socialism" or, in the supposed best interest of the socialism of the future, lays stress on a proper "balance" between criticizing the problematic aspects of the past and respect for its "positive side."

In practice there is an interconnection between the described types of glasnost: the openness needed for economic efficiency presupposes openness of debates about social problems which, in turn, calls for a greater degree of openness in political matters. This interconnection explains the gradual process of the actual extension of glasnost from one area of application to another, e.g., from disclosure of the widespread incidence of bureaucratic "pull," preferential treatment, corruption, etc. to social issues (such as the situation of church and religion in the USSR, the relations between the various nationalities in the Soviet Union, etc.) to occasional revelations on state functions. However, the fundamental criterion by which to gauge glasnost is the extent of the debate allowed on the power structure itself. It is precisely in that area that glasnost remains rather unimpressive.

Glasnost and its limits are neither defined nor protected by law. It is regulated by the so-called *neglasnye* directives, i.e., either oral or intended for internal circulation but not available to the public at large. Such directives can restrict the scope of glasnost or manipulate it at will. The fact that there are no guaranteed rights of exercising glasnost renders the official campaign of glasnost rather ineffectual as it feeds the popular suspicion that all the talk about glasnost amounts to no more than a clever political ploy. Restricted to half-measures, glasnost indeed becomes a semantic game of sorts aimed at making people believe that they are free. For no real freedom of opinion can exist when permission for expressing oneself freely has to be first obtained from the authorities. Freedom, by definition, means that no prior permission to use it is needed.

Not only does glasnost not offer any defense against the arbitrary will of the Soviet rulers, but it also can never develop into really full disclosures that would contradict the very nature of the regime with its all-pervasive secrecy and rampant disinformation. What really merits attention is not so much what the Soviet leadership professes or what it allows to be publicized but rather the reasons for its selective authorization of public debate. It will then be seen that glasnost seeks (rather in vain) to deceive the people as well as to circumvent, (and to the extent possible, nullify) the laws that govern socialist society without prejudicing the socialist essence of that society.

Imposed from above by the authorities and maintained under their control, the policies of glasnost are artificial and incompatible with what communism is all about. But these policies may nevertheless bring Soviet leadership some success, even if only temporary. In the long run, however, glasnost may gain momentum of its own and get out of control. In that case, leadership figures and institutions (including the regime as such) that were originally intended to be immune to the probings of glasnost may end up being exposed and denounced.

If glasnost does not go this far, Gorbachev's opponents can take advantage of it for such purposes as the formulation of a new opposition to him. In that case the Soviet leader might respond by turning glasnost into genuine freedom of opinion and expression. This would, however, amount to Gorbachev's transcending the boundaries of the system and its ideology and to the end of the absolute rule of the party.

An alternate scenario would be the gradual curtailment of glasnost by restricting the range of permissible expression. That would again silence political opposition in the USSR. But that would be nothing new in Soviet history.

Glasnost is today an inalienable feature of the normal spiritual and moral atmosphere in society which enables people to more profoundly comprehend what we have gone through in the past, what is going on in the present, what we are striving for, and what plans we have for the future, and thus help them conscientiously participate in reconstruction. (M. S. Gorbachev, Perestroika i novoe myshlenie dlya nashey strany i vsego mira [Reconstruction and the new thinking for our country and the whole world], Moscow: Izd. politicheskoy literatury, 1987, p. 72)

Everywhere we are hearing about glasnost and democracy in the life of Soviet society as if they were new phenomena. Does this mean that during the preceding 70 years the Soviet people lacked glasnost? (Pravda, 12 October 1987)

Glasnost, it seems to me, is not a particularly apt substitute for such a broad, all-encompassing concept as democracy. When it (glasnost) totally enters our life, we will have no desire to indulge in settling old scores, muckraking, and scapegoating instead of engaging in a truly free exchange of opinions, views, and ideas. Some people end up understanding glasnost as the right to administer a slap to everyone who does not please them. (Literaturnaya gazeta, no. 37, 9 September 1987)

Glorious (*Slavny*). A term of praise that is intermediate on the scale of exaltation, less exalted than "great" or "historic" but more honorific than "leading." Typically, the successes of the Soviet (or another socialist country's) economy, or individual or collective accomplishments, are described as "glorious." Although the term is vague, it is not applied unselectively. Glorious events are generally those related to the history of the CPSU, the Soviet state, or world communism such as the "glorious jubilee" (*slavnaya godovshchina*) of the Paris Commune or of the "virgin lands epic." An anniversary, however important, is not considered glorious if the commemorated event is not part of communist history, or if the Soviet leaders prefer to forget it. Thus, when the anniversaries of the French Revolution or the American Revolution are mentioned, their "failures" or "limitations" are always noted. By definition, such revolutions are not glorious.

The phrase "glorious date" (*slavnaya data*), may, however, be used in reference to any event that in Soviet eyes is "progressive," even though not part of communist history. It is warranted if, in the Soviet scale of values, the event rated high as do Soviet feats of arms or the annexation of various nations to tsarist Russia.

Often the adjective "glorious" is applied to something in the Soviet Union that is not actually treated with respect, such as the "Glorious Working Class" and the "Glorious Factory Collective." Likewise, the proletariat is proclaimed the "Glorious Hegemon" of the communist revolution. In such instances, the adjective merely pays lip-service to an outmoded cliché of Marxist ideology. The widely used phrase "the glorious party" (*slavnaya partiya*) refers only to the Soviet Communist Party. Other communist parties may be "leading," "progressive," or even "great," but only one can be "glorious."

During these days there arrive in the Kremlin in Moscow from all over the Soviet land reports about the glorious labor achievements of the heroic working class of the land of the Soviets, of the glorious peasants of the collective farms and of the national intelligentsia. (Sovetskaya kul'tura, no. 3, 1978, p. 1)

Celebrating . . . the glorious historical date-the fiftieth anniversary of the first 5-year plan-the Soviet people are experiencing the rousing feeling of pride in their native land. (Agitator, no. 8, 1979, p. 8)

The worldwide peace movement has written more than a few bright and glorious pages in the struggle of peoples for a lasting just peace, for detente, an end to the arms race and disarmament. (Za rubezhom, no. 18, 1979, p. 14)

Good Tradition (*Dobraya traditsiya*). Propagandistic appellation for the customs, public activities, and patterned interactions that the authorities find worthy of publicity and encouragement. Phenomena defined as "Good traditions" are by no means typical of or traditional in Soviet society. Thus, although it is asserted that the participation of city and town dwellers in helping collective farmers is a good tradition, in reality such participation is compulsory. It is true that the coercion applied by the party authorities to recruit "volunteers" can be described as a Soviet "tradition," but the "goodness" of this tradition remains problematic. In many cases, the meaning of this phrase is quite vague, as in the following examples: "It has become a good tradition to celebrate labor holidays" (*trudovye prazdniki*), or "A serious attitude to performed work is a good tradition."

The artificial forms of social and economic behavior that the Soviet authorities impose are often attributed to popular initiative and referred to as good traditions. In this way a sense of identification of the citizen with the state is promoted in the popular consciousness and the necessary equated with the desirable. Occasionally, such innovative good traditions may even be indirectly traceable to precedents in the pre-Soviet Russian cultural tradition, precedents having nothing in common either with the "unity of the party and the people" or with "communist consciousness."

The word "tradition" (*traditsiya*) is seldom used in Soviet propaganda without such positive adjectives as "good" (*dobraya*), "fine" (*khoroshaya*), or "glorious" (*slavnaya*). Soviet citizens assume that customs not thus qualified, religious customs for example, should be considered "not good," i.e., harmful, inhumane, or antisocial.

Although imposition of artificial good traditions runs counter to the genuine needs of the public, it does have a limited success due to people's deprivation of and yearning for some traditions, any traditions. However, the impact of the distortion of genuine traditions is anomic since the moral and humanitarian contents inherent in these traditions stand no chance of surviving their cooptation by the regime.

The All-Union Young Writers' Conference proved its worth and became one of our good traditions. (Literaturnaya gazeta, 21 March 1979, p. 2)

Donating part of our pay and personal savings to the cause of peace has become a good tradition in the USSR. (Agitator, no. 22, 1983, p. 38)

Helping the toilers of the countryside with the grain harvest has become a good tradition among Moscow transport workers. (Sotsialisticheskaya industriya, 4 May 1978, p. 3)

Great Confidence (*Vysokoe doverie*). A formula referring to mutual relations between the party leadership and the Soviet people. This term reflects the distinct social hierarchy of Soviet society, topped by the party, the actions of which the people are supposed to appreciate as reflecting great confidence in them and filled out by the subjugated masses whose relation to the party i simply described as confidence *tout court*.

Manipulation of these two categories of "confidence" creates the impression that due to the spiritual affinity and political solidarity of the ruled with the rulers, there are no essential differences between them. The thus supposed community of feelings and interests is intended to obfuscate the distinction between great confidence and plain confidence, which in fact reflects the inequalities in power relationships between the party and society, between the authorities and the man on the street. Clearly the party's great confidence in the people costs the party nothing as it deprives the party of not a whit of its authority. The party, which is supposed to have great confidence in the people, lords over them while the people, with their alleged simple "confidence" in the party, in any case have no say.

He said that this great confidence is totally vested in the glorious Communist Party and its Leninist Central Committee. (Izvestiya, 9 February 1979)

It is [a sign of] great confidence [in a person if] he is to be elevated to the highest state administrative body in the country. (Komsomol'skaya pravda, 11 February 1979)

On the fourth of March 1984, Soviet citizens will go to the pooling booths in order to give their vote to those in whom they have decided to invest their great confidence. (Izvestiya, 19 December 1983, p. 1)

Group A and Group B (*Gruppa "A" i gruppa "B"*). A phrase used to distinguish two basic categories of industrial production in the Soviet Union. Group A refers to branches of industry that manufacture the means of industrial development (heavy industry), while Group B refers to the production of consumer goods.

It should be noted that production in Group A serves as a major indicator of the economic progress of the state, hence Group B always receives comparatively less attention, its growth consistently lagging behind Group A's, in terms of both quantity and quality of goods. Thus, only every fourth worker is now employed in light industry and food processing industries, and these absorb no more than 12 to 13 percent of capital investment. This disproportion in the allocation of productive resources is explained by "the law of priority development of the means of production" that was "discovered" by Marxist political economy.

The persistence in applying this "law" has led and continues to lead to the recurring shortages of foodstuffs and essential commodities, the constant frustration of consumers, and, in certain periods of Soviet history to famine and mass starvation. Therefore, the very distinction of Group A and Group B in Soviet industry is indicative of the Soviet authorities' neglect of the people's elementary needs. However, this has never hindered party leaders from proclaiming that the priority development of heavy industry is proof of their "continuous concern" for the growth of the people's standard of living.

By the mid-1980s, an increase in the rate of production of consumer goods is undeniable. To judge from the major indicators, however, the development of Group A continues to outpace the growth in Group B. As a result, in terms of the supply of consumer goods and vital services, the USSR still ranks among the least developed of the industrialized nations of the contemporary world.

[Seventy-four] percent of all industrial products are classified as Group A. (Agitator, no. 19, 1980, p. 24)

Four-fifths of Group A production comprises the means of production, i.e., raw and prefabricated materials, fuels and energy. (Agitator, no. 19, 1980, p. 25)

Today special attention is being paid in the whole country to Group B production. (Bakinsky rabochy, 31 January 1984, p. 3)

Guards of Labor (*Gvardeytsy truda*). Term of commendation applied to workers and peasants said to be most progressive-minded, conscientious, and disciplined representatives of their classes. The term is symptomatic of the communist penchant for applying military concepts to things that are inherently civilian. Other examples are "old guard" (*staraya gvardiya*) and "the vanguard of the party" (*partiynaya gvardiya*). Literally, the term "guards" refers to soldiers from crack army units. The meaning of "guards of labor" is thus formed by analogy.

When Soviet propaganda speaks of ordinary people as guards of labor, it intends to disseminate an idealized notion of the Soviet worker as a selfless, resilient, and industrious human being who is deeply dedicated to the regime and who therefore can serve as a model to be emulated by all Soviet people.

Since the term is intended to convey the notion of high productivity, there are many specific kinds of guards of labor including "guards of the wheat fields" (*gvardeytsy khlebnykh poley*), "guards of the army of construction workers" (*gvardeytsy armii stroiteley*), "guards of oil exploration" (*gvardeytsy nefteprokhodki*), etc.

The eternal motto of the guards of labor is ceaseless study: ceaseless pursuit of general education, the mastering of politics and ideology and the raising of the level of professional competence and general culture. (Agitator, no. 12, 1978, p. 3)

The example of those patriots—the guards of labor—is an inspiring one. (Agitator, no. 22, 1983, p. 12)

H

Hands off (*Ruki proch ot*). A term expressing the demand for noninterference in the affairs of nations. The expression was introduced and became entrenched in Soviet political language during the civil war in Russia, when British workers founded an organization called "Hands Off Soviet Russia." This call was quickly adopted as a slogan intended to give expression to "proletarian solidarity."

Later the phrase developed into an all-purpose warning against anyone with designs on the USSR or regimes supported by it. "Hands off" is extensively used in newspaper headlines and on posters at demonstrations and rallies.

Hands off Afghanistan! (Krasnaya zvezda, 27 June 1979, p. 2)

Hands off Grenada! (Komsomol'skaya pravda, 28 October 1983, p. 3)

Hazing (*Dedovshchina* literally, being a grandfather). A euphemistic expression for the attitudes, practices, and customs of the humiliating of new recruits in the Soviet armed forces. The essence of hazing can be understood and evaluated only within the general context of the makeup of the Soviet army. The whole system of breaking in and training soldiers is designed to transform soldiers into inert, passive beings, unable to make any independent decisions, prepared for unquestioning obedience and absolute submission. This state of affairs dates back to pre-revolutionary Russia, where the army cultivated a spirit of inhuman discipline by the rod. The Soviet state extended this idea of the suppression of personality in the army, making it into the principle that a rank and file soldier is not a human being.

From the first days of his military service, the Soviet recruit finds himself under extreme conditions imposed in order to test his strength and endurance. Night exercises, watches, long marches, and cross country runs in the cold of winter and heat of summer do not so much train his body as destroy his character. He is expected to forget his previous habits and preferences, and to fuse into one amorphous collective. He has to submit to orders that paralyze his will and ability to think and completely determine his life. He is overwhelmed by a sense of anxiety, uncertainty, and lack of confidence in himself that do not leave him for a minute. He is forced to get undressed and lie down to sleep immediately upon order and he has to get up at the same frantic pace and to put on his uniform in no more than half a minute. The drabness and wretchedness of military life dull and sap his spirit. The soldiers must relieve themselves and wash up on command and march in line to the poorly equipped and shabby dining room, where they are seated strictly according to rank—sergeants, corporals, privates.

Any expression of dissatisfaction is suppressed and punished immediately. Insufficient zeal or inefficiency result in extra night duties and details. For disobedience and negligence, one is sent to military prison, to the punishment cell, where there is no possibility either to wash or to sleep (instead of beds and mattresses there are bare boards) or for any privacy (all movements are observed by the guard). Pent-up anger often overcomes reason. Soldiers seek relief from this tension, which ultimately is expressed in ugly forms—rage, drunkenness, brawls, and, especially, the humiliation of new recruits, inexperienced and not yet able to cope with the cruel and cynical environment in which they find themselves.

Officially, in the Soviet army servicemen are subordinated to each other according to rank or position. Along with the system of subordination, however, there exists an unofficial order of authority that takes into account a completely different pecking order, based on term of service, according to which there is a hierarchy of four grades.

In the highest are soldiers in the last year of service—the "veterans" or, as they are informally called, "old-timers" (*stariki*) or "grandfathers" (*dedy*—hence the term *dedovschina*). Below them are soldiers who have behind them the first year of service—"half-fighters" (*poluboytsy*—this term reflects their transitional status, i.e., the fact that they are no longer novices but not yet veterans). Then come the soldiers who have served at least half a year and who therefore have had time to experience the burden of military service. These are the so-called "youngsters" (*molodye*). Finally, there are those fresh from civilian life, the new conscripts, derogatorily called "sprats" (*salagi*—by analogy with the small, timorous fish). There is yet another category among the soldiers (but not a separate group) that is composed of those servicemen who, because of their stupidity, lack of will, cowardice, or sickness, do not fit into one of the four categories, and therefore, do not enjoy any privileges or protection from their buddies. They are constantly—right up to their demobilization—subjected to humiliation, insults, and violence.

Within every group the soldiers are equal. They have equal rights or, rather, are equal in regard to lack of rights. Military rank and post do not correspond to the soldier's informal status, so that a private, a squad commander, a sergeant, and a corporal can all find themselves on the same level of subordination. On the other hand, the second system of command is not entirely separated from the first one, and in fact it often supplements the former. In the group of "old-timers," naturally, there are more sergeants, and the sergeant-major, standing over all of them, is never appointed from among the first-year soldiers. Nevertheless, the informal system of power in the army significantly differs from the formal one—having its own traditions and rules.

In civilian life, a soldier may be a worker, a collective farmer, a student, a journalist, an engineer, a doctor, a promising intellectual or a pleasure-seeking mediocrity, a spoiled child from a well-to-do family or the sole support of his old mother. But once mobilized, he immediately loses his familial and individual features and becomes one of the "sprats." Now, on whim of the "grandfather," he must wash the latter's socks, clean his trousers, make his bed, sew on the collar to his tunic, take his place on guard duty, or wash dishes, clean the barracks, eat the remains of his food, fetch vodka for him, and even cover for him when he is inebriated. As a reward for his obedience and suffering, after half a year of service he is promoted to the category of "youngsters," which will save him from many, but not all, humiliations. As earlier, he will remain at the beck and call (*na pobegushkakh*) of the "old-timers," but for the dirtiest and most thankless jobs he will be replaced by the "sprats" from the new recruits.

The promotion of a soldier to the next "rank," from "sprat" to "youngster," is conducted in a simple manner: "half-fighters" hold his hands and a "grandfather" beats him three times on the shoulder with his belt, stick, or any other heavy item at hand. This initiation ritual takes place twice more, when a soldier is promoted from "youngster" to "half-fighter" and from there to "old-timer."

There, his sufferings will end and he himself will insult new recruits—just as others used to insult him or even more cruelly and cynically when, toward the end of his term of service, military life will be quite hateful to him. To arrange a "warm-up" for the "sprats," he will wrap them in a blanket, tie them up, roll them across the floor and throw them, crazed with fright, out of the window. If the novice is lucky, he will not break an arm or leg but merely get off with some bruises. Or, the "grandfather" and his friends may play another prank, blindfolding some unfortunate victim, with the whole squad beating him over the head until he recognizes who beat him last. A further prank is called the "bicycle": it entails putting cotton between the legs of a sleeping novice and setting it on fire. However, one is not allowed to complain. Such are the rules of the "game." Those who do not accept them because of their pride are in for trouble. They will be "educated" quite mercilessly. They will be humiliated in many ways—by being urinated upon at night, by having cockroaches thrown into their food, by being beaten into unconsciousness, by having hot or icy water poured over them or by being awakened by a burning match thrust into their face.

Young soldiers, exhausted by constant suffering and harassment, limit their movements and forego speaking openly and laughing aloud. If they smile in the presence of "old-timers," they do it timidly and servilely. Their appearance cannot be confused with that of veteran soldiers, who have almost civilian haircuts, moustaches and whiskers, concertina-like Wellington boots (*sapogi garmoshkoi*), their hands inside the pockets of their narrow slacks, and close-fitting tunics. No contrast can be more glaring than that between them and the "sprats"—with their crewcuts and their clothes black from cleaning floors and crawling on the ground during drills.

But mercy is not sought or expected. Those who inflict humiliation are doing to others as was done unto them. They must face all the hardships of military life until they mature and themselves become "grandfathers." Then their turn will come to vent their own pain and bitterness in full measure upon the fresh "reinforcements." Sadism, both inflicted and suffered, creates a sense of community so that the term of service does not seem so interminable. Endurance takes the place of happiness in the military service as in Soviet life as a whole. The latter projects onto the army its relentless and cruel mores, its callousness and soullessness. Only in small measure does the term "hazing" reflect the perverted nature of Soviet society. But the officially accepted synonym of that term—"extra-statutory relationships"—is removed even farther from reality. Such relationships should rather be called "extra-

human." It is the latter term that indeed characterizes both Soviet society and its army.

> Hazing has become a current social problem. (Nedelya, no. 15, 1988, p. 8)

> Hazing is a humiliation of those who have served less time than you have. (Izvestiya, 11 August 1988, p. 3)

> Hazing has long ago been allowed to penetrate military units; today it has become a major "enemy" of military collectives. (Komsomol'-skaya pravda, 23 July 1988, p. 2)

Headquarters (*Shtab*). A symbolic and prestigious way of referring to a supervisory body with a specific responsibility. Headquarters can be either temporary or permanent. Temporary headquarters are established at plants, construction sites, factories, or collective and state farms in order to organize and coordinate activity during crucial working periods for a given industry. "Work Rush Headquarters" (*shtab trudovogo shturma*) and "Summer Harvest Headquarters" (*shtab letney strady*) are two examples of this practice. Headquarters are also set up for the purpose of conducting various propaganda campaigns. For example, there are "Holiday Headquarters" (*shtab vykhodnogo dnya*) to promote "communist leisure" and "Consumer Courtesy Headquarters" (*shtab bor'by za vezhlivost'*) to encourage polite service to shoppers.

Permanent headquarters are established to increase production. These are: "Headquarters of Socialist Competition" (*shtab sotsialisticheskogo sorevnovaniya*), usually launched by party bureaus at factories and plants, or "Harvest Campaign Headquarters" (*shtab bor'by za urozhay*) set up by the regional party committees in the countryside. These represent field or operational headquarters, subordinate to the "Supreme Headquarters" (*vysshy shtab*), as the Central Committee is often colloquially called—which is not surprising, since it maintains total political and ideological control over the country. Directly below the Supreme Headquarters are "High Headquarters" (*vy-*

sokie shtaby), consisting of the Council of Ministers, Gosplan (the State Planning Committee), and the Academy of Sciences. These rule over a whole mass of subordinate agencies, whether ministries, departments, enterprises, or research institutes. The proliferation and penetration of headquarters into all walks of Soviet life help create a "militant" (*boevaya*) political atmosphere of "vigilance" and ideological mobilization.

The very word "headquarters" is an ever-present reminder that the orders and directives of the party leadership must be obeyed immediately with the same precision and absence of second thought that soldiers display when following orders by their superiors. Military symbolism is usually attached to key political, industrial, and social institutions of Soviet society. However, this term is frequently applied to less important or peripheral matters such as "The Headquarters for Planting Trees and Shrubs in the Region" (*shtab po ozeleneniyu rayona*) or "The Repair Work Headquarters" (*shtab remont-nykh rabot*).

> The party is the vanguard of the working class, its primary stronghold and military headquarters. (Istoriya VKP(B), Kratky kurs [History of the All-Union Communist Party of the Bolsheviks, brief course]; Moscow: Publishing House for Political Literature, 1950, p. 344)

> . . . A headquarters to combat failures to meet schedules is operating at the plant. (Agitator, no. 12, 1978, p. 11)

> The chief engineer has assumed a leading role in establishing a headquarters for minimizing waste at the trust. Similar headquarters are functioning in all workshops and all branches. (Agitator, no. 21, 1983, p. 8)

Hegemony of the Proletariat (*Gegemoniya proletariata*). A doctrine that upholds the leading role of the working class in the socialist revolution and that has been adopted by the Communist party to justify its unlimited power in Soviet society. Initially, the concept was used to buttress the idea that the establishment of a free, democratic society, the goal for which humanity had been struggling for centuries, could be realized by the seizure of political power by the proletariat.

Marxism, however, has always set certain limits to hegemony of the proletariat by subordinating the working class to the Communist party. Lenin restricted the role assigned to the workers even further by saying that the proletariat could assume the leadership in the Revolution only while struggling in the ranks of its vanguard, the Communist party. Thus, instead of implying that the Communist party will yield to the workers' will, the hegemony of the proletariat was made conditional on the latter's subservience to the party's edicts (*prednacherta-niya*). In itself, the proletariat came to be seen as a class that was "backward and conservative" (Marx) or compromised by "petit bourgeois tendencies" (Lenin).

Once they had seized power, the communists opposed workers' efforts to preserve the freedoms they had been attempting to wrest from tsarism and ultimately won in February 1917. Slowly but surely, the proletariat was subordinated to the state and the workers transformed into the party's "transmission belts" (*privodnye remni*). This process occurred in a succession of stages. Politically active workers (who sought to free the proletariat from the tutelage of the Bolsheviks) were subject to repression. This is what happened to the "Workers' Party" (organized in 1920–21) for demanding independence from the Bolsheviks. Furthermore, trade union leaders were replaced; public demonstrations were violently dispersed in 1920 and 1921. In 1922, the leaders of the "Workers' Opposition" were expelled from the Communist party; strikes were banned and trade-union debates were curtailed. These policies remained intact throughout Stalin's reign and have survived relatively unchanged to the present day.

Until the late 1950s, the doctrine of hegemony of the proletariat as presented in official publications conformed rather closely to its original formulation in classical Marxist writings. The most important aim of the "class-hegemon" (*klass-gegemon*) after a successful socialist revolution was to be the formation of the "dictatorship of the proletariat" (*diktatura proletariata*). However, in recent decades, the dictatorship of the proletariat has tended to be de-emphasized as a goal of "class-hegemon." Instead, the concept of the hegemony of the proletariat implied a stress on "the extensiveness of the proletariat's class bonds" and "the diversity of its forms." Concomitant to the redefinition of the hegemony of the proletariat, reservations began to be voiced about the "degree of maturity" (*stepen' zrelosti*) of the working class itself, its "ability" to lead Revolutionary struggles, and the level of "development" of other classes. The implication that the communists could draw on the support of more "mature" classes when and where the working class lacked "consciousness" and the ability to lead the struggle amounted to stripping the concept of hegemony of the proletariat of all its original meaning. Yet the redefinition is perfectly understandable in the light of the domestic and international circumstances under which it took place.

Whereas during the October Revolution, the civil war, and "war communism" (*voenny kommunizm*) it was necessary to recruit shock troops in the battle against "class enemies," modern Soviet society depends for the achievement of its aims more on the experienced and well qualified intelligentsia than on the proletariat. Lacking economic and legal advantages over other social groups and having failed to gain the power and benefits promised by the Revolution, the working class has ceased to be the regime's power base. This fact has forced the communists in their ideological formulations to bring the former "hegemon" within the same social framework assigned to all other Soviet subjects in the system of the "state of all the people" (*obshchenarodnoe gosudarstvo*).

In international propaganda, the "class-hegemon" and the hegemony of the proletariat were replaced by such concepts as "class bonds," "national movements," and "national fronts." This became necessary because of the USSR's support for underde-veloped countries that lacked a substantial working class. Nevertheless, the communists continue to pay lip service to Marxist slogans by implying that the "international working class and the world socialist system are a joint hegemonic force in the worldwide anti-imperialist struggle." The role of the USSR in this scheme is that of the leading force within the world socialist system, and the role of the CPSU is that of the "vanguard" of the Soviet state, i.e., of "the state of all the people." By such a formulation, a recognizable continuity with Marxist phraseology has been preserved.

However, the Communist party of the USSR has a competitor for leadership of the world socialist system: the Communist party of China. The latter has advanced a different ideological model, revolving around the concept of "the worldwide proletariat" (*mirovoy proletariat*), according to which the role of the "world proletariat" in the contemporary world is played by the population of "poor" countries already liberated or in the process of being liberated from colonialism. In its bid for world domination, the Communist party of China has cast itself as the leader of all these "poor" countries.

It was Lenin who first thought of the underdeveloped countries of Asia and Africa as being of equal importance to the proletariat of the industrialized countries. He even went on to prophesy that the "East will bury the West in the pit which the West has dug for itself" (in the same manner, he expected the proletariat to serve as "undertakers" for the bourgeoisie). It would seem that the long-term evolution of the concept of the hegemony of the proletariat was, in its major outlines, preprogrammed by Marxism at the time when the communist movement was still at its formative stage.

The only innovation in the vocabulary of communism in this context is "hegemonism" (*gegemonizm*), derived from proletarian "hegemony." This word entered the lexicon of world communism in the 1960s, when the Chinese communists gave it ideological currency in their unrelenting exposures of the post-Stalin CPSU leadership's design for world domination. The Soviet Communist party lost no time in responding in kind with accusations of "hegemonism" against the Chinese leaders themselves.

> Under the leadership of the Communist Party of China the hegemony of the proletariat secured the victory of the People's revolution and the establishment of the People's Republic of China. (*Bol'shaya sovetskaya entsiklopediya* [Great Soviet encyclopedia]; Moscow: The Encyclopedia Publishing House, 1950, 2d ed., vol. 10, p. 312)

> The hegemony of the proletariat in the bourgeois revolution with the union of the proletariat and the peasantry should have developed into the hegemony of the proletariat in a socialist revolution with the union of the proletariat and other working and exploited masses. . . . (*Istoriya V K P (b)*, *Kratky kurs* [History of the All Union Communist Party of the Bolsheviks, brief course]; Moscow: Publishing House for Political Literature, 1950, p. 72)

> Lenin [and] the Bolsheviks firmly insisted at the Congress on the main thing which guaranteed the success of the revolutionary struggle: the establishment of the hegemony of the proletariat. (Partiynaya zhizn', no. 16, 1973, p. 8)

Help to the Countryside (*Pomoshch' selu*). The compulsory recruitment of urban residents for temporary agricultural work. Official propaganda presents "help to the countryside" as evidence of the communist civic spirit that moves Soviet citizens to selflessly volunteer for work on collective or state farms. Each year, party organizations send hundreds of thousands of factory or office workers, students, and even schoolchildren to farms as help to the countryside. Mobilization of this manpower is conducted during harvest times (from late summer to early fall) and is accompanied by strident propaganda. Besides being an economic measure, help to the countryside is a propaganda technique meant to facilitate the disappearance of social barriers between town and country and between physical and mental labor. What the propaganda carefully avoids mentioning is that urban residents must be recruited for

agricultural labor only because of the inefficiency entailed by the involuntary work of collective farmers. Since slogans alone are clearly unable to provide sufficient motivation, those who dodge their assignment for help to the countryside face severe disciplinary measures: they are prevented from joining the party, refused job promotions, and expelled from the universities.

Urban residents employed as helpers to the countryside receive no additional wages. They continue to draw their normal salaries, which means that help to the countryside is subsidized entirely from the budgets of industrial enterprises and institutions.

Following the conversion of collective and state farms, as well as urban enterprises, to the system of self-financing, the situation is bound to change. This presents a problem: who will pay for the work days, which in 1988 alone reached 300 million? It is quite possible that ideological considerations will continue to outweigh questions of practical expediency. Meanwhile, the phrase "help to the countryside" is a term employed only in official documents and in the press. However, in colloquial speech it has come to be increasingly replaced by the phrase "agricultural duty" (*sel'skaya povinnost'*), which expresses much more accurately the real compulsory nature of help to the countryside.

> The resolutions of the July Plenum of the Central Committee of the CPSU generated a new surge of popular energy. From this, we feel entitled to draw the conclusion that help to the countryside must be concrete and effective. (Sotsialisticheskaya industriya, 6 August 1978, p. 1)

> The buro of the Provincial Party committee of Kharkov has approved the socialist obligations undertaken by a number of leading collectives with the intention of strengthening help to the countryside. (Ibid.)

> Help to the toilers of the countryside still goes on, even though the harvest is mostly over. On Monday, representatives of urban industrial enterprises went to pick apples. (Sovetskaya Moldaviya, 25 October 1979)

Heroism (*Geroizm*). A mode of conduct presented as a moral ideal of communist society that requires of the individual constant readiness for an impressive feat and for a life of activism under particularly difficult, even dangerous conditions. Marxism links heroism with turning points in history—times when the social process is susceptible to disruptions that make the fulfillment of a historically predetermined task contingent on the ability of individual groups—via particular physical, spiritual, and moral exertions in order to overcome exceptionally adverse circumstances. The Soviet epoch is viewed as being a period when opportunities for heroism abound. Not only heroism on the part of individuals but also sacrifices by the entire nation are demanded for the sake of building communism. Since individual heroism is not always subject to administrative control and cannot be produced by the party leadership upon command, it often depends on fortuitous factors. The government's aim, therefore, is to transform spontaneous personal feats into a controlled and sanctioned heroism of the masses.

In practice, such remote-controlled heroism amounts to self-sacrifice extracted under pressure. This phenomenon leads to the paradox of a supposedly happy, classless society established at the expense of the individual happiness of its members. The resolution of this paradox is seen by the communists in heroism and self-sacrifice. The personal feat plays the role of a spark for nationwide heroism. The hero (*geroy*) must accept exclusive responsibility for overcoming a particularly onerous or complicated problem. However, since the individual hero is expected to spark mass heroism, the exceptionality of his deeds ceases to be exceptional when the government imposes it as a universal moral norm for everyone to emulate. In this regard, Lenin noted that the triumph of a new society is not something that can be achieved by a single burst of heroism, but only by the heroism of persistent, protracted, and tedious work (Lenin, Sochineniya [Works], vol. 29; Moscow: Publishing House of Political Literature, 4th ed., 1950, p. 390).

During the civil war, heroism was understood as self-sacrifice in the name of Soviet rule. During the first Five-Year plans, heroism was equated with asceticism and self-denial. During the period of collectivization, the concept was identified with mercilessness toward those who refused to join the collective farms. During World War II, as during the civil war, the salvation of the Soviet regime was won at the price of the sacrificial immolation of millions of people. In the postwar years, bravery and endurance were again in demand as traits conducive to survival under conditions of continuing "temporary difficulties."

The prerogative for determining the meaning of heroism lies with the authorities. In 1935, the title "Hero of the Soviet Union" (*Geroy Sovetskogo Soyuza* was instituted for bravery and exploits of valor in war. In 1938, the title "Hero of Socialist Labor" (*Geroy Sotsialisticheskogo Truda*) was instituted to mark outstanding service to the country's economic development. Thousands of those heroes emerged, each portrayed as a true patriot and faithful follower of the party. The hero was supposed to die in the name of Stalin during wartime, give his or her all in labor on communist constructions, and do his or her utmost to protect state property in peacetime. The feats of such people are cited as evidence of communism's greatness in accordance with the formula "the party is the inspirer and organizer of the exploits of the people which embody heroism."

In reality, there is little room left for heroism in Soviet life today. Rigid norms of behavior preclude any genuine heroism. The very concept of heroism has been emasculated by party dogmatism. A person upon whom the title "hero" is bestowed has often performed no heroic deed whatsoever, but may receive the title on his birthday or another occasion merely in return for displaying loyalty and/or diligence. The title can be conferred more than once on the same person; for example, Khrushchev was three times and Brezhnev five times declared a hero.

With time, the awarding of the title came to be used as a token to be disbursed or withheld according to political considerations. Thus, the title was awarded to Nasser and Castro, who had not performed any heroic deeds for the Soviet cause, while Sakharov was administratively deprived of his thrice-crowned "heroism" as soon as he began to speak out against abuses of legality in the Soviet Union. At the end of the 1940s, the Chinese people was called heroic (*geroichesky*), but after 1960, when their concept of communism was found to differ from that of the Soviets, it seemed they were not heroic after all. Likewise, the Czechoslovak, Polish, and Yugoslav nations could at times be referred to as "heroic," while at other times be referred to quite differently, depending on the nature of the USSR's relations with these states at a given time.

The devaluation of the concept of heroism is proportional to the frequency of its use and abuse. The adjective "heroic" has been applied to a wide range of phenomena, such as initiative, labor, behavior, fate, and even ordinary daily life. All these have little to do with heroism as commonly understood but much to do with values stressed by the Soviet propaganda machine.

In its essence, Soviet heroism is quite inhuman and amoral. Millions of human lives have been sacrificed by the authorities in the name of illusory ideals for the real purpose of maintaining and strengthening their regime. Senseless exploits and unnecessary sacrifices continue to be encouraged. The vast suffering thus incurred receives its ultimate reward in the elevation of the Soviet people to the rank of a "nation of heroes" (*strana geroev*).

> Soviet man exemplifies bravery and steadfastness, labor and military heroism. (Agitator, no. 17, 1978, p. 2)

> The heroic essence of Soviet man's character, his active civic stance, and his high level of patriotic consciousness are unfailing. (Literaturnaya gazeta, 24 April 1981, p. 2)

> The efforts of the Party, the bravery and stead-

> fastness of the Red Army, and the heroism of the whole Soviet nation resulted in Moscow's not only resisting but throwing back the enemy from its walls. (Izvestiya, 2 October 1981, p. 3)

Heterodox Thinkers (*Inakomyslyashchie*). People whose thinking deviates from that officially sanctioned as appropriate for the Soviet mindset. The term "heterodox thinkers" is quite broad, including people who express various forms of opposition and protest, e.g., political rebels and fighters for free emigration, nationalists and religious sectarians, as well as people who simply refuse to be shackled by communist dogma. The term contains an inherent contradiction. On the one hand it presupposes the ability (and desire) to think differently than the authorities do. On the other hand, the latter do not really think, but merely apply the rigid mental stereotypes of Marxism and thus shape realities of life in accordance with their political ambitions or perceived needs of society.

Heterodox thinking gained currency in the 1960s, when the liberal movement arose in response to the reforms of Khrushchev as a consequence of de-Stalinization, which went further than the authorities intended and under the impact of the first tentative Soviet contacts with the West. Most surprisingly and paradoxically, however, the communist regime itself began subsequently to promote heterodox thinking and to create "enemies" of the state in order to suit various domestic and foreign policy considerations.

Among heterodox thinkers, religious believers have always been persecuted in the USSR. The distribution of religious literature may lead to arrest, internal exile, or incarceration in a mental hospital. In the 1970s and 1980s, a wave of repression was unleashed against other heterodox thinkers, such as underground proponents of a liberal version of socialism, founders and members of free professional trade unions, feminists, practitioners of yoga, and anyone else who refused to surrender his or her independence of judgment. Demonstrations in honor of International Human Rights Day, expressions of solidarity with political prisoners, and meetings with foreigners are all sufficiently independent actions to warrant punishment. Campaigners for national rights in Latvia, Georgia, Armenia, the Ukraine, and other republics have been falsely accused of promoting nationalism, advocating secession from the USSR, or participating in the human rights movement, which is likewise considered "not appropriate for socialism." A prominent place among the heterodox is reserved for the "perennial enemies of Soviet rule"—the Zionists, whose frequent scapegoating is intended to provide suitable "explanations" for various deviations from the party's "general line" or obstacles in the development of communism. "Socialist patriotism" is supposed to shine brightly, by contrast, against the obscurantism of Zionist heterodoxy.

By the early 1980s, the impression was created that the policy of "partially open borders," aiming at "getting rid" of "volatile" and "undependable" elements, was recognized as counterproductive and thereby terminated.

In reality, however, emigration of the Jews and of the Germans as well is too complex a phenomenon to assess it in terms of a simple result. It had to do with the international prestige of the state, if only because emigration fostered the hopes for the revival of "peaceful coexistence" and because it could help to assuage the thirst of the Soviet economy for Western technology. Furthermore, emigration did not take place in social isolation. It affected various Soviet domestic conditions and was affected by them in turn.

Had the USSR decided to entirely close its borders to emigration, it would of necessity have to offer the Jews some rights and to create at least a simulation of Jewish cultural life. This could only lead to complications, as other minorities (e.g., the Greeks, Kurds, Chinese, and Koreans) could take a hint and demand national autonomy and equality for themselves as well. Problems could also ensue with the "fraternal" peoples, like the Ukrainians, Belorussians, Lithuanians, Estonians, Georgians, etc., whose inequality vis-à-vis the Russians could seem less humiliating or galling when compared to the almost complete denial of any rights to Jews. Thus, the removal of the "Jewish brick" from the entire artwork of discriminatory finesse entailed the danger of undermining the whole construction. A national chain reaction could be sparked, which in the end could prove fatal to the regime.

This is what made the Soviet authorities prefer to buy peace and simultaneously gain political capital at the relatively low price of allowing emigration rather than arousing the trampled-on national identities. This is also why emigration gradually rose in the second half of the 1980s, even if not as precipitously as under Brezhnev in the 1970s. At the same time one hears in the Soviet Union that the departure of Jews from the "socialist homeland is liable to bring irreparable harm to the cause of building communism." There is some truth to such a view. The massive exodus did make some openings in the Chinese wall, which the Soviet system had erected to isolate itself from the outside world. But through the same opening there flowed enormous quantities of modern Western technology, the latest equipment, and millions of tons of grain. Hence, what the communist regime lost in its totalitarian homogeneity and ideological uniformity was, in the end, well compensated by gains in its stability and strength. The Soviet state has always been prepared to barter its communist principles for material advantages. The question is what—or who—will in the next decade be put by the Soviets onto the counter for bargaining with the West.

For a considerable time, the communist regime was not able to completely suppress the intellectual and moral resistance movement that had been spawned by Khrushchev's reforms. In order to put an end to the ferment in Soviet society, it would have had to overcome its own inhibitions and revert to Stalin's methods of permanent, totalitarian terror. Yet the party *nomenklatura* did not allow the Soviet leadership to make such a reversal because it recognized that unlimited arbitrary rule would threaten not only its privileges but also its own skin. The precedent existed: in the 1930s, the proletarian revolution, after defeating and crushing its real and imaginary opponents, moved with the tacit consent of the party ruling clique (*verkhushka*) to annihilate its own leaders. Mindful of this precedent, the *nomenklatura* opted against its repeat.

In this way, a surrealistic situation emerged: a struggle between opposing forces (the partocracy and the opposition) has resulted in their unity. They have needed each other to survive. This mutual dependence, however, could not last forever. It had to be terminated either through the destruction of the opposition or through the destruction of the partocracy. But the symmetry between the two has its limits. The fall of the partocracy does not need to entail the disappearance of the opposition, which, under certain circumstances, might then even gain strength. A total liquidation of the opposition, by contrast, would inevitably require the removal of the existing party ruling clique and its replacement by another *nomenklatura* capable of being the "guiding and determining force of society."

Like the present partocracy, such a future *nomenklatura* would have to strut its feathers as the Marxist "vanguard of progress," forging the "last social revolution in history." For the sake of ideological legitimacy, it would then again have to invent some heterodox thinkers to use them as counterexamples to its own virtues. But once the term appears, the phenomenon is bound to appear as well. Intellectual and moral opposition to the Soviet system has an assured existence.

In the present evolution of the Soviet Union, however, there are no signs of incipient destruction of either partocracy or the opposition. A middle road has been pursued instead. The partocracy adopted revolutionary slogans that, however, stop short of calling for a revolution and in this way managed to keep the leadership of the state firmly in its hands. All that it had to do was to maneuver a bit by fixing the composition of the country's elites to make room there for certain circles of the intelligentsia and to somewhat increase the rights of the representative organs of power. The social base that nourished heterodox thinkers and provided oral support for their ideas was somewhat undermined by such cooptations. A contributory role in achieving this effect was played by young technocrats—educated, liberal, enterprising careerists who have constituted Gorbachev's base of support. They sought to ideologically substantiate an essentially pragmatic (but convenient for themselves) argument that Gorbachev's reforms, although palliative, inconsistent, and contradictory, are the only alternative to stagnation, as under Brezhnev. Therefore, without completely sharing Gorbachev's goals, they give him full support in his struggle against the conservatives. But the technocrats were not alone in seeking to clip the wings of the genuinely heterodox opposition. Some liberal intellectual circles, which had for years opposed the communist ideology, but in a way that was shallow and incurred no particular risks, were also anxious to find for themselves a niche in the reconstituted elite. They were anxious to cooperate with Gorbachev's leadership, oblivious of its role in the routing and discrediting of heterodox thinkers prior to their coming to power.

But the heterodox thinkers did not disappear without a trace. Their ideas affected deeply the hearts and minds of many people. As a movement, they seem to have been disarmed after the authorities coopted its slogans, bending their content to suit their own purposes. However, the heterodox thinkers were also betrayed by the masses, which considered both the ends and the means of the struggle as too exacting and risk-laden. Soviet people are still fearful of clashing with the regime; nevertheless, the dissident movement of heterodox thinkers, far from disappearing from the scene, has for the moment receded, waiting in the wings and watching Gorbachev's reforms, which had driven them to the margins. But as soon as these reforms are stymied, the movement may likely be impelled to reappear and grow again.

. . . In a note dealing with (the use of) psychiatric hospitals to "cure" heterodox thinkers the author writes that this is not a new development. The tsars resorted to exactly the same method in order to shut the mouths of dissidents. (Posev, no. 11, 1974, p. 61)

The reprisals against so-called heterodox thinkers in the USSR have been carried on for many years. (Posev, no. 10, 1977, p. 19)

Recently a number of bourgeois states unleashed a political campaign in "defense of human rights," linking this campaign with the issues of emigration from the USSR and the so-called "heterodox thinkers." (Belaya Kniga [White book]; Moscow: Publishing House for Juristic Literature, 1979, p. 9)

At present no task is probably more critical for the very success of perestroika than developing a sensible tolerance toward heterodox thinking. (Moskovskie novosti, no. 37, 11 September 1988, p. 13)

Historic Decisions (*Istoricheskie resheniya*). Those decisions of the Soviet leadership which are declared to have a particular urgency and importance for the development of communist society. The phrase is applied to decisions of All-Union Party Congresses, conferences, and Central Committee Plenums, but not to decisions of the state or party apparatus of the various republics, provinces, and regions.

During the years of "the cult of the personality," the phrase was used to describe Stalin's edicts. After his death, it was increasingly employed in reference to edicts of the Soviet Union's collective leadership. The frequent reference to historic decisions serves to reaffirm the privileged position of the party oligarchy within Soviet society and to stress its status and social position.

After every change in Soviet policies, one set of historic decisions is replaced by another that is declared to be as consequential and as permanently binding as the preceding one had been. Decisions of CPSU Congresses, for example, are usually called "historic" only until subsequent Party Congresses, which may make new historic decisions. A change in party leadership can also lead to historic decisions' losing their historic status. Thus Stalin's historic decisions were rejected by Khrushchev, and the historic decisions of Khrushchev were harshly censured by his successors after his ouster. After the death of Brezhnev, it became clear that all the historic decisions of his authorship led the country into stagnation.

The working class, the peasantry and the nation's intelligentsia are focusing all their energy on translating into practice the historic decisions of the XXV Congress of CPSU. (Literaturnaya gazeta, 5 November 1970, p. 1)

Carrying out the historic decisions of the XXV Congress of the CPSU, the collective of House Building Combine No. 33, which had entered the All-Union socialist competition for raising the efficiency of industry and the quality of manufactured goods, successfully fulfilled its obligations. (Izvestiya, 6 January 1979, p. 1)

The further strengthening of ties between science and industry is a sure guarantee of the fulfillment of the directives of the XXVI Party Congress. (Izvestiya, 23 August 1981, p. 3)

History (*Istoriya*). Communist policies projected into the past. In Soviet doctrine, history as a science has no objective content but expresses the tastes and preferences of the ruling classes. The latter form historical concepts and determine how they relate to the needs of society. History is true only to the extent to which it is considered so by the ruling classes. As a particular ruling class leaves the arena of history, historical phenomena receive a new interpretation.

Soviet propaganda, drawing on such a philosophy of history, selects only those facts which demonstrate the progressive nature of communism and the inevitability of the advent of the communist era. All knowledge of events inconsonant with this viewpoint is suppressed. Each new ruler revises history and creates a niche for his or her own greatness. Gorbachev is no exception. The only difference is that he has his own way of revising history: by bringing out of oblivion dozens of people who were consigned there by his predecessors and assertively assuming a place of honor in the gallery of characters he has assembled.

The most striking aspect of Gorbachev's version of history is the boldness with which he is restoring the past. During the last one and one-half to two years, the founding figures of Soviet history such as Trotsky, Zinoviev, Kamenev, Bukharin, Voznesensky, and hundreds of others have been restored to Soviet memory. Soviet citizens began to learn many new and astounding facts. They were told of Stalin's power grab in 1929, presented with quite detailed knowledge of the tragedies of industrialization and collectivization in the 1930s, and confronted with a more positive image of Khrushchev than the one they had been used to.

The boldness of such revelations would indeed be worthy of respect were it not for the fact that once again a "new truth" is being presented, for whose sake facts are once again being distorted and hushed up while dates are being adjusted. New idols are being hauled onto the pedestal in place of old ones; new dogmas are being preached in place of old ones already discarded.

All this is being done in an atmosphere of great excitement, in the spirit of *perestroika*. The highest value is placed on strident denunciations of Stalinism, while historical study is, as before, tendentiously selective in its recognition of only those facts which please the current leadership. As before, one-sided interpretations of the past are being fostered. The only difference is that condemnation may replace commendation, or vice versa, but this is still no harbinger of truth. The point is not so much that all crimes are now being attributed to Stalin's alleged "antisocialism." Rather, the point is that historical studies are still pervaded by the spirit of utility, their conclusions bent to political circumstances.

A whole array of "craftsmen" skilled in fashioning history are waiting to prepare the most sensational of historical accounts according to request. They are ready to highlight any theme given to them by putting the thoughts of Gorbachev into Lenin's mouth. The idea is not original, of course. In another time and under different circumstances, the same historians attributed to Lenin ideas that would please Stalin, then Khrushchev, and then Brezhnev, Andropov, and Chernenko.

The servants of Soviet propaganda, great masters of falsification, are proclaimers of "personal perestroika"—of personal reform, and are really utilizing glasnost to further the aims of the new ruling oligarchy and their own personal advancement.

Today, anyone who wants to can interpret the history of the Party and the state. Matters have reached a point where various authors are discussing collectivization and industrialization, and are setting generations against each other, they are putting into doubt the achievements of the Soviet regime during the years of the cult of the personality. (Agitator, no. 13, 1988, p. 35)

A scientific approach to the history of Soviet society is one of the basic prerequisites for a more realistic, as well as a more comprehensive understanding of socialism and of the changing character of society. (Agitator, no. 3, 1988, p. 3)

Not by chance has perestroika on which, as M. Gorbachev has observed, the fate of socialism depends, contributed so much to arousing the interest of the public in history. (Nedelya, no. 15, 1988, p. 2)

Hullabaloo (*Shumikha*). Event highly disproved of by Soviet authorities. Although the term is used (in the sense of idle boasting and imaginary accomplishment) in relation to Soviet society, "hullabaloo" usually refers to such Western democratic processes as election campaigns, protest movements, and demonstrations whenever they do not conform to Soviet interests. The word then serves to cast doubt on the authenticity of what it attempts to discredit, without offering any solid evidence or valid arguments to prove its point.

A social phenomenon need not be pervasive or widespread in order to be labelled hullabaloo. The only precondition of the use of the term is the incompatibility of the phenomenon described with Soviet values or Soviet notions. Thus, for example, statements of protest voiced by reputable spokesmen of mass nationalist movements, as well as of individual dissenters, are discounted on the ground of their being nothing more than hullabaloo.

The sarcastic intention of the invective may be reinforced by the use of such adjectives as "unhealthy" (*nezdorovy*), "demagogic" (*demagogichesky*), and "notorious" (*preslovuty*). Phrases such as "unnecessary hullabaloo" (*nenuzhnaya shumikha*) and "pompous hullabaloo" (*paradnaya shumikha*) are also in common use.

A whole family of words based on the same Russian root as hullabaloo is routinely marshalled in order to discredit Western politics: for example, *shum* (noise), *shumny* (noisy), and *shumet'* (to make noise). This has led to the use of such awkward expressions as "to wail noisily" (*shumno vopit'*) or "to shout noisily" (*shumno krichat'*).

To the hullabaloo about the "Soviet military threat" there has been added the hullabaloo—at least at the same decibel level—about the "Soviet Union's violation of human rights." (Novoe vremya, no. 50, 1978, p. 20)

One wonders why those who raise a propaganda hullabaloo about the "violation of human rights" in Socialist countries do not first look at the domestic situation of their own societies. (I. N. Rozhko, Sotsialistichesky obraz zhizni i pravo (The socialist way of life and the law); Moscow: Zhanie Publishing House, 1979, p. 45)

. . . A great hullabaloo is being made about how the USA is supposedly "falling behind" in one or another military or military-technological field. (Za rubezhom, no. 51, 1979, p. 17)

I

Idealism (*Ideynost'*). Willingness to sacrifice self-interest for a higher moral goal, i.e., communism. In its Soviet version, the concept of idealism is artificially constricted, as it implies nothing regarding individual consciousness or activity beyond the bounds of Marxist dogma. The quality of the goals and their relation to human social needs depend exclusively on the interests of the Soviet authorities. Commitment to any ideals other than communism is not considered idealism but is rather termed "unprincipledness," "reaction," or "lack of idealism."

Only communist idealism is considered the true idealism and the driving force for the development of Soviet society. Communist idealism reflects optimism about the achievability of a perfect society and faith in humanism, heroism, and self-sacrifice. The encouragement of communist idealism is regarded as a most important task of communist upbringing and is associated with creativity, innovation, the transformation of life, and struggle for the realization of the "bright" goals of a classless society. Lack of idealism, by contrast, is equated with unscrupulousness, hypocrisy, cynicism, stagnation, bureaucratism, and political narrow-mindedness.

In reality, Soviet society can in no way be said to exemplify idealism. Certainly, idealism is not remarkable among the party leadership, in the government appartus that obsequiously implements the leadership's policies, or among the many millions of the party rank-and-file on whose acquiescence communist rule relies. The path to success in Soviet society, to high government posts, honors, and prosperity, is paved not by faith in communist ideals but by unquestioning obedience and readiness to accept whatever the party says. Soviet idealism, therefore, amounts not only to the conscious and deliberate subordination of self to the totalitarian regime but also to hypocritical justification of one's conformity and careerism.

> Idealism . . . means the fight for realizing the interests of all mankind and creating a better social system, which we call Communism. (M. I. Kalinin, O molodezhi [On youth], Collected Articles and Speeches; Moscow, 1969, p. 246)

> The criteria for the value of our artistic works were and remain Party idealism and consummate skill, truth in representing the life of the people, future-orientation and the degree of impact on the masses. (Sovetskaya kul'tura, no. 9, 1979, p. 2)

> Ideological cadres must present an image of Communist idealism and morality, making exacting demands on themselves and taking responsibility for carrying out their assigned tasks. (Agitator, no. 22, 1983, p. 2)

Ideology (*Ideologiya*). A system of ideas that is viewed as the expression of class interests and attitudes. Two basic ideologies are presumed to exist in any society, that of the "ruling class" and that of "the exploited." The ideology of the class which makes historic progress is the true one. In our time, such a class is the proletariat and those social classes and groups which align themselves with it to jointly build a most progressive society while destroying capitalism. All other ideologies, whether national, religious, or political, are considered reactionary and serving the interests of capitalism.

Communists do not accept the diversity of viewpoints that exists in the contemporary world. In a dichotomous manner, on the basis of political circumstance rather than ideological criteria, they divide existing ideological currents into "progressive" and "reactionary," into "anticapitalist" and "bourgeois." Any segment of opinion whose advocates look to the Soviet Union for support or reflect its influence is classified as a "progressive ideology" (*peredovaya ideologiya*).

Communist ideology—in its official Soviet version—is declared to be scientific by virtue of its reliance on "the only true" doctrine: Marxism. The core of this doctrine consists of theories of successive socioeconomic "formations" and class struggle. Any changes in the tenets of Marxism are permitted only with the authorization of the Central Committee of the CPSU. Any ideology lacking the party's authorization and referred to as "supra-party" (*nadpartiynaya*) ideology, is declared to be a revision of the communist "legacy" and harshly denounced as a manifestation of anti-Sovietism.

> While still in the conditions of a bourgeois society, the working class is creating its own ideology, its own views on politics, literature, and art, appreciating all the best of what world culture has amassed. Politicians, moralists, and aesthetic formalists are not capable of understanding its views. This indicates only the overall limitations of the bourgeois world view, and in no way implies that the proletariat's own outlook is bankrupt. Whether bourgeois ideologists like it or not, culture always has a political nature in a class society. (Antisovetizm na sluzhbe imperializma [Anti-Sovietism in the service of imperialism]; Moscow: Mysl' Publishing House, 1976, p. 101)

> A clash is taking place between two worlds and two major ideologies which personify two opposing social systems. (Mezhdunarodnaya zhizn', no. 7, 1983, p. 12)

> The social system, ideology and fundamental interests of classes ruling socialist and capitalist countries are mutually antagonistic. (Agitator, no. 19, 1983, p. 38)

Immortal (*Bessmertny*). An attribute ascribed to the ideas of Marxism-Leninism, to the Communist Party of the Soviet Union, and to the activities of officially recognized theoreticians and leaders of communism. The religious idea of the immortality of God and of the soul has been diverted by Soviet propaganda for use as an attribute of the Communist party and its policies. By implication, the latter are also uniquely infallible, presumably in view of their "scientific" char-

acter. Communist propaganda stresses the immortality of Marxist ideology in its efforts to convince people to accept and recognize it as ultimate and enduring truth. Significantly, no attempt is made to demonstrate on what foundations the quality of immortality (bessmertie) rests, nor to show how immortality can express itself in practice. Arguments are replaced by illogical slogans or axioms like "the party's ideas are immortal because they are true!" or "Lenin's name is immortal!" Such formulas are supposed to be self-evident and accepted accordingly. The assumption behind the slogans about immortality is the belief of the party leaders that the Soviet people lack sophistication to question what the party tells them.

The paradoxical removal from Stalin of his immortal status taught the Soviet leaders to be more circumspect about bestowing immortality. Some of Khrushchev's ideas, which were advertised at the time as having perpetual validity, were later acknowledged as wrong. After Khrushchev's fall, the title "immortal" tended to be restricted to the founders of communism: Marx, Engels, and Lenin. Yet Marxist ideology remains immortal irrespective of changes of personalities in the top Soviet leadership. Its immortality is unassailable, unaffected by any possible repudiations of the teachings of this or that ruler or by the bursts of "reform" of Gorbachev.

Similarly, the party is immortal and infallible. Even if some of its members or leaders may be wrong, the party can never be. The mausoleum in Moscow containing the embalmed remains of Lenin serves as a reminder of the immortality of the party that he founded and as an illustration of the propaganda cliché that "Lenin is *always* with us [emphasis added]."

> Immortal heroism and courage were displayed by the working people of the Ukraine, (and) by all Soviet people also during the period of reconstruction of the national economy which had been wrecked by the war. (Izvestiya, 9 October 1979, p. 3)

The time which has elapsed since the war years enables us to appreciate more deeply and more fully the immortal heroism of the warriors who went to their death in the name of life, freedom, independence and honor of their beloved Homeland, (and) in the name of socialism. (Kommunist vooruzhennykh sil, no. 9, 1980, p. 33)

. . . We are indebted to the wise leadership of our Party, and its Leninist Central Committee headed by the brilliant follower of the immortal cause of the Great Lenin, the dear to us all Comrade Leonid Ilich Brezhnev. (Izvestiya, 28 February 1981, p. 6)

Imperialism (*Imperializm*). The highest stage of development of capitalism, said to be characterized by the concentration of capital, the unlimited power of monopolies, and the maximum centralization of industrial production and banking. Imperialism means two things at the same time: a process of impoverishment and social decay and a drive toward the use of military force and conquest. Imperialism is said to be a "dying capitalism" that had earlier partitioned the world and is now seeking to repartition it through war.

Thus, the social and political realities that existed at the turn of the century are considered by the Soviets to represent imperialism. However, in a broader sense, the label "imperialism" is ritualistically applied almost always when Western society is spoken of. And, in the broadest sense, the same term is widely used to describe *any* regime of which the Soviets disapprove.

The word "imperialism" can be encountered in numerous phrases used to denounce political systems that, according to communist propaganda, constitute a threat to "peace and democracy." The "camp of imperialism" (*lager' imperializma*) and "international imperialism" (*mezhdunarodny imperializm*) are collective terms for all those industrially developed countries whose policies are objectionable to the USSR. The owners and managers of large enterprises and corporations in these countries are called "sharks of imperialism" (*akuly imperializma*), while their political spokesmen are called "stooges," "henchmen," "hirelings," and even "troubadours of imperialism" (*prispeshniki, stavlenniki, naimity, trubadury imperializma*). Their activities are branded as "intrigues of imperialism" (*proiski imperializma*).

The rote repetition by Soviet propaganda of classical Marxist views about the decay and downfall of capitalism is positively absurd today, when the so-called "imperialist" system has quite outlived predictions of its demise and contrasts sharply with the perilous condition of "real" and "mature socialism" (*real'ny, zrely sotsializm*). Since the word "imperialism" has lost much of its force, perhaps through overuse, Soviet ideologists, in order to restore the proper opprobrium to this concept, have resorted to rhetorical elaborations, such as "fascist imperialism" (*fashistsky imperializm*), "imperialism thirsting for gain and power" (*zhazhdushchy nazhivy i vlasti*), and "Imperialism: the stronghold of bloodthirsty regimes!" (*oplot krovavykh rezhimov*).

Imperialism is frequently equated with "militarism." An arms race, the instigation of armed conflicts, and preparations for a world war are all viewed as characteristic manifestations of imperialism.

In the Soviet lexicon, imperialism is also equated with "colonialism." Communist propaganda claims that national oppression and racial discrimination are integral features of imperialism, which by its very nature is opposed to the independent existence of other nations and bent on subjugating them to its will.

The imperialist nature of Soviet domestic and foreign policies has obviously not been commented on in the Soviet media. The constant focusing of attention on the imperialism of others may be seen as a ploy to distract attention from this paramount feature of the communist regime.

Although imperialism has lost its dominant role in international relations, the danger of destructive wars has still not passed. (Pravda, 1 February 1981, p. 4)

Imperialism has severely complicated the scenario of global affairs over the past decade. (Izvestiya, 17 October 1983, p. 3)

Imperialism is embroiling itself ever more deeply in a mesh of insoluble domestic and international antagonisms, cataclysms, and conflicts. (Agitator, no. 20, 1983, p. 40)

Implacability (*Neprimirimost'*). The refusal to tolerate anything declared to be hostile and alien to the Soviet system. Implacability is an attitude that the Soviet man is educated to internalize. In particular, he learns to be implacable toward bourgeois ideology (*burzhuaznaya ideologiya*), including its influence on Soviet society; "relics of the past" (*perezhitki proshlogo*), in popular attitudes and behavior; religious beliefs; and Western art. The Soviet people are also exhorted to manifest implacable opposition toward drunkenness, hooliganism, corruption, and parasitism.

Once internalized, an implacable attitude amounts to a virtual siege mentality marked by fear of "hostile encirclement" (*vrazheskoe okruzhenie*), diffuse suspiciousness, intolerance, and contempt for others. This personality syndrome, a combination of intolerance, response inflexibility, fear of the different, and conformity has become typical of the Soviet personality.

Exhortations to display implacability usually intensify during special propaganda campaigns, such as those which Stalin waged against "enemies of the people" (*vragi naroda*) and the "cosmopolitans" (*kosmopolity*). However, in deference to political circumstances, such as detente or power struggles inside the Kremlin, such exhortations can be toned down or replaced by others.

Concrete goals for the upbringing of Soviet citizens in the spirit of Communist idealism, high moral principles, and an implacable attitude toward hostile ideology and bourgeois morality are defined within the framework of Congresses and Plenums of the Central Committee. (Kommunist, no. 8, 1979, p. 27).

The social activism of the literary hero is displayed in his implacable attitude toward manifestations of petty bourgeois consumer psychology and his active struggle against it. (Literaturnaya gazeta, 1 July 1981, p. 2)

Impose (*Navyazat'*). To make a country or people accept decisions, opinions, or policies contrary to their interest. The word is used to censure methods claimed to be characteristic of capitalist societies and their business and military circles and are thus, by definition, reactionary. Typical phrases are: "to impose dangerous decisions" (*opasnye resheniya*), "to impose a military budget" (*voenny budzhet*), or "to impose plans for deploying nuclear weapons" (*plany razmeshcheniya yadernogo oruzhiya*).

Traditionally, the verb "to impose" signifies "to foist something off on someone," or "to act with force of deceit." When used in a political context, the term emphasizes the violence that, in an overt or covert form, is supposedly inherent in Western society—as opposed to the "beneficial" and "noncoercive" policies of the Soviet leadership, which allegedly would never "impose" anything on its people and enjoys their support and confidence.

To impose conjures up the image of the massive manipulation of popular opinion alleged to be practiced in capitalist countries—as if this practice were alien to the communist world.

The military industrial corporations that through their henchmen and governments direct the policies of the most powerful capitalist countries are imposing increasingly mammoth military budgets on the population. (Za rubezhom, no. 18, 1979, p. 2)

The BBC imposes on . . . its listeners the interpretation of events it requires. (Za rubezhom, no. 28, 1979, p. 15)

The Pentagon continues to impose on its West European NATO partners plans for the deployment of various types of nuclear missiles on their territory. (Sovetskaya kul'tura, 18 July 1979)

Inflation (*Inflyatsiya*). A reaction of the market to a surplus of money in circulation. The Soviet interpretation of inflation roughly corresponds to the generally accepted meaning in that it is explained by the excess of state spending over its revenues as caused by various economic crises in society and by the arms race. However, in the USSR the term has normally been applied only to bourgeois societies and, in any case, not to Soviet society. Until quite recently in the USSR it was claimed that "the socialist economy does not know inflation" (*Kratkiy slovar-spravochnik agitatora i politinformatora* [Short dictionary-reference book of the propagandist and political instructor], Moscow: Publishing House of Political Literature, 1980, p. 271).

A reevaluation of the concept and phenomenon of inflation occurred in connection with prestroika—unexpectedly and rapidly. A forgotten and taboo word suddenly became fashionable. It suggested some kind of social evil: repulsive, fearsome, intimidating, responsible for all the misfortunes and problems of Soviet economy. Propagandist drums sounded the alarm, calling upon society to close its ranks in the struggle against inflation. In the face of it, fear is instilled and passions aroused. A means of halting, breaking, and overcoming it is desperately sought. Words of warning are uttered to the effect that inflation is a result of the liberal reforms and *glasnost*. And nobody is able (or dares?) to explain that inflation in the Soviet Union is an old, neglected, and chronic illness. Society came down with this disease right after the Communist Revolution, when the market disintegrated and upon its wreckage and ruins there emerged an ugly extraeconomic creation: the socialist apportionment (*razverstka*). However, the free market did not disappear completely. It became "black," in other words, it went underground (cf. "black market"). For some time, the mad gallop of inflation was slowed down or even stopped by means of the NEP (New Economic Policy, cf.). NEP was able to halt—at least temporarily—the most inhuman form of the apportionment in the countryside, the "food apportionment" (*prodrazverstka*—the forcible confiscation of grain from the peasants). But it did not affect its single, integrated, and ramified centralistic system: set-

ting of the wholesale and retail prices, rationing of food, barter exchanges, payments in kind to enterprises, and apportionment of material and technical supply, capital assets, subsidies, etc.

Such "apportionment" continued to flourish for the first seventy years of the Soviet state and developed in a single, comprehensive body for the management and regulation of the economy and society. This body was so powerful and resilient that when, during the turning points of Soviet history (in 1953, with Khrushchev; in 1964, with Kosygin; and in 1985, with Gorbachev), some of its most repulsive elements were uprooted, it was resurrected again with slight modifications at best, since the system (and the idea) of apportionment itself was left intact. Whenever any distortion was discovered in the Soviet economy—for example, a shortage of food—it was corrected by another distortion, e.g., raising prices, so that within the overall structure of the apportionment everything remained well-adjusted and smooth.

The apportionment could never be said to contain any superfluous or alien element, since what was superfluous and harmful for the economy was the system itself. Without completely destroying the system, it would be impossible to get rid of parts of it. It was for that reason that immediately after the NEP the allotment was resurrected before it had time to expire. Yet this was done in a subtle, unobtrusive way, where the word "apportionment" was carefully avoided in public pronouncements, while the idea itself remained and was slowly but surely entrenched within Soviet society.

The blame for the total imposition of the apportionment is now being placed entirely on Stalin. This is wrong. Stalin lacked the education and knowledge needed in order to invent the apportionment. Stalin was a pragmatist; he simply concocted the ideology from the shreds of ideas developed by his political opponents, having first exterminated the latter to prevent anyone from claiming his "copyright." There was only one predecessor whose coauthorship of the apportionment Stalin never denied—and that was Lenin.

Like Lenin, Stalin relied not on the people—the workers and peasants—but on the communist bureaucrats as the mainstay of his power. It was their interests that the apportionment expressed and defended by redistributing economic goods in such a way that the choicest morsels fell to the bureaucracy, while the workers had to satisfy themselves with the leftovers. Nevertheless, there were also certain differences between the two leaders: Lenin viewed the party as the base of the ruling class, while Stalin practically removed the party from the corridors of power. This explains Lenin's encouragement of the NEP for the sake of consolidating the party and Stalin's drive to end the NEP as soon as possible—so as to strengthen and entrench autocracy and dictatorship. Thus Lenin was the real forefather of the apportionment, while Stalin was just its rescuer and guardian.

During both leaders' lifetimes, as well as afterwards, the apportionment depersonalized labor and depressed labor costs, leading to anarchy and runaway inflation, theoretically justified by presumed economic laws. Such "laws" were also used to explain the constant rise of prices in the country, both of the retail prices raised under the guise of numerous monetary reforms and the wholesale prices, i.e., procurement and purchase prices that soared after Stalin's death, from 1953 onwards. As a result, productivity started to decline, while revenues (in the nominal, monetary sense) continued to grow. It was only several years later, in the mid-1950s, that the Soviet currency lost its value, becoming almost useless for buying anything.

Khrushchev devised an ingenuous way of extorting money from the populace. He forced collective farms to purchase used and no longer usable agricultural machinery under the guise of liquidating the MTS (Machine-Tractor Stations), and then he "bought" the urban residents by stocking the stores with imported goods, for which he paid in gold and natural resources without giving a second thought as to their depletion. This tem-

porarily improved the country's balance of payments, yet failed to eradicate inflation since its prime economic cause, the apportionment, remained intact. After Khrushchev's downfall in 1965, the syphoning off of funds into the industrial and agricultural sectors was renewed on an even greater scale. This policy was auxiliary to the apportionment, and together they sparked soaring inflation.

It cannot be denied that the Soviet government attempted to curb inflation, but in doing so it invariably fell back on the use of force and harsh economic pressure. Thus, on two occasions, on the eve of World War II in 1940 and soon after its end, in 1947, enormous amounts of money, almost 50 percent of its total volume, were withdrawn from circulation. Store shelves began to "groan" under the weight of the new plenty. Yet this prosperity was a sham. The volume of consumer products did not in fact increase; what did increase was people's poverty. Indeed, it reached proportions so overwhelming that the government was forced between 1947 and 1953 to reduce the outrageously high prices. To be sure, gimmicks were resorted to in the process: the losses suffered by the national budget due to the price decreases were totally made up by compulsory annual subscriptions to government bonds. Thereupon the "black market" was flooded by yet another commodity, the bonds that were sold for 70 to 80 percent below their nominal value—a good indicator of people's views about the reliability and solvency of their government.

Nevertheless, Soviet people retained their nostalgia for the times of reduced prices. Their selective memory blocked out the suffering and hardship of those years, while idealizing the "consumer paradise" of no queues (cf.) and a wide selection of products, even if unaffordable.

The yearning for the times of Stalin grew during the 1960s, when various commodities began to disappear one by one. By the 1980s, inflation reached 20 percent while, for the expensive high demand items such as coffee, delicacies, chocolate, jewelry, shoes, clothing, and cars, the rate of inflation ranged between 100 and 200 percent.

Soviet people are in dire need of the most basic consumer goods, but they are unable to use their money. They have the means to buy, but nothing is available. The stores are empty. The unsatisfied demand has led to a uniquely Soviet phenomenon of money surpluses (*zatovarivanie*) in private hands. The Soviet population has saved up around 400 billion rubles—creating an illusion of general prosperity. Even if everyone did not work for a year, this surplus of money could not be spent. In fact, most people do not work; they merely give the impression of working. As the saying goes in the USSR, "the government pretends to be paying us, and we pretend to be working." This situation quite naturally discourages any inclination for honest work or professional self-improvement.

Attempts to stimulate production are undertaken by the government in full accordance with its principles. It makes use of that same allotment, i.e., distribution of the so-called "free" social and cultural services that have been first made unavailable in the market: medical services, education, and insurance. Their arbitrary and artificial "nationalization" results in their poor quality and inadequacy; they are free only in the sense of being worth little. This also opens up limitless possibilities of their abuse; indeed, these services are often dispensed illegally, in exchange for large sums of money. Nothing is ever "free" in the economy, everything is in recompense for labor. The so-called "free" social services are really covered by the surplus extracted from the very same workers who receive these services. Still, this does not hinder the government from claiming the role of benefactor, generous dispenser of concern and care. Thus, if there is anything free, or almost free, in the Soviet Union, it is human labor, which finances the services received by people as well as the services purloined from them for redistribution to the ruling elite.

The illusory free services are nurtured by the low remuneration for labor. In fact, this phenomenon is one form of socialist allotment that deprives the people of what is their due and rechannels it into the pockets of the powers-that-be. Yet it is not only the result of allotment but also one of its main causes, as it creates the basis for the widespread and all-pervasive system of compulsory labor. This results in creeping inflation of incomes, which leads to inflation of prices, which in turn requires salary increases, which again results in further inflation. Such is the vicious circle engendered by Soviet inflation. There is only one way to break it: by doing away with the allotment system and creating a free market.

A. Deryabin opposes the increases of retail prices for vital customer goods. He points out the possibility of balancing the budget by regulating monetary circulation, by decreasing the total volume of money circulated, which should effectively defeat inflation. (Nash sovremennik, no. 12, 1987, p. 158)

The first signs of inflation appeared in 1987. (Moskovskie novosti, no. 3, 15 January 1988, p. 10)

In view of the current economic complications, our attention is increasingly focused on monetary inflation. It is depicted as some terrible genie that has burst out of a bottle, which we are urged to chase back in (through what magic spells, I wonder) and cork the bottle. (Ogonek, no. 51, December 1988, p. 9)

Informal Group(s) (*Neformal'nye ob"edineniya*). Voluntary social groups that formed and exist outside Soviet official institutions and in opposition to official values. The adjective "informal" refers to lack of official status of the groups in question and to the fact that their activity remains legally unregulated. Freedom from legal regulation makes informal groups attractive to various segments of Soviet society; they provide outlets for self-expression, for sharing individual interests and tastes, for arguing viewpoints, and for promoting personal enthusiasms and desires for involvement. In a word, for much that the state curbs, stifles, and silences. However, their legally undefined status also makes the informal group vulnerable in any confrontation with officialdom and its "organs." The authorities can restrict or curtail their independence by intimidation or by cooptation. An offensive by the state against informal groups could well be fatal for the latter—by forcing them to surrender their independence and lose their spontaneity, i.e., all that accounts for their attraction in the eyes of a broad public. But there is another possibility—that the authorities might decide to tolerate them, begin to conduct a dialogue with them, and exhibit willingness to compromise with them.

The first postwar attempt to form informal groups in the Soviet Union took place in the late 1950s. On the crest of the Khrushchev "thaw," social life revived. Then it became clear that formal organizations such as the Pioneers, the *Komsomol* (cf.), etc. were too artificial creations to be able to provide facilities for satisfying the social and psychological needs of the masses. Their role was too narrow: limited to integrating individuals into communist society, regardless of the changing historical conditions. Whatever self-realization of individuals there was took place outside such organizations and reflected a strong sense of a "we" versus "them" mentality, a rejection of "their" ideas imposed by society and perceived as alien to "us" by many individuals. A number of the latter sought commonality with fellows with views like their own in a movement that suggested a reawakening of suppressed views and feelings.

The authorities attempted to "regulate" such groups that arose spontaneously and, by providing them with guidelines, channel their activity into safe currents of a "new romanticism" that encouraged searching for meaning via travel (within the USSR), exploration of interest in the world and in oneself, the development of the full potentialities of the individual, etc. Under the aegis of *Komsomol*, pseudo-informal facilities were established—for example, youth cafés or clubs and activities of various types, such as group quiz contests, meetings with interesting personalities, amateur song fests, etc.

But even at this time there were initiatives to move beyond such limited frameworks toward informal groups. Cases in point were the fans of popular balladeers like Okudzhava, Vizbor, Kim, and Vysotsky, or those interested in the past who met to discuss the Russian cultural and philosophical heritage. Such groups did not attempt to resolve social problems, but they contributed to peoples' mental emancipation from official ideology.

The authorities again attempted to provide an alternative to popular initiatives. In the early 1960s, they launched the Communard movement, an organization of senior students and workers, encouraged to stand up against "those who obstruct the building of a socialist society."

The majority of Soviet citizens remained indifferent to the Communard exhortations, such as class loyalty. More attractive for them were the values of personal love, simplicity, naturalness, and sincerity in human relations, which were antithetical to the officially espoused public-orientation, with its exultatory *partiynost* (cf.) and hypocritical demagoguery. Such personalistic attitudes were typical of the "hippie" movement that arose in the USSR in the late 1960s as an echo of a similar movement in the West. The bulk of Soviet hippies came from student and bohemian milieus, i.e., from the new generation of intelligentsia.

During this period there arose another informal group—that of rock music fans. Rock music, untraditional, emotion-laden, accessible, and striking a note of protest, continues to be a major ingredient of the Soviet youth subculture. For many, the informal group served as a vehicle for mental emancipation, as it freed them from the need to constantly lie, to perform in conformity with the dictates of society. Informal groups permitted them to breathe freely for a while, sharing tastes, views, and aspirations with others of compatible dispositions.

The split of personality, as manifested by the contrast between one's behavior at work, in the classroom, at *Komsomol* or party meetings, and antithetical behavior among groups of friends sharing common views and values, led to schizophrenic thinking and a dual behavioral standard. Under conditions of strict social control, Soviet citizens behave as required, showing themselves to be good, even "model" citizens, while among their peers they try their best to salvage whatever personal integrity they retain in defiance of the regime's best efforts to destroy it. Anything conceivable would be evaluated from mutually conflicting perspectives, depending on whether at that particular moment one was inside or outside of one's intimate peer groups.

In the early 1980s, stagnation of Soviet society resulted in the formation of a wide assortment of informal groups. As a rule, they sprang up in the major cities and immediately sought to distinguish themselves by their dress, slang, and special interests. In the Soviet context they stand out by their cosmopolitan orientation, noticeable even in the groups' names, like "rockers," "breakers," "pacifists," "metallists," etc. However, the similarity of these Soviet groups to their various Western counterparts is only partial since the former also have many indigenous features.

The structure of most informal groups is similar: a small nucleus of enthusiastic devotees, a broader ring of active members who support the groups's ideals, abide by its norms, and perform its rituals—and the more numerous circle of sympathizers loosely affiliated with the groups who, as a rule, are less interested in its ideology and more in its symbols. It is difficult to estimate the number of such groups in the USSR since in the wake of perestroika (cf.) they appear and disappear in constant flux. Some of the more popular or more notorious ones will now be described.

The "fan" movement (in Russian, the *fanaty*, i.e., fanatic or devoted supporters of specific sports teams) appeared for the first time in the early 1970s and gained much popularity by the 1980s. The purpose of such groups is to feverishly support their respective teams (such activity affords an opportunity for the release of pent-up emotions). Fan groups are comprised of attention-seeking youths who noisily parade before and after sports events wearing the colors of their team. For many fans the interest in sports is basically a pretext for having a good time.

Another very popular informal group is the *rokery*, or devotees of rock music. They are subdivided into several subgroups: the *bitlomeny* (the Beatles fans), the *khardrokery* (hard rock fans), the *metallisty* (the fans of heavy metal music), and the like. The membership of these groups consists mainly of high school, college, and P.T.U. (Industrial Training School) students; but one also finds older members, including young professionals, teachers, artists, etc. They distinguish themselves by their appearance, many of them dressing in the punk style, with their hair spiked high and dyed a variety of colors and their garb and even bodies adorned with metallic decorations such as pins, chains, dog collars, and studded bracelets.

An offshoot of the *rokery* are the *breikery*, the practitioners of breakdance, which includes elements of gymnastics or acrobatics. These too dress to shock: the high-style *breikery* wear dark glasses and gloves while their more "plebeian" brethren wear sports outfits. The bulk of "breakers" are P.T.U. students who are seeking an outlet for their emotional and physical energies.

Quite different is the attitude of various groups of nonconformists. They have a keen interest in intellectual pursuits, although its specific nature varies from one group to another. The older generation of creative intelligentsia believes that in a society without freedom the only place one can find freedom is the inner spiritual world, which should be cultivated and perfected accordingly. The partisans of such ideas shun all officially encouraged social activism and instead engage in a quest for true self through mysticism, religion, or drugs. They usually can be recognized by their long hair, beards and headbands as well as nonconventional garb with an idiosyncratic symbolism. They are prone to travel, their wanderings often taking them to exotic Central Asia and beyond to the Altai and the Tien Shan Mountains, where they may engage in meditation.

Another group of nonconformists adheres

to a system of beliefs and refers to itself as *lyudi sistemy* or *sistematiki*—"system people." Their declared goal is a quest for self-realization through spiritual liberation. Their high appreciation of literature and art attracts many young people, as does the tolerance that characterizes their attitude toward discordant views. The *sistematiki* also attract middle-aged and older people, including party members who are bored with the onerous and dull public activity that they are compelled to perform.

Close to the *sistematiki* are the pacifists who call for the renunciation of violence in international relations. They believe that the United States *and* the USSR are equally responsible for world tensions, since they consider that all political systems rely on force. Such a view, insofar as it is critical of the West, conforms closely to official Soviet ideology; but its parallel critique of the USSR borders on outright dissent. It should therefore come as no surprise that pacifist circles breed and nurture a number of varieties of dissidence. The pacifists try to stage antiwar demonstrations independent of those staged by the authorities for their own purposes. The more determined and radical pacifists refuse to serve in the Soviet armed forces in open defiance of Soviet law. The garb of the pacifists, like that of the *sistematiki*, differs little from that of other nonconformists. They too tend to wear long air and head bands and original ornaments, along with the near-obligatory jeans adorned with appropriate emblems. The one distinctive feature of the pacifist dress is often a backpack or canvas pouch.

In stark contrast to the nonconformists are the *lyubery*. This group has adapted to Soviet society and its dominant mindset so thoroughly that it has caused the authorities embarrassment, when Soviet society began to somewhat alter its profile via perestroika. The *lyubery* are "normal" Soviet people, intolerant of all views that challenge theirs, which they uphold as absolute truths. The roots of this movement lie in the official Soviet doctrine that Soviet ideology has universal validity as the key to understanding reality. The members of this group are righteous, at least by Soviet standards. They practice sports in facilities they themselves build. They neither smoke nor drink: they fancy themselves as ideologically "pure" as well. Accordingly, their goal is to "purify" society from elements pursuing ways of life alien to communism, e.g., hippies, punks, breakers, etc. They consider such categories a disgrace to the Soviet people. Not only are the *lyubery*'s attitudes very "Soviet," but so are their deeds. They engage in "preventive" violence against those who do not share their views. However, recently their methods have become too crude and impolitic for the Soviet authorities. In the evenings and on their days off, they leave their headquarters in a suburb of Moscow named Lyubertsy (hence their name) to go into the capital. With athletic skills acquired in their training in calisthenics, karate, boxing, and other sports, colorfully dressed in checkered trousers and narrow black ties, they proceed to beat up people they catch adorned with bracelets and chains, with hair locks dyed different colors or with shoulder-length hair. Their habit of ganging up on outnumbered victims also reflects the Soviet theory and practice of acting from "a position of strength." Another of their quintessentially Soviet habits is to appeal to public opinion: when they beat up a hippy or a punk, they invite passersby to admire the results of the "reeducation" they are administering. As a rule, their actions indeed receive the approbation of passersby. It is a common belief in the USSR that youth groups should be left to settle accounts between themselves: particularly when "correctly thinking" groups win over those succumbing to "incorrect" ideas.

The *lyubery* are so well organized that they can be suspected of receiving advice and support from outside. They are divided into gangs, each led by a leader. The prerequisites for membership are strict. One has to be an experienced brawler and only the fiercest and strongest "applicants" are admitted. No such group would be complete without an anthem. The *lyubery*'s runs as follows:

We were born and grew up in Lyubertsy
The heart of brute physical force,
And we believe that our dream will come true—
That Lyubertsy will become the heart of Russia.

Such songs sound familiar as an echo of the days of fascism. The *lyubery* could with justice be called fascists except that an even more full-fledged fascist informal group exists in the Soviet Union. Although little information is available about them, it is known that they adhere to the ideals of Nazism and celebrate the birthday of Hitler with demonstrations and acts of violence. Some facts concerning their composition and activities are also known. They often meet in places associated with Russian national-religious history, such as the Kazan Cathedral in Leningrad. They tend to wear skull-insigniaed jackets, mostly of the kind worn by the P.T.U. students from the ranks of which the bulk of these fascists come. Their activity has thus far been mainly confined to desecrating Jewish graves, making night raids on parks to commit acts of vandalism, such as smashing statues, painting swastikas on automobiles and house walls, and intimidating children and the elderly. They assume the names of leading Nazis, e.g., Hess, Roehm, etc. They write up recommendations for each other in the fascist style, noting "purity" of Slavic ancestry, social origin, and religion. Their ultimate goal appears to be the installation in the USSR of a dictatorship drawing its inspiration from the philosophy of Nietzsche and the views of Hitler. One fact of note is that many members of this fascist fraternity are members in good standing of Komsomol and yet have no qualms about committing acts of obvious hooliganism, such as attacking solitary passersby and forcing them to shout "Heil Hitler" or kiss their hands. Their systematic training in violent tactics suggests that these youngsters have benefitted from the advice of older people, possibly members of *Pamyat'*, one of the most notorious of the informal groups in the USSR.

Pamyat' (Memory), or, as its members refer to themselves "Society for the Preservation of Historical Monuments" (*pamyatniki*), was originally committed to the cultivation of Russian national culture, its antiquities, architecture, and the tradition-honored names of towns, cities, and regions. It began as an officially sanctioned group concerned with the preservation of the Russian national heritage. Among the actions sponsored by this group were attempts to preserve various historical sites and monuments. However, *Pamyat'* soon moved to a position of outright Russian nationalism, chauvinism, and anti-Semitism, which received support from a segment of Soviet public opinion, including from among the artistic and scientific intelligentsia, the party, the armed forces, and the KGB. The wide support it received was due to *Pamyat*'s clever adaptations to the shifts in Soviet policy. Today it espouses democratization (cf.) in order, its members claim, to disclose the real culprits, i.e., Jews, Masons, sympathizers with the West, those responsible for the setbacks of perestroika (cf.), and the "bureaucratic" and other "enemies" of democratization.

Such a position radically differs from the way glasnost (cf.) is understood by another informal group comprising unofficial publishing organizations that are calling for the abolition of censorship and freer access to copying machines. This group is supported by a large number of different informal groups concerned with a variety of specialized interests ranging from ecological groups confederated under their umbrella organization *Epitsentr* (Epicenter) to youth groups like *Optimisty* (The Optimists), all united in demanding freedom of debate on both domestic and foreign policy issues. In a nutshell, the philosophy of such informal groups is that all that is not expressly forbidden by law should be permitted.

The activity of the independent publishers has encouraged the emergence of dozens of other groups that have joined the fray in an effort to stir up the Soviet political establishment. The most active of these are the socialist informal groups, which maintain numerous discussion forums at which industrial, political, historical, and other issues are debated. Although not all these groups are committed to socialist ideology, they all utilize socialist rhetoric in criticizing Soviet institutions and practices. The most publicized action by a group of this type was the attempt to hold a protest meeting in support of the dismissed head of the Moscow city party organization, Boris Yeltsin. This meeting ultimately did not take place, but the initiative was much appreciated among broad circles of the capital's intelligentsia. Sensing public support, activists from the socialist clubs took to the streets of Moscow to collect signatures in support of Yeltsin.

The actions of the socialist informal groups represent a kind of balancing act: they recognize the leading role of the party while looking forward to "socialist pluralism." The latter aspiration may well put them in danger of losing official tolerance. In the meantime, their activity nevertheless establishes an important precedent as it tests the possibilities and limits of glasnost.

Under the conditions of an authoritarian society, all informal groups, even those concerned with avant-garde music or popular dance, necessarily assume a political character. In the arguments and clashes of opinion and expressions of conflicting values, one perceives efforts to reevaluate the past and change the present. Even the most reactionary informal groups display some rationality in their concerns, if not in the logic of their arguments or their means of action. For example, despite its chauvinism, *Pamyat'* reflects the desire of its members to restore the pride of the Russian people, while the fascist youth groups, albeit in a perverted way, are expressing their dissatisfaction with the existing socialist regime and social conditions it has created.

Thus, the informal groups are unique social interstices or cultural-political havens, where Soviet citizens, overexposed to indoctrination as they are, can seek emotional respite from official hypocrisy. For many, experimenting with informal groups eventually yields to social and political conformity, to being "good" Soviet citizens, good workers, or good professionals. However, at least some informal group members take a

different path—that of political protest, which provides them with a life purpose that in their society can be found nowhere else.

Passions flare around the so-called informal groups. The problem with them is not just their extravagant appearance. To that we have gotten used even if we do not approve it. Gradually one comes to recognize that the behavior of the "children" is largely due to failures of their "fathers" to educate them properly. . . . (Sotsiologicheskie issledovaniya, September–October, 1987, p. 56).

In Moscow and some other cities the informal group Pamyat' is increasingly making waves. (Izvestiya, 3 June 1987, p. 3)

Inactivity, lack of principle, formalism—this is why our numerous societies today are taken seriously by practically no one, neither the authorities in power nor the population. It is hardly surprising that alongside them here and there are arising various informal groups. (Komsomol'skaya pravda, 8 December 1987, p. 1).

Initiative (*Pochin*). An understanding or activity inspired by the authorities. The term "initiative" entered the core political vocabulary in the 1920s, when it was given a new lease on life by Lenin's definition of the *subbotnik* (cf.) as a "great" and subsequently a real "communist" initiative. Since then, the term has continued to expand to embrace such concepts as socialist competition (cf.), production obligations, the introduction of new technology, and so on. In fact, the word is an ideological soap bubble devoid of any real contents. Innovations promoted by the Soviet authorities as popular initiatives do not take root in Soviet society. Nevertheless, the socialist system persists in developing new initiatives, with *perestroika* and *glasnost* as the latest instances. In fact, Soviet socialism itself was an initiative undertaken by a handful of revolutionaries, which, despite its being at odds with much of reality, has managed to survive for more than seventy years.

The miners of the country have always been in the vanguard of socialist competition, leading the way in many patriotic initiatives. (Agitator, no. 14, 1978, p. 46)

Great Initiative. We have long been familiar with this all-inclusive formula of Lenin. (Literaturnaya gazeta, April 22 1981, p. 1)

The valuable initiatives and undertakings of the advanced workers are inspired by concern for the interests of society. (Izvestiya, 8 December 1983)

Innovator (*Novator*). A worker or employee who, in connection with his professional activities, introduces or adapts new standards, ideas, or methods that the authorities approve. A whole range of words was coined to refer to Soviet innovators during the formative years of the communist regime in the USSR. These included "shock-worker" (*udarnik*), "Stakhanovite" (*stakhanovets*), "rationalizer" (*ratsionalizator*), and "guardsman of labor" (*gvardeets truda*). Although each of these terms is characteristic of a particular stage of Soviet history, they all had the same purpose: to teach people to respect labor and to feel devotion to the party, which was supposedly so concerned about the development and improvement of production.

The Soviet leadership requires factory managements to provide ongoing reports on the activities of innovators. At production enterprises, meetings are often held to appraise the achievements of shock-workers and rationalizers. Even clubs and councils of innovators have been set up. Although innovation (*novatorstvo*) is encouraged and publicized, in reality it only operates on a superficial level as ideological window dressing. Innovators may receive wide publicity, but they have no real impact on the growth of labor productivity, or on the level of sophistication of industrial engineering.

The image of innovator as an exemplar is nontheless assiduously cultivated by Soviet propaganda. Innovators are portrayed as disciplined people with organizational skills who constantly overfulfill plans and norms and manufacture high-quality products, using all production reserves.

There do actually exist in the USSR many experienced, well-qualified, creative workers capable of developing and perfecting production processes. However, they are not looked upon by the Soviet leaders with favor. By virture of their qualities, they present a danger to the centralized administrative system, which cannot tolerate any individuality, orginality, or independence. Initiative (*initsiativa*) is channelled by the authorities into strictly supervised mass "campaigns" and is thus frustrated and suppressed. Officially approved innovation begins where real innovation ends. Far from reducing the workers' alienation from production, it intensifies their alienation; creative efforts are drowned in the noise of party rhetoric, and in the process human individuality is cheapened. The moral degradation of the worker is supposedly compensated for by bestowing upon him or her the honorific title of innovator and its concomitant slight material benefits and honors.

The scope of the concept of innovator is constantly being expanded to include additional spheres of activity. Some loyal, though not outstanding, scientists are declared to be innovators, and some writers and artists are also proclaimed innovators—provided their works do not transgress the binding canons of "socialist realism." Departure from these canons is considered "formalism," and its practitioners are considered to be guilty of apoliticality and lack of ideological consciousness. Thus, the concept of innovator in science, the arts, and industry alike masks a reality of ignorance, homogeneity, and dullness.

The innovators' motto "A personal contribution makes a collective success!" must become the moral norm for everyone's work. (Agitator, no. 14, 1983, p. 38)

The widespread introduction of innovators' achievements more often than not requires little expense and at the same time promises a significant increase in production. (Pravda, 25 December 1983, p. 2)

Intelligentsia (*Intelligentsia*). A social group disdainfully referred to in the Soviet Union as a social stratum. This way of defining the intelligentsia reflects not only an ironic, condescending attitude toward it, but also the hostility and fear it awakens in the Soviet regime. The process of the communists' alienation from the intelligentsia began immediately after the Revolution, no matter how much that revolution was initiated and carried out by the intelligentsia, which constituted the overwhelming majority of Lenin's party. The first Bolshevik government was also recruited from the ranks of the déclassé intelligentsia. Yet already in the 1920s, as the communists began to consolidate their power, Soviet policies came to be determined by those who were unfamiliar with and even hostile to intellectual endeavor— self-satisfied and cynical dogmatists. The party and the intelligentsia become two distinct and opposing concepts. The public mind was gradually brainwashed into forming a distorted stereotype of the *intelligent* (intellectual) as a pathetic, useless figure, plaqued by chronic doubt and hostile to the proletariat.

Citizens of intelligentsia extraction began to be discriminated against whenever they wanted to enter a university, find a job, or, most importantly, join the party. The latter worked according to a rigid quota: the proportion of the intelligentsia within the party had to be equal to their proportion within society. Thus, the intelligentsia was doomed to physical, intellectual, and, above all, political extinction. The modern-day Soviet heroes came from among the anti-intellectuals who proudly professed that "We didn't go to any fancy universities." The word "professor" acquired the sarcastic connotation of a useless eccentric out of touch with reality, while the notion of intelligentsia was customarily linked to the adjective "decayed" so much so that the two become virtually interchangable.

The process of distortion of the notion and nature of the intelligentsia in the Soviet Union was unique and far from accidental. The independent, free-thinking and freedom-loving members of the intelligentsia were a valuable, indeed an indispensible, asset to the Bolsheviks in their quest for power. Yet as soon as the latter achieved their goal, they began to consistently shoulder the intelligentsia out of the new society. The very integrity, honesty, and civic spirit that were indispensable during the Revolution turned out to be unwanted and even dangerous as soon as the Soviet leaders began to establish their dictatorship.

At first members of the intelligentsia were ridiculed, then harassed and intimidated, and finally, in their entirety, prosecuted. In essence, the political trials staged by Stalin can be described as reprisals directed against the intelligentsia. The numerous enemies of the regime, whether Trotskyites, "followers of Zinoviev and Bukharin," or "deviationists," were clearly prosecuted as representatives of the intelligentsia in various guises.

Members of the opposition were invariably presented as "enemies of the people (cf. "enemy of the people"), and in the name of the people the regime undertook to strangle the intelligentsia. Instances of mass purges and persecution of the intelligentsia occurred in the late 1930s as well, but they began and gained momentum much earlier. The first blow was delivered in 1922, when Lenin deported one hundred sixty prominent scientists, writers, artists, and actors from the country. They were branded as "fellow-travellers" of the Revolution, another derogatory and distinctly Soviet appellation for the intelligentsia.

The country lost some of its greatest thinkers, such as Sorokin, Berdyayev, Frank, and scores of others. The country's intellectual progress was paralyzed for decades, but the communists achieved their objective. The intelligentsia was intimidated to such an extent that even its spiritual and moral leaders swallowed their pride and offered their services to the new regime. Gorky was one of the first to break down. The man who so shortly before had denounced the autocracy with torrents of vehemence and rage suddenly began to justify and even eulogize the rule of terror. He was soon joined by Aleksey Tolstoy, Kuprin, and thousands of other intellectuals. Some of them sold themselves for privileges, others collapsed under the pressure of the communists, even going to the extreme of admitting their own social inadequacy and glorifying obedience and conformity.

Having lost its distinct qualities of moral integrity and passion for self-perfection and truth, the Russian intelligentsia in effect ceased to exist. It was replaced by pseudointellectuals, who were subservient and easily seduced into compromise, immorality, and even crime. This surrogate for the intelligentsia was formed and assembled by the Soviet system like a piece of machinery according to blueprints. Anyone found unfit for standardization and regimentation was shipped off for "remolding" to labor camps and prisons.

The intelligentsia is a social stratum made up of people professionally engaged in intellectual work. (Politichesky slovar', [The political dictionary], Moscow; The State Publishing House of Political Literature, 1956, p. 207)

Persons with an intelligentsia background began to face various obstacles when trying to enroll in institutes of higher learning, and were doomed to intellectual extinction. (Ogonek, no. 49, December 1988, p. 6)

Discreditation of the intelligentsia also took place earlier, but against this background it assumed the nature of a pogrom: the trumped-up trials of the 1930s were trials of representatives of the Party, scientific and military intelligentsia. . . . (Izvestiya, 18 January 1989, p. 3)

The old intelligentsia was replaced by narrow specialists who gained the official status of the "Soviet intelligentsia." (Ibid.)

Internationalism (*Internatsionalizm*). A major tenet of communist ideology and communist politics or practice that asserts that the fundamental interests of the working masses are the same all over the world. The theoretical foundations of internationalism were elaborated by Marx and Engels. Their creed was encapsulated in the famous slogan: "Proletarians of all countries, unite." In 1864, the First International was formed, from the outset committed to internationalism: a concept entailing class-conscious-

ness, equality, and the solidarity of all workers. The leaders of the subsequent Second International deviated from these commitments to the point of supporting the nationalism of their own respective countries. Subsequently, in 1919, the Bolsheviks set up their own Third International, the "Comintern." Nominally the headquarters of the international proletarian movement, the Comintern was in reality Moscow's tool for pursuing its global expansionist aspirations.

To conform to the altered goals of communism as a worldwide movement, internationalism needed to be interpreted as "proletarian" and "socialist" in nature. In the Soviet Union, "proletarian" internationalism refers to the identity of the class interests of the proletariat throughout the world, whereas "socialist" internationalism refers to relationships between various classes and the communist parties of socialist countries.

Epistemologically, internationalism is rooted in the Marxist theory of the incompatibility and irreconcilability of the class interests of the bourgeoisie and those of the proletariat. The theory maintains that the workers living in all capitalist countries suffer enough degradation and oppression, both at work and after working hours, to share the following political goals: the overthrow of capitalism, the establishment of a communist dictatorship, and the building of a classless society.

The political and moral doctrines of internationalism, as formulated by Marx and developed by Lenin, gradually lost their revolutionary content and came to be used as ideological justifications for the Bolshevik seizure of power. The call for the unity "of the oppressed peoples of the world" was sufficiently successful to mobilize international brigades to fight with the Red Army during the Soviet Civil War of 1918–21. The slogan of proletarian solidarity was used as a cover for the forced incorporation into the Soviet state of other nations through the medium of the formation of a "Federative Union of Republics." The independence of the Ukrainians, Transcaucasians, and Central Asians was suppressed by force in the name of internationalism. Later, Estonia, Latvia, and Lithuania were also annexed by the Soviet state under the pretext that "fraternal nations" needed to be "unified" in the spirit of internationalism.

Stalin's claim about the possibility of "building socialism in one single country" (*postroenie sotsializma v odnoy otdel'no vzyatoy strane*) precipitated the further ideological and political degeneration of internationalism. With the Soviet road to socialism being declared to be the model of "real" Marxism, the communist leadership was able to claim the unlimited right to interfere in the internal affairs of the communist parties of other countries. Some communist parties were dissolved and some were reorganized to conform to Soviet interests: those leaders who voiced any disagreements with Moscow were arrested and physically annihilated. Between 1948 and 1952, the KGB concocted highly publicized political trials in communist countries: the Rajk affair in Hungary, the Kostov affair in Bulgaria, and the Slansky affair in Czechoslovakia. Tito, who managed to elude such treatment by the Kremlin, was declared a traitor and a fascist; China for many years was declared an accomplice of global imperialism; and Albania, on much the same grounds, was expelled from the socialist camp.

As a result, the cleavages in the international communist movement magnified as various attempts to throw off Soviet domination followed one another. At the same time the international cooperation of Western workers' parties and trade unions was increasingly distancing itself from Soviet politics.

Internationalism is the most trusty principle of Communists' actions, and their powerful, battle-tested weapon. (Kommunist, no. 10, 1979, p. 7)

The essence of socialist internationalism is the sincere and conscientious desire for mutual understanding and trust, as well as a respectful attitude to others' experience, and strict observance of the principles of equality and independence. (Kommunist, no. 10, 1979, p. 7)

Karl Marx's internationalism and strict democratism are displayed most forcefully precisely where he mentions the oppressed and exploited peoples of the East. (Mezhdunarodnaya zhizn', no. 7, 1983, p. 13)

Intraparty Democracy (*Vnutripartiynaya demokratiya*). A formula providing for the participation of communists in the party decision-making process and implementation of decisions. The concept of intraparty democracy was expounded by Lenin, who elaborated its most important principles: appointments by elections from the top to the bottom of the party apparatus, accountability, a corporate spirit, criticism, and self-criticism. Clearly apparent beyond these formal stipulations, which were not altogether devoid of a certain recognition of the freedom of thought, was the aim of limiting democracy in Soviet society for the exclusive benefit of a single select caste, the party members. But the attempt to separate the party from society and to isolate it from social processes affecting the entire population proved to be a failure. The totalitarian nature of the regime had consigned the aims of intraparty democracy to the realm of fiction. It very quickly turned out that the communists can be as deprived of rights as all other Soviet citizens. Denied any legal protections, the communists were dragged into the terror machine and either mentally broken or physically crushed by it. So absolute was the reign of terror that even within the party there was no way in which intraparty matters could be influenced by party members. Personal opinions were completely disregarded and, in the staffing of party organs, the number of candidates put forward never exceeded the number of vacant positions. In the lower party organizations, it was still somehow possible to discuss candidates or even reject them, but in the upper echelons of the party the candidates selected by the higher-ups were always unanimously accepted and elected.

Party accounting and reporting came to be a mere formality. Speakers at party meetings were selected by prior arrangement, and the main lines of their speeches, decisions, and resolutions were fixed well in advance.

Criticism of leaders was completely out of the question. Senior party officials encouraged criticism only of their juniors or of those who had earlier been demoted (or who had died). Thus, Andropov permitted criticism of Brezhnev, Brezhnev of Khrushchev, Khrushchev of Stalin, etc. And thus it has been through all the years the party has been in power.

As for "self-criticism," it is encouraged, but on condition that it take place only at the lowest rung of the party hierarchy. There have been no cases in Soviet history of any public confessions voluntarily coming from the mouth of an incumbent leader.

The concept of collective leadership has also proved to be a failure. The Communist Party of the Soviet Union operates as an autocracy. The decisive factor is not the will of the party members but the opinion of the first secretary. He or she is always the absolute master of his or her district, town, province, or republic. "Collective leadership" manifests itself only in the unanimous approval of the decisions of the general secretary.

Neither is intraparty democracy manifested by "the activity of the masses" (*aktivnost' mass*). Right up to recent times, Soviet communists have remained passive and indifferent. All that was expected from them was their voluntary submission to the authority of the leadership in the name of ruthless "party discipline." Infractions of that discipline ended up in expulsion from the party and dismissal from work.

One principle of intraparty democracy, however, has been realized in practice, even if only under the threat of most severe punishments. It was "the unity of the party ranks and the inadmissibility of opposition and factionalism." The function of this principle has been to conceal, explain, and justify terror and massive purges within the party.

The apparent unanimity (or rather, unanimous obedience) of party members led the Soviet state in its seventieth year of existence into a deep social crisis and political quagmire. Life in the country is plagued by corruption and decay. Cynicism, hypocrisy, and apathy had become routine. The economy, paralyzed by administrative dictates, was on the point of collapse. As a result, the regime was obliged to reconsider and revise Lenin's concept of intraparty democracy. Soviet leaders resorted to more moderate and open policies: open discussion of candidates running in elections to party committees and a secret ballot were permitted.

This change, which could have been a hallmark capable of bringing about an overhaul of the entire structure of intraparty democracy, in fact did no more than refurbish this structure. This became apparent as soon as the procedure of electing delegates to the party conventions was raised.

Until 1961, there had been a rule stipulating that the candidate who gained the largest number of votes won. Then, in a tough intraparty struggle, Khrushchev repudiated this principle in order to please the party apparatus. In effect, anyone who received more than 50 percent (under the procedure allowing voting for plural candidates) was automatically elected. Of necessity, the size of party committees was expanded to accomodate all those who had passed the 50-percent mark.

In such an electoral system, the leaders—who never failed to receive more than 50 percent of the votes—became uncontrollable. Essentially, such elections amounted to a mere vote of confidence. This system still holds, even under Gorbachev. All those who receive more than 50 percent of the votes become members of the elected party organs—or else new elections are scheduled. In other words, party members are forced to elect the "right" leaders by attrition.

Nevertheless, Gorbachev's modest liberalizing measures sparked powerful pressures for democratization. At the party conference in Moscow in the summer of 1988, criticism of the Soviet leadership was unexpectedly heard. For the first time in many years, the usual surface unanimity of opinion was not apparent. The civic consciousness of party members, which now turns out to have not been completely destroyed, threatens at any moment to burst out of the narrow confines of intraparty democracy as practiced to date.

Much now depends on Gorbachev's perestroika, on whether it is a temporary tactic in his struggle for power and for regime stabilization or whether it really reflects a new worldview on his part. One way or another, it cannot be both these things at once. Or, rather, if it is both things at once, it cannot last much longer, because in that case one of them is sure to paralyze and in the end swallow up the other.

> The unity of the Party rank and file is to a large extent determined by the CPSU's tireless striving for the development of intra-Party democracy, of the innovative spirit and the activist commitment (aktivnost') of Communists, as well as for the strengthening of Party discipline and raising of demands imposed on each member of the Party. (Kommunist, no. 17, 1980, p. 15)

> The Central Committee's decree has tremendous political significance. This significance lies primarily in the help it has rendered to Party organizations in the task of reorienting themselves toward the goals of intra-Party democracy. (Ogonek, no. 8, 1987, p. 19)

> Measures must be planned and enacted for increasing intra-Party democracy so that all members of the CPSU may work in an atmosphere of Party comradeship. . . . (Resolution of the 19th All-Union Party Conference of the CPSU. Izvestiya, 5 July 1988, p. 2)

Isolated (*Otdel'ny*). An attribute used by the Soviet authorities to emphasize the singularity and atypicality of social phenomena that contradict socialist ideology. The scope of this term is quite broad. Since communist society is held to be antithetical to antisocial conduct, all instances of such conduct are portrayed as isolated phenomena ascribable to "relics of the past," shortcomings in the upbringing of an individual, the influence of Western ideology, or some similar cause.

In reality, the use of the term "isolated" conceals the true extent of vice and crime in Soviet society, where drunkenness, drug addiction, prostitution, vandalism, all varieties of fakery (*ochkovtiratel'stvo*), bribery, and pilfering are the norm rather than the exception. By labelling these evils "isolated" phenomena, the Soviet authorities seek not only to whitewash Soviet life but also to find individual scapegoats (e.g., incompetent officials or morally unstable persons, who either had fallen under the influence of bourgeois ideology/values or fallen prey to egotistical impulses) for the blemishes on the moral countenance of the USSR. Isolated cases by definition do not reflect the whole. If the Central Committee of the CPSU reports on isolated shortcomings in planning, the implication is that, on the whole, work in the country is satisfactory. When reference is made to some "lazy" managers, it is assumed that no one but them must be speedily condemned and replaced.

Thus, the existence of isolated shortcomings is acknowledged. The fate of an isolated official, who is blamed for these isolated shortcomings, is not enviable. He or she is certain to be dismissed from his or her position. In short, the practice of excoriating isolated phenomena is intended to leave the foundation of the Soviet system intact.

In certain circumstances, communist ideology does treat isolated cases as social models. Mention of the high productivity of "isolated" workers (i.e., "select" workers) is a case in point. Their achievements are glorified. By implication, their fellow workers stand rebuked for not having achieved the same high level of productivity.

The term is rarely used in reference to political life in the West. However, when the Soviets wish to praise the "progressive" nature of a public figure, they may speak of "isolated voices of reason" (in Europe) or "isolated far-sighted politicians" (in Germany).

On some occasions, isolated, in its more usual negative sense, is replaced by "certain" (*nekotory*), which in phrases like "certain leaders" (*nekotorye rukovoditeli*) or "certain party officials" (*nekotorye partiynye rabotniki*) is a term of reproof, meaning simply that these leaders or officials displease the Soviet authorities.

. . . With the aid of isolated hostile persons foreign nationalist organizations distribute among us anti-Soviet literature and pornographic publications. (Kommunist, no. 5, 1979, p. 47.

One encounters incidents of incorrect attitudes of isolated responsible officials to critical remarks in the press. (Chelovek i zakon, no. 8, 1979, p. 10)

The highest appraisal is given in cases when each person works at the set pace, and not when isolated workers overfulfill set tasks. (Agitator, no. 15, 1979, p. 2)

Itinerants (*Gastrolery*). Groups of youths engaging in antisocial activities. These groups exhibit many characteristics of organized crime: conspiratorial behavior, a developed system of communication, special funds, and a leadership system. However, they also have unique features, the first of which is the nature of their activity. Their criminal pursuits take place outside their place of residence and the location of their organization. They go out *na gastroli* (literally "on tour"), i.e., making the rounds (hence their names *gastrolery*) to many cities or resort areas having relatively high standards of living. A second distinguishing feature of the itinerants is their age; they are mostly youths, boys and girls no older than 18. They may be armed with knives, brass knuckles, and often pistols but rarely use them because, if caught *flagrante delicto*, they could be charged with armed robbery. Finally, in a curious reflection of their youthful romanticism, itinerants claim that their thefts are not thefts but a way of bringing about social justice by redistributing property in a more rational and fair way than is done by the state.

Organized crime or the mafia (cf.) in the Soviet Union quite naturally have found a way to take advantage of the itinerants: when the police or other law enforcement agencies begin to get on their trail, they execute a diversionary tactic by provoking gang fights between groups of itinerants at the clubs, discotheques, or public squares where they hang out. The mafia also hires youth for risky operations. They are useful, for example, for involvement in "wet jobs," which may well lead to murder, like bank robberies or thefts of goods from freight trains. The objectives and logistics of such operations are carefully worked out by the mafia chieftains, while the execution is often assigned to the itinerants. In the event that the latter are caught, their punishment is likely to be relatively mild due to their age. The youths are tempted by money, sex, and the attractions of an easy, debauched life. Their adolescent consciences are often not strong enough to withstand such temptations. Thus they became itinerants. However, much of the blame for their deviant choices can be pinned on Soviet society, its failures to practice what it preaches, and the vast gaps between rich and poor. Hence, in the main cities and the provinces, in the inner cities, and—especially in the new housing projects that have already become or are on their way to becoming slums—the youth gangs and bands of itinerants are proliferating.

The "organizers" who send the itinerants out on tour (and the latter often do not see the former) work very effectively in forming juvenile criminal bands. (Moskovskie novosti, no. 7, 12 February 1989, p. 7)

J

Journeyer (*Viziter*). A traveler whose mission is undesirable from the perspective of Soviet interests. The term has a sarcastic connotation due to its association with the aristocratic custom of undertaking journeys out of idleness or boredom. It is used to discredit both the person and his or her purpose. The negative connotation of the term is enhanced by the similarity to other foreign-derived Russian words generated by the suffix "er" (pronounced "yor") with derogatory overtones: *pozer* (faker), *rezoner* (sophist), *fantazer* (idle dreamer), *doktriner* (doctrinaire), etc.

Emissaries of the Soviet Union and countries allied with the Soviet Union are never referred to by this term. Instead, they are called "emissaries of friendship" or "of peace" (*poslantsy druzhby*, *mira*) or simply as "guests" (*gosti*), i.e., by terms that have the connotation of trustworthiness. Since Soviet policy undergoes rapid reversals, so does the manner of referring to particular personalities. Depending on his or her relations with the USSR and the fickle sympathies of the Soviet leaders, the very same person, whether a political leader like Tito, a writer like Howard Fast, or a scholar like Roger Garaudy, may be referred to at one time as a "journeyer" and at another as a "guest."

The latest journeyer, the Minister of Foreign Affairs of the Chinese People's Republic . . . is today arriving in the British capital on an official visit. (Pravda, 11 October 1978)

Among the journeyers to be found there were correspondents of the English magazines and journals: Times, The Sunday Times, The Daily Telegraph, reporters from the BBC and television, American reporters from The Washington Post, The New York Times and also their colleagues from the Federal Republic of Germany, Portugal, Italy and, of course, Pretoria. (Izvestiya, 17 October 1983, p. 3)

Komsomol (*Komsomol*). An abbreviation of "Communist Youth League" (*Kommunistichesky Soyuz Molodezhi*), the mass organization of CPSU youth founded in 1918. The structure of the Komsomol is an exact replica of the structure of the party. Like the party, the Komsomol is organized both along territorial and industrial branch lines. Primary Komsomol cells are established in factories and institutions, military units, and places of learning; they report to regional, city, and provincial committees of the Komsomol. The highest Komsomol body, the Central Committee (nominally a congress) selects a secretariat and a "buro."

The admission procedure has become formalized. Youngsters join the Komsomol in corpore, whether as grade schoolers or as members of labor collectives. Although positive motivation for joining the Komsomol is usually lacking, fear is an incentive. By refusing to join, a youth may forfeit later admission to a university or jeopardize his or her career. Membership in the Komsomol helps advance one's career, particularly in the civil service and, even more so, in the party. The corridors of power within the party apparatus are filled with those who, when young, were Komsomol activists; many are now ministers or chairmen of state committees. Leaders of the Komsomol (as well as of the party) perished in Stalin's purges before they could advance far in their bureaucratic careers. The first six Komsomol leaders met this fate. Their successors, however, were luckier. They advanced quite rapidly to the top echelons of the Central Committee and the KGB. In Brezhnev's last years, a new type of Komsomol *apparatchik* emerged with a rather obsequious and submissive character. It was then that the party tightened its control over the Komsomol even further via aging functionaries who were too old to make successful party careers but who were paradoxically appointed first secretaries of the Communist Youth League. It should be noted that two former Komsomol leaders, Andropov and Gorbachev, did succeed in becoming head of the Soviet Union.

With the ascent of Gorbachev to power, the Komsomol became somewhat reanimated. Like other institutions in Soviet society, it appeared to be affected by perestroika. However, it stood not in the vanguard of reforms but rather trailed behind them, obsequiously deferring to the party leadership. Alienation of Soviet youth from the Komsomol is still intense. The average youngster seeks means of self-expression in informal groups (cf.) of all kinds rather than in the Komsomol. The membership of a vast proportion of Soviet youth (more than forty million) in the Komsomol can only be attributed to their reluctance to consummate their alienation from it formally, after having parted with it spiritually.

> Every year thousands of young patriots, in response to the call of the Party [and] Leninist Komsomol are streaming into the ranks of those who are transforming vast areas of Siberia, the Far East and the non-black soil regions. . . . (Komsomol'skaya pravda, 15 April 1980, p. 1)

> In short, I believe that nothing of concern to youth should be permitted to be left outside the scope of the Komsomol's activity. (Komsomol'skaya pravda, 27 October 1983, p. 2)

> The strength of our Komsomol, the source of its energy and inspiration . . . are based on everyday Party guidance. (Kommunist vooruzhennykh sil, no. 6, 1984, p. 26)

Kremlin Ration (*Kremlevsky paek*). An allocation of foodstuffs distributed monthly to leading Soviet officials in addition to their salaries. The practice of allocating Kremlin rations to the Soviet elite dates back to the 1920s. Following the Revolution, Lenin introduced the system of wage-leveling (*urav-nilovka*) so that the salaries of party officials did not exceed those of a skilled worker. For many years, the communists did not dare to contradict the principle of equal pay, as once expounded by the Paris Commune. In a state based on the dictatorship of the proletariat (cf.), no one had the right to earn more than the workers. Initially, the only exceptions to this rule were made in the case of foreigners and "bourgeois" experts, imported to work in Soviet institutions. However, adherence to this principle proved to be impossible. To supplement their meager salaries, party and government officials resorted to theft and bribe-taking. At the same time, qualified professionals began leaving party and government employ to work for private employers.

Thus a compromise became necessary; the principle of wage-leveling remained but nomenklatura (cf.) officials began receiving Kremlin rations in addition to their salaries. During the famine period, Kremlin rations were distributed in kind, but by the early 1930s, they had assumed the form of monetary allotments. Top national officials received thirty-two roubles and provincial and regional officials eighteen roubles. Moreover, these were not ordinary Soviet roubles, which as a result of the inflation and commodity shortages lost almost all of their purchasing power, but roubles linked to the official price of gold (one rouble equal to one gram).

With time, the USSR gradually began to abandon the idea of income equalization. The salary of a leading party functionary, a high state official, a scientist, or high-ranking army officer became five or six times the average wage of a worker. Despite those changes, one tradition has survived. In addition to their salaries, members of the Soviet elite continue to collect their Kremlin rations in roubles linked to the value of gold on the basis of the same exchange rate (one rouble per one gram of gold) that was current in the 1920s! Thus, over and above his

or her basic salary, a high Soviet official receives credit with purchasing power of either two hundred or four hundred roubles, depending on his or her status. To add to the inequality, officials have access to closed shops (*zakrytye magaziny*) (cf.), where they can purchase according to their allotment from a vast assortment of high-quality foodstuffs at fixed prices and avoid having to shop in regular food stores.

> [They] get the kremlevsky paek, the Kremlin ration—enough food to feed their families luxuriously every month—free. . . . Old Bolsheviks . . . now on pension get their Kremlin ration at a special shop in a three-story building on Komsomol Lane. (Hedrick Smith, The Russians, New York: Ballantine, 1976, p. 32)

Kulak(s) (*Kulak(i)*). Rural entrepreneurs possessing land or commercial assets. In Russian, the word *kulak* means "fist," i.e., tightly closed hand, which is often associated with the notions of selfishness, greed, and miserliness. The coining of the term "kulak" was not incidental since in popular consciousness the success of farmers who managed to amass a considerable amount of land and develop it was evidently attributed to "tight-fisted" qualities of their character rather than to their industriousness.

The kulak class formed comparatively late in Russia, where serfdom had persisted until the mid–nineteenth century. However, it had already appeared within the framework of feudalism, in connection with the development of the production of marketable agricultural produce, and greatly expanded as soon as capitalism made inroads into Russia. The number of the kulaks grew fastest in those agricultural regions where enterprises employing hired labor were widely established. Gradually, the proportion of kulaks within the total population became significant: by 1913, they numbered twenty million, or 13 percent, of the total population. However, their economic importance was far greater than their numbers, as is proven by the fact that in pre-Revolutionary Russia they produced 50 percent of the marketable grain.

The kulaks were quite loyal to the Communist Revolution after the latter gave them—as to all the peasantry—what they demanded: namely the abolition of gentry landownership, effected by the decree on land of 25 October 1917. However, what for the peasants and the kulaks was the ultimate goal of the Revolution, for the communists was merely an intermediate stage. The latter took power not in order to benefit the people but to create a new Soviet man and a new Soviet society that would ideally suit their partisan purposes. In furthering these goals, they acted like foreign invaders in a conquered country, determined to shove communism down society's throat by whatever force and violence they deemed necessary.

Under such conditions, conflict between the kulaks and the Soviet authorities became inevitable. The latter demanded from the former grain, essentially without any recompense, first for feeding the urban proletariat, then for maintaining an army many million strong.

In 1918, an uprising broke out in the countryside. It was not only (and not mainly) the kulaks, who arose against the Bolsheviks, but the entire peasantry suffering from hunger and from the arbitrariness of the central authorities, who refused to provide soldiers for the Revolution. Peasant revolts involved a significant part of the rural population. In some regions, 40 to 60 percent of the male population took part, a proportion far exceeding that of the kulak population. However, the communists were not ready to recognize the existence of a war between the peasant village (which demanded the removal of the Bolsheviks from power, the convening of a Constituent Assembly, and an end to the "red terror") and the proletarian city. Such a war would have marked the collapse of the myth of the popular Revolution. This is why the communists began to refer to any opposition to their rule or dissatisfaction with their policies as being generated or incited by the kulaks. For this reason, the concept of the kulak has never been defined precisely by the communists. Even today, it still remains vague. Precisely due to its imprecision, the term became a

handy tool of propagandistic manipulation by the regime.

During the period of civil war (1918–20) and collectivization (1927–30), it was estimated that there were about 20 millions kulaks (i.e., ca. two to three millions peasant family farms), but by the time the fury of the class struggle abated during the period of NEP (cf.), the number of kulaks in the country turned out to be scarcely six to eight million—or just over one million households.

Whatever the fluctuation in estimates, one rule remained constant: "the enemy is the kulak." When, in the 1920s, the communists proceeded to a more liberal economic policy, the formula assumed the somewhat mitigated form: "The kulak is an enemy." This simple linguistic inversion was pregnant with profound implications as it presupposed the existence of enemies of the communist regime other than the kulaks. During NEP, the kulaks remained deprived persons (cf.), lacking political rights, barred from holding any public office, living as if on a volcano in fear of the morrow. Still, once they acquitted themselves of compulsory food deliveries in quotas determined by the state, the kulaks had the right to dispose of the remaining harvest as they wished, either by keeping it for personal use or selling it on the free market. This policy brought remarkable results: in 1922, post-Revolutionary Russia could for the first time not only meet domestic demand for grain but also begin to export grain, as it did before the Revolution. However, the Bolshevik party was not interested in a return to pre-Revolutionary affluence. It was not established nor fit to coexist with the people. It could exist and thrive only at the expense of the people.

The system required victims and hence the fate of the kulaks was sealed, since the communists saw in them the hated specter of the old world, the very symbol of successful entrepreneurship, which they had resolved—in the name of the welfare of the people—to eliminate by their Revolution once and for all. So in 1929, the party leadership moved from a policy of restricting the kulaks to a policy of liquidating them as a class. Within several months tens of millions of people lost their lives or were exiled. Needless to say, huge masses of people who were not kulaks were killed or exiled. Included in their number were industrious peasants, who by their hard work had managed to make a good living, or poor peasants, who still possessed a decent hut or a few head of livestock. The ostracism and persecution of all of them was justified by their being categorized as accomplices of the kulaks, "*podkulachniki*" in Russian (literally "proto-kulaks"), an absurd term, devised by the authorities for that purpose. Since nobody had any idea who the "kulak," let alone the "proto-kulak," was, the authorities could safely determine their number by quotas for each republic, province, or region. Such quotas, ranging between 5 and 7 percent of the region's population (although at times, in practice, even reaching 10 percent or more, since local party activists often wanted to exceed their quotas in displays of "Revolutionary consciousness"), then served as the basis for the area's "dekulakization."

From late 1929 until mid-1930, more than 300,000 peasant families, amounting to almost one and one-half million people, were imprisoned, exiled, or shot. Special instructions (of 30 January and 1 February 1930) were issued to step up the process of dekulakization further in the following months. Those who put up determined opposition to the socialist reforms in the rural areas were arrested and either executed in jail or dispatched to concentration camps. The peasants, who limited themselves to passive resistance, were permanently exiled to distant regions of the country. Transported in unheated cattle cars thousands of kilometers from their home, the exiles were dumped onto the steppe or rough taiga without food, means of subsistence, or tools. Some were assigned to digging ore or coal from ironhard earth, others to cutting timber or erecting electropower stations. All of them were said to be "building communism." They died by the hundreds of thousands, even millions, with the first victims being the children,

women, and the elderly. This was the first genocide in history directed against the authorities' own ethnic kin rather than against a foreign people. It occurred in peacetime, yet it was carried out by military means—by special units of the army, jointly with duly mobilized party and Komosol (cf.) members, implementing a carefully designed strategy serving several well-defined goals.

The first goal was to use the confiscated kulak property as a material base for the establishment of collective farms. The financial resources gained from the confiscations amounted to approximately 40 percent of the collective farms' indivisible funds. The second—probably the main goal—was to break the peasants' spirit of rebellion by suppressing the more enterprising elements among the rural population. But there was an additional goal: to deliver a warning to anyone who might ever dare to show any independence, ever disagree with the authorities, ever oppose them in anything and, at that time in particular, resist enrollment in a collective farm (cf.).

Stalin said, liquidate the kulaks as a class. The party, already accustomed to understanding communist newspeak well, interpreted the words of its leader as an order to physically annihilate them. And they were annihilated: the toll of collectivization reached ten million peasants tortured or killed by hunger. This figure is not an estimate. It was cited by Stalin in conversation with Churchill ten years after the event. Stalin was not ashamed to admit this, since the liquidation of the kulaks had crucial implications for the stability of the Soviet leader's position and of the system itself. Stalin could consolidate his power in the Kremlin, expand it and carry out his policies owing to the fact that he first crushed the opposition of the peasantry and thus gained a monopoly on economic as well as political power.

The liquidation of the kulaks as a class was carried out under conditions of a hard struggle against the kulaks who put up fierce resistance to the collectivization of peasant farmsteads, and against their direct agents, the right-wing restorers of capitalism. (Bol'shaya Sovetskaya entsiklopediya [The great Soviet encyclopedia], Moscow: Gosudarstvennoe izd-stvo B.S.E., 1953, vol. 24, p. 10).

As a result of the policy followed by the Soviet Union in restricting and eventually getting rid of the kulaks, their economic clout was significantly reduced. The proportion of the kulaks in the total peasant economy and agricultural production fell appreciably. (Kratkaya istoriya SSSR [Short history of the USSR], Moscow: Izd-stvo "Nauka," 1978, p. 227)

If the peasant preferred collectivization to the life of a kulak, if he was prepared to, and often did, include among the kulaks hardy farmers of medium means, if he approved the removal from the villages of the most well-off, free-market-thriving peasants, this was an indication that he himself was still in a pre-bourgeois state. (Novy mir, no. 11, 1987, p. 181).

L

Labor Collective (*Trudovoy kollektiv*). A group of people working together who are portrayed in Soviet propaganda as an entity endowed with an almost mystical aura created by their joint work. The activities of labor collectives in the Soviet Union are now regulated by a special law (enacted in July 1983) that claims to lay the foundation for Soviet-style self-management. Although this law is portrayed as being the fruit of a national debate, in which 110 million Soviet citizens (the entire adult population of the country) took part, it is difficult to imagine a more biting satire on communist democracy than the official accounts of the process. As the story goes, "130,000 amendments to and remarks on the draft law" were made at the "1,230,000 meetings" held for this purpose; approximately 0.05 percent of these were actually, even partially, incorporated into the law.

The law itself broadens the scope of the rights accorded to labor collectives, but on closer examination these rights stand revealed as nothing more than convenient fictions:

—The right to nominate candidates means nothing when it is the party that proposes the candidates for nomination;

—Participation in planning is a sham so long as it means rubber-stamping party decisions; and

—The regulation of the internal management of any enterprise is in fact done by the administration.

In effect, the majority of these so-called rights are actually duties. The "right" to implement party decisions, the "right" to enforce compliance with laws and government decrees, the "right" to fulfill contractual agreements, and the "right" to raise efficiency levels are all a far cry from real rights. Perhaps the most disturbing "right" is the one that makes it a duty to punish slack workers: to dismiss them, demote them, deny them bonuses or leave, or drop them from the lists of those in line to receive "living space" (cf).

The labor collectives are also required to cultivate their own gardens to supply their workers with food (and thus free the state of its most burdensome responsibility). They are also charged with sending their "foremost producers" (*peredoviki proizvodstva*) to study at secondary and postsecondary educational institutions, after which they will be required to return to and remain at their current places of employment. Furthermore, labor collectives are charged with promoting a counterplan (*vstrechny plan*, cf.) and, "when necessary," with "raising the question" of calling to account people "who have failed to fulfill obligations of collective agreements" (between administration and trade unions). Needless to say, "a question" cannot be "raised" except via the usual channels—the party bureau or local trade union committee, or the council of workers collectives, which is considered the highest organ of worker self-management and is accorded, in correspondence with the Law on State Enterprises, rather extensive rights and powers. However, the councils are headed by directors of enterprises and high officials; the heads of economic and social departments are seated in the councils ex officio as their permanent members. So, instead of representing and defending the interests of the workers, the councils became silent, spineless organs attached to the administration of enterprises, subservient to its will and controlled by it. The trade unions (cf.) were not without blame for this: perceiving the councils as rivals, they were not cooperative. Moreover, the struggle of the enterprises for survival under the new conditions of self-supporting economy (*khozraschet*, cf.) and self-financing could aggravate the conflict of interests between the management and council of labor collectives of an enterprise, leading to a clash such as that which erupted in late 1987 at the Yaroslavl Engine Manufacturing Plant where, at the end of their shift, the workers took to the streets with placards protesting the autocratic methods of management. Their discontent stemmed from the fact that the management, without consulting the workers, ordered them to work on most Saturdays. This specific case, however, signals a broader problem. The workers of this enterprise, as of thousands of others, are in a double bind due to the conflicting goals of Gorbachev's new economic reforms. On the one hand, the reforms call for active worker involvement in settling production problems; on the other, they leave the administration with no option but to rely on old methods of management that, in contrast to the new methods being hailed, at least guarantee partial fulfillment of production targets.

In order to create a semblance of democracy (and simultaneously to muffle public dissatisfaction), one of the articles of labor collective law envisages the participation of workers in discussions about the appointment of top officials. However, it also stipulates that their participation in these decisions must proceed "in accordance with the legislation of the USSR." Given the facts that Soviet legislation does not provide for such an eventuality and that it revolves around the concept of "democratic centralism" (cf.)— a concept inimical to self-management—this "right" is reduced to mere wordplay.

In respect to the "opinion" of the labor collective about whether or not to remove a manager, the law states that it must be reviewed by the relevant "public organizations," i.e., by the much-vaunted Soviet trio of party organization, Komsomol (cf.), and trade unions. It can be expected that common sense and the sad experience of the past will help the workers resist the temptation to take any advantage of these "democratic" innovations.

The Soviet authorities enacted the law in order to show that their economy is still capable of growth and development, that the Soviet economic model is not completely bankrupt. Actually, that remains to be seen since in the 1980s the Soviet Union has shown no significant economic development. Rather, it seems to be marking time with the same old problems recurring with the effect of preventing progress. If Gorbachev's advent portended some promise of economic progress, this promise has yet to be fulfilled.

> The labor collective is the main cell of our society. Here members are united by a common goal, with conscious discipline and a high sense of responsibility for attaining the objectives of the national economy. (Agitator, no. 13, 1979, p. 22)

> The cardinal task of raising the productivity of labor is the key goal of the labor collectives. The Soviet law on labor collectives markedly expands the rights of teams, granting them a much broader range of opportunity. (Agitator, no. 4, 1984, p. 3)

Landmark (*Vekha*). An event or occurrence in public or private life that is presented as momentous for the development of Soviet society. Ideological perspective may arbitrarily alter historical perspective. Thus a mundane fact of everyday life, for example, the milk yield of a Soviet milkmaid, may be described as a landmark in economic development, while an event as remarkable as the landing of an American astronaut on the moon may be presented as being not very significant.

The concept of landmark relates to a specific time reference point on a continuum defined by the Soviet authorities. When the term is used in reference to the Soviet state, "landmark" generally denotes a point on the road of the USSR toward a classless society. In reference to a person, the continuum would be "communist self-perfection."

The concept of the inevitability of the advent of communism calls for presenting reality in the most glowing terms. The term "landmark" helps in this, especially when accompanied by expressive qualifications such as "substantial" (*krupny*), "bright" (*yarky*), "visible" (*zrimy*), "heroic" (*geroichesky*), or "joyful" (*radostny*).

> The European [Security] Confererence and its concluding statement, drawn up during the meeting in Helsinki . . . was a great landmark. (Agitator, no. 6, 1979, p. 7)

> The highest forum [the upcoming Party Congress] of Soviet Communists will be an important landmark in the struggle for peace and international cooperation. (Izvestiya, 28 February 1981, p. 11)

> The concept of collective security that was engendered in our country in 1933 became an important landmark on the road to implementing Lenin's strategy for peace. (Mezhdunarodnaya zhizn', no. 7, 1983, p. 6)

Leninist (*Leninsky*). An appellation applied to any social or intellectual activity or goal that communist ideology holds in respect and considers significant. Like other terms derived from Lenin's name, such as "Lenin's follower" (*Leninets*) and (*Leniniana*), the adjective "Leninist" gained wide currency during the period when the worship of "personalities" was encouraged. Earlier, during the years of the consolidation of Soviet rule, the term had merely served as a value-neutral indication of authorship by the leader of the Russian revolution. "Leninist works," "Leninist plan," or "Leninist ideas" then meant quite simply Lenin's works, plan, and ideas, respectively.

After Lenin's death, "Leninist" began to be employed in the sweepingly broad sense defined at the opening of this entry. The phrase "Leninist methods" (*Leninskie metody*) typifies the semantic evolution that the adjective underwent. At the outset, the phrase meant no more than measures applied by Lenin. After the leader's death, it came to denote methods he "would have adopted," had he been alive, or methods perceived as being in the spirit of his teachings and actions. Subsequently, the phrase came to refer to methods considered worthy of Lenin's name. Finally, it came to refer to all conceivable varieties of methods, including ones

totally alien to Lenin, as long as they served the objectives of the Soviet leadership. Thus, lip service is paid to the memory of the cherished leader while advantage is taken of his name in order to enhance his successors' authority.

In communist newspeak, "Leninist course" (*kurs*), "Leninist policy" (*politika*), and "Leninist principles" (*printsipy*) refer to a course, policy, and principles that cannot be challenged, cannot be rejected, and cannot be replaced by any alternatives. There are virtually no limits to the use of the adjective, and there are solid ideological grounds for using it as often as possible. Official propaganda draws constant benefit from invoking Lenin's name to make Soviet citizens trust and respect the ossified dogmas of Marxism as well as whatever actions the party apparatus at a given moment decides to take.

Such abuse of Lenin's name yields handsome political payoffs. Anything done by the party is defined as Leninist; indeed the words "party" and "Leninist" are often equated. The history of the USSR abounds in instances where mutually incompatible or conflicting policies or ideas were both described as Leninist.

Stalin always disguised his aims by claiming loyalty to Lenin and by presenting himself as the latter's true "disciple and comrade-in-arms." Khrushchev also called himself and his program Leninist, while criticizing Stalin and attempting to change the structure of Soviet society. After he renounced Khrushchev's reforms, Brezhnev no less emphatically insisted on calling his own ventures in organizational reform Leninist. Andropov, while advocating and practicing Stalin's methods, claimed Lenin's mantle during his contest for top leadership. Andropov's successor Chernenko also claimed descent from Lenin. Gorbachev has done the same—by attempting to establish a direct Leninist connection linking him with the first Soviet leader directly without the mediation of intermediaries.

"Leninist" has thus become a universal term for anything done by the party or in the party's name. Named after Lenin are countless hospitals, factories, collective farms, and institutions in every corner of the USSR. There is a bewildering variety of items to which the adjective "Leninist" can be and actually is applied: e.g., "Leninist attitude" (*otnoshenie*), "Leninist style" (*stil'*), "Leninist norms" (*normy*), "Leninist comprehension" (*ponimanie*), "Leninist principledness" (*printsipial'nost'*), "Leninist friendship" (*druzhba*), or "Leninist knowledge," (*znanie*).

However, the most solid connection that has been established is the association of "Leninist" with the party. The extent of this connection is suggested by the verse of the Revolutionary Soviet poet Mayakovsky to the effect that "When we say the Party, we mean Lenin." This "meaning" was subsequently extended so that any invocation of the party would automatically "mean" first Stalin, then in turn, Khrushchev, Brezhnev, Andropov, and Chernenko, and now Gorbachev. Nevertheless, the party continues to be referred to as Leninist to preserve the chain of tradition and legitimacy.

The diversity of applications of the term "Leninist" provides communist propaganda with unlimited possibilities to create and disseminate various myths and fictions, the specifics of which depend upon the will of successive rulers and their tactics at any stage of the "building of communism."

During a difficult time for the country there appeared the Leninist slogan: work like a Communist (Party member). (Literaturnaya gazeta, 22 April 1981, p. 1)

History has strikingly confirmed the correctness of the Leninist idea. (Agitator, no. 23, 1982, p. 20)

Failures and mistakes were allowed in the organization and development of various kinds of social relations, [but] the main cause of deformations which made revolutionary perestroika imperative was the retreat from Leninist principles of Party and government life. (Druzhba narodov, no. 6, 1988, p. 193)

Life-Generating (*Zhivotvorny*). One of the qualities attributed to the teachings of Marx-

ism-Leninism. The term is used in such phrases as "life-generating source," (*zhivotvorny istochnik*), "*life-generating foundations,*" (*zhivotvornye osnovy*), "life-generating forces," (*zhivotvornye sily*), "life-generating ideas," (*zhivotvornye idei*), and "life-generating doctrine" (*zhivotvornoe uchenie*).

The term is used to portray communism as a creative idea capable of transforming society. It is a foregone conclusion that no ideas or doctrines produced in the West deserve to be described as life-generating. Instead, the products of Western minds tend to be described by loaded adjectives like "rotten" (*zagnivayushchy*), "sterile" (*besplodny*), "moribund" (*umirayushchy*), or "stillborn" (*mertvorozhdenny*), as in "sterile theories" (*besplodnye teorii*), "stillborn ideas" (*mertvorozhdennye idei*), "rotton regime" (*zagnivayushchi stroy*), or the like.

Can the capitalist system possibly resist the life-generating sources from which socialism draws its strength? (Kommunist, no. 8, 1978, p. 92)

The life-generating concepts of Soviet patriotism and internationalism have been increasingly influencing peoples' consciousness. (Agitator, no. 4, 1979, p. 5)

Science has become for us today the life-generating source of technological, economic, and social progress, as well as of the improvement of spiritual culture and human welfare. (Agitator, no. 5, 1981, p. 13)

Living Space (*Zhilploshchad'*, an abbreviation of the two words "*Zhilaya ploshchad'*"). Any kind of living space or accommodations: a house, apartment, room, or even a part or corner of a room. There are three kinds of living space in the USSR: state housing, cooperative housing, and private housing. In cities and towns, up to 80 percent of housing belongs to the state. This can be rented, but not bought or sold. About 20 percent of the urban population lives in cooperative apartments (*kooperativnye kvartiry*) and private housing built by state building enterprises with the money of the future occupants. The majority of rural dwellers and a small number of town residents own their living space, such as rooms, apartments, or small houses.

Many urban residents (including students, young professionals, young couples, etc.) do not have their own living space and rent a room or a corner of a room. The rent for a room or even a corner usually ranges in the vicinity of 20 to 25 percent of the lodger's salary.

Housing construction constantly lags behind demand, unable to catch up with the constant growth of the urban population. Thus a large proportion of city-dwellers continues to live in "communal apartments" (*kommunal'nye kvartiry*) that sprang up after the Revolution. The pretentious name "communal" (*kommunal'ny*) has a double meaning, as it refers both to shared living space and to the supposed social and spiritual ties between the codwellers. In popular speech, such "communal apartments" are often referred to in a highly derogatory manner by their initials "K.K." (pronounced "kaka"), which in Russian, as in English, is suggestive of defecation. As a rule, a communal apartment is occupied by several families, usually three or four, sometimes even more. Each family has one room, in rare instances two, while the kitchen, toilet, and bathroom are used by all. The first meaning of the term "communal" (shared premises) is therefore a reality, but the second (social ties in the sense of shared aims, mutual support, or common interests) is a complete fiction. Life in a restricted space where water, electricity, gas, and toilet facilities are shared becomes intolerable. There is no privacy and quiet; each lodger is under constant pressure to comply with this or that wish of his or her flatmate. Communal apartments are often shared by people of totally different social background, age, nationality, culture, and lifestyle. Under such circumstances, conflicts and clashes, not infrequently turning violent (the recourse to knives being more typical than to firearms), are inevitable. A comparatively low rent (which, according to Soviet propaganda, is the lowest in the world)

is collected by the authorities for the occupancy of premises hardly deserving the name of apartments.

Soviet propaganda, which asserts that the housing problem has been solved long ago in the USSR, avoids using the term "communal apartment" (not to mention room or corner), since that would reveal the acuteness and the unresolvability of the housing crisis. With deliberate vagueness, all kinds of communal accommodations are summarily referred to as living space.

The living space norm per individual is nine square meters. Anything in excess of that is either requisitioned or else must be paid for by a surcharge. Everyone whose living space is below the norm is entitled to more. However, the chances for obtaining additional living space are very poor. The waiting period is usually many years, sometimes even decades, after registration. Incidentally, the distribution of living space through one's work place or via local bodies such as regional executive committees (*rayispolkomy*) is proportional to the employee's "importance," with special favors falling upon party activists, the "best industrial workers" (*peredoviki proizvodstva*), and trade-union activists.

Members of the Soviet privileged class, including scientists, writers, artists, and army officers, are entitled to additional living space. As for the Soviet "elite," it is subject to no living space norms or waiting periods. Its members possess comfortable apartments, private houses, and sometimes a dacha (cf.), in the countryside.

In recent years, the ruling class has shown a certain preference for downtown private residences, hidden from public view behind the facades of high-rise buildings. Such an apartment is virtually a house in its own right, with two stories linked by a wooden spiral staircase and a private elevator, along with an abundance of rooms with fireplaces. Depending on the occupant's taste, walls can be demolished and new ones built, stone columns can be erected, and kitchen and bathroom fixtures can be exchanged at will. The rooms can be very spacious—up to several times the normal Soviet size. Such a residence can provide its occupants with unheard of comforts, but, lest it arouse too much envy, it does not differ in external appearance from the common drabness of Soviet apartment housing projects.

The luxury of the residences of the privileged class is a closely guarded secret, protected not only by high walls and anonymous facades but by strict security measures. Guards are posted. The identity of all entrants is carefully checked to the point that even mailmen have to show special passes. Visitors are ushered through a succession of guarded entrances, once the consent of a resident to receive them is obtained.

From the Soviet point of view it is quite natural to isolate the elite from the commoners. It is not desirable to mix social classes in the same apartment house. Apartments could hardly be shared, for example, by an arrogant party dignitary and a modest teacher, a famous writer and a journalistic beginner, an army general and a factory worker, people dining at a sumptuous table and those who must content themselves with frozen meat and plain potatoes, or high officials brought home in limousines and those who return home in overcrowded subways or buses. Soviet housing policy is therefore ideologically motivated. It instills respect if a high official is protected from the masses by high walls, or even better, by barbed wire and private garden behind it. It is hoped that the people will not find out how their leaders live, what they earn, or with whom they deal. Only without their finding this out can the illusion of a society of equal opportunity possibly be maintained.

In 1957 in the cities and workers' settlements, occupancy was taken of housing with a total living space of 48.4 million sq. meters. . . . This is significantly more than was constructed during the first or the second Five-Year Plan, and considerably exceeds the total combined living space of such cities as Kiev, Baku, Kharkov, Gorky, Sverdlovsk and Chelyabinsk. (SSSR kak on est' [The USSR as it is. A popular illustrated reference book]; Moscow: Publishing House for Political Literature, 1959, p. 275)

In our country 268 t of steel, 1.9 million kw/h of electric power, 232 t of cement, and 205 square meters of living space are produced every minute. (Kommunist, Kalendar'-spravochnik 1977 [Communist, reference calendar 1977]; Moscow: Publishing House for Political Literature, 1976, p. 56)

Despite the tremendous amount of housing construction, the amount of total living space to which each individual urban resident is entitled is growing relatively slowly. (Agitator, no. 10, 1978, p. 489)

M

Mafia (*Mafiya*). A clandestine criminal organization resorting to blackmail, violence and murder, known for its close links with government authorities, the public prosecutor's office, and the judiciary. From the Soviet standpoint, mafias exist only in the West, in particular in Italy and the United States. This concept has become entrenched in the Soviet way of thinking to such an extent that any mention of the term immediately evokes the image of the capitalist world, as depicted by communist propaganda, ridden with corruption and terror. In relation to Soviet realities, it is acceptable to use the term "mafia" in its figurative sense alone, in exposing its particular ("isolated") vices and shortcomings: influence peddling, protection racketeering, the pursuit of corporate interests, etc.

However, mafia, far from being a figure of speech, is a widespread factor in Soviet reality, sharing properties with its free-world counterpart. The only distinct feature of the Soviet mafia stems from the fact that Soviet society, unlike the Western one, has no built-in immunity against it. Morality is undermined by ideological relativism that places communist objectives above humanitarian or religious values. Ordinary social controls have been paralyzed by totalitarian terror and replaced by naked coercion. Alongside the political power hierarchy, modeled in its image, there emerges a parallel mafia hierarchy.

Since the mafia originated and took shape during the recent decades, it would be quite appropriate to view it as a product of the advanced Socialist period in the Soviet Union's development. Prior to the Revolution, mafias did not exist. Tsarist Russia did not manage to "evolve" beyond ordinary crime perpetrated by a vivid menagerie of picturesque rogues, burglars, con men and embezzlers, yet never elevating crime to the government level. The mafia was also nonexistent during the early years of the Soviet regime. Gangs of thieves and robbers may have given rise to a series of fascinating social (as well as literary) scenarios, yet they fell short of consolidating into organized crime and infiltrating the government apparatus. There were only isolated cases of bribery among Soviet officials, not because they were constrained by Revolutionary ethics—they had none—but because of the undeveloped character of social relations. The surplus product of Socialism was then so puny that it was incapable of supporting the growth of the mafia.

The advance of the mafia was also checked in the years of Stalin's rule. Mass terror and all-pervading fear prevented the emergence of "white collar" corruption, even though it did not hinder the rise and spread of ordinary crime toward which the regime displayed tolerance and even occasional lenience. There was a certain community of interests between political and criminal gangsterism, as best evidenced by the privileged status enjoyed by convicted thieves in labor camps. Employed as guards and instructors in penal colonies and prisons, they were entrusted with their inside management. Criminals were socially closer to the regime than any other elements who have fallen from grace, be they workers, peasants, and even former members of the power elite, from reprobate peoples' comissars to wayward commanding officers. This was because criminals were quite sensitive to the spirit of the Soviet times, adapting themselves and adopting in their own right the regime's inexorable laws and staying away from politics. Dealing brutally with anyone expressing "heterodox" opinions, they created the outward appearance of popular rule to the point of holding assemblies and establishing mutual aid funds. They, in fact, were the most independent people in the country, spared the hardships—unemployment, hunger, privation—suffered by the rest of the population, and facing no danger of being punished—in their own midst—for uttering an indiscreet word. The Criminal Code treated them with leniency: they were rarely given the death sentence, and they had a better chance of being pardoned than political prisoners.

While it was hardly possible to be enamored of the existing tyranny, one could find ways to turn it to one's advantage. Thus, as soon as the economy began to improve and stabilize, the country saw the first signs of the mafia. This happened right after World War II as a result of the Soviet people's first encounter with the outside world. Another factor that contributed to the emergence of the mafia was the new direction of state terror. The regime was kept quite busy dealing with the millions of its new victims—entire nations (albeit small ones, like the Ingush, the Balkars, the Crimean Tatars, the Kalmyks, and others), in addition to prisoners of war returning from fascist captivity. The government had no time for prosecuting economic crime. This provided the ideal opportunity for the mafia to surface. It was still undeveloped, badly organized, hastily knocked together; its separate links still in the process of spontaneous birth and chaotic disintegration, its yearly turnover measured by a ridiculously small (by present standards) sum—a few hundred million rubles. It became a nationwide phenomenon only later, after Stalin's death, in the 1960s. It was then that within the mafia there arose its first notorious (if not yet universally recognized) "godfathers," like Rokotov and Faibishchenko.

In another ten years, the Soviet mafia surfaced and openly proclaimed its existence. The plundered millions were no longer a matter of shame that had to be hidden away; they were not invested in multistory mansions, foreign cars, and valuables. Public money was openly and freely shifted to private individuals—to the underground shops, factories, and enterprises, which, in the guise of government workshops, manufactured illegal products. They also bilked the state of considerable amounts of raw materials. This gave rise to a new economic elite—Soviet-style millionaires: "*tsekhoviki*" ("shop workers"), the leaders and promoters of the Soviet countereconomy.

The ordinary criminals reacted to the mafia befittingly by intensifying organized criminal activity. Mafia millionaires became targets for attacks by groups of gangsters who burned their houses, country dachas, and cars and who blackmailed, tortured, and kidnapped until they were allowed to share the millionaires' profits. Thereafter huge sums of money began to flow into the criminal world in quantities it had not known throughout Soviet history. This immediately transformed the criminal milieu, giving rise to crime bosses who could now afford to keep large staffs of bodyguards and hitmen.

The relationship between the illicit business and the gangsters was initially antagonistic, but it ended in speedy reconciliation. The compromise was reached in the mid-1970s, at a joint convention that took place in the northern Caucasus, where the "*tsekhoviki*" agreed to "contribute" 10 percent of their profits to the racketeers, who would in turn supply protection and insurance. Thus united, the criminal world began to hand over part of their joint profits to government officials in order to secure impunity and illegal acquisition of raw materials. It was thus that the Soviet mafia was eventually formed, comprised of three separate segments of organized crime. First, there was the industrial segment, which constituted the foundation where multimillion-rouble fortunes were made and consisted of thousands of black market (countereconomy) workshops. This segment was protected from below by the segments of organized gangsters and from above by the party and government apparatus.

However, this structure was not immutable. The "top," not always content with the passive role of patrons of crime, would occasionally take the initiative and proceed to organize criminal ventures of its own. The party and state apparatchiki founded underground enterprises and formed gangs, skillfully disguised, vicious and greedy, whose job it was to buy and sell position appointments and procure and handle bribes and favors. Unwilling to be excluded from the action, the gangsters at the "bottom" were clearly dissatisfied with being reduced to the role of mere watchmen. Some of them demanded, and often obtained, a reassignment of roles, replacing the managers of business at the helm of the economy and dictating their will to the ruling elite. Corrupt government and party officials (and virtually all of them were corrupt), including the highest ranking ones, such as Politburo members Aliev and Kunaev, or the Minister of Internal Affairs Shchelokov, had influence only among their formal subordinates. The mafia boses did not consider them their equals. They looked down on those bureaucrats while paying them generous sums in exchange for favors. They often charged them with humiliating tasks. Even the all-powerful ruler of Uzbekistan—Rashidov—was forced more than once to fly to Moscow in order to settle some shady affairs, such as getting out of jail a *chaikhanshchik* (the owner of a teahouse in Central Asia) or a physical education instructor, who actually were "godfathers" (or, as they say in the USSR, "authority figures") within the mafia. The mafia makes skillful use of the method of stick and carrot, bribery and blackmail, procuring prostitutes for the leaders' offspring, corrupting them with drugs and gambling, seducing and compromising their wives. Such methods proved so successful that they were applied to Brezhnev's own family. His children and son-in-law (not to mention his deputies and secretaries), and possibly Brezhnev himself, felt prey to mafia entrapment.

Murder and terrorism are not essential operations of the Soviet criminal world, although they are sporadically resorted to, whenever deemed necessary, against anyone who tries to challenge the mafia. The power and influence of the mafia, however, rests on money. Enormous sums, amounting to billions of rubles, flow from the countereconomy and professional crime to the "special fund" ("*obshchak*"). From this fund payoffs are made to the police and the public prosecutor's office, and the salaries of government and party officials are supplemented. This fund is also used for the welfare of mafia members to bribe the administration of prisons and labor-camps, smuggle vodka to their inmates, support their families, provide medical treatment and financial aid to convicts after their release, and assist them in buying clothes and apartments. From the same fund there also comes money for capital investments in underground enterprises and, as of late, cooperatives.

Along with the changing nature of organized crime, there has been a change in the very appearance of the Soviet "*blatar*" (racketeer). Today, his image differs sharply from that of a suspicious-looking character, untidy and unshaven, with cloth cap pulled low over his eyes, a cigarette hanging from a corner of his mouth, and a switchblade inside his leather boots. His conventional appearance conveys a totally different impression: he looks just like a member of the Soviet intelligentsia—an engineer or a scientist—except perhaps being dressed somewhat more exquisitely and with better taste. He is polite, well-mannered, and dignified.

This image corresponds to a deeply transformed mafia of today, which resembles any respectable Soviet institution. It is now characterized by a stable structure, clear organization, and rigid hierarchy, with bosses (who, according to the Soviet statistics, number from two to three thousand), treasurers, and hitmen. The mafia also has a well developed network of agents who connect it with various levels of the power structure, such as the public prosecutor's office, the militia, the courts, the government, the party, and the economic management. It has even spread its "tentacles" into the fields of science and art. In those areas it quite measures up to the mafia of the West. It does, however, lag behind its Western counterpart in one respect: its international connections are insufficiently developed due to the tight controls at Soviet borders. Accordingly, it experiences some difficulties with "laundering" its capital (since the banks are a government monopoly). However, recently there have been signs of progress in this area as well. The policy of *perestroika* has enabled the Soviet mafia to join the international drug trafficking and created favorable conditions for legalizing profits from it by means of private enterprises, which serve as "fronts."

In conformity with the distinction indicated above between the three segments of organized crime in the USSR, the latter can now be described as functioning on three different levels. The lowest level consists of those criminals who have not yet gained access to the ruling elite. On the second level are those who have already begun to establish temporary contacts with the government apparatus, which as yet stops short of permanent cooperation. The third level is represented by cliques, which simultaneously operate in the sphere of government administration, economy, and the underworld. These are powerful groupings that function as networks, where the strongest and most advanced mafiosi oversee the activities of their various less organized and influential subordinates. The total size of that level of organized crime vacillates between three and four thousand. All parts of this network are governed by a complicated system of seniority, complete with a "table of ranks" defining the superiors and subordinates. Each part of the network has its assigned territory and exercises exclusive control over a specified sphere of influence, such as the countereconomy, prostitution, gambling, and various other rackets. Such units do not show any inclination to merge, although regular cooperation and coordination goes on between them. There has also been a noticeable increase in the mafia's involvement in political power struggles. Gradually, the mafia usurps the positions of the *nomenklatura* (cf.) itself, while the *nomenklatura*, out of vanity and greed, facilitates this process.

As long as the *nomenklatura* was in a position to take advantage of the countereconomy, and in this way to reap, by means of bribery, multimillion-rouble profits, it could afford not to mingle with the underworld. That situation changed with Gorbachev's coming to power. His expanding struggle against corruption slammed shut many doors of access to wealth. Forced to look for new channels for amassing wealth, the *nomenklatura* found them by openly offering its services to the mafia. The *nomenklatura* found itself even more dependent on the mafia when Gorbachev violated its customary immunity. This forced it to seek the mafia's support and protection, and the latter did not hesitate to use any means (including murder) to keep its faithful representatives in positions of power. In return, the *nomenklatura* showered mafia members with honorary titles, science degrees, and high state awards—and even promoted them to the key government positions. As a result, in many of the country's areas, regions, and even republics (Azerbaijan, Uzbekistan, Kazakhstan, Tadzhikistan, and the Krasnodar Territory), the real executive power passed to the mafia's hands. This "promotion" of crime has affected every segment of Soviet society, nourished by the growing unemployment, instability, and hopelessness of life in general. Each day thousands of Soviet people contribute to the mafia by stealing from others' pockets or becoming dealers, gamblers, or prostitutes. The most capable and dynamic of these, having sized up the situation, join the world of crime. With luck, they will start climbing its ladder. Those who are intelligent, energetic, and callous enough will end up managing the most crucial sectors of government administration: first the economy and then politics. They will then begin to evade any accountability and simply enjoy their power and wealth.

The mafia itself, unabashed and undaunted, is beginning to come out into the open. The urban scene witnesses virtual demonstrations of its power as in the luxurious and triumphant funeral processions of mafia bosses. Then, streets and squares are filled with thousands of people arriving from all over the country: men wearing light-colored felt hats, buttoned-up worsted overcoats, and white boots with high heels in the style of Chicago gangsters of the 1920s; the women wearing tight leather suits or mink coats. Hundreds of wreaths are displayed, and red carnations are ostentatiously scattered along the route. Upon observing such parades, conducted in utter contempt of the organs of law enforcement, the ordinary Soviet citizen may well wonder whether the authorities can find ways to cope with the mafia. Fifty years ago, no such doubts could have arisen: a few hundred thousand people connected with the mafia (and an equal number of innocent bystanders) would have been shot, and order would thus be restored. Today, such a simple solution is not available. In order to crush the mafia, Gorbachev would have to dismantle the socialist system itself, which serves as its ideal habitat.

> As recently as five years ago . . . a question as to the existence of the mafia in our country would cause the heads of Soviet MVD (Ministry of Internal Affairs) to raise their brows in surprise and smile condescendingly: "Have you been reading detective stories?" (Literaturnaya gazeta, 20 July 1988, p. 13).

> . . . Mafia chieftains do not limit themselves to the internal struggle for spheres of criminal influence; sooner or later, the firmly established "Godfathers" join, and quite actively at that, the political struggles. (Literaturnaya gazeta, 17 August 1988, p. 13).

> When such a highly-esteemed organ as Literaturnaya gazeta raises the issue of the mafia in the USSR, we do not mean to include as members of the mafia the persons convicted, even if on repeated occasions, for the so-called ordinary crimes, i.e., burglars, pickpockets, hooligans, muggers, swindlers, rapists, and so on. (Literaturnaya gazeta, 28 September 1988, p. 13).

> . . . At the same time the word "mafia" was becoming firmly entrenched in our vernacular. (Moskovskie novosti, 25 September 1988, p. 14).

Military Clique (*Voenshchina*). The military circles of a foreign state opposing Soviet pol-

icy. A military clique is seen as a reactionary force reflecting the militaristic aspirations of imperialism and exerting pressure on the governments of various countries to oppose communism and suppress pro-Soviet social movements. The negative connotation of the term is conveyed by the suffix "shchina" which in Russian expresses contempt for a designated quality. Examples are: *podenshchina* (subsistence on menial odd jobs), *oblomovshchina* (apathy, the term derived from the main hero of Goncharov's novel *Oblomov*), *lakeyshchina* (servility, kowtowing), *derevenshchina* (provinciality, babbitry), *dostoevshchina* and *eseninshchina* (two terms which refer disparagingly to the spiritual depths respectively immortalized by Dostoevsky and the poet Esenin).

The expressiveness of "military clique" may be strengthened by adjectives like "diehard" (*makhrovy*), "reactionary" (*reaktsionny*), or "reckless" (*bezrassudny*). Alternatively, the names of countries considered unfriendly to the USSR may serve as qualifying adjectives: e.g., the Israeli military clique, the American military clique. The derogatory connotation of the term is so strong that its reiteration in reference to this or that country casts opprobrium on the country itself, on its social structure, or on its national culture.

The top military figures of communist countries or of states that fall within the Soviet sphere of influence are never referred to as military cliques but only as "military circles" (*voennye krugi*) or "armed forces" (*vooruzhennye sily*). Predictably, the "armed forces" of the Soviet bloc countries are described as not being involved in politics, their role allegedly being limited to guarding unwaveringly the achievements of socialism and peace and defending the interests of "national liberation movements." "Military circles" are said to operate under strict control of the party, being assigned the unassuming role of advisory or expert teams to provide input into the political decision-making process, as reflected in the phrases "The military circles of the USSR consider . . ." or "In the opinion of Soviet military circles . . ."

Of course, this is far from the truth. Actually, top commanders of communist armies actively interfere in political life. For example, the ouster of Beria and the dismissal of Khrushshev and the accessions to power of Brezhnev, Andropov, and Chernenko were carried out with the cooperation of the Soviet military clique. Pressures from "military circles" also influence foreign policy and are largely responsible for the militarization of the country.

These facts make it rather hard to sustain the theoretical distinction between the military cliques of the free world and the military circles of communist states.

The UN General Assembly registered a sharp protest against the brazen acts of the Israeli military clique that carried out the aggression in Lebanon. . . . (Komsomol'skaya pravda, 19 December 1982, p. 3)

The American military clique is about to deploy intermediate range nuclear weapons in Europe. (Pravda, 16 October 1983, p. 5)

The perfidy and barbarity of the American military clique as displayed during the invasion of Grenada evoked a mighty wave of indignation on every continent. (Izvestiya, 20 December 1983, p. 4)

Mobilization (*Mobilizatsiya*). The activation of the human skills, capabilities, and creative potentialities of individuals and collectives and of material resources for the performance of tasks determined and assigned by the communist leadership. The word "mobilization" entered political usage from the military vocabulary. Subsequently, it became widely used in everyday speech in such contexts at "mobilization of the masses," "mobilization of the population," "mobilization of cadres," "mobilization of youth," "mobilization of reserves," "mobilization of all the toilers," and "mobilization of progressive forces." The term implies the image of Soviet society as a military camp organized by the party "headquarters" under war conditions.

The Soviet people are urged to display heroism and self-sacrifice in order to overcome hardships. Soviet citizens are mobilized, for example, for the "struggle" to prevent "poor harvest" (*bor'ba s neurozhaem*), to launch an "offensive" (*nastuplenie*) against the taiga, and to carry out sowing "campaigns" (*posevnaya kampaniya*). With time, the concept of mobilization has become a cliché. In effect, the term has ceased to be understood as a signal for prompt action; it now tends to be used as a code word signalling the political requirements of the moment (as determined by the authorities), which invariably imply an additional burden to be borne by the populace.

The very discussion of so many vital questions . . . has undoubtedly promoted better work at all stages of the agricultural cycle, as well as the mobilization of field and farm laborers in order to fulfil the tasks laid down for the 1st year of the Tenth Five Year Plan. (Izvestiya, 19 September 1980)

The main task here is reliance on the masses, as well as efficient mobilization of the activist ranks, together with all the resources and opportunities provided by the population. (Izvestiya, 2 October 1981)

The foremost task is to mobilize the working masses in order to successfully complete this year's plans and to establish a smooth rhythm of work from the first days of January. (Pravda, 21 December 1983, p. 1)

Moral and Political Unity (*Moral'no-politicheskoe edinstvo*). An idealized description of the relationships between different classes and social groups in Soviet society, implying the existence of a consensus among them. It is claimed that after the elimination of hostile classes and with the building of socialism, Soviet society is becoming completely homogeneous. Internal contradictions, conflicts, and clashes of private interests are said to be unknown in it. Moral and political unity is declared to have become the driving force behind the development of the state.

The doctrine of moral and political unity is based on the Marxist concept of private property as the cause of social cataclysms, of the split of society into hostile classes, of irreconcilable political and economic struggles, of national discord, and of massive impoverishment. Consequently, the abolition of private property through the expropriation of industry and the nationalization of capital is perceived as resolving all class-rooted contradictions and creating the preconditions of socialism.

However, there are inequities in Soviet society, even though their class nature is submerged. It is true that all the major classes—the workers, the peasants, and the intelligentsia—are not in conflict, in that they are equally exploited by the ruling party oligarchy.

The primary source of the contradictions in Soviet society is the relationship between the state and the people. The inhumanity of the former pervades the social and spiritual life of the country, including production processes, relations between Soviet nationalities, and interpersonal morality. The slogan of moral and political unity was designed to portray currents and movements of opposition as alien to the unity of the Soviet system, as mental "relics of the past," (cf.) or as the results of bourgeois ideology penetrating the USSR from abroad.

Such driving forces as the moral-political unity of Soviet society, the friendship of the peoples of the USSR, and Soviet patriotism have developed on the basis of the commonality. (I. Stalin, Voprosy leninizma [Questions of Leninism]; 2d edition, 1952, p. 629)

Today, we have achieved such a high level in the development of the economy and social relationships, such a high degree of moral-political unity in Soviet society that a firm basis can be created for . . . greatly increasing the material and spiritual resources of the country. (Kommunist, no. 15, October 1979, p. 24)

The bloc of Communists and unaffiliated establishes the foundations for the moral-political unity of Soviet society. (Komsomol'skya pravda, 4 March 1984, p. 1)

Nakhalstroy (Literally, brazen construction). Unauthorized residential buildings and barracks unlawfully erected on city outskirts. "Nakhalstroy" is a word mainly in colloquial speech. It is made up of two words—*nakhal* (brazen) and *stroy* (construction). The press and official agencies are reluctant to use it, replacing it with a more neutral term, with less of a deprecatory connotation—samostroy" (housing built on one's own initiative). Nakhalstroy emphasizes the absence of a permit for construction, and therefore its openly unlawful character, while "samostroy" simply focuses on the private initiative.

Both terms are often alternately used in the same sources, depending on the author's intention of which aspect to emphasize. Yet for all the verbal gymnastics, the phenomenon remains the same.

The word "nakhalstroy" has been derived by way of analogy with official abbreviations, such as *gosstroy* (state construction), *tekhstroy* (technical construction), etc. The term is old: it appeared immediately after the Revolution, when the cities were flooded by the rural population escaping hunger and unemployment and having no place to live. The outskirts of cities and towns soon were filled with unauthorized structures built in a slapdash manner from clay, wood, and pieces of old iron. These were typical slums, squalid and sunk in mud. However, since in theory there could be no slums under socialism, the existence of nakhalstroy has not been recognized. The lots on which it is built are defined as vacant. It is not supposed to exist, and not registered officially, even though these unauthorized residential sites of every Soviet city (with the possible exception of Moscow, the country's political showcase) are populated by many thousands of people—approximately 4 to 5 percent of all the inhabitants. Even if one agrees on a conservative estimate of 3 percent—still, with the urban population numbering two hundred million, one receives the total of 6 million people residing in nakhalstroy dwellings. Most of them are young couples (often with many children), who no longer wish to live with their parents, or new arrivals from the countryside unwilling to live in squalid, poorly equipped workers' dormitories. (The latter sharply contrast with party workers' dormitories, which are bright and offer modern conveniences and considerable comfort).

As a rule, nakhalstroy houses are not separate structures scattered all over the city. Rather, they form compact and separate urban neighborhoods or microregions. Because they lack hospitals and schools, the hospitals and schools located in adjacent areas are chronically overcrowded, having to accommodate not only the registered residents, but also the supposedly nonexistent nakhalstroy housing dwellers. Likewise, nakhalstroy housing areas have no stores, public transportation, or even taxi service because the drivers refuse to take the chance of ruining their cars on the bumpy roads. It is impossible to call a doctor or an ambulance, and there are no telephone lines there. Nakhalstroy housing is the scene of countless personal tragedies unknown to ordinary city-dwellers. A woman in labor cannot be taken to a hospital; a dying man cannot receive medical help or even a burial. To families without a residence permit (which the nakhalstroy housing-dwellers do not have), the cementery management will not assign a burial plot. There is no post office, with the effect that many letters and urgent telegrams get lost. Nor can people there receive home subscriptions to papers or journals. Yet the people bear it all. They recognize the futility of complaining: they are outlaws; they can be evicted or have their structures demolished at any moment. Their unsightly structures stick out like sore thumbs against the skyline of socialist cities threatening to draw the ire of the authorities. A rare outsider that happens to wander into such a neighborhood will immediately draw the wary glances of its residents. They may think, could this be a housing inspector with an eviction notice?

Occasionally, nakhalstroy housing residents gather the courage to connect water to their buildings and win the privilege of paying electric bills: a weak and illusory guarantee of their legitimization. The authorities treat nakhalstroy housing-dwellers in an inconsistent manner, sometimes ignoring them, sometimes subjecting them to lightning raids, complete with bringing in bulldozers and razing one house after another. Meanwhile, during the lulls in between the bursts of government activity, new nakhalstroy housing springs up, electric cables are installed, and roads are covered with crushed brick to make them just barely passable in inclement weather.

Like many other problems long left unsolved, nakhalstroy housing is being slowly recognized as having the right to exist. The likelihood of demolition of the supposedly "temporary" structures becomes more remote; they are gradually absorbed into the city and begin to affect its life. This still does not mean that they cannot be demolished. This may well happen when the master plan of urban development reaches the supposedly vacant lots. Although they have been long filled by nakhalstroy housing, so densely spaced that there is one family every few square meters, officially, they are still considered uninhabited. This is why the police, reinforced by bulldozers, may once again overrun nakhalstroy housing sites and raze them. The state is not obliged to provide housing or compensation to the homeless, and it will certainly not put off the demolition of nakhalstroy housing until its residents' turn has finally come to receive an apartment. As this overview has illustrated, the prospects and consequences of Soviet urbanization are hardly promising.

> It is hard to believe that this is still the capital. Such little streets run through its outskirts almost everywhere. The city people have a colorful name for them, which fits even if it is somewhat vulgar—nakhalstroy. (Trud, 19 August 1988, p. 2)

> Every city, especially a Southern one, regardless of its size and importance, inevitably reaches a point when it becomes surrounded with spontaneously erected residential settlements. The reasons for their rise are known—the perpetual, traditional housing shortage, growing worse from one five-year plan to the next, and inducing people to use unlawful means to meet their needs. Nakhalstroy is not officially recognized by anyone. The land on which it stands is considered vacant, the structures are not registered anywhere. (ibid.)

> In Sumgait [after the pogroms against the Armenians] the process has begun of clearing the so-called Nakhalstroy. (Vyshka, 26 October 1988, p. 3)

Neighborhood Profile (*Sotsial'ny pasport mikrorayona*). A dossier compiled on the residents of a given area for the purpose of surveillance. Neighborhood profiles contain abundant information on the residents: year and place of birth, nationality, marital status, and place of work. They also include personal information, such as type of work, interests, living conditions, and convictions and detentions by the police. The material is based on various sources: personal files at work, house registers (special logs for the registration of tenants), and information elicited from neighbors, co-workers, and functionaries of party organizations. All this information is included in neighborhood profiles, together with statistical data on neighborhood crime. Of particular importance are the data concerning residents considered dangerous to society—in other words, to the authorities.

Officially, neighborhood profiles are supposed to contribute to the "healing of moral climate" (*ozdorovlenie moral'nogo klimata*) of neighborhoods with up to 10,000 inhabitants. This entails the registration of individuals whom the authorities term "antisocial elements" (*antisotsialnye elementy*), such as drug addicts, hooligans, and thieves. The main purpose of neighborhood profiles is surveillance: keeping tabs on unreliable nonconformists or dissidents.

Massive surveillance and massive informing are needed to feed the neighborhood profiles with information. For these purposes, the services of an enormous number of people, particularly pensioners, are enlisted. They are aided in this process by the *druzhinniki* detachments of civilian guards, which assist the militia that operate out of special bases for the preservation of public order.

Neighborhood profiles are usually compiled only for large cities, since political discontent in small workers' settlements and rural areas has not yet flared up, even though antisocial behavior—hooliganism and drunkenness—is no less widespread there than in the large industrial centers.

> In creating neighborhood profiles, our goal was to go beyond the collection of statistical data and to obtain pictures of the social and psychological character of neighborhoods by observing and by talking with the people. (Agitator, no. 18, 1978, p. 37)

> In order to diversify the methods of reaching different population groups, Party organizations are studying the composition of residents, as reflected in neighborhood profiles. (Agitator, no. 12, 1979, p. 21)

New Economic Policy (NEP) (*Novaya ekonomicheskaya politika*). A complex of agrarian and industrial reforms carried out in the Soviet Union in the 1920s. The decision to carry out a New Economic Policy and its announcement at the Tenth Party Congress on 15 March 1921 indicated a retreat of the Soviet authorities from their policy of the immediate building of communism. Their plan to make "a great leap forward" into a communist society had not worked. They had not succeeded in forcing the people to work under the militarized administration regime in forced labor camps touted as "schools of labor," which in fact were concentration camps. The envisioned utopia became a society with mass hunger, peasant revolts, and worker discontent. The hopelessness of the situation prompted Lenin to admit the error of his four-year-long experiment in War Communism (cf.), which had cost the country millions of victims.

The transition to a New Economic Policy was dictated by the low productivity of forced labor, which led the authorities to search out new paths to a classless society: material incentives and the differential pay scales in proportion to the amount and quality of one's work.

The first measures of the New Economic Policy were in agriculture. The forced deliveries of agricultural products (which in practice meant their requisitioning from the peasants) were replaced by a tax in kind. In fact, what was at issue was not the total magnitude of the state's share, which approximately corresponded to previous amounts taken (in grain, the total was 240 million poods annually), but the alleviation of the arbitrariness of forced expropriation. Taxation meant the existence of impersonal norms, above which the peasants were allowed to sell or use themselves whatever remained after the tax was collected.

The introduction of the New Economic Policy was an adaptation to circumstances. The disasters caused by War Communism forced Lenin to take a "step backward" to cope with reality. Communist ideas, which had been the only ones voiced in public in the Soviet republic since 1917, lost their monopoly. The new policy opened vistas for some forms of capitalism. Small- and medium-sized industries were reprivatized, private trade was permitted and it was revived. Soviet citizens gained the opportunity to do "comparative shopping," to choose between the goods of the state or those of a private entrepreneur.

Money came back into wide circulation, and the previous class structure was partially restored, with the existence of capitalists (*nepmany*, *kuptsy*), and peasants—the wealthy ones (*kulaki*), well-off ones (*serednyaki*), and poor ones (*batraki*), as well as workers, employees in Soviet institutions, and a new intelligentsia composed of members of both the former intelligentsia and new Soviet technocrats. In Soviet cities, gambling and auctions indicated that a wealthy class had emerged as did automobiles and horse-drawn carriages, carrying people in fur coats and jewelry.

Remembering a means of protest they had practised in the recent tsarist past, workers attempted to strike. Waves of discontent and unrest swept the country, particularly affecting the peasantry. In short, there was a spontaneous, uncontrolled drive to restore pluralism in the country. There was, however, one surprise: the proletariat, which was supposed to be the carrier of the Revolution, became marginal to the point of near-extinction, when heavy industry was virtually destroyed. The Communist party, after finding itself in the position of the vanguard of a hardly-existing class, became the vanguard of the party bureaucracy, that is, of a creation of its own making. Still, the economy was developing. In 1922–23, for the first time since 1917, the country was not only able to meet domestic demand for grain, but could also begin exporting it. At the same time plentiful supplies of food and goods appeared in the stores.

Another portent of the times was the simultaneous liberalization of the economy and the frightful police terror: the New Economic Policy and the CheKa (the secret police, now known as the KGB) were like the magnetic poles of the period. Entrepreneurs had opportunities to make money and things to spend it on, but they lived in fear from day to day as they were denied basic human rights. (This is the origin of the term *lishentsy*—which meant those [thus] deprived.) Yet hope sprang eternal that the already incipient stage of revolution heralded a coexistence of communism with capitalism that might be turbulent but would still allow private enterprise to survive.

In 1923, industrial enterprises, spurred by the desire for profit, raised the prices for their goods. A disproportion (referred to in Russian as *nozhnitsy*—"scissors") arose between their prices and the prices of agricultural products. The authorities sought to solve this problem by calling on the peasants to "enrich themselves"—another slogan of the New Economic Policy. Thereupon the area of land under cultivation rose dramatically, by 1924 reaching 80 percent of the prewar level. Industry also grew, although not as much as the leaders hoped. However, growth was still impressive, particularly in small industry which did not require major capital investment.

Yet another problem cropped up at this time. In the course of the New Economic Policy, unemployment increased by a factor of eight, from 150,000 in 1921 to 1,200,000 in 1927.

On the crest of the New Economic Policy, the prohibition of alcohol (the "dry law") was repealed and state monopoly of the production and sale of alcoholic beverages was established. Apparently, Stalin's reasoning went as follows: if the masses can't be supplied with sufficient food, they at least should be provided with sufficient drink. This was one consideration for repealing the prohibition. Another was that the state desperately needed whatever money the population had managed to amass. Here, another gem of Stalin's "Revolutionary" logic was invoked: bondage of the masses to alcohol was preferable to the bondage of the state to foreign capital.

To summarize—there were drawbacks, but the successes of the New Economic Policy were undeniable. It facilitated the revival of the economy ravaged by war and revolution, and it provided food to the people.

However, these were not the communists' goals. Their Revolution was not for the sake of such goals, but for the sake of a new society totally subordinated to their will. To justify their hopes, they needed a new brand of humanity, obedient, submissive, and malleable. Having made their putsch in the name of a Revolutionary class, which did not exist, the Bolsheviks needed to form a new class. For this purpose, they had to first renounce the New Economic Policy, which had outlived its utility and thereby had to be liquidated. From 1926 onward, the New Economic Policy began to be gradually stifled. Its days were numbered. The system created by force could not be reconciled with normality. It could not dispense with intimidation and terror. In a crisis, it could put aside such methods for a while, but it was bound to reemploy them as soon as the crisis had passed. The Soviet ruling apparat was unsuitable for functioning under conditions of social peace as opposed to those of civil war. During the New Economic Policy, this apparat became paralyzed by corruption and dissipation. In order to save this bureaucracy and itself along with it, the communist government reverted to the use of violence.

From then on, violence would be the trump card in the big game played out to establish a communist society. The period of courting the popular masses was over.

In order to accelerate progress toward socialism, the party resolved to send thousands of party members to the countryside. Their assignment was to force the peasantry to join collective farms and, in the process, to requisition grain. They searched for grain just as they did during War Communism, smashing walls, breaking into cellars, vandalizing, and burning down peasant huts. This took place in 1929. In December of that year, the New Economic Policy was officially declared defunct. Soviet history moved back to its accustomed track of terror and violence that it would maintain until its next digression into liberalization.

> . . . new economic policy was a special policy of the Soviet state in the transitional period from capitalism to socialism. It was intended to strengthen the economic unity of the working class and the peasantry, to provide both with material incentives for developing the economy, to allow a limited degree of capitalism while preserving the commanding heights of the economy in the hands of the proletarian state. (Kratkaya istoriya SSSR [Short history of the USSR], part 2, p. 142. Moscow: Izd. "Nauka," 1978.)

The transition of the country onto the path of new economic policy was basically achieved during the period between the Xth and XIth Party Congresses when the administrative apparatus was reorganized and industry shifted to a self-supporting basis. (Sovetskaya istoricheskaya entsiklopediya [Soviet historical encyclopedia], vol. 10, Moscow: Izd. "Sovetskaya entsiklopediya," 1967, p. 262.)

> New economic policy marked a sharp break with the immediate past. It was a kind of revolution in economic thinking. For the first time the question was directly posed: what should a socialist economy be like not under extraordinary, but under normal conditions of human existence? (Novy mir, no. 6, 1987, p. 143.)

New Political Thinking (*Novoe politicheskoe myshlenie*). Soviet foreign policy doctrine derived from the assumption that the world is single, integral, and indivisible. New political thinking is based on a critical reassessment of the Soviet Union's role in today's world, which recognizes that Soviet options are not unlimited. New political thinking overturns a number of previously "infallible" tenets of communist faith, such as the possibility of surviving a nuclear war, nuclear intimidation, the relation of force and revolution and struggle rather than coexistence.

What is being proposed is to place at the center of international relations a principle that is quite close to that of Christian ethics and to the categorical imperative of Kant— that of relating to the needs and interests of other states (and their citizens) as if they were one's own. The doctrine that rests on such foundations appears compelling but is not free of inner contradictions. It implies that all political and ideological problems of the contemporary world can be solved by peaceful means. No conceivable social or economic conflicts can justify the recourse to armed force. What their solution requires, instead, is open-minded thinking, searching for alternatives, and sober, realistic assessment of the dynamics of international relations. The doctrine calls for rationalism in foreign policy: for determining the real bones of contention, the "basic links" (in Lenin's terms) in interstate conflicts, and addressing them without preconceptions. The purpose of this rationality is to save "all humanity" from the dangers of confrontation and the arms race.

The new approach to international relations does not mark any change in the essential features of Soviet foreign policy. What has changed is merely Soviet rhetoric. New political thinking is thus not a new Soviet policy but merely a new philosophical wrapping for the old policy: one resting on the notion of class struggle. It merely replaces an offensive rhetoric of class struggle with a milder, more civilized rhetoric.

Most of the concepts on which new political thinking is based are too abstract to be understood by the Soviet leaders in all their implications. History has mocked their unsuccessful attempts to direct its course: hence, against its will, the Soviet leadership has been forced to renounce many of its previously cherished views. It was compelled, for example, to revise its evaluation of the capitalist system, by admitting, pace Marx, that it has not lost its viability. Likewise, the timetable for world revolution had to be indefinitely postponed. Although the Third World is in ferment, it appears to be in no hurry to model itself on communist experience. Nor does the Soviet Union have any reason to be sanguine about the socialist camp, where disunity prevails. All this has encouraged Gorbachev to work out a new strategy. Hence the new political thinking, and hence its pithy slogans, such as:

—In the nuclear age the very survival of humanity can no longer be taken for granted.
—Nuclear war cannot be won.
—Foreign policy can no longer be pursued from imperial positions.
—Ways of thinking and ways of acting must be based on a rejection of the resort to force.
—International relations must be humanized.
—Security cannot be achieved by military means.
—Security is indivisible.
—The advanced countries must elaborate and support joint programs of development.

—Military doctrines must be defensive only.
—Political positions must be freed from ideological intolerance.

However, this version of the Ten Commandments, according to Gorbachev, is not all that there is to new political thinking. Occasionally, one also hears exhortations about the need for transcending the interests of the "systems," represented by the two superpowers. The most interesting of these is the claimed priority of the interests of all humanity over class interests. This clashes with Marxism, which since its beginnings has stressed class conflict and viewed all progress as dependent on the struggle of the working class, which was destined to free itself and, in so doing, free all mankind from exploitation. New political thinking finds that this Marxist teaching has been rendered suspect by the threat of nuclear war, and it revises it accordingly.

The position of new political thinking on the interrelationship between war and revolution does not jibe well with Marxism either. New political thinking refuses to see war as a fuse for revolution, and instead conditions prospects for social progress on success in establishing global peace. The causal link between war and revolution, strong in classical Marxism, is hereby weakened. This, however, does not finally resolve the problem, but only postpones it until such time as the Soviet Union catches up economically with the West. Then, the causal link will reappear.

New political thinking does not apply to the underdeveloped and developing regions of the world. The special conditions of the nuclear age do not obtain there. In that part of the world, new political thinking anticipates the possibility (and occasionally even the necessity) of encouraging revolutions by force.

In this respect, Western Europe and the United States are another matter, since any conflict there has a clear potential of developing into a global one. In relation to these, the Soviet Union is prepared to renounce (at least temporarily) the image of the implacable enemy, which during its seventy years proved to be highly serviceable in justifying the huge Soviet military buildup and in explaining away the social and economic chaos in the USSR. Yet the USSR requires an "enemy" to hold itself together: if none is obvious, one has to be uncovered. For a while, this can be an "internal" enemy such as corruption, drug addiction, or alcoholism—i.e., the phenomena currently spotlighted as barriers to perestroika (cf.). But when perestroika fails, or at least when its failure can no longer be concealed, scapegoats will have to be found abroad, since finding them at home would amount to admitting that the system is unreformable. The West may well be cast into the role of the "bad guy."

In the meanwhile, the Soviet leadership has inferiority feelings toward the West. Hence its bid to obtain Western support and approval as tokens of recognition of the "rightness" of its new political course. In his desire to please the West, Gorbachev is presently promising to follow the principles of new political thinking. However, he fails to realize that principles of thinking are neither old nor new, that in fact they are timeless. What can and must be new are assessments of current conditions that the Soviet leadership still continue to view in terms of antiquated concepts and formulas. What is new is their flexibility, their shrewd mode of coping with today's problems, which serves their political interests well.

> The fundamental principle of new political thinking is simple: nuclear war can not be a means of achieving any conceivable political, economic, or ideological goals. (M. S. Gorbachev, Perestroika i novoe myshlenie dlya nashey strany i vsego mira, [Perestroika and new thinking for our country and the whole world], Moscow: Izd. politicheskoy literatury, 1987, p. 143).

> The need for new ways of political thinking also stems from the fact that too many of the old ways of thinking are not only unacceptable today but also dangerous in the extreme. (Sotsiologicheskie issledovaniya, no. 3, 1986, p. 5).

Next Generation of Communists (*Kommunisticheskaya smena*). A term for Soviet youth that is indicative of the hopes and intentions of the authorities. The phrase "the next generation of communists," used constantly to refer to young Soviet citizens, seeks to bridge the Soviet generation gap with the cement of communist ideology. It portrays Soviet youth as the inheritors of a predetermined future, which is taken for granted to be communist. There are, however, a number of factors that work to pull these young people away from the future planned for them.

There is considerable resentment among the youth that, despite a prolonged adolescence spent as disciples of the party and Komsomol and lengthy vocational and ideological training, much of their training turns out to have been out-of-date or irrelevant. Few prestigious positions are available to them, and advancement is slow.

The long training period gives Soviet youth an opportunity to form strong interpersonal bonds with each other. Adult influence is minimal, and even the Komsomol has little success in reaching the young. Thus teenagers in the Soviet Union, as elsewhere, turn to their own peer group for a social milieu free of hypocrisy and cant, with the frequent result that alternative subcultures surface whose values are at odds with communist society at large. Programmed, in essense, to be robots, many young people turn away in revulsion from the propagandistic platitudes of those in positions of authority and seek alternative affiliations or life-styles to express their individuality and creativity. The best and boldest of them join dissident groups, while others find their way to the criminal underground. Interestingly, in this respect there is much in common between working-class youth and the privileged offspring of the ruling class, despite the latter's affluence and opportunities for advancement. Although they are expected to be a bulwark of the regime, the privileged youths have grown increasingly pessimistic.

Realizing that the appeal of communism has worn thin, the government has somewhat retreated from its authoritarian posture to rely increasingly on the latest techniques of manipulative persuasion. Since Soviet young people, like their peers elsewhere, are very media-oriented, the Soviet authorities attempt to impose a unifying set of values on them by means of the mass media. It seems unlikely, however, that this approach will be successful in the face of the realities of Soviet life.

Soviet youth has not yet reached beyond spontaneous rebelliousness to set out concrete demands for social change. If and when that does happen, as it well may, what was supposed to be the next generation of communists could become the generation that will replace communism with a different social system.

> Never, even in the most difficult days in the history of our country did the Party lose sight of the young generation. The next generation of Communists has always been its foremost concern. (V. Ivanov, V partiynom rukovodstve—sila komsomola [In the party leadership lies the driving force of the Komsomol]; Moscow: Publishing House for Political Literature, 1981, p. 5)

> Veterans assure the Party, its Central Committee and the Politburo of the CPSU that all their efforts, knowledge and experience will be directed toward the upbringing of the young generation of Soviet people, our next generation of Communist fighters. (Partiynaya zhizn', no. 17, 1983, p. 3)

> Party organizations of our district are paying constant attention to the upbringing of the next generation of Communists. (Chelovek budushchego rozhdaetsya segodnya [The man of the future is being born today]: Moscow: Moscow Worker Publishers, 1984, p. 146).

Nomenklatura (*Nomenklatura*). (1) A list of the top posts that defines the place and the rights of its holders within Soviet society. (2) The ruling stratum of Soviet society. Numerous researchers have attempted to penetrate the intricacies and to interpret the structure and dynamics of the nomenklatura. However, the closed nature of Soviet society and official secrecy have given birth to numerous misconceptions, such as the interpretation of nomenklatura as the nervous system of the Soviet regime or as a secret network of the most influential officeholders who determine the way the Soviet people live. Besides being emotionally loaded, these and similar definitions at best take into account only selected aspects of the nomenklatura without revealing what is most essential about it and how it operates.

There is nothing mysterious about the nomenklatura. In essence, it is a group of official positions that can be filled only by decisions of party organizations. Depending on the nature of the positions, their status, and their public significance (in other words, depending on their power), nomenklatura positions are divided as follows: the CC CPSU, the party central committees of the republics, and the territorial, provincial, city and regional party committees.

Within each category listed, there are subdivisions: the nomenklatura of the Central Committee of the CPSU is subdivided into the nomenklaturas of the Politburo, the Secretariat, and of the Central Committee departments. Analogous divisions can be found in the nomenklaturas of republic, provincial, city, and regional party committees.

Included in nomenklaturas are all positions of any significance, whether party, public, state, economic, or scientific. It follows that the nomenklatura is an instrumentality that helps the party organizations (or, more accurately, the ruling communist bureaucratic class acting in the name of the party) bring every facet of social and political life in the country under its control. Thus the nomenklatura is the Soviet elite's chief tool for gratifying its ambition to maximize its own power, an ambition disguised by the repetition of slogans like "the party is the driving force of Soviet society."

The concept of the nomenklatura arose in the process of Stalin's decimation of "Lenin's party" and the formation of a new communist class. Stalin lacked the qualities required for a party leader: he was neither a prominent theoretician nor a gifted speaker. Yet his perfect mastery of the art of political manipulation enabled him to gradually isolate the bulk of the party from its leaders,

Lenin's outstanding comrades-in-arms. He replaced the power of ideas within the party by the idea of power, in whose service he put all of his intelligence, natural cunning, and extraordinary memory. Stalin invented the system of nomenklatura to use as a primary vehicle in his quest for power. This system caused a drastic change in the nature of relations within the top party echelons, which began to be filled not with leaders elected at congresses and plenums and exercising independence and freedom in their judgements, but with people promoted by Stalin and totally loyal to him.

The Organization and Assignments Department of the Central Committee, founded while Lenin was still alive, was transformed by Stalin into a nomenklatura production unit. In 1923, this department, on Stalin's instructions, sent over ten thousand party workers to the peripheral regions of the USSR, placing them in positions of authority. This department also channelled party cadres in the opposite direction, from the periphery to the center. The department functioned like clockwork: it approved and assigned party committee secretaries throughout the country; from these locations the secretaries then selected congress delegates favored by Stalin; the delegates in turn elected the "proper" Central Committee members, who proceeded to select a Politburo obedient to Stalin's will and dedicated to the task of churning out new party cadres loyal to Stalin.

Thus the circle of nomenklatura was both expanded and closed. The principle of dedication to the party was replaced by that of dedication to the General Secretary (cf.). In 1924, the party ceased to exist as a revolutionary force. It was destroyed from within, adulterated beyond recognition by the multimillion infusion of new members, illiterate and conformist, who flooded the party at Stalin's bidding. The ratio of highly educated, professional members began to rapidly decrease; in 1925, it was less than 5 percent, and by 1929, it had fallen to a mere 1 percent. The party's profile and character were now set by the Stalinist cadres, made up of declassé workers and peasants and farm laborers. By 1930, they made up 90 percent of all party members; out of that number, 80 percent had finished primary school only, while the educational attainment of the other 20 percent was defined as "incomplete secondary."

The party "fledglings," malleable and self-seeking, began to devour the backbone of the party, the Leninist old guard. These young upstarts were used by Stalin as his main ally in his struggle for power. But Stalin knew that an ally with frustrated ambitions is highly unreliable, and so he spared no efforts in awarding them privileges and posts, and fattened them up on the so-called "Kremlin rations" (cf.). While millions starved to death, the rising nomenklatura gorged itself with caviar and salmon and wore fur hats and padded sheepskin coats generously distributed to the delegates of party plenums and congresses.

It wasn't enough for Stalin to lift the nomenklatura above the people. He also had to hermetically isolate it from them, so as to make it utterly and permanently dependent on the system and on himself. He abolished the *partmaksimum* (the maximum wage paid to party workers) and placed the nomenklatura in an artificial "*spetsmir*"—i.e., a "special world" of exclusive shops, sanitariums, hospitals, and even cemeteries in which members of the nomenklatura alone could be buried. The ordinary Soviet citizen could penetrate this wonder world of privileges neither when alive nor in the afterlife.

The nomenklatura, insulated and secure within this cocoonlike world, had no way of gauging the people's needs and reactions, preferring staged party and industrial meetings with "*spets-massy*," or selected "representatives" of the people, to any direct contact with the real masses. Hence its incompetence in managing the country, which it concealed by hunting for scapegoats or "enemies of the people." Thus, the purges were not only needed by Stalin in order to crush the opposition, but also to benefit the nomenklatura. The victims of the first political trials were top industrial managers accused of bad judgment in setting the planning targets (either too high or too low) and thus undermining the economy.

This search for people to blame for economic failures continued to expand, swallowing ever new victims—peasants, workers, and members of the intelligentsia (cf.). Soviet society, originally intended to incarnate the "bright future" (cf.), became a giant concentration camp with millions of inmates whose compulsory labor was used to build socialism. It was the latter who built the largest projects of "Stalin's five-year plans," such as the White Sea-Baltic Canal, the Dneproges (the giant hydroelectric power station on the river Dnieper), and the Magnitogorsk metallurgical combine.

Ration coupons and queues (cf.) became a steady fixture of Soviet life. In order to distract the masses from hunger and ruin, Stalin tried to secure their compliance by flattery, and he pretended concern for their well-being. While the nomenklatura luxuriated behind high *dacha* (cf.) fences, the workers suffered and died from hunger and poverty. Yet they were glorified in the press, praised in public, awarded honorary titles— e.g., "distinguished milkmaid," "tractor-driver," "swine-breeder," etc. Single individuals were picked out from the faceless mass, proclaimed *udarniki* (shock-workers) or Stakhanovites (cf.) and showered with decorations and titles. Yet even they were excluded from any participation in politics. Governing the country remained the sole prerogative of the nomenklatura, functioning according to a strict hierarchical order and rigid, military-like discipline.

"Party workers should be selected so as to make the key position held by people capable of accepting and implementing Party resolutions," stated Stalin. He elaborated: "The ranks of our Party, meaning its higher ranks [i.e., the nomenklatura] number three to four thousand top leaders. I would call them the Party's High Command. The next layer consists of 30–40 thousand middle-level functionaries. These are our commissioned officers. Further down are 100–150 thousand lowest Party officials. These are, so to speak, our Party's non-commissioned offi-

cers." [I. V. Stalin, *Sochineniya* (Works), Moscow: Izd-vo politicheskoy literatury, 1950, Vol. 9, p. 147.]

This frank and revealing statement was made by Stalin in 1927. Over the next sixty years, the basic structure of the nomenklatura remained virtually unchanged. Its army-like hierarchy is still the same; only its scale has changed. Its ranks have long reached the million mark, continuing to grow and expand. As always, the nomenklatura's main concern is not with real work but with pretending to work hard. The main thing is to create an impression, to be noticeable. This explains the endless flow of initiatives, pledges and reports, as well as the office lights burning late into the night, to prove that night watches are held and telephones are diligently manned. The bosses must know that the nomenklatura is always alert and ready to perform as required.

The nomenklatura is not interested in painstaking work. Its members display a totally self-centered attitude. Their imagination is busy inventing slogans and staging ideological charades. When faced with any nonstandard situation demanding originality and initiative, the nomenklatura is immobilized. In order to hide its embarassment or, rather, inferiority complex, it falls back on arrogance, rudeness, and inaccessibility. It constantly seeks to boost its self-esteem, and it does so by accumulating luxury and wealth and making trips abroad. There, rather than back home, it seeks recognition and respect. While vociferously condemning capitalist society, the nomenklatura in fact pays court to it and emulates it.

There is no provision for the nomenklatura in the constitution of the USSR. The only formal basis for its existence is the secret directive "On the procedure for the selection of leadership ranks" of the Central Committee of the CPSU. Updated systematically, this directive defines and regulates with precision the manner in which people are appointed to posts of significance in the state administrative system. The nomenklatura affects all the instruments of Soviet power by defining the pattern of direct and indirect interaction between the Politburo, the Central Committee, army headquarters, and the KGB. Thus the nomenklatura is the party rulers' chief tool for gratifying their ambition to maximize their own power, an ambition disguised by the repetition of slogans like "the will of the party" (*volya Partii*), or "The party is the driving force of Soviet society" (*Partiya—dvizhushchaya sila sovetskogo obshchestva*).

Although different nomenklaturas exist, the same hierarchical principle is observed at all levels. This principle determines the social position of each member of the Soviet ruling class and the privileges to which the appointee of each nomenklatura is entitled. Politburo members, Central Committee secretaries, and ministers are at the very top of this hierarchy, and they receive the most generous salaries and fringe benefits accordingly. In addition to special allowances for entertainment and clothing, they are provided with special medical care, and, in addition to salaries, they receive sums of money in gold—indexed rubles that have a far higher purchasing power than the ordinary ruble. Members of the lower-ranking nomenklaturas have few perks and privileges, but, in terms of status and material prosperity, they still rank far above any other group of professionals. This is why the nomenklatura appointees *in corpore* stand above the rest of society as a ruling class, albeit internally stratified into an elite and several gradations of membership. (The gradations extend from the party downward to the government, the Komsomol, the trade unions, the military, the industrial cadres, and the artistic nomenklaturas). By virtue of their control over the whole system of official appointments, party nomenklatura members are in the position to fill the most prestigious and best-paying posts with their own people. Naturally, fierce competition for these positions goes on constantly in the corridors of power.

Nomenklatura cadres are trained in special, privileged educational institutions: in the Higher Party School, the Diplomatic Academy, the Academy of National Economy, the Academy of the Ministry of For-

eign Affairs; in the higher schools of the KGB and the MVD (Ministry of Internal Affairs); and in the Institute of International Relations and the Institute for Foreign Trade. The nomenklatura appointees always enjoyed the support of and leniency from the nomenklatura hierarchy, and, as long as they remained with the nomenklatura framework, they stood above the laws of the land. (Under Gorbachev, this might have changed somewhat). They have been allowed to waste public resources and even to be involved in crimes. The severest punishment appointees were likely to receive was demotion one step down the nomenklatura hierarchy, and as long as they remained swimming in the "waters" of the nomenklatura at whatever depth, there was still a chance to reach the shores of leadership—if political winds were favorable. In sum, the opportunities of nomenklatura appointees for self-aggrandizement were virtually unlimited, provided they followed orders strictly, displayed obsequiousness toward superiors, and had a modicum of shrewdness and ingenuity.

The power of the nomenklatura was shaken under Gorbachev. Many of its privileges have become targets of vehement public attacks. The most egregious of the nomenklatura's transgressions have been revealed by Soviet newspapers. High nomenklatura figures, who had until quite recently appeared to be unassailable and, as secretaries of republic or provincial party committees or ministers, did not have to concern themselves with legality, suddenly found themselves under criminal investigation. However, it soon became clear that the fire was not being directed at the nomenklatura as a class but only at its representatives, whose political careers were in decline, who were compromised by their close ties to Brezhnev, or who had failed to demonstrate the loyalty that the new leadership required. As the purges and personnel changes subsided, the fervor in denouncing the nomenklatura subsided as well. It became more or less clear that Gorbachev could not afford to undermine the prestige and power of the nomenklatura without simultaneously undermining the foundations of his own authority. He had to preserve a nomenklatura vigorous enough to replenish its own ranks after any loss.

Finally, the existence of an established system for appointing and reshuffling nomenklatura officials totally subordinates the whole society to the Communist party. It helps conceal the resemblance of such a system of governance to Sicilian or Corsican mafias and it precludes all accountability. There is nothing in this system analogous to penalties for political miscalculations and failures, such as the downfall or electoral rejection of governments in free countries. The nomenklatura assures that the party leadership will not fall, no matter what it does.

> The Party bodies have a nomenklatura of cadres, that is, a range of posts whose powers and responsibilities are subject to the express opinion of the committee. (Partiynaya zhizn', no. 23, December 1980, p. 25)

> A list exists of the nomenklatura posts of the Party committee, but exists only formally, since appointment to and discharge from these posts is not discussed at meetings of the Party committee. (Sotsialisticheskaya industriya, 1 August 1982, p. 2)

> Practically every day we overhear conversations, especially in downtown Moscow, which use the by now familiar phrases like "Ivan Ivanovich has joined the nomenklatura," "This is a nomenklatura post," or "the nomenklatura roster." (Ogonek, no. 3, January 1989, p. 12).

Notorious (*Preslovuty*). An evaluation of and reaction to events and acts that conflict with the interests of the Soviet leadership. Since these interests do not remain constant, the term "notorious" is a dynamic concept. Its use depends on the political and social circumstances prevailing at any given moment. Thus, in the recent past any manifestation of private enterprise was labeled "notorious," as were any attempts to introduce free market elements into the Soviet economy. Yet, with a change in Soviet policies there came a corresponding change in the attitude toward these phenomena. It turned out that private enterprise and free market not only do not contradict the socialist system, but, on the contrary, contribute to its development and advancement.

At the same time, there is a certain category of values that to this day evokes consistently negative response in the Soviet Union and will, in all likelihood, continue to do so. Such notions as freedom, democracy, equality, and progress, in the genuine and wide-ranging sense as understood and practiced in the West, continue to be branded by the Soviet propaganda with the same old "notorious" label.

> The notorious pluralism, so extolled by the supporters of the bourgeois forms of democracy . . . turns out to be far from a paradise. (Novoe vremya, no. 26, 1977, p. 18)

> The notorious popular capitalism . . . collapsed under the powerful impact of strikes and popular demonstrations of the 1950s. (Sbornik, Srazhayushcheesya iskusstvo [Collection, art under arms]; Moscow: Znanie Publishing House, 1977, p. 3)

> One would like to know why the authors of the notorious propaganda hullaballoo about the "infringement of human rights" in the socialist countries do not acquaint themselves with the conditions Soviet society lives under? (Sotsialistichesky obraz zhizni i pravo [Socialist way of life and law]; Moscow: Znanie Publishing House, 1979, p. 45)

O

Ongoing Production Meeting (*Postoyanno-deistvuyushchee proizvodstvennoe sovesh-chanie*). Consultative organ controlled by the administration but designed to create the impression of workers' self-management. Production meetings came into practice in the USSR in the 1920s. At the onset they took place under the aegis of the trade unions, but later began to be convened and controlled by the management. As a rule, these meetings discussed secondary issues, such as labor discipline and outcomes of socialist competition (cf.), taking only nominal part in discussing state plans, the possibilities of accelerating production, and improving efficiency.

From the late 1950s onward, production meetings became ongoing institutions, maintained to create the fiction of workers' self-management in the Soviet Union. In fact, the prerogatives of ongoing production meetings were as limited as before, and their methods of deliberation precluded any free debate or objective inquiry. The meetings were never held spontaneously, but were planned in advance and staged according to the party organization's detailed scenario in which roles were assigned and decisions made beforehand.

By 1984, more than 150,000 ongoing production meetings existed in the Soviet Union. Since then, there has been drastic decline in their numbers and importance. Gorbachev's policy of perestroika required real workers' self-management, no longer camouflaged by the fiction of ongoing production meetings.

The decisions of the ongoing production meeting help yield solutions to complex problems and thus improve work results. (Ekonomicheskaya gazeta, no. 6, 1983, p. 13)

It dawned on him that it was the last day of the month, the day of the ongoing production meeting. (Novy mir, no. 1, 1984, p. 117)

Opinions (*Mneniya*). Informal, illegal or extralegal secret directives of party leaders based on political considerations. The USSR is an ideocratic state in that all social phenomena and decisions must conform to communist ideology. When reality refuses to fit this ideology, the latter needs to be supplemented or modified. Opinions are the medium of such covert modification, since the dogmas of scientific communism cannot be openly negated. Prompted by the exigencies of the moment, opinions are issued in those cases when it is not possible to give a communist interpretation, explanation, or substantiation to party policies. The issuance of opinions provides the authorities with some relief from the discomfort of doctrinal uncertainty.

One very important dogma in need of revision is that of internationalism, which commands equality for all Soviet ethnic groups. Basically irrelevant as a factor in Soviet policy, it is only taken out of the ideological closet on ceremonial occasions. Although this is public knowledge, the partocracy cannot openly sanction militant Russian nationalism without flying in the face of Leninism. Therefore it resolves the dilemma by secretly disseminating appropriate opinions. For example, there are no official instructions on quotas for admission to institutes of higher education or for certain jobs, but opinions do exist (camouflaged by anti-Zionist rhetoric) to the effect that for Jews, restrictions in these areas are needed. Although the details of these quotas are not uniform, the opinion that Jews should not be employed in the central apparatus of the KGB, the Ministry of Foreign Affairs, the Procurator's Office, and the Ministry of Foreign Trade would seem to be universally followed. For all other nationalities (except Slavic ones), the same opinion suggests a proportional representation rather than total exclusion.

Opinions trickle down from the summits of power in the form of verbal remarks and hints. They are deliberately vague and thus can be revised or even retracted without difficulty.

To be able to implement an opinion correctly seems to require appropriate "class feeling" (*klassovoe chut'e*) and "party conscience" (*partiynaya sovest'*). Since they are informal, opinions, such as the quotas on the admission of Jews to universities, cannot be appealed.

Sometimes opinions contradict each other. For example, one opinion welcomes and encourages provincial specialists to work in Moscow (thus emphasizing the transnational profile of the capital) while another opinion (intent on preserving the Russian character of the city) complains that not enough is being done to prevent an influx of residents of the non-Russian republics to Moscow. In the face of the dilemma of how to resolve the problem of Moscow's "ethnic quota" on the basis of some reasonable compromise, opinions resolve it at the expense of the "outsiders" by hinting that it is the representatives of the Soviet ethnic groups, which have their population centers elsewhere, who present the major threat to the capital's Russian identity. At the same time, in regard to the ethnic composition of Moscow, the authorities display some democratic restraint since there is the danger that if they lean too much in the direction of "Great Russian" chauvinism, they will be accused in subsequent opinions of ignoring Leninist principles. Opinions regulated all aspects of Soviet life, including those which Soviet laws do not cover, such as conduct of Soviet citizens abroad, family relations, and customs and tastes. For example, for a long time it was considered dangerous to associate with foreigners or inappropriate to wear narrow trousers or have beards.

Opinions are mentioned by ordinary citizens throughout the Soviet Union in whispers, and with respect and a touch of puzzlement, thus, often unintentionally, imparting to them an aura of mystery. With Gorbachev's reforms the role of "opinions"

as a regulator of social behavior weakened considerably. In the Soviet Union an attempt is being made to build a society based on law and not on "opinions." Nevertheless, "opinions" still influence the behavior of Soviet people in politics and in daily life, but to a lesser extent than previously.

> . . . Korytov hinted . . . that there exists such an opinion there . . . . (A. Zinoviev, Svetloe budushchee [Bright future]; Lausanne: Editions l'Age d'Homme, 1978, p. 224)

> People who take opinions for official decisions are fools! Opinions lead their own elusive lives, independent of the leadership, scattered in the air as it were, but they are there! (V. Kormer, Krot istorii [The mole of history]; Paris: YMCA Press, 1979, p. 13)

> Opinions expressed in letters, proposals and suggestions are reflected in the resolutions of the Central Committee of the Communist Party of the Soviet Union and the Council of Ministers of the USSR, as well as in the statements by Party and government leaders. (Kommunist, no. 17, 1980, p. 23)

Opportunism (*Opportunizm*). Revision of the philosophical principles of Marxism, or political practices considered to conflict with Soviet interests. Soviet propaganda depicts as opportunism any doctrine hostile to communism, which disorients the working masses and is contrary to their class interests.

Soviet ideology distinguishes between right-wing opportunism and left-wing opportunism. The former is defined as a theoretical model that revolves around the view that capitalism will naturally evolve into socialism and makes a fetish of the spontaneous workers' movement. The assumptions of right-wing opportunism are the belief in the possibility of cross-class collaboration, the rejection of the dictatorship of the proletariat, and the renunciation of the class struggle. Left-wing opportunism is portrayed as an adventurist doctrine that advocates terror as a way of making revolutions and leapfrogging over stages of historical development.

The Soviets trace both right-wing and left-wing opportunism to the interests of different social groups in capitalist society from which they spread, infecting the proletariat and its party. Right-wing opportunism supposedly appeals to a middle-class mentality that wishes to avoid revolution in order to hang on to its privileges. Left-wing opportunism is supposed to derive from the mind-set of alienated and socially marginal people who (unlike the communists) are too individualistic to be capable of waging class war in an organized fashion. According to Marxist theory, they seek salvation from constant oppression in an "extremist" revolutionary praxis, which deviates from the ideological program laid down by Marx.

Under the inspiration of Marx and Engels, communism has since its inception been waging a struggle against opportunism. Its battle against ideological deviation reached a high point during World War I and the subsequent Bolshevik coup in Russia. Then, from 1917 onward, the communists again and again undertook an exhausting struggle against the myriad forms of opportunism they detected around them.

With the creation of the Comintern in 1919, right-wing opportunism was proclaimed the number one enemy of the workers' movement. Identified as the ideology of social democracy and totally incompatible with Leninism, right-wing opportunism was defined as denying the necessity of proletarian revolution and of socialization of private property, and as advocating instead individual freedom and moral perfection. In the process of the bolshevization of the Comintern, affiliated parties and reformists who spoke out in favor of revising Marxist dogma were expelled and, whenever feasible, subjected to repression in the USSR.

In the course of "building" socialism in the USSR, a bitter and persistent struggle was also waged against left-wing opportunism. The methods and resources used were the same as those employed in the struggle against right-wing opportunism: they ranged from expulsion from the party to public political trials. The persecution of left-wing opportunists was even extended beyond the

borders of the USSR to the Comintern apparatus and foreign communist parties.

Lenin and Stalin's concept of opportunism was imposed upon foreign communist parties, where it provided the basis for bloody purges. The slightest deviation from "the general line" of Moscow (which claimed to speak for the entire "world communist movement") was condemned and severely punished.

After Stalin's death, opportunism was reassessed. The view that right-wing opportunism was a more dangerous enemy than fascism or imperialism was dropped. At the Twentieth Congress of the CPSU in 1956, the desirability of a rapprochement of communists with right-wing socialist parties and trade unions was suggested. Nevertheless, the Soviet leadership's attitude toward democratic parties and free trade unions for many years had not changed much, and the traditional notion that such parties and trade unions are opportunist has been retained until the present time.

In the 1960s, left-wing opportunism was proclaimed to be the main danger to the communist movement, when a number of "socialist countries" (China, Albania, and North Korea) refused to blindly follow Soviet dictates. The same countries (rather than right-wing opportunists) were additionally accused of destabilizing the communist movement and breaking ranks with the Soviet Union. Left-wing opportunists were also said to have alienated themselves from international communism and to have espoused policies of adventurism "mixed with great-power chauvinism."

In the 1970s, the concepts of right-wing and left-wing opportunism were slowly losing any real meaning. Political views that had once received Soviet sanction as being Marxist-Leninist (they might have differed in terminology but not in essence from those preached by the Kremlin leadership) were now castigated as varieties of opportunism. For example, left-wing opportunist ideas of fomenting revolutionary upheavals as a universal means of seizing power were officially approved and adopted (albeit with certain reservations) at the Twentieth Congress of the CPSU. This development went hand in hand with the branding of the parliamentary road to socialism as a manifestation of right-wing opportunism, even though the Soviet Communist party program called for more or less the same thing.

Faithful to the teachings of the communist "classics," Soviet mass propaganda has continued to reiterate that "the further development of the international Communist movement and of the worldwide socialist system calls for a struggle against all manifestations of opportunism." And yet, modern "Leninism" has been "enriched" precisely through its assimilation of concepts once branded as right-wing opportunism or bourgeois deviation. In general, theoretical positions once defined as right-wing opportunism or bourgeois ideas have received official Soviet sanction. Soviet sociology has come to adopt a refurbished model of state-monopoly capitalism first put forward by the "opportunist" Karl Kautsky. Moreover, the social democratic praxis of attaining power by parliamentary means on behalf of the proletariat and the concept of the "state of all the people" have now been incorporated into communist ideology. However, the transplantation of democratic principles into the body of Soviet philosophy could not dispense with verbal disguise. The ruse of terminological substitution was used in order to escape the ideological opprobrium once attached to the ideas now adopted.

Thus, the ideological quest has never totally abated. It could be pursued timidly, cautiously, inconsistently, and in keeping with Marxist verities, until prestroika and glasnost have recently permitted it to come out of the Soviet closet. Thereupon it transpired that socialism could come in various forms and find different applications in different social structures and that there is real socialist content in policies of social democratic parties, heretofore said to be based on unabashed opportunism.

The acknowledgment that forms of socialism might vary could not fail to exercise an impact on the contents attached to the

term "opportunism." Although it continues by inertia to resound with Leninist overtones, its meaning has been altered. Today, it is only opposition to Soviet policy, irrespective of the ideological identity of the opponent, that merits labelling its proponent as opportunist.

> The whole struggle of our Party, and of the workers' movement in Europe in general should be directed against opportunism. This is not a trend, a movement, this thing [opportunism] has now become an organized tool of bourgeois [elements] within the workers' movement. (Lenin, Sochineniya [Works], 4th ed., vol. 35; Moscow: Publishing House for Political Literature, 1951, p. 152)

> Opportunism is sometimes manifested in attempts to cling to certain concepts of Marxism which have already become obsolete, and transform them into dogma . . . . (Istoriya VKP(b), Kratky kurs [History of the All-Union Communist Party of the Bolsheviks, brief course]; Moscow: Publishing House for Political Literature, 1950, p. 342)

> Maoism is one of the obvious examples of opportunism in an ugly stage of decay when opportunism and social-chauvinism have reached "full bloom" and become allied with imperialism. (Mezhdunarodnaya zhizn', no. 12, 1979, p. 24)

Output Norm (*Norma vyrabotki*). The government-imposed quota of daily industrial shift output; also, the volume of industrial output. More than one-half of all Soviet industrial workers work on the basis of the output norm, while in the construction industry, the number rises to four-fifths. Those who work according to this system are called "pieceworkers" (sdel'shchiki)—and they are paid accordingly. Workers' pay packets do not necessary correspond to their output norm, however. They can be higher if the output norm is over-fulfilled or lower if it is not. Fixed-time workers, however, operate not according to output norms but according to job assignments that specify the volume of production required for a given shift.

The necessity of fulfilling the output norm becomes apparent to anyone during the very first days of employment. Not only his or her own interests, but those of his or her employer and even those of the country as a whole are inextricably linked to the output norm, although in a distorted and contradictory fashion. Theoretically, the output norm should be economically sound and readily attainable by an industrious, skilled worker. In reality, however, Soviet industry, with only minor exceptions, functions on the basis of overly low output norms, which can be easily over-fulfilled by at least 20 and sometimes as much as 50 percent, not only by qualified workers but even by unskilled workers. These norms are low because they were set on the basis of impressionistic estimates and were not supported by any measurements. Other norms simply failed to keep pace with technological improvements and higher productivity facilitated by them. In any case, they provide industry with an illusion of well-being. If the percentage of overfulfilled output norms could be considered evidence, then practically a majority of Soviet industrial workers would be shockworkers (*udarniki*) or model-workers (*peredoviki*) who continually manage to overfulfill their shares in quarterly, yearly, and five-yearly plans, while their factories continually underproduce, fail to meet their assignments, and are afflicted by stagnation.

The practice of artificial lowering of the output norm undermines labor discipline and worker morale. Workers' earnings grow on account of new production technology rather than improved worker performance. Thus, even without any doctoring of their work performance records, they gradually cease to earn even the wages they are paid. Only a socialist enterprise can operate on the basis of unearned income without incurring insolvency. This is because socialist enterprises start by underpaying their workers by as much as 90 percent. The resulting surplus is so big that it can easily accomodate inefficiency and low productivity of work.

This covert form of labor exploitation is not the only cause of relatively low output norms. They are also nurtured by the very structure of Soviet industry, whose development has for years consisted of building new plants rather than developing and improving already existing enterprises. As a result, not all vacant jobs in industry can be filled by the labor force available. This provides workers with a wide choice of employment, hence lowering their interest in job stability. Under these circumstances, attracting and keeping skilled workers in industry has become quite a problem. Solving it by improving working conditions would require too much effort. This is why Soviet enterprises resort to rewarding workers with what by strict standards of industrial accounting would amount to unearned income.

The pervasiveness of lowered output norms explains why the growth in wages nearly always precedes growth in productivity. The result is that the population accumulates money but does not have available goods, foodstuffs, or services to spend it on.

Another aspect of the same phenomenon is the use of drastically variant output norms by the same factories. In workers' parlance, output norms can be good (i.e., advantageous) or bad (disadvantageous). The former are obviously the ones that have been lowered, while the latter, although raised, are economically sounder. Their unequal allocation among different collectives of workers causes friction and labor disputes.

There are two reasons for the imposition of unrealistically high output norms as against the common pattern of artificially lowered norms. The first is simply incompetence on the part of managers, who try to achieve higher productivity by lowering piecework pay rates. The second reason is tactical. Disproportions between output norms can be a perfect means of manipulating workers into submission. Obliging workers will then receive lowered output norms, while their more rebellious colleagues get the augmented ones. In this way, any manifestation of independence on a worker's part can be speedily suppressed, while workers as a whole learn not to "stick their necks out" and to avoid real efforts.

In implementing perestroika, the Soviet leadership is trying to provide industry with "scientifically"-based output norms. Such attempts are cautious and seemingly non-coercive, however, and are intended to prevent unrest. A well-tried formula is used, whereby workers and entire work brigades are conditioned to "spontaneously" propose that norms be increased without waiting for a review of antiquated output norms in use. Pay rates are being widely changed, and workers who propose higher norms are awarded generous bonuses on account of the expected cost savings. The broad mass of workers, meanwhile, is exploited even more.

Pieceworkers, who amount to more than half of all our industrial workers and four fifths of those in construction, learn the meaning of the output norm in their very first days of employment. (Agitator, no. 8, 1988, p. 40)

The transition to new methods of labor remuneration is most often achieved simply by lowering pay scales or by reviewing output norms, without taking into account the opportunities offered by technology and good labor organization. (Agitator, no. 2, 1988, p. 7)

Paradox (*Paradoks*). An unexpected opinion at variance with conventional wisdom. Although the word "paradox" derives from antiquity, when it was used to describe things contrary to logic, at no time before the advent of the Soviet era has there been such an obvious rejection of logical thinking. Not only has this happened within the confines of communist doctrine, where self-contradictory statements have always abounded, e.g., "the dictatorship of the proletariat is the highest level of democracy," "democratic centralism," "peaceful coexistence is a form of ideological struggle," and others, but also in everyday life with its contradictory "outcomes."

The social homogeneity in Soviet society was achieved by the destruction of "class enemy" categories—the aristocracy, the clergy, the kulaks—and by mass persecution of the intelligentsia. The "union" (Lenin's term) of the two "friendly" classes, the proletariat and peasantry, entailed the harshest possible oppression and exploitation of the rural population. Every Soviet leader, each one in his own way, has created new paradoxes in the life of the country. Khrushchev outspokenly criticized Stalin's cult of personality (cf.) in order to enhance his own personality cult, while Gorbachev is trying to bring about the separation of party and state functions by fusing party and state positions. It is totally illogical to attempt to delimit the responsibilities of the party and the state by proposing a joint chairmanship for them in the form of a "secretary-chairman." But people have to accept such paradoxes in keeping with the traditions of Soviet society, whereby peace often means war, friendship means hatred, internationalism means nationalism, and so on.

It is forgotten, however, that steering the ship of state towards an ideology [espousing] a tax in kind is at this stage much more difficult than in the early 1920s. It would appear to be a paradox. Then, there was poverty and destruction. . . . Now, there is none of this. (Ogonek, no. 34, August, 1988, p. 7)

But what prevented Dunaevsky from composing a full-fledged song of praise for Stalin, if he idolized him so much? We know that he never tried it: neither in the 1940s nor the 1950s. There is a paradox in this. Some unconscious [signal] in his romantic psyche must have cautioned him against creative falsehood. (Ogonek, no. 30, July, 1988, p. 23).

Parasite (*Tuneyadets*). A person who lives off someone else's labor. A parasite is an organism that uses another "host" organism as its habitat and depends on it for sustenance and survival, while causing it serious damage. The term also has a metaphorical meaning, wherein it refers to a human being, living off someone else's labor or resources. In the Soviet Union, this metaphorical meaning has additional connotations. The Soviet concept derives from the communist worldview, which defines labor as "an act of glory, heroism and valor" (Stalin), and from Soviet jurisprudence, which regards any form of departure from "socially useful" work as a serious criminal offense. According to these criteria, not every type of work is recognized as socially useful, but only work in state-owned industry or agriculture and in certain cases (when special authorization ["a patent"] is granted) in private or cooperative enterprise.

Business conducted without official sanction—in private handicrafts or creative occupations like teaching, translating, literature, and art, for example—is not considered socially useful, thereby offering almost unlimited opportunities for arbitrary uses of the "parasite" label. Forced into this category, as necessity dictates, are practitioners of various vocations and professions, who have incurred the displeasure of the author-ities. The label is used particularly often to discredit dissidents, who are then duly ar-rested, tried, and banished from big cities. Many well-known writers and gifted artists have been branded with this appellation, in-cluding Yosif Brodsky, who eventually won the Nobel Prize for Literature. (In 1964, he was sentenced to five years of hard labor for "nonparticipation in socially useful work.")

New developments have created new op-portunities for labeling a person as a para-site. In order to implement its plan for speeding up economic growth, the party needed huge amounts of cheap labor. This is why in 1987, in Moscow alone, 70,000 peo-ple were forcefully employed in state indus-try. In 1988, their number already soared to 80,000, which means that in yet another year it could well reach 100,000. In any event, the country's labor laws (comprised of over 12,000 decrees and clarifications) make this likely.

The observance of work discipline is con-ceived of as a strict constitutional duty in the Soviet Union. This makes it possible to ex-pand the flexible scope of "social parasit-ism" even further. Thus, this scope includes speculators, embezzlers, bribe-takers, and various other categories, depending on the content of current propaganda campaigns. Perestroika has again called for parasitism to be uprooted. Today, it is no longer re-garded as a "relic of the past," but rather as a present-day "scandalous" phenomenon. Its "scandalousness" is predicated on the as-sumption that parasitism is the antithesis of socialism. This antithesis, far from being a textbook concept, has been coexisting along-side and indeed within socialism despite "its alien nature." The destructive role of the parasite was once again reassessed, this time against the background of "the era of stag-nation" of the Brezhnev years. It was de-termined to combat it by rectifying "the spineless" and amorphous legislation said to have been incapable of effectively making people work.

Once again, after parasitism had been out of the limelight for a while, the press began to talk about the reeducation of parasites.

The classics were enlisted into the campaign. It was recalled that in the works of Marx and Engels, the word "labor" occurred more fre-quently than "capital." The utterances of "the founders of scientific communism" were judged not sufficiently effective, however. And so the public was bombarded with quotes from eminent Russian thinkers—Belinsky, Dobrolyubov, Chernyshevsky and even No-vikov, who emphasized (in the eighteenth century and in a different context, to be sure) the indispensability of labor, to the point of choosing the phrase "They work while you eat their labor" as an epigraph for his jour-nal.

Such measures were clearly insufficient to affect the "moral well-being" of the Soviet people. Next to be enlisted in the battle was "public opinion" (*obshchestvennost'*), which could be easily incited to the extremes of hatred and malice toward people whose en-ergy earned them successes. Upon official instigation, the press was flooded with let-ters. As a result, the concept of the parasite turned out to encompass a successful neigh-bor living off the same stairway ("he has a more spacious and better furnished apart-ment, which one can't get on his earnings"), an industrious and capable work colleague ("he gets promoted too quickly, which proves that he has unearned income, well placed friends, and the right connections"), and the like. And so the word "parasite" has come to include varieties of surprising designates. In an atmosphere thus created, anyone who is disliked or envied can be referred to as a parasite.

A parasite of a particularly repulsive variety is a social being who lives off the work of others. (Agitator, no. 19, 1987, p. 29)

In 1964 the judge Savel'eva sentenced Yosif Brodsky. She convicted him of parasitism. He was just a poet. . . . (Ogonek, no. 31, July 1988, p. 26)

When they speak of this social pathology, they give the impression that they are making no distinction between a professional criminal, a hired hand (shabashnik), and a demoralized classical parasite. (Sotsiologicheskie issledovaniya, no. 3, 1988, p. 147)

Partocracy (*Kommunisticheskaya byurokratiya*). The new ruling class that was formed and raised to power by the Revolution and subsequent radical restructuring of Soviet society. Historically, the partocracy in the Soviet Union was formed from the classes that supported the socialist Revolution—the proletariat, peasantry, and intelligentsia—plus a conglomeration of people from various social backgrounds who joined them. Since 1917, depending on the historical and cultural characteristics of a given communist country, the proletariat may or may not form a proportionate segment of the ruling class.

The partocracy's attitudes toward the proletariat have passed through various stages as the party advanced toward power. As long as the communists were competing for power, they were forced to look to the proletariat for support in their professed aim of destroying capitalism. Under the conditions of the political "interregnum" (1917–18), when the Russian bourgeoisie and nobility had lost the reins of power and the partocracy had not yet taken them up, the myth was fabricated that the interests of the partocracy and of the proletariat coincided.

Once the communists came to power, however, they apparently no longer needed to speak in the voice of the workers. The "dictatorship of the proletariat" remained as an ornament disguising new, distinctly communist forms of class domination. The accumulation of economic power by the new ruling class, pursued through forced industrialization and forcible collectivization, generated contradictions between the working masses and the communist authorities that made them antagonists. The goal of the new communist class was its complete political, economic, cultural, and ideological control over society. The realization of this goal was bound to lead the partocracy into conflict with the proletarian intelligentsia that had arisen on the crest of the October Revolution.

Thus the Leninist Bolshevik Guard was exterminated in prisons and forced labor camps as soon as their ideals clashed with the aims of Stalin. On the corpses of the Old Bolshevik guard a new power structure arose, comprising members of the ruling elite whose power increased as the stratification of communist society deepened.

In the past, the emergence of new ruling classes resulted from corresponding economic realities, but the rise of the partocracy deviates from this pattern. The communist partocracy had neither economic power nor roots and support in society at large. It began by seizing political power and only then proceeded to lay the foundations of its economic power. Once power was firmly in the hands of the partocracy, professed communist ideals became mere window-dressing, displayed for propaganda purposes. The partocrats (*partokraty*) soon changed from revolutionaries to reactionaries, as can be expected from a ruling class that has become firmly entrenched in power.

The communist ruling class is highly party-oriented. Only party members can hold high public and political posts. This fact is responsible for the common misconception that party membership (and it alone) is the path to privilege, power, and influence in Soviet society. Such a view is a gross oversimplification.

Actually, the new ruling class holds sway in both party and government, as well as in the police and even in science. The real connection between this class and the party is that the latter provides legitimacy to the former's existence. By professing its adherence to the party's program, statutes and regulations, the partocracy establishes for itself a raison d'etre. For the partocracy, the invocation of the party's name is a formality, by means of which it can identify itself with the party, or rather, identify the party with itself.

Because the partocracy has concentrated absolute power in its own hands, not shared with any other class, it follows that it has no allies in Soviet society, the least so among the workers or peasants. This is why the reallocation of national income (and, therefore, the determination of wage levels) can in the USSR be entirely arbitrary, conforming merely to the partocracy's class interests. The same class interests determine the directions of economic development for the country.

The communist ruling class is a pyramid with a clearly defined social and political hierarchy. The party elite forms the top of this pyramid. The governmental elite is one step down from the top. The position of other elite groups depends on the degree of their connections with the party apparatus. This is the case with the scientific, trade-union, artistic, and literary elites, as well as with a tiny elite of professional public figures. The described ranking reflects the character and functions of the various elites, their role in Soviet society, and the degree of their influence on policy decision-making. But the partocracy is divided up horizontally as well as vertically. Different elites coexist at the same hierarchal level within an elaborate network of mutual interconnections. The top rank of the hierarchy, which comprises the most privileged segment of the ruling class, includes not only secretaries of the Central Committee of the CPSU and first secretaries of republic party committees but, due to their power and prestige, also selected representatives of other elites like directors of major ministries, of the Procurator's Office, and of the High Court—plus editors-in-chief of the most important newspapers, presidents of academies of sciences, top army staff and chairmen of artists' unions and associations.

Directly below this group are the deputies of the above-listed officials who translate Soviet policy into practice. They are communists of the new type who began their political career after World War II. This group comprises the heads of the departments of the Central Committee of the CPSU, the Supreme Soviet and the Council of Ministers, heads of the Komsomol organizations and trade-union chiefs, first deputy ministers, and other top party or government officials. The third rank from the top is composed of party bureaucrats, heads of every conceivable type of state institution (eco-

nomic, industrial, medical, and educational), high officials of republic councils of ministers, the Procurator's Office, the High Court, and the KGB on the republic and provincial levels. It also includes renowned scientists, plus writers and artists who hold state awards and honors.

Officials of prestigious organizations and institutions make up the fourth and lowest rank of the partocratic hierarchy. Although in no way distinguished, they have won a modicum of renown by mere virtue of their involvement in organizations that command a certain status. They are instructors, inspectors, responsible organizers of party committees, members of artists' unions, top economic managers, professors, journalists of party newspapers, and the worker-peasant "aristocracy" delegated to the Supreme Soviet and party committees.

All ranks of the ruling class participate to some degree in the political life of the country. Those at the bottom level of the pyramid, and even of the less than influential third level, however, do not participate in actual decision-making. The management of state affairs is in the sole hands of the first rank, assisted by the second—the elite of top government organs, such as the Council of Ministers, the Supreme Soviet of the USSR, the KGB, the army, the Procurator General's Office, etc. As far as the setting of the political course of the country is concerned, not even the first rank in its entirety has a role in its formulation. National policy formulation is the exclusive prerogative of the no more than thirty-strong body of Politburo members and Central Committee CPSU secretaries. The top government elite only plans concrete methods for implementing the policies determined at the top level, while the third- and fourth-rankers actually implement these policies and bring them down to the level of the masses. One might compare the two lower ranks to preparatory schools, where those about to assume power learn the skills they will need to rule. All appointments to high office are in the hands of the top party elite. There are a great number of social roles or masks in the USSR, like those of the prime minister, the president of the Academy of Sciences, the chairman of the all-powerful KGB or of a modest artists' union—behind all of them one finds the partocrat.

Formerly, in Lenin's day, the dictates of the partocracy were carried out indirectly via representative government organs—the soviets. Later, under Stalin, the secret police was used to implement these dictates. Under the successors, from Khrushchev to Chernenko, the rule of the partocracy has been revealed overtly, while the prerogatives of executive and legislative bodies of the state have been flouted and trampled. Gorbachev decided to once again revert to the system of "political masks," namely to separate the prerogatives of party and state organs in order to strengthen the authority and influence of the partocracy. In line with this idea, he ruled that first secretaries of party committees (from district level up to general secretary) have to assume functions of chairmen of the respective level of executive soviets as well. In this way the power of the partocracy would certainly not be weakened; if anything, it would be more solidly concentrated in the hands of the party elite.

However, the problem of the partocracy as a class is that (at least to date) it does not have the right to pass on its power and privilege to its children. This limitation stems from ideology and is the price paid for the need to rely on ideology to camouflage the partocrats' egotistical desires and self-serving policies.

Although it is not possible to bequeath to one's offspring lifelong rank and benefits, property can be bequeathed to children and grandchildren. Thus, in the Soviet Union the perpetuation of power begins with the accumulation of capital; money guarantees acceptance into an institute of higher learning and also buys one a prestigious position and a high income: a correspondent member of the Academy of Sciences receives 350 rubles per month until he or she dies in addition to a salary, while the corresponding sum for a full member is 500 rubles. Academicians have at their disposal dachas (cf.), closed stores

(cf.), and automobiles. The major difference between the privileges of the academic and party elites is that the former's status is less glamorous but more dependable. Such stability is quite attractive for Soviet officials, who have to worry about losing status due to intrigues or disfavor of their superiors. Hence many members of the partocracy hastened to find for themselves sinecures in the Academy of Sciences: under Khrushchev and Brezhnev they amounted to 15 percent of the total membership of the Academy, while with the generous assent of Gorbachev they now amount to 20 percent. The status thus gained can in turn be converted back into wealth.

In this way, the Soviet partocracy frees itself from the restraints imposed on it by ideology and finds in capital a technique for perpetuating privilege, influence and, ultimately, access to power. Thus it becomes the dominant class in the full sense of the word, with a monopoly on property and a permanent hold on inherited power. The process is circular: social status yields academic status yields wealth yields social status.

However, this cycle was unexpectedly broken by Gorbachev. He took advantage of the partocracy's inclination to prostitute itself in order to reshape it. He ousted from it those Brezhnev-appointed holdovers whose loyalty he could not count on. Thus the country temporarily became exposed to scandal-mongering publicity over criminal trials featuring members of the party elite— with ministers and provincial and city party secretaries as defendants. Much of the private life-style of the partocracy, including its unprincipledness and cynicism, were thus revealed to the public. However, a tight veil was still maintained over the fact that the partocracy's abuses have their clear source in the system of distribution of power. As long as this system is maintained, the partocracy's potential for corruption and abuse of power remains intact and likely to recur in coming generations of partocrats.

The aristocratization of the partocracy and the preservation of its homogeneity is attained via endogamy. The closed social world of the elite circles forms a marriage market that sets up barriers against aspiring out-group entrants. Thus, the Soviet ruling class isolates itself. It has income hidden from others' eyes with its concealed villas off-limits to outsiders, special schools closed to the general public, special closed institutes, special closed stores, and endogamous marriages—a completely insulated way of life.

It is a free and easy life. The partocracy would be the last to fear that, once they had scaled the social heights, they might find there a vacuum; or that once they had succeeded in amassing a fortune, they might not know what to spend it on; or that having attained the ultimate in success, they may have to pay a price in return; or that there may be a sad aspect to a life consisting of a pursuit of vanities. Such concerns are totally alien to them.

Is the partocracy happy? To answer in the negative would be to judge the matter from a non-Soviet perspective. After all, its members have won a contest in which the loser was the entire nation.

> Our worst internal enemy is a Communist bureaucrat [partokrat] who occupies an important . . . Soviet position. (V. I. Lenin, Sochineniya [Works], 4th ed., vol. 33; Moscow: State Publishing House for Political Literature, 1951, p. 199)

> The struggle to the end, to complete victory over bureaucratism [partocracy] is possible only when the whole population participates in governing. (V. I. Lenin, Sochineniya [Works], 4th ed., vol. 26; Moscow: State Publishing House for Political Literature, 1949, p. 425)

> Aren't all the objective students of the Soviet system in agreement that precisely this system is a "class society" . . . due primarily to the emergence at its tip of a partocracy, of the very new class of which Trotsky had written in his time, and Djilas in our time. (Vremya i my, no. 75, New York, 1983, p. 125)

Party (*Partiya*). The Communist Party of the Soviet Union. Following the Bolshevik coup, as the regime moved toward a one-party system by suppressing all other political parties, the term "party" without qualifying adjectives began to mean the Communist party.

Russian dictionaries list many meanings of the word *partiya*, but since the formation of the Soviet language, unless the context indicates otherwise, "party" means the CPSU. Thus people were conditioned to the notion that no political parties except the CPSU could exist, could ever have existed, or could exist in the future. However, it turned out that the party could not isolate itself from the fever of reform which seized Soviet society under Gorbachev. Under intense pressures from below exerted by large masses of people deeply influenced by the scale of political shake-ups occurring in Eastern Europe, the February 1990 Plenum of the Central Committee of the CPSU, was compelled to announce that the Party was prepared to renounce its monopoly on power. Only the future will tell whether this announcement will have any practical meaning.

While being a ruling party, the CPSU operates as if it were an underground organization. The Leninist organizational structure of the party has remained intact since the Revolution, in spite of the fact that it was set up by Lenin as an illegal political organization in an underdeveloped country that was just emerging out of feudalism and autocracy. As the ruling body of a modern state, it continues to act on the basis of clandestinely conveyed secret instructions that override the laws of the land.

The propaganda image of the party is unique. The concept of the indivisibility of the Soviet people and "their" party is continually dinned into the national consciousness. The spiritual aspirations of the party and the public are held to be identical. This is supposed to obviate the need for the Communist party to seek and receive a popular mandate. The full name—Communist Party of the Soviet Union—is employed only in official documents and reports. The use of the unadorned word "party" suggests a sense of intimacy and evokes feelings of love and loyalty from Soviet citizens. The propaganda machine has not been lax in extolling the party's central place in communist society or in making clear its tremendous power. In fact, a veritable cult of the CPSU is being promoted, with the party presented as virtually a sovereign ruler over the country, in complete disregard of the fact that the Soviet constitution stipulates otherwise.

The party is said to have a special role to fulfill: both in Russia and in the world at large. The success of the October Revolution is seen as the direct results of "the infinite experience, unrelenting militancy, and glorious history of the party." The victory over fascism in World War II is ascribed primarily, if not exclusively, to the "party's great organizational and mobilizational strength," and the Soviet conquest of space to the "wisdom of the party's far-sighted policies." The transformation of a "backward state" (i.e., tsarist Russia) into the "most advanced industrial power on earth" is seen as the greatest achievement of the party. Making and preserving peace throughout the world is portrayed as the party's "major concern." Finally, party policies are said to be based on "a profound knowledge of the objective laws of social development."

Indeed, anything viewed as positive and progressive in Soviet society, whether in the past or the future, is identified with the party. The omnipotence and omniscience of the party are emphasized and extolled constantly. The party is presented as a powerful "life-generating" force endowed with quite extraordinary moral and political qualities. It is "progressive," "leading," "mighty," "righteous," "devoted," "selfless," "ironclad" (in its determination), "tempered" (in struggles), and, in fact, appears surrounded by an almost supernatural aura. Every citizen of the state is not only expected to honor and cherish the party but also to idolize it. This explains why the party is said to be "dear," "beloved," and "of our own flesh and blood."

In the Soviet view, the party is far from being an ordinary political organization. It is a focus of strength towering high above the entire social system: the only place where truth is fully comprehended and determined. Therefore, the party is not reducible to its members, not even to its leaders, who may rise and fall. Crimes may be committed by them, but the party remains above reproach. It is a manifestation of a higher order of rationality. It is "the intellect, dignity and conscience of our times" (*um, chest' i sovest' nashey epokhi*). Of course, the superior wisdom, humanity, and justice of the party is reflected in its leaders. They are thus endowed with quite extraordinary qualities, which include unerring righteousness and the gift of historical foresight. They know in advance the course of social and political development that humanity will take.

At the outset of Soviet rule, religion was declared to be the opium of the people. God was toppled out of heaven and "smashed" along with all other superstitions. The advent of a society governed by the objective laws of materialism signalled the end of reliance on miracles. But the communists proved incapable of ruling society without recourse to a new brand of spiritual "opium." A new, communist theocracy was created that, after it had reneged on its promise of democracy, needed arguments to justify its claims to power and for that purpose established the cult of the party. And when that cult was insufficient, the cult of the leader—Stalin—was created. However, despite the great efforts of the Soviet propaganda machine, it soon became apparent that without the party, without the huge and powerful bureaucracy (party, secret police, and military bodies—depending on the changing political course of the party), no single person could control the totalitarian state.

During the Stalinist period, the mystical halo of the party always hovered above Joseph Stalin's head, and Stalin could become Stalin only because ideology created in Soviet society a whole class of people with Stalinist social instincts. In effect, the personality cult around Stalin was no more than a form of the impersonal cult of the party. The void left by Stalin's demise made it necessary for his successors to depersonalize and strengthen the cult of the party so as to legitimize their own succession. Circumspectly, the new Soviet rulers admitted that particular power-holders, i.e., individual party leaders, can err. In this way, people's faith was diverted toward an object that could not err—the party, which, for all its facelessness, did not remain impersonal because it had leaders through whom it spoke.

Thus new religion developed in the Soviet Union, replacing the long-suppressed belief in the supernatural. The party had its own holy trinity—Marx, Engels, and Lenin—whose writings replaced the Bible. Illuminated by the greatness of this "trinity" and its teachings, there followed the "apostles": Khrushchev, Brezhnev, Andropov, Chernenko, and now Gorbachev, served by the less exalted riffraff of the far-flung party apparat. Only the place of "hell" in the communist "religion" is not settled; it remains moot whether to relegate the "sinful" Stalin there, to abolish it as inconsistent with Marxist doctrine, or to preserve it as a threat and warning to future leaders.

In contrast to the apostles of Christianity, the communist apostles are not above ordinary human weaknesses. They have the right to err and commit crimes with impunity, because they are in advance absolved of all guilt by the party. The holy word of Marx is their Old Testament, and the gospel according to Lenin is their New Testament. The party is revered as the truest incarnation of the holy trinity's ideas, and therefore, by definition, as the repository of infinite wisdom that infallibly acts in the best interest and expresses the fondest hopes of the working masses who, in the USSR, have escaped the hell of capitalism and are standing on the threshold of communist redemption.

For its inquisition, the party has the KGB (formerly the *Cheka*). The priests and missionaries of the Soviet faith are the officials dealing with ideology, who determine which actions and thoughts of Soviet citizens are worthy and which unworthy, which correct and which incorrect or blasphemous. Like priests of the church in the past, the ideological functionaries have the right to censure, excommunicate, and mete out punishment.

According to party statutes, members of the party are free to leave its ranks if they so decide. In reality, this is not so simple. Leaving the party voluntarily brands one with the Soviet mark of Cain, unleashing the severest of punishments and ostracisms. This sin is considered a grievous, mortal sin. It is the exclusive prerogative of the party to select and reject its members. Traditionally, the party has exercised this prerogative of eliminating members through purges. Since the CPSU took power in 1917, millions of party members have been expelled.

The party has also built its own houses of worship. The most lavish buildings in the Soviet Union are those belonging to party committees. The Lenin Mausoleum serves as the party's most sacred shrine, located in the very heart of the capital. Tens of thousands of deceived (or simply bored and curious) Soviet citizens are herded into pilgrimages there every day.

Loyalty to the party, as well as love and worship of it, are favorite themes of Soviet propaganda. Awe and respect for the party is encouraged by fear of deviating from its holy writs. The word "party" has given birth to many Soviet neologisms, such as *partiyny* (belonging to the party) *partiynost'* (party spirit) and *partiets* (party member).

The Communist Party of the Soviet Union successfully unites the progressive, most consciencious section of the working class, of the collective farm peasantry and of the intelligentsia of the USSR. (Kommunist, Kalendar–spravochnik [Communist, a reference calendar for 1977]; Moscow: Publishing House for Political Literature, 1976, p. 36)

Under the guidance of the Communist Party, the toiling masses of our country are successfully transforming into reality the great tasks defined by the XXV Congress of the CPSU. (Agitator, no. 1, 1979, p. 21)

In the period of mature socialism the national policy of the Party, along with the education of the masses in internationalism, are assuming certain new features. . . . (Problemy mira i sotsializma, no. 1, 1980, p. 6)

Party Functionary (*Partiyny rabotnik*). An official of one of the numerous organs of power within the Communist party. In the Soviet Union there is a huge and ramified network of educational institutions geared for turning out professional party functionaries. Both the Higher Party School and the Academy of Social Sciences in Moscow are part of this network; they train functionaries operating at the national level, while party schools in the republics train lower-ranking party functionaries. University graduates, graduates of KGB and MVD (Ministry of Internal Affairs) schools, of the Foreign Service and International Relations Academies, and of the Institute of Commerce are also often recruited for party work.

In the Soviet Union, party work is the surest path to career opportunities. The future is promising for graduates of these schools. Long-term service is rewarded with a high salary and manifold rights and privileges. In due time, party workers are also guaranteed an opportunity to be transferred to such other desirable areas as the diplomatic service, science-related activity, production-management, etc. A district committee instructor may be appointed director of a factory or school, a city committee instructor is considered eligible to become a director of a major administration, and a Central Committee instructor a deputy minister. In other words, the opportunities of party functionaries for job-switching are excellent.

Transfers of this kind may superficially seem to have many advantages, but they carry a price. For instance, if a party functionary moves into the industrial sector, he will be able to supplement his income through graft and thus improve his financial situation quite rapidly. However, such a move will also mean that his days as a member of the privileged party caste are over. His responsibilities in political or production work will be more concrete and possibly also much more exacting than before, and he will certainly operate under much higher tension. Yet, if he knows how to maintain contacts, he may be able to secure his return to the party apparatus and even obtain a position higher than the one he originally held. For example, if

he becomes a Central Committee instructor, he might request transfer to a position of "independent" authority, such as a secretaryship in a provincial committee—already an elite position, qualifying its incumbent for membership in the Central Committee or in the Supreme Soviet.

Of course, this party functionary must first prove himself as secretary of a provincial or city committee, but if he serves his superiors in the manner required, if he is attentive to their whims and desires, he can count on his due reward and excellent prospects for future promotion. From a "local prince" or "governor general" of a province, he may rise to a position closer to the "throne," becoming the head of a department or even a Central Committee Secretary. There, if he takes the proper precautions and avoids being hurt by intrigues, he may one day even become a member of the Politburo. This would mean gaining immortality during his lifetime, as his portraits would be carried in celebrations, he would be invited to join the honorary presidium at important meetings, and he would receive "resounding applause turning into an ovation" wherever he appeared.

Although this can happen, it does not always. Often obstacles crop up, such as the inability to get along with a boss or adapt to a given political situation. Both these situations call for scapegoats, which means that a party functionary may suddenly be relegated to obscurity or abandoned to the wolves as an example for others. In order not to tempt fate, the better educated and more prescient Central Committee instructors learn from the experience of fallen colleagues and step off the party "conveyer-belt" in time. Cleverly exploiting their unlimited power and influence, they see to it that they are awarded advanced scientific degrees—first a candidate's degree, and then a doctor's degree. As soon as a good academic opening comes up, they transfer out of party work and assume the directorship of a scientific research institute, a position that in a short time will guarantee their promotion to membership in the Academy of Sciences of the USSR. This is very prestigious in itself. Besides, if the former party functionary remains ambitious, the possibility always exists that an academician nurtured in party work may be summoned back to the Central Committee. If this happens, the least that he can expect is a department headship or a secretaryship. These are just a few of the trails that may bring a party functionary to the peaks of power. Those who are vainglorious and, especially, who dislike systematic work or lack competence for it may find party work to their liking. Party functionaries at all levels are essentially dilettantes who may have diplomas or study certificates but not real competence. Basically, they are educational failures: engineers manqués, journalists manqués, scientists manqués.

This situation reflects not so much the low aptitude of party functionaries as the process by which the partocracy recruits new entrants to its ranks. Only those willing to surrender their aspirations for professional competence of the sake of party-mindedness have a chance. This process of selection begins early in an individual's life—in the Komsomol. It may happen, of course, that the secretary of a local Komsomol or party organization is a competent specialist. But the atmosphere of party work is deleterious to the pursuit of professional interests by anyone. From the moment one is appointed a party functionary, one's whole attention and all one's activities begin to revolve around a single focus: the party. The party functionary is always in a state of feverish activity, always exhorting and spouting slogans, always trying to win people to the cause, always publicly exposing something, always giving speeches at sundry meetings and forums that rehash newspaper editorials and party directives.

A low-ranking party functionary, caught up in the whirlpool of hectic activity, constantly rushing from one meeting to the next, has few opportunities to advance his education. His professional competence is bound to steadily decline as party work becomes the only thing that provides him with a social role and status. If he fails in his capacity of party functionary, his way back to industry or science will be agonizing. He may find that, while climbing up the party ladder, he has forgotten everything of real substance that he once knew. As he realizes that beyond party work he has no place in society, he feels trapped in partocracy for the rest of his life. His readiness to keep his mouth shut about his real opinions, to relinquish his convictions and principles, and to defer to the authority of party directives and circulars is a natural consequence of this realization.

As a result, the functionary is likely to lose much of his human sensitivity and inner values. These are replaced by pride in what is still available to him: his party career. To this he will sacrifice whatever traces remain of honor and conscience, so that when he finds himself in a position of real power deciding matters of life-or-death import to others, he will already be egocentric, rigid and callous, no longer capable of an unbiased perception of, or balanced judgment about, anything unrelated to his personal egotistic ambitions. Intrigues, balancing acts, and mutual backstabbing—all motivated by the drive to get and keep status—will exhaust his mental energies and sedate his conscience, while the gratification of his appetite for delicacies from special government stores will help him visualize the living conditions of ordinary people only on the basis of dim recollections or newspaper accounts. If the thought suddenly bursts on him, he thrusts it aside as rapidly and absolutely as possible, lest it disturb his peace of mind or awaken his conscience. He is well aware that a party functionary with a conscience is in a very dangerous situation.

The party functionary does not easily forget an insult, and he nurses grudges against anyone who ever slighted him. He knows how to take revenge subtly, even elegantly, and in a wily manner. He treats people with consideration at least ostensibly, while setting traps for rivals until they get caught. A real diplomat, he doesn't show all his trumps and does not reveal his true nature even to himself. He is always able to justify to himself every deed he commits so that he never suffers from any contradiction between this outward behavior and inner standards. This inner harmony is never disturbed by doubt, guilt, or uncertainty. His acting skills are so finely developed that sometimes he does not even know whether he is pretending or acting genuinely. He is unaffected by his reputation because he knows that in the Soviet Union there is no such thing as public opinion. The fate of others depends on his character traits and motivations. He decides matters as if in a one-man show theater, where everybody else is a silent extra or merely stands in the wings. He dictates while others perform under his dictation. Under such conditions, politics in the USSR becomes transformed into psychology, and life into something irrational, governed by unpredictable motives and instincts.

Of course, the party functionary does not easily or quickly ascend a pedestal and become famous. As a rule, the path to power takes him through humiliating servitude.

The party functionary must be like a cormorant, who, its neck throttled by the fisherman's hands, can breathe but cannot swallow the fish in its beak. The cormorant obediently brings the fish to its master's boat, and from time to time the fisherman rewards its work by loosening his grip and allowing the bird to swallow the captured fish.

Top party functionaries look with leniency when their junior associates, just beginning their careers, grab a slice of the pie (e.g., a bribe) bigger than their due. Strictly speaking, there is nothing wrong in it: on the contrary, a party functionary who would not take bribes would be suspect. He will be forgiven provided that he sticks to the sacred, unbreakable rule: when being "fed" by the two hands—of the party bureaucracy and of black-market business—he must be unquestioningly loyal and obedient only to the former. It does not mean that one's membership in the partocracy implies the obligation to unfailingly fulfill every one of its directives. But he must consistently apply the partocracy's interest as the basic criterion in making decisions.

An important feature of party work is the accumulation of privileges that buy power. In other words, power in the USSR has a cumulative character: the more power a party functionary has, the more opportunities he also has for expanding its scope. His entire activity revolves around accumulation of personal power. Principles, convictions, ideas may concern him, but only when convenient. It is because to renounce power would mean to renounce oneself, to lose everything and rapidly roll down the social ladder. Insofar as power determines the motives of his actions, the party functionary is not the master of his destiny. A hierarchical system of this type resembles a monarchy, although absolute rather than enlightened, since no one in the USSR is an independent subject. Even party functionaries lack independence. They are tied to each other by an unbreakable chain of mutual favors and wirepulling and by shared feelings of hostility toward the ordinary people.

17,000 party functionaries were dispatched to the villages to help the collective farms by working in political sections. (Istoriya VKPb, Kratky kurs [History of the All-Union Communist Party of the Bolsheviks, brief course]; Moscow: State Publishing House for Political Literature, 1950, p. 303.

L. I. Brezhnev noted that personal contact with the working people enriched the party functionary, strengthened his contact with life, and helped him to recognize at first sight, so to speak, what people think, need, and are interested in. (Kommunist, no. 17, 1980, p. 24)

A woman minister, a woman cosmonaut, a woman member [of a soviet], director, manager, [or] party functionary. (Bakinsky rabochy, 23 February 1984, p. 3)

Party Member (*Partiets*). A term for a member of the Communist party. The term "party member" became current in the 1920s and was connected with the increased social stratification then taking place in the Soviet Union. To the officially recognized classes of Soviet society—the workers loyal to the regime, the hired farm hands who were sympathetic to it, the dissatisfied and alienated peasants, and the hostile clergy—there was added a new stratum of privileged party members, out of which there arose and was consolidated a new ruling communist class.

Although apparent synonyms, "party member" and "member of the party" (*chlen partii*) did not always have precisely the same meaning. In the 1920s and 1930s, the latter term referred merely to formal membership while the former implied that a particular person is not merely a party member but a reliable and tireless revolutionary.

However, with changes in Soviet society, the situation of party members changed. As membership in the party expanded, a closed social elite emerged within the party. The result was that the rank-and-file party member lost his or her privileged position, and the term lost its original connotation. It came to denote mere party membership. Gradually, "party member" was replaced in common speech by "member of the party," the former term being retained only in propaganda discourse. Although membership in the Communist party is a certificate of particular loyalty to the regime, it is not enough to elevate a person into the ruling elite or secure special privileges. Thus there are many members of the party who are no better off than the tens of millions of unaffiliated Soviet citizens.

Motives for and circumstances of joining the Communist party vary. For example, the leadership sets recruitment quotas for a certain number of workers, some taken straight from the lathe into the party, and, for social balance, peasants. Such people are then "invited" to apply for party membership. To reject such an invitation without a plausible explanation would be foolish since it would make a person highly suspect in the eyes of the authorities. In order not to forfeit the chance for some semblance of tranquillity, many people have little choice but to join, even though they know that membership entails the boredom of compulsory attendance at endless meetings and the strain of compulsory performance of various "social assignments" (*obshchestvennye nagruzki*). Officials are included in those groups for which

membership in the party is compulsory. Every supervisory position in the USSR corresponds directly to a specific rung in the party hierarchy, e.g., a minister has to be a member (or a candidate member) of the Central Committee of the party, the head of a department or trust must be a member of a city or regional party committee, while a chief engineer, senior project designer, or high-ranking scientist must be at least a simple member in good standing. Membership in the party in these cases may not necessarily be a matter of career advancement—although advancement is impossible without it—but is first and foremost a prerequisite of job security.

There are many who join the party simply to promote their career ambitions, though they may soon learn that membership does not automatically open the way to membership in the Soviet elite. It takes years of diligent work in public affairs and strict adherence to a code of self-effacement and self-abasement for a citizen to prove him- or herself reliable enough to be allowed to reach the rungs of elite hierarchy.

Entrance to the party represents a kind of "purgatory," which a Soviet citizen may enter in hopes of rising higher, although, by itself this step does not guarantee a successful career in the communist "hereafter."

Party members criticized themselves during discussion of problems of organizational and Party work. (Partiynaya zhizn', no. 21, 1983, p. 43)

. . . in order to be a really active ideology-inspired Party fighter, every party member must constantly be engaged in raising the level of his political education. . . . (Partiynaya zhizn', no. 22, 1983, p. 12)

Party-Mindedness (*Partiynost'*). (1) An attribute of work indicating that it reflects a communist ideological orientation. (2) A social, class-based criterion of the conformity of scientific theories and works of art to the dictates of the communist authorities and Marxist doctrine. The concept of party-mindedness, discussed and justified by Lenin in his 1905 article entitled "Party Organization and Party Literature," was initially intended for the sole purpose of evaluating propagandistic literature. Such literature was to be under the control of party organizations and faithful to the party program. After the October Revolution, the "correct" class and ideological perspective began to be required indiscriminately of a whole gamut of artistic creation, past and present. It quickly became accepted as a universally applicable and indispensable critical yardstick for all social phenomena (See A. Lunacharsky, *Lenin i literaturovedenie* [Lenin and literary criticism], Moscow, 1932).

Party-mindedness demands that "reality" be presented and interpreted according to the communist worldview. Thus, the contradictory and multifaceted aspects of the world, perceived in the categories of party-mindedness, are reduced to the simplistic and predetermined. The paradoxical nature of human existence and universal moral values are suppressed in favor of a rigid mindset used to buttress a worldview crude enough to be encapsulated in slogans. Social phenomena not compatible with this mindset are either unknown or largely incomprehensible to those who have it.

Although party-mindedness is an artificial creation, it nevertheless is used as the standard by which every aspect of life is judged. Scientific theories and hypotheses have to be first and foremost party-minded. They are initially evaluated in terms of their correspondence to the Marxist canon. Evaluation in terms of their validity and explanatory or predictive power comes second, if at all.

Considering the party monopoly over ideas, it is not surprising that party-mindedness has often led to repression. A striking case in point is the postwar developments in Soviet biology that resulted in the destruction of numerous research centers and academic institutions and the dismissal of a number of prominent scientists from their posts. The devastating effects of party-mindedness were by no means confined to biology; every branch of intellectual pursuit, including philosophy, political economy, psychology, history, and sociology felt the force of its tyranny. Although military considerations forced the authorities to give physicists a certain degree of experimental freedom, even in this field a party-minded crusade eventually attacked such "idealistic" disciplines as the theory of relativity, quantum physics, and cybernetics.

In the arts, party-mindedness demanded a pseudorealism that programmatically precluded the presentation of what the Communist party considered undesirable and therefore termed "atypical." Verisimilitude was demanded—but with the proviso that content must be "typical" (*tipichesky*). Hence a distinction was posited between "reality"—the random facts of life, isolated, and of minor significance—and "truth"—ideologically sanctioned, "typical" facts, proclaimed as *truth* in *Pravda*. According to party-mindedness, only this kind of truth constitutes fit subject matter for an artist.

This narrowly utilitarian approach to art and the superimposition of the categories of historical materialism onto aesthetics straitjacketed creative endeavor and turned art into a form of party work. To statisfy the requirements of this "work," canons of socialist realism were established. Unapproved art forms (such as lyric verse, satirical theater, modernist music, structural analysis of literature, and abstract art) were forced to lead a precarious subterranean existence.

Many outstanding Soviet artists who did not conform to the dictates of party-mindedness were punished. Artists as gifted and diverse as Akhmatova, Tsvetaeva, Zoshchenko, Solzhenitsyn, Galich, Tartkovsky, and Brodsky, were silenced, incarcerated, or forced into exile. Hundreds of other important artists, poets, writers, directors, and musicians shared a similar fate.

The demand for party-mindedness deprives the artist in the Soviet Union of the right to an individual style or vision and leaves him or her a choice between bowing to the party or discontinuing artistic work. However, there is a third way that many Soviet writers have opted for to escape party dictates, that is, to turn to genres, e.g., translation, national epic, and folklore, where party interference is less pervasive. Yet creative artists cannot even take refuge in historical works as party watchdogs ensure that the past reflects their own understanding of the present. The Central Committee departments, which deal with propaganda, agitation, and science and which ensure that party-mindedness rules, are foremost among the plethora of organizations that vigilantly oversee all artistic work. Without their approval, no novel, painting, film, or symphony can reach the public.

However, Gorbachev's "thaw" of glasnost, which extricated from oblivion many outstanding names in art and literature, has in no way done away with party-mindedness. The latter has merely changed its profile, like other aspects of Gorbachev's rule: it is less blatant and more subtle than the previous version. The new Soviet leadership is magnanimous toward artists, who are no longer alive and hence not dangerous. Such veneration of famous corpses is convenient, since it enhances the liberal reputation of current government policies. Thus, Gumilev, Pasternak, Grossman, Chagall, and others have been posthumously enrolled in the service of perestroika.

The basic idea of party-mindedness, namely the claim that the party has the right to guide the intellectual life of the country, remains unchallenged. Beyond the borders of the USSR, party-mindedness found its expression in the form of the generalization of the October Revolution's experience. This experience was packaged in the form of dogmatic teachings forcefully foisted onto the countries of Eastern Europe, i.e., countries with different social structures and different historical experiences than the Soviet one. This led to collective criminal trials (of Kostov in Bulgaria, of Rajk in Hungary, of Patraskianu in Romania, of Slansky in Czechoslovakia) and to formidable economic stagnation.

In diplomacy, party-mindedness was expressed in the excommunication of Yugoslavia from the communist camp and the stig-matization of its leaders as fascists. To protect the holy cow of party-mindedness, tanks were sent in 1968 to crush Czech communists who sought for their country its own model of socialism, and ten years later to invade Afghanistan in order to bring a state, located outside the bounds of the socialist camp, to accept all the norms of Soviet politics.

Finally, party-mindedness means a dictatorship of the Soviet Communist party that is enforced by all possible means in art, intellectual life, and politics.

> Materialism can be said to include party-mindedness (and therefore) it requires that the evaluation of events be made directly and frankly from the point of view of a specific social group. (V. I. Lenin, Sochineniya [Works] 4th ed. vol. 1; Moscow: Publishing House for Political Literature, 1941, pp. 380–81)

> This victory is the result of the consolidation and perfecting of the democratic principles guiding the conduct of the Party and government. It has involved intense ideological work based on the principles of party-mindedness, class character, scientific outlook and civic consciousness. . . . (Agitator, no. 14, 1983, p. 12)

> The Party respects talent, but under no circumstances can talents forgo the Leninist principles of party-mindedness and the popular roots of literature. (Partiynaya zhizn', no. 17, 1983, p. 64)

Patriotism (*Patriotizm*). A mode of behavior and an attitudinal pattern inculcated in Soviet citizens. Soviet propaganda views patriotism as a sociopsychological phenomenon. Its moral value is to be assessed separately for each concrete socioeconomic context in which it appears. Thus, in exploitative societies (as all noncommunist societies by definition are), patriotism is rife with contradiction as love for the homeland coexists with hatred of the ruling regime. Under such conditions, patriotic sentiments of the masses only reach their full pitch during periods of historical dislocation. But it is precisely at such times that the working masses are said to have the right, or more correctly, the obligation, to reject patriotism when it comes at their expense or is contrary to their interests. In other words, in a conflict between homeland and class struggle, communism accords priority to the latter as Marx and Engels said: "The proletarians have no fatherland."

This formula, however, no longer holds when the communists have their own fatherland. In this fatherland, patriotism had to be rehabilitated as a positive national sentiment that would manifest itself in service and devotion to the Soviet communist state. In a remarkable about-face, the interests of the socialist homeland were proclaimed to coincide somehow with the aspirations of the international working-class movement, and the slogan "The proletarians have no fatherland" was replaced by the slogan "The Soviet Union is the fatherland of the world proletariat."

Previously irreconcilable, socialist patriotism and communist internationalism were thus proclaimed to be identical. This transformation occurred at the beginning of World War II as the culmination of the sustained effort to free patriotism from all its "bourgeois" connotations. When that was done, nothing hindered the appeal to popular patriotic emotions in the call to the defense of the communist state. During the war, the manipulation of the Soviet peoples' patriotic feelings did not stop short of typical great-power chauvinism. The Soviet people were taught that their country was superior to all others. Russian history was used to justify communist expansionism. Historical parallels were cited to legitimize the actions of the Soviet leaders. In fact, not only the Russian princes' liberation of their country from Mongol rule but even the colonial subjugation of Siberia by Ermak and the aggressive wars of Ivan the Terrible, Peter the First, and Catherine the Second were extolled as models for Soviet patriotism. However, the historical background was intended as an auxiliary prop for the "national form" of Soviet patrotism, the "contents" of which, in all circumstances, were required to remain "socialist."

Patriotism is frequently modified by attributes such as "Soviet" (*sovetsky*) or "socialist" (*sotsialistichesky*)—which in effect are equated. Soviet patriotism implies unquestioning loyalty to the party and the Soviet state. Since in the communist worldview devotion to the communist system, the Communist party, and the Soviet government together are substituted for love of one's native land and culture, all dissatisfaction with the regime is considered antipatriotic.

In practice, Soviet patriotism is used to embrace a multitude of actions. For example, it is patriotic to do one's military duty or to participate in socialist competition. Antipatriotic behavior can range from dodging military service and refusing to work beyond the limits of one's strength to dissenting from prescribed patterns of thinking or even marrying a foreigner. Via the equation of homeland with the Soviet system, the authorities label all opposition to the regime as irreconcilable with patriotism.

In order to blur the basic connection between patriotism and ethnicity, Soviet propagandists resort to the term "mass patriotism," which is intended to associate patriotism with enthusiasm for concrete projects, such as the cultivation of virgin lands or the construction of large industrial complexes.

Patriotic clichés abound. For instance, the phrases "patriotic undertaking" (*patrioticheskoe nachinanie*) and "patriotic initiative" (*patriotichesky pochin*) are used to denote any undertakings sponsored by the authorities, such as donating blood to medical institutions or working on holidays without remuneration. However, regardless of context, the ideological intent of the term is clear: the natural feeling of love for homeland must be replaced by love, however inauthentic, for communist values, including love for the party and the state.

The Peace Foundation unites people with clearly expressed patriotic sentiments and internationalist sympathies. . . . (Izvestiya, 26 September 1981, p. 3)

In a Soviet person patriotism and loyalty to the Fatherland are inseparable from love for the socialist system. (Agitator, no. 22, 1983, p. 10)

The author studies the character of the Soviet people with the same depth and seriousness and shows how the mighty spirit of national patriotism was revealed in our Fatherland's most difficult hour. (Izvestiya, 14 October 1983, p. 5)

Patronage (*Shefstvo*). Regular assistance in furthering production or educational goals rendered by one enterprise or individual to another enterprise or individual. The most widespread form of patronage is the participation of urban residents in agricultural work. In the early years of the Soviet regime, members of the intelligentsia taught the peasants to read and write, thereby attempting to raise the latter's political literacy (*politgramota*). Later, workers and employees were mobilized to work in fields and farms in attempts to make up for the scarcity of rural manpower and the inability (or unwillingness) of the peasants to complete their assignments.

Whole enterprises are often being recruited for patronage. Government agencies send employees to villages where they work without remuneration to help the collective farms fulfill their plans. Likewise, experienced workers assume sponsorship of youths, instructing them in work skills and familiarizing them with the latest technology.

Even famous scientists and artists are forced to assume "patronage obligations," such as visiting various enterprises to give lectures and concerts intended not merely to entertain the audience but also to educate it in the spirit required by the authorities.

In recent years, the flow of services in the reverse direction, i.e., from "protégés" (*podshefny*) to "patrons" (*shefy*), has become a factor of considerable significance. The protégé organizations assume certain obligations in relation to their patrons. These include supplying the patrons with food, fruit, and vegetables directly to patron enterprises (which helps at least these fortunates cope with general shortages), with the understanding that such supplies are not supposed to adversely affect planned deliveries to the state.

By taking part in discussions that follow each performance of the patrons, the "protégé" workers not only evaluate what they just saw or heard but also exercise ideological supervision over the performers by, it is claimed, spontaneously evincing their sound communist consciousness (*zdorovoe kommunisticheskoe nachalo*).

This process is used to give the appearance of a unity between the "toilers in the fields and factories" (*truzheniki polei i zavodov*) and the "toilers in the arts and sciences" (*truzheniki iskusstva i nauki*), and also to support the party demand that works of art should be readily comprehensible to common laborers—which, in fact, means that art should suit the interests of the party. This controlled interaction of patrons and protégés is employed by the Soviet authorities as a means of ideological indoctrination, political pressure, and administrative control.

By imposing patronage and assigning patrons, the authorities have succeeded in adding yet another agency of social control to the already existing ones.

Factory collectives have assumed patronage over schoolchildren. (Agitator, no. 22, 1983, p. 54)

Patronage of the construction of the "Komsomolskoe" settlement has been assumed by toilers of the provincial center. (Izvestiya, 3 December 1983, p. 1)

Often there are cases when patrons from the cities not only dig potatoes or bind flax but also milk cows. (Pravda, 13 December 1983, p. 3)

Peaceful Coexistence (*Mirnoe sosushchestvovanie*). A political slogan suggesting the renunciation of war as an instrument of foreign policy. The doctrine of peaceful coexistence was first formulated by Lenin as an alternative to worldwide communist revolution. The striking features of this doctrine were its inconsistency and duplicity. What the phrase "peaceful coexistence" seemed to imply was the recognition of t'ie right of nations to decide their own destiny independently and to have their sovereignty and territorial integrity respected by other nations. Yet peaceful coexistence was simultaneously regarded as a major form of class struggle. The Bolsheviks overcame this inherent contradiction with the aid of dialectics. They broadened the concept of peaceful coexistence in the direction of "internationalism," which they interpreted in such a way as to permit and even justify the Soviet Union's interference in other countries' internal affairs as well as to instigate Communist wars of "liberation" (*osvoboditel'nye voiny*). However, at the same time, the concept of peaceful coexistence was also restricted, so as not to be applied to ideology and thereby not hinder Moscow from waging permanent ideological warfare against the Free World.

The hypocrisy of the doctrine of peaceful coexistence stands best revealed in the well-known quip of Lenin that the capitalists "will sell us the rope with which to hang them." Far from being just a joke, the quip served Lenin and his successors as a policy assumption that the outside world should be manipulated into surrendering or committing suicide.

Lenin used to stress the view that the capitalists of the whole world and their governments would close their eyes to reality in their race to capture the Soviet market. He said they would grant credits that would enable the USSR to support communist parties in their own countries. By providing materials and technology that the USSR lacked, they would rebuild Soviet military industry, which later would facilitate a Soviet victory over its suppliers. In other words, the capitalist profiteers would commit suicide. However, it turned out that the USSR has not yet been able to hoist this rope and hang world capitalism with it. During the protracted competition with the West, the USSR has seen its economy seriously decline along with its social welfare and intellectual energies. The Soviet Union has not been able to "digest" new countries that fell into the sphere of their political influence during the period

of peaceful coexistence. The USSR was also faced with the prospect of an arms race in space, which threatened to reduce the technologically lagging Soviet Union to the status of second-rate power. In order to conceal its strategic powerlessness (at the time when its domestic crisis could no longer be concealed), Moscow has attempted to revive its policy of peaceful coexistence. The new Soviet leadership apparently realizes that the West must still remember the tragic experiences of the previous period of peaceful coexistence, which was marked by bloody wars and "peace settlements," such as prevailed in Vietnam, Cambodia, Ethiopia, Angola, Nicaragua, and Afghanistan—and hence it is offering a new, modified version of peaceful coexistence wrapped in attractive, humanitarian packaging. It is freed of ideological intolerance: the slogan launched was "the interest in survival shared by the whole world," which marked a clear departure from Leninism that put class interests above that of humanity as a whole. The new policy called for seeing the planet and its population as an indivisible entity and for the pursuit of foreign policy for the sake of not just national but also global goals.

The next step away from Leninism was the rejection of the image of the enemy, which had been cultivated by the communists to indoctrinate their ranks in hatred for the bourgeoisie and to heat them up for combat. Also reassessed was the idea of the competition between bipolar social systems that had been viewed as bound to lead inevitably to the ultimate victory of socialism over capitalism. The very phrase "victory of socialism" is now admitted to be flawed in that it could be taken to suggest implacability, fanaticism, and intolerance. It is now being proposed to accept political pluralism in the world as a sign of cultural diversity of humanity, which should be accepted and appreciated by all countries. The professed rejection of war as a means of spreading revolution is indeed a logical corollary of such a worldview. Perhaps the most profound departure from the traditional concept of peaceful coexistence lies in the philosophical implications of the "new political thinking" doctrine that the new Soviet leadership now expounds and advocates openly. The doctrine breaks radically with the theory of "scientific communism" while drawing from the intellectual heritage of the eighteenth century philosophy.

The combined ideas of peaceful coexistence and new political thinking may indeed be beneficial for humanity unless Gorbachev or his successors get involved in a kind of "struggle for peace" capable of desolating the whole earth.

> The struggle for wide international recognition and the introduction into international practice of the Leninist idea of peaceful coexistence occupied a central role in Soviet diplomatic efforts. (Mezhdunarodnaya zhizn', no. 9, 1979, p. 19)

> . . . objective opportunities and socio-political forces exist that are capable of preventing a slide into a new Cold War and of securing a normalized, peaceful coexistence for states with diverse social systems. (Pravda, 1 February 1982)

> The deputies to the highest organ of power in the course of personal contacts with parliamentarians of other countries, and delegations of the Supreme Soviet during their missions abroad, consistently defended the idea of peaceful coexistence of states and attacked the aims of aggressive circles in the United States and its allies. (Izvestiya, 19 December 1983, p. 1)

Peasant (*Krest'yanin*). (1) A person of inferior social rank, usually engaged in farm labor. (2) Somebody believed rude, unsophisticated or uneducated. Deliberate efforts have been made to push the word "peasant" out of circulation and replace it with "*kolkhoznik*" (collective farmer) or "*kolkhoz* peasantry." In terms of scope, however, the word "*kolkhoznik*" is narrower than "peasant," since it excludes those who work on state farms (*sovkhozy*), as well as those few private land cultivators who do exist. When a more comprehensive term for people working the land is needed, the blunt expression "rural laborer" (*sel'sky truzh-*

enik) is resorted to. In short, every effort is made to avoid using the word "peasant," even when the word fits. The only reason for this circumlocution is that the authorities associate the word with the image of the unruly, ungovernable *muzhik* class that has more than once rebelled against the regime.

The attitude of Soviet communists toward the peasants has been ambivalent. On the one hand, they recognize that the peasant typifies the nation as a whole by virtue of his forthright, proud, and anarchic nature. On the other hand, they look down at his presumed backwardness, obstinacy, dull-wittedness, and resistance to progress. This view of the peasantry is traceable to the mainstream current of Russian literature and social thought. The works of Pushkin, Turgenev, and Gorky are replete with praise for the hard-working, patient, and steadfast peasant, while not ignoring his or her common vices: drunkenness and passivity. The same authors also stressed that the peasants' earthy wisdom and good nature often made them morally superior to the intelligentsia. Their opinions stemmed not so much from detached judgement as from their own feelings of social inferiority (Pushkin and Turgenev) or class solidarity (Gorky).

Russian intellectuals and utopians tried to overcome the social barriers dividing them from the peasants. As part of the program of "going to the people," as advocated by the *zemlya i volya* (Land and Freedom) movement in the late nineteenth century, thousands of them flocked to the countryside to educate, heal, and generally concern themselves with the peasantry. But they were to be disappointed, for the muzhiks were not ready to accept their radical views. Society as a whole began to despair about the peasant, creating attitudes that provided fertile ground for the spread of Marxist doctrine, which provided ideological justification for the view that the peasant could never be regarded as the country's hope for the future.

Marx and Engels liked to speak of the "idiocy of rural life," while their Russian disciple, Plekhanov, saw the muzhik as "an unfeeling beast of burden." Lenin pointed out his "wild and mean individualist spirit," while for Stalin the peasants were "the refuse of humanity." None of them limited themselves to such epithets, however. They all tried to discover the historical role of the peasant in political development.

Basically, what Marxism did was to convert the populist illusions about the "prototypical peasant" into a no less delusory image of an idealized proletariat. As a result, no one accurately gauged the aspirations of either the workers or the peasants. This failure led to the formulation of the totally unrealistic theory of "socialist" revolution, according to which any society aspiring to progress would split into two hostile classes, the bourgoisie and the proletariat. In between them would be the peasantry, who were destined either to side with the workers, if they were to remain deprived, or to supplement the ranks of the capitalists, if they were to grow rich.

Communist policy toward the peasantry was always based on the perception that they were an intermediate social stratum. The communists never cared about their needs and were interested only in their social function, i.e., whose side they would take in the Revolution. The attitude of Lenin and of all subsequent Soviet leaders toward the peasantry depended on their assessments. For Lenin, the peasant was alternately "a property owner" or "a laborer." The peasant, he contended, suffered from adversity and exploitation, yet still remained "an entrepreneur." Lenin used to say that the peasant's petty production gives birth to capitalism spontaneously and on a massive scale. Lenin did not confine himself to talking. He was determined to exploit the peasantry for the sake of socialist reconstruction. True, he believed that in the end peasantry was bound to disappear from the stage of history, and as a true-blue Marxist he was anxious to precipitate that process.

Lenin pronounced the well-to-do peasants (kulaks, cf.) against whom he attempted to incite the envy and ire of the poor peasants, to be enemies of the party and the proletariat. To cheer the hearts of the unfortunates whom the Revolution had driven into greater poverty than ever, an impression was created that a utopian, classless society was just around the corner and that all that was needed to build it was just one last effort—destruction of the kulaks. The rich peasants were subjected to crippling taxation, declared to be lishentsy ("deprived persons," cf.) and stripped of all their rights. Still, Lenin's earthly paradise failed to materialize, and so the battlefront against the peasants was broadened. If Lenin's policies regarding the peasants can be considered inconsistent and vacillating, his comrades-in-arms can hardly be described as hesitant. Zinoviev, for example, declared: "Ninety out of a hundred million people must follow us. To the rest we have nothing to say. They must be liquidated." Even by conservative estimates in his number of peasant victims, Stalin outstripped Zinoviev's "recommendation."

The antipeasant terror in the Soviet Union would eventually be considered "normal" for a socialist society. It was therefore replicated in China, Cambodia, and, in a milder form, in Cuba and Eastern Europe. In the USSR, the terror against peasants can be divided into three periods. The first period, a prologue to what was to happen next, lasted from 1918 to 1922. It claimed five million peasant victims, shot for "sabotage" and "anti-Soviet activity," in addition to seven million who died in the chaos and poverty caused by the civil war. The second period encompassed 1929 and 1930, when countrydwellers were hit by a double blow: the kulaks were liquidated as a class, either physically or by being exiled to Siberia, and the peasantry was crushed and totally subjugated to the state by the collectivization of agriculture. The cost of this "revolution from above" is estimated at six and one half million deaths. The denouement of the third stage of the terror unfolded from 1932 to 1933, again at the cost of millions of lives. It consisted of starving the peasants to death by purposefully engineered famine. The new *kolkhozy* were stripped of all their produce and crippled by extortionate taxes. In the party's assessment, however, the task remained uncompleted, and scattered attempts to complete it continued until the outbreak of World War II.

Thus, the peasantry paid for the attempt to put Marxist ideas into practice by the destruction of 25 percent of its ranks. They had to die in order to permit the Soviet leadership to carry through its dreams of building a new society and test its theories that distinctions between peasants and workers, and between the city and the countryside, are bound to disappear irreversibly.

The so-called kulaks often happened to be decent people while the poor peasants could be dregs of society and parasites. (Literaturnaya gazeta, no. 34, 24 August 1988, p. 5)

. . . and after Stalin's article appeared, kolkhoz and village soviet chairmen, and members of the government began to oppress the peasants. (Pravda, 21 August 1988, p. 2)

The peasants have, nevertheless, come a long way during the period of Soviet rule. How far we would all have advanced if the muzhiks had not been crushed and tormented? (Izvestiya, 13 August 1988, p. 3)

Pension (*Pensiya*). Form of social security provided on grounds of age, disability, or loss of the main family breadwinner. The average pension in the USSR is 87 rubles/month, which just barely exceeds the poverty line of 70 rubles and enables no one to make ends meet. For food alone, a person needs to spend a minimum of 70 to 80 rubles, and even this on the condition that he is able to obtain foodstuffs at set prices in state stores. But he needs at least 20 rubles for the rental of his one-room apartment, 5 rubles for transportation, 10 rubles for domestic expenses (e.g., repairs), 10 rubles for clothing, and at least 10 rubles for medication and/or entertainment. Such a minimal budget amounts to 125 to 130 rubles monthly.

However, there does exist in the Soviet Union a segment of the aged population that lives somewhat more comfortably. This is a group of 500,000 special pensioners. For the members who are former party or government officials, the special pension amounts to 240 rubles for national posts, 160 for republic ones, and 140 for local ones. Also among the privileged are 100,000 retirees who receive military pensions, which amount to more than half of their salaries, and tens of thousands of diplomaed doctors of science and professors, who receive a minimum of 160 rubles.

Yet all of these together—retired party and government officials, ex-officers, and ex-academics—comprise less than 2 percent of the 38 million-strong army of Soviet pensioners. The remainder live in destitution and undernourishment: 29 million pensioners receive less than 90 rubles monthly, while another 8 million between 90 and 120 rubles. Furthermore, their living standard is constantly declining due to inflation pegged at 4 to 5 percent annually. Unlike many other countries, in the USSR pensions are linked neither to the standard of living nor to the index of consumer prices.

Pensions in the Soviet Union amount to less than half the average salary, to 42 percent of it, to be precise, while in the West they amount to 50 to 80 percent of a worker's income. A Soviet pension is obviously inadequate to allow an elderly person to maintain his or her former living standard, which itself ranked only 49th among the developed countries in the world. As if this were not bad enough, the situation of others is even worse: pensions of invalids range from 26 to 41 rubles, those of collective farmers amount to 40 rubles, and those of families who have lost their breadwinner to 31 rubles.

Thus, the pension of invalids with third class ailments who have not completed their work probation period amounts to 20 rubles per month. (Moskovskie novosti, no. 2, 8 January 1989, p. 3)

My mother received a small collective farm pension of 50 rubles and during the last three years of her life she lived with me. (Ogonek, no. 14, April, 1989, p. 3)

People's Jurors/Jury (*Narodyne zasedateli*). Citizens participating in criminal or civil trial hearings. The people's jurors for district and city courts are elected by open vote at their places of work or residence for 2½-year terms, while the jurors for military tribunals are elected at servicemen's meetings for terms of the same duration. The people's jurors for the highest courts—provincial, republic, and supreme—are elected by the respective Soviets for terms of five years. Essentially, all these elections are only a formality, since the candidates are picked in advance by the party committee, with a single candidate for each seat.

The jury's powers are just as nominal. Professional judges are always able to impose their will on the jury. The jury is not qualified to formulate a proper verdict, one that would include an analysis of the evidence and the presented arguments, and thus it has no choice but to comply with the judge's instructions. More importantly, the judge represents the awe-inspiring power and authority of the government, while the jury members represent no one but themselves and the favor of the invisible hand "up there" that selected them for participation in court proceedings.

The passive role of the people's jury led to their being nicknamed "*kivaly*"—a derogatory word literally translatable as "those who nod their heads in assent." Their apathy and helplessness are one of the causes of the arbitrariness of the Soviet courts, which often punish the innocent while, under the pressure of phone calls from the authorities, acquitting criminals. The courts also tend to follow the changing direction of political winds in zealous haste to rubberstamp the verdicts determined in advance.

The tragic protracted exposure to legal despotism has in the recent years increasingly prompted Soviet citizens to challenge this miscarriage of justice. Finding no support in the annals of Soviet law, they turned to Russian history to the practice of jury trial (*prisyazhny sud*), which had been introduced in Russia more than a century ago, in 1864. It turned out that tsarist judicial practice corresponded to the spirit of contemporary Soviet democratic reforms. Still, so-

cialist rhetoric had to be paid its due, and so the term "people's representatives" (*narodnye predstaviteli*) was introduced. Supposedly, the "people's representatives," unlike the people's jury, were to be totally independent of the judge. Even more than that, the judge's decisions were to be based on the judgment of the representatives, whose deliberation and conclusions were supposed to determine the outcome of the trial.

Needless to say, "people's representatives" are incapable of solving many judicial problems. In order to democratize the Soviet legal procedure, one would have to begin with restructuring the system of criminal investigation in a way designed to make it impossible for the public prosecutor's office to supervise its own operations, concretely to conduct investigations, and at the same time to determine their legality. Yet it is indeed advisable to substitute people's jury with "people's representatives," i.e., to confer on the latter all the authority that the former had possessed in theory. This would revolutionize the entire judicial system in the Soviet Union as the investigators, prosecutors, defense counsels, and judges alike would cease to treat legal proceedings as a superfluous ritual with a predetermined outcome. The law would then become the instrument of justice and legality in the way it had been before it became bound by the shackles of Soviet ideology.

> In the USSR, members of the people's jury for district and city courts are elected at general meetings held at their place of work or residence . . . . (Sovetsky entsiklopedichesky slovar [Soviet encyclopedic dictionary], published by "Sovetskaya Entsiklopediya," Moscow, 1981, p. 872)

> That is precisely why the bench, in addition to the judge, also includes two members of the people's representatives, and all three are absolutely equal before the law. (Moskovskie novosti, 23 October 1988, p.12)

Perestroika (*Reconstruction*). In the broad sense: qualitative changes of a social system, the introduction and development of new forms and methods of administration with the aim of improving its functioning and operation; in a narrower sense: the transformation of (specifically) Soviet governmental structure, economic management and social policies. The term "perestroika" first appeared in Russian in the eighteenth century as a literal translation of the Latin *reconstructio* (*re* into the Russian *pere* and *constructio* into *stroenie*.) The meaning of the term then corresponded directly to the meaning of its constituent elements: it meant rebuilding, re-equipping. In the late 1980s, during the period of social reforms inaugurated by Gorbachev, the meaning of the term became broader. A first, it referred to various measures intended to produce optimal economic effects by means of advanced technology at minimum cost in terms of time, effort, and resources. Subsequently, the term has been extended to also encompass social relations and civic virtues. In this context, the authorities have attributed to it "revolutionary" content.

The latter, "revolutionary" meaning of perestroika clashes with its original meaning, which implies the existence of preserved foundations. As Marxists understand it, revolution entails a radical overhaul of the social and political structure, concretely the overthrow of an old regime and the establishment of a new one, usually by armed uprising sparked by a legitimacy crisis and a wave of popular discontent. The new meaning also remains at odds with the real character of the changes occurring today in the USSR. The very foundation of Soviet society—Soviet socialism—remains entirely unaffected by all of the reforms Gorbachev has launched.

Conceptually, perestroika is close to within-the-system "reform," which affects only some aspects of society, its polity, or institutions, while preserving the system itself. Like reform, perestroika occurs when the ruling class (in the USSR, the Communist party elite), usually under popular pressure, embarks on various intrasystemic transformation, ultimately in order to maintain or consolidate its power.

Yet perestroika is not entirely coextensive with "reform," since a reform can be radical while perestroika (thus far at least) can not. It is closer to "evolution" or amelioration, that is, gradual change within the communist system aimed at modernization and improved functioning of its institutions, such as state monopoly of property, one-party rule, or central planning. The striking features of perestroika are cautious, gradual, and planned change, implemented by the socialist state on its own initiative and under the guidance of the party. The only thing revolutionary about perestroika is that it resembles what is commonly described as *revolution from above*. But even here the resemblance is more apparent than real, since, after the current changes, all power remains in the hand of the party exactly as was the case before. Power has not even been redistributed *within* the ruling class: it remains concentrated to the point of virtual monopoly in the hands of the highest echelon of the elite—the partocracy (cf.).

Despite the crucial disclaimer just noted, there is something revolutionary about perestroika. It is revolutionary in a semantic sense: it marks a devaluation, a "deradicalization" of "revolution" as a key Marxist concept. Perestroika redefines the concept of revolution so that it no longer implacably requires class struggle but may even entail class cooperation within the confines of a single social formation with the goal of revitalizing rather than destroying it.

This reevaluation of old ideological verities occurred neither suddenly nor arbitrarily. Beginning with the 1970s, Soviet society found itself in a completely novel situation—its rates of economic development began to fall precipitously, its social problems mounted and became acute, its spiritual values began to be covertly eroded, and alcoholism and drug addiction increased until they posed a tangible threat of social disintegration. Decadent, corrupt party leaders were losing control over social developments, while in both ideology and high culture inertia and stagnation held sway.

The connection between one's labor and one's level of consumption was totally lost.

National income began to seriously decline until it reached the level of deep economic stagnation. At a certain stage, attempts were made to halt or at least slow down this process by increasing investment and building new production units. However, such extensive methods of developing the economy were frustrated by bureaucratic inertia and incompetent management. The Soviet workforce, browbeaten, exploited, and deprived in the extreme, could not be induced by any incentive to work conscientiously. Attempts to co-opt some of them by privileges or awards only helped stir up more discontent among the masses of others who resented the further social inequalities. It was clear that Soviet society was in dire straits.

However, this was by no means the first crisis in Soviet history. Since 1917, it had undergone a number of social tremors starting with the period of War Communism. Then the authorities tried to impose elements of a classless society, equalization of wages and some forms of workers' self-government. Lenin succeeded in overcoming the crisis of this period by adopting his New Economic Policy (NEP, cf.), which tolerated a certain degree of economic liberalism and democracy. Another grave crisis began in the 1930s, when Stalin made Soviet society bear the brunt of his forced industrialization and forced collectivization of agriculture. This social crisis, spurred by massive repression carried out by means unequalled in their inhumanity, continued until the early 1950s.

After Stalin's death, Soviet leaders began to lead Soviet society onto the path of change, but with great caution. No radical steps that might transform society were undertaken. Their policies did not imply a rejection of socialism, but rather a reaffirmation of the Soviet brand of socialism with all its inner contradictions and endemic problems. This explains why they could not succeed in overcoming the malignancies inherent in the Soviet system. The root of the problem lay not in any subjective or personal failures of Soviet leaders but in the nature of the diverse barriers to social change that Soviet socialism erected and continues to erect. These barriers, whether political or economic, are responsible for the dearth of distributive justice and social equality.

The survival of any social system (or of any natural organism for that matter) depends on its ability to heal or revitalize itself. This crucial ability was gradually lost, as a result of which Soviet socialism began disintegrating, first economically and then socially. Soviet ideology was no longer helpful in sustaining the Soviet system's survival capacity. There remained one possible way of saving that system: an organ transplantation in the medical sense of the term. For organs of a social system healthier than the Soviet one (i.e., a free market, cost accountability, pricing reflecting market values, etc.) could still be transplanted into the Soviet system. Perestroika is in fact the name of such a transplantation, but it is a euphemistic one, its euphemism intended to avoid an open discrediting of communist ideology.

Although it is closely connected with social development, acceleration (cf.), and improvement of social conditions, in its contents perestroika is not to be equated with these processes. Perestroika amounts to transforming the social structure, politics, and culture of the USSR. It presupposes improving economic administration, increasing discipline, and introducing more responsibility and better organization. However, these measures are by themselves insufficient to revitalize Soviet society. Thus perestroika fosters new ways of reorganizing the economy and the material base of production, reassigning investment priorities; it calls for the introduction of advanced (computerized) systems of management. Perestroika also entails a reorientation from building new enterprises to modernizing the equipment of existing ones, saving resources, and improving the quality of manufactures.

Various reforms attempted in the Soviet Union by previous leaders were stymied by petrified production relations and the entrenched interests of existing institutions and organizations. Two previous attempts at perestroika, the reforms of Khrushchev in 1956 and of Kosygin in 1966, failed. But Khrushchev and Kosygin attempted to change Soviet society before it was politically ripe for it. Gorbachev's perestroika, by contrast, is occurring in a different political context: it was launched when urgent need for radical change was already commonly recognized in the USSR. Such changes were required with— or without—Gorbachev. Without them, the prospects for the vast and rich Soviet Union have been correctly assessed as dim.

Under Gorbachev, perestroika very quickly expanded from the economy to the social sphere, since it is in the latter area that the key to its success lies. But social change is unimaginable except through the medium of significant changes in the way people think and in their style and methods of work. It is also unimaginable without the implementation of certain constitutional rights, which had existed on paper but not in practice and without the implementation of glasnost (cf.).

The aim of perestroika is not only to improve the performance of government institutions but also to remold the patterns of citizens' behavior. The Soviet leadership has finally come to understand that no real social and economic change is possible without the removal of multitudinous institutional barriers, without a mobilization of human effort, and without some consideration for the interests of labor collectives and various interest groups. Perestroika also calls for a reevaluation of the traditional Soviet ideological commitment to the Soviet brand of social "security"—i.e., a commitment that had always been the Soviet Union's pride. Perestroika threatens to deprive millions of workers of their relative security, which has thus far only shielded them from the ordinary pressures of everyday life and thereby generated widespread apathy. Despite their inability or unwillingness to do good work or their drinking and shirking on the job, the masses of laborers manage, although with difficulty, to make ends meet. The system has guaranteed them employment; but it also "guaranteed" that anyone who performed his or her work industriously would have to content him- or herself with a pitiful salary and near-poverty.

Perestroika raises expectations in regard to the workers' performance and assigns them greater responsibility. It denies them the automatic right to survive even if they work badly. Simultaneously, it exposes the privileges that are enjoyed by the Soviet elite and, although it does not propose to eliminate them, it tends to restrict them to the select few.

While attempting to optimalize the performance of social and production collectives, perestroika provides the political leadership with opportunities for correcting its performance by means of encouraging democratization (cf.). Thus it is the actual practice rather than the theory of perestroika that is fostering the values of self-management (however restricted) and openness to criticism (though directed). This process also allows the Soviet authorities to approach their real problems more comprehensively and to implement reforms, including the assessment of costs and benefits and the incorporation of such assessments into the new system of management.

The perestroika-based reforms entail the gradual transition from purely administrative techniques of industrial management to economically-informed ones such as full cost-accountability and self-financing, and they make personal income proportional to the productivity of one's work. Perestroika is expected to last ten to twelve years, i.e., until the end of the present century. Much less well-defined than the time schedule is the destination point of perestroika, i.e., the social structure that is intended to emerge under the impact of now ongoing changes. No concrete blueprints have been provided, rather a general outline has been mooted, namely the building of a modern socialism, more efficient, more dynamic, and more humane than the one now in operation. To sum up, perestroika represents yet another alternative to communism, one that the present Soviet leadership can be expected to exploit propagandistically during the time it stays in power.

At present, that leadership is keenly concerned with making its reforms irreversible.

They envisage the continuation of perestroika for a minimum of five years, and they hope that at the end of that time reversal to old ways will no longer be possible, since stagnation of political institutions will by then be overcome, the economy will be revitalized, dependable and effective mechanisms of social acceleration (cf.) will have been created, self-management and workers' initiative will have taken root, and inner discipline and orderly behavior will have become the norm.

However, none of these aims should be construed as meaning that perestroika would mark the end of the totalitarian system. Rather, its goal is to leave the foundation of the Soviet edifice, one-party rule, intact and merely to renovate the economic pillars and the ideological roof of that edifice. This means that power in the Soviet Union will remain in the hands of the party bureaucrats, who will either foster or hamper perestroika, depending on their corporate interests. Consequently, the ultimate fate of perestroika is in question. Adverse consequences may well appear not only in the more distant future, but also in the immediate future, since perestroika already faces firm and widespread opposition. The most active segment of this opposition consists of several thousand holders of top national or republic posts in the party hierarchy who came to power under Gorbachev's predecessors. The possible success of perestroika can only spell their demise as their careers are bound to be terminated by a purge intended to open the door to supporters of the new leadership. No less a threat to perestroika is posed by the whole bureaucratic estate of hundreds of thousands of influential party functionaries and high government officials. They have grown fat on the fruits of corruption and learned to expect them as their due. For them, perestroika means the loss of at least some of their privileges, the most important of which is the absence of effective oversight, i.e., their immunity to criticism. Such bureaucrats are unlikely to be at the forefront of opposition to Gorbachev because they are too disunited and too dominated by the power

and authority of the top leadership. However, they would support and join a revolt against Gorbachev with relish if and when it started.

Another serious obstacle to perestroika is posed by the several million-strong economic bureaucracy. These cadres have long ago ceased taking any initiative. They are incapable of generating any ideas and even of learning anything new, as that requires an intellectual effort, which for some would be too demanding while for others downright impossible to make. Although they support perestroika verbally, they have no idea how to implement it in their own bailiwicks and therefore undermine it—with unrealistic projects, promises that cannot be kept, customary write-ups (*pripiski*, cf.), etc. The common skepticism of Soviet toilers, workers, and peasants about perestroika precludes their enthusiastic endorsement of it. They have little faith in the merits of the measures touted by Gorbachev & Co. They are adopting a wait and see stance. Moreover, their doubts are tinged with fear: it is difficult for them to endure without vodka (cf. anti–alcohol campaign) and they suspect that labor discipline and ceaseless supervision will make their lives even more onerous.

Determined support for perestroika cannot even be found among the officials at the very top of the power pyramid, the members of the Politburo and the secretaries of the Central Committee. They support it, but only as long as it brings results and suits their own corporate interests. At the first signs of its collapse—in the event of its proving disappointing or in the event of an authority crisis—they will be the first to oppose it.

In the meanwhile, however, serious social change is taking place. Malignant layers of "mature" or even "superannuated" socialism are being removed. Political rigidity, spiritual petrification, and dogmatism become discredited. People undergo transformations: they are made to learn new social commitments, attachments, emotions; they are given an opportunity to speak without fear and to think instead of sloganeering.

This process is occurring, but slowly, gradually, hesitantly, and with setbacks.

The goal of perestroika is not to change the system itself but to mend it. Its aim is not the transformation of the regime but its revitalization. However, Gorbachev has already gone farther in the process and done more than all his predecessors, including Khrushchev. Khrushchev's policies were directed against a by-product of the system—the Stalinist cult of personality. In other words, these policies merely affected the subject of history. In contrast, Gorbachev has already transcended the level of historical subjectivity. His perestroika concerns itself with the object of history: but precisely because of that it poses a threat to the integrity of the system. Hence the discrepancy between its design and its unintended effects. Subjectively, perestroika was meant to repair the system. By carrying it out, Gorbachev is modernizing this system, getting it in step with the age, and suffusing it with flexibility and dynamism. But objectively, perestroika also undermines the system, its political foundations, and the social structure.

This contradiction between the subjective intention and the objective consequences of perestroika can be expected to soon pose a painful dilemma to Gorbachev. He might then put a halt to perestroika out of fear that it will imperil the regime. In that case he would inaugurate a phase of political reaction. But he might alternatively extend perestroika: in that case he might inaugurate genuinely revolutionary transformation of his society. The latter development is, however, rather unlikely since the sociopolitical structure of the state as well as the entire cultural "superstructure" (its morality, attitudes, worldview, etc.) all remain unaffected by perestroika. Emphases in the system are changing, but not yet the system itself. Its repressive totalitarian essence has begun to shift to low gear and has more moderate manifestations, but it has not been permanently altered. At any time it might be shifted again into a higher gear.

In other words, the process of perestroika has not set in motion qualitative, basic changes, but only ones of secondary importance. Yet a quantitative change may conceivably be, at a certain point, transformed into a qualitative one. In that case, perestroika would pursue its own independent course beyond any communist framework, thus engendering irreparable schisms within the monolithic Soviet society. Once things go this far, the Soviet leadership itself would be compelled to undergo a radical transformation.

One should, however, beware of confusing the changes in the meaning of the concept of perestroika with the changes in the meaning of the phenomenon in itself. Yet perestroika ultimately may develop a dynamic of its own: the call by Gorbachev for a revolution within the framework of the 1917 Revolution may engender "counterrevolutionary" developments that would challenge the foundations of the communist edifice laid by Lenin and his associates.

. . . at issue are processes of an extreme importance to our country. Too much depends on the success of perestroika to allow even the slightest relaxation in our concentration on it. (Perestroika neotlozhna, ona kasaetsya vsekh i vo vsem. Sbornik materialov o poezdke M. S. Gorbacheva na dal'niy vostok 25–31 iyulya 1986 [Perestroika is urgent, it affects everyone and everything. A collection of materials from M. S. Gorbachev's trip to the (Soviet) Far East from 25–31 July 1986], Moscow, 1986, p. 36)

Perestroika is the determined overcoming of stagnation and the destruction of braking mechanisms, the creation of a dependable and effective mechanism of accelerating the socioeconomic development of society, and fostering in the latter of greater dynamism. (M. S. Gorbachev, Perestroika i novoe myshlenie dlya nashey strany i vsego mira [Reconstruction and a new thinking for our country and the whole world], Moscow: Izd. politicheskoy literatury, 1987, p. 20)

Perestroika can be considered revolutionary not in the political sense, in which it means a socio-political resolution aiming at a regime change, but in a dialectical, socio-philosophical sense where it means a leap forward in social development. (V. Semenov, Voprosy filosofii, no. 1, 1987, p. 22)

Personal Case (*Personal'noe delo*). Hearing conducted by a party organization to deal with a misconduct of a party member who has violated party discipline or the criminal law. Although Soviet dictionaries and encyclopedias do not include the phrase "personal case," the phenomenon is of major significance. Of prime importance is the fact that party members are granted a kind of immunity whereby no criminal investigation can be initiated against them without the knowledge and consent of their party organization. They can be brought to trial only after a city or district party committee determines their liability for prosecution. Moreover, party members are not arrested until after they have been expelled from the party. There are very rare exceptions to this rule, when expulsion from the CPSU is carried out in absentia, upon the recommendation of the procurator's office and under the authority of the city or district party committee.

Paragraph 12 of the CPSU statute states that "if a member of the Party commits a criminal offense, he must be expelled from the Party and stand trial in accordance with the law." Yet it is the party and not the judiciary that decides whether or not the person has committed a crime, and if so, what punishment he or she deserves. In cases where the party organization considers a public trial ill-advised, it reviews the case in camera, and, in conformity with the CPSU statutes, opens a personal case on the member in question.

Such cases are first reviewed by primary party organizations and then, if necessary, by special party investigatory organizations, such as the Central Committee's Party-Control Committee or party commissions operating at the level of district, city, regional, provincial, territorial, or republic committees.

The proceedings of personal cases are secret. They are extralegal and are usually the result of secret directives from above. Party commissions are staffed by party investigators whose unlimited powers put them above the state procurator's office and also allow them to subordinate the latter to their (or rather, to the party's) will.

In constitutional terms, the delegation of law enforcement powers to a political organization, such as the Communist party, indicates that the latter stands above the law. Practically, the existence of such "private" law enforcement facilities enables the Soviet leadership to conceal the crimes of members of the party from public knowledge and thereby both preserve the reputations of criminals in high places and keep the name of the party unsullied by scandal.

As a rule, a personal case is set up for hearing in response to the initiative of an anonymous letter received by party headquarters or on the basis of information of an investigative agency.

In Soviet propaganda jargon, the hearing of a personal case by a primary party organization board as hailed as "the effective means of comradely control over the conscientious fulfillment by a Communist of his obligations." In colloquial speech, it is simply called "repentance." If the repentance is not considered sufficient or if the offense under investigation is very serious, then, with the approval of either the city or district party organization, the personal case is brought before a closed meeting of a party organization. In certain cases, a superior party body examines a particular personal case and makes recommendations to the party organization, either for punishment or for leniency.

There are two categories of misconduct that warrant the hearing of a personal case. The first involves infringements of discipline, such as absenteeism from party meetings and political study groups, nonpayment of membership dues, other violations of party discipline, or engaging in behavior considered antisocial, such as drunkenness, hooliganism, or adultery. Personal cases of this type are used for educational purposes and carry no threat of expulsion. Since the shortcomings of an individual party member have a bearing upon his or her entire workplace or party discipline, they are not considered his or her own private affair but rather "a problem affecting collective interests." Accordingly, the party organization requires reeducation of its errant members. Under this banner, the party encourages denunciations of fellow party members and interference in their private lives.

The second category of misconduct involves abuse of office—bribery, theft, illegal transactions, reporting nonexistent achievements in plan fulfillment. As a rule, these are not offenses committed by the rank-and-file membership, and thus they lead to personal cases relatively rarely, basically when a party member breaks the rules of the game, as by failing to share his or her ill-gotten gains with higher ups or by allowing his or her misdeeds to become public knowledge. In the latter case, the party is quick to dissociate itself from the offender by defining his or her personal case as a "private affair which does not reflect upon the party." Thus, the concept of "private affair" serves as a convenient way of telling the masses that corruption is occasional rather than widespread. In reality, graft is caused less by individual traits of party members than by the system of status and privilege from which all party members benefit.

Over the past few years, the number of new stories in the Soviet press about delinquent communists has clearly increased. Cases of infractions of discipline at work, drunken and disorderly behavior, the embezzlement of state funds, and bribery are reported with the frequency of natural disasters. In the five years since Gorbachev has been general secretary, hundreds of thousands of party members have been expelled. Also, seminars on procedural methods related to personal cases and the struggle against corruption were set up for secretaries of primary party organizations.

The party metes out punishment according to the gravity of the offense. Personal cases involving violation of discipline are treated with relative indulgence; those found guilty are advised to mend their ways, and the affair usually ends there. However, if a personal case is of a criminal nature, demotion, expulsion, or referral for criminal prosecution are not unusual. The disposition of such cases usually depends more on the position occupied by the party member and his or her connections in the party apparatus than on the degree of his or her actual culpability. Sometimes the handling of such cases reflects current developments in party policy. For example, when a campaign against a given type of offense is being waged, harsher than usual punishment of party members may be meted out for the edification of the public. Normally, however, it is the cases of rank-and-file members that are referred for criminal prosecution. Heads of the regional-, city-, or republic-scale enterprises are rarely prosecuted, and top party leaders, as a rule, are not prosecuted, highlighting the fact that the party is not subject to the jurisdiction of courts of law.

Highly publicized trials, like those currently taking place under Gorbachev, are the exception that proves the rule. First, they concern leaders who had fallen out of power or had been compromised by their closeness to Brezhnev. Secondly, such political has-been can neither defend themselves nor implicate their accusers, who, no less than they, have been involved in crimes.

There is a standard procedure for hearing personal cases at party meetings. Everything is determined in advance; speeches and decisions are drafted well before the meetings get under way. Nevertheless, attendance at such meetings is high, since they offer some break from the boredom and monotony of regular meetings.

Although at one time criticism and self-criticism were considered to be a source of the party's strength and militancy, over the years they have become an empty ritual of denunciation and defamation of the culprit, a symbolic demonstration of the depth of his or her moral degradation. The script of a personal case requires that the accused play his or her allotted part and vigorously condemn him- or herself. If one attempts to justify one's actions, this is considered a challenge to the authority of the party. Denunciation of associates and promises to improve one's behavior are also part of one's role. One's guilt is not in question. The only chance of mitigating the verdict lies in appealing to the mercy of one's judges. Absence of ill intent, ignorance, or human weakness can be cited as extenuating circumstances, provided the culprit acts the penitent. All this is an act. Fear turns wayward communists into archhypocrites. Their duplicity reflects the general character of Soviet society, in which there are two moralities: one for communists and another for the common people. Communist morality is grandiloquent but sham, while the ordinary Soviet citizens try to preserve at least the remnants of moral values common to all mankind. Thus, the actual feelings and thoughts of those accused are probably entirely different from the platitudes they are forced to mouth in their slavish bid for leniency. Alienated from the official Marxist ethic, resentful of the "collective" that has turned them into small cogs in the state machine, their self-pity is so great that they probably do not even recognize their complicity in their own humiliation.

Party organizations not only punish offenders but also administer "prescriptions" for their "rehabilitation" (*ispravlenie*). Self-abasement and promises of future obedience on the part of the confessed offender are not taken as a guarantee that he will "mend his ways," but rather as an indication that he will be more cautious and more cunning in the future. Therefore he is assigned new party tasks or other means of proving himself a "reformed" man. For the party, ordinary hypocrisy is not enough: it requires that hypocrisy become a deeply ingrained habit, a virtual second nature.

Thus it turns out that the hearing of personal cases, which is considered an important means of political education, is actually a training course for hypocrites. These sanctimonious displays are referred to in party propaganda as "means of raising the consciousness of party members." The verdicts of these party "courts" carry more weight than those of the courts of law since ex-convicts are not prevented from reintegrating themselves into Soviet society, while those who are expelled from the party are marked

for life. Dismissed from their positions, or, if fortunate, only demoted in rank, the expellees become social pariahs. The only way out of this position is reinstatement in the party, but this involves repeated humiliation, in numerous hearings, endless penance, and reiterated demonstrations of party loyalty. They need to find sponsors to vouch for them and are also required to undergo a second "candidacy" period before any party organization will consent to readmit the penitent. Of all party procedures, rehabilitation thus embodies most fully the characteristics Lenin required for the "new type" (*novy tip*) party that it be monolithic in structure and martial in discipline.

> The hearing of a personal case consists of the discussion of the unseemly conduct of a Communist at a Party bureau, a Party committee, or a Party meeting. (Partiynaya zhizn', no. 17, 1979, p. 74).

> I am willing to postpone the hearing of the personal case of the Communist Tokarev until he returns to work. (Partiynaya zhizn' no. 21, 1979, p. 70)

> When one ponders these personal cases, one realizes that a penalty meted out to a Communist by the Party nearly always indicated that something has been overlooked by the Party organization . . . . (Kommunist vooruzhennykh sil, no. 22, 1979, p. 43)

Personal Socialist Obligations (*Lichnye sotsialisticheskie obyazatel'stva*). The obligations of all Soviet employees to increase the productivity and efficiency of their labor. Soviet industrial enterprises work according to plans approved by government authorities and carrying the full force of law. However, in order to make up for waste stemming from faulty organization of production, the party leadership strives to induce Soviet workers to perform above and beyond plan quotas (*vneplanovye zadaniya*) by assuming additional personal socialist obligations. Although inspired by management, such efforts are described as "voluntary initiatives" (*dobrovol'nye pochiny*) on the part of progressive and conscientious workers, encouraged by symbolic rewards such as diplomas, citations on the "board of honor," or the conferral of titles such as "Best Steel Worker" (*luchshy stalevar*), "Best Milkmaid" (*luchshaya doyarka*), or "Outstanding Producer" (*otlichnik proizvodstva*).

The ideological function of personal socialist obligations is to make Soviet workers exert their maximum psychological, intellectual, and physical energy. Personal socialist obligations help intensify exploitation, since the resulting increased performance becomes the basis for reviewing and boosting production norms. The authorities claim that personal socialist obligations are fulfilled because of improvements in organization of labor and production methods.

"Personal obligations of collectives" (*Lichnye obyazatel'stva kollektivov*) have been introduced parallel to personal socialist obligations. Their purpose is to enmesh the workers in a network of mutual and collective responsibilities. Each member of a production team is supposed to take on individual tasks that become an integral part of the team's tasks. It follows that the team member must see to it that his or her fellows work as demanded.

In reality, personal socialist obligations are purely formal in character and are not carried out. Imposed on the occasion of anniversaries, jubilees, and other commemorations, they have little impact on Soviet productivity.

> 1,860 workers have assumed personal socialist obligations. (Agitator, no. 11, 1978, p. 8)

> This progressive collective fulfilled its own socialist obligations with honor. It completed its five-year plan in three and a half years. (Zarya vostoka, 18 July 1979)

> Of the 250,000 Moscow workers who assumed personal [socialist] obligations to fulfill their task for the five-year plan by April 11, 1980, over 30,000 have already kept their promises. (Agitator, no. 23, 1979, p. 17)

Planning (*Planirovanie, Plan*). The system of centralized management and control of the national economy. Economic planning includes determination of basic directions and targets of production development and strict control over their achievement.

Planning of the work of enterprises, hailed as the most important social innovation and scientific discovery of the twentieth century, began to be practiced in the USSR in 1921. The adoption of "Goelro," the plan for countrywide electrification, was the most famous example of large-scale planning. From 1929 onward, national five-year plans have followed each other in succession, transforming the economy of the country into a totalitarian system governed from a single center. Extraordinary nationwide significance is attributed to these plans, and immense resources, time, and effort are expended on their drafting. Before assuming the force of law, the state plan traverses a long and complex path. The Politburo of the CPSU and the Council of Ministers outline the basic direction and set the major targets for development of the national economy for a given period of time. The main guidelines for production, labor, finance, industrial construction, technological innovation, and delivery of supplies and equipment are based on these targets.

The State Planning Committee (*Gosplan SSR*) elaborates a general draft plan for the development of the entire national economy on the basis of the main guidelines and of draft plans submitted by republics and ministries. The draft is then submitted to higher party authorities for approval. After it is approved by the Central Committee of the CPSU and by the Council of Ministers, the national economic plan is referred to the Supreme Soviet of the USSR, whose task is to enact it into law. From then on, the plan acquires the authority of a legally binding norm for all ministries and departments in the Soviet Union. The production and technological, as well as financial, plans for every Soviet enterprise are adjusted to conform to the state plan. The state plan is made concrete through the system of various guidelines: quantitative (volume of production), qualitative (growth in labor productivity and profitability), kind (type of output produced and services), and cost (commodities for sale, gross income, production costs, etc.).

One of the main tasks of the state plan is to achieve a balance between the production of goods and their consumption, that is, between aggregate labor and aggregate wages as expressed in available consumer goods. In other words, the state plan is directed toward balancing production and consumption. Therefore, plan targets are elaborated in terms of "gross output" (*po valu*) estimates, that is, in such terms as rubles, tons, kilometers, cubic meters, and liters. True, plans listing "assortment" or types of goods to be manufactured also exist, but the fulfillment of production tasks—right up to Gorbachev's reform of 1988—has been estimated mainly in terms of gross input. An innovation of perestroika is the evaluation of an enterprises's success on the basis of profits, revenues, and rentability, i.e., in terms of market categories.

Much depends on the fulfillment of the plan: the current assets available to an industrial enterprise, the sums it can assign for the benefit of its employees, bonuses, and last but not least, its reputation. This explains why the manager of a Soviet factory or plant is concerned neither with the quality of its production nor with its marketability. Above all else, he or she is concerned with meeting quantitative criteria of plan fulfillment, seeing to it that the plan is fulfilled (preferably slightly overfulfilled) by hook or by crook. This is usually achieved by concentrating on goods that are "easy to produce"—expensive and unprofitable ones.

Apart from five-year plans, there also exist other types of state plans: current, annual, long-range, and longitudinal (fifteen years or more). The managers of all branches of the national economy—according to the new law on state enterprises—are obligated to compile their own plans (annual, quarterly, and monthly), which are then approved by party organizations. These plans are generally overblown and unreliable. Moreover, capable and experienced Soviet managers know how to circumvent the rigid requirements and pad their figures. If they refuse to do so, their factory's plan will inevitably be unfulfilled, with many unpleasant consequences, including the denial of bonuses to its working force.

The determination to plan everything and everywhere means that the drafting of plans extends over many months or even years. During this time, even quotas that originally may have been perfectly sensible become outdated and loss their relevance. Yet revisions in the plans are forbidden, since any change not envisaged in advance, and thus not included in the state plan, undermines the principle of centralized and directed control of the economy. As a result, planning turns into a senseless game divorced from the real needs of the national economy. The complexities and paradoxes of planning continue to appear even within the strategy of economic reform. While opposition is expressed to the regulation of enterprises, there is comprehensive regulation of economic activity as a whole—in terms of perestroika—which covers the whole fifteen-year period up to the year 2000.

The term " plan" is normally used jointly with attributes intended to stress its importance and reliability, such as: "united" (*ediny*), "constructive" (*sozidatel'ny*), "long-range" (*perspektivny*), "creative" (*tvorchesky*), "grand" (*velichestvenny*), and "general" (*general'ny*).

National economic planning is possible only where there is a socialist mode of production and common ownership of the basic means of production. (Kratky ekonomichesky slovar' [A concise economic dictionary], Moscow: Publishing House for Political Literature, 1958, p. 237)

The practical implementation of measures for improving planning is bound to lead to major changes in the whole system of controls over the national economy. (Kommunist, no. 17, 1980, p. 28)

The State plan for 1984 must become a crucial step in the implementation of the resolutions of the XXVI Party Congress and of the subsequent Plena of the Central Committee of the CPSU. (Pravda, 17 December 1983, p. 1)

Political Avant-Gardism (*Politichesky avangardizm*). A concept that recently emerged out of the depths of the Soviet conservative consciousness to discredit the proponents of any radical social reforms (cf. perestroika). The term's condescendingly sarcastic overtones derive from the analogy with avant-garde art, which, in the Soviet view, is a negative phenomenon in contemporary art as it clashes with the "positive" tendencies of "realism" and "materialism." When used in politics rather than in art, avant-gardism is equated with adventurism, which denotes the lack of a "correct" understanding of existing realities and constraints.

The appearance of the term "political avant-gardism" reflects, on the semantic-philosophical level, a certain stage in the ongoing struggle for power in the Kremlin. The stage in question was that of late 1987. It was marked by the clash between the two views of perestroika, the milder and self-contradictory one of Gorbachev and the more coherent and radical of Boris Yeltsin, former head of the Moscow city party organization and member of the new Supreme Soviet. Yeltsin views perestroika as an opportunity for a genuine democratization of Soviet society, for overhauling the entire social system. For Gorbachev, however, perestroika was more importantly a tool for consolidating his own power, for purging foes and replacing them by his own men. Gorbachev's approach to perestroika was based on his reliance on the power of Soviet bureaucracy and his belief that it was capable of solving all problems without having to leave the office or the speaker's podium. Yeltsin, on the other hand, went to the people rather than contenting himself with speaking at party forums. He liked meeting regularly with the working people on the streets of his city or in their factory workplaces. He hoped to thus mobilize them for active participation in social transformations.

Gorbachev is a dyed-in-the-wool party *apparatchik*. During his political rise, he was so preoccupied with quantifiable goods and values that he is now incapable of understanding that concern about the people may assume forms other than benevolent patronage or philanthropy. The outlook of Gorbachev was based on a conservative orientation characteristic of the party bureaucracy, which fears the prospect of a popular power. His outlook was cramped by Lenin's notion of tactical political concessions or "retreats," which, on more than one occasion in Soviet history, turned out to be (in Lenin's term) "one step forward, two steps backward." Gorbachev is daunted by the fear of losing control over his economic reforms. In his mind, this threat is tantamount to that of a new social revolution. This fear prompts him to slow the pace of the reforms he has launched so that they can be guaranteed to proceed smoothly, without threat to either himself or the system.

Surprisingly (i.e., for society but not for Gorbachev), such fears led Gorbachev to the first purge of personnel, which he himself had only recently elevated to positions of influence. The first victim turned out to be Yeltsin. To oust him quietly was, however, not enough: it was necessary to ideologically brand his views in order to prevent the rise of other Yeltsins. In the Soviet Union, no one is permitted to be more progressive than the general secretary. It is particularly impermissible for anyone close to him to aspire to the mantle (and laurels) of the originator of perestroika. Only the general secretary can be the "general." Others can only be his proconsuls or aides-de-camp. As in "socialist realism" (cf.) Soviet politics leaves room in its drama for only one single hero. All others can only perform the role of extras or spectators, and this they are expected to do with enthusiasm. Yeltsin did not understand, or he refused to comply with, the conventions of a one-man show. He wanted to appear in Gorbachev's play, but in the role of a hero in his own right: as a protagonist of reforms fighting against powerful and dangerous ranks of the party nomenklatura (cf.), which was entrenched in the capital's party committees and ministries. Yeltsin dared to create a popular movement with the potential of transforming the masses from a passive crowd of spectators into a conscious and responsive political force for reform that might eventually push both the general secretary and the party bureaucracy along with him to the sidelines.

Such were the social psychological origins of the concept of political avant-gardism. But there was more to the history of the concept as far as the underlying ideology was concerned. There was a subtle connection with traditional communist rhetoric. First, political avant-gardism was presented as an authoritarian (and therefore anti-Marxist) tendency because it supposedly relied on force. Second, Yeltsin himself (despite his constant appeals to public opinion) was declared an avant-gardist on the assumption that he wanted to reach the goals of perestroika in "one or two leaps" while ignoring the constraints that posited the need for a more gradual implementation. Third, political avant-gardism was branded as objectively "conservative" on the presumption that its methods, which were doomed to lead to failure, would discredit the idea of reform and would thus serve the interests of the opponents of reform.

Opprobrious political connotations were also attached to this concept. The political avant-gardists were pictured as proponents of the "castigation of party cadres." Their views were unceremoniously likened to those of Stalin and Trotsky. Through such innuendo, Yeltsin appeared in the minds of the gullible Soviet citizens as a partisan of repression. Finally, in order to remove all doubt about the "truth" of such fabrications, it was alleged that political avant-gardists were intent on gaining power over the country by resorting to political terror by constant and merciless exposure of all opponents of reform.

The problem with such a contention was that political avant-gardism had appeared and crystallized as a political tendency under the auspices of the *new* policy of Gorbachev. Yeltsin was a product of this policy even if, as it appeared, not an approved one. Hence the guarded and euphemistic terms in which political avant-gardism was criticized. The danger it posed to "the case of socialism"

was noted, yet the qualification immediately followed that its supporters include a number of "sincere communists" and "capable administrators." While giving considerable theoretical currency to the concept, the Soviet leadership had no intention of depersonalizing perestroika. The goal was rather to sever its connection with Yeltsin and to permanently link it with Gorbachev.

> The more I think about such a situation, the more obvious it is that we encounter here one of the most dangerous phenomena of perestroika, namely that fact that avant-gardism has some support among the workers. . . . Such attitudes are a breeding ground for political avant-gardism. (Moskovskie novosti, no. 51, 20 December 1987, p. 15)

> There is more and more talk today, particularly in the press, about the avant-gardists and conservatives of perestroika. The implication runs that society is split with the top leadership of the country, the media, the artistic intelligentsia, the workers and peasant masses on the one side and, an army of white collar workers . . . on the other. . . . (Moskovskie novosti, no. 5, 31 January 1988, p. 7)

> As we recall, at the October Pleunum avant-gardism was condemned. (Moskovskie novosti, no. 6, 7 February 1988, p. 13).

Political Information (*Politinformatsiya*, abbreviation of *politicheskaya informatsiya*). Means of disseminating and inculcating communist ideas and values. Political information is one of the basic means of party propaganda securing the involvement of Soviet citizens in social and political activities and the control of the masses. The Soviet leadership uses political information to acquaint the public with, and indoctrinate it in, the ideas, views, and values it deems suitable and thus to guide the masses appropriately on domestic and foreign policy issues.

In the USSR, there is an institutionalized function of political information carried out by "agitators" or "political explainers" (*politicheskie informatory*). They are responsible for all the industrial enterprises, offices, and institutes in the country. For this work, party committees select people who are considered to be devoted to communist ideas. Then these select candidates receive special training. Political information agitators in the USSR number more than five million. In addition to their selection and training, the extent and amount of their experience is also important. All their activities are carefully supervised. Political information agitators have at their disposal material prepared by the Central Committee. They are also supplied with lists of recommended literature on each relevant topic. The journals *Kommunist* (Communist), *Partiynaya zhizn'* (Party life), *Agitator* (Agitator, i.e., propagandist) and *Mezhdunarodnaya zhizn'* (International life) publish instructional material for them.

The content and form of political information are in a constant state of flux, changing with the demands and aims of the political leadership. The most widespread form of political information is a short talk lasting between ten and thirty minutes, which is delivered at places of work during working time. On such occasions, the audience generally learns nothing new. The talks are punctuated by crude assertions phrased in the form of slogans or "theses." Their appeal is primarily emotional, only secondarily intellectual. The same slogans are repeated endlessly, so as to create reliable mental stereotypes around which the thinking of Soviet citizens can revolve.

In the USSR, political information continues the Stalinist traditions of omitting or distorting truth out of fear of objective analysis of events and phenomena. However, in a modern society, even one in which ideology is as dominant as it is in the Soviet Union, it is difficult to confine all political and cultural thought to a few defined-in-advance fundamental ideas. This has become particularly difficult now that a degree of glasnost (cf.) is in vogue and people have been encouraged to express their own opinions. Some Soviet citizens have begun to turn to a broad range of sources, including archives, until recently completely off-limits, in order to gain access to knowledge missing from political information. Also recently, the Soviet press has begun to illuminate many aspects of life

in their problem-ridden complexity. But most Soviet citizens, accustomed as they are to double-think, never reveal their true attitude toward information from official sources. What they usually do is to take part in a game of political information in which both the agitators and their uncomplaining audience cooperate in a performance that neither believes in. In this sense, political information agitators are merely playing the game in the style the party demands. However, there does exist quite a significant category of people in Soviet society—comprised primarily of special and party pensioners and of active-duty and retired military men—who perceive the concealing or distortion of information by political information as a wise tactical strategy of the Soviet authorities, necessitated by the complex tasks of "building communism" or by the changing circumstances of international relations.

While some people respond to political information with a degree of scepticism, the prevailing attitude toward it is one of indifference. This is understandable. Exposure to the same propaganda stereotypes from early childhood can well have a numbing effect.

In the late 1980s, after the Twenty-seventh Congress of the CPSU, the authorities made attempts to improve the quality of political information, to make it more concrete and persuasive. These attempts failed, as the defects of political information are more closely related to its content than to its presentation. Political information cannot be effective as long as the mass media are subject to censorship, but the Soviet regime cannot dispense with censorship without undermining its own foundations and principles. The party apparatus has repeatedly called for improving the quality of political information, specifically for increasing its coherence and relevance to changing realities. Yet, none of this has ever materialized. The nature of political information and the methods of its dissemination have remained unchanged. All contemporary problems continue to be viewed through an ideological prism.

In the labor teams of collective and state farms the political information talks were conducted, during which the experience of an advanced master of machine-milking was revealed in detail. (Agitator, no. 11, 1978, p. 14)

On the day following the opening of the Congress, Alexander Vasilevich conducted a political information session in his shop. (Partiynaya zhizn', no. 8, 1981, p. 6)

Some Party Bureaus regularly fail to post memos to notify collectives in advance of a forthcoming lecture, meeting or political information session. (Partiynaya zhizn', no. 17, 1983 p. 69)

Pricing (*Tsenoobrazovanie*). The process of fixing the prices of goods and services. The specific concept of pricing, though seemingly detached from the realities of everyday life, reflects the severe problems and deep contradictions that rend the socialist economy. The major among those problems are the lack of a balanced state budget, a severe shortage of goods, inflation, and unstable currency. All of them were in one way or another attributable to Soviet pricing policy, which distinguished itself by its arbitrariness, disregard for supply and demand forces, and for the production costs. In the past, the last factor was totally ignored; nowadays, in the context of today's reforms, it is overemphasized, rousing exaggerated hopes and expectations. The new pricing system is by itself expected to promote conditions necessary for the development and smooth operation of self-supporting enterprises and to transform unprofitable industries into highly efficient organizations, regardless of the quality of their management. Yet it is delusory to think that pricing alone can make up for economic ignorance and inferior technology.

Attempts are being made to restructure pricing by taking into consideration real, socially necessary production expenses, which until very recently were almost completely financed by surplus extracted and various taxes, which aggravated labor exploitation by a factor of two or three. Apart from constituting one of the major defects of socialist pricing policy, such practices were responsible for the inequitable distribution of income.

The imbalance between the money supply and industrial output led to the accumulation of enormous sums in private pockets, hundreds of billions of rubles, for which no commodities could be purchased. Concurrently, piles of totally unwanted goods grew in the stores. The stocks of unsold goods have grown threefold over the past fifteen years. Such waste is a direct result of the faulty accounting mechanism, which, instead of considering demand as a factor, is oriented towards the *val* i.e., gross output, used instead of profit as an indicator of industrial efficiency. The losses so incurred must be covered by constant price rises: of retail as well as wholesale prices. Retail price increases since 1970 have amounted to 5.7 percent for meat, 3.5 percent for milk and milk products, 22.6 percent for pastry and sweets, 79.1 percent for shoes, 182 percent for furniture, and 193 percent for cars.

Pricing, which takes into account socially necessary labor costs, is now seen as the best way out of economic stagnation. Straightforward solutions to complex problems are very typical of Soviet thinking. In his time, Lenin sought a panaceum or "key" that would "heal" the backward economy of the country and also found it in the socially necessary labor-cost-based pricing. But socially necessary costs are an abstraction. They have no objective existence apart from specific industries and their operations, which vary from enterprise to enterprise. In certain branches of industry, in oil and gas, for example, the difference between the selling and cost price can be more than a hundredfold, while in other branches, such as light industry and food production, the difference does not exceed a factor of two or three. Thus, the question arises of how much of their cost is really socially necessary. Up till now, Soviet economists have not come up with the answer. Nevertheless, they view the transition of enterprises to the self-supporting status as a go-ahead for reviewing prices—in an upward direction, of course. But price increases, by virtue of not being dictated by social considerations, inevitably lead to a spiral of new price increases as long as production lags behind.

The State Pricing Committee (*Goskomtsen*) came up with the following proposals: first, wholesale prices are to be reviewed no later than 1990, since industrial deficit, accumulated by self-supporting enterprises, already exceeds one hundred billion rubles; second, beginning with the next five-year plan in 1992, price projections for the construction industry, planning and purchase prices for agriculture are to be increased; third, commercial retail prices are to be raised, in conformity with what is called "balanced prices" or "agreed prices". As a result, there is to be an increase in the price of foodstuffs, which in 1988 were subsidized by the government to the tune of sixty billion rubles.

Economic development is, therefore, perceived as depending not so much on better social relationships but rather on devising a new pricing system. In other words, the public will have to pay for technological progress in industry. Concepts of social justice are today being sacrificed to economic expediency. The main aim of Gorbachev's reforms is to provide the Soviet economy with real incentives for achieving greater industrial efficiency. Questions of human welfare are accorded a very low priority. Furthermore, whenever welfare is considered at all, it is conceived of in general terms, without taking into account the interests of specific groups of people, such as the low paid, pensioners, or students. Nor is account taken of people on a "fixed income," for whom overtime work does not mean extra pay. Nor is attention given to the fact that material well-being depends not only on income but also on provisions for those family members who cannot be gainfully employed.

The predictions of the incentive effect on the proposed price increases on industry and supplies are likely to be erroneous, as they fail to sufficiently take into account more complex economic relationships. The point is that in themselves, higher prices do not lead to increases in raw materials or manufactures. They can as well lead to a new distribution of material benefits, perpetuating old social imbalances and inequalities.

In many large Soviet cities, consumer goods and food products most in demand are now distributed at factories. If their prices were to be raised significantly, they would surface on the shelves of ordinary stores (no longer "under the counter")—but in the capacity of museum exhibits, coveted yet unobtainable by ordinary people unable to pay for them. At the same time, those with unearned wealth will be perfectly able to get hold of them freely. Social polarization will increase, and given the lack of competition and constant shortages on the Soviet consumer market, prices will skyrocket and the door to inflation will be wide open. Controlled inflation, as called for by Soviet economics, will not materialize.

Retail price increases require another form of compensating the workers by raising their wages and thus increasing production costs, which are bound to push prices upward even more, thus making inflation uncontrollable. Demand, instead of being curbed, would thus be stepped up, as people would feverishly buy up goods in expectation of price raises.

The democratization of pricing, now a much talked about subject in the Soviet Union, essentially means its bureaucratization. Factories are beginning to look for ways of increasing profits on their production by raising prices rather than by reducing costs. The domination of consumption by production remains in force. Artificial attempts to bring Soviet prices closer to their world level are also unrealistic. The only realistic way to break this vicious circle is to increase the competitiveness of Soviet products, to change the content of Soviet exports by including more manufactures in place of raw materials, and to increase the country's participation in the international division of labor. The Soviet Union should not produce goods that can be bought more cheaply on the world market.

There is no doubt that Soviet domestic trade should be affected by prices on the world market. This should, however, be the natural result of industrial development rather than of administrative fiat. For this to happen, the expenditure accounting system must be first straightened out. Surprising as it may be, in the Soviet Union it often happens that no one knows exactly what the real cost of producing a given item is. Existing documentation is so intricate that it gives no possibility of assessing real costs, let alone subsidiary expenses. Most important of all, the tendency to stabilize industry by raising prices must be abandoned.

Prerequisite to creating an efficient managerial model is the exact opposite of what has been done until now, namely the decline rather than the rise of wholesale prices. If this were to happen, industrial workers might certainly find it difficult to keep their salaries, but their standard of living would not fall, as the rates would remain stable. Also, state allowances would then prove to be unnecessary.

The law of value cannot be abolished arbitrarily. Yet it is this law rather than any political circumstances that determines the dynamics of the relationship between labor costs and prices. Reduction in labor costs necessarily leads to the lowering of prices. Concurrently, the composition of the workforce should be structured in accordance with advanced methods of work organization rather than with the backward Soviet ways of organizing labor, which inevitably lead to overpricing the finished products. With modern organization of labor, for instance in agriculture, the costs of production can be cut by a factor of between five and ten, even in the absence of new manufacturing technology. Unless the supply of goods can be brought into line with consumer demand, there is no point in discussing a reduction of retail prices. Retail prices must be adapted to labor productivity and remuneration. Labor productivity must rise faster than wages, while wages must grow more rapidly than retail prices.

Given today's pricing system, however, and the tremendous shortages on the consumer market, a member of a cooperative quite often finds himself with a gold mine and earns an income which bears no relation to labor expenses. (Novoe vremya, no. 51, 18 December 1987, p. 28)

Today we are faced with the task of reconstructing our pricing system on principles which truthfully reflect all socially necessary expenses and not just the expenses of a particular branch or factory. (Agitator, no. 3, 1988, p. 39)

Our pricing must reflect the characteristics of the socialist market. Prices of key items, on which the dynamics of the general level of prices depend and which are the backbone of the whole pricing system, must be centrally controlled by the state. (Agitator, no. 2, 1988, p. 5)

Privileges (*Privilegii*). Benefits awarded to certain categories of employees, in addition to their regular wages. In the USSR, privileges have almost always a covert character, so much so that Soviet dictionaries obfuscate the connection between privilege and position by associating privileges with earned or deserved benefits, as in the case of the benefits enjoyed by invalids or war veterans, (see S. I. Ozhegov, Dictionary of the Russian Language, Moscow, 1977, p. 540). Consequently, an image of social equality in the USSR has been created, whereby a responsible official supposedly earns only two or three times as much as a skilled worker. The fact that such an official's salary goes together with privileges that, in terms of their monetary value exceed his or her salary by a factor of five, six or seven, is conveniently suppressed.

Money is not the key to the matter, for it is quite understandable that a person in a position of authority and influence should be paid more than his or her subordinates. Rather, the essence of privileges lies in the way the income differences are accentuated. Privileges (including their scale) depend not on one's work but on one's hierarchical rank. By virtue of providing benefits that are unobtainable by everyone else, privileges automatically qualify their bearers for membership in a wealth elite. Given Soviet commodity shortages, the bestowal of privileges is tantamount to one's exclusive possession of special rights and nearly unlimited opportunities for further advancement. Official vehicles at their disposal, apartments in individually designed buildings located in fashionable districts, dachas provided by the state, hospitals and polyclinics for the exclusive use by the elite, all evoke respect and deference. High prestige is attached to acquiring goods from shops and delicatessens, which are closed to the general public (hence their name, "closed stores" (cf.)), to receiving special travel services in public transport, railway stations, and airports, to the opportunity to purchase hard to obtain books, or to priority in distribution of theater and cinema tickets. It seems as if some clever minds are constantly thinking up new privileges for the elite—special beaches, restricted leisure grounds, and, surely the most original innovation, special elevators for the exclusive use of bigwigs in high offices.

One of the essential characteristics of privileges is that their existence is not to be admitted in public. The monopolization of goods and services by the ruling classes means that an increasing amount of resources is diverted from the public domain. Concurrently, the secrecy surrounding the privileges, which has no basis in law, ensures that they will be abused and that abuses will remain hidden. Like official positions, titles, academic degrees, etc., privileges are sold in the USSR. A privileged license plate number (which has the power of exempting the driver from the jurisdiction of the traffic authorities), a place at a "government" rest house, or registration at a closed (government) retail establishment all command high prices. Who can afford them? Those with plenty of money, top figures in the black market (cf.), and organized crime. They are prepared to pay for such privileges, and the country's leaders are ready to sell them.

In the glasnost era, privileges have ceased to be a forbidden subject for discussion. Under Gorbachev, the impression is being created that the rule of law holds supreme in the USSR. This requires that privileges either be abolished or legitimized. Thus public discussion of privileges has begun (or rather, has been inspired from above). The very act of raising the matter in public was an unexpected and daring step. Due to this, Gorbachev could achieve his primary aim of presenting himself to the nation as a judicious ruler and as a champion of justice and equality. At the same time, he could thereby promote another aim, which was to set the people against the sluggish and greedy bureaucracy. This was intended to break the bureaucracy's pride, intimidate it, and thus mold it into a fawning and compliant tool.

Criticism of privileges began within confines strictly delineated by the government: as officials were told, "*Perestroika* must begin with oneself." Privileges were suddenly being described as "remnants of feudalism"; the prevailing "barter" system of exchanging goods and services was being criticized because under prevailing conditions of shortages (cf.), it is not sufficient to have money. One must also have the privilege of elite access to items or services in short supply.

As criticism of privileges intensified, it began to affect the inert and resistant party-administrative sector. Questions were asked as to why someone who works badly eats well, while someone who works hard has nothing to eat. It then became clear that privileges are easy to confer but hard to take away: their holders, with all their corporate interests and ideology, had power in society. Yet to ignore the popular mood was hardly possible either. Thus, timid, palliative measures were taken to curtail privileges. Several thousand junior managers were deprived of official cars, while in some districts government stores and rest homes were closed. But privileges remain, now talked about openly and on the way to being legitimized. Accordingly, public opinion is being encouraged to accept the view that there is nothing out of the ordinary about privileges. Factories as well as government institutions have commissaries, it is noted. (The fact that manufacturing plants hand out a meager monthly ration, while party committees offer their employees delicacies in abundance, is conveniently ignored.)

Similarly, the existence of government hospitals and sanatoria is legitimized on the ground that kolkhozniks, oil-workers, and miners have their own health centers. And so the rhetorical question is often asked, Why should party officials not also have theirs? The people are also expected to sympathize with high-ranking officials, who are more vulnerable to heart attacks than others.

There is no hope, therefore, that the communist class will voluntarily renounce its privileges. In any case, such hypothetical voluntary action would be beside the point. To do away with privileges, one would first have to abolish shortages. This could only be done by changing the organization of the retail trade and granting workers more economic freedoms. This, however, would in turn entail an overhaul of the whole system. In the meantime, the Soviet leadership cannot make up their minds about whether to initiate the radical reforms that would be required for this purpose. Therefore, the issue of the communists' most important privilege, their monopoly on power, has never been raised.

> Very revealing is the fact that practically all respondents assessed some privileges as fair and others as unfair. (Moskovskie novosti, no. 27, 3 July 1988)

> The need for certain privileges and their inviolability have been firmly instilled in our consciousness. We have resigned ourselves to these scandalous examples of social injustice, and only some outstanding event (such as the construction of a government maternity hospital), is capable of arousing us to a semblance of protest. Even then we just talk and after a while quiet down. But the government maternity hospital, government pediatric polyclinic and government, health centers will remain with us. (Ogonek, no. 27, July, 1988, p. 3)

> He works from 8 a.m. to 10 p.m., six days a week. He gets 430 rubles (370 after deductions and dues), plus a 100 for overtime, a government dacha in summer and access to a commissary. It is sad and embarassing to mention this, but rumors about the fabulous privileges of the "aristocracy" are just so much. . . . (Literaturnaya gazeta, no. 28, 13 July 1988, p. 3)

Progressive (*Progressivny*). In the wide sense: in keeping with the communist Weltanschauung; in the narrow sense: corresponding to Soviet interests. In both senses, the notion of progressive is based on a primitive interpretation of historical development, assuming that the USSR is the spearhead of humanity's historical progress. Hence, everything in the USSR, whether the economy or political system, education or health services, science, literature, or the arts is by definition progressive. Obviously, such a definition bears no relevance to real achievements but is instead a useful demagogic device to conceal failures stemming from the incompetence of the CPSU in handling the economy or from its interference in cultural affairs.

The content of the term "progressive" is not only devoid of objective meaning, but it vacillates in accordance with the zigzags of Soviet policy. The nearly twenty years of Brezhnev's rule were proclaimed progressive, but under Gorbachev the Soviet people "discovered" that it has been a period of stagnation and decline.

The "progressiveness' label (*progressivnost'*) is also applied to events in international politics. Communist regimes are proclaimed to be "very" progressive. Pro-Soviet governments are simply progressive, while states that lie within the sphere of Soviet influence are declared to be "following the path of progress." However, if any of these countries should distance itself from the Soviet brand of communism, the honor of being progressive is withdrawn. This happened at different times with Albania, China, and Yugoslavia. Conversely, the same honor is bestowed upon political movements (and their leaderships) throughout the world if they contribute to the Soviet goal of undermining the foundations of democratic states, as do the "progressive" Palestinian Liberation Organization, Irish Republican Army, and Japanese Red Army.

> The solidarity of the CPSU with the progressive forces in the developing world expresses itself in various forms. (Mirovaya ekonomika

i mezhdunarodnye otnosheniya, no. 2, 1980, p. 17)

On April 22, of this year, the Soviet people, the peoples of the countries of the socialist community and all of progressive humanity will celebrate the 110th anniversary of Lenin's birth. (Partiynaya zhizn, no. 4, 1980, p. 3)

Progressive writers unite the power of the word which conveys glorious ideals with their professional tasks. (Pravda, 14 October 1983, p. 3)

Propaganda (*Propaganda*). The organized dissemination of communist ideology for the purpose of indoctrinating the masses with the communist worldview. The basic contents of Soviet propaganda are Marxist philosophy, the international political situation, party decisions, and resolutions, while its aim is to instill a uniform code of thought and behavior in the minds of the public.

Propaganda has many means at its disposal, ranging from the mass media to educational indoctrination. To keep the public under their control, the authorities rely on propaganda alternated with constant political intimidation.

Propaganda is one of the most effective tools of the Soviet regime. Its efficacy is guaranteed by its monopoly. It does not have to compete with any rival source of information or any rival ideology, and therefore cannot possibly be challenged. This explains why Soviet propaganda has succeeded in deluding the naive, who are taken in by the "brilliant future" promised to them under communism. The image of this brilliant future is one of liberty, equality, fraternity, secure peace throughout the world, guaranteed employment, free education, and guaranteed old-age pensions. Soviet propaganda proclaims that communism is the protector of children and the family, calls for the "stigmatization" (*kleymit' pozorom*) of graft, drunkenness, and vandalism. It is not so simple to realize that all these lofty notions are but a facade, manufactured by Soviet propaganda. Its actual aim is that of indoctrinating the masses with views and ideas rigidly linked to the "general line" pursued

at any given moment by the party. To achieve this purpose, Soviet propaganda employs a diverse and elaborate mythology.

One propaganda myth extols the Soviet system as the most advanced and progressive in the world. Extensive use is made of legends about the party (those are ageless within the Soviet time-continuum), as well as about its leaders (those are less durable, expiring together with the given leader). Yet each new leader brought them back to life according to the same old pattern: outstanding individuals, selflessly devoted to the pursuit of the people's good. All of them, during their lifetime, were depicted as true Marxists, continuing Lenin's legacy, men whose political acumen and infinite wisdom were matched by their unassuming behavior in everyday life. Someone whose rights "happened" to be flouted could be expected to find such leaders very willing to redress any wrongs.

Among other illusions that have been fostered by propaganda, the most common is the idea of "further perfection," "further successes," "further growth," and "further achievements" of the Soviet economy, science, and culture. This bogus language, backed by an abundance of spurious figures and distorted reports, never allowed the public to forget that the land of the Soviets was triumphantly marching forward. It is true that recently there has been a shift towards more "modest" language, no longer exalting the triumph of the already developed socialism but rather the building of democratic socialism. Such "modesty" has its reasons: it reinterprets the past, declaring Stalin a political gangster, accusing Khrushchev of inconsistency, blaming Brezhnev, Andropov, and Chernenko for social stagnation—all in order to link Gorbachev directly to Lenin, to the sources of the Revolution. Yet mythology has not been abandoned. It continues to brainwash the people via the use of laconic imperatives such as "The party and the people are one!" or "The Party is Our Helmsman!"

At the same time, the Soviet propaganda apparatus is flexible enough to accommodate all the vicissitudes of communist history. The slogan "worldwide revolution" (*vsemirnaya revolyutsiya*), current in the 1920s, was eventually succeeded by the idea of peaceful coexistence. Appeals to come to terms with privations in the name of world revolution were replaced by promises of material prosperity and affluence, at first by the 1980s (the Khrushchev program), then by the 1990s (the "Food program"), and finally by the year 2000, at the completion of *perestroika*. Calls for the total abolition of private property were replaced by cautious encouragement of individual initiative in industry and agriculture, urgent steps that had to be made in order to salvage the remains of the ruined economy.

Soviet propaganda has ample recourse to hypocrisy to bridge the abyss between ideological mirages and real life. Fearful and morally and mentally cowed, Soviet people have no alternative but to rely on official communist sources and to believe the most absurd claims of communist propaganda. They commonly believe, for example, that Stalin's terror and the struggle against "enemies of the people" were necessary in order to save the Revolution; or that the Soviet invasions of Hungary in 1956, of Czechoslovakia in 1968, and of Afghanistan in 1979 were staged at the request of the peoples of these countries; or that the suppression of popular discontent in Poland in 1981 was a fulfillment by the USSR of previously assumed obligations toward its allies; etc. The unavoidable consequence of the steady exposure to communist propaganda is a split personality and constant recourse to double-evaluative standards. In public, Soviet citizens use an array of propaganda clichés, but in private, they ridicule and reject these same clichés. Without wanting to, however, they accomodate themselves to myths they don't believe in, and they come to live by them.

Since "political information" (*politinformatsiya*) does not always succeed in eliminating doubt and discontent, propaganda is forced to employ well-tried techniques of "tension reduction." Cautiously voiced critical comments implying the acknowledgement of wrongs in the USSR appear in the mass media periodically. This "democratic" ploy allows the authorities to channel discontent in the direction they choose. At the same time, the Soviet public is constantly reminded that the party is ever vigilant in its defense of legality, that all shortcomings will be remedied, and that guilty parties will be punished. The most common propaganda ploy to pacify the public is to report that those responsible for evils have been found and exposed. The categories of guilty parties may vary depending on the circumstances: they may be interventionists, oppositionists, factionalists, Trotskyists "of all shades," saboteurs, spies and wreckers, imperialist "saber-rattlers," "enemies of the people," agents of foreign intelligence services, cosmopolitans, dissidents, or Zionists, as well as idlers, loafers, grafters, absentees (cf. absenteeism), or parasites (cf.). The latest invention is "enemies of perestroika" who are blamed for the unsuccessful reforms and the inefficient attempts at introducing new methods of economic management.

The indoctrinative success of Soviet propaganda has produced a phenomenon unique in the twentieth century, namely "Homo Sovieticus." Easily controlled, he is ready to do whatever he is told. Despite the obsolete and hackneyed nature of its conceptual framework, or perhaps because of it, Soviet propaganda has indisputably succeeded in creating this new communist "species," which can exist both within and beyond the borders of the Soviet Union, and which encompasses people of many nationalities and different age groups. Its efficiency has reached unprecedented proportions today, when Gorbachev's reforms are hailed as the revelation of the century, seen by the Western public as a positive step toward creating a better world, a world without war, strife, and antagonisms.

Imperalist propaganda prates about the "Soviet threat. (Izvestiya, 12 March 1983, p. 1)

Open meetings held by Communists in district schools have met with impressive results. Their aim has been to spread propaganda about the

Soviet way of life among senior pupils. (Agitator, no. 4, 1984, p. 48)

Prostitution (*Prostitutsiya*). A profession that Soviet officialdom long claimed to have ceased to exist in the USSR. As everywhere else, prostitution has always existed in Russia. Since the establishment of Soviet power in 1917, however, the regime has influenced both the Soviet concept and practice of prostitution. In the early days of the communist regime, prostitution was regarded as a relic of the capitalist society of exploiters and was subsequently declared as having been "completely done away with" at the end of the 1930s, when the USSR was proclaimed as being on the verge of entering a classless society. This reflected Lenin's viewpoint that in a country where socialism had triumphed, there was no place for prostitution. Accordingly, if there was no place for it, it could not possibly exist. Hence, punishments for prostitution were deleted from the Soviet criminal code, and right up to the mid-1980s its existence was never officially admitted. By then, it was no longer possible to suppress the subject, not only because of glasnost, but chiefly out of fear of AIDS, after 275 cases of that disease were recorded in the USSR in 1987. Other reasons for giving more attention to prostitution were the epidemic of conventional veneral diseases, which in 1987 afflicted 350,000 people, and the effect on public morals as 15 percent of prostitutes were found to be schoolgirls no older than seventeen.

Once the decision was taken to tackle this sensitive and embarassing subject, Soviet propaganda had to make the difficult choice of the means of conducting the campaign against prostitution. Should it be vilified as immoral? But then, it was no more immoral than bribe-taking and speculation. Should it be presented as a source of unearned income? But what the prostitute sells is not state property. Should she be made detestable in the eyes of the public? Impossible. In the Soviet Union, there is no room for the pre-Revolutionary notion of a prostitute as a victim of an imperfect society, as a "fallen woman," someone whom some humanists even elevated to the status of a martyr. In fact, a Soviet prostitute arouses exactly the opposite feelings in a society of unhappy, overstrained workers, who suffer from low wages, perpetual debts, and frustrated ambitions. Far from evoking compassion, a prostitute, with her extravagant, idle, bohemian existence, arouses the envy of millions of people. Prostitution is not only a fully respectable but even a prestigious profession. Indeed, it ranked ninth in an occupational prestige study: between a top manager and a salesman, above such well paid professions as diplomat, teacher, taxi driver, car mechanic, and butcher (*Sotsiologicheskie issledovaniya*, no. 6, 1987, p. 64).

Prostitution is as common in the USSR as it is envied. There are at least 100,000 professional prostitutes, in addition to at least one million amateurs who practice the oldest profession either intermittently or only during some part of their working life. The professional prostitute, however, has some specific Soviet requirements to deal with. Most of the women involved are forced to undertake some kind of conventional work, or at least register themselves as if engaged in one. Their reason for holding two jobs is not economic: a successful prostitute can in one hour's time earn as much as an average worker does in a month. The reason for her second "job" is that a woman who neither works nor is supported by parents or husband is banished from society, exiled from the city, and punished by "reeducation" through hard physical labor.

Prostitution is obviously a young woman's profession. Seventy percent of prostitutes are under the age of 30, and they usually come from an average (or, to be more accurate, typically Soviet) family background, from the working class or intelligentsia. Seventy-five percent of prostitutes have a partial or complete high school education. In other words, most Soviet prostitutes can by no means be defined as belonging to the "lower classes" or the underworld. The reason behind their self-degradation, therefore, should be sought not in lack of education or unsettled family background, but in the values of Soviet society, which subverts conventional notions of social justice.

In the USSR, prostitution is a result of the contrast between a woman's position in society and her unfulfilled aspiration for self-expression. Life for a woman in the Soviet Union means a miserly wage (120–30 rubles a month) or an even more meager scholarship (40–50 rubles) and an unsettled, wretched existence in a communal apartment or corner in a dormitory, together with outrageously high prices—150 rubles for a pair of shoes, 200 for a woolen suit, and 250 to 300 for a coat. In addition, one has also to take into account the virtual impossibility of escaping from the provinces and obtaining a residence permit (*propiska*, cf.) in a big city. It is hardly surprising therefore, that every second girl student and every third female worker finds it hard to resist the temptation when offered a meal in a good restaurant (or its equivalent) after being accosted on a street or in the park. What is surprising is that more women do not go in for prostitution.

For what defenses against it does a young Soviet woman have? Religion is suppressed and degraded, while few believe in morality. Her only choice is between a professional career and success with men. Either way, a woman's prestige and self-esteem depend on how she looks and dresses. In the USSR, failures are not pitied and the consumption-oriented public does not show tolerance to those who fail to look stylish.

Soviet women begin to slide into prostitution gradually. At first, they are passed around among friends. They try not to maintain intimate relations with numerous partners simultaneously, in order to avoid looking "cheap." Later, they often work together in tandem with girlfriends, receiving remuneration in the form of gifts. They start to take money—between 20 and 40 rubles a night—only in the third stage. Subsequently, they start to pursue clients in restaurants and hotels and end up using the services of a pimp. Finally, when they start losing their looks, they have to take to the streets unless they manage to get married or change their occupation in time. However, any form of prostitution is far more remunerative than the average wage. Even a streetwalker earns at least 20 to 30 rubles a day.

Still, it is by no means easy to make a fortune from prostitution. Only 8 percent of Soviet prostitutes profess to live well or very well. This category includes the so-called "currency prostitutes" (*valyutnye prostitutki*) whose clients include foreigners. They are chic women who frequent the bars of big hotels and take in 100 or 200 dollars a night. To see such earnings in the right perspective, it should be realized that on the Soviet black market a dollar costs four to five times its official exchange rate. Most importantly, foreign currency gives them access to shops for foreigners, while currency speculation increases their income twofold or threefold. "Currency prostitutes" have to pay for their privileged working conditions, of course, by supplying information to the KGB. The advantage of this is that it protects them from harassment by the police. As a result, those with this "protection" have no need to pretend that they hold a legal job and can indulge in a little "business" on the side (usually in narcotics), with the full knowledge of the security services. To practice their trade and to maximize profits, they need apartments and cars of their own. Due to their links with the authorities they can and do buy cooperative apartments and the best cars.

Twenty-five percent of Soviet prostitutes enjoy a higher than average standard of living, with private apartments and none of the usual concerns of making ends meet. But 40 percent are not so well off. Even if they have enough to eat, they are far from prosperous and live in communal apartments or dormitories. Seventeen percent can be classified as hard-up, although not yet quite on the poverty line. The deprivations they experience, however, can well be a cause rather than an effect of their chosen life style.

Boring and degrading work generating a sense of life's purposelessness provides fertile ground for social pathology. Yet these factors alone are not the root cause of prostitution. The root cause of all the rampant depravity in the USSR is the lack of any connection between high consumption standards and both the nature and amount of work handed over. The prevailing spirit of stick-at-nothing acquisitiveness does not favor asking any questions about the price paid for comforts or methods used to gain them. Morality is thus replaced by a calculus. As a result, there is no opprobrium attached to prostitution. As long as a prostitute makes good, leading a carefree existence, society does not condemn her. People only turn their back on her when she is down and out. Only then does the state suddenly begin to express concern about "morality".

A few timid, inconsequential attempts have been made to restrict prostitution. In 1988 (at the time of writing, only in the Russian Federation), penalties for prostitution were introduced: a warning or fine of up to 100 rubles for a first conviction and a fine of up to 200 rubles for a second conviction within one year. Such feeble and purely administrative measures are not going to deter anyone from prostitution. Yet from the sociological viewpoint, it is significant that the existence of prostitution has fully been acknowledged in the Soviet Union and is now considered a crime.

> Once they finally took up such a delicate topic as prostitution and made a bit of noise about it among the public, the mass media very quickly lost their enthusiasm for the subject. (Sotsiologicheskie issledovaniya, no. 6, 1987, p. 61)

> I believe that the rush to decriminalize prostitution 30 years ago was premature. (Trud, 31 July 1987, p. 4)

> The pernicious influence of prostitution is spreading as fast as an epidemic, while we keep arguing whether it is time to define it as a crime, and about how to differentiate between a professional prostitute and a non-prostitute. (Trud, 31 July 1987, p. 4)

Psychological Warfare (*Psikhologicheskaya voyna*). The attempt to control people's minds and behavior with the help of such techniques as blackmail, provocation, intimida-

tion, and disinformation. In Soviet ideology, psychological warfare and the policies contributing to it were long considered to be a form of class struggle. On the assumption that capitalist society is divided into hostile classes, the working class was expected to wage ideological war against the bourgeoisie. But it eventually became apparent that in the workers' movement itself there was a struggle underway between Leninism and its various heresies—"right-wing" (*pravy*) and "left-wing" (*levy*) deviationism, dogmatism, revisionism, and opportunism.

The Soviet Union differentiates between psychological warfare and ideological struggle. The latter, according to Soviet propaganda, has an objective basis in the class structure of contemporary society and does not conflict with the possibility of peaceful coexistence between nations. Detente does not and cannot invalidate the laws of the class struggle. Under conditions of detente Communists are not expected to be reconciled to capitalist exploitation nor monopolists to become supporters of revolution. It follows that ideological struggle does not encroach on the sovereignty of independent states.

In contrast to ideological struggle, psychological warfare is understood by communists to be a deliberate response to the goals of imperialism. Psychological sabotage is seen as a prerequisite and prologue to military intervention and, hence, is understood as a violation of generally accepted international norms. Psychological warfare flouts sovereignty and implies interference in the internal affairs of other states.

There are also differences between ideological struggle and psychological warfare in regard to their respective methods. Ideological struggle seeks to impose a fixed system of values in order to generate desired patterns of social behavior. This is why ideological struggle is conceived of as a struggle between ideas, concepts, and worldviews. Psychological warfare, by contrast, attempts to propagate fallacious stereotypes in order to confuse political opponents and intimidate, deceive, and arouse panic. The aim of psychological warfare is to foment discontent.

However, in the USSR the demarcation line between ideological struggle and psychological warfare was construed differently for some time. Whereas ideological struggle encompassed the Soviet propaganda campaign against the West, including all the auxiliary theoretical manipulation and ideological sabotage practised for this purpose, psychological warfare, implying something to be condemned as in violation of international norms, was exclusively used in reference to any form of criticism of the Soviet system, even if it amounted to nothing more than an unbiased and objective factual account.

Since psychological warfare was not held in high repute throughout the world, the Soviet leadership had a reason to avoid relying on it, at least too openly. The purpose was served by presenting Soviet policies as peace-loving exactly when they really aimed at undermining detente; by extolling noninterference in the internal affairs of other countries while demanding for communists the freedom to sow confusion and discontent anywhere; and by calling for tolerance while insisting on the irreconcilability of antagonistic ideologies. While professing lofty ideals, the Soviet leaders developed new strategies of psychological warfare. Some of the more subtle of these are considered below.

1. Stirring up discontent: An idealized image of the USSR as a flourishing society has been fostered in the West by various channels, e.g., Western communist parties, liberal and pacifist circles, and similar groups. This has been contrasted with life in an open society, whose real and imaginary problems are depicted as being both malignant and intractable. The Soviet leadership believed, not without reason, that people of democratic countries might become receptive to communist views and ideas. The apocalyptic pictures of the West churned out by the communist propaganda machine were also exploited for domestic consumption. By comparing the USSR with the "doomed West," Soviet reality was made to appear tolerable

in spite of its profound political and economic problems, absence of civil rights, and exploitation of labor.

2. Manipulation of information: This involved diverting attention from major events or issues to less important ones. For example, the paeans of praise for free Soviet education and medical services camouflage the fact that they cost the Soviet people 40 percent of their wages, which the state duly deducts each month for the so-called public funds (*obshchestvennye fondy*). In the West, on the other hand, the cost of these services comes to less than 10 to 12 percent of a working person's wages. Thus, the Soviet people must pay 3 to 4 times more for educating their children and obtaining medical services than they really cost. However, the Soviet leadership correctly assumes that the structure of Soviet society does not lend itself easily to an outsider's comprehension. And indeed, communist demagogy about free education and free access to medical services did strike a responsive chord in public opinion beyond the Soviet borders.

3. Stereotyping of consciousness: This involved the molding of an automatic mental reaction to classes of events in order to make people apply the same evaluative criteria to different types of information. In effect, interpretation and evaluation became mechanical operations. Through recourse to crude ideological equations (e.g., socialism = freedom, capitalism = slavery, socialism = work, capitalism = unemployment), the communists sought to influence people directly, without necessarily affecting their deeper assumptions about the world.

There were other complex subversive propaganda methods used by the communist press in the West as in the Soviet Union. They included the juxtaposition of items, which might be innocuous when read separately, but which tend to have a prejudicial effect when read in juxtaposition. For example, an ordinary report on rearmament side by side with a story about the atomic bombing of Japan evoked a different response than would the first report separately. Another method entailed influencing the unconscious through visual perception. In the simplest manipulation, by placing provocative photographs in close proximity to a given text, propagandists sought to provide terms of reference for the readers' interpretation. A description of economic depression, side by side with pictures of successful and prosperous businessmen, or stories about how millionaires live, placed near pictures of down and out unemployed workers, were just two examples of such juxtaposition.

The ills of Western society were often exposed and continue to be exposed through the publication of critical reports from the Western press. By and large, Soviet readers receive only extracts or summaries of such reports; their content is presented as typical and reflecting the very essence of the "capitalist way of life" (*kapitalistichesky obraz zhizni*). The objective is to arouse discontent, uncertainty, suspicion, and distrust, which the Soviet Union hopes will ultimately lead to ideological confusion in the West and prompt a search for political alternatives.

The Soviet Union is eager to engage in polemics with the West, even though such polemics often have an unanticipated, boomerang effect. The West is dragged into discussions involving the comparison of democratic systems not with concrete communist countries, but with their projected theoretical utopias. This technique of unbalanced comparisons, which has been particularly cultivated under Gorbachev via various radio and television programs (including joint East-West satellite broadcasts), encourages Soviet propaganda to broaden the scale of psychological warfare so as to involve tens, even hundreds, of millions of mostly apolitical people. These are the most significant fronts on which Soviet psychological warfare operates. But psychological warfare is also being fought from defensive positions, where the purpose is to prevent dissemination of liberal, democratic, and humanistic ideas in Soviet society, where they would threaten the survival of communism. This purpose calls for the application of a strategy and tactics to destroy intellectual independence, create mental stereotypes,

present the world through the prism of official ideology, and rectify ideological deviations from communist dogma—via "reeducation" when necessary. The Soviet Union has no need for objective information; it does need to present information in a way that will further its goals.

Psychological warfare, whether offensive or defensive, is conducted by the state and party propaganda bureaucracies, the press, radio, and television, and through art and literature. Its cost amounts to hundreds of billions of rubles—more than the budget of any single Soviet ministry. Nevertheless, the new Soviet leadership was compelled to begin to retreat on a number of psychological warfare fronts, but not for economic reasons—since the USSR never spared its resources when world revolution was at stake. Ideological retreat was imperative as a price for the development and extension of a new detente. However, the propaganda regiments and units leading the psychological warfare were not demobilized but merely removed from the front. When required, they will again be deployed against the West. The battle will be waged as fiercely and mercilessly as in the past, since the Soviet psychological warfare mentality has not changed. The conduct of psychological warfare continues to find ample reflection in the Soviet language. For example, the mass media are defined as a "means of influencing the minds and souls of the people," who are thereby "mobilized" for the war of ideas; propaganda workers are described as "fighters" on the "front of mass agitation," and their task is defined as "decisively repulsing" the ideological "enemy."

Washington is stepping up psychological warfare against the socialist states. (Pravda, 8 October 1983, p. 5)

An important role in conducting psychological warfare is assigned to NATO agencies. (Pravda, 28 November 1983, p. 6)

The armed forces of the US have special psychological warfare units for strategic and tactical purposes. (Ibid.)

Public Work (*Obshchestvennaya rabota*). Unpaid work that serves the political, cultural, or professional requirements of the state. This service is obligatory and facilitates the imposition of intellectual and social control over Soviet citizens. The most prestigious form of public work is that performed in party, Komsomol, and trade-union organizations. Propaganda and agitation are important components of public work, which includes anything from service in the *druzhiny* (civilian militia) to the training provided to beginners by experienced workers in factories, schools, and collective farms, training that is known as "patronage" (cf.), (*shefstvo*) or "tutorship" (*nastavnichestvo*). Public work may become institutionalized with time, or may remain temporary, which means that it is carried out periodically or for a limited time.

Soviet citizens perform public work in their free time, as well as during working hours. In either case, they are not paid, receiving instead moral rewards in the form of certificates and expressions of gratitude. Particularly "outstanding" public workers (*obshchestvenniki*) are occasionally rewarded with inexpensive gifts, such as books, albums, or picture postcard collections; or they may be given free placement in a rest home or sanitarium. Participation in public work is regarded as evidence of Soviet citizens' high degree of civic responsibility, ideological awareness, and political involvement. Refusal to carry out public work is looked upon with suspicion or even held to be an act of disloyalty to the country. Thus, the bulk of the population, from schoolchildren to pensioners, feel obliged to perform public work, despite the fact that it cuts heavily into their free time. Some professionals involved in the humanities, writers, and artists are in this respect no exception. In fact, they devote much of their free time to such activity.

They participate in public work by providing experienced professional manpower for the ideological indoctrination of the population: giving lectures, organizing seminars, and administering peoples' universities.

Soviet citizens do not display any enthusiasm for public work but are aware that their career advancement may often depend on it. For those who wish to make a career in the party, public work can be a launching pad. Many Komsomol, party committee, and trade-union officials are also recruited from the ranks of public workers) *obshchestvenniki*), who distinguish themselves in zeal.

But public work is essentially a parody of civic initiative. Under the guise of offering the opportunity to make a worthwhile contribution to society, it thrusts Soviet citizens into a world of politicized activity that leaves them no time for independent thought or individual pursuits.

Colloquially, public work is referred to as a "public burden" (*obshchestvennaya nagruzka*) or simply "the burden" (*nagruzka*); these terms reveal the true attitude of the Soviet people toward obligations imposed on them without their consent.

I am frequently asked whether it is difficult to combine professional and public work. . . . However, I believe that a good team foreman has not only the opportunity but also the obligation to be a good agitator. (Agitator no. 15, 1978, p. 23)

The team foreman never fails to give his free time for public work. He is a member of the Party "buro," and he does on-the-spot inspections for the Committee for Conserving Metal. (Agitator, no. 9, 1979, p. 58).

This Communist has assumed public duties which might well be performed by two persons instead of one! He is a deputy of (our Party) organization, a chairman of the court of honor of young officers, and a member of the Komsomol "buro" of our unit. . . . (Sovetsky voin, no. 11, 1979, p. 24)

Q

Quality Seal (*Znak kachestva*). Certification conferred on goods proclaimed to conform to international standards. A quality seal was for the first time awarded in 1967 to an electric motor produced by the Vladimir Ilyich Factory in Moscow. By 1986, tens of thousands of different types of products manufactured in the Soviet Union were thus honored. The emblem of the quality seal is a pennant catapulted from the Soviet *sputnik* to the moon. Its validity extends for two years for consumer goods and up to three years for industrial equipment. When the validity period is about to expire, the product is retested. If found wanting, its certification can be annulled.

Quality seals were introduced in the hope of stimulating improvements and rationalizations in Soviet industry, whose products notoriously fail to live up to standards both internationally and at home. Shunned in foreign markets, such products depress the overall volume of exports, and this in turn brings chronic shortages of convertible currency. Quality improvements, however, are frustrated by the organization and structure of the Soviet economy, i.e., by the centralized planning, which is devoid of flexibility and versatility, by the absence of high-quality raw materials and modern equipment and, above all else, by the lack of incentives capable of making the producer concerned about what he or she produces. Raising the price of a product awarded a quality seal has proved ineffective because the proportion of quality seal articles within the overall industrial output is too small to have a major effect. In 1979, it amounted to 13 percent; in the first half of 1983, to 14 percent of total output; and by late 1988, it was down to 9 percent, despite the fact that many manufacturing concerns, particularly those in heavy industry, prefer to recommend their by-products, rather than main-line production items, for a quality seal. (In the case of machine-building plants, such by-products include home refrigerators, sauce pans, or wire, and in agricultural machinery plants, they include rakes and shovels.) It is significant that many articles lose their quality seal in retests, especially when external, state quality control is introduced.

Scientifically regulated quality control of industrial products is impossible under the conditions prevailing in Soviet society. One of the reasons for this is that for the sake of propaganda, the proportion of products with a quality seal must be increased from each planning year to the next and from each five-year plan to the next, regardless of whether the quality standards are actually improving.

> . . . several hundred articles usually lose their quality seal every year. Light industry has the dubious honor of being a leader in this field. (Agitator, no. 21, 1979, p. 34)

> The value of goods produced with a quality seal was three million rubles in excess of the plan. (Pravda, 13 December 1983, p. 2)

Questionnaire Form (*Anketa*). A questionnaire designed to elicit personal information. A questionnaire form is more than just a random assortment of questions. It is carefully designed so as to reveal the fullest possible picture of a respondent. The questions are not only meant to look into one's personal background—family name, first name, patronymic, year and place of birth—but also to reveal the respondent's social profile.

The item "social origin" is intended to determine the extent of one's political loyalty. Working-class origin designates the respondent as "one of us"; peasant origin is a little less trustworthy; while a person of intelligentsia extraction is considered unreliable and warranting suspicion. Such suspicions operate in the process of admission into the party. The Soviet Communist Party has long ceased to be the vanguard of the working class; it has become a bureaucratic springboard to power by means of which the most conformist and unscrupulous, after thorough ideological brainwashing, advance to the top. Many Soviet leaders sought to "improve" their biography by retroactively claiming worker origins. Proletarian descent was considered proof of one's belonging to the communist aristocracy, even though no social class in the Soviet Union has been more deprived than the working class.

Multiple layers of bearers of rank and privilege have developed in the USSR. In this context, the issue of "social origin" acquires particular significance, not literal but vicarious, as it reveals one's family status. If one's family ranks sufficiently high within the elite circles, one has wide possibilities for upward social mobility. This makes it easier to understand the typically Soviet expression, "This person has a good questionnaire form." In other words, one's educational attainment or innate talent do not count for that much. The main criterion is that of meeting the requirements of a "good" questionnaire form. Its manifold questions are intended not only to expose the respondent's own personal life but also ito shed maximum light on the respondent's family, both nuclear and extended. In the past, respondents were asked whether they had served in the White army or worked for the Provisional Government, and whether they or their families had ever been deprived of voting rights. Today's questions include such details as e.g., had the respondent ever been a prisoner-of-war or resided on territories occupied by the enemy, and if so, where, when, and under what circumstances had he or she been "liberated." Another standard question asks whether a person has relatives or friends in capitalist countries.

There are also tricky questions, seemingly innocent, yet dangerous in their implications. The most loaded among them is that of nationality. Some nations are granted the full range of political rights (the Slavs); others (national minorities who have their own republics) have restricted rights; while the third group (Jews, Crimean Tatars, and Germans) are subject to even more stringent restrictions. This discrimination, however, sometimes has paradoxical side-effects: membership in an "inferior" national group occasionally may become an advantage. A member of a discriminated nationality occasionally gets preferential treatment in being hired or sent abroad, so as to prove that the USSR is indeed a "brotherhood of nations."

The reforms carried out by the Soviet leadership have not reformed the questionnaire form, which, for example, still retains the question: "Have you ever been abroad and if so, where, when, and for what purpose?" The question seems incongruous in view of the fact that foreign travel, be it for business or pleasure, has become a common phenomenon. Yet the way the question is formulated, with its implicit suggestion of approbrium attached to a foreign travelling, is far from accidental. Politics may change, but people are believed to remain the same and therefore should be subjected to maximal controls. In fact, the questionnaire form is supposed to function as a sort of an administrative X-ray machine, providing the information to ensure that the crucial positions are occupied by those whose "political health" profile is most appropriate. However, like other strictly administrative measures, questionnaire forms proved powerless in preventing corruption, protectionism, and nepotism. For one thing, questionnaire forms help eliminate exactly the kind of people that might be relied upon for not giving in to corruption and for willingness to take risks in efforts to stamp it out.

In the USSR, more power and importance are attached to questionnaire forms than to their respondents as persons. Thousands of Soviet people cower in fear each time they have to fill out a questionnaire, for they sense the presence of a Big Brother behind it. They know that it is Big Brother who, on the basis of their answers, will determine whether they deserve a job, a promotion, or a trip abroad and will thus shape their future.

> Questionnaire forms come in different forms. Some are straightforward, others more complex, and then there are some which you can make neither head or tail of. The difficulty of a questionnaire form grows in direct proportion to the importance of the job which the respondent is applying for. (Radio Liberty: Research Bulletin, 19 June 1984, p. 1)

> I noticed a questionnaire form. No, not a sociological questionnaire but an application form. The kind a citizen must fill out in order to get a job or have his passport stamped. (Moskovskie novosti, no. 31, 31 July 1988, p. 3)

Queue (*Ochered'*). Line or list of people waiting for foodstuffs, consumer goods, or services. Queues first appeared during the early years of the Soviet state, when the process of the building of socialism (*postroenie sotsializma*) brought about the country's economic disintegration, marked by widespread shortages of basic commodities. From then on, queues have been an integral part of the Soviet experience. Waiting in queues, Soviet citizens each year waste more than eighty billion man-hours (which is equivalent to the work of 40 to 45 million people annually.

The vast number of queues that form every day and every hour in the Soviet Union is beyond count or classification. They can be roughly classified as belonging to one of four types: spontaneous, administrative, shortage-related, and invisible. Moreover, each of these queues can be subdivided into two categories: "live" queues and queues on paper. The first may range in size from a dozen to several thousand people and in length from several meters to a kilometer, extending throughout a whole residential district. The queues on paper are compiled and kept by official institutions—by trade enterprises or state bodies. Such queues can comprise tens or hundreds of thousands of names.

Spontaneous queues are not something distinctly Soviet. In all modern countries, there are queues for various types of entertainment: sports events, theatrical perform-

ances, films, concerts, etc. Since waiting in such queues is not a prerequisite of human survival, they are voluntary in character and selective in composition, depending on interests, tastes, and preferences of the queuers.

Administrative queues in the Soviet Union are for apartments, hospital admissions, top jobs, etc. Usually they assume the form of lists; this usually frees people from the necessity of breathing down each others' necks or from standing in the cold or in a downpour. That is their advantage, but there is a disadvantage to such queues as well. People can know their number in line, but knowing one's number is neither meaningful nor dependable knowledge. Those with "influence," or with resources to offer a bribe, will always move ahead of others, closer to the objective. Administrative queuing can involve months or even years of waiting, and it ultimately may even be futile. An apartment may never be obtained, a telephone never installed, furniture or an automobile never purchased.

The queue for apartments is the most unusual type and, at the same time, it reveals something about Soviet life in general. Such a queues can be entered at the city or district executive committee or at one's place of work. Entry does not simply depend on one's intention but also on one's eligibility for an apartment, which the applicant must prove. For that purpose, a number of points need to be certified. There has to be less than six square meters of "living space" (cf.) per person in his living quarters (unless the apartment is substandard in terms of hygiene or safety—e.g., with leaking ceilings or unsafe walls—or his quarters must be scheduled for immediate demolition). Needless to say, certification of such circumstances requires waiting in a number of other queues, whether live or paper ones, for an appointment with the head of the housing administration, with the housing supervisor, with the public health physician, with the architect, etc. This may last excruciatingly long. And it still does not necessarily follow that the applicant is in the position to receive and assemble all the requisite documents. However, the resolution of the problem is to be found in the very concept of "going for an appointment." On the face of it, the phrase may seem absurd since no one "goes for" an appointment but is summoned to it: in theory to be welcomed there and received hospitably. Still, the phrase has some meaning. Soviet officials indeed "receive" people, but they are more interested in receiving "gifts," either in cash or in valuables. Without such "gifts," an appointment with an applicant can be delayed interminably or never materialize. But as a proof of the applicant's goodwill, a "gift" must be first offered to the official's secretary, who controls access to the boss. Needless to say, such proof of "goodwill" must be sufficiently convincing. Only when it is does the applicant succeed in winning for himself a promising place in the queue for the appointment. At this stage, a new hitch might occur. The official may stop receiving people for the day or longer before the applicant's turn comes or even just when it was about to come. This means further waiting, as happens quite often in administrative queues.

Shortage-related queues are subject to somewhat different rules. Although bread is no longer in short supply in the USSR, other staples like meat, butter, cheese, fruit, and vegetables are; and so is clothing and footware, not to mention prestige items like jewelry or cosmetics, or luxuries like carpets or cars.

However, queues are formed not only for goods in short supply, but also for those that are available. This is partly because of the shortages of manpower: salespeople, cashiers, delivery truckers, etc. Another reason, however, is that queuing for available goods opens the way to speculation and fraud. Sales personnel can pad their pockets and cheat their customers on weight or quality of merchandise they sell.

Queues are not disappearing. Considerable numbers of people have a stake in their continued existence. The stake is not just financial. There is also a matter of establishing "right" connections and rising to high social status via mutual exchange of favors.

Hence the phenomenon of invisible queues in the Soviet Union. They are invisible in the sense that one does not literally queue up for a hotel room or a reservation at a sanitarium. Yet, practically the whole nation is figuratively in queues for such desired prizes, for who does not dream of staying in fine accomodations while on a business trip or of getting some rest and recreation? However, reservations in hotels or at sanitariums are usually available to those who need them least, that is, to the members of the Soviet elite who anyway never have to wait in Soviet queues for anything. The queue embodies the system of privileges and confirms the elite's raison d'être. If Heroes of Socialist Labor and deputies of the Supreme Soviet, for example, are served or receive goods out of turn, then all other Soviet citizens are ordained to receive goods and services only by waiting in queue. Hence, "they also serve who only stand and wait": they *wait* in queues and their waiting *serves* to elevate the status of those who enjoy the privilege of not having to wait.

In the "paper" or "administrative" type of queue, a person's name is entered on a waiting list. This is the common procedure for obtaining anything substantial: an apartment, a car, a hospital bed, imported furniture, admission to a rest home, a handmade carpet, the installation of a telephone, and many other kinds of purchases of services. The waiting period in such cases ranges from a few weeks to a few years.

Soviet queues have an inner dynamics of their own. Interpersonal tension and conflict, even if not always obvious, are rife. Queues also have "laws" of their own. For example, if a person is fortunate enough to make it to the head of the queue, and there is something left, he is allowed only a limited quantity of the goods for his own use and not for resale. Each product then has its own quota: e.g., 400 grams of butter, 1.5 kilograms of meat, 2 kilograms of cereals or sugar, one bottle of milk, one pair of gloves, two tickets to the theater or a concert, one carpet, one overcoat. In addition, in order to make a single purchase, one must stand in three different queues! The first one is for selection of the item, the second is for payment, and the third in order to receive one's purchase. Volunteers often take it upon themselves to organize the queue; they make lists, give out numbered tags or mark the number of people's places in indelible ink on the palms of their hands, conduct roll calls, and keep order. Anyone not present at the queue site during a number check loses his place. Quarrels and even physical fights periodically break out in queues. The animosity of purchasers subsides only as they approach the sales counter and their attention focuses on the purchase at hand.

For Soviet citizens, the queue has become not only a tradition-honored necessity, but also an inner need. Without a queue, they will not buy anything just because the lack of demand will for them be a prima facie proof of substandard quality. On the other hand, they will rush to queue up even when they do not require what is being sold in the queue. The crowd psychology is at work here: there must be a reason. Act like others first, later perhaps a rationale will appear.

The social structure and composition of queues reflects the hierarchy inherent in Soviet society. People who queue for products are on the lowest rung of the Soviet social ladder. They are workers, rank and file officials, professionals without a big reputation. Such people do not have the privilege of exchanging their money for goods (*otovarit'sya*) in closed stores (cf.). Some factories distribute goods to their workforce, and these workers thus do not have to join queues. In contrast, the rural population must queue, traveling hundreds of kilometers—either individually or in organized groups in buses—to shop in town.

Queues have their "long-standing" impact on personality formation. A typical queuer is always tired, irritable, and aggressive. His eyes are often glazed. In a queue, the Soviet citizen, whatever his or her occupation or background, assumes the characteristic identity of a queue-member. If he succeeds in making a purchase, he reacts with the same jubilation as other "winners," and if he fails

(because the desired item has been sold out or the store has closed), he feels the same frustration as other "losers."

Queues are not only an integral part of Soviet life, they are also one of the props of the regime. The shortages of foodstuffs and consumer goods in the USSR are a cleverly organized and subtle ploy to restrain popular discontent. In fact, they are even more effective in some ways than police surveillance and administrative control. Paradoxically, standing in a queue provides an outlet for social dissatisfaction; the denial of civil and political rights is forgotten in the face of the satisfaction a consumer experiences when he manages to buy an article in short supply. Thus the attainment of such a prize allows one unfortunate to elevate himself a little above his fellow unfortunates.

Reflecting this phenomenon of Soviet life, a queue jargon has developed containing expressions such as "they threw out" (*vybrosili*), which means "they put on sale;" "it sufficed" (*dostalos'*), or "it did not suffice" (*ne dostalos'*), which means that the supplies of a given product lasted or did not last; "to stand through a queue" (*vystoyat' ochered'*), which means to make a purchase; "to pull away" (*otorvat'*), which means to buy; and to "take up a queue" (*zanyat' ochered*), which means to take a place in a queue.

Likewise, the queue has given birth to a number of aphorisms, e.g., "No queue means no goods," "A non-live (i.e., on paper) queue lives longer than a live one," "The queue is a good form of publicity," and "The longer one queues, the more one buys." There is also a witty quip that relates to an aspect of the Gorbachev era: "The queue is an informal organization [cf.] based on affinity of interest."

The word "queue" has also given birth to some characteristic neologisms. One of the most recent, thus far not listed in Soviet dictionaries, is "ocherednik" (queuer), meaning a person who has been waiting for years to obtain an apartment.

The queue is a staple element of Soviet culture, providing the "inspiration" for countless stories, cartoons, and anecdotes.

If the queue were to disappear from Soviet society overnight, Soviet culture would be impoverished. However, such a prospect is not in the cards. The queue is too entrenched as an institution.

> I live near the jewelry shop, and I see the queues which usually form two or three hours before opening time. The most eager buyers even spend the night in nearby telephone booths. (Komsomol'skaya pravda, 16 October 1980, p. 4)

> In general there are reception hours for the public in a regional social security office on only four out of five working days, and even then only from 9 a.m. to 1 p.m. With queues it is the same! (Izvestiya, 13 October 1983, p. 2)

> The larger the store, the more customers and the longer the queues. (Izvestiya, 12 January 1984, p. 2)

> Still the most terrible thing is not these usual queues in which you at least know who is last, but the invisible queues where you can stand your whole life without getting anything. (Literaturnaya gazeta, 20 April 1988, p. 14)

R

Racket (*Reket*). Blackmail and extortion accomplished by force or threat of force. The term "racket" became recognized as applying to Soviet society only recently—in the context of perestroika. Until then it was exclusively used in the USSR to castigate bourgeois society—particularly the American one—its mores, and way of life. That was the way it appeared in Soviet dictionaries: "RACKET—in the USA blackmail, violence, forcible extortion type of gangsterism" (Kratky politichesky slovar. [Concise political dictionary], Moscow: Publishing House of Political Literature, 1978, p. 335).

In fact, rackets have existed in the Soviet Union throughout its entire history, and especially from the time drug addiction and underground business (cf. Black Market) first appeared. However, the structure of rackets has changed over time. When the Soviet regime was established, rackets were a new phenomenon engaged in by amateurs or beginners, each of whom chose his particular business in tune with his "vocation:" some shook down prostitutes, others reaped profits from the black market, sometimes via the protection racket, still others sold drugs.

Rackets became organized and solidified in the late 1950s as organized crime expanded and grew stronger. They came to be run by recognized leaders and have clear structures. Huge groups were formed implying clear division of labor: the bosses plan operations, the "fingerers" target victims, their women play the role of decoys or lures, and the operators or "combat staff" work over the victims, either psychologically or physically. Sufficiently intimidated, black marketeers rarely complain to law enforcement agencies. The racketeers know this and use it to their advantage.

Disguised in police uniforms, the operators appear in the apartments of black marketeers or other fat cats and, brandishing guns or other weapons, demand "your money, your valuables, or your life." If such threats do not work, the *tsekhoviki* (i.e., black market millionaires) are taken for a ride out of town and, in some deserted place, beaten until they agree to disclose the location of their treasures. From that point, they are in the racketeers' pockets, or, rather, vice versa: the racketeers have regular access to their pockets. Of course, they utilize each victim to gain access to his "business associates."

In principle, Soviet racketeering differs little from its Western counterpart. Nevertheless, there are some differences. The Soviet racketeer alone is not criminal; the social environment is not less criminal. The victims forced to pay "protection tax" are themselves lawbreakers; otherwise they would not have amassed the profits "taxed" in such a peculiar way. This feature of Soviet rackets is rather unique. The racketeers push their way into the world of illegal business and, once they get hold of compromising evidence, they start blackmailing heads of supply depots, directors of markets and stores, who thus join the ranks of vulnerable victims, including prostitutes. Of course, these businessmen and these "business women" do not turn to the police for redress of their grievances because there they would meet with something worse than "taxes," namely humiliating interrogations and severe penalties. The racketeers, who often fleece their victims seven times over, are prepared to protect them from the authorities.

In view of this, the attitude of the Soviet "business community" toward racketeering tends to be more respectful than its attitude toward the authorities. The "businessmen" do not fear the law; they can buy their way out of legal difficulties. It is much more difficult to escape the clutches of the racketeers and more dangerous to try. The latter have extended their tentacles into all parts of the second economy (cf.), right up to members of the government involved in financial wheeling and dealing. But they wouldn't miss a small trick either, not even neglecting the petty profits that can be accrued by "taxing" the proceeds of petty crooks like those who engage in the "shell game" (in Russia, thimbles are often used in place of nuts) or who con simpletons on street corners who hope to guess under which "shell" the ten-ruble note is hidden; or "currency exchange" swindlers operating at commission stores, where they can relieve their customers of quite significant sums by palming off on them "dummy" wads of money, with rubles on the outside and just paper on the inside.

Some racket operations became somewhat obstructed in 1987, when the government began to close down the "Berezka" (cf.) stores. This put out of work masses of speculators and buyers and sellers of foreign export bank checks and, along with these, hordes of con men and extortionists who had gotten used to making an easy living. But then to the rescue came the expansion of the cooperatives (cf.)—cafés, restaurants, sewing workshops, and kiosks—on which the racketeers soon succeeded in laying their hands. Similar fates befell the sellers of homemade produce at markets, train stations, and subway stops. All these people are forced to pay protection money or be beaten and have their merchandise commandeered.

The growth of the cooperatives gave a real boost to racketeering. As profits began to reach six- and seven-digit figures, the social base of racketeering began to expand. Until quite recently, the bosses of the criminal underground viewed racketeering with scorn, finding extortion incompatible with their thieves' honor and prejudicial to their status. However, when some racketeers became millionaires, the bosses decided to reconsider the matter. As a consequence of their "new thinking," the nature of racketeering has undergone some alteration. It has become subtler, cleaner, more refined, less prone to blood and gore. Every cooperative is now assessed and assigned a "tax rate" accordingly. In this way, cooperatives are forced into illegality, income concealment, purchasing stolen equipment, obtaining supplies of raw materials "on the side," and consequent inflation of the prices of their goods or services. Without overpricing, they will not survive in a society in which racketeers set the rules.

On this border territory between lawfulness and lawlessness, the cooperatives have fathered a new type of distinctly Soviet racketeering, namely government racketeering. In Soviet society, cooperatives do not command respect, but rather envy or contempt toward an institution believed by almost everyone to be transitory and ultimately doomed. No official, no matter how petty, is ready to help them without getting something for him- or herself. Taking bribes from cooperatives has become so common that officials no longer have any qualms or apprehensions about it. They accept them openly, without even being ashamed to count their takings in public. This means that the idea of free enterprise has died stillborn in the Soviet Union.

> In general I would like to emphasize that . . . the commercial and communal food-provisioning cooperatives have been suffering and will keep suffering. (Ogonek, no. 5, January–February 1989, p. 18)

Radiosaboteurs (*Radiodiversanty*). Personnel of foreign radio stations broadcasting to the Soviet Union. The term initially appeared in the late 1940s when, anxious to preserve their information monopoly, Soviet authorities began to assiduously jam foreign radio stations. This was accompanied by attempts to discredit foreign broadcasters, especially those who used the languages of Soviet peoples, by labelling them "radiosaboteurs." This concept reveals the extent of the authorities' fear of uncontrolled and independent information capable of disrupting their reliable and well-oiled propaganda machine designed to filter and select all data.

For many years, Soviet society remained

hermetically isolated. Infiltration of uncensored or ideologically unprocessed information threatened it with inevitable disintegration. Comparisons and analogies between the Soviet Union and the West were a definite taboo. The communist press issued frequent reports on the billions spent by the United States on weapons, while passing over in silence the huge Soviet military budget. Similarly, Soviet citizens were told at length and often about the Palestinian resistance to Israeli rule, while anti-Soviet resistance in Afghanistan only rated a brief and occasional mention.

The halt in the jamming of foreign radio stations in 1988, without doubt an important step on the road to glasnost, resulted in a kind of informational shock. The Soviet citizen was swamped with utterly surprising facts, he learned to his amazement about the practice of destroying surplus produce in the West, while his own country is plagued with chronic shortages; or he discovered that unemployment benefits in Western countries exceed many-fold the average Soviet salary. Much of this flood of information could not be digested by minds conditioned by political indoctrination. Thus, Soviet propaganda made an effort to organize and channel this flow of data according to current requirements. By dealing out the truth in little doses, Soviet authorities now try to discredit Western broadcasters themselves rather than the Western mass media, as they did in the past. Depending on their age and social origins, foreign broadcasters are depicted as accomplices of Hitler who managed to escape punishment, as blatant anti-Semites (for his own purposes, Gorbachev may be willing to appear as a defender of the Jews), or as brazen revanchists (*naglye revanshisty*) and warmongers (cf.). Together, they are subsumed under the all-embracing category of radiosaboteurs.

Many delegates stated that their countries are subject to similar types of radiosabotage. (Sotsialisticheskaya industriya, 13 November 1982, p. 3)

The most criminal and shameful action of the radiosaboteurs is that, having surpassed the limits of perfidy, they are now using all the resources at their disposal to enlist Kazakhs under the banner of their vaunted 'liberty'. Their particular target among the Kazakhs are the young and those living abroad. (Kazakhstanskaya pravda, 18 December 1983, p. 3)

Reactionary (*Reaktsionny*). The Soviet term for the obsolete, i.e., antisocialist, classes. Actions, events, or theories are branded "reactionary" when they have no place within the scheme of historical progress as the communists conceive of it. Hence democratic regimes and institutions, religions, idealistic philosophies, abstract art, and various scientific theories are all termed reactionary. In general, the label has been used in accordance with dialectical pragmatism, depending on the changing political winds, and the needs and political preferences of Soviet leaders.

In the Soviet domestic context, the term is used relatively seldom, since it is viewed as incompatible with the socialist concepts and ideas. The only exception is nationalist manifestations as well as religious sects and movements unrecognized by the government. These are branded as reactionary.

The emotional force of the term is enhanced by the use of such qualifying adverbs as "extremely" (*kraine*), "openly" (*otkrovenno*), "utterly" (*naibolee*), etc.

It is not difficult to see the mobilization of imperialist reactionary forces, bent on opposing positive developments in international relations. . . . Their aim is to test the strength of the edifice of detente. (Kommunist, no. 16, 1978, p. 17)

. . . the bourgeoisie, abetted by reactionary leaders of the trade unions of the capitalist countries, has succeeded in setting different segments of the working class against each other and in splitting the international trade union movement. (Problemy mira i sotsializma, no. 3, 1980, p. 10)

Recreant (*Pererozhdenets*). A term used by the authorities to brand individuals who renounce their Marxist worldview and, under the influence of "bourgeois ideology," display behavior inappropriate for Soviet citizens. Communist propaganda attributes recreancy to the insuperable contradiction between consciousness and being, whereby individual consciousness lags behind social being. This interpretation stems from the view that human nature is corrupt and therefore must be held in check. The remedy is seen in state control and regulation, which supposedly benefit the common good by producing the servile obedience and blind compliance communists deem necessary for social progress.

Although living in a "healthy and beneficent" socialist environment, individuals are considered liable to fall prey to "relics of the past" (*perezhitki proshlogo*, cf.). Petit bourgeois attitudes or the desire for private ownership can make inroads into the minds of people who have "not kept pace with reality." Bourgeois ideological sabotage and the pervasive influence of capitalist psychology are presented as "dangers" threatening Soviet life. The party faithful are told to maintain their vigilance at all times, lest these temptations lure them into recreancy.

However, recreancy really owes its existence not to external factors but to Soviet policies. Forced labor, exploitation, and the call for mindless conformism cannot fail to provoke a reaction. In the final analysis, in his rejection of communist morality and of the hypocrisy and inhumanity of Soviet ideology, the "recreant" affirms a kind of human dignity totally alien to the leaders of the USSR. And for that, he is punished.

The malice and unscrupulousness of these bourgeois recreants knows no bounds. They hate our Party and all those honorable people who labor strenuously to build socialism with the fury of renegades. (Ushakov, Tolkovy slovar' russkogo yazyka [Explanatory dictionary of the Russian language], Moscow: State Publishing House for Foreign and Soviet Peoples' Dictionaries, vol. 3, 1939, p. 189)

By his clamor about Party recreancy, Trotsky endeavored to conceal his own recreancy and his anti-Party schemes. (Istoriya VKPb, Kratky kurs [History of the All-Union Communist Party (Bolsheviks) Brief course], Moscow:

Publishing House for Political Literature, 1950, p. 254)

At the plenum, the former first secretary of the Sevastopol Party gorkom (city committee) A. Smolyannikov . . . announced from the podium that the harsh punishment of recreants, like the former employee of the Department for the Fight against Theft of Socialist Property Ya. Kubov, was supported by the people of Sevastopol. (Pravda, 22 March 1989, p. 6)

Registration (*Propiska*). A residence permit (localized to city or rural settlement, specifying actual address), which each Soviet citizen must obtain from the police. The purpose of the procedure is to restrict the population's mobility and employment options. A registration system involving the maintenance of police files on the entire population was first instituted in 1932 in the wake of the rural famine and forced collectivization of that period and the mass migration of peasants to urban centers that it produced. Ostensibly to regulate and improve census-taking methods, the true aim of the policy was to shield the towns and, in particular, the capital from an influx of peasants; it also allowed the authorities to control the movement of the population and ferret out people who were in hiding.

The registration system is regulated by specific legislation. Upon reaching the age of sixteen, inhabitants of cities and workers' settlements are issued internal passports that must bear a registration stamp. A citizen who leaves his or her address for more than three days or moves to a new home—even if it is around the block from his or her former one—must register his or her movements at the local police station. If registration is refused, the rejected applicant has twenty-four hours to leave his or her place of residence—whether temporary or permanent. Delays are punished by a fine or by imprisonment. Failure to register or to obtain a passport is a serious criminal offense, punishable by a heavy fine or imprisonment for up to two years.

Not that long ago, in comparative terms of Russian history (in the 1920s), none other than Lenin branded the internal passport as a shameful feature of tsarism. The communists prided themselves on the fact that Soviet law did not recognize a passport system. Freedom of movement and residence were considered key achievements of the new regime. The internal passport was introduced in 1932, simultaneously with registration. They were provided with a communist rationale, in terms of blocking the movement of the kulaks (cf.) to the city, where they might disguise themselves and disappear into the general population and take advantage of their anonymity in order to rob stores or set factories on fire.

Inhabitants of rural areas—with the exception of the Moscow and Kaliningrad provinces and the Baltic region—are not issued internal passports. (This was the law until 1974, and has remained unofficial practice since.) Without a passport, a peasant does not have the right to leave his or her collective farm, settle in a city, or obtain work outside the collective farm.

There is little difference in this respect between the social order of the USSR and that which existed in imperial Russia prior to 1861. Serfs were the property of landowners in the same way that collective farmers are the property of their collective farms or rural councils (soviets). Likewise, runaway serfs were apprehended and sent back to the country by the police just as collective farmers who are caught without passports by the militia are sent back today. But necessity is still the mother of invention. In the past, peasants bought their freedom from landowners; after paying "quit rent" (*obrok*), they left for the towns. Today, collective farm workers make their way out of agricultural servitude by bribing the chairman of the rural soviet with a bottle of vodka and heading for one of the industrial sites, where they can hope to somehow obtain work and a registration stamp.

The system of internal passport controls deeply affects the way Soviet citizens live their lives. People do not seek work on the basis of vocational suitability but rather on the basis of where they can register. Inhabitants of cities, afraid of losing their registration permits and consequently their apartments, refuse to budge from their cities of residence, thus remaining for their whole lives stuck in the place where they were born.

A registration permit has become so indispensable that without it, it is impossible to go to college, place a child in school or kindergarten, obtain an apartment, get an appointment in a clinic, be hospitalized, or simply negotiate one's way across the bureaucratic minefield of everyday life. It grants the authorities control over the lives not only of individuals but even of entire peoples. The Crimean Tatars are a case of point. Deported from Crimea in 1944, they have been trying to return to their native lands ever since, but to no avail. In spite of the fact that steady employment would be available to them in both collective and state-owned farms there, they have persistently been refused registration permits.

Personal considerations and personal desires are irrelevant in the registration procedure. Sometimes children are refused registration with their parents, or parents are not permitted to register with their children. Registration for residence in Moscow, Leningrad, and capitals of union republics have been legally banned for many years, unless it is warranted by employment considerations. It is quite difficult to gain such employment opportunities, as they can only be provided by enterprises that have registration "quotas," e.g., party organizations, military plants, and enterprises that require unskilled labor. If a person is fired, he or she automatically loses his or her "quota" registration. Thus on the path of the migration of the population (a process that in most cases is quite positive), the state erects administrative barriers aimed at artificially holding back the expansion of the large cities. This attempt is fruitless. The Soviet citizen is capable of finding many roundabout routes of getting from the country to the city, from small towns to many major industrial centers. Among the means employed are fictitious marriages (which help explain the unusually high percentage of divorces), bribes, and favors, which contribute to the flourishing of corruption (cf.).

The limitations in regard to registration have been accompanied by a paradox. A problem has developed with its converse, *vypiska*, or permission for residents to leave a city with the right to return to it. Once they manage to establish themselves in a city, Soviet citizens aspire with all their energy to remain there. As a result, they often lose the opportunity to gain satisfaction in work, career, or family life.

Since many have invested so much and even paid a high price for this privilege, the fear of leaving the city without the possibility of returning to it prompts hundreds of thousands of specialists who are quite superfluous in the city (e.g., agronomists, veterinarians, and experts in animal husbandry and agricultural development, whose services would be such a boon to the countryside) to refuse to leave urban areas. However, the possibility of freely leaving one's residence with the right to return to it would not only yield economic benefit; it is also an individual's elementary democratic right.

Nor are Soviet arguments about the social nonutility of uncontrolled, unorganized migration very convincing. They, in fact, lead to absurd decisions and regulations. One of them was an attempt to tie rural youth in Central Asia to rural regions where there was already tremendous overpopulation and covert or even (a rare phenomenon in the USSR) overt unemployment. In Uzbekistan alone, the number of unemployed (excluding women and invalids) amounts to one million.

Administrative limitations and restrictions on freedom of residence due to the registration system are a harmful "relic of the past," not of the capitalist nor even of the serfdom-feudal past but a legacy of Stalinism, with its cruel and implacable state despotism. Only a modern autocratic state could be so determined to prevent people from settling in border areas or in the "closed regime" cities like Kaliningrad, Sevastopol, Vladivostok, and Severomorsk, or in settlements or regions where secret work was being carried out in nuclear fission, the production of strategic weapons, or the extraction of precious metals.

Former convicts are restricted in their choice of domicile and are forbidden to register in a large city for several years. They are not allowed to live within a radius of 101 kilometers from Moscow or within a radius of 50 to 70 kilometers from any capital of a republic. The registration system (which hardly affects the Soviet elite) offers considerable possibilities for arbitrariness. Perhaps this might explain its retention in fairly recent legislation. A new law of 1975 granted the Ministry of the Interior even greater control over Soviet individuals through the use of coded information, which provides any interested bureaucrat with ample biographical data (e.g., family status, social mobility, profession, work record) on the passport holder via his or her passport number. With this addition, the task of controlling people has become much easier.

In order to receive registration (be registered) in a settlement area located in a border zone, one must obtain special permission from the organs of internal affairs. (Sobranie postanovleny pravitel'stva SSSR [Collected decrees of the government of the USSR], no. 19, Moscow, 1974)

At the police department he was informed that he had to leave Moscow soon since he had a registration for Leningrad. (Posev, no. 7, 1976, p. 12)

You can buy living space only via a cooperative, and the cooperative is accepting only people with permanent registration. (Posev, no. 8, 1980, p. 37)

After presentation of the documents to the [internal] passport division, the question of registration will be taken up at a session of the executive committee (Izvestiya, 17 February 1990, p. 6)

Rehabilitation (*Reabilitatsiya*). (1) Restoration of lapsed functions of an organism. (2) Restoration of someone's reputation. (3) Judicial restoration of legal rights. In Soviet practice, the latter meaning is the most widespread. It is most often used even in a more specific sense referring to (the usually post-humous) exoneration of victims of Stalin's tyranny. The rehabilitation of Soviet citizens illegally condemned during Stalin's rule began in the second half of the 1950s. At that time, approximately 100,000 people were released from incarceration and returned to their families and to work. Approximately 200,000 more were exonerated posthumously on account of the lack of any evidence of the crime for which they had been executed. However, as compared to the scale of the Stalinist terror, which left more than twenty million people confined in prisons and camps and at least two million executed, the scale of rehabilitation was quite minuscule. It benefited primarily government functionaries and party activists.

Thirty years had to pass, and the Kremlin leadership had to change several times, before the Soviet regime recognized that justice must be restored universally rather than selectively. For that purpose, one had to stop talking of specific cases of judicial errors and of distortions on the part of the authorities and begin instead to talk of mass scale despotism. That, however, would pose a dilemma: how could the convictions of tens of millions of people be reviewed? If each case were to be examined, it would take years. Hence it was decided to summarily define as illegal decisions of extra-judicial organs such as the "troikas" (cf.) and other "special commissions" as well as all convictions of people whose names had been simply placed on quota lists for prosecution. This was a convenient solution as it made it unnecessary to review each individual case of rehabilitation separately. But the solution was unjust. It did not include hundreds of thousands who had been executed without any proceedings whatever in the torture chambers of the Cheka or millions of victims of pre-Stalin terror between 1917 and 1924.

Likewise unsatisfactory was the material compensation granted to people after their rehabilitation beginning in 1956. Such compensation amounts to the equivalent of two months' salary from the last work place plus a symbolic sum (up to 500 rubles), suppos-edly to compensate for "confiscated property." The Soviet leaders believe that moral recompense is more important (and less expensive) than a financial one. Hence they have decided to give their support to the idea of erecting in Moscow a monument to the victims of Stalin's terror. They hope the monument will exculpate them and their regime from responsibility for that ghastly past.

The rehabilitation of Soviet people illegally condemned during the Stalin terror proceeded after the XXth Party Congress. (Moskovskie novosti, no. 3, 15 January 1989, p. 1)

We say much and write much about rehabilitation, but the time has come to begin to talk about rehabilitating the Party. (Ogonek, no. 14, April 1989, p. 3)

Relics of the Past (*Perezhitki proshlogo*). Views, morals, and traditions that conflict with those officially prescribed. The term "relics of the past" encompasses a wide variety of beliefs, attitudes, and behavior patterns. Depending on political expediency, either feudalism or capitalism is blamed for their existence. Being at odds with Soviet ideology, they are held to be antisocial (e.g., acts of cruelty, violence, cynicism, vandalism) or anti-Soviet (e.g., lack of principles, political apathy, careerism). In the official Soviet view, the advanced industrial democracies of the West belong to the "past," and the social systems and ideologies they have produced are considered relics. The historical future, on the other hand, allegedly belongs to the USSR. The ossified, conservative regime and its nineteenth-century-based ideology are described as "progressive" formations against which all else must be measured and will be found wanting.

This historical attitude enabled the Soviet poet Mayakovsky to say of his visit to the United States, the home of the scientific and technological revolution of the twentieth century, "I rushed seven thousand miles forward, but went seven years backwards!" From the same perspective, long outdated doctrines of Marxism-Leninism are hailed for helping "to define the main directions of socio-economic and political development for long years ahead."

Soviet ideology constantly manipulates history to distance itself from the origins of social phenomena it deems negative. Thus, far from bearing any responsibility for hypocrisy in international affairs or domestic corruption, the Soviet Union in its propaganda is shown combating these evils with all the strength it can muster. The survival of relics of the past into the present era is explained by the influence of "capitalist encirclement" on supposedly "isolated," insufficiently "Sovietized" individuals. The expression "birthmarks of capitalism" (*rodimye pyatna kapitalizma*) for many years served as the semantic equivalent of relics of the past. By referring to the "birth" of Soviet society from a capitalist one, this expression helped lay the blame for the faults of Soviet society on the matrix out of which it emerged.

In recent years, it has become increasingly difficult for communist propaganda to explain away antisocial behavior and the erosion of conventional morals as relics of the past, since that past is now generations away. At the same time, blaming the capitalist West for these phenomena lacks credibility when censorship is strict and borders remain sealed. Nor does it sound convincing to argue today that relics of the past owe their continued existence to the time lag between social reality and individual consciousness, which may not have caught up with this reality. Rather than admit that the relics of the past are an integral element of the Soviet system, Soviet propaganda attributes them to temporary economic difficulties, failures to follow or implement ideology, and breaches (invariably "isolated") of socialist legality and deviations from the party line (whose perpetrators should be severely punished).

Attempts to overcome relics of the past have thus far proven totally ineffective. They have consisted for the most part of empty slogans, such as calls for a struggle against bourgeois values and nationalistic prejudices and for greater vigilance (under the guidance of the party) in opposing such values on the part of individuals, the educational system, and society at large. Timid and cautious demands to eliminate the "objective" conditions that give rise to relics of the past are occasionally mooted. The problem is, however, that the "objective conditions" are really part and parcel of the communist system. Thus it is scarcely logical that the consequences of the latter be attributed to the past.

In propaganda messages, typically cited conditions are production failures and instances of faulty management or organization of labor, and of lack of vigilance. Attention is called to particular cases, which might be remedied or improved. Perhaps the CPSU leadership will rectify such failures, but it will scarcely rectify the systemic features or underlying causes responsible for the major failures of communist society. This guarantees that relics of the past will be reproduced in the future.

> The new image of the Soviet man, his Communist morals and weltanschauung are confirmed in his consistent and uncompromising struggle with the relics of the past. As is known, we often feel the pain of such inherited social "ulcers" which are fundamentally alien to socialism, such as a negligent attitude toward labor, lack of discipline, interest in profit, or disruptions of the norms of socialist communal life. (Agitator, no. 17, 1978, p. 7)

> We should fight systematically and unrelentingly, using all means of propaganda and upbringing . . . to liquidate the distorted relics of the past which are hostile to socialism and yet often encountered in our life. (Agitator, no. 10, 1979, p. 4)

Renegade (*Otshchepenets*). A person in conflict with Soviet society. The original meaning of the word," an apostate from the church and faith," was borrowed to refer to dissenters from Marxist ideology and the party. The term "renegade" in its new context thus came to signify anyone viewed as an "apostate" from the Marxist-Leninist faith and perforce as a traitor to socialism and the Soviet Motherland.

No one who disagrees with the regime

escapes being labelled a renegade. Open opponents of the regime, human rights campaigners advocating adherence to Soviet laws and the constitution, and even adherents of "pure" Leninism are thus all branded with the same stigma. Nonconformist scientists, writers, and artists were frequently branded as renegades as well. The "traitorous" connotation of this term made it very useful for propagandistic labelling of a wide range of "deviants," real and purported. In recent years, "renegade" has been applied to those responsible for the period of stagnation, i.e., Brezhenev's rule. Still, its use is restricted to the official language: in colloquial Russian the word is hardly ever encountered.

There are still various types of renegades who choose the path of malicious denigration of the Soviet way of life. . . . (Pravda, 23 February 1979)

In 1980, the government announced to all renegades "If you want to leave, nobody is stopping you." (Novoe vremya, 1 January 1984, p. 10)

Political naivete, distorted adventurist motives, an illusory and totally amoral desire to live it up at the expense of others and contribute nothing to society sums up the motivations of renegades. (Komsomol'skaya pravda, 25 January 1984, p. 2)

Report (*Raport*). A self-congratulatory communication about the fulfillment of goals or other achievements, addressed by industrial enterprises and institutions to the party or Soviet government authorities. Typically, a report deals with one of the following: "work achievements," "the start-up of a newly completed industrial plant," "successful" completion of a harvesting campaign, and scientific discoveries or overfulfilled quotas, e.g., for milk production.

A constant flow of reports is encouraged by the authorities, yet the press presents such reports as indications of the working people's gratitude to the party. The reports ostensibly confirm the involvement of the workers and real communication between the working masses and their government.

Like many other terms of the Soviet language, the word "report" is taken from military usage. Its transfer to civilian usage reflects the party's efforts to indoctrinate Soviet society in values of army life, such as strict discipline, unquestioning obedience to superiors, and execution of orders without fail. An atmosphere of constant mobilization and discipline is thus created.

Only achievements are reported. There is no place in the report to dwell on disruptions of the production process or resultant failures to fulfill the plans. These are either concealed or minimized.

With the passing of each day the intense competition is growing for the privilege of signing the report of the Don working people to the XXVIth Congress of the CPSU. (Partiynaya zhizn', no. 21, November 1980, p. 18)

With every day the flood of work reports to the Congress is increasing. With deep emotions the workers, collective farmers and intelligentsia dedicate their achievements to the Party forum. (Pravda, 20 February 1981, p. 1)

Reports on fulfillment of plans of the delivery of grain to the government and on the fulfillment of related socialist obligations are arriving from the Bashkir and Udmurt Autonomous Soviet Socialist Republics. . . . (Pravda, 14 October 1983, p. 1)

Ruling Clique (*Verkhushka*). Pejorative term for political and military leaders of foreign states that are out of favor with the Soviet authorities. In contemporary Russian, the word *verkhushka* clearly expresses contempt, e.g., "the ruling clique of the bourgeois class," "Tel Aviv ruling clique," "the military ruling clique of NATO." However, in the 1920s it was still possible to use the term neutrally, as when the question was raised: "How should the Party and the *verkhushka* be run in the future?" (*Pravda*, no. 297, 1925).

The term *verkhushka* is close in meaning to the word *verkhi*, "top leadership." While ideological manipulation has transformed ruling clique into a term of opprobrium, the same is not true for "top leadership." Thus one commonly finds phrases like "conference of top leadership" (*soveshchanie v verkhakh*), "meeting of top leadership" (*vstrecha v verkhakh*), and "consensus within the top leadership" (*dogovorennost' v verkhakh*). *Verkhi* is also used to substitute for the word *lidery* ("leaders") whenever the Soviet government seeks rapprochement with leaders of the countries it previously scorned and vilified.

During the whole period of the military dictatorship in Argentina, for example, the government of that country was invariably referred to in the Soviet press as a ruling clique. However, during the conflict between Britain and Argentina (the Falklands-Malvinas War of 1982), when the strategic interests of the USSR and Argentina to some degree coincided, the Argentine ruling clique was suddenly transformed into a "top leadership." But the transformation can go in the opposite direction as well, as when the Egyptian government, which was definitely a "top leadership" in Nasser's days, became a ruling clique when relationships with the USSR cooled after his death.

Communist and procommunist leaderships are referred to neither as a ruling clique nor a "top leadership." For them the deferential term "governing body" (*rukovodstvo*) is reserved. The latter suggests associations with nobility of aims, creativity in devising solutions to problems, and concern with the welfare of the people.

The rabbinic ruling clique in the West has placed religion at the service of Zionism. . . . (G. G. Bakanursky, *Iudaizm i sovremennost'* [Judaism and the world today], Moscow: Znanie Publishing House, 1978, p. 64)

The criminal activities of the Beijing ruling clique were universally condemned by the peoples of the whole world. (*Mezhdunarodnaya zhizn'*, no. 4, 1979, p. 102)

The BBC was created as a tool of the conservatively oriented ruling clique. (*Za rubezhom*, no. 2, 1979, p. 15)

Rumors (*Slukhi*). Unsubstantiated pieces of information. At first glance, the reason for the rise and spread of rumors in the Soviet

Union appears rather obvious: Soviet society suffers from a constant shortage of reliable information. Hence the anticipation that the progress of glasnost (cf.) is bound to reduce the role of rumors as a source of information.

Undoubtedly the lack of information contributes to the surfeit of rumors, but it is not their only cause. The claim that lack of information causes rumors is an overstatement. It is more justified to say that rumors indicate that information is lacking. Still, the immediate cause of rumors in the USSR is not so much the absence of information as the existence of unsatisfied demand for it, the unquenched thirst for a certain kind of knowledge.

Any state, even the most democratic one, will always be short of indisputable, exhaustive, and exact information. Yet in no other developed society is information so poor and distorted as in the Soviet socialist state. Here, entire domains of public affairs are inaccessible to public knowledge: the decision-making process, foreign policy, and the life-style and customs of the ruling elite. In short, it would be easier to enumerate the kinds of information that reach the public than to determine what is withheld and concealed. That explains the constant demand for rumors. The common public, however, is not excited by just any rumors but only by those that have some direct or indirect bearing on its interests or are somehow related to its expectations.

Among the rumors currently circulating in the Soviet Union, the latest and perhaps the most widespread is the talk of an impending devaluation of the ruble. This is not exactly a rumor but a partly substantiated expectation. It was spurred by the government's preparations for huge price increases that are going to hurt primarily the lower-paid workers. Or, in another instance of a rumor: during 1988, a mass dismissal of employees was expected to take place—eight million people being the projected figure. Again, this was grounded on actual facts, such as the reduction of government personnel. In spite of the government's attempts to refute these rumors, people continue to believe them. What is more, the rumors' credibility grows in direct proportion to the insistence with which they are denied.

Rumors in the Soviet Union are rarely spontaneous. More often than not the government is behind them. In a society devoid of free public opinion, rumors function as a sort of feedback, informing the authorities about the probable public response to government decisions under consideration. This makes it possible to sound out consequences of government plans. Rumors about devaluation and dismissals are good cases in point. Both measures were repeatedly discussed on the highest level in Moscow and analyzed more than once by prominent scientists weighing the pros and cons of an economic reform. Only the danger of public unrest and fear of the situation getting out of control forced the Soviet leaders to abandon such schemes. Still, the mistrust remained.

Certain rumors have a totally "disinterested" character. They constitute a sort of "art for art's sake" by merely catering to the demand for rumors. A case in point is the rumors about the ostentatious habits of Gorbachev's wife Raisa and her passion for expensive clothes, jewelry, and gifts. According to such rumors, while in England, Mrs. Gorbachev talked the Queen into presenting her with a set of famous jewels, and in France she managed to obtain expensive gifts from the companies Christian Dior and Cartier. Such rumors are interesting as reflections of the popular image of Soviet leaders' wives. Such beliefs cannot be just described as products of idle fancy; they provide an insight into Soviet reality. The ordinary Soviet man-in-the-street thinks as follows: Brezhnev's wife and daughter excelled in greed and egomania, so why should the wife of the new leader be any different? After all, like all her predecessors, she is beyond all criticism and above the law. Besides, her greed has been substantiated by some facts: as secretary of the Soviet Culture Fund (a volunteer position), she apparently was ready to accept a salary double that of a professor.

Another common kind are "purposeful" rumors intended to bring someone into disrepute or undermine his or her credibility. Such rumors circulate on all levels of Soviet social structure, since they are a handy means of discrediting the intended targets, be they a successful competitor, disagreeable boss, or talented colleague. Soviet leaders themselves are not averse to using this method, in which case they cease to be plain rumors and become part of politics. Shortly before the downfall of Communist party secretary Romanov, there appeared rumors of his planned attempt to escape with a mistress on a yacht to Sweden. This was not that unlikely as it might have seemed, since the Soviet elite easily forget about their ideals and principles as soon as they come into conflict with their private interests; except for the fact that the very same tale had been heard prior to the removal of V. Tolstikov, whom Romanov replaced in the post of first secretary of the Leningrad District Party Committee. On that occasion, the same details were reported: "found in the state of intoxication," "in the company of a loose woman," and "with no identity papers." Geographical detail was also the same—a yacht was supposed to have been spotted in the Gulf of Finland, outside the Soviet territorial waters.

The claim that rumors supposedly originate under primitive social conditions and spread among uneducated people is not necessarily true. It is true, however, that the Soviet public is not used to critical thinking and to questioning and analyzing situations independently (i.e., without party directives). If anything, it is used to relying on authority blindly. All this creates favorable conditions for rumors. The drabness of Soviet life and its monotony make people a captive audience for all sorts of rumors. There are countless numbers of most incredible rumors, such as the story about Nancy Reagan at a Kremlin reception trying to abscond with a golden teaspoon from an antique collection. Such rumors may be ridiculous but not meaningless, as they represent a "response" of sorts to the rumors about Gorbachev's wife. The rumor about Nancy Reagan is not free of ideological overtones. It was meant to sow seeds of mistrust toward the American president: How can he be trusted if his wife behaved like that?

Of course, such fabrications convince only a few. There has recently been some change for the better, as far as the attitude of the Soviet public to rumors is concerned. This newly-learned ability to think a little more critically works in particular in cases of rumors that to all appearances are inspired by the government. However, in the absence of authentic democracy, rumors continue to be an organic trait of Soviet society.

It would seem that the advent of glasnost should put an end to rumors. In fact, however, their list is still long-starting with the monetary reform. . . . (Moskovskie novosti, no. 11, 13 March 1988).

Where else, if not in queues, can we have a chat and exchange the latest news and the current rumors? (Literaturnaya gazeta, no. 31, 3 August 1988, p. 16).

The city is humming with rumors about Armenians being murdered and beaten, and subjected to all kinds of indignities. (Vyshka, 13 July 1988, p. 3)

Saber Rattling (*Bryatsat' oruzhiem*). The term is used in the same sense as in English but is applied exclusively to the foreign policies of states and military blocs hostile to the USSR. In Russian, the term first appeared in military jargon and then was adopted into the language of ideology. Its use is intended as a constant reminder of an ever-present armed threat looming over the "communist camp." Soviet military preparations, deliveries of weapons to various countries, and the concentration of armed forces along the borders of sovereign states are never referred to as saber rattling but are always described by such formulas as "the taking of steps necessary for guaranteeing the security of the Soviet state."

> The fondest hopes of the people of the United States, as of all other peoples of the world, are tied to peace, and to the search for it through negotiations: not saber rattling. (Literaturnaya gazeta, 29 October 1970, p. 9)

> Imperialism and reaction take up the defense of the most rotten regimes which are hated by their own peoples, and keep saber rattling while resorting to brute force against developing countries. (Izvestiya, 25 October 1980, p. 5)

> American imperialism and its accomplices in various parts of the world, showing utter contempt for the peace-loving hopes of people of good will, brazenly engage in saber rattling [and] fanning the flames of war. (Literaturnaya gazeta, 1 July 1981, p. 1)

Samizdat. Literature produced by private, dissident sources. The word "samizdat" came into prominence in the 1960s, but the concept of samizdat, the dissemination of literature that has not been passed by the censor, had been known in Russia for a long time before, from at least as far back as the mid-eighteenth century. However, the phenomenon became widespread only after the Revolution. Samizdat took on large-scale proportions in the last twenty years, when the works of many writers and poets were typewritten and duplicated by hand in hundreds of copies. It was then that samizdat began to encompass not just fiction but also scientific disquisitions and commentaries on current affairs. Samizdat magazines, collections of articles, and almanacs appeared, including *Sintaksis*, *Feniks*, *Bumerang*, *Metropol'*, and *Katalog*.

Another form of samizdat was *magnitizdat*. It began to appear during the last twenty years and consists of novels, stories, essays, and, in particular, poems recorded on magnetic tape and then copied and distributed in hundreds and thousands of copies. The songs of Galich, Vysotsky, and Okudzhava were disseminated in this manner.

The development of samizdat was also enhanced by the publication in the West of works that were banned in the USSR. A new media form analogous to samizdat thus appeared, receiving the name *tamizdat*—the publication abroad of writers and scholars living in the USSR. *Tamizdat* to some extent influenced Soviet policy toward literature. After appearing in *tamizdat*, the works of numerous authors that had not appeared in the USSR were often unexpectedly allowed to appear there. But current Soviet literary policy also has had an effect on *tamizdat*. Glasnost has denied foreign publishers an opportunity to publish books that originally may have been written with an "eye" on them, at least as a possible option.

An element of reciprocity exists between samizdat and officially authorized literature. Samizdat feeds official literature with ideas and styles, while the latter "leaves" for the former those works which do not conform (or at least not completely conform) to the current party line on literature.

Western propaganda is trying to destroy our system from the outside by smuggling into the USSR anti-Soviet literature printed in Russian by various disreputable publishers in the pay of the CIA. . . . These are presented as works which are illicitly circulated here, in the so-called samizdat (Komsomol'skaya pravda, 5 May 1981, p. 2)

In addition to publishing new authors, unknown even to the state security services, samizdat, in its early years, also published works of Tsvetayeva, Pasternak, Akhmatova and Mandelshtam. This was the best possible recommendation for this new publishing venture. (Kontinent, no. 1, 1984, p. 155)

A letter from Minsk, signed by several members of the Writers Union of the USSR who work in the republic, was published in Literaturnaya gazeta under the heading "Director and samizdat." (Literaturnaya gazeta, 27 August 1988, p. 7)

Scientific Degrees and Titles (*Nauchnye stepeni i zvaniya*). Official status symbols indicating ranks in social prestige, work position, and academic qualification. The Soviet scientific hierarchy has a dual system of degrees: on the one hand, *kandidat* and doctor of science; on the other hand, *dotsent* and professor. "Candidate of Science" (*kandidat nauk*) corresponds to a Ph.D. in the West, but the degree of "Doctor of Science" (*doktor nauk*) has no counterpart. At this point, the similarity between Soviet and foreign scientific degrees breaks down. In the free world, the third scientific degree (Ph.D.) is conferred by a university and requires the consent of three scholars who are conversant with the subject matter of a thesis. In the USSR, a *kandidat* degree is only formally conferred by the Scientific Council of a higher educational establishment or scientific institute. In practice, it is awarded by a special governmental agency attached to the Council of Ministers of the USSR, the VAK (*Vysshaya Attestatsionnaya Komissiya*—Higher Examination Board). As far as doctoral degrees are concerned, Scientific Councils do not even have the nominal right to confer them. Their recommendations have a purely advisory character. Decisions are made by the VAK alone.

The conferral of both degrees is a complex, drawn-out, and multistage procedure. To obtain the degree of "Candidate of Science," three examinations called "candidate minimum" (*kandidatsky minimum*) must first be passed. These are exams in philosophy, a foreign language, and the candidate's particular field of specialization. For the philosophy exam, a compulsory selection of quotations from Lenin and the current Soviet leader have to be known by heart as an important indicator of the candidate's loyalty and ideological background. The foreign language exam is superficial. There is no need to really know the language—it is quite sufficient to be able to understand a page of text, with the help of a dictionary. All that is needed for the science exam is the ability to smartly rehash textbook basics.

Passing the "candidate minimum" is the first step on the road to obtaining the degree. The next stage is to write a thesis. This is a text of several hundred pages (never less than a hundred), devoid of any innovative ideas. The sole major requirement is "dissertationality." The meaning of this is quite clear—the thesis must be moderately well written, must not offend anyone considered to be an authority, and must not be controversial. A sloppily written thesis may be accepted if it is submitted by a sufficiently influential official or by a candidate who holds a high party or state position. Many Soviet political figures or their relatives have entered the scientific world via such an academic shortcut.

Once a thesis has been completed, it must be defended. This process is also broken down into a number of stages. It begins with the predefense, an examination and approval of the work by a meeting of the department or subfaculty, where the thesis was written. There can be either a single predefense, if the candidate defends his or her thesis at the institution where he or she wrote it, or two, if it is to be also defended at another scientific establishment that is more qualified to evaluate part of the work.

The predefense is more important than the defense, since there the official defense opponents are nominated (it is important for the "defender" that they should be personally known to him and easy to satisfy). At this predefense stage, an external subfaculty of the department is assigned to assess the thesis formally and officially. The opponents' appointment is a formality. Two of them, a doctor and a *kandidat*, are needed for a "candidate" thesis and three (all doctors) for a doctoral thesis. Their function is to sit in at the defense and express their opinion.

The defense itself is a charade. The decision of the Scientific Council has already been made in advance and its members usually doze or chat while waiting for voting. The procedure is a standard one. The candidate's biography, scientific, and work record are read out. Then the candidate himself comes forward and expounds the contents of his thesis. Subsequently, the opponents express their opinions. Then the opinions of outside evaluators who had been contacted by the defender are introduced. Finally the vote takes place. The thesis-defender's file, crammed with documents—forms, minutes of proceedings, and certificates—is then sent to the VAK, where the already defended scientific works are discussed in great secrecy behind closed doors. No one knows who sits on its board of experts or how they are selected.

The VAK has all the attributes of a typical Soviet institution: a complex hierarchy, clear-cut subordination, as well as a host of departments and offshoots. For many years, the institution formed part of the Ministry of Higher and Special Secondary Education and was chaired by a minister. Since 1974, however, it passed into the purview of the Council of Ministers, to be headed by one of the premier's deputies. From then on, as chairman of this influential organization, the official concerned has been responsible for convening the plenum of the VAK, which is comprised of between forty and sixty scientists representing every field of specialization, who in turn make up the panels of experts whose task is to evaluate the theses.

Yet one more part of the bureaucratic structure involved is the presidium of the VAK. This office coordinates the activity of the VAK's secretariat, which carries out the organization's everyday work, and every few months convenes the General (or "Major") Plenum, which is attended by representatives of departmental ("Minor") plena. The VAK presidium is responsible for procedural questions, confirming new directives, and approving additional regulations and changes in the procedure of defending theses. Another of its functions is to supervise the activity of boards of experts, which assess the defended theses. Theses are examined in a quite arbitrary manner, not regulated by any rules. A board has the right to send a *kandidat* thesis for assessment by one of its reviewers or can recommend it to be approved immediately. In the latter case, the presidium automatically rubberstamps the decision and the examinee becomes a "Candidate of Science."

Doctoral theses must be presented for assessment by a reviewer. But much depends here on the attitude of the board of experts. If it has nothing against the author of a dissertation, it selects favorably disposed opponents. But if there is any ill feeling involved, the reviewer is approached in a manner that will ensure that the candidate's thesis is blocked. For this to happen, all that is necessary is a hint that "there is an opinion up there" that the thesis warrants careful examination. The ears of the habitually servile and fawning members of the board of experts are acutely sensitive to such hints (if they come from sufficiently influential persons) in favor or against a thesis. If the "opinion up there" is favorable, the thesis will pass through all the corridors of the VAK within a month.

The hierarchy of scientific degrees in the Soviet Union is augmented and reinforced by the hierarchy of academic employment functions. A *kandidat* at a higher educational institute is usually linked to the status of *dotsent*, while a doctor is linked to the status of professor. They are confirmed in these appointments by the VAK on the recommendation of the Scientific Councils. This is also not subject to any norms or objective criteria. Everything depends on the goodwill of the higher-ups, thereby leaving wide scope for arbitrariness, blackmail, and intimidation of scientific employees.

The unfortunate impact of the VAK upon the advancement of science is obvious to all, including the Soviets. Yet the agency exists and is thriving because in the USSR the interests of the authorities are more important than progress and social prosperity.

The conferral of degrees is accompanied by the acquisition of substantial privileges. Climbing the rungs of the scientific hierarchy also provides the opportunity for climbing in terms of one's social standing. "Candidates" and doctors, lecturers and professors belong to the lower ranks of the ruling class, while the few of them who enter the Academy of Sciences may play a direct role in designing major government policies. In the Soviet Union, basic government functions such as the allocation of resources or the administration of the country do not require knowledge and expertise. What matters in personnel selection is the degree of loyalty and devotion to the regime. Against this background the main function of the VAK becomes apparent: to serve as a filter for preventing the upward mobility of independent, thoughtful people and an inverted funnel for accelerating the mobility of those prepared to carry out any demand received from higher-ups.

> Scientists who have the academic degree of Doctor of Science can still become "consultants" with symbolic pay . . . Scientific employees who have the degree of Kandidat and are sometimes also genuine experts have no such opportunity. (Ogonek, no. 34, August 1988, p. 5)

> Last fall, four employees of . . . [research institutes]—Professor G. Ishchenko, Dotsent G. Astaf'yev, and Candidates of Science V. Zigizmund and T. Khadzhibaeva—appealed to the Secretary of the Central Committee of the Communist Party of Uzbekistans pointing to the extremely unhealthy situation in . . . [their work places]. (Ogonek, no. 33, August 1988, p. 25)

Scientific Worker (*Nauchny sotrudnik*). A person occupying a post in a scientific-research institute. The positions of scientific workers in the Soviet Union are strictly differentiated in junior, senior, and directorial ranks. Over the fifteen-year period from 1970 to 1985, the number of scientific workers in the USSR doubled; and by 1988, they numbered more than 1½ million. Scientific workers are considered to be "workers on the ideological front" (*rabotniki ideologicheskogo fronta*) and are selected and appointed (after being thoroughly investigated) by the party organization of the relevant institute. Then each worker, in accordance with his or her academic degree and position, is assigned to the appropriate category of the party nomenklatura—district, city, or national. A junior scientific worker is assigned to the nomenklatura of the party district committee, while senior and directorial ones (with a candidate of science degree or doctoral degree, which is higher than a Ph.D. in the West) are named to the nomenklatura of the city party committee. The head of a department, deputy director, or research secretary of an institute is named to the nomenklatura of the provincial party committee, while the director of an institute belongs to the nomenklatura of the Central Committee.

A scientific worker with a degree has more freedom of choice as to the direction of his research, and, no less important, his position relieves him of material deprivation. After the defense of his candidate degree dissertation, a scientific worker's salary doubles, and after the awarding of the doctorate it quadruples. His privileges grow just as rapidly, which is extremely important in a country where almost everything is in short supply, big reputations no less than food products or other merchandise.

A scientific worker with a diploma is guaranteed a secure place among the scientific Brahmins. The highest of these do not overexert themselves; labor by sweat of one's brow is the lot of workers who have no degrees. Usually the "diplomaed" scientific workers receive decent housing, the opportunity to purchase imported furniture, and eventually a car—the symbol of respectability and of having made it in Soviet society. Thus, an advanced academic degree in the Soviet Union has a similar function to the title of nobility in tsarist Russia.

The salary of a junior scientific worker without a degree but employed in an academic institute is approximately 120–40 rubles per month; with a candidate's degree, it rises to 220–50 rubles; that of a senior scientific worker with a candidate degree is 300–40 rubles, while a doctorate yields 420–50 rubles. The salary of a directorial scientific worker (usually with a doctoral degree) is 470–550 rubles.

Those who are doctors of science receive special medical services in special academic medical centers, clinics, and hospitals. Their health is viewed as an important resource of the state. In many republics, they have available to them the medical facilities of the Fourth (the Kremlin) Directorate of the Ministry of Health. They are also eligible for an annual stay at a rest home or sanitarium.

Work in Soviet research centers proceeds at a furious pace. Scientific workers are being turned out as on an assembly line. Both young and not so young people, who already have one degree, slave over dissertations (required for candidate degrees and doctorates). The paramount goal is to obtain a degree. To paraphrase the nineteenth-century poet Nekrasov, who said, "You don't have to be a poet, but a citizen you must be," the motto is, "You don't have to be a scientist, but a candidate degree you must have!" During the first year of postgraduate study a dissertation topic is decided on. During the second year, examinations on three mandatory disciplines have to be passed (*kandidatsky minimum*) (cf. "scientific degrees and titles"). What then remains is to publish articles and defend one's dissertation. Once this threshold is crossed, and one has the candidate degree, the future is unlimited. Such, at least, is the general rule. However, Jews who for some reason are today foolhardy enough to try to make a career in science have much less chance of getting a degree and finding success in a scientific-research

institute. This is because of a secret decree that sets employment quotas for Jewish scientists in various types of scientific establishments.

The basic requirement for a degree-seeker is a command of research technique. Originality is not required, to the point that one is well advised not to show any, or at least to camouflage it cleverly with Marxist terminology and references to the recognized authorities of science. If one exhibits originality of thought, one risks the envy of the less gifted. The result is that dissertations usually reflect diligence far more than originality or erudition.

The time is now past when Soviet scientists wrote dissertations individually. Now, the department, section, or laboratory to which the degree-seeker is attached performs a considerable part of the work for him or her. Experiments, observations, measurements, and operations that by their very nature are collective provide the basis of the dissertations, as is often true in the West. But in the USSR, scientific collectivism assumes a peculiar form: first, the collective works for the degree-seeker, then after the latter gets his degree, he works to help others obtain theirs.

Success or failure often depends on factors other than the quality of the dissertations. Decisive factors at this stage tend to be personal connections or the scientific reputations of one's official adviser (*rukovoditel'*).

The direction of scientific research is often determined arbitrarily. The choice may have nothing to do with the real needs and potential of research, but rather stems from mere guesses about what kind of research the upcoming party directives are likely to demand to suit the needs of the latest political campaign.

Scientific institutes operate in an atmosphere of routine and all-pervasive "whitewashing." Their work plans include as many direct practical utilitarian projects as possible, simply because it is easy to receive large grants for such projects. Much of this grant money will then fill out the budget of the institute, permitting it to carry out projects not yielding immediate benefits to the economy. The plans describe expected results in a nontechnical style so that the bureaucrats in appropriate ministries and at the Department of Science of the Central Committee of the CPSU can understand them and appreciate their value. They are also formulated in such a way that, no matter what the actual results, they can be described as "successful."

Soviet hypocrisy flourishes in scientific research institutes. Socialist competition (*sotsialisticheskoe sorevnovanie*, cf.), Komsomol control, the board of honor (*doska pocheta*, cf.)—all these reveal how fully "Soviet" these institutes are. It is only natural that within this setting even honest and talented scientific workers eventually just go through the motions and learn to perform their investigations as if they were bureaucratic formalities to be finished off with dispatch. The lack of any sensible purpose of much research contributes to the same effect.

According to the Charter of the Academy of Sciences, vacant positions of scientific workers are filled by elections held by the research councils of the institutes. In reality, the outcomes of the competitions are predetermined by the board of directors and the party bureau, which invariably give preference to party members, especially to former party functionaries. Out-of-favor party functionaries often need quiet sinecures in non-"hot spots." The position of a scientific worker suits this purpose ideally. It guarantees a respectable occupation in addition to a fine salary. And if such a scientific worker happens to return to power and influence eventually, he is expected not to forget his former benefactors. Therefore, an experienced director of a scientific institute tries to establish good connections in high places within the government. He helps one apparatchik write his dissertation, helps another finish a book, and places the daughter, son, or son-in-law of a third in a graduate program. Because of such exchanges of favors, the Soviet party and state apparatus surpass all other government bureaucracies of the world in

the proportion of employees with scientific degrees.

These "diplomaed" (according to need) party functionaries provide cadres of directors for research institutions. Such directors can help ensure that scientific work is conducted and reported in consonance with official ideology and that science is channelled in directions desired by the party. Such direction ensures the mass aspect of Soviet science, i.e., the availability of masses of "qualified" scientists. It allows the speedy dismissal of any "dissenting" scientific worker and his replacement by a more trusty one.

> . . . Scientific workers must orient themselves more toward the future, . . . keeping their fingers on the pulse of trends just beginning to be apparent. (Voprosy filosofii, no. 7, 1983, p. 22)

> Over the course of several decades already before the war but particularly after it, the number of scientific workers in the USSR grew by leaps and bounds. (Literaturnaya gazeta, 7 March 1984, p. 10)

> Moscow is the major scientific center where almost one-fourth of all the scientific workers of the country are employed. (Kommunist, no. 2, 1984, p. 18)

Scourge (*Bich*). A misfit; someone resented by society. The social downfall of someone labelled a scourge of society (hence the term) is determined by the paradoxes of Soviet existence, by the lack of protection of individual rights, by the grueling and poorly paid labor, and by the low standard of living. Among the scourges, people who have been excluded from the normal networks of social relations of family, neighborhood, and work environment, one finds a cross section of Soviet society: workers and peasants, physicians, engineers, academics, and journalists.

After losing their apartments as a result of divorce of a job change, or after changing profession either voluntarily or due to low salary or conflict with the bosses, such people hire themselves out for temporary, often seasonal work in the North, in Siberia, or in the Soviet Far East—in the hope of being able to begin a new life. Seasonal work on shipboard or in gold or uranium mines enables people within a few months to earn two to three thousand rubles, the equivalent of an average annual Soviet salary and, hence, referred to as "long rubles." However, such work cripples people both physically and morally; it strips them from their moorings and sets them adrift. The work is exhausting, twelve to fourteen hours a day, under conditions of constant danger—from radiation or cave-ins in the mines or from storms at sea—in cramped quarters, with a number of people stuffed into a rough barrack or tiny cabin, and no social benefits in the future to compensate for present suffering.

After having amassed a considerable sum of money in order to set himself on his feet materially or to realize such a cherished dream as buying a car or building a cooperative apartment, a person of this type seldom manages to put his wealth to good use. As a rule, he is no longer able to return to his previous place of residence due to the denial of a residence permit (cf. "registration"), while the prospect of settling for a pitiful existence on a collective farm (cf.) or state farm does not hold any attraction after he has been "spoiled" by the high wages he has managed to earn. Although he may have money, he is without home, family, and future. With the loss of his previous ties, finding himself physically and morally banished from normal "respectable" society, he seeks a substitute in the company of down-and-outers, cynical and antisocial like himself. The hard labor he performed had deposited in his soul a load of bitterness and humiliation and weakened his resistance to merely following his instinctual drives. Now he tends to be attracted to drinking out of desperation, to drinking sprees that eat up his savings until he has no resources left to live on, and he either joins a gang of thieves or becomes involved in theft on his own. He thus becomes a scourge, taking revenge on society for his lost life.

There are hundreds of thousands of such marginal people in the Soviet Union. Not all of them are failures; their ranks are swelled by ex-convicts who cannot adjust to life "on the outside" and country people who became deracinated due to the impoverishment of the villages. However, the main pool of "recruits" for scourges comes from the millions of young people who have been mobilized for Komsomol projects like the huge construction projects for "building communism" in the Soviet Far East. There they waste their strength and youth. They end up as homeless, unskilled, demoralized, mentally devastated, tragic parodies of slogans like "We are building BAM [the Trans-Baikal Railway] and BAM is building us," which in reality should be paraphrased, "BAM is our construction, BAM is our destruction." In return for their exhausting work and broken lives, society provides them with money—for as long as they are capable of working. Then it rejects and forgets them. They become social outcasts, without employment or permanent residence, harassed or pursued by the police in their hideouts and in the railway stations where they often find shelter in the absence of any alternative.

For me it was more important to find out how a scourge becomes a scourge, to understand the logic of this phenomenon. (Moskovskie novosti, no. 10, 5 March 1989, p. 15)

Second Economy (*Vtoraya ekonomika*). Including "**Shadow Economy**" (*tenevaya ekonomika*), totality of production relations based on infractions of law and circumventions of the existing state economic system. The second economy is not a specifically Soviet phenomenon but in Soviet society it originated with the peculiarities of Soviet socialism, such as shortages of goods and services, inflexibility of management, the ideologically determined distribution of goods, and centralized planning and management of production. All Soviet enterprises have been compelled to rely on illegal operations in order to meet plan targets, secure supplies of hard to obtain essentials, and sell their production. Thus the second economy has a symbiotic relationship with the overt Soviet economy. The former fulfills useful and even vital social functions for the latter. The second economy functions like a lubricant for the state machinery: without it, society would grind to a halt. It redistributes what has been plundered by the state in a way somewhat more equitable than the original allocations. It takes part of the national product from the exploiting ruling class and returns it to the exploited people. It provides society with consumer goods and foodstuffs that the state is unable to provide. It also creates a network of interpersonal ties and relationships running from the top of society to the bottom, which are crucial for its normal existence and compensate for rampant injustice and illegality.

The second economy exists in the Soviet Union both outside the state economy (in the form of self-employed labor and small group contract work) and within the very depths of the state sector, as well as in major state and collective-cooperative enterprises in the form of clandestinely pursued business activities.

One variety of the second economy is visible and lends itself to study. It consists of huge numbers of artisans (according to the most conservative estimates, numbering more than twenty million) who act either as single individuals or small workshop teams and who offer to the population a broad range of goods and services from clothing, footwear, and household utensils in short supply to repairs of apartments and automobiles. The bulk of such work is done in response to demand in rural areas. Tens of millions of square meters of living space (cf.) and social facilities are being thus constructed in the countryside, including houses, collective farm structures, pigsties, garages, clubs, and roads. Under most unfavorable conditions—constant administrative harassment and criminal persecution—this variety of the second economy has proven its vitality and efficiency, responding faster than state industry to rapidly changing demand, helping to overcome the dictate of the state producer over the individual consumer, and, no less importantly, providing the population, which had

not found outlets for its energies and skills in collectivized production, with opportunities to use its skills and knowledge profitably.

Another variety of the second economy, which is kept carefully concealed from sight, is an inevitable sequel of or supplement to the socialist "first" economy. In view of its inseparability from the first economy, there are good grounds for calling it the shadow economy. Its very existence, after all, is dependent upon the Soviet system of production, with its impersonal state property and total alienation of the workers from the results of their labor. While the overt variety of the second economy rests on conscientiously performed work of private producers, the covert variety—the shadow economy—rests on corruption, pilferage, and embezzlement.

While private entrepreneurship, lawful or unlawful, responds to demand for goods in short supply, with the shadow economy, this is not the case. The latter, parasitically attached to the official Soviet economy, takes advantage of its sluggishness, inertia, centralization, and dependence on bureaucratic fiat.

The origins of the shadow economy lie in the workforce's adaptation to the state command economy behind the propagandistic facade of which it began to assume distorted forms. Such adaptations evolved only gradually. At an early stage, typical were various activities in the indeterminate zone between legality and illegality. This usually consisted of various sorts of manipulations of the plan that were easy to understand and explain, at least on the surface. For instance, using informal personal contacts, production managers colluded with ministers so that they would be assigned easily attainable plan targets, adjusted to less than full production capacities. Such deals were far from disinterested, since overfulfillment of the artificially lowered targets was rewarded by bonuses or other material benefits. There still was a kind of "social" motivation involved, since the benefits were shared: workers received higher income, the managers got promotions, and the top authorities gained plaudits that could serve as springboards to some public office. It goes without saying that such informal favors as adjusting plan targets was not done for free. They posited the need for banquets, picnics, parties, etc. with all the requisite expenditure. The latter couldn't, of course, be borne by the very modest salaries. Therefore, funds from state coffers are used. In this case not only the "hand" that gives the allocation in expectation of a "reward" is generous, so is the one that is on the take. The latter, in fact, helps itself to funds that more than cover expenses; thus something is left over after the required payoff for the satisfaction of the takers' often expensive pleasures and growing "requirements," such as a new car, a well-furnished apartment, or a suitably comfortable dacha (cf.).

However, the holes in the budget need to be somehow covered. This is how the underground entrepreneurship comes into the picture, by taking raw materials unrecorded in the plan and producing out of them goods unrecorded in the plan. This is how the shadow economy made its appearance in one branch of industry after another—light industry, the food industry, the chemical industry, and subsequently machine building, the machine-tool industry, etc.—until it pervaded all of Soviet industry. There exist many ways of selling clandestinely produced goods: they can be sold for cash in retail outlets or exchanged on the wholesale market for other goods. Profits are split proportionally in relation to the risk of detection, one part going to those who produce the goods and the other to those who market them. Such operations are concealed by faked bookkeeping—legal production is registered in enterprise reports and integrated into state plans, while illegal goods are not recorded anywhere. Documentation related to any stage of their processing is eventually carefully shredded. One thing that remained constant was the "game" of lowering plan targets for enterprises involved in the shadow economy. Not only did the thus lowered targets yield considerable opportunities for illegal sales of raw materials (which were received in huge quantities

disproportionate with what is needed to meet the lowered production targets), but they also served as a leverage to intensify exploitation of workers. In enterprises involved in the shadow economy, the workers are subject to two kinds of exploitation—with their salaries comprising only a minimal proportion of the value of the goods they produce, they are grossly underpaid by the state. And, in addition to that, they are badly cheated by the factory wheelers and dealers who make them produce goods not intended to be recorded in their factories' output. But the profiteering administrators know how to pacify the workers and suppress their discontent. They do it not at their own cost, but at the cost of the state: by lowering the norms, raising professional ratings, paying for work not done, etc. The risk of those involved in the shadow economy is minimal, since bribing party and government leaders, the police, and employees of the prosecutor's office averts the danger of detection and prosecution. The purpose of the bribes is in such cases to receive timely warnings of the imminent checkups of the enterprises' accountancy.

The shadow economy operates under conditions so favorable that at times it can afford token concessions to public interest. Sometimes production plans are not lowered. At other times, when officialdom's demand for "heroic" labor performance runs high, the profiteers may respond to the call in an effort to raise the prestige of their enterprises. On such occasions all stops are pulled out—with everyone thrown in to action, "storming," overtime, and night shifts. However, their main contribution to "achievements" is via write-ups (cf.).

Here we have another by-product of the shadow economy: fictional economic values worth no more than the paper they are written on. There is massive reporting of things that do not exist in reality, e.g., millions of tons of cotton reported as harvested, supposed hundreds of thousands of cubic meters of lumber, kilometers of unbuilt roads and unlaid railroad lines, etc.

The Soviet authorities cannot bring themselves to attack the shadow economy, since it brings such handsome benefits to the party and government hierarchy of all levels, in conformity with the principle of distribution proportional to one's place in the political pecking order. Countermeasures have aimed mainly against the expansion of exactly that form of the second economy which is relatively productive and socially advantageous, that is, self-employed labor. Moreover, the measures against the second economy resorted to so far have been mainly punitive. Thus, tradesmen are being subject to oppressive taxation or confiscation of property while the public is taught to scorn their pursuits and lifestyles. Eventually, the realization dawned on the authorities that such a struggle was pointless: small group production could not be done away with, since it all-too-easily adapted to the fluctuations of socialist policy. Finally, the Soviet leadership decided to decriminalize self-employed labor and thus allow it to emerge out of the underground in order to make it subservient to the state.

However, the purpose of subjecting self-employed labor to state control was not attained primarily for sociopsychological reasons. The Soviet citizen is sceptical about the durability of a liberal policy in regard to self-employed labor. He or she fears that the time of permissiveness will soon come to an end. Such fears are well-grounded, since the authorities reiterate that self-employed labor is basically needed until state enterprises become mature enough to provide all that the population demands. In other words, self-employed labor is said to be assigned a merely temporary and transitional role in providing the Soviet market with goods and services in demand. There are other reasons self-employed labor is not going to have smooth sailing with socialism. There still exist commodities and services not included in the list of what self-employed labor is permitted to provide. Such "omitted" commodities and services are a taboo of sorts, since all that is not explicitly permitted by Soviet law is forbidden. And, in addition to all that, bureaucratic arbitrariness, red tape, procras-

tination in case-processing, and erection of all kinds of senseless obstacles are sure to exact their toll from self-employed labor. Contrary to what one might assume, it will certainly not be enough to obtain a license in order to engage in a self-employed labor venture. One will also have to obtain the premises, raw materials, and the like. These are things that in the USSR always entail an exorbitant effort, expense, and amount of time.

But the main impediment to the legalization of individual production, services, or small workshops has to do with the ways the second economy is linked to the shadow economy. This link is essential because reliance on the shadow economy's channels is prerequisite for obtaining raw materials and marketing.

It follows that in order to truly decriminalize self-employed labor, one would also have to decriminalize the shadow economy along with all its corrupt business practices. Decriminalization of only one of its sectors, that of individual labor activity, won't do.

The shadow economy exists both outside the socially organized sector (in the so-called "second economy") and in its midst. (Ogonek, no. 51, 1987, p. 26)

He speaks about corruption and mutual backscratching in various walks of life in Armenia, and about the shadow economy which has attained vast dimensions. (Moskovskie novosti, no. 6, 7 February 1988, p. 3)

This branch of industry finds it difficult to meet its plan targets at the time when the scope of operations of the shadow economy is increasing. (Izvestiya, 29 January 1988, p. 3)

The period of stagnation engendered not only a "shadow economy" but also a "shadow administration." (Izvestiya, 16 January 1988, p. 3)

Security Clearance (*Dopusk*, literally "access"). A document allowing access to participation in secret work and to classified materials. Security Clearances are issued by the secret (first) department within Soviet enterprises and institutions, on recommendation of the management. The latter has in any given case to explain why a clearance or its renewal is needed.

There are several levels of security clearances. The most common one provides employees with access (thus the name) to projects and studies marked with the initials DSP (*Dlya Sluzhebnogo Pol'zovaniya*—"For Official Use Only"). Such materials cannot be taken outside or published by the media. However, foreign books and articles containing views and evaluations contradicting the official line also often receive the DSP seal. Then they are often published in the USSR in restricted circulation (in violation of the international copyright law), but not for public sale. Occasionally, instead of "DSP," such publications may be stamped "DNB" (*Dlya Nauchnykh Bibliotek*—"For Scientific Libraries Only"), in which case limited numbers of them can be sold, but only to security clearance holders.

The next type of security clearance is called "form number two." It provides access to materials marked "*Sekretno*" ("Secret"). All materials bearing this stamp are kept in the safes of the first department, which has a special catalogue with the item's title, publication date, name of its author or editor, the number of copies, and the terms of use. This type of clearance is used in factories working for the military as well as in most military and police research. The loss of any such materials, or their borrowing without approval of the first department, is a serious crime, investigated by the KGB and carrying the maximum penalty of eight years imprisonment.

Particularly trusted individuals may receive the third type of security clearance giving them access to materials marked "SS" (*Sovershenno Sekretno*—"Top Secret"). This applies to space research, development of new strategic weapons, operational plans of the General Staff, most KGB assignments abroad, and some of the instructions and resolutions of the Politburo and the Secretariat of the Central Committee.

The fourth and highest level of security clearance is held only by an extremely narrow circle of people directly linked to the Politburo or involved in overseeing the activities of the Defense Council and the General Staff.

In most cases, however, the veil of secrecy is drawn not so much over military and state secrets as over the backwardness of Soviet science and industry and the rigidity and incompetence of the government. This is the kind of information that is strictly guarded in secrecy.

> They check the documents of every visitor, their special security clearances. . . . (L. Vladimirov, *Rossiya bez prikras i umolchaniy* [Russia without embellishments and omissions], Frankfurt AM: Possev-Verlag, 1969, p. 135)

> I took the paper out of the boss' hands, examined its contents and asked him what this was all about. It turned out that it involved a security clearance for secret work. ("22," 1979, no. 9, p. 101)

> However, even the fruit of intellectual endeavor can be kept under seven locks in the secret archives, to which security clearance is not easy to obtain. (*Russkaya mysl'*, 9 February 1984, p. 6)

Self-Employment (*Individual'naya trudovaya deyatel'nost'*). Work performed outside the public sector of Soviet economy. Self-employment in privately-owned but state-controlled workshops was legally authorized only in 1987, but it always existed in the USSR. Even when it was not legally authorized by the state (as it is now, under the 1987 "Self-employment Law") and essentially clandestine, it played a vital role in the country's economic development. During the last five-year plan, self-employment produced goods and services worth approximately 12 to 14 billion rubles, which was equivalent to one-third of the total cost of services provided by state and public agencies for pay. About half of all apartment repairs and a third of household utensil repairs are carried out by the self-employed. Collective farmers markets, which are one of the types of self-employment, account for 20 percent of total sales of foodstuffs. And in rural areas, self-employed temporary construction brigades (cf. temporary laborer—*shabashnik*) carry out nearly 20 percent of all building-installation work.

Because of the virtual uncontrollability of self-employment, it poses a problem for the state in the form of lost tax revenues. (For every officially registered self-employed person ["*individual'shchik*"] in 1987, there were a dozen who lacked the necessary permits). In the service sector, this well-established "small economy" (*malaya ekonomika*), far from being really small, has made significant inroads into breaking the state's monopoly on industry and trade. This was why in 1987 the government decided to legalize self-employment and thus to bring it into the "socialist" fold. It had no choice, in fact, since the "small" economy had begun to close ranks with the "second economy" (cf.), leading to massive embezzlement and corruption in state enterprises. The situation had reached a point were the self-employed were competing with the state in different kinds of industrial production and in such vital areas of the economy as fuel and electricity generation.

The government decided that abuses in self-employment were caused by porous legislation. There is sufficient truth in it, but only in the sense that scarce raw materials could not possibly be obtained in any legal manner. Certain forms of self-employment were banned without real justification, while in other sectors the self-employed utilized loopholes in the law and began to function quite openly. It became clear that if self-employment was performing a vital function, it could not possibly be abolished. The government was therefore faced with the choice of either letting self-employment flourish without any controls, in flagrant contradiction of Soviet socialist principles, or curtailing it and subordinating it to the requirements of the state.

The legalization of self-employment posed an ideological dilemma, since its spirit of private entrepreneurship had to be reconciled with the state monopoly on the economy. The problem was "solved" by telling the public that self-employment could in no way be construed as "private enterprise." One could speak of petty private property as being the basis for self-employment, it was explained, only if the latter were the sole or main source of personal income. Given the circumstances, it was decided to encourage self-employment as a secondary occupation. As such, it had to consist of single individual or family labor but, under no circumstances, of hired labor. The third clause of the "Self-employment Law" stated that self-employment could be practiced by "those employed in state industry after their regular working hours."

The government, realizing that these provisions were quite unrealistic, amended the law to permit self-employment of persons not employed in the public production sector, but only under exceptional circumstances as defined by the state. In practice, however, exceptional circumstances turned out to be not so exceptional, as self-employment was becoming the sole occupation no longer of housewives or pensioners but of dynamic young people. In addition, self-employment began to attract a stream of highly qualified university and college graduates who, instead of earning a miserly salary in their fields, preferred "to make money" by repairing cars and apartments, tailoring, or growing vegetables.

The gain of such enterprising graduates proved to be society's loss, as investment in higher education was proving unredeemed and the prestige of intellectual professions was declining. This became even more pronounced when doctors, engineers, and teachers began to "play hooky," performing their self-employment chores on working time. It is common in the USSR to attribute such conduct to greed. But this is beside the point; for the fact remains that in the public sector of the economy there are also millions of university graduates performing unskilled jobs, with the same economic effect as a result.

The high earnings of the self-employed are regarded as a sign of the "unsocialist" and "nonproductive" nature of self-employment. The Soviet Union has still not totally renounced its commitment to egalitarianism: hence the idea of imposing progressive taxation on the self-employed on the assumption that they exploit market conjuncture to arbitrarily impose prices, bearing no relation to either raw materials or labor investment.

Realizing the advantages and disadvantages of self-employment, the Soviet government may be expected to be wary in using its powers to punish or pardon the self-employed as it deems fit. It has to be wary, since the "small economy" contributes significantly to the development of the state and to satisfying the consumer demand. Meanwhile, therefore, Soviet leaders have decided to respond to the "challenge" of self-employment by quite unexpectedly recognizing it as "a completely socialist form of production."

> Self-employment has always existed in our country. Under the conditions of socialist economy there is basically nothing new nor unusual in its existence. (Kommunist, no. 18, 1986, p. 24)

> Although enough time has passed for everyone to be convinced of the fact that self-employment is a completely socialist form of economic activity, the issue is still intensely debated. (Agitator, no. 7, 1988, p. 38)

> A self-employee department has been opened in the "Moskva" department store. It accepts goods from anyone who is authorized to produce them. I went there and was shocked at the exhibition of poor taste and clumsy workmanship. Who buys these goods? The sales assistants sighed: People do buy them, as the adjacent departments are empty! (Literaturnaya gazeta, 1 January 1988, p. 12)

Self-Sacrifice (*Samootverzhennost'*). Ideologically motivated selflessness in the service of communism. This term connotes the self-abnegation and even self-effacement that the Soviet people have been called upon to exhibit not only in exceptional circumstances like war, famine, and natural disaster, but also in everyday life: at work, in interpersonal relations, and in public activities. The demand for and expectation of self-sacrifice

has not abated since the establishment of the Soviet state seventy years ago, and it reveals the essential inhumanity of the Soviet regime, the cynicism and hypocrisy with which it proclaims "all for man, all in the name of man."

There is a good reason for constant appeals for self-sacrifice. Given the existing conditions of poor management, beggarly wages, and constant lack of such necessities as transportation, raw materials, and equipment, everyone's simply doing his or her job will not suffice to save the situation. Only self-sacrificial work, work to the limit of one's strength, "blitz-work" with little respite, may possibly avail. The demand for self-sacrifice in public activities is intended to conceal the emptiness, drabness, and hardship of Soviet life.

From the ideological point of view, the emphasis on self-sacrifice is supposed both to acclaim and inspire the people. However, the overuse of calls for self-sacrifice has stripped them of effectiveness. When the people hear phrases like "sacrificial labor" (*samootverzhenny trud*) or "self-sacrificing toilers-fighters for communism" (*samootverzhennye truzheniki-bortsy za kommunizm*) applied to themselves or their lives, they tend to relate to them with sarcasm and the disbelief that comes from experience.

> The golden hands of self-sacrificing toilers are responsible for creating all material and spiritual values. (Agitator, no. 1, 1979, p. 37)

> Self-sacrificial labor, concern for the common welfare and for an individual distinguish all the candidates. . . . (Pravda, 25 February 1979, p. 2)

> Self-sacrificial labor has formed the harmonious character of the personality of the epoch of mature socialism. (Izvestiya, 12 March 1984, p. 3)

Self-Supporting Economy (*Khozraschet—khozyaystvenny raschet*). Computation of workers' wages as a direct function of the ultimate effects of their work, now practiced as a managerial method in socialist economy. The principles of the self-supporting economy were first formulated by Lenin. Despite constant subsequent revamping, these principles never approached the basic tenets of Gorbachev's present-day economic policy: enterprise independence, self-supporting, self-financing, and self-administration. In contrast to the past, Gorbachev's ideas are hardly pure theoretical constructs. In 1987, they received the full force of the law in new legislation relating to state enterprises, and they were established as norms of economic management.

An important feature of the present version of the self-supporting economy is the increasing independence granted to industrial enterprises, which allows them considerable discretion in devising production plans and concluding contractual agreements. Naturally, in a country where centralized control still reigns supreme, there are limits to the independence of workers collectives. Actually, the limits on independence depend on the amount of state commissions that always take first priority and often exhaust their entire production capacity. But in addition to that, targets and objectives of Soviet state planning also set limits on local independence. Nevertheless the self-supporting economy does allow industrial plants considerable discretion in allocating their profits as they see fit, whether into production growth or welfare facilities or improvement of work organization.

The two basic principles of the present-day self-supporting economy are self-support and self-financing. Although close in meaning, these are in fact two different concepts. The former refers to plain return of the invested value and the latter to development and expansion. Both imply, however, that factories have to rely only on the means they have earned. Thus, workers' collectives are taught to dispense with government subsidies. If the resources available prove to be insufficient, the collectives can obtain bank loans. In such an event, they are responsible for putting the bank credit to the best possible use. This means that once each factory within a given industrial sector receives its due allocation from the national "purse," it can no longer in the event of financial distress rely on obtaining funds from the pool of other factories.

The aim of this policy is admirable: to make enterprises cover their costs with their own earnings. But under Soviet command-planning it just does not work. Industry, as long as it has to follow orders from above, cannot make effective use of the much-vaunted self-supporting economy principles; in particular, the subordination of factories to central authority does not go together with their reliance on incentives for higher productivity. Workers' collectives are still obliged to execute government commissions, while the government is no doubt concerned about the quality of their work, but also about keeping their wage levels low. The self-supporting economy has merely led to a cosmetic change without in any way affecting the wage-levelling philosophy of Soviet economics. The last principle of the self-supporting economy, "self-management," is also ineffectual. It purports to allow the workers at industrial plants to elect their own management, establish workers' councils, and freely discuss managerial decisions. All of this has completely failed to materialize, however.

The following two models of the self-supporting economy's possible implementation will show the inherent inconsistency and contradictoriness of its underlying assumptions.

The first model deals with the distribution of profits, which approximately follows the procedures typical for the Soviet economy. Production costs, particularly wage costs, are deducted from the revenues. Only afterwards are the profits calculated. From these, the enterprise pays its obligations to the state and/or interest on bank credits. Only the remainder (if anything is left) can go into the production fund, creation of material incentives, workers' welfare, or reserves.

The second model deals with the distribution of revenues as normally practiced by private enterprise. First to be covered by a factory's revenues are its material production expenses, then its obligations to the state and the banks. Only the remainder is counted as profit. The latter is then apportioned in a way far from traditional. To begin with, two funds are serviced, the welfare fund and the development fund; then a reserve is set aside, and salaries come on the bottom of the line.

These different models of the self-supporting economy have generated variant responses. The first model took root in the Soviet Union relatively painlessly. It proved to be attractive because of its cautious approach: regardless of how a collective worked, it was assured of its wages. Even if no profits were earned and targets not met, the only thing affected (but not necessarily decisively) was development. This version of the self-supporting economy is generally preferred, since Soviet economy does not work smoothly because since state planning agencies are inefficient and raw material and equipment supplies are undependable. This implies, however, that an industry's manufacturing costs may grow and its earnings may fall, but wages will not be affected. A worker will never know what is happening in his or her factor, for this version of the self-supporting economy totally isolates him or her from hard economic facts. There is every basis, therefore, for viewing the described mode of production not as profit-distributive, but as "cost-intensive," in the sense that it guides collective efforts toward expenditure growth rather than decrease for the sake of increasing the volume of production and sales.

The second model of the self-supporting economy was adopted largely in order to overcome the shortcomings of the first. It is rather single-mindedly preoccupied with the factor of income. Income can be earned by properly exploiting available resources as well as by cutting production costs, while improving quality and consequently also raising prices. It follows that in this version of the self-supporting economy, a worker's responsibility for the ultimate results of his activity and the knowledge of his self-interest begin to count. Being concerned about his paycheck, he perforce becomes concerned

with the nature of contracts that his enterprise undertakes, for the simple reason that the latter affects the former. This mode of production does not depend on the mere bulk of goods produced and therefore does not warrant rushing the workers to perform more without regard to the cost and possible waste. Personal responsibility on the part of the worker thus becomes a factor. A sense of ownership begins to develop in him and he ceases viewing himself as just a salaried employee. His wages begin to be indeed earned; instead of being categorized merely as production costs, they become the outcome of his work. This second version of the self-supporting economy has only one drawback—it is alien to the character of Soviet economy and is thereby bound to be rejected. Nonetheless, the opposite development cannot be precluded in advance either. If the last described model is nevertheless accepted and consistently followed through, it is the existing Soviet economic system that would have to be rejected.

It cannot be said that self-support is a concept unknown to our economy and to our managerial cadres. The current situation is notable for the fact that the principles of self-supporting economy are not theoretical assumptions or wishful thinking. They are incorporated into the Law of State Enterprises (Organizations) of the USSR and have become the pillars of the new economic policy. (Agitator, no. 4, 1988, p. 25)

Self-supporting economy is a system of economic relationships between society and industrial enterprises (organizations), between different enterprises and between their component units (workshops, parcels of land, brigades, teams). (Agitator, no. 6, 1988, p. 38)

Only under true self-supporting economy will the permanent workers' collectives recognize the disadvantage of hiring temporary workers under the present terms of remunerating their labor. (Sotsial'nye issledovaniya, no. 6, 1987, p. 94)

Shortage (*Defitsit*). Unavailability or scarcity of foodstuffs, industrial goods, or public services attributable to structural factors operating in the Soviet economy. Communist propaganda long explained the occurrence of shortages either by historical factors, like the devastation of the country during the Revolution and wars, or by constantly rising demand for goods and services. In order to stress Soviet economic achievements and minimize the significance of the shortages, the present standard of living is often calculated in reference to the standard obtaining in 1913.

The real reasons for shortages, however, have to do not with the difficulties of growth but with the very nature and structure of Soviet society. The system of centralized planning, the militarization of the economy, the alienation of the worker from the products of his labor, his lack of interest in the quality and quantity of what he produces, and the defective organization of management are all relevant factors. The attribution of shortages to the particular nature of the Soviet people and their constantly rising consumer expectations is false.

The economic potentialities of a society depend on the division of labor within its production system and among the factors of production, and it is precisely in these areas that the gross malfunctions of the Soviet economy and its contradictions have become apparent. The best qualified manpower was withdrawn from light industry, agriculture, services, etc. and assigned to military industry according to the priorities of the Soviet leadership and its global ambitions. Such a manpower policy creates production lags. While production in military industry is fairly satisfactory, in civilian industries it is declining, occasionally even coming to a virtual standstill.

Shortages also resulted from the totally unfounded assumptions used to make estimates and forecasts in the absence of any serious research on either productive potential or the absorptive capacity of the market. Social needs were calculated not by the intrinsic dynamics of social development but by extrinsically imposed political objectives. The usual maldistribution of manpower between sectors and the deliberate use of unreliable indicators entailed waste. Characteristic also were insufficient mechanization of production, management so primitive that it recalled preindustrial forms, and, consequently, a constant demand for unskilled labor. All these factors together combined to create and continue to create permanent shortages, making them an inevitable feature of the "Soviet way of life" (*Sovetsky obraz zhizni*, cf.).

For a long time, Soviet propagandists attempted to justify shortages on the grounds that they actually contribute to raising the efficiency and profitability of production. They reasoned that shortages performed an almost humanitarian function, as, for example, the manpower shortage encouraging managers to consider workers as human beings, which in turn is claimed to lead to the improvement of the scientific organization of labor and improvement of working conditions. However, putting the problem in the terms that the Soviets do indicates categorization of the individual as a commodity, along with butter, meat, clothing, soap, and textiles.

The Soviet Union has constantly struggled against severe shortages in manpower: compulsory labor instruction in the schools was introduced and youth were mobilized for major industrial projects ("building communism"). As far as shortages of foodstuffs and goods are concerned, campaigns against them were conducted with far less regularity and consistency, taking place only at times when these assumed threatening proportions. Such a campaign was launched by the government in the late 1970s, under the banners "Struggle against Speculators" and "Raise a Firm Barrier against Inefficiency and Negligence." Something similar can be observed in the Soviet Union in the late 1980s, but with one difference. Awareness has finally dawned that shortages are a product of the paradoxes of the Soviet socialist system of the command economy and of strict central planning. This simple truth is now being officially admitted in the USSR.

However, understanding of the cause of shortages has not yet produced ideas of how they can be overcome. Gorbachev's economic reforms are being undermined in the corridors of Soviet bureaucracy, which inhibits the development of a "socialist market"—its tentative attempts to establish cooperatives and allow individual and family contractors the possibility of negotiating and concluding deals with consumers and supplies and of making a free choice of trade partners.

Since the 1930s, and USSR has been divided into a number of supply zones. The first zone is comprised of Moscow, Leningrad, and several cities of the Baltic republics and the Ukraine that are visited by foreign tourists. In these locations, supplies are relatively abundant, at least by Soviet standards. The second zone comprises the capitals of Union republics and large industrial centers. In this zone, supplies are irregular and shortages recurrent. The third zone comprises industrial towns and settlements in the provinces and regions. There, staple food products are distributed at places of employment. In retail outlets, goods are available only via ration cards of special coupons.

Permanent shortages force Soviet citizens to spend a considerable part of their lives in lines in front of shops. Queueing (cf.) has thus become a permanent feature of Soviet everday life. The few who are not required to waste time queueing are the members of the small elite (the nomenklatura, cf.) at the very top of the social pyramid. They have access to closed stores (*zakrytye magaziny*, cf.) or closed distribution centers (*zakrytye raspredeliteli*) that are provided with abundant assortments of goods, foods, and services.

The sales personnel . . . managed to sell under the counter more than half of the shortage goods which they received. (Sotsialisticheskaya industriya, 17 August 1982, p. 4)

It is clear that by putting aside goods for themselves (and) for "important" people, sharpies engaged in commerce are creating shortages artificially. (Agitator, no. 20, 1983, p. 24)

For a long time it was generally considered that the transition to wholesale trade was possible only after elimination of shortages. However, it is precisely the system of distributing resources according to ration cards that creates shortages. (Izvestiya, 9 July 1988, p. 1)

So-Called (*Tak nazyvaemy*). A phrase used to evoke scorn, which has evolved into a clichéd formula for discrediting whatever and whomever the Soviet authorities wish to castigate. The term is used to cast doubt on the existence of a host of most diverse phenomena, ranging from the so-called "Jewish problem" (*evreysky vopros*) in the USSR to the so-called "Soviet military threat" (*sovetskaya voennaya ugroza*).

"So-called" encompasses a broad semantic range, which includes both "unreal" (*ne nastoyashchy*) and "self-proclaimed" (*samozvanny*). For example, by referring to many emigré journals as "so-called publications" (*tak nazyvaemye izdaniya*), the communist press refuses to recognize them as bona fide literary works. Similarly, by referring to Soviet dissidents as "so-called heterodox thinkers" (*tak nazyvaemye inakomyslyashchie*), the authorities seek to create the impression that they are not real thinkers and represent no one but themselves. The term "so-called" has such a derogatory connotation that it is considered superfluous to provide proof for the suspicion it raises.

To further enhance the condemnatory impact of this term, Soviet propaganda often places its referent in quotation marks. Thus, one reads, for example, about the "so-called 'infringement' " of human rights in the USSR.

The organs of bourgeois propaganda . . . are doing their utmost to exaggerate the issue of the so-called "violations" of rights and freedoms of the individual in the USSR and other socialist countries. (Kommunist, no. 5, 1979, p. 45)

The United States Information Agency and the CIA are directing a number of so-called "social" centers [which are, in reality—AUTHOR] for psychological warfare. (Pravda, 28 November 1983, p. 6)

Socialist Competition (*Sotsialisticheskoe sorevnovanie*). A method of developing the Soviet economy that is also viewed as a means of promoting communist education. The key idea of socialist competition is the use of contest methods of production. However, this attempt to find a substitute for capitalist competition is contrived and from the outset doomed to failure. A person's participation in socialist competition stems from one of two motives: enthusiasm or fear. Enthusiasm was common for the generation that lived during the early post-Revolutionary years. People then lived in poverty and even died from starvation, but they sincerely believed that they were creating a paradise for posterity. Self-sacrificial enthusiasm was enhanced by the mass media, which extolled the first "blitz-work" initiatives.

However, with the expiration of Revolutionary euphoria, enthusiasm flagged and fear came to the fore. Numerous purge trials of the 1930s (the Shakhty case and many others) attributed all shortcomings in production to sabotage and deliberate wrecking. Socialist competition was instituted by administrative fiat. Numerous government-sponsored, obviously contrived "movements" (*dvizheniya*) forcibly flung the workers into maelstroms of competition named after their heroes, e.g., "Stakhanovite" (cf.) (*Stakhanovskoe*), "Izotov" (*Izotovskoe*), and others. During World War II, socialist competition was conducted under the slogan of "everything for victory" (*vse dlya pobedy*), urging a worn-out population, already suffering from the hardships of wartime and an intolerable workload, to work still harder, beyond their twelve-hour shifts. Fearing that accusations of "aiding the enemy" might be lodged against them if they did not cooperate, workers "volunteered" to yield part of their meager earnings to the state to "help the front."

By the 1950s, work enthusiasm was completely dead and only fear remained, but fear of a different kind. It was not so much fear of the state security organs (which had lost some of their clout and had come to be despised even more than in the past) as economic fears that kept socialist competition going. Every six months, Soviet enterprises raised their production quotas while real

wages steadily declined. This was held to be in accordance with one of Stalin's oracular interpretations of communist economic "laws," to the effect that productivity must increase at a faster rate than wages.

In the 1980s, socialist competition began to concern itself increasingly with matters of efficiency of production and improving the quality of the goods produced. But this is an exercise in futility. Soviet citizens have become cynical about newspaper slogans and assurances of how beautiful life is in the USSR. Yet the flywheel of socialist competition continues to rotate, propelling itself by its own inertia.

Socialist competition is not a smooth process. Moving by fits and starts, it goes into full gear only when the time left to meet the production quota begins to run out and work-blitz tactics must be employed to meet the deadline.

This is why in many factories and plants socialist competition has merely a symbolic existence. Signs are posted in workshops announcing "We will celebrate . . ." (*Vstretim*!) an anniversary, a birthday, a party Congress—any event will do—"with new work records." Then, for such "celebrations," work teams or model workers (those with no record of causing damage or work stoppages) are selected and featured in a propaganda blitz, which also includes "reports" of party committees about workers increasing their productivity and accelerating the rate of technological progress "in response to the call." Needless to say, in spite of all the hullabaloo about socialist competition, efficiency is not improved and technological progress is not stepped up. The only place where socialist competition actually works is in the field of disinformation—the underlying principle being that the more said about victories achieved, the more "successful" the competition.

Another function of socialist competition is to set some workers against others. Victimization of individuals allows the government to manipulate the dissatisfaction of the workers into "safe" channels. Thus socialist competition highlights not only duly honored victors, but also losers who are scapegoated as being responsible for low productivity and failures in meeting production quotas.

In stock Soviet rhetoric, propaganda posters castigate those who have failed to live up to expectations. The formula is to cast "shame" (*pozor*) on the "culprits" in such phrases as "shame on . . . for disrupting . . . harming . . . failing to accomplish . . . ," and so forth.

Socialist competition has a distinct scenario. The first stage consists of establishing preconditions for socialist competition by undertaking "socialist obligations." The trade-union organization of an enterprise is involved. Concrete obligations are undertaken and schedules for their fulfillment are set. The workers are not consulted, but rather are presented with a list of "socialist" and personal objectives to be met by a certain date. The second stage, the socialist competition itself, is no less a mystery to the workers. They find out about its progress from regularly published reports on the "enthusiasm of workers of the towns and villages," "counter plans" (*vstrechnye plany*), and "labor watches" (*trudovye vakhty*).

During the concluding third stage of socialist competition, the results are tallied. This is very important for enterprise management, since bonuses, awards, and other benefits are dependent on them. The outcomes are computed on the basis of concocted reports. Fabrication begins at the level of basic component unit of industrial enterprise (team or shop) and then spreads throughout the entire bulky hierarchy of the Soviet industrial production system.

> Socialist competition is now spreading throughout the country, heralding the successful completion of the tenth five-year plan and the XXVIth Party Congress in a worthy manner. (Literaturnaya gazeta, 22 October 1980, p. 2)

> The drive for a Communist attitude to work entails a high degree of socialist competition. (Agitator, no. 20, 1983, p. 15)

> . . . the creativity of the working people of

Moscow has been manifest in the energy with which they engage in socialist competition. (Izvestiya, 26 October 1983, p. 2)

Socialist Pluralism (*Sotsialistichesky plyuralizm*). A new philosophical category intended to reconcile the existing diversity in the world with Marxist scheme of social development. The appearance and advocacy of the concept of socialist pluralism can be accounted for by the need to adopt bolder approaches to reality capable of providing a plausible ideological case for Gorbachev's reforms. The term "pluralism" was long used in the Soviet Union in the context of "bourgeois pluralism," always with negative connotations. It was presented as an "idealist" doctrine, which in the era of imperialism was transformed into a major concept of bourgeois philosophy and sociology, to be countered by the concept of "dialectical-materialist monism."

However, on the eve of the 1990s, the concept of pluralism suddenly acquired previously unnoticed characteristics. It turned out that diverse patterns of intellectual and social development did not pose a challenge to socialism and to its economic, political, and social aims and ideals. Hence the phrase "socialist pluralism" gained currency, despite the fact that, if taken literally, it could sound like a contradiction in terms. For the contradiction between socialism and pluralism is pervasive, both when the two terms are meant as worldviews and when they are meant as descriptions of existing social and economic realities.

Marxism is based on monist, mono-factorial thinking, whereas pluralism presupposes an interplay of ideologies. Furthermore, the concept of socialist pluralism hardly corresponds to the realities of Soviet intellectual life, where a virtual ban on the expression and elaboration of antisocialist theories and views still holds. Hence the bounds of socialist pluralism are quite narrow. What is permitted is the expression of diverse views about socialism. This explains why one does not talk simply about "pluralism" but about "socialist pluralism." In this form, socialist pluralism is advocated both by Soviet conservatives and by cautious liberals who support glasnost and perestroika.

Socialist pluralism does not jibe with the principle of "democratic centralism" (cf.), long pronounced to govern Soviet politics. Yet characteristically, the latter concept is no less blatant a contradiction in terms than socialist pluralism.

"Pluralism" presupposes freedom for heterodox thinkers (cf.) and intellectual dissidence. However, the still current Soviet practice is to punish people first and investigate their cases afterward, which means that one who fails to shout "yea" at the right time will soon thereafter be shouting "help!" The Soviet consciousness is immobile, drawing not on "pluralism" but rather on doublethink.

The prerequisite of pluralism is the democratic structure of the state. However, a diversity of autonomous and independent social institutions is not what one encounters in the history of socialism. Hence, even in theory, socialist pluralism does not envisage a division of authority; it does not affect the single-party system that remains the very essence of Soviet socialism; nor does it pose any challenge to that system. Socialist pluralism substitutes a pluralism of views for a pluralism of policy options, reducing the former to the contrived choice between more left-wing and more right-wing possibilities within socialist orthodoxy. This is the basis for the claim that a genuine debate about possible policy directions is being conducted in the USSR. A leftist policy is interpreted as the advocacy of "more" socialism—i.e., the defense of public ownership of the means of production and the increase of the role of the state in the regulation of the economy and society. A rightist policy is not adverse to certain features of capitalism (now abashedly admitted to be universal and "common to all humanity"), such as commercial or financial relations and democratic forms of authority. In other words, leftist policy aims at pure socialism while rightist policy aims at a socialism adulterated by ingredients of capitalism.

At this point, the question arises as to whether pluralism may at all exist under socialism. The answer is that it may, but not in the form envisaged by the proponents of socialist pluralism.

In its history, socialism has assumed various forms: tyrannical socialism, as in Soviet Russia during the period of "War Communism" (cf.) or in its most highly developed form in Campuchea under the Khmer Rouge; despotic socialism, as in the USSR of Stalin; totalitarian socialism, as under Khrushchev and Brezhnev; and, finally, authoritarian socialism, as is now developing under Gorbachev. The latter may further develop into an authoritarian-democratic socialism if the liberal reforms now being pursued in the Soviet Union turn out to be successful. However, fully democratic socialism is a functional impossibility in the Soviet Union. The Soviet state may proceed along a socialist path or it may evolve into a democratic one, but it cannot follow both at once.

This does not mean that either development would be straightforward or linear. Even a sharp turn of Soviet society towards a democratized economy would not necessarily mean an analogous direction in social relations. Under certain conditions a rightward lurch in economy engendering a leftward lurch in social relations would be quite possible. Economic pluralism may yet prove to require a political totalitarianism to ensure the regime's stability. Something of that sort already occurred once in Soviet history, when Lenin increased repression and banned factionalism within the party in order to protect his New Economic Policy (cf.).

The model of socialist pluralism does not envisage the existence of a political opposition, nor of any party other than that of the communists. It is claimed that socialist pluralism does not incorporate any social antagonisms because it exists and expresses itself within the confines of a single party as a movement aiming at its internal democratization. Such an approach to pluralism not only contradicts its essence but also does not correspond to present Soviet realities, such as the development of cooperative, family, and private property—in addition to state property. When strengthened and expanded, these new forms of property are bound to seek ways and means of political expressions. Various segments of the population, whose income and life-styles depend on private enterprise, eventually can be expected to make their political influence felt. As a result, diverse political tendencies are already beginning to appear in the form of various, as yet still informal, organizations. In the future, this process is certain to intensify. If not halted by force, it will portend the end of the single-party power monopoly in the USSR.

In fact, such a monopoly has never been perfect. The party always had to share its power: during Stalin's rule, with the security organs, under Khrushchev with the army, under Brezhnev with both these institutions, as well as with the organized crime mafia (cf.). The latter, after neutralizing the government apparatus, gained effective control of key power positions.

The struggle for power intensified under Gorbachev. Four institutional contestants to power emerged. The first was the party leadership (headed by the general secretary [cf.]), comprising proponents of reform who sought to free socialism from its "army-regimented deformation." The second was the party bureaucracy, which opposed change and was incapable of carrying the reforms through. The third was the millions of party rank and file, an inert, initiative-avoiding mass taught by long years of totalitarianism to be submissive and await orders from above. If they are ordered to pursue reform, they will do so to the best of their limited ability, and if ordered to the barricades to oppose them, they will go there. The fourth potential force is the ordinary people, who are adopting a wait-and-see attitude toward perestroika.

The conclusion of this struggle, which will determine the development of Soviet society for many years to come, will ultimately depend on whether the ordinary people support or reject Gorbachev and his reforms. But at the same time a very significant role will be played by the three other forces who

are in a state of constant flux. The party bureaucracy, which panicked when Gorbachev came to power, has gradually recovered. Well versed in political maneuvering, it is actively undermining perestroika. Within the party a split has also taken place. Its most active part, consisting of members of the intelligentsia, trust and support Gorbachev, while its working class and peasant-originating membership, anxious to forestall a further drop in their living standards, lacks confidence in perestroika and makes its opposition to it clear.

The greatest support for reform came from the highest echelon of the party, where the general secretary has succeeded in installing his faithfuls. However, even here support cannot be assumed to be permanent. Any crisis or failure in the economy, intensification of ethnic discontent, or foreign policy setbacks might undermine Gorbachev's authority. This is why socialist pluralism belongs to the realm of rhetoric rather than action. Mechanisms for translating it into reality are simply lacking.

> Hence, one can speak of the historical development of socialist pluralism and even of its specific periodization, in accordance with the basic stages of the transitional period and of the building of socialism as a whole. (Sotsiologicheskie issledovaniya, no. 5, September-October 1983, p. 23)

Socialist Realism (*Sotsialistichesky realizm*). The style officially approved in Soviet art, hailed for its expression of class and party perspectives. The term first appeared in 1932, when the Soviet leaders were seeking a way to define the dialectic-historical method in literature, a formulation that would bind the writers to follow the party line while in a way allowing the expression of common aesthetic standards. Several suggestions were made. The new method was first referred to as revolutionary, monumental, tendentious, social, and proletarian—until the term "socialist realism" (coined by I. Gronsky, the chairman of the Organization Committee of the Union of Writers of the USSR) was settled on. This term contained all that was required: an aesthetic category—"realism"—and a political one—"socialism," indicated by the adjective "socialist." In October 1932, this term was adopted and approved at the highest level. Stalin referred to it approvingly at a meeting with writers, and it was immediately proclaimed a universal definition of the artistic method prescribed for Soviet literature and, subsequently, for all Soviet art.

The main principle of socialist realism is the portrayal of reality in its "revolutionary development," i.e., from the communist, future-oriented perspective. Socialist realism's ideals are embodied in a particular type of modern hero and formalized in a strict set of requirements. The latter include the espousal of "idealism," "populism," "party-mindedness," and optimism, at least in regard to history in the long run, and they entail the rejection of all "formalism," "naturalism," and "subjectivism."

Socialist realism is a kind of hyperrealism that has been sufficiently fluid and flexible to accommodate innumerable "servants of the muses," both in the Soviet Union and elsewhere. Socialist realist convention dictates that communism can be described in a manner ranging from the extremely positive to the ecstatic. Portrayals of contemporary Soviet life are not considered complete unless they include panegyrics on the glories of living in a classless society. Dealing with the past calls for a more complicated approach, since the Soviet future must somehow be implied as the inevitable outcome of human history.

Socialist realism gives artists leeway to express their views, provided that they portray life in a Marxist manner, as synonymous with class struggle, and provided they show that communism cannot fail to produce happy outcomes. If an author chooses a tragic theme for his or her work, communism must be shown to prevail and in its triumph mitigate any grief for those who fell by the wayside in their struggle to bring about the communist future. Satire is reserved for embodiments of bourgeois morality and petit bourgeois traits said to have survived into the

Soviet era. Soviet realist poetry must passionately laud the *status quo*, replete with moralistic exhortations echoing the "program of the CPSU."

Socialist realism is used to endow even such an apparently mundane activity as the construction of a factory, the opening up of a mine, or the reaping of a harvest with deep spiritual significance. Such achievements are portrayed not merely as studding the "road to communism" with glorious landmarks, but also as forging the soul of the "new man."

This "new man" is the embodiment of the "positive hero" hailed by Gorky: pure of heart, educated, reliable. Ignorance, apathy, and treacherousness have disappeared, and minor flaws are admitted only to allow the protagonist the opportunity of correcting them in his untiring quest for moral and political impeccability.

In socialist realism, the "positive" hero is not expected to be typical of any social or psychological reality, but he must be politically unimpeachable. When socialist realism was made the standard, verisimilitude went by the boards to the point that in the 1940s and 1950s, internal conflict was excluded from the domain of Soviet drama. What remained was a continuum of virtue, wherein "upright" qualities or characters were allowed to clash with the "outstanding": "The good struggles with the better" (*bor'ba khoroshego s luchshim*). Thus, "drama" was bound to remain lifeless and static. Although parading as art, socialist realism is basically intended to help the party carry out its goals. Artistic interests were, from the early days of socialist realism, subordinated to the dictates of the party. Writers, who in Stalin's phrase had become "engineers of human souls," (*inzhenery chelovecheskikh dush*) were conscripted into the ranks of propagandists and thus "freed" from the exigencies of the creative imagination. In works of socialist realism, fidelity to reality was limited at the outset by requirements entailed in Soviet upbringing (cf.), while style and characters were basically chosen for reasons of political expediency.

Socialist realism answered the "social demand" of succeeding periods: thus, industrialization evoked paeans to productivity, the war to effusions of patriotism, and the postwar period to moral concerns. The aim of Soviet art was declared to be didactic, pure, and simple; yet, required to glorify the revolutionary past and the communist future, it lacked the means for dealing with the actual present.

The theory of socialist realism calls for the comprehensibility of art by the public at large. Thus, even if the contents of art duly conform to doctrinal specifications, any search for new forms or styles of expression is decried as antistate activity. However, "deceit for a higher purpose" (*vozvyshenny obman*) and "revolutionary romanticism" (*revolyutsionny romantizm*), no matter how they distort reality, are smiled upon.

What socialist realism fails to do is to explain why Soviet life needs to be embellished if it is already so attractive. Furthermore, if socialist realism is possible, why not "feudal" or "burgeois" realism? The contradictions of socialist realism are irresolvable. Its socialist ideology precludes its being realistic, for if it were realistic, it would not remain socialist. In actuality, such art has proved to be not entirely socialist and entirely not realistic, and it satisfied neither artistic nor political requirements. This situation finds its reflection in the public polemic now underway in the Soviet Union, which typifies the range of concerns under glasnost. This dispute is less interesting for its content than for its style and form: what is at issue is not the liberation of art from socialist realism, i.e., from party dictate, but the definition or modification of the doctrine's name. The issue is whether the traditional formulations are consistent with the new requirements of the Soviet leadership.

What socialist realism has undeniably achieved is the creation of a language of its own. What has happened is that a match has been made between the Soviet language and the literary approach advocated by socialist realism. They have been tailored for each other.

The literature and art of socialist realism make a great contribution to the enrichment of the spiritual life of the workers and to their education in Communist ideals. (Voprosy filosofii, no. 7, 1983, p. 45)

The method of socialist realism demands from the artist a class approach to the study and depiction of life. (Ogonek, no. 6, 1984, p. 28)

Socially Useful Labor (*Obshchestvenno-polezny trud*). Any work in socialist industry or agriculture that is officially presented as serving the common good. The phrase "socially useful labor" is intended to contrast the virtue of labor performed in state-run enterprises (plants, factories, collective farms, or state farms) with the supposed social insignificance of the work carried out outside the system of state regulation and planning, on private agricultural plots, or in home crafts.

Socially useful labor is portrayed as the basis of economic progress as well as the most important formative influence shaping the character of Soviet individuals. Labor outside the state sector is often held to be motivated by greed for personal gain even at the expense of the public. Soviet pundits argue that the workers' alienation from his or her labor has been overcome in the process of building a communist society. By virtue of taking an active role in the organization and management of industry and by reaping the fruits of his or her labors, the Soviet worker is said to live an unalienated life.

In reality, however, the Soviet working people have absolutely no say in the management of the institutions that employ them and, therefore, no control over the products of their labor, which the state disposes of as it pleases. The new law on state enterprises adopted under Gorbachev gives the workers nominal control over their workplaces. In fact, the ruling party bureaucracy keeps a tight hold on the reins of industry, exploiting economic resources for the aggrandizement of the military-industrial complex and for the bureaucrats' own personal profit. Needless to say, the Soviet public must foot the bill to the point of incurring enormous sacrifices.

In other words, the ostensibly socially organized labor is not in reality socially useful.

Household work, child care, and standing for hours in queues for products—by and large considered female chores—are not recognized as socially useful labor. Were they to be, and were the state to grant some form of fiscal renumeration for this work, this might draw women away from what is officially considered to be socially useful labor. However, every potential female worker is needed to make inefficient Soviet industry even marginally successful. In 1988, women made up more than half of the country's working population. In general, women are treated as a commodity: they tend to be employed in some of the hardest and most dangerous types of work, including mining, construction, road-building, and drilling. With family income falling short of what is officially recognized as subsistence level, many women, mostly mothers, are compelled to accept any work they can find and thus often perform tasks for which they are not physically suited.

Apathy, waste, and primitive organization seem to be endemic to socially useful labor. Negligence and petty theft are rife. The productivity and efficiency in state-run industries are markedly lower than in the private sector. More than a third of all agricultural production in the USSR comes from private plots, which amount to less than 3 percent of all the lands under cultivation and hardly benefit from fertilizers or modern technology. Handicraft workshops and cooperatives (cf.), in which less than 2 percent of the population are employed, provide the country with 6 percent of its manufactured goods. In other words, labor, which for a long time was not officially recognized as useful and which under the current economic reforms is only partially recognized as socially useful labor, has proven itself to be not only socially valuable but, indeed, socially indispensable.

> The experience of the Soviet Union and other socialist countries has irrefutably demonstrated that the liberation of women and their active participation in socially useful labor and in the administration of the state are not only

possible and feasible, but are also the inevitable precondition of economic and social progress in general. (Zhenshchiny mira, no. 1, 1976, p. 14)

> Some organs of the right-wing bourgeois press saw a "limitation on democracy and freedom" even in the constitutional provision stating that the refusal of socially useful labor is incompatible with the principles of socialist society. (Chelovek i zakon, no. 6, 1978, p. 24)

Soul (*Dusha*). Man's spiritual world as perceived through the prism of communist ideology. The word "soul" in its Soviet understanding lacks transcendental reference and is used in the sense of "feeling" in such phrases as "to speak soulfully" (*govorit' s dushoy*) and "to put one's soul into a matter" (*vlozhit' dushu v delo*). Soul is used to define people's attitude toward work, public activity, study, and the collective in a sense roughly synonymous with "passionately" (*goryacho*), "with enthusiasm" (*s uvlecheniem*), and "with feeling" (*s chuvstvom*).

The word "soul" appears also in contexts where it would suffice to simply speak of a conscientious attitude toward a given thing or process. By playing on the traditional meaning of the term, Soviet propaganda pursues a variety of ideological and pragmatic goals. On the one hand, religion is subverted when a term referring to supramaterial values is reduced to a prosaic, material level. Yet, at the same time, borrowing a concept from religion elevates mundane things by vesting them with apparent significance and profundity.

The citizen is exhorted to relate to state property "with his soul" (*s dushoy*) as if the property were really his, and to work "with his soul" even if the work is so hard that it taxes his strength to the limit and lowers his self-respect.

Last but not least, the use of the term "soul" is intended to counter apathy by arousing people's enthusiasm to emulate fictional heroes who soulfully and masterfully (i.e., in strict conformity with the canons of socialist realism) acquit themselves of their tasks as production workers or public-spirited citizens.

On this foundation there has arisen and will prevail a new historic community of people, the Soviet people, in which everyone will give part of his soul to the common effort. (Sovetskaya kul'tura, 2 June 1978, p. 3)

Every year one sees more and more of such construction which are built with soul. (Krasnaya zvezda, 2 June 1981, p. 4)

If we want to farm worker to be a person with a soul we also must relate to him with soul. (Pravda, 25 December 1983, p. 3)

Soviet People (*Sovetsky narod*). A collection of diverse national groups at various levels of social and cultural development proclaimed as having been welded together into a new human community with common interests and aspirations. Historically, the entity of the Soviet people began with the October coup; socially, it emerged with the establishment of socialist relations between national groups; geographically, it is coextensive with the boundaries of the Soviet Union—the last empire in the world where nations and national minorities are being liquidated by being deprived not only of their independence but also of their national distinctiveness, cultures, customs, and values. In this empire, ideological uniformity is substituted for national uniqueness.

Soviet propaganda presents the notion of Soviet people as a sort of abstraction, an embodiment of the universal communist spirit. The term "Soviet people" is a kind of ideological shorthand for the alleged communist success in uniting different "socialist nations" into a single economic and political unit.

The origin of the concept of the Soviet people is traceable to two slogans: "Workers of the World, Unite" and "Oppressed Nations of the World, Unite." However, soon after the socialist Revolution, values expressed by these slogans were revealed as mutually incompatible. Lenin left no room for doubt on this score. "The proletariat," he wrote, "must not do anything that might bolster nationalisms. On the contrary, it supports everything that will help wipe out national distinctions and barriers between na-

tions" (Lenin, *Sochineniya* [Works], 4th ed., vol. 20. Moscow: Publishing House for Political Literature, 1948, p. 19). By 1920, it had become apparent that there was certainly no bolstering of national consciousness. (Nor was there an elimination of differences between nations, but this did not become obvious until much later.)

In keeping with their objectives, the Bolsheviks tried to export the communist revolution abroad, but the proletariat of the world remained uninterested. After a series of abortive proletarian revolutions in Europe, communists were left with no choice but to consolidate the revolution in their own country. However, in seeking to manipulate the aspirations of different oppressed peoples, the communists encountered an insurmountable contradiction. Theoretically, "proletarian solidarity" was supposed to be internationalist, transcending ethnic boundaries. Yet, if the communists were to manage national awakenings, they needed to be aware of unique national characteristics. This contradiction persists to the present day. In order to create a Soviet society, communist leaders had to weld together various disintegrated national fragments of Russia into a cohesive whole. But in order to bring them together, they had to offer them some a semblance of independence.

The Union was modelled on the Russian Federative Republic. In this federation, although it was multinational in itself, the Russian element was predominant, and its predominance was a prototype of the socialist figure. Although political autonomy was soon completely suppressed, the cultural distinctiveness of the republics and autonomous regions was emphasized. Newly recognized indigenous groups sprung up on the political landscape overnight. Native cadres of communists were organized; indigenous languages were rapidly and needlessly promoted (even if they had previously been spoken by only a few thousand people); cultures were invented; peoples were divided and united into artificial formations.

However, the existence of a conglomerate of even mildly independent Soviet republics was soon perceived to conflict with the foundations of communist rule. The few national rights won in the 1920s were completely withdrawn by the mid-1930s. Parading as a "Union" and owing its existence to forced unification, a new colonial empire rose.

The means chosen to solve the nationality problem was the liquidation of nations via the creation of a new historical entity, the Soviet people. As practical steps toward establishing this new historical entity, indigenous national cultures were suppressed, while russification was forcibly imposed everywhere. The Soviet state came to increasingly resemble its tsarist predecessor, being multinational in theory and antinational in practice. The Russian nation was declared the "elderly brother," while the other nations became either "middle" or "younger" ones. The life-styles, traditions, and beliefs of the latter increasingly filled with Russian content while their original national features were retained only in the externals. With time, however, the common Russian cultural content began to dissipate until it became a sterile form, while the national elements of culture gained momentum and strength to the point of becoming its very substance. Thus the Soviet people broken down before it could form itself, whereas its constituent entities have retained their identities. Now the Baltic nations clamor to regain their national sovereignty; the Armenians demand new borders and the reunification with Nagorny Karabakh; and the Ukrainians and Belorussians express dissatisfaction over the suppression of their national cultures. The ferment has extended to include the Muslim periphery, and finally has even affected the Russian Republic. Apparently, even the Russian people feel themselves suffocated by the attempt to create the Soviet people as a "new human community," sensing that it only stifles their national spirit by depriving them, along with other peoples, of their identity and historical traditions.

Gorbachev has proved to be quite unprepared in the face of the development of national unrest. His policy has been a reactive one, lacking a clear conception or plan. In effect, he has consistently been lagging behind events. This situation derives from his unrealistic belief that the nationalities problem can be resolved within the framework of an "improved" socialism. However, Soviet socialism can only be dismantled not reformed. Since Gorbachev is not yet ready to admit this, his reactions to challenges posited by recent inter-ethnic violence are half-measures. He is attempting to appease nationalist passions within the network of state institutions established by Lenin. Only if this system is done away with can solutions be found to the nationality problems of the Armenians, Ossetians, and other peoples with contested ethnic territories and boundaries.

> The Soviet people is a people of exemplary courage, industriousness, tolerance [and] generosity. It is a great, heroic people which does not boast of its achievements, but does not minimize them either. (Agitator, no. 23, 1982, p. 14)

> The Soviet people is preparing for its most glorious holiday, the anniversary of the Great October revolution. (Agitator, no. 19, 1983, p. 20)

> The Soviet people shouts a resolute "No!" to the ominous intent of the forces of imperialism to push the world into the abyss of nuclear catastrophe. (Pravda, 1 December 1983, p. 1)

Soviet Way of Life (*Sovetsky obraz zhizni*). The totality of social and moral forms of behavior of the Soviet people. The "Soviet way of life" is not equivalent to the concept of "way of life in the Soviet state" (*obraz zhizni v sovetskom gosudarstve*). The former refers to the peculiar pattern of life common to all Soviet citizens, and the latter to the position an individual occupies in the system of government administration and production, with the understanding that all rights and duties are determined by position. Thus, it may perhaps be more advisable to speak not of one but of many patterns and ways of life in the Soviet Union.

Above all else, the Soviet way of life refers to the general atmosphere that shapes the Soviet man: his materialist worldview, his subconscious, his political intolerance, his double moral standards and his doublethink. It also refers to his subservience to authority and his leader-worship. The peculiar character traits of the Soviet man have been processed, polished, and assembled on the conveyor belt of the socialist machine that works by simple and crude rules: "he who is not with us is against us" (*kto ne s nami— tot protiv nas*); "if the enemy does not surrender, he has to be annihilated" (*esli vrag ne sdaetsya—ego unichtozhayut*); "Whatever serves communism is true and just"(*pravdivo i spravedlivo vse chto sluzhit kommunizmu*); "the great goal justifies any means" (*velikaya tsel' opravdyvaet lyubye sredstva*).

The Soviet people were promised (in the program of the Communist party adopted under Khrushchev) that the 1970s would be years of plenty. Yet on the eve of the 1990s, under Gorbachev it is now clear that living standards in the USSR rank twenty-fourth in the world, almost twice as low as the rank of tsarist Russia in its time. And in terms of national income per capita, the USSR is still further behind, ranking twenty-ninth in the world. Furthermore, more than one-third of the state wage fund (which is the main source of people's income) is distributed among 10 percent of the population. The breakdown of this 10 percent is as follows: party and government functionaries, 3 percent; officers and generals, 2 percent; scientific workers, 2 percent, industrial and agricultural managers, 3 percent. Average income is 200 or more rubles, but if one takes into account various indirect supplements to salary, e.g., special rations, free public transportation for deputies to soviets, cars for personal use, the right to buy commodities or goods in closed stores (cf.) for hard currency, etc., then the average income is more than 300 rubles. In no way does this imply that members of the Soviet elite receive more than they merit, but these figures give a notion of how badly others are underpaid. In the USSR, people are rewarded for loyal service, not hard work. The closer an elite member is to the corridors of power, the more generous is his or her renumeration. The utility of occupational and intellectual qualifications is irrelevant. What is important is only loyalty to the regime and proximity to the leadership.

Conversely, the further removed a person is from the levers of the ruling mechanism, the smaller is his or her contribution to the only thing that counts: the strengthening of the regime. Consequently, the person's income and opportunities are proportionately low. Here again, the public utility of his or her labor is not a relevant factor.

The average monthly income per capita of 22 percent of the population (the intelligentsia and part of the working class) is approximately 100 rubles, while that of 35 percent is less than 100 rubles. The latter figure, however, when broken down, reveals that 25 percent of the population (students and pensioners) receive 55 rubles per month, while the remaining 10 percent receive a bare 70 rubles.

It should not be assumed that the authorities are pleased with these income figures. After all, the workers and peasants comprise the classes upon which the prosperity of the regime largely depends. Therefore, the regime is interested in their work and would like them to earn more. But there a vicious circle appears: low productivity of labor means low wages, which leads to low productivity, and so forth. A Soviet paradox captures this phenomenon with extraordinary clarity. The authorities pretend to pay workers a wage, and the workers pretend to work. The authorities are, of course, well aware of this situation, but have no choice but to acquiesce to it. The social equilibrium is too precarious, and the masses are feared, since they are known to have nothing to lose.

But it is not only incidents of disobedience and expressions of dissatisfaction that the authorities fear. Communist ideology itself is bound to raise fears, since it teaches that the impoverished proletariat and the peasantry are the spearheads of revolution.

But the communist regime has found a solution: The Soviet people are granted a basic minimum security. Everyone is guaranteed a job—a guarantee that has resulted in the emergence of millions of superfluous jobs—and a roof over his or her head. Six to seven square meters of living space is dirt-cheap, and many municipal services are practically free of charge. Yet working people cannot expect a decent living standard because no substantial rise in living standards is possible without radical social and political reforms that not even the current reform-minded Soviet leadership of Gorbachev is willing to carry out. Accordingly, the Soviet Union is lagging further and further behind the social and economic development of other twentieth-century industrial states. By standards of Marxist theory, the country is ripe for a revolution. It could be argued that the partocracy (cf.) has created its own grave diggers in the working classes. There is a clash of interest between productive relations and productive forces—the proletariat does not want to continue living in the old way and the ruling elite does not know how to rule in a new way. Still there is not yet a revolutionary situation in the USSR, and it can hardly be predicted when one might appear.

There are, under Gorbachev, no mass arrests in the Soviet Union and no massive repression. But permanent tension prevails. Women are worn out by hard work plus housekeeping drudgery after working hours. Children have to cope with school curricula that are often meaningless. Men are exhausted by moonlighting at second jobs. People are eking out difficult lives rather than really living, and even the leadership is nervous and restless, haunted by fear of the populace. Necessities cannot be purchased at subsidized prices in state-run stores but must be acquired either by waiting in long queues or for exorbitant prices on the black market. Free and readily available medical services are a propagandistic myth. In theory, health care is socialized; in practice, however, Soviet citizens not only pay indirectly for their hospital stay but must also supplement at their own expense the food, medication, and treatment received there. Likewise, in practice it is impossible to obtain free placement in a rest home.

For all these reasons, the Soviet way of life increasingly acquires criminal-underworld characteristics. The state rips off the citizen and the citizen rips off the state. Money-grubbing and satisfying one's needs at the expense of others are pervasive. The social fabric is in bad shape. The virus of crime is everywhere. Spread by the corrupt and selfish party autocrats, it infects those who serve the power hierarchy, and it manages to contaminate even those who normally behave decently but under exceptional circumstances commit acts of a criminal nature. This last category encompasses virtually the entire Soviet society.

While such criminality extends to all Soviet republics, cities, and provinces, it would be absurd to attribute it to a national characteristic of the Soviet people rather than to the Soviet way of life. Crime is obviously traceable to the falseness and unreality of officially proclaimed social achievements, such as the building of "developed socialism" (in its contemporary incarnation—democratic socialism) and the overcoming of the difference between mental and physical labor and between the cities and the countryside. In reality, in place of supposed equality, in this kingdom of fictions, the most tangible things are social status and money. They are the sole actors that determine a man's prestige and his place in society. Any vertical mobility depends on one's status. Status opens the gates not only to the accumulation of quantitative benefits (money, privilege) but also to the trappings of prestige and power. One's housing, one's car, one's access to scarce commodities—all depend on one's post and one's standing in the official hierarchy.

Official morals preach proven ways of achieving these same goals: studying hard, diligence, obedience, and, above all else, hard work. A citizen is constantly exhorted to work hard in order to receive recognition, renown, and esteem. However, those who give credence to such exhortations soon discover that the realities are more complex. They discover, for instance, that the way to prosperity for them is blocked because of their lack of proper "connections." Or that, contrary to all the moral rhetoric, prosperity can be secured only by unlawful means. It is precisely this latter reality that is directly responsible for the spread of criminality, since it encourages the use of any means as long as they are conducive to one's goal, without a second thought about their morality or lawfulness. Deceit, corruption, and shady transactions become a major and, eventually, the universal behavior pattern.

In their race for power and money, the Soviet people willingly and routinely overstep the boundaries of law, assuming, not without good reason, that this is the only way to rapid success. As a consequence, swindling, graft, and bribery flourish on a massive scale as vehicles to power, well-being, and material security. Everything the Soviet man owns or uses—his apartment, furniture, clothing, food, car, all the paraphernalia of his everyday life from the cradle to the grave—has in all probability been acquired by unlawful (or marginally lawful) means. In such a system, crime becomes a concrete expression of domestic policy simply because the domestic policy engenders and encourages crime. In some environments, political power is the precondition of economic corruption; in others, corruption is a precondition for ascent to power.

After they have embarked on the path to crime, Soviet people very often come to the perfectly valid realization that the methods by which they are enriching themselves are in no way different from those resorted to by the Soviet leaders. Furthermore, they soon come to realize that their only chance of escaping criminal responsibility lies in employing criminal means to raise their social status.

The enemy resorts to perfidy and slander, blackmail and corruption, seizing any opportunity to take advantage of our slightest miscalculation, error or misconception about the Soviet way of life. (Literaturnaya gazeta, 1 July 1981, p. 3)

Our reality provides the amplest evidence of the Soviet way of life representing the efflo-rescence of the spiritual forces of the people and the advancement of human welfare. (Pravda, 21 December 1982, p. 1)

The Soviet way of life is the concrete embodiment of the lofty spiritual values and ideals of socialism. (Agitator, no. 23, 1982, p. 35)

Special Archives (*Spetskhrany*). Files containing information carefully concealed from the public. Special archives were established in Soviet institutions and organizations in the early 1920s. Their formation exalted the status of the elect few to secrets of the realm. The main function of special archives was to conceal from the public at large information that was or could become prejudicial to the system and its leaders. The latter consideration was particularly important as the people were supposed to see their leaders as free of any blemishes. Anything that might stain their reputations was consigned to oblivion, usually through the medium of the special archives.

The aura of mystery was so pervasive that even someone like Stalin could be regarded as a superman. He would have continued to have been so perceived—if it had not been for Khrushchev, who began to dismantle the "cult of personality" (cf.) of Stalin, perhaps too strenuously and, especially, too early, as witnesses and victims of Stalin's crimes were still alive. The superman was thus felled from his lofty pedestal. Yet the pedestal of the party remained intact, historical evidence notwithstanding. In order to buttress it, state archives made partly accessible, under Khrushchev, were sealed once again. In addition to the millions of old documents, many protocols and official resolutions of various party conclaves, which had not previously been secret, were then consigned to secrecy. The authorities who disliked Khrushchev's interference were determined to prevent any further meddling. So piles of various documents were transferred to places of "limited access," where it was prohibited to copy them or write down their contents. This was explained in typical Soviet fashion, by claiming that "it was not possible to control the flow of information." It was quite easy to circumvent the law, which guaranteed the citizens an access to the archives "in the interest of the development of the economy, science, and culture." The guardians of the Soviet archives were breaching the law, not for the first time; the practice was common since the days of Lenin.

In 1918, a decree was passed about the centralization of all archives in a single government agency and their accessibility to the public. However, two years later, the access stipulation was amended. A new law restricted it considerably. Shortly thereafter, various agencies began to withdraw their files from the state archives and to establish archives of their own. In 1939, all archives, including those of scientific and historical institutions, were transferred to the NKVD. They were removed from there only in 1961, when a separate Department of Archives of the Council of Ministers of the USSR was established. Even then, however, the state security organs retained charge of secret archives, including the special archives. Charged with their oversight were usually Chekists (cf. Cheka), who had not succeeded in making careers in other KGB activities.

Every important or influential government body of any sort in the Soviet Union has its own archives and among them, special archives to which access is strictly limited. In the most powerful institutions, like the KGB, the Ministry of Internal Affairs, the Ministry of Foreign Affairs, and the Ministry of Defense, archives are enveloped in such secrecy that even their own heads do not have easy access to them. Politburo sanction is needed in order to open any of these archives to the public. Such extreme precautions are dictated not by any technological or military secrets the archives might contain; many such secrets have with time become obsolete anyway. But the documents do contain endless revelations of the arbitrariness of the authorities, of trumped-up trials, and international provocations authorized by Soviet leaders. For such secrets, the Soviet authorities allow no statute of limitations.

Special archives account for at least 50 percent of all Soviet official documents. Even glasnost has not been able to open them. Despite partial democratization of society and political reform, the law on state archives was drafted in great secrecy. When it was gazetted, it turned out that the keepers of the archives were still empowered to grant or deny access to their special archives section. In twelve ministries and other government agencies, the files are still being kept separate from the central archives. The only innovation in the new law was then expiration of secrecy after a period of fifty years. Yet even this ruling lacks meaning, since the declassification procedures are not operationally defined: it is not stipulated who is in charge of what and how things need to be done. Such obfuscation of a legal matter is, of course, not fortuitous. The Soviet authorities know well that by controlling the past, they control the present and determine the future. They also know that in any distribution of power, with perestroika or without it, that future will belong to them.

I would like to inform the uninitiated of the continuing existence of a broad network of special archives. They were established in the late 1920s not only in libraries, but also in every major archive. Over the decades huge masses of documentation were filed in them and continue to be filed. . . . (Ogonek, no. 2, January 1989, p. 10)

Special Schools (*Spetsial'nye shkoly*; abbreviated *spetsshkoly*). An extensive system of schools for the children of the Soviet elite. The children of the Soviet elite commence their institutional education at the age of six, when they pass from the kindergartens of the Central Committee, Council of Ministers, and KGB into special schools. These schools provide a superior general education, plus training in the manners, speech, dress, and demeanor appropriate for members of the upper echelons of Soviet society. Here, also, the personal ties are formed that will ensure that these young people are surrounded throughout their lives with people of their own social backgrounds.

The special schools have luxurious features that other schools lack. For example, some of them have excellent gymnasiums and swimming pools, facilities that are not the norm for Soviet schools. The curriculum of the special school is more comprehensive than that of ordinary schools, the classes are less crowded, and professional competence of the teachers is higher.

Extraordinary efforts are made to encourage individual talents. Noted artists are brought in to instruct those showing ability at drawing, and leading actors instruct children whose forte is acting. There are specialized schools for training in foreign languages and "schools for talented children" (*shkoly dlya odarennykh detey*) in the fields of music, mathematics, physics, and art. These schools are ostensibly open to everyone, but the overwhelming majority of the pupils are from elite families. Typically, they are driven home by the family chauffeur at the end of the school day.

The special schools give today's young elite a better education than their fathers received in the old system of party schools, which provided a highly politicized education. They nevertheless perform basically the same function: enculturating the next generation of Soviet leaders. Among the values explicitly taught are communist ideology and communist morals. At the same time, the students are indirectly taught additional values— that one's position in society is all-important, that their position in society is superior, and that no one is good enough to be their friend except the scion of a prominent party or government functionary or of a top KGB official. Children of doctors or engineers are not adequate. On meeting another child for the first time, the immediate question of a special school pupil is "Who is your father?"— meaning "What is your father's position?"

These children absorb easily the idea that, in order for life to be worthwhile, they must succeed in finding their own place as adults in the small charmed circle of those who live well in the Soviet Union. They are given every assistance in doing so. Despite the intense competition for places in institutions of higher education, special school students

have little concern about being admitted. Many of them are accepted into universities by special arrangement. Also, the superior foreign language training they receive greatly improves their chances of being admitted to high-status institutions of higher learning, like the Institute of Foreign Trade, the Institute of International Relations, and the Higher Academy for the Diplomatic Service.

It is little wonder that the self-assurance of these young people tends toward arrogance, or that many of them learn to be unscrupulous in pursuit of status, money, and perquisites. Special schools turn out precisely the kind of people the authorities need. In the future, these graduates will be bound by common experiences, share worldviews, exchange mutual favors. They will become accustomed to respecting each other though not as complete equals (How can there be complete equality between the daughter of a Central Committee secretary and the son of a plain general, or the son of a much-honored writer and the daughter of a chairman of a mere district council executive committee?). Their experience will eventually lead them to identification with the ruling class and to serving its interests. Such children, who grow up together, trust each other, and are personally close to each other, will understand the needs of their peers.

The young people from elite families begin their life paths with the backing of highly placed, well-off, and esteemed parents or relatives. At the family table, they hear conversations between people who determine policy. In this way they will gradually learn how things are done and themselves gain the desire to make history. Eventually they will have a good chance of gratifying such desires, since the distribution of high government positions largely depends on the kind of personal and family connections that they possess.

Behind the scenes arrangements for filling prestigious posts are one of the forms of informal cooperation between influential families. In every sphere of his activity, the young member of the elite meets people to whom he is linked in one way or another via family ties or other contacts. At every step he finds trust and support. Wherever he goes, he will find buddies ready to do favors for him.

His appearance and behavior immediately make him recognizable as one who has graduated from a special school. His acquaintances and friends can certify that he is one of the "in" people. He lives in a luxuriously furnished flat in a special building, while the vast majority of his fellow citizens live in crowded and poorly appointed apartments. His clothing, even if intentionally neglected, has a cut and style (it is either custom-made or imported) that distinguishes him from his social inferiors. He is an honored guest at social events like lavish parties and elite picnics. There he has the opportunity to gain confidence in terms of his behavior and self-expression.

The graduates of special schools (and of the privileged higher institutes of learning) are bound together by the shared awareness of their membership in the ruling class, in a category of people accustomed to exercising power. After graduation from school and their chosen institutes of higher learning, the children of the elite work at party committees, in ministries, or in security organs, or they go into the diplomatic service. No matter where they go or what they do, their futures are secure. Sitting in leather armchairs, surrounded by prominent and influential officials—many of whom are old school friends or relatives—they will mingle in a milieu that takes power for granted and uses it to shape Soviet society and form government policy.

> . . . There are no contradictions between the aims of the upper classes and the aims of education since the upper class children are being educated in special schools to which ordinary children have no access. (Posev, no. 2, 1974, p. 46)

> I discussed the film "The Last Escape" at the Slantsevskaya special school where it was screened. (Agitator, no. 3, 1984, p. 45)

Special Settlers (*Spetspereselentsy*). Nations that were branded as traitors, exiled from

their home territories, and denied the right to return to them as punishment for alleged collaboration with the enemy. Until quite recently in the Soviet Union, this term was officially taboo, and the nations in question were almost never mentioned in official statistics or reports, despite the fact that they amounted to many millions. Via innuendo and fabrication, the public was inculcated with the view that the special settlers were enemies who had betrayed the "socialist homeland." The communist regime carefully devised a long-range plan for the resettlement of the Soviet nations, with the aim of creating homogenous ethnically compact territories, which would be easy and convenient to control and, if need be, to suppress. The first attempt at nationwide repression or, as Solzhenitsyn termed it, "removal," took place in the USSR in 1937 in regard to the Koreans.

Only subsequently did the ethnic terror machine begin to go into gear, and there were still fits and starts to be smoothed out. The resettlement of the two-hundred-thousand-strong Korean community from the Soviet Far East to Soviet Central Asia was announced ahead of time, and those slated for resettlement were allowed to take with them necessities, valuables, and family heirlooms. Furthermore, the authorities paid them allowances to help them reestablish themselves in the new location. The allowances amounted to 300 million rubles, a significant figure at that time. But by 1941 and the resettlement of the Germans, the mechanism of repression was already working with precision and without mercy. In one night, three million people were evicted from their homes and dispatched many thousands of kilometers away: across the Urals to Siberia, the Caspian steppe, or to the wastes of Uzbekistan. Tens of thousands perished en route from hunger and disease. Yet even under wartime conditions, the rope of violence against "suspect" nations was not drawn into a choking noose. The Germans were given twenty-four hours' advance notice to collect their belongings and were permitted to take with them warm clothing and food.

The Second World War—the Great Patriotic War in Soviet terminology—increased the scope and ethnic terror as the regime gained experience. Repressions were planned and executed masterfully and mercilessy like assaults on an enemy. In 1943 and 1944, thousands of families of Chechens, Ingushes, Karachais, and Balkars in the Northern Caucasus; Crimean Tatars on the Crimean peninsula; the Meskhi in the Transcaucasus; and the Kalmyks along the Volga were surrounded by NKVD troops. Roused from their beds, stricken with fear, these people—mainly women and children, since their husbands and sons were off fighting the war—were within minutes packed into vehicles that took them to cattle cars in which they were dispatched eastward. A third of the total two million special settlers perished from hunger or disease during the endless journey, or subsequently from grueling work on cotton plantations in the taiga, coal mines, or various extractions sites. These were the most terrible years in the fate of these nations. Uprooted from the lands where for centuries they had cultivated their unique ways of life, they lost their culture, their traditions, and their languages. And yet, despite everything, many of them believed that their grievous conditions were due to a mistake or the criminal intent of someone like Beria. Most ironically, they turned to Stalin, hoping that he would redress their grievances.

In "response" the great leader relieved their loneliness by dispatching to exile destinations a second flood of special settlers comprised of frontline soldiers, both officers and lower ranks, party members, and non-members who were "rewarded" for the Soviet military victory by being sent into exile for a grim "family reunion."

The new nationwide resettlements followed suit. One hundred thousand Greeks became special settlers, punished for the "crimes" of their brothers in Greece, who in 1945 failed to carry out the local communist revolution to a successful conclusion. Three million Jews were being slated for a similar fate. Their "resettlement" was scheduled for 1953. The intention was to pin on them collective blame for the "murderers in white robes," i.e., the alleged deeds of mostly Jewish physicians falsely accused of poisoning high party officials. The plan was to dispatch of poisoning high party officials. The plan was to dispatch the Soviet Jews to the inhospitable Ussuri region in the Soviet Far East for no other reason than their failure to justify "Soviet confidence" in their loyalty. Yet another reason for their exile was also proffered: to "protect" the Jews from the "just" wrath of the people.

The death of Stalin nipped these plans in the bud. However, for several years more, right up to the 1956 Special Decree of the Supreme Soviet of the USSR, the Kurds, Kalmyks, Karachais, Chechens, Balkars, Greeks, Meskhi, Germans, and Crimean Tatars were still considered special settlers. In 1956, most of them were permitted to return to their territories, with the exception of the Meskhi, Germans, and Crimean Tatars, who were not. They were doomed to remain where the will of the tyrant had driven them. The conditions were somewhat improved: strict surveillance was removed and they were allowed to pursue higher education. However, they were warned that any attempts to have their confiscated property restored or to return to their home territories would be futile.

The following year, a resolution was passed to restore the autonomous republics and provices of the Chechens, Ingushes, Kalmyks, Karachais, and Balkars—with the Germans, Crimean Tatars, and Meskhi again being discriminated against. These three peoples remained branded as criminals on the basis of some individual incidents of collaboration with the Nazi occupiers. This absurd exercize in collective criminal responsibility was specifically applied to the Crimean Tatars, as if other relevant factors did not exist, as if almost the whole male population of 60,000 Crimean Tatars were not fighting the Germans at the front, and as if approximately half of that number had not fallen on battlefields. The Meskhi and Germans were in no position to "collaborate" with the enemy, since the Nazis never invaded their home territories. The blame and misfortune of the Soviet Germans consisted in their "blood ties" with the invaders, notwithstanding the weakness of such "ties" after they had been living in Russia for more than two hundred years. But in Stalin's eyes, the Russian Germans "might" have sympathized with their blood cousins. The "crime" of the Meskhi derived from the fact that they once, also long ago, had come from Turkey, a country which, although neutral in World War II, was suspected by Moscow of leaning to the side of Germany.

After another ten years, it became more and more difficult for the Soviet regime to maintain three million Germans, 700,000 Crimean Tatars, and 120,000 Meskhi under a cloud of suspicion. Hence in 1967, a new decree was issued entitled "On the citizens of Tatar nationality who lived in the Crimea," but which also related to the Germans and Meskhi. The decree freed these people from the opprobrium attached to their supposed "treason," but not because the charge was admitted to be unjustified, but because, as the decree stated," a new generation has entered labor and political activity." In other words, no doubt was expressed in regard to crimes committed, but it was merely asserted that a new generation bore no responsibility for them.

The authorities continued to use all means possible to prevent the return of these special settlers to their homeland. The means varied. With regard to the Crimean Tatars, the pretext was that "the Crimean province had already been resettled by others." With regard to the Meskhi, the excuses were that "there was a lack of living quarters and that the border regions necessitated strict controls over resident populations." With regard to the Germans, "economic" reasons were cited to the effect that their return would be unfeasible. It was considered more "economically" advantageous to keep them on the collective farms (cf.) and state farms of Siberia, which were suffering from an acute manpower shortage.

The 1967 decree was halfhearted and inconsistent. It did not envisage the organized resettlement of these people on their home territories or the granting to them of the same housing or other rights enjoyed by other nationalities. Consequently, they found a solution to their legal discrimination that was quite unforeseen by and unpleasing to the authorities. The Germans, who had made a significant contribution to the development of Russia, began streaming toward their ancestral homeland, Germany. The Meskhi dispersed throughout the Soviet Union so that when, finally, in 1986, they were granted permission to return to Georgia, there was practically no one left to return, since hardly anyone apart from the elderly remained in their exile settlements. Only the Crimean Tatars continued to stubbornly fight for their right to return home. The most desperate made their way to the Crimea, resolved to live there without work and "registration" (*propiska* cf.), under constant threat of eviction. The Crimean Tatars keep demonstrating, staging hunger strikes and protests, and writing collective protest letters and communiques to the press that recount the sorrows and sufferings of their nation of six million. Now, like the Germans, they are beginning to have hope: the new Kremlin leadership, which has condemned the ideology and practice of Stalinism, may pay heed to their national aspirations. Possibly, the near future may bring an end to their suffering and deprivation of rights.

He started speculating with certificates which he distributed to special settlers. (Komsomol-'skaya pravda, 5 April 1989, p. 2)

According to data on the Khlopkovy Gulag [the cotton-growing labor colonies] one third of the 400,000 special settlers died. (Moskovskie novosti, no. 15, 9 April 1989, p. 13)

Speculation (*Spekulyatsiya*). Purchasing and reselling various commodities with the aim of profiting from the difference between the purchase and resale price. In theory, any kind of commercial transaction can be regarded as speculation, for it always involves the idea of making a profit by "juggling" prices, especially wholesale, retail, and seasonal prices. Earnings obtained from such "speculation" can be regarded as reward for the risk and as compensation for the loss incurred in the event of a lack of demand for a given good. In the broader sense of the term, industry, too, is not free of such speculation as it aims to sell its products in the way that will best serve its interests by providing a rapid return on the expenses incurred in the manufacture of these products.

The Soviet state makes full use of its expertise in speculation. For the state, it is an important method of getting rich at the expense of the masses of the people. Either openly or surreptitiously, the prices of consumer goods and of imported products are constantly raised. The state also does good business by exploiting price fluctuations on the world market by buying up and reselling gold, oil, sugar, cotton, etc. Indeed, speculation is an essential component of most, if not all of the Soviet Union's international trade deals. These transactions are usually based on barter rather than on currency payments. Thus the USSR barters its raw materials and, sometimes, weaponry for imports of much-needed Western machinery and high technology. This business is profitable because the goods are exchanged on the basis of artificially inflated prices of Soviet raw materials. All that does not hinder Soviet officialdom from claiming that speculation exists only in capitalist and underdeveloped countries. In the USSR, it supposedly persists solely as one of the so-called "relics of the past" or "temporary difficulties" against which a fierce struggle is ceaselessly waged.

Immediately after the Revolution, the Soviet government declared speculation to be a major evil. The Soviet leadership had then no intention to permit its citizens to reclaim their right to engage in free trade, which it had denied them. Any form of trade, after all, was proclaimed to be the monopoly of the state. Anyone trying to encroach on this monopoly was labelled "an economic saboteur," to be, as Lenin threatened, "shot on the spot." Although merciless, this policy

was not devoid of some rationality. Speculation ripped off the Communist regime of always badly needed money and, no less importantly, it redistributed wealth in a way straying from the communist concept of redistribution "according to the social class," conceived of as the regime's primary means of winning the support of the masses.

Later on, the Soviet regime found for itself new and, as it turned out, more preferred enemies than the speculators: still-surviving members of the propertied classes, striking workers, rebellious peasants, intellectuals, and members of the party elite, whom the government had appointed to run the country. As a result, speculation for a while became a less urgent problem. It was not forgotten, however, and, when recalled during comparatively peaceful periods, it was blamed for wrecking the socialist economy and leading to chaos in industry. Needless to say, speculation was also said to be responsible for the shortages of consumer goods. There certainly was a link between the two, but it was the opposite of that which was officially proclaimed: far from creating shortages, speculation was itself created by shortages.

The most recent figures available show that in 1987 Soviet speculators earned 1½ billion rubles. This effectively means that family budgets were on aggregate reduced by this sum, without any corresponding material compensation. And so the paradoxical situation has arisen wherein a Soviet worker, who scarcely manages to see himself through to the end of the month on his miserly salary, is prepared, or obliged, to buy many essential items for far more than their posted prices.

In a country where there are constant commodity shortages, speculation performs the useful role of satisfying to some extent consumer demand, thus reducing the deprivation of all concerned. There is no basis, therefore, for viewing the speculator as "parasite." Far from living on unearned income, he works without respite and without any of the normally guaranteed work conditions. He gets up in the middle of the night in order to take his place at the head of the queue for short-supply goods and is constantly searching for opportunities. He is always contriving ways to make a profit in the interstices of the Soviet system.

Nor does the Soviet speculator in any way resemble the shady, repulsive character depicted by Soviet propaganda. In reality, he is an ordinary person with more than a modicum of intelligence, initiative, energy, and inventiveness. Without these qualities, he would never be able to pull off complicated deals, such as buying up and reselling vast quantities of fruit and vegetables. Without being thoroughly acquainted with the laws of Soviet supply and demand, he would not be capable of dealing with vast quantities of merchandise, such as, for example, when he purchases thousands of cubic meters of timber, delivers it to a *kolkhoz* (cf. collective farm) in exchange for grain, which he then sells to other enterprises, winding up with a handsome profit of several hundred thousand rubles in the process (see *Agitator*, no. 6, 1988, p. 21).

Naturally, small-scale speculators working on a profit margin of just a few hundred rubles flourish alongside the big operators in such places as *kolkhoz* markets, shops, and theater box offices. *Melochevka*, as minor speculation is known, is the preserve of those with low incomes—pensioners, students, housewives, and seasonal agricultural workers. The case of the seasonal agricultural workers is interesting in that they are driven to speculation by the state itself. Like many other workers, they are paid for their labors in the fields in kind, by so called "natural remuneration" (*natural'noe voznagrazhdenie*, also known as "natural payment"—*natural'naya oplata*).

"Natural remuneration" is a typically Soviet device. Instead of money, agricultural workers are paid with produce, with tens or hundreds of kilograms of grain, fruit, or vegetables. This suits the *kolkhoz* and *sovkhoz*, which usually have no storage facilities. It also suits the workers, for they are thus given the chance to make a profit on sales of the produce. For a long time, the state vacillated over whether or not to regard as speculation

(and consequently, whether or not to define as a crime) the sale at markets of agricultural produce at inflated prices when this produce was obtained by *kolkhoz*- and *sovkhoz*-employed workers in the form of "natural remuneration" for their labor.

A solution to this quandary was found by modifying the traditional definition of speculation by order of the Presidium of the Supreme Soviet of the USSR on 21 July 1985. According to the new definition, if the sale was conducted "for profit," it qualified as speculation. If it was done merely for the purpose of realizing "surplus" earnings, it was considered "work activity" (*trudovaya deyatel'nost'*). The ambiguity inherent in this decree reflects the ambiguities of life in the Soviet Union. On the one hand, the urgent need to solve the food supply problem forces the government to encourage private enterprise in the supply of produce. On the other hand, the sale of produce according to free market forces, that is, according to prices negotiated between the buyer and seller, clashes with the communist worldview and make state controls redundant, thus establishing a highly dangerous precedent.

Certainly, the government could not stand by and watch the free markets empty so that the population would not have fruit, vegetables, meat, and poultry. (Free markets account for a quarter of the nationwide consumption of these foodstuffs). Yet at the same time, it recoiled from relaxing its monopoly on trade even to the slightest extent.

In May 1986, the Council of Ministers passed a resolution aimed at tightening up the rules of market trading, leading to stricter regulation of anyone dealing with the sale of agricultural produce. Fines and other liabilities for speculation were concurrently increased. As a result, sales of produce at markets fell in 1987 by 8 percent. Another result of the attack on speculation was the growth of organized crime at *kolkhoz* markets, leading to threats of violence against vendors and to spiralling prices. Whenever a newcomer who refused to pay protection money appeared among the vendors, he was immediately dealt with by being savagely beaten or murdered. There was no point in complaining to the authorities, for the long arm of the Soviet mafia extends right up to the party leadership and totally encompasses the police.

Compulsory administrative measures for combatting speculation can therefore be described as quite useless, for its root cause lies in the very structure of Soviet society. When that structure is changed rather than simply tinkered with, i.e., when free trade is officially sanctioned and forced labor is abolished, speculation will disappear of its own accord, at least in the ugly forms in which it exists today.

> Speculation is a very great danger to society. Lenin, in his time, took a particularly harsh view of speculators. "A speculator," he wrote, "is a pirateer of trade, breaker of [our] monopoly. He is our chief 'internal' enemy, the enemy of the Soviet regime's economic undertakings." (Agitator, no. 6, 1988, p. 21)

> People who had grain, tillers of the soil, were exiled for "speculation," or for "hoarding and resale." (Komsomol'skaya pravda, 21 August 1988, p. 2)

Stakhanovite (*Stakhanovsky*). Term characterizing both methods of organization of labor and productive units that are considered progressive and model workers, equipped with the latest technology, and who set production records. The term "Stakhanovite" was coined in 1935. In a speech on 4 May 1935, Stalin described the cadres as the most valuable and decisive resource of the production process. Sensing the demands of the "historical moment" and divining which way the winds of the party "general line" were blowing, the management of a Donbass mine initiated the colossal hoax of the miner Stakhanov's record productivity. During the night of 30 to 31 August 1935, coal miner Aleksey Stakhanov was reported to have attained an output of 102 tons of coals instead of the usual 7 tons, thus exceeding the norm 14.5 times. Nineteen days later, he claimed (or the management claimed on his behalf) an output of 227 tons, thus exceeding the accepted norm 32.5 times. The "Stakhan-

ovite initiative" (*Stakhanovsky pochin*) was taken advantage of by the government to step up exploitation of the workers.

From that moment on it was taken for granted that "obsolete" (*ustarevshie*) quotas would be overfulfilled—if not by 32.5 times, then at least threefold or fourfold. Otherwise, the workers and, particularly, management would run the risk of prosecution for sabotage or economic counterrevolution (cf.).

The Stakhanovite mania spread over the entire country. Stakhanovites appeared (or, more precisely, were created) everywhere: there was Krivonos in railway transport, Busygin in the automobile industry, Smetanin in footwear, the Vinogradov sisters in the textile industry—who instead of operating twenty-six weaving machines took on 216—and Demchenko in agriculture.

There were also "Stakhanovite children" (*Stakhanovskie deti*). One Uzbek schoolgirl decided she would pick cotton with both hands (which had not been the practice previously). As a result she outstripped the entire brigade. The Stakhanovite movement and its various manifestations, such as "blitzing" (*shturmy*), or "fulfilling plans ahead of schedule" (*dosrochny pusk*), or "shock-watches" (*udarnaya vakhta*) were hailed by the Soviet press. The year 1936 was proclaimed Stakhanovite Year, and Stakhanovite brigades and shops were organized for the dual purposes of raising labor productivity and outdoing each other in "socialist competition" (cf. *sotsialisticheskoe sorevnovanie*).

The party apparatus organized and promoted Stakhanovite records and was willing to resort to every method at its disposal for the sake of the industrialization of the Soviet economy. Hence the drive for "labor enthusiasm" (*trudovoy entuziazm*). Endeavoring to fulfill obviously unreal state plans, the authorities recruited as many workers as they could to take part in socialist competition. The mass media turned the Stakhanovites into celebrities; propaganda presented them as representing a new and ideal type of worker who sacrificed his or her personal interests to serve the state.

The Stakhanovite initiative and its offshoots were totally fraudulent. Productivity records were fabricated in the backrooms of party headquarters and the editorial offices of newspapers. For a few workers, special conditions were created. In reality, creating new records required so massive a commitment of production resources that many factories subsequently suffered from severe disruption of their work as a result.

A special resolution passed by the Plenum of the Central Committee of the VKP(b) (the All-Union Communist Party of the Bolsheviks) in 1935 called for the transition from individual Stakhanovite records to the mass escalation of productivity by means of the introduction of Stakhanovite work methods. Stakhanovite schools were opened (which in the 1950s were renamed "schools of advanced work methods"); leading workers assumed "patronage" (cf. *shefstvo*) over workers who were not fulfilling their quotas; and Stakhanovite shifts and units were introduced. In the 1960s to 1970s, these were renamed "communist" shifts and units. The purpose of these measures was to raise the productivity of labor through extremes of exploitation. This was also achieved by the tried and true method of increasing norms of output and reducing rates of payment. In the process, the living standards of the workers actually deteriorated while productivity did not increase. Thus two years after the Stakhanovite "records" were made, the national plan of coal production still remained unfulfilled; nor was there any noticeable increase in productivity in any other branches of the national economy.

The failures incurred in the process of industrialization of the country were attributed by the party leaders to acts of the "enemies of the people" (*vragi naroda*, cf. Enemy of the People) and "wreckers" (*vrediteli*), while the deep-rooted flaws in the very system of labor relations itself did not come in for criticism. Stakhanovites frequently were featured in show trials, which highlighted the "exposure of wreckers" (*razoblachenie vrediteley*).

Such scapegoating proved to be of no help. Nor did other draconian methods. In 1938, a labor code was enacted that prohibited workers from changing jobs. Being more than twenty minutes late for work was punished by six months of corrective labor (which usually meant working at one's original work place but with the 25 percent of one's wages deducted as a fine). When tardiness was repeated for a second time, the violator was sent to a forced-labor camp.

The enormous meat-grinder of the Stakhanovite movement destroyed the lives of hundreds of thousands of workers. Some of them were hailed on the pages of newspapers and had honors heaped upon them until new "heroes of labor" appeared on the scene and the originals were no longer needed. As a rule, yesterday's Stakhanovite hero ended up as an inveterate drunkard or a burnt-out idler. There were also some who failed to adapt themselves to changing party requirements in time and paid for it with their freedom or their lives.

In 1975, the fortieth anniversary of the Stakhanovite movement was triumphantly celebrated in the USSR. Although Aleksey Stakhanov was still alive, he was living in a hospital in a state of mental breakdown and alcohol-induced depression.

The Soviet language also contains the nouns *stakhanovets/stakhanovka*—male/female Stakhanovite worker, which is close in meaning to *udarnik/udarnitsa*—male/female "shock-worker" but has additional implications that are lacking in the latter term. *Stakhanovets* refers to a shock-worker who is not only actively involved in socialist competition (cf.) but is also an inspirer of a "nationwide movement" for increasing labor productivity via mastery of new technology.

As noted above, Stakhanovite labor failed to produce a boost in the Soviet economy. Everything contributed to the movement's discreditation: the fraudulent output-recording practices ("whitewashing," cf.), the contrived enthusiasm that in reality covered the stagnation and mismanagement of Soviet industry, and, finally, the personality of the typical Stakhanovite—often an alcoholic—who was exploited by the authorities. In the 1950s and 1960s, the term "Stakhanovite" (along with "Stakhanovite teams" and the "Stakhanovite movement") virtually disappeared from usage, being replaced by such phrases as "shock-worker of communist labor" or "communist labor team" (cf.).

But although the terminology changed, the purpose of driving productivity upwards by any means has remained. This means that exploitation and the alienation of the workers from their work have also remained. The multitude of "new" movements cropping up after the Stakhanovite one had faded were indistinguishable from their predecessor, save that their cynical nature was even more apparent.

In the 1970s, for example, there was the innovation referred to as "for yourself and for that lad" (*za sebya i za togo parnya*). It meant that each work team had to have included in its list of members the name of a soldier who had been killed at the front in the Great Patriotic War. The workers had to meet not only their own production quotas but also an additional quota, and since the dead soldier could not collect his wages, the State did. This clever strategem led to many anecdotes about "that lad."

In many of the "movements" or supposed innovations in Soviet society, the only thing that is new are the figures: for the Nineteenth Party Conference there were fifty blitz-work watches; for the Twentieth, one can safely predict 100 blitz-work watches.

The creation of such new "movements" is becoming increasingly difficult for the communist regime. It is harder and harder to find ways to inspire the people. Here the idea of the Stakhanovite movement—in the period of the Gorbachev reforms—once again, perhaps in a slightly updated version, offers a model for increasing productivity at the state's behest.

The Stakhanovite movement is an example of our people's mastering new technology and constantly increasing productivity. (Istoriya

VKP(b), kratky kurs [History of the All-Union Communist Party (Bolsheviks), brief course], Moscow: State Publishing House for Political Literature, 1950, p. 323.

. . . Stakhanovites are the prime movers of our industry and the Stakhanovite movement represents the future of our industry. . . . (Ibid., p. 324)

State Apparatus (*Gosapparat*). The totality of Soviet governmental institutions and their employees. The term "state apparatus" usually refers to ministries and departments as well as those who head them: ministers, chairmen of state committees, and their deputies. In short, the word refers to what nominally is the country's highest echelon of authority (nominally because the political decision-making process is the sole responsibility of the party organs). The sole area of authority and the sole responsibility of the state apparatus is to implement these decisions.

The peculiarity of the Soviet state apparatus lies in the anonymous way in which it functions, a consequence of the Soviet social system's lack of regard for individual initiative. The origin of this attitude is the Stalinist notion of people as cogs in the social system. There is no need to pay any attention to them as long as they continue to function. This attitude resulted in taboos regarding their private life and social conduct. For the system, which left no place for independent action, private life was irrelevant. The activity of state officials at all levels was strictly regulated. Loyalty and a "proper" background were chief credentials for any managerial post. Once a bureaucrat took up such a post, it would be many years before he or she left it.

A biographical survey of heads of ministries, state committees, and their deputies during the 1970s and 1980s shows that the average period of incumbency exceeded eighteen years. Fifty percent of these bureaucrats stayed tied to their desks for twenty-three years or more, literally growing into the state apparatus and becoming, by virtue of their "meritorious service," mouthpieces of the unchanging (and hidebound) administration, totally imbued with the bureaucratic spirit and entrenched in office routine. All the content of their activity was subordinated to one single aim: holding on to their portfolios. Losing it (unless they were prompted), would signal the end of their career.

Officially, ministers' and state committee chairmen's terms of office are, of course, strictly limited—to be terminated at the beginning of the first session of the new Supreme Soviet, which is reelected each five years. But as a rule, senior state administrators in the Soviet Union remain in office for a second, third, fourth, and even fifth term—until they die or fall from favor. The staffing of the government is summarily confirmed by the Supreme Soviet (according to a list submitted by the Central Committee of the Communist Party of the Soviet Union) without any discussion of the candidates.

A study of the careers of senior state officials reveals that their progress is either linear or zigzag. The former is typified by progress in one, e.g., the economic sector. Here, a career is typically begun at an enterprise, then, following a series of promotions, culminates in the post of deputy-minister or minister. The distinguishing feature of a career that progresses along a zigzag path is that advancement is spurred by moving into the party or *Komsomol* apparatus. In such a case, vertical progress is very rapid, often jumping several intermediate stages and finally crowned by an appointment as minister. The overwhelming majority of Soviet ministers have traversed this latter path. They became deputy-ministers when they were in their forties and after ten or fifteen years were appointed as ministers.

This career pattern led to a situation where every minister, devoted exclusively to the interests of the department he controlled, aspired to expand his area of authority in order to get hold of more material resources and to increase his staff and his production funds. As a result, the state's material resources were squandered, but the minister's authority, power, and influence increased.

In addition, new ways of getting rich appeared. Ministers and their deputies did not want to be mere cogs. They were still human beings, and typically Soviet at that. They sought and found ways to "grease palms," turning government service into the mutual exchange of favors and privileges.

Gorbachev decided to hold the managers of the Brezhnev era responsible for this "era of inertia and stagnation" and to concurrently attribute the failure of his perestroika to their incompetence and their opposition to his reforms. Thus began a mass dismissal of ministers. By 1989, more than 70 percent of the Council of Ministers had been replaced (it cannot be determined how many of them had fallen victim to a power struggle).

Being age 56 on the average, the new ministers proved to be considerably younger than their predecessors. Like their predecessors, however, they had a long record of at least twenty years of party service. They had higher educations: twenty-one of them even had a Doctor of Sciences degree. This was fully in keeping with the spirit of former times, when even the Minister of Internal Affairs (MVD), General Shchelokov, had the degree of Doctor of Economic Sciences.

The most important point, however, is that 55 percent of the ministers were recruited from among deputy-ministers and 40 percent had held managerial positions in the party organs, while only 20 percent came from industry or the diplomatic service. These statistics can be used to conjecture that most of them are likely to remain devotees of the old methods of administration. For all the talk about mysterious conservative forces allegedly sabotaging Gorbachev's reforms, there is nothing mysterious about them. It is precisely the men who owe their careers to Gorbachev who are responsible for mounting obstructions and causing delays to Gorbachev's reforms. Old-fashioned administrative habits will not die out easily.

Nevertheless, only the present appointment policy can assure Gorbachev of a stable government. He is bound to surround himself with those who are dependent on him and subject to his will. Meanwhile, the transformation of society can wait. He is not the first Soviet leader (and certainly will not be the last) to sacrifice principles for power. Nevertheless, he has won the reputation of a zealous denouncer of bureaucracy and its inability to "timely and fully appreciate the necessity for change."

What qualities should be characteristic of people—ministers and chairman of state committees—who occupy the highest post in the state apparatus? (Ogonek, no. 31, July 1988, p. 6)

. . . economic reform would be realized considerably better were it not for the tenacious conservatism of the administrative apparatus. Those in charge are stubbornly clinging to their views. (Pravda, 6 July 1988, p. 1)

The government apparatus remains unwarrantedly cumbersome. The actions of a considerable part of it are out of touch with the needs and interests of society. (Izvestiya, 5 July 1988, p. 2)

State Approval (*Gospriemka*). A means used in the Soviet economy to test and appraise the quality of industrial production. The institution of state approval is taken from the example of the military industries. State approval is subject neither to the authority of the management of industry, whose production is under state control, nor of the ministry that administers a given industrial sector. The personnel of state approval operate within the framework of the USSR State Committee of Standards. In enterprises where this means is employed, the committee has permanent representatives who are highly qualified staff.

Certain organizational and psychological difficulties were encountered when state approval was first implemented in the USSR. Primarily, these problems consisted of filling the state approval apparatus with specialists, providing these specialists with testing equipment they needed, and compiling technical documentation. The psychological problems encountered in the process turned out to be even more forbidding. State ap-

proval is opposed on many grounds. It is blamed for excessive production requirements, as a result of which factories are thrown into disarray and plans are disrupted. Attempts are made to have the bulk of finished products put up for state approval at the end of each month, in the knowledge that prerequisites to it are likely to be lowered when conditions become hectic. Or it may happen that state approval inspectors find themselves under pressure of threats and requests from the management; or else it may happen that management neither hinders nor helps state approval inspectors, ensuring that the latter clash with workers, which could thus be considered responsible for factory stoppages.

To some extent, the work of state approval inspectors duplicates the tasks of Technical Control Departments (*Otdely Tekhnicheskogo Kontrolya*—OTK) in factories, but it does have its own special features. OTKs have no independence and are tied to the stipulations of the plan by the prospect of bonuses. State approval, by contrast, is not dependent on the work record of an enterprise and does not have to "stand to attention" in front of management. OTKs are responsible for supervising the quality of articles during the process of their manufacturing, while state approval tests finished products. However, both deal with the problem of quality, a thorn in the flesh of Soviet industry.

Had the frequency of Soviet propaganda terms used during the 1970s ever been computed, "quality" might well rank first. Soviet enterprises hold special "Quality Days," "Quality Weeks," "Quality Quarters of the Year," and even "Quality Five-Year Plan Periods." "Quality Brigades" as well as "Quality Collectives" have been formed. A special "Quality Seal" (cf.) (*znak kachestva*) is awarded to the best products, those which conform to "world standards."

In view of all this attention to the problem, one might suppose that the problem of industrial quality in the Soviet Union has been resolved more or less satisfactorily. Ten years after the quality campaigning started, however, when many verities have begun to be put under the magnifying glass, it transpires that the average quality of Soviet goods continues to be extremely low. In effect, the "attack on" (or "campaign for") quality has had to start literally from scratch. Here, the use of such military terms as "attack" and "campaign," which under other circumstances might have been quite inspirational, became glaringly insufficient. The help of the army—in deeds, not in rhetoric—had to be enlisted by directly emulating its experience and methods in testing and appraising the output of military industries. This is how the phenomenon of state approval originally appeared in Soviet society and in the Soviet lexicon.

State approval was not the only nor even the main administrative device transferred from military to civilian industry. In the 1960s, civilian plants borrowed from the military the work system known as "network scheduling" (*setevoy grafik*), and, most recently, in the post-state approval era, the supercentralized program of special-purpose planning. Neither system was invented in the Soviet Union. Based on systems analysis and an approach involving cooperation between different branches of industry, they were first employed in the American economy and only then borrowed by the Soviet defense industry. In May 1986, when the massive tide of "gross output" (*val*—an indicator of industrial efficiency, to replace profit) began to flood the few islands of high quality in civilian industry, the decision was taken to stem the flow by using state approval, which again meant borrowing from "the military experience."

This decision was tough but daring. Immediately, a severe blow was dealt to the reputation of such prestigious Soviet Enterprises as "Dinamo," "Krasny Proletary," and many other factories, which previously had been proclaimed models to emulate for the whole of industry. During the first ten days of state approval's operation, its inspectors were unable to approve the quality of even a single lathe. In Moscow, state approval revealed that out of 709 factories that had introduced complex quality control systems, 60 to 65 percent were manufacturing products below the required technical standards. The reason was the long-established custom of bowing to the idol of gross output.

The rule by which Soviet industry worked was to increase production, to adhere to the plan, and to fulfill the plan at any cost. But following the adoption of state approval in the first half of 1987, substandard products worth nine billion rubles were returned for further processing, concurrently with an overall increase of twenty two billion rubles in the value of industrial output. In 1988, 2,200 production combines and enterprises went over to the state approval system. During January of that year, 1,700 metal-cutting lathes (20.5 percent of those produced) were rejected as below standard, as were 26,900 tape recorders (21 percent), 41,800 televisions (7.22 percent), 296,000 watches (15.1 percent), 910,000 knitted items (11.8 percent), and the like.

It was then that the limitations of state approval became clear. Although state approval is capable of revealing negligence on the part of management, at times even to the extent of elaborating on the reasons for failures in the production process and stoppages, it can do nothing to prevent or correct such failures. It can force an enterprise to observe state-imposed standards, but is not empowered to change or upgrade them, even when they are responsible for the detected quality defects.

But possibly the crucial flaw of state approval relates to the limits of its potential effectiveness in the long run: even if it is capable of boosting productivity and performing accuracy for a while, a strict system of control by itself cannot assure higher production quality for any length of time. The reason is that with time, the directors of plants adapt themselves to the new rules and learn to circumvent them.

State approval contains an inherent contradiction. To begin with, it carries the threat of the abolition of pay bonuses. This is equivalent to a drop in earnings, which adversely affects worker motivation. Secondly, the battle for higher quality disrupts production plans, which is incompatible with the general party line that production needs to grow. The third contradiction is that failure to make a profit leads to the closure of enterprises, with consequent unemployment and the disaffection it generates. (Within the next few years, unemployment in the USSR is likely to reach eight million, while by the year 2000 it could reach twenty million.) To conclude, instead of entering a period of comparative stability, the Soviet system is now confronting a whole maze of inner contradictions and social conflicts.

> State approval has already been operative for two years. Generated by perestroika, it is concerning itself with the subject of quality, thus contributing to raising industrial efficiency. (Agitator, no. 11, 1988, p. 32)

> The state approval program in our country is being expanded. Don't your think that this will give rise to an overblown and quite superfluous staff of officials, who will duplicate the existing Technical Control Departments (OTK)? Don't we already have enough free loaders in every shape and form? . . . . (Novoe vremya, no. 49, 4 December 1987, p. 23)

> The aim of state approval is to provide a firm barrier against defective production, but without trespassing on the turf of the Technical Control Department. (Agitator, no. 2, 1987, p. 12)

State of All the People (*Obshchenarodnoe gosudarstvo*). A polity that Soviet propaganda presents as the natural outgrowth of the dictatorship of the proletariat (cf.). The state of all the people is proclaimed to be a political system wherein power is allocated in conformity with the will of all strata of Soviet society, in contrast to the dictatorship of the proletariat, which is said to represent mainly the interests of the working class.

The concept of the Soviet state as belonging to "all the people" was first introduced by Nikita Khrushchev under pressure from European communists, who found the term "dictatorship of the proletariat" impolitic and contrary to their interests. At that time the truth about the dictatorship of the proletariat in its Stalinist form was already widely known, and it adversely affected the popularity of the idea of communist revolution. Soviet ideology was thus given the task of providing arguments that would admit the possibility of a parliamentary accession of communists to power. The concept of the state of all the people was therefore born in an attempt to repudiate the traditional communist notion of violence as a precondition of a communist state.

The political climate of detente, which in the 1960s reigned supreme, provided the Soviet government with incentives to publicly renounce its violent ideology, of which the idea of the dictatorship of the proletariat was a constituent part. Khrushchev's domestic policy considerations (his opposition did not allow him to proclaim that the transition to a new, democratic form of government was already in the making) also contributed to the use of the term.

The concept of the state of all the people was a direct borrowing from Western sociology—to be exact, from precisely those assumptions of Western sociology which in the past had been subject to particularly biting Soviet criticism—and was incorporated into Marxist philosophy. However, neither wishing nor daring to completely break the continuity with the Leninist doctrine of the state, the Soviet leadership insisted that the state of all the people was a natural outgrowth of it and, moreover, that the aims and objectives of the two were the same. Soviet ideology keeps reiterating that the state of all the people represents the interests of all the people simply because all the classes of communist society share the interests and goals of the "revolutionary" proletariat.

In harmony with Khrushchev's promise of a full-fledged communist society for the current generation, the state of all the people was hailed as a driving force toward a classless society. To make this propaganda minimally credible, some secondary functions of the state, like educational adminstration or petty crime control, were (without any success) entrusted to public associations for their implementation.

However, this extension of responsibility to official public associations (e.g., trade unions, soviets) led to their even greater subjugation to the state. At the same time, genuine public associations, like independent trade unions, independent peace groups, groups supporting a political prisoners' fund, or creative groups of nonconformist writers, were being crushed by the KGB. The state hailed as the state of all the people turned out to be no less a state against all the people than its dictatorship-of-the-proletariat predecessor. The continuity between the state of all the people and the dictatorship of the proletariat manifested itself after the fall of Khrushchev in the intensification of persecution of religion and dissidence, in the encouragement of informing, and the use of extra-judicial repression.

Under Stalin, power was concentrated in the hands of the party oligarchy supported by the secret police and the army. Under the state of all the people, and system and power structure have not changed, although some subsidiary adaptations have been made in the system: the partocracy has been transformed from top authority into guiding force, while the KGB and army have become power-sharers with it. Finally, although the political police are no longer omnipotent, the state of all the people has not lost its police character.

> The formation of the state of all the people is a major step on the way from state government to popular self-government. (V. G. Afanas'ev, Nauchnoe upravlenie obshchestvom [Scientific governance of society], Moscow: Publishing House for Political Literature, 1968, p. 335)

> A new historical entity of the Soviet people has been created and transformed into reality in the USSR. This consists of the socialist unity of the working people of diverse nationalities, of the laborers in industry, agriculture, culture, of workers engaged in both physical and mental labor. Their unity is an indication of how deep-rooted is the expansion of the social base of the Soviet state; of how, in the state of mature socialism, the USSR is becoming the state of all the people. (Sovetsky soyuz, politiko-ekonomichesky spravochnik. [The Soviet Union, a political and economic reference book] Moscow: Publishing House for Political Literature, 1975, p. 44)

> The dictatorship-of-the-proletariat state is being transformed into the socialist state of all the people which has the mandate of the entire society. At the same time, proletarian democracy is being transformed into socialist democracy of all the people. (Kommunist, no. 8, 1979, p. 125)

State Order (*Goszakaz*). Directives and norms determining the volume and the nature of industrial production required for delivery to the state. The phenomenon of the state order (and the term itself) appeared in the context of perestroika, specifically in the process of reforming the socialist system with its centralized command economy, whereby planned production targets were imposed upon enterprises by central management. For many years, this system was the basis and backbone of the Soviet economy. The plan (cf. planning) was elaborated in detail. It could be fiercely debated, but in the end it had to be officially approved. Once approved, it commanded ceaseless effort to fulfill and overfulfill it. The activities of party, Komsomol (cf.), and trade-union organizations revolved around this effort.

However, in 1987, in the course of the reforms carried in the Soviet Union, there came a moment when it was resolved to reject directive plan targets and to replace them with state orders, which would set for every enterprise the volume of mandatory deliveries to the state. State orders were seen as a new instrument for the management of the centralized Soviet economy, which would enable it, by means of providing some measure of flexibility, to satisfy the minimal needs of the society.

In fact, state orders are an old rather than a new institution. To begin with, the way the problem is posed is old. The talk about the minimum need of the state is vague enough to include any kind of performance, in production or otherwise. Notions to that effect derive from the conviction that without state orders there would be chaos. The deeper roots of such notions, however, lie in habituation to the command system of management and in blind faith in the party's exclusive knowledge of what is needed for social development.

Radical reform is not feasible if only economic means are employed and if only management structure is affected. Radical reform can succeed only if it really affects society. The present reform, however, is slowed and stopped on the threshold by its unwillingness to part with ideological dogma. It is claimed that perestroika should be implemented concurrently with the fulfillment of the state plans. But since the plan is mandatory (and hence implies perfection), the question arises as to why perestroika is needed. Furthermore, how is it possible, since perestroika would make millions of workers redundant, and unemployment is not an acceptable option.

An exit from such dead ends and conflicts is being sought in an extension of state orders, which are gradually assuming the same level of detail as the plans did formerly. In 1989, state orders determined the production of most consumer goods and foodstuffs, embracing the total production of sugar, oil, cotton, and wool; all defense, petroleum, and cement industries; a large part of the heavy machinery and aviation industries; production; capital and housing construction; and 90 percent of railway transport, 80 percent of auto manufacturing, and more than 95 percent of tractor and combine production.

Even irrespective of the state orders as strictly imposed by the State Planning Committee (*Gosplan*), enterprises are not independent. They still cannot freely dispose of production surpluses left after delivery quotas are met. Mandatory deliveries are imposed by ministries, state committees (*goskomitety*), and central (administration) boards (*glavki*). Moreover, they must be strictly carried out—regardless of their consequences for enterprises. Orders must be strictly obeyed, as in the past, although now they may be discussed first. In the past, the Soviet economy resembled an unenlightened

monarchy; now, with state orders, it resembles an enlightened one.

> The state order for food and manufactured consumer goods is excessively large just where, it would seem, the share of a state order should be minimal. (Ogonek, no. 44, October 1988, p. 15)

> Think about it, what does it mean when the state order confers 105%, or 100%, or even 95% of production? This means the end of self-supporting economy, the end of self-financing. (Strana i mir, no. 4, July-August 1988, p. 46)

> All delegates attacked attempts of the State Planning Committee and of the ministries to strangle the Enterprise Law while it was still in the cradle. To strangle it with state orders. (Ogonek, no. 50, December 1988, p. 13)

Stigmatize (*Kleimit' pozorom*). A phrase used to condemn and expose opponents of the Soviet regime. The phrase is primarily used in reference to hostile foreign forces, such as capitalism, international reaction, and Zionism, to call attention to the alleged danger of the "encirclement" (*okruzhenie*). Forces inside the country that oppose the Soviet leadership are also considered to require "exposure" (*razoblachenie*). Any deviation from the political line of the party, and any view or tendency at variance with official ideology or morality, are described as requiring stigmatization.

Stigmatization is carried out through the medium of various propaganda campaigns and involves the symbolic participation of the "Soviet public" (*sovetskaya obshchestvennost'*), (that is, of approved "representatives of the people") and of the media. The institution of public humiliation has several rationales. It serves to intimidate the victim, to isolate him socially, to deprive him of potential support, and, last but not least, to force others to become accomplices in this victimization rather than letting them remain mute witnesses. The outcome is an all-pervasive atmosphere of terror, social tension, and suspicion.

Throughout Soviet history, the party apparatus has given short shrift to social groups and individuals whose ideas and opinions were out of line with the way the regime wanted them to think. During Stalin's purges, mass hysteria was whipped up in order to expose "enemies of the people" (*vragi naroda*), (cf. "enemy of the people") "wreckers" (*vrediteli*), "saboteurs" (*diversanty*), and "traitors" (*izmenniki*). They were condemned in the name of "the unity of the party and the people" (*edinstvo partii i naroda*), and people were called upon to stigmatize them for "Trotskyism" (*Trotskizm*), "right deviationism" (*pravy uklon*), "Menshevik idealism" (*menshevistsky idealizm*), "rootless cosmopolitanism" (*bezrodny kosmopolitizm*), or "Weisman-Morgan theories" (*Veismanizm-Morganizm*) in agriculture, to mention only a few of the most notorious cases. It should be borne in mind that each of these and similar stigmatizations resulted in a long list of casualties of police terror.

In the post-Stalin era, the regnant vocabulary of hate had become outmoded; it was therefore superseded by a new wave of lexical clichés, such as "anti-Soviet person" (*antisovetchik*), "ideological saboteur" (*ideologichesky diversant*), "renegade" (cf. *otshchepenets*), and "parasite" (cf. *tuneyadets*). In the 1970s, it was the "accomplices of international imperialism," that is, domestic enemies in the persons of dissidents, while in the 1980s, it is the "enemies of perestroika" who have been singled out for stigmatization.

The hysterical public outcries aroused are supposed to demonstrate that the regime's repressive policies reflect a popular mandate. By stigmatizing the enemies of the Soviet authorities, the popular masses are supposed to be expressing their own will.

Representatives of a special UN Committee . . . stigmatized the South African Republic's undeclared war against newly independent African states. (Pravda, 2 February 1981, p. 1)

A call to writers and representatives of the cultural world contains an appeal to open people's eyes to the dangers threatening peace and to stigmatize those who are today pushing mankind toward the abyss. (Literaturnaya gazeta, 15 July 1981, p. 2)

Peoples of the world are stigmatizing the evil deeds of the Begin clique, of international Zionism. (Agitator, no. 12, 1983, p. 61)

Stilyagi ("Punks"). People who wear flashy clothes and seek to imitate Western modes of behavior, or what they perceive as such. The phenomenon and concept of the stilyagi first appeared in the 1950s when, after the dark, lackluster days of Stalinism, the first glimmers of liberalization appeared in Soviet society. Foreigners began to tour the country, at first in small groups and, subsequently, in large numbers after the Moscow Youth Festival in 1957. This gave Soviet citizens, mainly young people, the opportunity as well as the inclination to emulate them by following their fashions in dress, hair styles, and dance styles. In short—to be different from everyone else and thus challenge, often spontaneously and unconsciously, the existing morality and social norms.

The tendency of the stilyagi to set themselves apart from the masses led to the creation of a special jargon, deliberately coarse and unguarded, which openly expressed contempt of the official parlance, filled as it was with stilted and meaningless clichés. This jargon was essentially the first manifestation of Soviet dissidence and therefore began to spread rapidly and successfully. It originated out of the fusion of several different linguistic formations. One kind of fusion consisted of the reinterpretation of already existing words. *Kadr* or *firmennaya devochka* (quality girl) meant an attractive women, *khata* (peasant hut) meant a vacant apartment, and *predki* (ancestors) meant parents. The second type of verbal fusion was influenced by criminal slang: *dokhodit'*, to die of hunger; *fartzevat'*, to trade; *telega*, squealing; and *bliny*, counterfeit gold coins.

Professional musical terminology also had an influence on the vocabulary of the stilyagi. This was no accident, for young Soviet citizens had no other model that they could emulate. The life of the senior party-state elite families was hidden behind high walls and fences. The lifestyle of those who served them, writers and artists, was alluring and romantic, but they too were distant and un-approachable, the object of myths and gossip, but unknown and poorly understood. The only available model for emulation that was out of the ordinary and imposed by no one was restaurant musicians. To be acquainted and occasionally to exchange a few words with them was considered a great honor.

The restaurant musicians enriched the slang of the stilyagi in many small ways, e.g., with *lobat'*, to play; *bashli*, money; *pokhilyat'*, to go; *kiryat'*, to have a drink; and *chuvak/chuvikha*, lad/girl. All these words and expressions led to the formation of a distinct dialect, which was rich, colorful, and expressive. This dialect helped them to identify each other and exchange signals, to prevent the uninitiated from understanding them, and to emphasize their distinctness and esotericity. Concurrently, it conveyed the sense of dissatisfaction with the Soviet way of life. Because of that, such expressiveness could be perceived as dangerous.

The stilyagi were expelled from educational institutions, driven out of the Komsomol, ridiculed and castigated in the press. But the very act of vilifying and humiliating them inadvertently helped popularize them. *Druzhinniki* (auxiliary, volunteer policemen) could grab them on the street and cut their long hair and beards by force or cut up their bell-bottoms. But all this only contributed to the growing attractiveness of the stilyagi for successive cohorts of the younger generation.

It is generally thought that the phenomenon and concept of the stilyagi exhausted themselves and gradually disappeared. The truth is that in the course of time, Soviet society has become more tolerant of forms of self-expression among its citizens. The word "stilyagi" has certainly lost its meaning when the particular style of dress, which the concept implies, is no longer regarded as seditious and merely sharply and cruelly ridiculed but not suppressed by force. Yet the concept of the stilyagi has persisted, being slightly adapted to the spirit of the times.

The appellation now applied to them is *tsentrovye meny* ("center men").

The lingo of the stilyagi has undergone a partial transformation, reflecting a new, more modern worldview. Their updated vocabulary has two sources: the way of life, customs, and traditions of the rapidly changing Soviet cities and the English language as it has been assimilated and adopted on the street. From the first source come such words as *poplavok* (buoy), badge of a higher educational institute; *pod gazom* (under the gas), tipsy; *nakhalovka* (cf. *nakhalstroy*), an illegal construction built by and for oneself; *bormotukha*, bad wine; and *kanareika* (canary), police car. There are also expressions, both full and amusingly abbreviated, which parody the language of bureaucrats, such as *TsU* (*tsennye ukazaniya*), valuable instructions; *ChP* (*chrezvychaynoe proisshestvie*), an exceptional event; *zakon podlosti* (the law of meanness), meaning the inevitability of nastiness; and *afganskiye konservy* (Afghan conserves), metal coffins of soldiers killed in Afghanistan.

In the contemporary stilyagi (or "center men") dialect, extensive use is also made of foreign (mainly English) words that are grammatically and phonetically adapted to Russian, such as *voch*, watch; *trauzery*, trousers; *shuzy*, shoes; *gai*, guy; *chif*, driver; *oldy, perenty*, parents; *laikat'*, to like; and *ringanut'*, to ring (telephone). So many mutilated foreign words have come into use in the USSR and their number is being so rapidly augmented, because of the popularity of the English language, that they merit separate study. These words, like the concept of the stilyagi, for all their vulgarity and coarseness, in a sense enrich the expressiveness and piquanterie of modern Russian, dried and "desalinated" by the steady overdose of ideological officialese. Also, such words somehow reflect the authentic experience of everyday life in the Soviet Union.

Many stilyagi words become part of everyday speech. They are figurative, emotional, and witty, having become not only functional but also highly popular, particularly those which poke fun at the Soviet way of life. Thus the word *vibrirovat'* (to vibrate) subtly describes the behavior of a Soviet citizen in the presence of authority—nervous and agitated; it does not just simply denote a phenomenon, but depicts its dynamics. Another example, *pakhat'* (to work, literally, to plough), succinctly conveys the nature and essence of Soviet citizens' work activity: hard, dismal, and thankless. The earthiness and unpretentiousness of many expressions in the language of the stilyagi testify to the depreciation of social values inherent in socialist reality. The stilyagi, as well as those Soviet citizens who have adopted their language, wish neither to be deceived nor to deceive. There is no cause for concern over the future of the Russian language. It is great and powerful enough to take its regenerative capacity for granted. If freed from its present political tutelage, it can be expected to soon rid itself of its accumulation of verbal refuse.

> . . . twenty or thirty years ago, a non-conventionally dressed young man was called a stilyaga, but now, in pseudo-English, he is a "center man." (Novy mir, no. 9, 1978, p. 73)

> The first stilyagi appeared. These were young people, dressed in an obtrusive, even overdone Western style as understood by them. (Obozrenie, no. 9, April 1984, p. 31)

Stooge (*Prispeshnik*). An accomplice ready to engage in amoral or antisocial activity. The term is commonly used in order to discredit any opponents of the Soviet regime ("imperialist stooges," "militaristic circles and their stooges," etc.).

The description of political opponents of the regime as stooges of some obscure forces is in keeping with the Soviet tradition of attributing ulterior and sinister motives to all such opponents, their supporters, and their sympathizers.

At the same time, the term clearly does not apply to the real enemy but only to his fellow traveler. This nuance is significant, as it offers hope that the stooge can be won over and used in the interests of the Soviet Union.

In meaning, "stooge" is virtually synonymous with "accessory" (*posobnik*) and "accomplice" (*soobshchnik*), i.e., with other words designed to create the stereotyped image of unprincipled henchmen, criminals, or reactionaries.

> Four years ago the Campuchean people crowned their century-old struggle against French colonialists, American imperialists and their reactionary stooges with victory. (Sovetskaya kul'tura, 17 April 1979, p. 1)

> The pressing task of all genuine Marxist-Leninist parties and all fighters for peace and progress is to pursue the struggle against the policy and ideology of the Peking leadership and the aggressive schemes not only of the imperialists but also of the Maoist stooges. (Kommunist, no. 11, 1980, p. 109)

> The Soviet people are so unanimous in support of the Declaration by Yu. V. Andropov, because it exposes the intentions of the Reagan administration and its stooges. (Agitator, no. 24, 1983, p. 6)

Struggle (*Bor'ba*). A term used to attribute to the Soviet way of life as having a dynamics, which it does not in fact have. The struggles for communist labor, for increasing work productivity, for fulfilling work plans, like other clichés, are intended to express the alleged dedication of the Soviet people to constructive and creative labor.

The struggle for communist conduct, or for the "new man," is intended to conceal the moral and spiritual decay of Soviet society, as manifested by its rampant bribery, theft, hooliganism, and alcoholism. Calls for uncompromising, fierce, and ruthless struggle (*besposhchadnaya bor'ba, surovaya bor'ba, zhestokaya bor'ba*) against internal enemies reveal the authorities' concern about the dissident movement and other forms of dissent.

The call for struggle against imperialism and international reaction and against the "influence of the West" reveals the expansionist ambitions of the Kremlin and, at the same time, its fear that contact with the Free World will lead to the discreditation of communist ideals and thus undermine communist faith. In a society that has long ago lost its revolutionary ideals, Soviet propaganda attempts to revive them by ascribing to the most mundane social phenomena the character of a struggle, or rivalry and competition. Struggle in sports (*sportivnaya bor'ba*) is also given a political coloration. Competitions are evaluated from an ideological perspective: victory in sports is viewed as an illustration of the superiority of the Soviet system, while defeat is considered an indication of weakness.

In such a context, the term "struggle" has lost its traditional meaning and now has begun to reflect not real life, but an ideological fiction. The apathy and social inertia of the Soviet people are thus disguised with exhortations and slogans.

> Constant and unwavering struggle [should be waged] against antisocial phenomena, spiritual pettiness, and its constant concomitants: drunkenness, hooliganism, infractions of labor discipline, and other immorality. (Partiyny zhurnal, 9 May 1979)

> Of course, for fishermen the struggle for quality [in their work] begins with the expedition itself. (Pravda, 15 December 1983, p. 2)

> The present elections are taking place at an important stage of the struggle to transform into reality the decisions of the XXVI Congress of the CPSU, [and] of the 11th five-year plan. (Izvestiya, 19 December, 1983, p. 1)

Struggle for Peace (*Bor'ba za mir*). A tool of Soviet policy that exploits people's fear of a third world war for the sake of covert interference in the internal affairs of independent states. The struggle for peace was officially launched by the Soviet government toward the end of the 1940s, during the period of the so-called Cold War. The slogan "struggle for peace" and the whole movement operating under that name was then used by Moscow to attempt to counter the U.S. monopoly of nuclear weapons by a ban on their use.

However, as early as the 1950s the slogan began to serve other purposes as well, such as diverting attention from the Soviet arms buildup, recruiting sympathizers with pacifism in the Free World, and arousing armed conflicts in areas of strategic importance. On one level, the conduct of the struggle for peace is not compatible with the fundamental tenet of Marxism-Leninism that the contradictions between socialism and capitalism are unresolvable and therefore wars between the two systems are inevitable. Khrushchev attempted to resolve the conflict between communist theory and social practice by elaborating the formula of peaceful coexistence between states with different political systems, thus shifting the class struggle from the realm of interstate relations to that of ideas. However, this "struggle of ideas" soon was expressed in praxis in the form of Soviet expansion into countries of the Third World. This took place under Brezhnev, who interpreted the struggle for peace in such a way that it excluded wars of "national liberation." This obfuscation discredited the term considerably.

An unexpected development in the use of this term occurred under Gorbachev, who has extended Marxism to the point of rejecting one of Marxism's crucial assumptions, namely the principle of class struggle in international relations. According to Gorbachev's "new thinking," common concerns of all of humanity—the preservation and consolidation of universal peace and prevention of nuclear war—come before class-specific goals: the promotion of socialist revolution.

The new philosophy of Soviet foreign policy redefines the objectives of the struggle for peace. It may lead to the encouragement of humanist tendencies in today's world. However, another possibility is as likely: that the changed slogans will fail to affect political realities at all.

> For the Soviet state the struggle for peace is not a temporary or circumstantial goal, but a basic principle observed in the fraternal unity with all states of the socialist community. (Pravda, 5 May 1981, p. 4)

> In the struggle for peace and socialist progress the unity and dynamism of the international

Communist movement—the most influential contemporary political force—have great significance." (Partiynaya zhizn', no. 19, 1982, p. 9)

The speakers note the vital importance of the struggle for peace. (Pravda, 16 October 1983, p. 5)

Subbotnik (*Subbotnik*). Collective work performed without compensation (the term is derived from the Russian *subbota*, Saturday). The first subbotnik in the Soviet Union was initiated by fifteen workers from the Moscow railyard, who on the night of Saturday, 12 April 1919, in response to the call of their party organization, repaired three steam locomotives. Lenin saw the initiative of the Moscow railroad workers as evidence that "sprouts" (*rostki*) of communism were extending their roots into working class life. Thus, the term "communist subbotniks" (*kommunisticheskie subbotniki*) came into being. Within a year, Lenin himself was taking part in a subbotnik in the Kremlin.

Since then, subbotniks have become an annual, or more frequent, event in Soviet life. Since 1979, All-Union subbotniks or *voskresniks* (Sunday subbotniks, from the Russian *voskresenie*, Sunday) have been carried out in accordance with a resolution of the Council of Ministers.

Subbotniks are organized and carried out under party auspices and timed to coincide with holidays or "commemoration dates" (cf. *znamenatel'nye daty*), such as the anniversary of the first subbotnik or Lenin's birthday. Subbotniks may be organized at industrial plants in order to make up for "disruptions" (*proryvy*) in the fulfillment of work plans or to prepare work sites. In any case, regardless of the objective, the initiative for subbotniks always comes from the administration and never from the "working masses" themselves, despite claims to the contrary.

Subbotniks necessitate planning involving different levels of the industrial and party hierarchy. The profits are estimated in advance. Their distribution is also determined in advance, the usual beneficiaries being military, industrial, and agricultural development.

Moreover, a subbotnik must be staged: the appropriate holiday atmosphere must be provided. Flags, loudspeakers, speeches, and a contrived joyful atmosphere are indispensable paraphernalia for the occasion. Since dodging a subbotnik is viewed as an antisocial or even treasonous act, overworked and underpaid Soviet citizens sacrifice their leisure time out of fear, not zeal. The accumulated resentment of the participants can later be drowned in drinking bouts, which the management of the enterprise involved secretly encourages.

Subbotniks are routinely followed by newspaper reports about their great benefit to the state economy. From these reports, the participants learn of their own "high political consciousness" (*vysokaya politicheskaya soznatel'nost'*) and "communist" attitude toward work. In reality, the contribution to the economy from subbotniks is highly problematic. At best they save money that would otherwise be paid out in wages. Theoretically, the capital thus saved could be reallocated for the development of the economy, where it not for the fact that the growth of the Soviet economy hinges not on capital but on an increase in the supply of raw materials and machinery. The ultimate purpose of subbotniks is not the development of production. It is not economic but rather ideological. Subbotniks are live demonstrations of "communist enthusiasm" at work and a means of indoctrinating the public to unstintingly obey orders from above.

The work-blitz commemorating the 25th anniversary of the patriotic movement culminated in a subbotnik carried out on the initiative of Communist labor collectives of Moscow. (Pravda, 16 October 1983, p. 1)

Many work collectives attain a high productivity of labor during subbotniks. (Agitator, no. 5, 1983, p. 31)

The working class of Leningrad marked the Communist subbotnik by doing outstanding work. (Izvestiya, 16 October 1982, p. 1)

Subsidiary Farming (*Podsobnoe khozyaystvo*). (1) Personal, private farming on a plot of land set aside for the personal use of rural inhabitants. (2) Factory-operated: agricultural departments at state enterprises or institutions. Private-plot farming (L.p.kh.— *Lichnoe priusadebnoe khozyaystvo*) is considered to be objectively necessary for socialism. However, the notion of exactly how necessary it was has varied from one stage of Soviet history to another. Private plot farming was accepted as an unavoidable concession to the peasants' fondness for private ownership but was subjected to numerous restrictions. Some of these restrictions were decidedly oppressive, particularly under Stalin, who enforced uniformization of production (collectivization) throughout Soviet agriculture. Khrushchev also did not stint in persecuting the peasantry. By so doing, he tried to reduce the distinction between the town and country as part of his grand design to bring the communist utopia one step closer.

Subsequently, when it became clear that the basic units of Soviet socialist agriculture, the *kolkhoz* and the *sovkhoz*, were unable to feed the nation, the government became more tolerant of private plot farming. Brezhnev discovered that it could be a great help in the production of milk, meat, and vegetables. He became obsessed with the idea of assigning factories and institutions the task of providing their employees with foodstuffs, thereby freeing the state from this responsibility, of which it could not acquit itself in any case.

In this way, private plot farming was introduced to industry under the name of factory subsidiary farming (*proizvodstvennoe podsobnoe khozyaystvo*—P.P.Kh.). Units of subsidiary farming were established in all kinds of factories and other institutions. A government decree in December 1978 announced that these units would be provided with land and allocated livestock, farming materials, and equipment. By early 1981, the country had nearly 80,000 enterprises with subsidiary farming units, which produced 450,000 tons of meat, more than a million tons of milk, 810 million eggs, and hundreds of thousands of tons of fruit and vegetables. When Gorbachev subjected Brezhnev's policies to scathing criticism, he could not deny that factory subsidiary farming was the latter's valuable innovation. He even improved on it to some extent by assigning each factory subsidiary farming unit the task of producing at least 20 kilograms of meat per worker. In addition to existing factory subsidiary farming units, he promoted the establishment of new types, e.g., the fruit and vegetable cooperatives. At the beginning of 1987, there were 47,000 of the latter, which by the combined efforts of around seven million urban families, grew 3½ million tons of potatoes and other vegetables as well as 700,000 tons of fruit.

The public began to be bombarded with the slogan "Provisioning the citizens is the job of the citizens themselves." The government's attention began to focus on the growth of private subsidiary farming units (which sometimes were even affectionately, although archaically, referred to as "farmsteads"), which in 1987 accounted for one-fourth of all agricultural production: 4.8 million tons of meat, 22 million tons of milk, 48 million tons of potatoes, and 15 million tons of fruit and vegetables. The total value of this produce amounted to 53.4 billion rubles. But the government's aim in encouraging this new form of agriculture, essentially consisting of regional self-sufficiency in food production, is still a long way from being achieved. This is primarily because subsidiary farming is regarded as a mere branch of Soviet agriculture, which otherwise is unreservedly dominated by the powerful (although unprofitable) *kolkhoz-sovkhoz* system.

An inevitable result of this state-owned farming system has been a steady decline in the agricultural work force. Between 1968 and 1988, its size shrank by three million to 49 million. This latter figure equals approximately one-half of the population of the countryside (Agitator, no. 13, 1988, p. 4).

The fall in *kolkhoz* and *sovkhoz* productivity came as no surprise to the country's leaders. What took them by surprise, however, was the slowdown in private plot farming production from 26 to 24 percent. The situation became even more worrisome when it was realized that cattle and poultry husbandry on private plots had undergone a particularly sharp decline. A third of all rural families had no livestock at all and therefore could not market any produce derived from it.

A quite ludicrous situation developed where the rural population, supposedly responsible for feeding the nation, were themselves becoming net food consumers rather than producers. The average *kolkhoz* family in 1986 purchased 32 kilograms of meat (compared to 20 kilograms in 1981), as well as tens of kilograms of fruit and vegetables from state or cooperative trading posts. One of the reasons for this absurdity was the low productivity of subsidiary farming units, which are usually very labor-intensive and use little in the way of modern agricultural equipment. Ninety percent of all their work is, in fact, done by hand. As a result, the average production of a private subsidiary farmer is worth no more than 1.15 rubles per hour, which is less than in the notoriously inefficient *kolkhoz* and *sovkhoz* farming system.

Another problem of private plot farmers is the difficulty they encounter in selling their produce. The network of cooperative trade buys less than 50 percent of their potato crop, 46 percent of their vegetables and just 28 percent of their fruit. The remainder they have to market by themselves.

The Soviet government has recently tried to deal with some of the imbalances affecting private plot farming by abolishing restrictions on the quantities of cattle and poultry they may keep. Private plot farmers have also been allowed to farm larger areas of land. The government's more tolerant attitude toward private plot farming, however, is aimed at stimulating the development of *kolkhozy* and *sovkhozy* rather than of subsidiary farming. Hence the size of private plots allowed and the quotas for livestock raised on them are linked to how the peasants acquit themselves of their working ob-

ligations as members of *kolkhozy* or *sovkhozy*. The same condition is also attached to the sale of horses to rural inhabitants and to granting them permission to build a house or farm buildings. In the final account, therefore, subsidiary farming can be described as just one more form of leverage by which the government hopes to improve the functioning of the Soviet socialist economy. In other words, *plus ça change, plus c'est la même chose.*

> . . . as was noted at the Fourth All-Union Congress of Kolkhozniks, the importance of private subsidiary farming in no way decreases under the conditions of the further development of cooperatives in the country. (Agitator, no. 13, 1988, p. 44)

> Subsidiary farming by industrial enterprises is an essential supplementary method of increasing the yield of agricultural produce. (Agitator, no. 2, 1988, p. 9)

> The highly unsatisfactory state of development of subsidiary farms of the ministry's enterprises in the Yaroslavl province is causing problems. (Agitator, no. 15, 1988, p. 33)

Surge of Political and Labor Enthusiasm (*Obstanovka politicheskogo i trudovogo pod''ema*). A propagandistic cliché designed to create a semblance of enthusiasm among the people and a modicum of popular support for the Soviet government. This long and vague phrase lacks any concrete content. It appears in a multitude of easily modifiable variations that can be split into parts, such as "the surge of great (enormous, high) political (moral, labor) enthusiasm (activity)." These vocabulary variations hardly affect the intended sense of the phrase or the purpose of using it. The talk about "political enthusiasm" (*politichesky pod''em*) is intended to imply popular enthusiasm for whatever the party is doing, and the talk about "labor enthusiasm" (*trudovoy pod''em*) always contains references to symbols of sudden spurts of popular energy in response to this or that political happening.

In fact, neither the party nor its policies are capable of generating any popular enthusiasm. The reason is simple: the Soviet people have from time immemorial been aware that their chances of influencing government policy are nil. This makes them completely indifferent about the social realities and polities of the country. To be sure, a degree of vitality has been injected by Gorbachev's perestroika. However, it would still be inappropriate to speak of any moral or political unity in the country—the path of the party and that of the people have diverged too much for that. At best there can only be a truce or short-lived coexistence between time.

> The Soviet people are preparing for elections by displaying a surge of political and labor enthusiasm . . . . (Agitator, no. 1, 1979, p. 20)

> The election campaign is accompanied by a surge of tremendous political and labor enthusiasm . . . . (Agitator, no. 4, 1979, p. 3)

> The Cuban people celebrated their national holiday in a spirit of high political enthusiasm and surge of fervor. (Izvestiya, 3 January 1982, p. 4)

Take the Grain (*Vzyat' khleb*). To bring in the grain harvest. The word "take" has in this context military overtones, as in "to take an enemy position . . . ." Inherent in the expression "to take the grain" is the sense of nature's hostile resistance to man's attempts to dominate it for his own purposes. The Russians, as it were, do not so much harvest grain as mount an attack on it. Hence the phrase "the frontline in the fight for grain" (*front bor'by za khleb*) for which all available human and transport resources are "mobilized"—another word borrowed from the military sphere. Reports on "battles for grain" are given in almost military-style communiqués in the press, over the radio, and on the late-night television news. It is as if the primary concern of the entire nation is to ensure that the grain harvest is completed successfully without waste and without losses.

This supposedly nationwide task is obstructed, however, not by the recalcitrance of nature but rather by the disorganization of the Soviet economy and inherent malfunctioning of Soviet socialist economic system, which alienates the agricultural laborer from the land he or she farms. The peasant has no interest in such notions as "to take the grain." He prefers instead to spend his time and energy in cultivating the tiny private plot that is his major source of livelihood (cf. subsidiary farming).

Collective and state farms are not capable of guaranteeing good grain storage. Grain has to be transported dozens and sometimes hundreds of kilometers from the location it is harvested to regional silos, with up to a third of its bulk being lost as it is hauled along bumpy, impassable roads—yet another third gets despoiled on its stalks because of the lack of manpower and harvesting equipment.

Although there is grain, it is going to be very "hard" grain. Taking it at a time of harvest failure, which is not uncommon in local agriculture, is no less difficult than in years of good harvest. (Izvestiya, 18 August 1988, p. 1)

It would be naive to think that grain can be taken with enthusiasm alone. The entire chain of agricultural production must be organized in a carefully planned manner. (Pravda, 14 February 1988, p. 2)

Taxes (*Nalogi*). Compulsory payments levied by the government on Soviet citizens and enterprises. Taxes can be direct, based on income and property, or indirect, added to the value of merchandise. Taxation that in the USSR remains an important source of government revenue is rather regressive, with the popular masses bearing most of its burden. It is useless to look for any objective or scientific criteria in the Soviet taxation system. Direct taxes in the Soviet Union are possibly the lowest in the world. Direct taxation, otherwise known as income tax, constitutes only 7.5 percent of national budget revenues. However, income tax is not collected equitably as part of the population is exempt from it.

Exemption from income tax is a kind of social benefit granted to certain groups, such as rural party officials, agricultural experts, chairmen of collective and state farms, Heroes of the Soviet Union and holders of the three orders of Honor. Government employees are taxed regressively; the higher they are in the hierarchy, the lower their taxes are. For the workers, the maximal tax-free salary is 70 rubles a month, while in the military the highest nontaxable salary is five times as high: 350 rubles. City and district executive committees are free to use their discretion in exempting private citizens from taxes. Thus the main burden of direct taxes falls upon ordinary workers, peasants, and government employees.

Surcharges, or indirect taxes, are another matter. Here the government is indiscriminately ruthless in robbing its citizens. In 1988, surcharges accounted for 59.1 percent of the national budget. While direct taxes decrease the average family income by 8.5 percent, surcharges take a 60-percent share. Their largest part is included into the prices of commodities, i.e., it comes from the consumers' pocket.

Retail prices of Soviet goods tend to be much higher than their wholesale prices. Many consumer items carry a markup of 300 to 500 percent. Thus, the Gorky automobile plant sells its Volga sedans to the government for 3,400 rubles each, while in the stores a private citizen pays 16,000 rubles for the same car. Markups of up to two or three times the wholesale price are also imposed on household appliances, refrigerators, washing machines, vacuum cleaners, television sets, and musical instruments. As to the food and consumer goods, production costs determine only the bottom prices, while the top asking price depends entirely on demand and supply. Commercial enterprises have a free hand in setting their prices. However, this only applies to the ordinary citizens. Members of the elite buy everything they need in special stores at discount prices.

However excessive the purchase taxes may be, they constitute only a small portion of the surcharges. The largest part is deducted from production profits, i.e., indirectly taken out of the workers' salaries. The consumer industry contributes 72 percent of its profits to the national budget, while in heavy industry this figure amounts to 90 percent. This accounts for the constant deficits in the government wage fund as well as for the meager investment in housing construction and social welfare.

Therefore, official claims concerning the huge welfare benefits that Soviet citizens receive have absolutely no grounds in reality. All the government-subsidized food and medical services, education, and social welfare return to the people only a tiny fraction of the monies raised by the government through direct and indirect taxation. Moreover, these services are dispensed with remarkable irregularity.

> Direct taxes decrease the average worker's family budget by 8.6 percent, while over 60 percent, according to my calculations, is deduced through surcharges. (Moskovskie novosti, 16 October 1988, p. 8)

> Under socialism taxation represents one of the methods of planned distribution and redistribution of part of the gross national product. (Sovetsky entsiklopedichesky slovar' [Soviet encyclopedic dictionary], Moscow: "Sovetskaya entsiklopedia" Publishers, 1981, p. 867)

> The Supreme Soviet of the USSR has passed a decree on the taxation of cooperatives. (Moskovskie novosti, 25 September 1988, p. 10)

Temporary Difficulties (*Vremennye trudnosti*). A phrase that, while attempting to gloss over, obliquely refers to the chronic shortage of goods and services. Temporary difficulties have been explained at various stages of Soviet history by war and its consequences, unfavorable climatic and other natural conditions, and bad harvests. The attribution of temporary difficulties to defects of the Soviet economic system is taboo. At most, the explanation may refer to the complexities of building communism or to "isolated" cases of incompetence among managers, shortcomings in the work of local authorities, etc.

Although the phrase "temporary difficulties" admits the existence of disruptions in the life of Soviet citizens, it is only to explain them away as merely temporary in nature. After seventy years of Soviet statehood, however, the disruptions keep recurring to the point where they have become an integral and permanent part of Soviet life. No other phenomenon in the USSR compares to temporary difficulties in permanency. Much as the people have become reconciled with time to putting up with constant "difficulties," the adjective "temporary" is commonly scorned as sheer propaganda. This is why temporary difficulties has been gradually replaced by "objective difficulties." (*ob'ektivnye trudnosti*). The latter term is thought to be more successful in concealing the underlying causes of the Soviet people's low standard of living and the shabbiness of their living conditions.

Every developing town encounters temporary difficulties: insufficient construction of new housing and lack of facilities in residential districts, delays in introducing social, cultural and other everyday amenities, and keeping the streets clean. (Agitator, no. 9, 1978, p. 36)

The Soviet Union in the past always successfully overcame temporary difficulties which arose from sudden breaks in the supply of a range of products for the West by establishing its own industries for manufacturing the goods in question. (Pravda, 29 February 1980, p. 3)

Temporary Laborer (*Shabashnik*). A person who hires him- or herself out for temporary seasonal work, usually in construction or agriculture. The term derives for the word "*shabash*," a popular slang word for termination of work, a break in work for rest, or work on the side in one's free time. The word may be derived from the Hebrew *Shabbat*, the Sabbath that in the Jewish tradition refers to the cessation of work and rest.

The word *shabashnik* is hardly ever used in literary Russian or in legal documents. Official documents, including work assignment sheets, employ the term "seasonal" or "temporary" laborer (*sezonny rabotnik* or *vremenny rabotnik*). In exceptional cases, official documents mention "the so-called *shabashnik*." Indeed, for thirty years the *shabashnik* has been a staple topic for the Soviet newspapers. He has been the perpetual "hero" of the Soviet newspaper columns devoted to court proceedings and satirical articles in popular magazines. The press has nothing good to say about the social value of his work and criticizes his high earnings. Naturally, such a high-handed approach both to the term and the reality behind it bears no relation to its real social function.

A single statistic for 1987 suffices to show the extent of the *shabashnik* phenomenon

and its role in the Soviet economy. During that year, 17 percent of all construction laborers through the USSR were *shabashniki*, and they carried out 25 percent of all ongoing construction work. They receive proportionally higher wages than full-time workers (40 to 50 percent more) but their higher earnings are commensurate with their far higher productivity. Typically, *shabashniki*, when engaged on a job, work for twelve or even fourteen hours a day. Contrary to widely held prejudices against them, they are therefore in no way overpaid. In addition, their earnings do not include the usual social benefits like retirement pensions or any kind of unemployment or incapacity allowance. Also, the time spent in *shabashnik* work is not officially recognized as work experience.

This explains exactly why Soviet economic managers prefer *shabashniki* to ordinary workers. The *shabashnik* does not make any demands on living accommodations, canteen facilities, transport to and from work, fuel and vegetable supplies for the winter, or access to rest home or medical facilities. Most important, he does not have to be pushed into working overtime. Neither does he have to be paid any overtime supplements, bonuses or "thirteenth [i.e., extra] month's" salary. The only disadvantage to employing *shabashniki* is that their higher than average pay, by exceeding officially prescribed rates, is theoretically illegal. But unless a plant manager is prepared to break the law to some extent, he will never be able to fulfill his planning targets. And these targets, based not on any scientific criteria but on an obscure precedent (the conditions under which they were once met are considered irrelevant), must be met unconditionally.

Soviet industrial managers are also obliged to work according to the long-discredited *val* (gross output) system. Conceptualizing the value of production in terms of gross output rather than profit produces severe strain as a vicious circle appears where even the quantitative targets, or development aims, become difficult to meet due to a lack of manpower contingent on too many diversified products and new projects that are being undertaken concurrently.

Consequently, economic planners have had no choice but to resort to *shabashniki* as their reserve of labor. These are not, of course, the usual surplus manpower that floods the Soviet labor market and consists of seasonal workers who drift to European Russia from the overpopulated and perennially unemployment-ridden Asian regions. And these are neither seasonal peasant workers who are willing to take on any job in the idle winter months nor graduates hoping to change their professions. True *shabashniki* are highly skilled and distinguished by their work discipline and ability to work in an organized manner.

Shabashniki, indeed, are model workers. Their initiative, dynamism, experience, and improved work methods have provided a precedent for the contractual production system, which, as Soviet economists now hope, will in the end save socialist industry. Indeed, the *shabashnik*'s skills and high productivity would appear to make him a model of workmanship in the public eye. Yet as individuals *shabashniki* remain disliked. With its characteristic suspiciousness, Soviet officialdom perceives the usually proud and independent *shabashnik*, who is unwilling to become an impersonal cog in the wheels of socialist industry, as an alien body in the system. Accordingly, the authorities instill in the public prejudice about the *shabashnik*'s alleged antisocial character: greed, mercenary nature, disregard for the law, and ability to snatch a larger slice of the national pie than is his due by "wangling for himself higher than official rates of payment." Such slurs have their basis in the fear that the *shabashnik*, by virtue of his independent attitude and his ability to deal on an equal footing with his state employers, might set a potentially seditious example for other workers.

To banish from workers' minds any thought of emulating the *shabashnik*'s style, the Soviet propaganda machine states emphatically that *shabashnik* labor methods, effective as they may be, cannot be applied to the proc-

ess of "accelerating" the economy. (The recurrent theme of "acceleration" [cf.] has now become virtually synonymous with economic development.) As an alternative to *shabashnik* activity, therefore, the authorities are promoting the labor contract (*podryad*, cf.). Contractual labor units cannot work efficiently, however, without being provided with all the necessary materials and equipment, and that is something that the Soviet economy is still incapable of providing. Thus, for want of anything more suitable, Soviet industrial managers continue to turn to the hard-working, well-disciplined *shabashniki*, who deliver what is expected from them with or without perestroika.

A temporary worker is called a shabashnik not just because money comes easy to him. The problem rather is that he earns too much relative to the work he performs. (Sotsiologicheskie issledovaniya, no. 6, 1987, p. 90)

In rural areas, after all, temporary construction brigades (whose members are sometimes called shabashniki) accounted for approximately eight percent of all building work. (Agitator, no. 7, 1988, p. 38)

Thaw (*Ottepel'*). A comparatively liberal period in the USSR following the death of Stalin. The word was first used in its metaphorical political sense in a poem composed by N. Zabolotsky and published in the magazine *Novy mir* in October 1953. Zabolotsky's poem was also the first sign of a cultural and political awakening in the Soviet Union of that time. One year later, Ilya Ehrenburg published a short story using the word as its title. Very soon thereafter, the word "thaw" in its new sense gained widespread currency and began to characterize official policy, which changed from that of terror to relative leniency. This policy proved to be inconsistent as it featured a number of contradictory tendencies: both conservatism and liberalism as well as an attempt to reinterpret the past from a critical angle, together with the desire to shield it from a profound ideological revision and moral reappraisal.

The thaw period, the eleven years from

1953 to 1964, consisted of several stages of rise, development, and fall. Its advent was characterized by the great (and often over-optimistic) expectations of democratization and humanization of Soviet society. The prospect of such developments was boosted by the Twentieth Congress of the CPSU, where Khrushchev's sharp attack on Stalin opened up the possibility for criticizing various previously unmentionable aspects of life in the Soviet Union: the wretched plight of the peasantry, the stagnation of agriculture, the backwardness of industry, and the low standard of living. The militarist concepts underlying Soviet foreign policy were revised and the foundations of detente were laid.

These were the headiest days of the thaw. Yet it proceeded with fits and starts. Under pressure from his colleagues, Khrushchev maneuvered, retreated, and then unexpectedly rushed forward, implementing reforms and allowing himself to once more raise the specter of his predecessor at the Twenty-second Congress of the CPSU in 1961. At that congress, he delivered his fiercest attack on Stalin ever. Afterwards, however, the thaw slowed down as Khrushchev began to cultivate his own personality cult with its own distinct features: the insistent advocacy of outmoded dogmas and a spirit of infallibility and arbitrariness. When Khrushchev fell, the thaw fell with him. The new Soviet government headed by Brezhnev regarded the thaw as a dangerous manifestation of "voluntarism," at that time the most terrible of all political crimes.

The "injection" medicine of Khrushchev's thaw had a strong effect: it even worked on those who longed for the days of Stalin. (Moskovskie novosti, no. 36, 4 September 1988, p. 8)

Remember that after 1956, during the "thaw," work in the (labor) colonies was still difficult. (Moskovskie novosti, no. 38, 18 September 1988, p. 11)

In the opinion of Ch. Aitmatov, who took to writing during the thaw period of the fifties, the current and by no means easy task is to carry out a real democratization. (Za rubezhom, no. 22, 1988, p. 12)

Trade Unions (*Profsoyuzy*). Professional organizations that operate within the Soviet government system and are controlled by the Communist party. Shortly after the October Coup, in the period of so-called War Communism (cf.) when the whole economy became state-managed, the already existing trade unions were transformed into tools of the party apparatus. Their programs formally stated that trade unions were to be administrative bodies enabling the working masses to exercise power. In fact, they first became administrative bodies in which the workers did not rule and then, later, administrative bodies that ruled over the workers.

War Communism was born from disaster and terminated in disaster. Industrial enterprises did not work. Due to hunger, many urban dwellers fled to the countryside while the dissatisfaction among the peasants grew into revolt. In the winter of 1920 to 1921, in order to prevent total economic collapse, several Soviet trade union leaders made an attempt, the first and last of its kind in the history of the USSR, to gain for the trade unions control over economic management. The dissatisfaction of trade-union activists with authoritarian and bureaucratic methods of industrial management led to the famous Trade Unions Debate, which reverberated throughout the Soviet Communist party. A demand was voiced to institute "Trade-Union Democracy" that would make trade unions independent of party dictate and state control.

The Bolsheviks considered the program submitted by the trade-union leaders in appropriate, ill-timed, and liable to hinder the transition to the New Economic Policy (cf.) that was then under way. Lenin, together with Trotsky, demanded expulsions or censure for the recalcitrant trade-union leadership. Ignorant of the real situation in the country and naively hoping to resolve the economic crisis by strictly administrative measures, Lenin remained totally bound by the communist frame of reference. He was afraid that if the trade unions (to which 90 percent of the unaffiliated workers belonged) were to appoint industrial managers, the party might become superfluous, even though he was compelled to acknowledge that the workers should be "somehow" defended from the state, lest they refuse to defend that state in adversity.

One of the paradoxes of the Bolshevik Revolution was the fact that it broke out in a predominantly peasant country, which meant that the dictatorship of the proletariat was largely instituted without a proletariat. Furthermore, the outcome of this revolution would prove to be particularly tragic for the proletariat. Although labor representatives tried to keep some balance between centralization from above and spontaneous initiative from the masses below, the Tenth Congress of the Soviet Communist Party in 1921 decided to absorb the trade unions into the administrative apparatus used by the authorities to control the working masses. As Lenin phrased it, the trade unions were to become "a transmission belt from the party to the masses."

The "nationalization" (*ogosudarstvlenie*, Trotsky's term) of the trade unions transformed them into an ordinary agency for the management of industry, thus freeing the party apparatus from the need to perform such administrative functions. Furthermore, by using the transformed trade unions, the CPSU was in a position to exploit the working masses in maximizing industrial production regardless of the human cost.

Trade-union membership presently numbers 142 million (comprising 80 million workers, 40 million technicians, engineers, and white collar workers, and 22 million peasants). Trade unions are organized according to branches of industry and are highly centralized. The highest trade-union body, the All-Union Central Council of Trade Unions (*Vsesoyuzny Tsentral'ny Sovet Professional'nykh Soyuzov*, abbreviated *VTsSPS*) is formally elected at trade-union congresses. There are more than thirty branch-based trade unions in the USSR, with local committees in all industrial enterprises and

institutions. The rights and duties of trade unions are stipulated in their statutes. Their basic statutory tasks are to organize and manage "socialist competition" (*sotsialisticheskoe sorevnovanie*, cf.) and see to it that the national economic plans are fulfilled. Trade unions members are exhorted to work conscientiously, observe state and labor discipline, raise their political consciousness, and attend meetings.

It is claimed that the trade unions observe certain democratic principles. It is true that there are rules for electing administrative bodies and appealing the decisions of lower authorities to higher ones. However, given the fact that the trade unions are completely subordinated to the party bureaucracy, all these regulations are merely exercises in formalism. Soviet trade unions do not have the right to call strikes; if strikes break out, it is *in spite* of the trade unions. (In May 1989 a new law was proposed that would give the labor unions the right to strike.) Soviet citizens cannot opt not to belong to a trade union without finding themselves unemployed or being denied disability allowance or admission to a sanitarium. Neither promotion nor job reassignment is possible without a trade-union recommendation.

The trade unions really have only punitive powers: they can prosecute their members in "comrades' courts" (*tovarishcheskie sudy*), which issue reprimands or reassign a worker to a lower-paying job. Trade unions can also deprive a worker of bonuses (in cooperation with management) and impose disciplinary measures. They carry out communist educational work, e.g., organizing lectures or group visits to the theater and exhibitions. In connection with the limited democratization of society under Gorbachev, trade unions now supervise the observance of labor laws and can raise the issue of improving working conditions, although only on terms that the party finds acceptable.

The trade unions have not yet reformed themselves: they have done little to really defend the interests of their more than 140 million members despite the fact that, in the spirit of the times, in early 1988 they hastened to adopt a resolution about "basic reform." This resolution in fact related not to social problems but to the accelerated introduction of a self-supporting economy. Once again, the workers, their labor, and their way of life were, as often previously, pushed to the periphery of trade-union concern.

According to Lenin, the trade unions are a "school of communism" (*shkola kommunizma*). If communism is equated with social apathy and alienation from the products of one's work, then Lenin was certainly right.

The numerous tasks facing Soviet trade unions require that their organizational and educational activities be further improved. (Komsomol'skaya pravda, December 1982, p. 1)

Already on the seventh day of the Great October Socialist Revolution the young state proclaimed freedom for trade unions. (Agitator, no. 18, 1983, p. 30)

In their defense of the rights and interests of the working people, the Soviet trade unions are invariably supported by the law. (Agitator, no. 18, 1983, p. 31)

Transform into Reality (*Pretvoryat' v zhizn'*, literally "to transform into life"). To implement the plans, decisions, and directives of the Soviet leadership. The word *pretvoryat'* ("to transform") was ordinarily encountered in Russian only in folklore and fairy tales. It was used there to describe the wondrous feats and powers of heroes of Russian epics, who determined the fate of ordinary mortals. The solemn expression "to transform into reality" sounds highfalutin. Soviet propaganda borrowed it from legendary history for one reason only: to impart to decisions of the party an aura of the wondrous or even the wonder-working.

"To transform into reality" is often used in reference to decisions of party congresses and plenums or state plans. Recently, the word has become devalued due to overuse, no longer referring exclusively to "landmark" decisions, but is also employed in reference to ordinary party activities, such as the activities of the republic, municipal, and even district party committees. The expres-

sion "to transform into reality" is supposed to lend a sense of importance to everyday tasks and convince the Soviet citizen that his or her dull, exhausting work is imbued with a higher significance. However, in reality the term is quite vague, and its continuing use stems from the growing indifference of the Soviet people and the failure of the Soviet government to provide for them a life of dignity.

The Soviet people are enthusiastically transforming into reality the decisions of the XXVth Congress of the CPSU. (Chelovek i zakon, no. 4, 1979, p. 5)

The transformation into reality of the edicts of the Party to a significant degree depends on a careful, respectful attitude toward everything created by the labor of the Soviet people. (Kommunist vooruzhennykh sil, no. 16, 1979, p. 28)

The past three years was a period of very active transformation into reality of the edicts of the XXVI Congress of the CPSU, the XXXth Congress of the Communist Party of Azerbaijan and the subsequent Plenums of the CC of the Party. (Vyshka, 16 December 1983, p. 2)

Troika (literally "threesome"). A three-man government body authorized to take extrajudicial punitive measures in absentia. The troika was founded in 1918, when it became apparent that the existing Soviet judiciary was unable to handle the flood of political and criminal cases. The institution survived until 1953.

The troika initially was an organ of territorial and provincial administration. It was comprised of the three top local leaders: the secretary of the party committee as chairman, and the heads of the Soviet executive committee and of the state security department as its two members. This body was granted extensive powers, including the right to sentence defendants to various terms of imprisonment and even to death. Cases were heard by a troika after a brief investigation conducted in the manner typical of that period: confessions were obtained with the help of blackmail and torture and were considered sufficient and often the only basis for the determination of guilt and punishment.

Soviet dictionaries never made any mention of the troika in this sense, citing instead the term's other meanings, such as three horses harnessed abreast, or a three-piece suit. All references to this word's sinister connotations were avoided.

In 1934, the troika emerged on the national and the republic levels. It was founded under the auspices of the All-Russian Central Executive Committee, the state's highest legislative body. According to its decision, the Soviet NKVD (People's Commissariat for Internal Affairs) was to include a Special Tribunal authorized to apply various administrative means, such as exile or imprisonment in corrective labor camps for terms not exceeding five years and deportation from the Soviet Union.

With the intensification of terror, the Special Tribunal had its authority extended to include the right to issue longer sentences, ranging from ten to fifteen and even twenty-five years. Later, prison terms gave way to a more favored verdict: execution by a firing squad. The Special Tribunal troikas were comprised of the deputy people's commissar (later to become deputy minister) of internal affairs, the head of the chief militia authority, and a representative of the given republic. The troikas wielded unlimited powers, unhindered by considerations of legality or state interest. The sole basis for their arbitrary rulings were reports of their informers or anonymous reports, used in compilation of "special files" and "memoranda." The Special Tribunal members would leaf through those documents, have a brief discussion, and then entered a laconic record to the effect that "upon hearing . . . it was resolved . . . .

The term "troika" originated in the Soviet period, while the institution of "Special Tribunal" is a legacy from Emperor Alexander III who, following his father's assassination by revolutionaries, founded an agency under that name. The agency was affiliated with the Ministry of Internal Affairs, and it was empowered to punish "enemies of the mon-

archy" without a trial. However, unlike its Soviet counterpart, it had no right to pronounce death sentences. The Soviet Special Tribunal, on the other hand, made extensive use of this prerogative, sending hundreds of thousands to execution by firing squad. This was possible due to the Special Tribunal's efficiency. In a few hours, it processed scores of cases, with such mind-boggling speed that the stenographers barely had time to enter the names of the condemned in the records.

Verdicts pronounced by the troika were not subject to appeal. They could only be rescinded by the troika itself, although not one sentence is known to have been rescinded. The prisoner would receive his verdict, sign it, and be sent directly to a labor camp or his death. Occasionally, the formal decision would arrive too late, when the prisoner had already been "liquidated." In such a case the investigator or the warden would add to the document a note, "Defendant informed of troika's decision."

The troika was the ideal vehicle of mass terror. It was answerable directly to Stalin. He would receive folders containing short summaries of the charges, examine them for any familiar names, and jot down numbers in the margins, where "one" meant death by firing squad, and "two" a ten-year prison term. These sentences were accepted without question and carried out immediately. All cases unmarked by Stalin were left at the troika's "discretion."

Parallel with the troika's activities, the Soviet government also staged highly publicized public trials, complete with shocking confessions and self-abasement. Yet these were only just a handful of carefully preselected showcases in the otherwise concealed process of the blatant disregard for law and the mass murders carried out by the troikas. This machinery of terror was set in motion by Stalin, the great Kremlin master. Yet responsibility for processing the countless victims lay in the hands of Stalin's apprentices, i.e., party and government functionaries of various ranks. The paradox inherent of these times was that the very same people, after having been the driving force of repression, eventually became its victims.

> While discussing the mechanism of repressions, we must not overlook that sinister organ called the troika. It existed in every republic, territory, and province. (Sotsiologicheskie issledovaniya, no. 3, 1988, p. 89)

> I was tried by the so-called troika. Three well-dressed young men were sitting behind a table placed on a high podium . . . . (Literaturnaya gazeta, no. 34, 24 August 1988, p. 12)

> N. Khrushchev had done a great thing by abolishing the Special Tribunals. (Komsomol'skaya pravda, 21 August 1988, p. 2)

> How many of such troikas were engaged in churning out sentences all over the country? Tens of thousands? Or maybe hundreds of thousands? (Literaturnaya gazeta, no. 34, 24 August 1988, p. 12)

Ulcers (*Yazvy*). A term used in reference to phenomena of capitalist society. The use of this word in Soviet propaganda rests on its metaphorical association with incurable evil or irreparable damage.

The word "ulcers" (usually in the plural) occurs in a relatively small set of standard phrases: "social ulcers" (*sotsial'nye yazvy*), "ulcers and iniquities" (*yazvy i poroki*), "the ulcers of unemployment" (*yazvy bezrabotitsy*), etc.

The use of the word "ulcers" harkens back to the Marxist-Leninist characterization of bourgeois society as incurably ill, rotten to the core, and historically doomed. The term is primarily applied to social ills like prostitution, poverty, unemployment, alcoholism, and drug addiction, but it is also used in reference to various other more general, allegedly systemic aspects of the Free World, as in the phrases "ulcers on the body of capitalism" (*yazvy na tele kapitalizma*), "fetid ulcers" (*yazvy kotorye smerdyat*), and "the ulcers of racist regimes" (*yazvy rasistskikh rezhimov*).

In the propaganda of the first decades of Soviet rule, the word "ulcers" was also applied to social processes in Soviet society that were held to be incompatible with communist ideology and with what was supposed to be the communist way of life. In such cases, the use of the term invariably implied the transitory character of the phenomenon being described.

As long as it was assumed that the USSR was in the process of building socialism, ideology could permit itself to speak of the presence of ulcers in Soviet society by presenting them as a "legacy" (*nasledie*) of the past or of capitalism, which was being kept alive by hostile elements not yet stamped out by the communist dictatorship. However, when the Kremlin leaders proclaimed with fanfare that socialism had already been built, the term "ulcers" was applied exclusively to social realities in noncommunist states. The "final victory of socialism in the USSR," hailed by the Soviet authorities in the 1960s, was proclaimed to have already cleared up all the sores of Soviet society. Although here and there a few blemishes remained, they were said to be "isolated shortcomings" (*otdel'nye nedostatki*) due to the "relics" (*perezhitki*) or "birthmarks" (*rodimye pyatna*) of the capitalist past. The Soviet Union's "healthy" social structure, "advanced" and "efficient" economy, "elevated" interpersonal relationships, alleged decent living standard, and humane morality were said to leave no room for "social ulcers."

However, ulcers were detected and were even diagnosed as "bleeding" when, under perestroika, a reevaluation of achieved social progress was made. It was then determined that in fact socialism had not yet been attained in the USSR. So once again, one now hears about the ulcers of Soviet society: corruption, drug addiction, prostitution, etc. In contrast to the past, however, the diagnosis no longer is optimistic, perhaps because people in the Soviet Union no longer believe that the failings of socialism "that is yet to be attained" can ever be cured.

. . . Our ideological opponents attempt to conceal exploitation and chronic unemployment, inhumanity and poverty-all of these ulcers on the capitalist organism which leave millions of people with no choice but to live off crime. (Voprosy filosofii, no. 11, 1978, p. 7)

They are incapable of justifying or concealing the terror, corruption, and other ulcers on the body of capitalism which grow more fetid each year. (Literaturnaya gazeta, 8 July 1981, p. 6)

Western television tries in every way possible to conceal or obscure ulcers and iniquities which are necessary features of the world ruled by capital. (Komsomol'skaya pravda, 27 October 1983, p. 2)

Unemployment (*Bezrabotitsa*). Involuntary idleness, presented by Soviet sociologists as a social phenomenon existing solely in capitalist societies, but which actually exists in the Soviet Union as well. The term "unemployment" is associated with an entire complex of conditions supposedly distinctive to imperialism: insecurity, homelessness, denial of rights, humiliation, and callous attitudes to those who are employed. Soviet press reports, as well as statistical and reference publications, omit any mention of "capitalist" unemployment allowances, their value, or their statutory duration. Consequently, Soviet readers have no way of knowing that the purchasing power of unemployment allowances in the West may well exceed that of the average salary in the USSR. Not knowing this, they readily perceive the unemployed in the capitalist world as helpless and defenseless unfortunates, abandoned to their fate.

Unemployment in the USSR can be declared nonexistent because it is never referred to as such. However one does find phrases like "inoccupation" (*nezanyatost'*), "labor inassignment" (*netrudoustroennost'*), "insufficient level of occupation" (*nedostatochny uroven' zanyatosti*), "nonexploitation of labor reserves" (*neispol'zovanie trudovykh rezervov*), and "reserves of unoccupied manpower" (*rezervy nezanyatoy rabochey sily*).

Athough this phenomenon is verbally camouflaged, its scale is large. For instance, at the March 1965 Plenum of the Central Committee of the CPSU, it was announced that in nonindustrial towns and settlements as many as 16 percent of employable males and 25 percent of employable females were "unoccupied." It should be noted that Gorbachev's economic reforms propose by 1990 to remove from the system of government production twenty to twenty-five million workers, which to a Western observer certainly sounds like unemployment.

The double standard in the usage of the term "unemployment" serves an ideological function: to make the Soviet people believe that unemployment is an unalterable feature of the "world of capitalist exploitation" but cannot and will not appear in any form in a communist country. The euphemisms for unemployment mentioned above are employed to convey the impression that the phenomena they refer to are transient, unimportant, and attributable to minor managerial failures. They could not possibly affect the essence of communism. Hence the low priority that the Soviet press assigns to coverage of the phenomena in question. The substitute terms for unemployment are used rather sparingly. They tend to appear in reports or speeches of party leaders and in other restricted communications not intended for the public at large. The only exception to this rule occurs during periods of personnel change in the top leadership. During such periods, the defeated leaders are as a rule blamed for economic mismanagement. To add substance to such accusations, unemployment, under its code names, may be discussed.

The term "unemployment" is likewise not applied to "friendly" socialist or developing countries. If, however, any such country attempts to shake off Soviet domination and defiantly pursue independent policies, unemployment is sure to appear there. Thus, for instance, as soon as relationships between the USSR and Yugoslavia began to sour, a considerable amount of reporting of mass unemployment in the latter country found its way into the Soviet press. Yet as soon as the relationship improved, Soviet readers were relieved of accounts of unemployment in Yugoslavia and might therefore presume it had disappeared there. Something similar happened with regard to China, where countless millions were reported by the Soviet press as being unemployed, but only after the Sino-Soviet rift appeared.

In characterizing Soviet society, the General Secretary of the CC of the CPSU, L. I. Brezhnev, noted that we have created a society not subject to the domination of monopolistic oligarchies, free of the fear of economic crises, of unemployment, and of other social cataclysms. (Kommunist, no. 10, 1976, p. 12)

The guarantee of full employment to the population, the absence of unemployment is a great achievement of socialism, a tremendous advantage of our country over capitalist society. (Agitator, no. 8, 1988, p. 12)

In late 1930 the last unemployed were taken off the Moscow and Leningrad labor exchanges. . . . For 60 years now we have not known unemployment, and there is no excuse for it to return. (Trud, 28 January 1988, p. 1)

Unity (*Splochennost'*). The community of interest that purportedly characterizes the relations between the Soviet people and the party. The word is also used in reference to cooperation between socialist states, parties, or groups. In its first meaning, "unity" is often combined with synonyms such as "*edinstvo*," unity, or "*edinodushie*," unanimity. In its second meaning, "unity" frequently appears with modifiers: "fraternal unity" (*bratskaya splochennost'*), "fighting unity" (*boevaya splochennost'*), "party unity" (*partiynaya splochennost'*), "international unity" (*internatsional'naya splochennost'*), and "class unity" (*klassovaya splochennost'*). Used with special frequency is the phrase "monolithic unity" (*monolitnaya splochennost'*).

"Unity" is often used together with nearsynonyms to emphasize the idea of community and cohesion: "solidarity and unity" (*edinstvo i splochennost'*), "unanimity and unity" (*edinodushie i splochennost'*).

Words of the same root as "unity" are widely used to form such Soviet clichés as "the united collective" (*splochenny kollektiv*) and "to unite their ranks" (*splotit' svoi ryady*).

We shall oppose the hostile maneuvers of imperialism with our boundless devotion to the ideals of Communism, and with the unyielding unity of the Soviet people behind the Party. (Pravda, 26 February 1981, p. 2)

The patriotism of the Soviet people and their unity with the Leninist Party are reliable guarantees that the resolutions of the XXVI Congress of the Communist Party of the Soviet

Union will be successfully implemented. (Izvestiya, 27 February 1981, p. 2)

The Congress called for the unity of all the progressive democratic forces of Israel in the face of the threat of Fascism. (Pravda, 16 February 1981, p. 4)

Unprecedented (*Nebyvaly*). A term of praise that can be applied to almost any aspect of Soviet life. In the Russian language, the word "unprecedented" has been used in its present sense only since 1917. Its usage was prompted by the need to surround the Communist Revolution with a mythical aura, to present it as an event without parallel in the history of the world. This is why any public activity, national policy, economic project, state plan, school reform, artistic creation— in short, any event—is declared unprecedented as long as it can in some way be construed as having a connection, however tenuous, with the Bolshevik Revolution.

An educated Russian is likely to associate this word with Russian folklore. In this way, party activities are linked with the heroic epics (*byliny*) of early Russian literature in which the mythic warriors (*bogatyri*) had unprecedented (although the word is not used explicitly, the idea is evident) physical prowess, resourcefulness, and courage. Thus every minor party-inspired undertaking that is called unprecedented is associated with epic qualities.

Other word with similar evocative qualities are "wondrous" (*udivitel'ny*), "marvelous" (*chudesny*), and "fabulous" (*skazochny*). These yield phrases like "wondrous upsurge," "marvelous successes," and "fabulous power," all of which have folklore and epic connotations.

The Communist Party and the Soviet state have created favorable and historically unprecedented social conditions for the development of education and culture of the peoples of the union and autonomous republics. (Agitator, no. 11, 1978, p. 42)

. . . in 1956 due to the development of virgin lands, the province delivered grain to the state in quantities unprecedented for that time . . . . (Izvestiya, 16 March 1979)

The speakers emphasize that the Congress is taking place in a situation of unprecedented exacerbation of the international situation. (Izvestiya, 9 December 1983, p. 4)

Upbringing, Soviet (*Sovetskoe vospitanie*). The transmission of the sociohistorical experience of communism to new generations with the aim of instilling in them communist values and aspirations. Soviet upbringing has two goals. The educational goal is to transmit to the future citizens the knowledge and skills needed by the state. The indoctrination goal is to impart knowledge of and devotion to communist principles. The clear priority assigned to the latter was stressed by Lenin: "In the entire process of bringing up, educating, and instructing contemporary youth it is imperative to concentrate on indoctrinating them with Communist morals" (V. I. Lenin, *Sochineniya* [Works], 4th ed., vol. 31, Izd-vo politicheskoy literatury, 1950, p. 266).

There is an inconsistency in the way Soviet upbringing is handled. On the one hand, its spiritual content is deliberately limited to what is considered required for instilling communist ideals; on the other hand, its forms of instruction (intellectual, manual, vocational, and physical) are very wide, perhaps wider than necessary. The foundations of this inconsistency can be traced back to the theories of Nadezhda Krupskaya (wife and comrade of Lenin), and Anton Makarenko (famous pedagogue who worked with homeless children). They both believed that training in skills without ideological upbringing is a means without an end, while ideological upbringing without modern training in skills is an end devoid of the means for its fulfillment.

The process as well as the content of Soviet upbringing are determined in accordance with political ideology. The curriculum, instructional methods, and structuring of the learning process are all designed in conformity with the tenets of the communist creed. Soviet teachers conform to this system by employing various methods, such as persuasion, encouragement, punishment, and a highly structured routine of work and rest. Illustrative of values stressed in Soviet upbringing is the importance of "life" education in the collective via the collective and for the collective. Soviet upbringing is also viewed as serving the "building of communism" (*postroenie kommunizma*). In the CPSU's program, this purpose is defined as the education of a "new person" who will be endowed with "spiritual richness, moral purity, and physical perfection" (*Programma KPSS* [Program of the CPSU], Moscow: Izd-vo politicheskoy literatury, 1956).

The Soviet educational system reflects a great disparity between instruction and upbringing. For example, scientific curricula are not compatible with the goals of the latter. Moral ideals espoused in the schools are remote from such fundamental realities of Soviet life as the low standard of living and the narrow range of civil liberties and permitted cultural expression. The hardships of everyday life give rise to feelings and views widely divergent from those which Soviet upbringing strives to mold. There is an attempt to bridge this gap by a manipulation of the educational process in such a way that curricular content is subordinated to the dictates of Marxist ideology and a spirit of devotion and obedience to authorities is cultivated. At least partially, this goal is achieved, especially since the influence of the school is reinforced by the influence of other socializing agencies that also seek to suppress mental traits and character dispositions that deviate from the professed "moral code" of Soviet society.

Soviet upbringing is hardly confined to schools, though these play a key role in the process. Numerous institutions outside the schools (*vneshkol'nye uchrezhdeniya*) are also involved in Soviet upbringing, such as Pioneer and Komsomol organizations, youth camps, "children's rooms" in police stations, and houses of culture. In a broad sense, Soviet upbringing is promoted by all political, cultural, and social institutions, including literature, the arts, the mass media, and labor organizations. Numerous educational and entertainment institutions (*kul'turnopros-vetitel'nye uchrezhdeniya*), such as clubs, libraries, and museums systematically contribute to the indoctrination of the adult population in the spirit of Soviet values.

Family upbringing must comply with the demands of Soviet upbringing. Parents ignoring these demands are liable to severe punishment, which may include the loss of parental rights and forced surrender of their children into the custody of more "loyal" families.

Regardless of the institutional auspices under which it is pursued, Soviet upbringing is always directed and controlled by the party. Accordingly, it seeks to prevent undesirable influences from affecting the minds of both its charges and of those in charge. The ultimate concern of Soviet upbringing is to instill its own version of the truth in the minds of Soviet citizens, particularly of the future citizens.

The Soviets pay particular attention to the question of the internationalist, ideological-political, labor, and moral upbringing of juveniles and youths. (Izvestiya, 13 October 1983, p. 3)

The most important task of upbringing is the formation of a working person. (Pravda, 15 October 1983, p. 1)

Internationalist education is one of the most effective forms of Communist upbringing. (Agitator, no. 6, 1983, p. 58)

V

Vanguard (*Avangard*). A party, social class, union, or organization that supports a communist regime and is considered a force for social progress. The term was originally borrowed from military usage. When used in political and ideological contexts, it is meant to stress the idea of "struggle" for "the bright future of mankind" (*svetloe budushchee cheloveschestva*), an "accelerated labor pace" (*udarny trud*), "socialist competition" (*sotsialisticheskoe sorevnovanie*), or the like. In such usages, it evokes associations with the never-ceasing class struggle in which the proletariat (and its communist vanguard) must fight against numerous enemies, both external (like "the world bourgeoisie," fascism, right and left revisionism, Trotskyism, Maoism, Zionism, etc.) and internal (like the agents, both covert and overt, of the above enemies operating in Soviet society). The attribution or denial of vanguard status to various social groups at various stages of the development of Soviet society is determined exclusively by the instructions of the CPSU. The CPSU itself is the prototypic vanguard. The vanguard of the Soviet working class, of the proletariat of the world, and of all "mankind." In its capacity as a vanguard movement, it takes an active part in various vanguard initiatives, like the attempt to cultivate the virgin lands (*osvoenie tseliny*), various pioneering enterprises (*pochiny*), or communist constructions (*stroyki kommunizma*). The stress on the Communist party as a vanguard is intended to remind the Soviet people that the CPSU remains their spiritual guide and political tutor. The existence of this vanguard is supposed to inspire the Soviet People to self-sacrificial efforts and help them not only to be satisfied with the present, but also to be confident about the future.

In turn, the Soviet working class is hailed (according to Marxist-Leninist doctrine) as the vanguard of the progressive forces of the world. In some contexts, all the workers of the Soviet Union are presented as the vanguard of the less "class-conscious" remainder of humanity. The Komsomol is also referred to as a vanguard. Further, sometimes the role of the vanguard in the building of communism is assigned to various industrial enterprises, collective farms, "accelerated Komsomol construction" projects (*udarnye Komsomol'skie stroyki*), "communist labor brigades," etc. Thus, it is apparent that any group of people or any institution can be referred to this way whenever it suits Soviet aims.

Such social or national groups as the World Peace Council, the International Youth League, Palestinian terrorist organizations, and the Sandinistas of Nicaragua are credited with being vanguards because of their pro-Soviet orientation. As soon as any such group or institution frees itself from Soviet tutelage, it ceases to be a vanguard. Practical matters of Soviet interest also influence which groups receive vanguard status.

A good example of the shifting criteria for recognition as a vanguard is the treatment of Iraqi political movements during the past fifteen years. At the end of the 1970s, the Ba'ath Party of Iraq was referred to as "the vanguard of the Arab nations." The sole basis for such a distinction was Baghdad's adherence to Moscow's line. In fact, the Communist Party of Iraq (which by Soviet ideological criteria *should* have been hailed as a vanguard) had been suppressed and driven underground by the Iraqi authorities. Ideological considerations came to the fore only when Iraq tried to break free of Kremlin influence; then Moscow suddenly recalled (at the Twenty-sixth Congress of the CPSU in 1980) that it was the Communist

Party of Iraq, and no longer the Ba'ath Party, that was the vanguard of the Arab working masses. Similarly, when Beijing challenged Soviet hegemony in the International Communist movement, the Chinese Communist Party, along with all other communist parties that gave it their support, were deprived of their vanguard status by the Soviet authorities. The American working class long ago fell from the vanguard when it remained indifferent to the attractions of Bolshevism.

The criteria for determining what is and what is not a vanguard are therefore totally arbitrary, but arbitrariness of standards in all regards has always been an essential trait of totalitarianism.

In [Socialist] competition the vanguard is always made up of Communists, advanced workers, and innovators in production. (Kommunist, no. 10, 1979, p. 45)

Like a pioneer in the vanguard the writer is the living conscience of society. (Literaturnaya gazeta, 8 July 1984, p. 15)

. . . we . . . are in the vanguard of the struggle of mankind against evil, violence, and exploitation. (Ibid.)

Vanguard Trooper (*Zastrel'shchik*). A person who is described by official propaganda as active, energetic, and resourceful, i.e., as embodying qualities useful to the authorities. Although the word (which literally means the bowman who is first to shoot his arrows) is archaic, it accurately reflects the Marxist-Leninist notion of history as a constant and uninterrupted struggle in which any new initiative or achievement is a "shot" at the enemy.

In the same vein, anything undesirable for the Soviet rulers is conceived of as a "blow" against socialism. Since those who deliver these "blows" can also be referred to as vanguard troopers (of class, psychological, or ideological warfare), the term can carry negative as well as positive connotations. It has a positive connotation when used in reference to the Soviet Union and countries of the communist camp, as in "vanguard troopers of socialist competition" (*zastrel'shchiki*

sorevnovaniya) or "vanguard troopers of progressive methods" (*zastrel'shchiki peredovogo opyta*), and a negative one when it refers to the West, as in "vanguard troopers of the arms race" (*zastrel'shchiki gonki vooruzheniya*) or "vanguard troopers of ideological subversion" (*zastrel'shchiki ideologicheskikh diversy*).

The countries of South-East Asia were fated to become the vanguard troopers in the postwar rise of the national-liberation movement. (B. Sinitsyn, Yugo-Vostochnaya Aziya: puti natsional'nogo vozrozhdeniya [South-East Asia: the path of national rebirth] Moscow: "Znanie" Publishers, 1978, p. 3)

The people are accustomed to regard us, their representatives, as vanguard troopers who introduce into production progressive labor methods, and as leaders in Socialist competition. (Agitator, no. 2, 1979, p. 38)

The Communists acted . . . as vanguard troopers in the introduction of strict order, organization, and discipline. (Partiynaya zhizn', no. 19, 1979, p. 52)

Veteran (*Veteran*). An official, worker, or party functionary with a long record of service, or a former soldier who fought in the war. All veterans are considered by the authorities to be stalwart supporters of the regime. Many Soviet veterans were awarded government honors, but their past services were soon forgotten and in their daily lives they encounter the same difficulties and deprivations as the vast majority of the Soviet population.

In 1978, thirty-three years after the end of World War II, the title of honor "Veteran of the Great Patriotic War" (*Veteran Velikoy Otechestvennoy Voiny*) was instituted. Similarly, in 1980, when a large proportion of those who might have qualified were no longer alive, there was finally enacted a "resolution for improving the material and living conditions of war veterans and invalids." This resolution conferred on them a number of benefits: the right to one free trip a year on the railroad, priority for admission to a rest home or sanitarium, and a 50 percent reduction in income tax. The Soviet government compensated for its long neglect of the soldiers to whom it owed its survival by granting them a few insubstantial benefits and handouts, along with tokens of appreciation and certificates of merit.

The title "Veteran of Labor" (*veteran truda*) is bestowed upon people who have worked in an industrial enterprise or an office for more than twenty years. In contrast to "War Veterans," these people do not enjoy any particular privileges. All the incentives they receive are symbolic. For example, their names appear from time to time on "Boards of Honor" (*doski pocheta*). When they retire, all they receive are words of gratitude and, in rare cases, a one-time allowance (*edinovremennoe posobie*).

"Party veterans" (*veterany partii*), however, occupy a special niche in Soviet society. These are party functionaries who have served the party faithfully for many decades and survived the purges and the terror. Official propaganda describes them as "the nation's invaluable asset" (*bestsenny fond naroda*) and "Lenin's cohorts" (*Leninskaya gvardiya*). They are granted special benefits: access to restricted shops several times a year (usually before national holidays) where they can buy scarce goods (*defitsitnye produkty*); treatment at special health care clinics; free admission twice a year to a sanitarium; pensions two to three times higher than the standard, etc.

In consequence of the benefits they receive, it is not surprising that many of these "party veterans" publicly praise the Soviet regime on radio and television and also carry out agitation work (*agitatsionnaya rabota*) among the people.

> The meeting of party and labor veterans with the leaders of the CPSU was held in a warm and comradely atmosphere. (Agitator, no. 18, 1983, p. 2)

> Meetings are regularly held between students and veterans who are heroes of the battles of the Great Patriotic War. (Agitator, 29 November 1983, p. 2)

> The Ministry of Defense of the USSR wished veterans of the Soviet armed forces good health,

happiness, and continuing success in their efforts to strengthen the military might of our beloved Motherland. (Vyshka, 16 December 1983, p. 2)

Vigilance (*Bditel'nost'*). Ability to recognize enemies of the Soviet order and to halt their activity. The need for vigilance is predicated on the concept of the historical development of human society as proceeding via class conflicts, and it stems from the division of the world into two opposing camps: that of imperialism and that of communism.

The term "vigilance" has been subject to some evolution parallel to the evolution of Soviet statehood. In the early years of the state, vigilance was used to refer to the ability to recognize and unmask class enemies, such as the bourgeoisie (*burzhuaziya*) or former landed gentry (*dvoryanstvo*). The then-current slogan, "A good Communist should be a good 'Chekist,'" indicates that vigilance was considered to be a crucial component of political consciousness.

During the period of the first Soviet Five Year Plans (the 1920s and 1930s), which was marked by mass terror, vigilance was referred to as a "weapon" in the struggle against "remnants of hostile elements" within the party. Stalin used vigilance as a tool to direct suspicion against his former associates and aids by branding them as "Trotskyites," "Bukharinites," "Zinovievites," etc., who were declared to be "enemies of the people," (cf. "enemy of the people") wreckers and traitors of the fatherland (*vragi naroda, vrediteli, izmenniki rodiny*), and then executed. The statutes of the CPSU emphasized vigilance as a supreme communist virtue, the "loss" of which merited expulsion from the party. The Soviet constitution of 1936 went so far as to define the loss of vigilance as a crime against the state, thus making vigilance not only a civic virtue, but also a civic duty.

The model of vigilance in the Soviet Union is the CPSU. All its past and present activities are described and interpreted as manifestations of vigilance directed against clever and insidious "enemies" of communism.

Lenin is said to have been inspired by vigilance (that is, by concern for preserving the unity of the party) when he split the social-democratic movement in Russia and severed his Bolshevik faction from it. Vigilance has been a handy means of preventing and suppressing all dissent within the party. The struggle of the party against "opportunism" and "revisionism" is also attributed to vigilance.

With time, the term "vigilance" began to be used with such qualifiers as "revolutionary" and "proletarian" (*revolyutsionnaya bditel'nost', proletarskaya bditel'nost'*). The elaborate terminology served to encourage fabricated political accusations. The term "vigilance" included the ability to detect and unmask noncommunist outlooks, deviations from the prescribed Soviet way of life, or interest in foreign culture and art—in other words, all weaknesses that are supposed to be capable of leading "insufficiently conscious" Soviet citizens onto the path of politically subversive antistate activity and bourgeois morality.

Although constant vigilance and the denunciation of wrongdoers are fundamental prerogatives of the KGB, the security apparatus alone cannot ensure the loyalty and allegiance of all the people. Since the long arm of the KGB cannot in every instance reach out to every Soviet citizen, each Soviet citizen, appropriately imbued with vigilance, is expected to reach out to the KGB by voluntarily serving as an informer.

The nationwide practice of informing on others is presented as an important form of communist vigilance, which helps Soviet society rid itself of alien elements. The demand for vigilance is ubiquitous: at the workplace, Soviet citizens are urged to uncover sabotage and embezzlement; in daily life, they are urged to look out for possible illegal or questionable sources of income (*netrudovye dokhody*) of their neighbors, acquaintances, and relatives; in school, they are urged not only to monitor the instructional program, but also the attitudes of teachers and pupils.

In the early 1980s, there was a broad call to supplement vigilance in regard to others

with vigilance in regard to oneself (*samobditel'nost*) and self-incrimination (*samodonositel'stvo*). This idea was first implemented by the party apparatus in Azerbaijan, where the Center for the Study of Social Opinion and Sociological Research of the Communist Party of this republic turned "to Communist Party members, Komsomol members, and all working people" with the call for informing party organs about any cases of embezzlement of socialist property or of bribe-taking, speculation, theft of private property, or other corrupt practices in which they were involved (*Bakinsky rabochy*, 13 August 1981, p. 1).

By virtue of inculcating into the members of society suspicion and distrust, and by virtue of encouraging hypocrisy and mendacity, universal vigilance creates a psychological atmosphere conducive to repression. In recent years, the authorities have been more cautious and circumspect in the recourse to force, but the machinery of terror—the KGB and the CPSU as the source of power—has been left intact. If at any time in the future the Soviet leadership considers it advisable to start operating this machine at full capacity, the victims of vigilance could again be numbered in the millions.

> It is particularly important . . . to display revolutionary vigilance to put . . . decisive resistance to anti-socialist forces. (Izvestiya, 23 August 1981, p. 1)

> We entered the year 1982 continuing to increase the defensive might of socialism and continuing to increase our vigilance. (Izvestiya, 3 January 1982, p. 4)

> The course of developments in the world arena obliges everyone to display an even higher degree of responsibility, discipline, and vigilance than before. (Pravda, 1 December 1983, p. 1)

Visible (*Zrimy*). An attribute intended to indicate that specific phenomena of Soviet life are to be accepted as significant and beyond question, and that these phenomena are seen by the authorities even though not necessarily by others. This term has acquired usefulness in the contemporary Soviet lexicon by the substitution of the literal meaning of "visible," as accessible to vision, for the figurative meaning: "obvious" or "self-evident." In the latter sense "visible" is used in such phrases as "visible features" (*zrimye cherty*), "visible landmarks" (*zrimye vekhi*), (cf. "landmark") "visible signs" (*zrimye primety*), "visible contribution" (*zrimy vklad*), "visible evidence" (*zrimoe svidetel'stvo*), or "visible connection" (*zrimaya svyaz'*). The term is often employed in highly self-congratulatory propaganda messages commending the communist leadership or extolling some aspect of Soviet reality.

Along with similar adjectives, such as "tangible" (*osyazaemy*) and "weighty" (*vesomy*), "visible" is used to buttress the myths of Soviet achievement and of the inevitability of communism. However, as the onset of the classless society is repeatedly postponed, the expression "visible features of communism" (*zrimye cherty kommunizma*) has lost credibility.

In its attempts to refurbish the legend of communism still to come, Soviet ideology has invented the term "developed socialism" (*razvity sotsializm*), later to be called "mature socialism" (*zrely sotsializm*), which had not been foreseen in classic Leninist doctrine. Accordingly, the use of the expression "visible features of communism" or its vaguer variant, "visible features of the new [era]" (*zrimye cherty novogo*), became more current as "communism within the lifetime of the present generation" discredited itself.

The adverb "visibly" (*zrimo*) is also widely used, for example, "visibly increased political activity." The more neutral "clearly" (*naglyadno*) and the more emphatic "with ones's own eyes" (*voochiyu*) have essentially the same meaning.

All these terms, "visible," "visibly," "with one's own eyes," and "clearly," function in the Soviet vocabulary as signals to indicate that the people do not have the right to dispute what is officially asserted, in defiance of nearly universal popular disbelief.

The glorious epic of the virgin lands project, that is already heralding the future, will never be forgotten and will always live in the memory of the people as a visible landmark of the second half of the twentieth century. (Krasnaya zvezda, 6 March 1979)

The Tenth Five Year Plan left visible traces on the land in Soviet Estonia. (Pravda, 1 February 1981, p. 2)

More than two hundred thousand KMAZ diesel vehicles working on the highways and construction sites are visible evidence of this. (Pravda, 17 February 1981, p. 1)

Voyage (*Voyazh*). A mission undertaken by a political leader or private individual for purposes considered irreconcilable with Soviet interests or displeasing to the Soviet rulers. The term "voyage" has an ironic connotation that highlights the allegedly dubious or dishonest purpose of the mission.

Soviet officials never undertake voyages; their travels are described by neutral terms such as "stay" (*prebyvanie*), or, alternatively, as visits (*vizity*), a term that is intended to convey a sense of the official importance of their mission.

The word "voyager" (*voyazher*) also has a derogatory connotation. It is applied to people whom the USSR wishes to brand as being involved in unacceptable activities or representing unacceptable values.

The stormy Mister Den, as American newspapers have nicknamed Den Xiao Ping, the Deputy of the State Council of the People's Republic of China, did not stint himself in the threats he made toward Vietnam during his voyage to the United States. (Mezhdunarodnaya zhizn', no. 4, 1979, p. 104)

The voyage of the American Vice-President (to the countries of Northern Europe) should be seen first and foremost as a prelude to the coming session . . . . (Izvestiya, 2 April 1979)

The Agency [i.e., the CIA] also notes the activity stirred up among various groupings hostile to Nicaragua connected with the voyage of Kissinger's team. (Izvestiya, 13 October 1983, p. 4)

Vyezdnoy/Vyezdnye (plural). Literally, "one who can exit"), a person officially authorized to travel abroad. In order to obtain this rare privilege a Soviet citizen must convince the authorities first, that he will come back, second, that he will not disclose state secrets, and third, that he will represent his country abroad with dignity and will not compromise it through immortal conduct.

Free foreign travel was abolished in Russia soon after the Revolution. During the brief period of the New Economic Policy (cf.), the Soviet borders became somewhat permeable, and it was possible to exit by paying the government the 400 ruble travel tax (an enormous sum in those times).

In 1925, a special statute was passed stipulating that "valid" reasons were required for foreign travel. The interpretation of these reasons was so restrictive and so entangled in a web of secret instructions that the "statute" supposed to permit foreign travel effectively banned it. Hence passage through the "gate" in the iron curtain became the exclusive privilege of those who demonstrated unwavering loyalty to the Soviet regime.

In the post-Stalin period (1959), the government enacted a new "exit statute," which was more liberal. From this time a Soviet citizen could go abroad not only on business trips, but also as a member of a tourist group. Ten years later it became possible to leave the USSR for temporary or permanent residence abroad in order to visit relatives or to be reunited with one's family. Still, "valid reasons" remained the necessary prerequisite. Such "reasons" did not necessarily need to be the real motives of travelling, but they needed to be recognized as valid by the authorities.

The total subjectivity of this stipulation gave the Soviet government unlimited scope for arbitrariness. For instance, foreign travel could be refused on the vague grounds of "security," without any further explanations. People who became such "refuseniks" lost opportunities for social mobility and were viewed as unfit for prestigious appointments and promotions. On the other hand, those classified as *vyezdnye* rapidly advanced up the social ladder and were granted various honors, degrees, titles, and awards. As a result, the term *"vyezdnoy"* was divested of its literal meaning and became an important indicator of social status.

In 1973, the Soviet Union ratified the International Convention on Human Rights, which specifically ruled that "Everyone has the right to leave any country, including his own." Still, for many years thereafter the Soviet government continued to deny its citizens this inalienable right. Along with that, it continued to divide its citizenry into the majority, for which the border remained an impassable wall, and the elite "nomenklatura" (cf.), which had the whole world at its disposal.

This situation remained unchanged until the period of perestroika. The new Soviet leadership, in its quest for popularity, began to reconsider many of the thus far inviolable privileges enjoyed by the chosen few. Its reforms also affected the *vyezdnoy* phenomenon. The procedure for obtaining permission to go abroad was relaxed and simplified. Thus, in order to seek permission to visit a foreign relative or friend, it became sufficient to submit an invitation. Yet the existence of relatives or friends abroad remained the necessary condition. Thus, the Soviet citizen was now free to travel anywhere . . . but still for "valid reasons" only. Moreover, freedom of movement is still hemmed in by the "considerations of state security" clause.

The Soviet concept and practice of secrecy still hamper the process of democratization. Since the state won't let out its secrets, and the citizens are enjoined to guard them zealously, an ordinary person is powerless to appeal such a decision worded as "foreign travel considered inexpedient." Under glasnost, the mouths of citizens may be open, but the ears of officialdom are not. Even the "Universal Declaration of Human Rights" is of no avail, for in the Soviet Union it is far from universal.

"Vladimir Alekseevich, sorry for being so personal, but are you vyezdnoy?" "Well, I often travel on business trips, so you might say I am vyezdnoy. Why, aren't you?" (Ogonek, no. 5, January 1989, p. 7)

War Communism (*Voenny kommunizm*). A formula for the Soviet policy of terror resorted to during the years 1917 – 20. In the Soviet Union, War Communism is presented as a temporary measure, dictated by the difficult conditions of the war period, and indispensable for providing for the defense of the country, effecting mass mobilization of the population, and supplying it with food. In reality, War Communism was devised as an attempt to by-pass various stages of social development (in contradiction to Marxist teachings) and to rapidly bring society to the stage of communism, i.e., to a classless system of production and distribution. According to the tenets of War Communism, the countryside had to hand over its grain to the city on a quota basis (via forced requisitioning). This grain was supposed to be apportioned among the workers and their vanguard (*avangard*), "the party," according to family size. All other classes and strata of society were left with the choice of either providing for themselves or starving to death.

The peasants, however, refused to give up their grain for the sake of "the bright future," and in May 1918 the government issued a decree on "grain conscription" (in addition to military conscription). This decree marked the beginning of War Communism as it opened the main front of the civil war — against the peasants, who suffered the onslaught of a 55,000-man army of supply units (*prodotryady*). The villagers, who were either well-disposed or adopting a wait-and-see attitude toward the Communist Revolution, were thus totally antagonized. They had no desire to starve, suffer the arbitrariness of the communists, or consent to the trampling of their rights. As a result, peasant revolts flared up throughout the country.

The first wave of peasant revolts swept through the central districts near Moscow at the very beginning of 1918. Subsequently, they spread to the Cossack provinces of the Don and the Transcaucasus. In 1919, the revolts spilled over into Ukraine and in 1920 reached Siberia. The extent, desperation, and strength of this popular resistance took the communists by surprise. They presumed the peasant attacks against them must have stemmed from a "misunderstanding" because "a better government than that of the Soviets could not be imagined."

But the peasants did imagine a better government: one without Bolsheviks, requisitions of produce, and terror. Not only did the uprisings spread more and more, their character changed from that of spontaneous outbursts to an organized struggle, waged by real armies. War is war, and hence the communist dictatorship struck at the peasants with full force. The "vengeful sword" of the dictatorship, the Extraordinary Commission (*Cheka*) was diverted from the struggle against counterrevolution to the struggle against the popular masses, which had supported the revolution. After the defeat of the Whites in 1920, the regular army also was brought into the fight against the peasants.

The attempt to totally break the resistance of the peasants failed, however, and they continued to evade the all-embracing grasp of the dictatorship. As before, grain had to be searched and requisitioned by forcibly entering the cellars, ploughing up vegetable patches, and relying on threats and reprisals, such as shooting the recalcitrant and taking hostages. Thus War Communism shaped the regime to come. The most outstanding feature of this regime was to be not so much the ruthlessness and cruelty of its laws, but the extent to which its own laws were flouted and disregarded.

The regime banished all classes from the

ranks of society, not even excepting the supposedly "ruling" class, the workers. All were deprived of their independent function in society and permitted to survive only to the extent to which they could be of use to the dictatorship. The party oppressed the people, driving them out of active politics and replacing the state apparatus with its own agencies. All those outside the party who refused to serve it were exterminated. All opposition, including that by the communists themselves, was totally suppressed and outlawed. The world was divided into antagonistic forces.

Nothing under the new regime could remain neutral, neither culture, science, nor education. Only what served the victory of communism was morally acceptable. Restoring the old system had meanwhile become impossible because, since all social groups were in a state of collapse, there was no force in the country capable of effecting such restoration. The old society had disappeared and a new one had not taken its place. The regime has never relented in its attempts to create that society by force.

In the hope of perpetuating War Communism as a system of government for many years, the regime speeded up the nationalization of industries, created agricultural communes, communalized aspects of daily life, instituted and intensified the militarization of labor, and abolished money, turning to a barter of goods and services. Meanwhile, however, the economy was disintegrating even further. Output fell by 12 percent every year, so that by 1921 it scarcely amounted to half the prewar level. Unemployment set in, leading the country into a new crisis, punctuated by workers' strikes. These occurred mainly in industrial districts traditionally considered bulwarks of Bolshevism, such as the Donbass and the Urals. But Moscow, Petrograd, Tula, Kiev, and Kharkov were also rocked by worker discontent.

The supposed "leader of the Revolution," the proletariat, began to come out against the communists, who in effect found themselves isolated. This became obvious when the Baltic Navy mutinied in March 1921, demanding new elections for the soviets ("soviets without communists") and the restoration of democracy ("freedom of speech and the press for workers and peasants"). The Kronstadt mutiny was a particularly grave challenge to the communist authority, which found itself confronted by a revolutionary army.

The regime had to be saved. Realizing this, Lenin admitted that War Communism had been a mistake. A mistake it was indeed, its magnitude measurable by two million casualties. Such was the cost of this attempt to build socialism in the Soviet Union. The birth and growth of socialism were in the end to cost Soviet society much more dearly, to the extent of fifty million killed and savagely persecuted. In 1921, when Lenin abandoned War Communism, he took "a step backward." Very soon, however, his successor, Stalin, was to take "two steps forward."

War communism — the economic policy of the Soviet state under the conditions of economic collapse and Civil War in the years 1918 – 1920 — meant the mobilization of all forces and resources for defense. (Sovetsky entsiklopedichesky slovar' [The Soviet encyclopedic dictionary], Moscow: "Sovetskaya Entsiklopediya" (Publishers), 1981, p. 238)

It would be embarrassing to recount, event by event, how after the Brest-Litovsk peace treaty the country made the transition to war communism . . . . (Literaturnaya gazeta, 13 July 1988, p. 12)

Selyunin seeks the roots of war communism also in the history of our fatherland, beginning with the sixteenth century, concretely with the time of Ivan the Terrible, who was so dear to Stalin . . . and of the so ardently appreciated Peter (the Great) who remains cherished by many of our countrymen. (Ogonek, no. 36, September 1988, p. 19)

Warmongers (*Podzhigateli voiny*; literally, war igniters). Political and public figures accused of escalating the arms race and increasing international tension. In its literal sense, the term is logically misleading: one does not ignite war. It is war itself that ignites, blows up, destroys, etc. Thus, it would be more logical to call warmongers "peace igniters" or "peace destroyers." However, Soviet propaganda, in this case as well as others, attaches little importance to common sense, striving instead to produce an intended psychological and emotional response. It is this task that the phrase carries out quite efficiently by triggering the stereotypical negative reaction of aversion, outrage, and indignation. In this context, the phrase first appeared in the USSR after the British "Curzon ultimatum" of 1932 to the Soviet government. Thereafter, the term "warmongers" was employed on numerous occasions, such as the break in Anglo-Soviet relations (1927–29) or the Munich Four Power Conference of 1938. However, the word began to enjoy its widest use only after World War II, during the period of the Cold War.

In the present era of Gorbachev, in line with his "new political thinking" (cf.), the term "warmongers" is avoided and its propagandistic use reduced. It began to be used less frequently against American and European political leaders, as well as against the former "Chinese hegemonists." Mutual understanding became the order of the day. Sakharov, the "internal" warmonger, was also rehabilitated and his authority effectively utilized by Moscow in establishing closer ties with the West. Israel proved to be less fortunate; its leaders are still branded as warmongers, although not as frequently as before. Still, it is too early to talk about this propaganda cliché being altogether discarded. Its continuing — even if now rare — use stems from Soviet propaganda's penchant for articulating its ideas with emotional rhetoric. In its literal meaning, the expression serves as a metaphor that conveys the notion of war as an act of arson capable of burning up the world and destroying all mankind. Soviet propaganda enhances the expressiveness of the invective even further by using it in such rhetorical phrases as "the aggressive intrigues of warmongers" (*aggressivnye proiski podzhigateley voiny*) or "the perfidious designs of warmongers" (*kovarnye zamysly podzhigateley voiny*).

In order to explain the motives behind the warmongers' actions, Soviet propaganda would invariably refer to the Marxist theory of the nature and causes of war. According to this theory, wars are products of social contradictions generated by the struggle between imperialist powers. This concept appeared fatalistic in its assumption that wars are inevitable. Gorbachev set out to review and modify this notion of war. He espoused a new political thinking that excluded war from modern life. This undeniably novel idea completely contradicts the communist worldview, according to which only objective reality, and not wishful thinking or good intentions, determine political outcomes. Gorbachev's idea can mean one of the two things: either that the Soviet leader has succumbed to idealism, a highly unlikely possibility, or that the Soviets have never really considered Western countries as warmongers, which seems more likely. If the latter is the case, it would mean that Soviet leaders have used the term in order to fabricate an image of the enemy and thereby to justify militaristic policies and expansionist aspirations of their own.

The Soviet Union has not entirely discarded this sort of apologetics, the best proof being that Lenin's distinction between just and unjust wars is still considered basically valid. Wars that benefit and are often encouraged by the Soviet Union are "just," while those that thwart its designs are "unjust." Thus, the concept of warmongers continues to be used as a political lightning rod that deflects the charges of militarism from the Soviet Union and rechannels them toward the West.

> The close and comprehensive political cooperation of the states of the socialist community in the economic, scientific-technical, cultural, and military fields is a pledge to enhance even further the strength and influence of socialism, the most reliable protection against any intrigues of warmongers. (Bakinsky rabochy, 7 November 1980, p. 1)

> The crucial political purpose of the struggle for peace is to expose the plans of the warmongers, and thus to nip them in the bud. (Za

rubezhom, no. 46, 7–13 November 1980, p. 8)

Let the US imperialists and their accomplices know that the Soviet people will do their utmost to frustrate the plans of these warmongers. (Agitator, no. 20, 1983, p. 44)

Watch (*Vakhta*). Pressured, exhausting work at Soviet enterprises done to commemorate some important or memorable occasion that is depicted as a display of enthusiasm and heroism (on the part of the working people). Borrowed from nautical terminology, the word "watch" suggests a parallel between the country and a ship, and between the population and its crew. On this "ship," strict discipline is enforced, unquestioning obedience to the will of the "captain" and his "officers" is demanded, and people are required to remain faithfully at their posts. The application of the watch concept to manual labor also helps romanticize Soviet citizens' lives, helping to conceal the drabness and squalor of their existence and provide symbolic compensation for their lack of job satisfaction.

While supposedly acclaiming the conscientiousness of the workers, the concept actually refers to a subtle form of ruthless exploitation: Soviet workers who "stand on watch" (*stat' na vakhtu*) are obliged to put in long hours of overtime and exert themselves to the limit under constant pressure.

"Watch" is often combined with adjectives that refer to the type of work involved, such as "labor watch" (*trudovaya vakhta*) and "sowing watch" (*posevnaya vakhta*), and to heroism in overfulfilling plans — referred to, in honor of the legendary Nikolay Stakhanov, as "Stakhanovite watch" (*stakhanovskaya vakhta* (cf. "stakhanovite"). Some adjectives refer to the period when a watch takes place, for example, "Pre-October watch" (*predoktyabr'skaya vakhta*) and "Pre-Congress watch" (*preds"ezdovskaya vakhta*), a reference to the increased work efforts before a party congress.

Thousands of workers in industrial enterprises, trade organizations, public transport, and service industries of the Soviet district of Kishinev mounted a labor watch on November 20, under the banner: "110 shock-working days on the 110th anniversary of Lenin's birth." (Sovetskaya Moldaviya, 21 November 1979, p. 1)

Our country mounted a watch in honor of the Party Congress. (Izvestiya, 28 February 1981, p. 1)

Our fleet is commendably mounting the watch of peace. (Literaturnaya gazeta, 22 July 1981, p. 1)

Whitewashing (*Ochkovtiratel'stvo*). Reporting of deliberate falsehoods on the performance of industrial enterprises and institutions. This metaphor means "throwing dust in someone's eyes," to "deceive," or to "delude." Whitewashing is a widespread phenomenon stemming from a number of causes: unrealistic plans, the heavy hand of bureaucracy, lack of organization and of diligence of labor collectives, and inadequate supplies of raw materials and equipment. For production shortfalls due to any of the above causes, the manager or director of the enterprise is liable to be punished. Whitewashing allows him to delay the punishment or to escape it entirely. This explains why whitewashing is fairly widespread in spite of being a punishable offense.

As a social phenomenon, whitewashing made its appearance in the USSR in the late 1920s. The difficulties encountered in carrying out the policy of universal collectivization prompted the responsible officials to cover themselves by mendacious reporting to the Central Committee. Evidence was fabricated in these reports so as to confirm the correctness of party policy in the countryside and present the performance of their authors in a favorable light. Gradually, a pattern established itself to the point of becoming an entrenched tradition. From above there issued instructions out of all touch with reality; from below there emanated reports of nonexistent achievements.

Officially, whitewashing has always been denounced; unofficially, everybody has an interest in whitewashing, from the ordinary worker to the director of the enterprise to the general secretary of the CPSU. For all of them, mendacious reporting is routine.

Gradually, elaborate whitewashing has become an integral part of Soviet life and an indispensable method of industrial management. Every Soviet institution, whether factory, collective farm (cf.), or research institute, plays around with fabricated facts and figures, especially in regard to fulfillment of targets, increases in productivity, savings of raw materials, and exploitation of manpower reserves. This information flows from lower ranking to higher ranking echelons of the apparatus. At the final count, data thus concocted are included in state plans and party directives. These plans and directives are then circulated widely, especially among managerial personnel, with the effect that their "implementation" leads to nationwide whitewashing. In turn such falsified data become the basis for new planning (cf.) targets, which are just as unattainable as previous ones and are thereby conducive to a new round of whitewashing.

Although the Soviet press now writes freely and widely about whitewashing, it rarely fingers the guilty parties, doing so only when an outcry has been raised or when the party was involved in yet another campaign against "write-ups" (cf.). Whitewashing is too extensive a practice to be remediable: it remains a basic component of the Soviet social compact whereby the rulers deceive the ruled and the ruled deceive the rulers.

> The Soviet way of life cannot be reconciled with efforts to obtain from the state as much as possible and to give as little as possible in exchange, with wastefulness and laziness at production sites, with petty consumerism, and with the evasion of public responsibility. The vices referred to often give rise to deception, whitewashing, theft, and embezzlement of socialist property. (Kommunist, no. 5, 1979, p. 20)

> The magazine Selsky mekhanizator, in issues 6 and 7 of the past year, was already reporting the practice of whitewashing in the Gagarin Trust. (Krokodil, no. 18, 1979, p. 4)

Following another failure to fulfill a plan, the

former director Goncherenko, together with the chief engineer Merzon, took advantage of the nonexistence of control on the part of the Party organization and decided to resort to whitewashing for the sake of having their enterprise designated as progressive. (Partiynaya zhizn', no. 4, 1980, p. 77)

Wise (*Mudry*). A routine description of communist leaders and their policies. The term first gained currency in Soviet parlance when it was used to extol Stalin, as in "wise Stalin," "the wise leader," and "the wise teacher." When this was deemed insufficient, other similar expressions were also introduced: "Stalin's wisdom" (*stalinskaya mudrost'*) and "Stalin, the friend and teacher of the peoples" (*Stalin — drug i uchitel' narodov*). The linking of "wise" with Stalin's name was intended to convey the image of this leader as the embodiment of absolute truth — a combination of truth and goodness, moral and intellectual perfection, infallibility, and a vast wealth of experience.

After Stalin's death, all the qualities associated with the term "wise" were transferred to the party and its "achievements," as in "the wise thinking of the party" (*mudraya mysl' partii*), "the wise words of the party" (*mudroe slovo partii*), and "the wise leadership of the party" (*mudroe rukovodstvo partii*). The phrase "wise policy of the party" (*mudraya politika partii*) was overused to the point of becoming a cliché. This phrase stressed the universal correctness of the party's decisions, that is, its infallibility, its superior comprehension of social processes, no matter how complex, and hence the accuracy of its predictions about the future.

Lenin and his policies were granted wisdom posthumously, as reflected in the phrases "Lenin's wise national program" (*mudraya leninskaya natsional'naya programma*) and "Lenin's wise words" (*mudroe leninskoe slovo*). In the 1970s, the adjective "wise" was lavished upon Leonid Brezhnev; subsequently the appellation was bestowed upon Andropov, Chernenko, and, most recently, Gorbachev. In addition to being wise, they were routinely described as being brilliant and experienced statesmen. This reverence should be seen not only as an indication of the revival of the cult of personality, but also as an attempt to invoke a sense of the continuity of current party policies with the Revolutionary tradition and in particular with Lenin, whose memory remains genuinely venerated by many Soviet citizens.

These massive successes were achieved by the working class, the collective farmers, and all the working masses of our country thanks to the daring decisions and wise policies of the Party and the government. (Istoriya VKPb, kratky kurs [History of the All-Union Communist Party of the Bolsheviks, brief course], Moscow: Publishing House for Political Literature, 1950, p. 314)

The workers and staff of the Yu. Kasimov Machine Building factory expressed . . . their full support for the wise domestic and foreign policy of the CPSU and . . . the Soviet government. (Vyshka, 7 February 1984, p. 1)

The working masses of Azerbaijan know that they are indebted for everything they have achieved to the wise leadership of our dear Communist Party. (Vyshka, 19 February 1984, p. 2)

Work-Blitz (*Shturmovshchina*). Frenzied rush work to meet planned production quotas. The term "work-blitz" has negative connotations in Soviet propaganda. In fact, work-blitzes are common in Soviet industry and construction. The seasonal nature of agricultural labor justifies the use of a different term — "the rush" (*strada*) — which, although it has a positive connotation, refers to essentially the same problem.

Work-blitzes are usually launched in a last-minute effort to meet production quotas before the end of the period (month, quarter, year) covered by the mandatory report. Constantly under the pressure of directives from above, often lacking adequate raw materials and manpower, Soviet industries have little chance to operate smoothly. Under these conditions, they cannot cope with the inevitable production disruptions (*proryvy*) without periodically overstraining manpower and resources. In such hectic periods

of overtime and night shifts, enterprises are compared to wartime front lines, with storming (*shturmovye*) detachments of workers rushing to "assault" (*brat' pristupom*) a given production target.

Work-blitzes have numerous drawbacks. The strain under which workers operate leads to interpersonal tensions that often disrupt the process of production. Moreover, overuse and abuse of machinery during work-blitz periods results in its damage and lowers the already low quality of manufactured goods. Soviet consumers in the know seek out goods (e.g., televisions, tape recorders, refrigerators) produced in the middle of a report period and avoid products manufactured during work-blitzes.

Work-blitzes are openly disparaged by the Soviet authorities, and the individual cases of labor mismanagement that are supposedly responsible for them are criticized. No one can openly acknowledge, however, that these last-minute rushes to meet quotas are the result of the Soviet economic system itself.

. . . the work-blitz is a system in its own right. When it comes, the load on equipment increases several times. There is no time to make efficient repairs or adopt safeguards. And what is the result? Some of the older machines go out of commission and new equipment is acquired, only to meet the same fate. (Sotsialisticheskaya industriya, 6 May 1977)

In the first 10-day period of the month, perhaps more than 20%, perhaps not even 15% of the monthly quota is met, making work-blitz in the last days of the month necessary. As a result many thousands of rubles are paid out in overtime. (Sotsialisticheskaya industriya, 8 August 1978, p. 2)

The drive to meet the quota at all costs, the hope that will-power always overcomes all obstacles, and the exclusive reliance on monetary incentives lead to work-blitzes, high personnel turnover, and an absence of discipline. (G. V. Romanov, Izbrannye rechi i stat'i, [Selected speeches and articles], Moscow: Publishing House for Political Literature, 1980, p. 35)

Write-Ups (*Pripiski*). Distorted, falsified data supplied by official Soviet bodies. As a social institution within the Soviet industrial system, the practice of write-ups originated during the formative years of the Socialist regime. Still, for many years this meaning was not included in the dictionaries, where the term was interpreted in its original sense, as an addition to something already written. Exaggerated reporting of plan fulfillment, increasing productivity, growth of prosperity, and so on was required in order to demonstrate nonexistent achievements in the building of socialism, to prove that the "general party line" was correct, and that the masses were enthusiastic.

Statistical information compiled at all levels of the Soviet bureaucratic hierarchy almost invariably sounds optimistic, regardless of whether it deals with the number of meetings or lectures held, production output, or harvest yields of collective farms. As a consequence of write-ups, official statistics nearly always testify to various successes and accomplishments, indicating that production targets have been met ahead of time, raw materials have been saved, and production rates have been high. Write-ups parallel the millions of posters that are prominently displayed to proclaim universal affluence, glowing work enthusiasm, and historic achievements.

Write-ups perform an important social function, making it possible to evade responsibility for failure to fulfill plans or for low productivity, to conceal embezzlement, to secure the favors of higher-ups, and to obtain bonuses. Still, write-ups should not be attributed to the penchant of Soviet leaders for abuse of office (no matter how the latter are corrupted by Soviet politics), but rather to state planning as a system.

Whatever field of activity it covers, whether industrial production, science, public work (*obshchestvennaya rabota*), or art, the plan assumes the status of law; it can in no way be revised in response to feedback coming from the production line. For failure to fulfill a plan, the responsible manager can be dismissed from work and even put on trial. Meanwhile, those who continue to be responsible for its fulfillment can do very little to improve matters. All their efforts are par-

alyzed by the inertia of the system, widespread apathy, continual disruptions in the supply of raw materials and equipment, primitive labor organization, and low wages. All these factors encourage the Soviet leaders to resort to write-ups.

The allegedly "broad-based" Soviet inventiveness (*massovoe sovetskoe izobretatel'stvo*) also reflects the write-up phenomenon. Industrial improvements devised by engineers are credited to workers. This is hailed as "fulfilling the plan of developing the innovation movement."

Resorting to write-ups has been elevated to the status of national policy. In the 1960s, in order to claim primacy in conquering space, the Soviet government squeezed three cosmonauts into a spaceship cabin designed for one. They came back nearly suffocated, but the goal was achieved as the world applauded the achievements of Soviet science. Moscow has been transformed into a show place, a giant Potemkin village. The city is more or less adequately supplied with goods and amenities, and apartment housing construction is relatively extensive — to the detriment of other regions of the country, where an acute shortage of living space prevails.

Write-ups also involve rank and file workers. Workers report production of nonexistent commodities, collective farmers report hectares of land that have never been cultivated or crops that have never been grown. Their involvement in the production of write-ups is voluntary, grounded in their understanding of their utility for both the bosses and themselves. Owing to write-ups, they have their wages increased and can obtain bonuses for "plan overfulfillment."

Write-ups comprise a total and all-embracing system, where more often than not a number of enterprises conspire in jointly fabricating them. One confirms the delivery of unproduced goods, another the receipt of unpaid money. All that is supported by the necessary accounting documents, including delivery reports, receipts, and statements of indebtedness.

The system of party and state control over the national economy contributes in its own way to the practice of write-ups. This system is based on an idolatry of quantitative indicators; it has yet to learn how to evaluate outputs reliably. It believes, for some reason, that production of a particular item has to be higher today than it was yesterday, and higher tomorrow (or reported higher tomorrow) than it is today. For the party and state bureaucrats, it is of no importance that warehouses are filled with unsold stocks, and that some items will never be in demand. The bureaucracy continues to operate; the "heroes" receive bonuses and tokens of appreciation.

By the beginning of the 1960s, write-ups assumed so massive a character that passing over the whole thing in silence was no longer possible. The Soviet government was forced to enact a decree "On Measures to Prevent Acts Intended to Deceive the State." Subsequently a campaign against write-ups was launched that culminated in countless dismissals from work and the prosecution of several hundred administrators and accountants. But like all campaigns, it was bound to last for a while and then expire. It ended as suddenly as it began. Needless to say, write-ups have survived the campaign, as was predictable in advance — in view of the fact that

the system, which has always done its best to encourage this practice, emerged from the campaign unchanged.

While write-ups are formally a punishable offense, actually they are a prerequisite for any managerial success. They are necessary and profitable on every rung of the social ladder, from the head of a workshop to the general secretary of the CPSU, because, by cumulatively piling fiction upon fiction all the way from the bottom to the top of the bureaucratic hierarchy, they convey a consistent impression of the prosperous advance of socialist society.

Write-ups cause great damage to the economy and to worker morale. Many such write-ups (some of them on quite a large scale) were uncovered at the metal construction plant in the town of Komsomolsk. (Partiynaya zhizn', no. 4, 1980, p. 77)

No sooner had National Control Commission started to investigate the Batetsky Trust than it turned out that the 22,000 rubles, 49 repaired tractors, and repairs done in exchange for spare parts in short supply existed only in write-ups. (Literaturnaya gazeta, 22 October 1980, p. 2)

Workers at the Kommunar plant say that write-ups in reports of production-plan fulfillment have become the established pattern there. (Sotsialisticheskaya industriya, 30 August 1982, p. 3)

Y

Youth (*Molodezh'*). Soviet youth—a sociodemographic grouping, comprised of those aged between fourteen and thirty or even thirty-two who have a specific social status, position in society, and function in the national division of labor. Until very recently, youth were not recognized as a distinct social stratum. They were viewed as nothing more than an age category and were not defined in terms of any sociological concepts. At best, superficial psychological definitions were applied to them. Thus, youth were supposed to be characterized by the rapid growth of individual differences or by the desire (and aptitude) for intimate affiliation with others. Such typical youth characteristics as a distinct social motivation pattern, an inclination toward self-examination, and impulsiveness (sometimes carried to the extreme) were deliberately ignored. Nor was any notice taken of the fact that the young tend to be less concerned about material comforts and security than older people.

In the Soviet Union, no reliable knowledge on the contemporary younger generation has ever been assembled. There are at least two reasons for this. The first is the objective difficulty of measuring, describing, and explaining the vast number of processes, tendencies, and phenomena relevant to the life of sixty-four million young men and women between the ages of fourteen and thirty, representing all kinds of professions and no less than one hundred nationalities. The second reason is that the authorities have not been particularly interested in the subject. They understand that any research on this subject can only bring to the fore questions to which they have no clear and convincing answers: for instance, questions concerning the meaning of life or the future direction of the country. As a result, a situation has evolved where, although it cannot be said that the subject of youth is unknown in the Soviet Union, it cannot be claimed that enough is known about it.

Discussion of youth used to lead to romantic stereotypes such as "our youth are good." Recently, with the advent of perestroika, this stereotype is often inverted, resulting in the belief that "our youth are bad." Sociological studies of Soviet youth (if they can be relied on) claim that 84 percent of Soviet citizens maintain the view that "our youth are good" (*Agitator*, no. 7, 1988, p. 8). At first glance, it may appear surprising that so many respondents expressed their satisfaction with youth. Yet what is really surprising is that 16 percent of respondents dared opine that "our youth are bad." Essentially, this reply reflects impatience with the common idealization of youth coupled with ignorance about them. Such ignorance encourages the denial of such widespread phenomena as the existence of drug addiction (affecting 10 percent of youth), prostitution (15 percent), political indifference (30 percent), nationalism (35 percent), egoism (36 percent), a lack of aims in life (40 percent), passivity (46 percent), and consumerism (51 percent) (see *Agitator*, no. 7, 1988, p. 9).

Soviet society is slowly and painstakingly divesting itself of its false image of its youth. This has happened only very recently, even through contradictions in the life of young Soviet citizens had become increasingly apparent much earlier, even in the 1950s. Then as now, Soviet youth were believed to have "gone wild," because of having it "too easy," without the need to support themselves. This was supposed to explain their taste for vodka and buying up anything that's around. Soviet youth indeed "goes wild" (rebels), but not because they "have it easy" (this is not and has never been the case in Soviet society), but because of their unfulfilled spiritual, intellectual, and emotional aspirations. Today's youth have no goals or ideals worth living or dying for. The results can be seen in the high incidence of escapism into the world of drug addiction and crime.

The authorities are now pursuing a senseless course of restraining youth by threats, restrictions, and prohibitions; it is senseless because throughout history, youth are always impulsive and inclined to take risks and seek thrills. This is also the aim of Soviet youth, even if pursued in a manner that is idiosyncratic and even brutal. They organize themselves into gangs and terrorize towns. In the USSR, fights between youth gangs are a tradition—apartment block against apartment block, street against street. They fought without particular enmity, until blood was drawn, and then soon made peace. For years, fist-fighting was a commonplace occurrence, an entrenched custom. It is no exaggeration to say that generation after generation of Soviet youth grew into manhood fighting their peers. Yet Soviet cities could usually sleep peacefully.

The rude awakening came in the 1970s when, at first in working class districts and then everywhere, armed gangs began to form. They blockade the streets and make short work of passersby. They set on people with iron bars, cripple them with chains, and are adept at fighting with knives and even bayonets. In every town, the gangs have their own way of going about their business: some gangs are active at night under the cover of darkness, while others operate during the daytime, pulling nylon stocking masks over their faces. All the gangs are characterized by discipline, organization, cohesion, and an inexplicable hatred of strangers. Another distinguishing feature is the mutual loyalty within gangs. They adhere to the Three Musketeers' principle of "one for all and all for one." And this is what may explain their popularity. Within Soviet society, made up of three hundred million isolated individuals devoid of any personal security, gang violence serves as a means of self-expression

and self-assertion within an accepting peer environment.

How have Soviet authorities responded to the needs of the youth? They began forming "alternative" operational detachments of young people. The goal was crime control, but these antigang gangs soon began flouting the law. A kind of curfew has been imposed on teenagers in certain towns in the Ural and Volga regions. After 9:00 P.M. they are banned from the streets, while the operational detachments mount searches, patrol the streets, and record the names of suspicious characters. In time, they have come to fulfill a policing function. No alternative opportunities for young people's activism have been created. While opposing the street gangs from a position of strength, the operational detachments have alienated themselves from young people and have lost the support of society.

Soviet society has been able to offer its youth nothing apart from curtailing their leisure time through various compulsory activities, reducing the number of exemptions from military service, or impelling youngsters to take jobs in "voluntary-compulsory" formations, which no adult would perform. This outright violation of individual freedom is called "labor education." Needless to say, far from instilling an appreciation of work, it only alienates from it.

Soviet youth do not see any connection between production and consumption. They rightly observe that those who earn a lot are not those who work hard, so the youth work out of necessity, in drudgery and despair, or in order to gain a record that will help them enter an institution of higher education. The authorities are trying to divert the energies of the youth to peripheral activities, such as protection of the environment or of historical sites or to disarmament campaigns. Youth are easily lured to such activities, but they also pose a challenge to society by demanding changes in the system of values and in the organization of industrial production—which society is not prepared for.

In the USSR, society is quick to resort to defensive reactions, allowing youth to study more and more years and thus maintaining them in the status of children, with their civic consciousness and development retarded. Soviet society talks about democracy, but its approach to youth is becoming less and less democratic. Society simply tells youth where and how must they "reconstruct" themselves (*perestroit'sya*)—or else. Compulsory education is shortened, youngsters are channeled to trade schools and dispatched to major industrial projects designated as "communist construction."

Youth have absorbed the hypocrisy of society at large and are repaying the latter generously in the form of "youth problems" and growing duplicity, hypocrisy, self-righteousness, and irresponsibility of their own. Thus, Soviet society gets the youth it deserves, but it is not the youth it would like to have. Hence complaints and misgivings about youth are rampant among Soviet adults.

As part of its exploitative attitude toward youth, society tries to win their favor via flattering declarations, such as "the role of youth in Soviet society is constantly growing"—for which there is absolutely no basis in fact. The role of youth is decreasing, not only quantitatively as a result of falling birth rates, but also in terms of their public roles. Soviet science too has "aged" in the sense that the number of young Soviet scientists has dropped almost threefold over the past decades. Youth's role in public administration has also diminished. Particularly significant in this respect is that the average age

of skilled workers and specialists in industry has risen considerably. The only place where the role of youth has actually grown is the Komsomol (cf.), and this has happened only because not belonging to the Komsomol is tantamount to challenging society as a whole. Both youth and the Komsomol have suffered as a result. Youth has placed itself in an even more vulnerable situation, while the Komsomol, having swallowed up forty million young people, has begun to stifle under its own weight, becoming unmanageable and losing its capacity for action. The original driving force of Komsomol activity—guarding the interests of society—has been finally and irrevocably lost, while Soviet youth, realizing that it has no future, has begun to sink into dejection and desperation.

Youth is a complex subject to study, a highly important topic for theoretical and practical consideration. To deal with youth is to deal with life as it unfolds rather than with an abstract future. (Agitator, no. 7, 1988, p. 8)

Alternative youth groups have arisen in order to defend teenagers against gangs. These groups in fact perform some police duties, and they enforce order in places crowds congregate, patrolling the streets etc. (Ogonek, no. 29, July 1988, p. 22)

Specific problems concerning youth began to arise in the 1960s, when the majority of parents spared youth from the need of going out to work early in their lives. It was then that some young people began to get hold of money for buying vodka and possessions. (Sotsiologicheskie issledovaniya, no. 1, 1988, p. 82)

Bibliography

Adams, Jan S. *Citizen Inspectors in the Soviet Union.* New York: Praeger, 1977.

Adomeit, Hannes. "Soviet Crisis Prevention and Management: Why and When Do the Soviet Leaders Take Risks?" *Orbis* 30 (Spring 1986): 42–64.

Aganbegyan, Abel. *The Economic Challenge of Perestroika.* Bloomington: Indiana University Press, 1988.

Agursky, Mikhail. *The Third Rome: National Bolshevism in the USSR.* Boulder, Colo.: Westview Press, 1988.

Alexeyeva, Ludmilla. *Soviet Dissent: Contemporary Movement for National, Religious and Human Rights.* Middletown, Conn.: Wesleyan University Press, 1985.

Baradat, Leon P. *Soviet Political Society.* Englewood Cliffs, N.J.: Prentice Hall, 1986.

Barghoorn, Frederick C., and Thomas F. Remington. *Politics in the USSR.* Boston: Little, Brown and Co., 1986.

Barry, Donald D., and Carol Barner-Barry. *Contemporary Soviet Politics.* 3d ed. Englewood Cliffs, N.J.: Prentice Hall, 1987.

Beissinger, Mark R. "In Search of Generations in Soviet Politics." *World Politics* 38 (January 1986): 288–314.

———. *Scientific Management, Socialist Discipline and Soviet Power.* Cambridge, Mass.: Harvard University Press, 1988.

Benningsen, Alexandre. "Islam in the Soviet Union." *Journal of South Asian and Middle Eastern Studies* 8 (Summer 1985): 115–33.

Bergson, Abram, and Herbert S. Levine, eds. *The Soviet Economy: Toward the Year 2000.* London: Allen and Unwin, 1983.

Bialer, Seweryn. *The Soviet Paradox: External Expansion, Internal Decline.* New York: Knopf, 1986.

———, ed. *Politics, Society and Nationality inside Gorbachev's Russia.* Boulder, Colo.: Westview Press, 1989.

Bialer, Seweryn, and Joan Afferica. "The Genesis of Gorbachev's World." *Foreign Affairs* 64 (3) (February 1986): 605–44.

Bialer, Seweryn, and Thane Gustafson, eds. *Russia at the Crossroads: The 26th Congress of the CPSU.* London: Allen and Unwin, 1982.

Birman, Igor. *Ekonimika Nedostach* (The scarcity economy). New York: Chalidze Publications, 1984.

Bittman, Ladislav. *The KGB and Soviet Disinformation: An Insider's View.* New York: Pergamon-Brassey's, 1985.

Bond, Daniel L., and Herbert S. Levine. "The Eleventh Five-Year Plan 1981–1985," In *Russia at the Crossroads: The 26th Congress of the CPSU,* edited by Seweryn Bialer and Thane Gustafson, 87–107. London: Allen and Unwin, 1982.

Bornstein, Morris. "Improving the Soviet Economic Mechanism." *Soviet Studies* 37 (January 1985): 1–30.

Bräker, Heinz. "Soviet Domestic Policy 1977–1979." In *The Soviet Union 1978–1979,* vol. 5, 3–11. New York and London: Holmes & Meier, 1980.

Breslauer, George. *Five Images of the Soviet Future.* Berkeley: University of California, Institute of International Studies, 1978.

———. "How to Think about the New Political Thinking." *Crossroads* 28 (1989): 53–59.

———. *Khrushchev and Brezhnev as Leaders: Building Authority in Soviet Politics.* London: Allen and Unwin, 1982.

———. "Khrushchev Reconsidered." *Problems of Communism* 25 (September–October 1976): 18–33.

Brown, Archie. "Gorbachev: New Man in the Kremlin." *Problems of Communism* 34 (May–June 1985): 1–23.

Brown, Archie, and J. Gray, eds. *Political Culture and Political Change in Communist States.* 2d ed. London: Macmillan, 1975.

Brown, Archie, and Kaser Michael, eds. *The Soviet Union since the Fall of Khrushchev.* New York: Free Press, 1975.

Brzezinski, Zbigniew. *The Grand Failure: The Birth and Death of Communism in the Twentieth Century.* New York: Charles Scribner's Sons, 1989.

Bunce, Valerie. *Do New Leaders Make a Difference? Executive Succession and Public Policy under Capitalism and Socialism.* Princeton, N.J.: Princeton University Press, 1981.

Bush, Keith. "Major Decree on Private Plots and Livestock Holdings." *Radio Liberty Research Bulletin* 38/81 (26 January 1981).

Butson, Thomas G. *Gorbachev: A Biography.* New York: Stein & Day, 1985.

Byrnes, Robert F., ed. *After Brezhnev: Sources of Soviet Conduct in the 1980s.* Bloomington: Indiana University Press, 1983.

Carrère d'Encausse, Helene. *Decline of an Empire: The Soviet Socialist Republics in Revolt.* New York: Newsweek Books, 1981.

Churchward, L. G. *Soviet Socialism: Social and Political Essays.* London: Kegan and Paul, 1988.

Cohen, Stephen F. *Rethinking the Soviet Experience.* Oxford: Oxford University Press, 1985.

———. *Sovieticus: American Perceptions and Soviet Realities.* New York: W. W. Norton, 1985.

Cohen, Stephen F., Alexander Rabinowitch, and Robert Sharlet, eds. *The Soviet Union since Stalin.* Bloomington: Indiana University Press, 1980.

Colton, Timothy J. *Commissars, Commanders and Civilian Authority: The Structure of Soviet Military Politics.* Cambridge, Mass.: Harvard University Press, 1979.

———. *The Dilemma of Reform in the Soviet Union.* Rev. ed. New York: Council on Foreign Relations, 1986.

Connor, Walter D. "Social Policy under Gorbachev." *Problems of Communism.* 35 (July–August 1986): 31–46.

Conquest, Robert. *The Great Terror.* London: Pelican Books, 1971.

———. *The Harvest of Sorrow: Soviet Collectivization and the Terror-Famine.* London: Hutchinson, 1986.

———. *The Last Empire: Nationality and the Soviet Future.* Stanford, Calif.: Hoover Institution Press, 1986.

Crossroads 24: Special Soviet Issue. 1987.

Crossroads 28: Symposium. "The USSR in the International System: The Impact of New Political Thinking." 1989.

Dallin, Alexander, and Condolezza Rice, eds. *The Gorbachev Era.* Stanford, Calif.: Stanford Alumni Association, 1986.

Desai, Padma. *Perestroika in Perspective.* Princeton, N.J.: Princeton University Press, 1989.

Diamond, Douglas B. "Soviet Agricultural Plans for 1981–1985." In *Russia at the Crossroads: The 26th Congress of the CPSU,* edited by Seweryn Bialer and Thane Gustafson, 108–20. London: Allen and Unwin, 1982.

Dibb, Paul. *The Soviet Union: Incomplete Superpower.* Urbana-Chicago: University of Illinois Press, 1986.

Dornberg, John. *Brezhnev: The Masks of Power.* New York: Basic Books, 1974.

Eklof, Ben. *Soviet Briefing: Gorbachev and the Reform Period.* Boulder, Colo.: Westview Press, 1988.

Elliot, Ianin. "And Now Chernenko." *Survey* 28 (Spring 1984): 5–8.

Fehér, Ferenc, Agnes Heller, and Gyorgyi Markus. *Dictatorship over Needs.* Oxford: Basil Blackwell, 1983.

Feiwel, George R. "Economic Performance and Reforms in the Soviet Union." In *Soviet Politics in the Brezhnev Era,* edited by Donald R. Kelley, 70–103. New York: Praeger, 1980.

Feldbrugge, F. J. M. *The Distinctiveness of Soviet Law.* Dordrecht: Martinus Nijhoff, 1987.

Fortescue, Stephen. *The Communist Party and Soviet Science.* Baltimore: Johns Hopkins University Press, 1987.

Fremeaux, Philippe, and Christine Durand. *Comprendre l'Economie Sovietique* (Understanding the Soviet Economy). Paris: Syros, 1985.

Friedberg, M., and H. Isham, eds. *Soviet Society under Gorbachev.* Armank, N.Y.: M. E. Sharpe, 1987.

Friedgut, Theodore H. *Integration of the Rural Sector into Soviet Society.* Jerusalem: Hebrew University, 1976.

———. *Political Participation in the USSR.* Princeton, N.J.: Princeton University Press, 1979.

Gati, Charles. "The Soviet Empire: Alive but Not Well." *Problems of Coummunism* 34 (March–April 1985): 73–86.

George V., and N. Manning. *Social Welfare and the Soviet Union.* London: Routledge and Kegan Paul, 1980.

Glazov, Yuri. *The Russian Mind since Stalin's Death.* Dordrecht, Boston, and Lancaster: D. Reidel Publ. Co., 1985.

Goldfarb, Jeffrey C. *Beyond Glasnost: The Post-Totalitarian Mind.* Chicago: University of Chicago Press, 1989.

Goldman, Marshall I. "Gorbachev and Economic Reform." *Foreign Affairs.* 64 (1) (Fall 1985): 56–73.

Goodman, Elliot R. "Gorbachev Takes Charge: Prospects for Soviet Society." *Survey* 29 (2) (Summer 1986): 202–17.

Graham, Loren R. *Science, Philosophy and Human Behavior in the Soviet Union.* New York: Columbia University Press, 1987.

Grancelli, Bruno. *Soviet Industrial Relations.* Winchester, Mass.: Allen and Unwin, 1987.

Grant, Nigel. *Soviet Education.* London: Penguin Books, 1979.

Green, Donald. "Capital Formation in the USSR: An Econometric Investigation of Bureaucratic Intervention in the Process of Capital Construction." *Review of Economics and Statistics* 60 (February 1978): 39–46.

Green, Leslie C. "Soviet Law in the 1980s." *Crossroads* 22 (1986): 83–89.

Greenberg, Linda Lubrano. "Soviet Science Policy and the Scientific Establishment," *Survey* 17 (Autumn 1971): 51–63.

Gripp, Richard. *The Political System of Communism.* New York: Dodd, Mead and Co., 1973.

Gunlicks, Arthur B., and John D. Treadway, eds. *The Soviet Union under Gorbachev: Assessing the First Year.* New York: Praeger, 1987.

Gustafson, Thane. *Reform in Soviet Politics.* New York: Cambridge University Press, 1981.

Gustafson, Thane, and Dawn Mann. "Gorbachev at the Helm: Building Power and Authority." *Problems of Communism* 35 (May–June 1986): 1–19.

Hammer, Darrell. *The USSR: The Politics of Oligarchy.* 2d ed. Boulder, Colo.: Westview Press, 1986.

Heitlinger, Alena. *Reproduction, Medicine, and the Socialist State.* New York: St. Martin's, 1987.

Herlemann, Horst, ed. *Quality of Life in the Soviet Union.* Boulder, Colo.: Westview Press, 1987.

Hewett, Ed A. "Gorbachev's Economic Strategy: A Preliminary Assessment." *Soviet Economy* 1 (October–December 1985): 285–305.

———. *Reforming the Soviet Economy: Equality versus Efficiency.* Washington: Brookings Institution, 1988.

Hill, Ronald J. *Soviet Politics, Political Science and Reform.* White Plains, N.Y.: M. E. Sharpe, 1980.

Hill, Ronald J., and Peter Frank. *The Soviet Communist Party.* 2d ed. London: Allen and Unwin, 1983.

Hoffman, Eric, and Robin F. Laird. *The Politics of Economic Modernization in the Soviet Union.* Ithaca, N.Y.: Cornell University Press, 1984.

———. *The Soviet Polity in the Modern Era.* Hawthorne, N.Y.: Aldine de Gruyter, 1984.

———. *Technocratic Socialism: The Soviet Union in the Advanced Industrial Era.* Durham N.C.: Duke University Press, 1985.

Hough, Jerry F. *The Soviet Union and Social Science Theory.* Cambridge, Mass.: Harvard University Press, 1977.

Hough, Jerry F., and Merle Fainsod. *How the Soviet Union Is Governed.* Cambridge, Mass.: Harvard University Press, 1979.

Hutchings, Raymond. *The Soviet Budget.* Albany, N.Y.: State University of New York Press, 1983.

Hyland, William G., "Kto Kogo in the Kremlin." *Problems of Communism.* 31 (January–February 1982): 17–26.

Ioffe, Olimpiad S. *Soviet Law and Soviet Reality.* Dordrecht: Martinus Nijhoff, 1985.

Johnson, D. Gale, and Karen McConnell Brooks. *Prospects for Soviet Agriculture in the 1980s.* Bloomington: Indiana University Press, 1983.

Jokay, Charles Z. "A Lion in Chains: The CPSU and the Soviet Military." *Crossroads* 24 (1987): 51–64.

Jones, Anthony, and William Moskoff. "New Cooperatives in the USSR." *Problems of Communism* 38 (November–December 1989): 27–39.

Jones, Ellen. *Red Army and Society.* London: Allen and Unwin, 1985.

Jones, Ellen, and Benjamin L. Woodbury. "Chernobyl and Glasnost." *Problems of Communism* 35 (November–December 1986): 28–39.

Jönsson, Christer. "The Superpower Factor in Soviet Foreign Policy Making." *Crossroads* 24 (1987): 17–28.

Jowitt, Kenneth. *Revolutionary Breakthroughs and National Development.* Berkeley: University of California Press, 1971.

Juviler, Peter, and Hiroshi Kimura. *Gorbachev's Reforms: U.S. and Japanese Assessments.* Hawthorne, N.Y.: Aldine de Gruyter, 1988.

Kanet, Roger. "New Political Thinking and Soviet Foreign Policy. *Crossroads* 28 (1989): 5–22.

Katsenelinboigen, Aron. *Soviet Economic Thought and Political Power in the USSR.* New York: Pergamon Press, 1980.

———. *Studies in Soviet Economic Planning.* White Plains, N.Y.: M. E. Sharpe, 1978.

Katz, Zev. *The Communications System in the USSR.* Cambridge, Mass.: Harvard University Press, 1971.

Katz, Zev, Rosemarie Rogers, and Frederic C. Harned, eds. *Handbook of Major Soviet Nationalities.* New York, 1975.

Kerblay, Basile. *Modern Soviet Society*, trans. Rupert Swyer. London: Methuen 1985.

Khrushchev, Nikita S. *Khrushchev Remembers*, edited and translated by Strobe Talbott. Vols. 1, 2. London: Penguin Books 1977.

Kirsch, Leonard. *Soviet Wages: Changes in Structure and Administration since 1956.* Cambridge, Mass.: MIT Press, 1972.

Kontorovich, Vladimir. "Discipline and Growth in the Soviet Economy." *Problems of Communism* 34 (November–December 1985): 18–31.

Kushnirsky, Fyodor I. "The Limits of Soviet Economic Reform." *Problems of Communism* 33 (July–August 1984): 33–43.

Lapidus, Gail W., ed. *Women, Work and Family in the Soviet Union.* Armonk, N.Y.: M. E. Sharpe, 1984.

Leonhardt, Wolfgang. *The Kremlin and the West: A Realistic Approach.* New York: Norton, 1986.

Levi, Arrigo. "The Evolution of the Soviet System." In *The Dilemmas of Change in Soviet Politics,* edited by Zbigniew Brezezinksi, 135–50. New York: Columbia University Press 1969.

Lewin, Moshe. *The Gorbachev Phenomenon: A Historical Interpretation.* Berkeley: University of Cornfina Press, 1988.

Littlejohn, Gary. *A Sociology of the Soviet Union.* New York: St. Martin's, 1984.

Matthews, Mervyn. *Privilege in the Soviet Union: A Study of Elite Life Styles under Communism.* London: Allen and Unwin, 1978.

McCauley, Martin. *The Soviet Union after Brezhnev.* London: Heinemann, 1983.

————, ed. *The Soviet Union under Gorbachev.* New York: St. Martin's, 1987.

Medish, Vadim. *The Soviet Union.* 3d ed. Englewood Cliffs, N.J. Prentice Hall, 1987.

Medvedev, Roy. *All Stalin's Men.* Translated by Harold Shukman. Oxford: Basil Blackwell, 1983.

Medvedev, Zhores. *Gorbachev.* New York: W. W. Norton & Co., 1986.

————. *Soviet Agriculture.* New York: W. W. Norton & Co., 1987.

Meissner, Boris. "Transition in the Kremlin." *Problems of Communism* 32 (January–February 1983): 8–17.

————. "The 26th Party Congress and Soviet Domestic Politics." *Problems of Communism* 30 (May–June 1981): 1–23

Menon, Rajan, and Daniel N. Nelson. *The Limits to Soviet Power.* Lexington, Mass.: Lexington Books, 1989.

Mickiewicz, Ellen. *Media and the Russian Public.* New York, 1981.

Millar, James R., and Elizabeth Clayton. *Quality of Life: Subjective Measures of Relative Satisfaction.* Soviet Interview Project Working Paper no. 9. Urbana-Champaign, Ill., February 1986. Mimeo.

Miller, Robert F. "The Politics of Policy Implementation in the USSR: Soviet Policies on Agricultural Integration under Brezhnev." *Soviet Studies* (April 1980): 171–94.

Mitchell, R. Judson. "The CPSU Politburo in 1990: A Projection." *Crossroads* 19 (1986): 21–44.

Mitchell, R. Judson, and Teresa Gee, eds. "The Soviet Succession Crisis and Its Aftermath." *Orbis* 29 (Summer 1985): 293–317.

Murphy, Patrick. "Soviet Shabasniki: Material Incentives at Work." *Problems of Communism* 34 (November–December 1985): 48–57.

Narkiewicz, Olga. *Soviet Leaders: From the Cult of Personality to Collective Rule.* Brighton, England: Wheatsheaf Books, 1986.

Nelson, Daniel C. *Elite-Mass Relations in Communist Systems.* London: MacMillan Press Ltd., 1988.

Nikolaevsky, Boris. *Power and the Soviet Elite.* New York: Praeger, 1965.

Nimitz, Nancy. "Reform and Technological Innovation in the Eleventh Five-Year Plan." In *Russia at the Crossroads: The 26th Congress of the CPSU,* edited by Seweryn Bialer and Thane Gustafson, 140–55. London: Allen and Unwin, 1982.

Nogee, Joseph L., ed. *Soviet Politics: Russa after Brezhnev.* New York: Praeger, 1985.

Nove, Alec. *The Economics of Feasible Socialism.* London: Allen and Unwin, 1983.

————. *Stalinism and After: The Road to Gorbachev.* 3d ed. Boston: Unwin and Hyman, 1989.

Odom, William E. "Soviet Force Posture: Dilemmas and Directions." *Problems of Communism* 34 (July–August 1985): 1–14.

Ozinga, James R., Thomas W. Casstevens, and Harold T. Casstevens II. "Circulation of Elites: The Politburo 1919–1987." *Crossroads* 27 (1989): 37–41.

Pankhurst, Jerry G., and Michael Paul Sacks, eds. *Contemporary Soviet Society: Sociological Perspectives.* New York: Praeger, 1980.

Parks, Michelle, and John L. Moore, eds. *The Soviet Union.* 2d ed. Washington, D.C.: Congressional Quarterly Inc., 1986.

Poljanski, Nikolai, and Alexander Rahr. *Gorbatschjow: der neue Mann* (Gorbachev: The new man). Munich: Verlag Universitas, 1986.

Porket, J. L. "Unemployment in the Midst of Labor Waste." *Survey* 29 (Spring 1985): 19–28.

Powell, David E. "The Soviet Alcohol Problem and Gorbachev's Solution." *Washington Quarterly* (Fall 1985): 5–15.

Rigby, T. H. "A Conceptual Approach to Authority, Power and Policy in the Soviet Union." In: *Authority, Power and Policy in the USSR,* edited by T. H. Rigby, Archie Brown, and Peter Reddaway, 9–30. New York: St. Martin's 1980.

Rigby, T. H., and R. F. Miller. *Political and Administrative Aspects of the Scientific and Technological Revolution in the USSR.* Canberra; Australian National University, 1976.

Rothberg, Abraham. *The Heirs of Stalin.* Ithaca, N.Y.: Cornell University Press, 1972.

Rubinstein, Joshua. *Soviet Dissidents: Their Struggle for Human Rights.* 2d ed, Boston: Beacon Press, 1985.

Rumer, Boris. "Realities of Gorbachev's Economic Program." *Problems of Communism* 35 (May–June 1986): 20–31.

————. "Structural Imblance in the Soviet Economy." *Problems of Communism* 33 (July–August 1984): 24–32.

Ryavec, Karl. *Implementation of Soviet Economic Reforms.* New York: Praeger, 1976.

Schroeder, Gertrude E. "The Slowdown in Soviet Industry 1976–1982." *Soviet Economy* 1 (January–March 1985): 42–74.

Scott, Harriet Fast, and William J. Scott. *The Armed Forces of the USSR.* Boulder, Colo.: Westview Press, 1979.

Shapiro, Leonard. *The Communist Party of the Soviet Union.* 2d ed. New York: Vintage Books, 1971.

Sheetz, Elizabeth C. "Stepped-Up Efforts to Curb

Dissent in the USSR." *Radio Liberty Research Bulletin* 164/77. New York: Radio Liberty, 12 July 1977.

Shelton, Judy. *The Coming Soviet Crash.* New York: Free Press, 1989.

Shlapentokh, Vladimir. *Public and Private Life of the Soviet People: Changing Values in Post-Stalin Russia.* New York: Oxford University Press, 1989.

Šik, Ota. *The Communist Power System.* New York: Praeger, 1984.

Simes, Dimitri K. "The Military and Militarism in Soviet Society." *International Security* 6 (Winter 1981–82): 123–43.

Solomon, Peter, Jr. *Soviet Criminologists and Criminal Policy: Specialists in Policy Making.* New York: Columbia University Press, 1978.

Spechler, Dina. "Permitted Dissent in the Decade after Stalin." In *The Dynamics of Soviet Politics,* edited by Paul Cooks, Robert Daniels, and Nancy Heer. Cambridge, Mass.: Harvard University Press, 1976.

Taubman, William. *Governing Soviet Cities.* New York: Praeger, 1973.

Thornton, Judith. "Chernobyl and Soviet Energy." *Problems of Communism* 35 (November–December 1986): 1–16.

Tomiak, J. J., ed. *Soviet Education in the 1980s.* London: Croom Helm, 1983.

Trump, Thomas M. "The Membership Dilemma of the CPSU: Impact on the Party Congress." *Crossroads* 24 (1987): 1–16.

United States Department of Agriculture. *Grains: USSR Grain Situation and Outlook.* Foreign Agricultural Circular. Washington, D.C.: Goverment Printing Office, May 1985.

Voslensky, Mikhail. *Nomenklatura: gospodstvuyuschy klass Sovetskogo Soyuza* (The nomenklatura: Ruling class of the Soviet Union). London: Overseas Publication Interchange, 1985.

Warhola, James. "The Role of Social Discipline in Soviet Management of Russian Nationalism." *Crossroads* 27 (1989): 55–65.

White, Stephen. "Propagating Communist Values in the USSR." *Problems of Communism* 34 (November–December 1985): 1–17.

Woll, Josephine. "Glasnost and Soviet Culture." *Problems of Communism* 38 (November–December 1989): 40–50.

Yanov, Alexander. *The Russian New Right.* Berkeley: University of California, Institute of International Studies, 1977.

Yanowitch, Murray. *Social and Political Inequality in the Soviet Union.* White Plains, N.Y. M. E. Sharpe, 1977.

———. *Work in the Soviet Union: Attitudes and Issues.* Armonk, N.Y.: M. E. Sharpe, 1985.

Zaslavsky, V., and R. J. Bryn. *Soviet-Jewish Emigration and Soviet Nationality Policy.* New York: St. Martin's 1983.

Zemtsov, Ilya. *Chernenko, the Last Bolshevik: The Soviet Union on the Eve of Perestroika.* New Brunswick, N.J.: Transaction Publishers, 1989.

———. *La corruption en Union Sovietique* (Corruption in the Soviet Union). Paris: Hachette, 1976.

———. *Policy Dilemmas and the Struggle for Power in the Kremlin: The Andropov Period.* Fairfax, Va.: Hero Books, 1985.

———. *Private Life of the Soviet Elite.* New York: Crane and Russak, 1985.

———. *Soviet Sociology.* Fairfax, Va.: Hero Books, 1985.

Zemtsov, Ilya, and John Farrar. *Gorbachev: The Man and the System.* New Brunswick, N.J.: Transaction Publishers, 1989.

Ziegler, Charles. "Issue Creation and Interest Groups in Soviet Environmental Policy: The Applicability of the State Corporatist Model." *Comparative Politics* 18 (2) (1986): 171–89.

Zlotnik, Marc D. "Chernenko's Platform." *Problems of Communism* 31 (November–December 1982): 70–75.

———. "Chernenko Succeeds." *Problems of Communism* 33 (March–April 1984): 17–31.

Index of Russian Terms

Index of Subjects and Names